How to read your star signs

The Only One-Volume Guide to
Your Sun, Moon and Rising Signs

Sasha Fenton

Thorsons

Thorsons
An Imprint of HarperCollins*Publishers*
77–85 Fulham Palace Road,
Hammersmith, London W6 8JB

First published by Thorsons as three volumes,
Sun Signs, Moon Signs and *Rising Signs*
This combined edition published 1998
5 7 9 10 8 6 4

A catalogue record for this book
is available from the British Library

ISBN 0 7225 3730 1

Printed and bound in Great Britain by
Creative Print and Design (Wales), Ebbw Vale

Contents

Rising Signs

Part One: Background

Part Two: Rising Sign-by-Sign

Part Three: Deeper and Deeper

Introduction

Over the past dozen or so years, many people have found their way into astrology by means of my books and now you can do so too with the aid of this trilogy of Sun, Moon and Rising signs. This three-in-one book contains much of the information that you will need to help you understand yourself and others by means of astrology. I remember when I first discovered astrology how it opened my eyes to the inner motivations of people and how it explained their peculiarities to me. Astrology made a confusing and frightening world far more comprehensible and easier to live in.

Astrology is not a difficult craft to get to grips with and nowadays the plethora of affordable software has eliminated the sweat of calculating a chart, leaving only the fun side of the subject. As your own interest develops, you will find plenty more books to help you on your way and very soon you will be happily analysing charts and teaching yourself about people, places and events in a particularly pleasant and enjoyable manner.

The Sun Sign book not only gives you the basic information about each sign but it also contains examples of twenty-four charts of famous people with their characteristics fully explained for you. The Moon Signs book shows the inner nature of feelings, emotions and reactions. Whatever may be on the outside, it is always worth looking at the Moon sign to see what a person's inner nature is all about. There is even a section on how to progress the Moon to see what phase of life any person is going through at any time. This simple technique takes you gently into the realm of predictive astrology. Rising Signs explains the ascendant in detail and it shows how this modifies the personality. In some cases, the Rising sign is a stronger influence than the Sun sign because it is often the first thing that one notices about a person. Many people look far more like their Rising sign than they do their Sun signs.

So with these three basic elements of astrology at your fingertips, you will be well on the way to understanding the subject as a whole and hopefully excited enough by it to take your studies a step or two further until you too are a competent astrologer. Good luck!

1

Sun signs

Aries

Come, cheer up, my lads, 'tis to glory we steer,
To add something more to this wonderful year;
to honour we call you, not press you like slaves,
For who are so free as the sons of the waves?
Heart of oak are our ships, heart of oak are our men,
We always are ready; Steady, boys, steady!
We'll fight and we'll conquer again and again.

Heart of Oak by Dr Boyces

A suitably courageous song for Aries.

Sign: The Ram

The ram is a strong animal whose task is to protect the females in its harem, fight other rams for supremacy and, of course, to fertilise the females in order to ensure the birth of all those lovely little lambs. Do Ariens, therefore, ride roughshod over everyone, guard their property ferociously, and chase every member of the opposite sex they come across? No, of course they don't! But then there's Patrick. Patrick has a wife and three children, a nice house in the country, a business and at least two lovely cars. He has an eye for a pretty secretary and at least one regular girl-friend living in a penthouse flat in town but this doesn't stop him trying to chat up at least one new female per day.

Ruling Planet: Mars

This planet is traditionally connected to the idea of war (however, Venus, which is associated with open enemies, is in its way an even more warlike planet). The Mars type is a natural leader with the courage, energy and originality necessary to inspire others. Mars is also associated with masculine sexuality and vitality.

Gender: Masculine

Masculine subjects are more likely to tackle a problem themselves than to hand it over to someone else to deal with. These subjects say what they mean and don't hesitate to push themselves or their children to the forefront.

Element: Fire

Fire sign people are optimists who have faith in the future. They are intuitive, often appearing to jump to conclusions. They are friendly, generous and youthful in spirit but they can be quick-tempered and irritable. All fire-sign people have the ability to begin large enterprises but may be less able to finish what they start or to handle the details which may be involved.

Quality: Cardinal

Cardinal people like to take their own decisions and can be quite stubborn and determined. They are ambitious, either for themselves or their families, and are not easily pushed around. Some are very powerful and competitive personalities. Many, especially Ariens and Capricornians, reach executive positions and are very adroit politically, in addition to being a little manipulative if it helps them to gain their objectives.

Some General Characteristics

Aries is the first sign of the zodiac and therefore represents the springtime of life. Ariens are considered to be straightforward, honest and enthusiastic about life. However, I can't help thinking that there are so many successful Arien politicians and would-be politicians that, despite their straightforward manner and approach, they can also be pretty crafty. At the time of writing, we have an Arien Prime Minister, John Major, in Britain. His closest competitor for the job was an Arien, Michael Heseltine. The leader of the opposition, Neil Kinnock, is yet another Arien and we should not forget that would-have-been politician, Jeffrey Archer and one we would all prefer to forget, Adolf Hitler. Of course, political leaders do come from all areas of the zodiac but Ariens or those who have very strong Aries features on their charts are well represented at or near the top of any organisation. This is odd in one way, because Ariens lack confidence and need a strong and supportive partner if they are going to get anywhere.

The more successful Ariens seem to have the knack of picking just the right sort of partner to support their aims.

The strongest Arien trait is competitiveness, and this exists even among those who don't appear competitive at first glance. The Arien may compete in the usual manner, by trying to be the most successful in his career or in hobbies, sports and games. Others push their children to succeed or push themselves to pass examinations in order to prove that they have intellectual superiority. On the subject of Arien competitiveness, I vividly remember an occasion where a group of psychics rented space at a 'psychic and mystic' exhibition. Plonked right at the front of the available space was the inevitable Arien, his table piled high with knick-knacks for sale, fake flowers flopping about everywhere, busily catching the eye of every passer-by who could be persuaded to have a consultation. At the end of the festival, the Arien, complete with the lion's share of the takings, rushed off home only to lose the lot to a couple of overgrown, but not yet independent, children and a rapacious spouse.

Ariens are quick on the uptake and impulsive in small ways, but they are not so quick to make major changes, preferring the security of a marriage, a settled home and a secure job. If marriage doesn't work out for them, they can happily live alone, thereby avoiding the possibility of dealing with matters of dependence. Most Ariens have many friends and acquaintances because they have an open and non-hostile manner and genuinely enjoy helping others. However, some Ariens have such an overwhelming personality that they frighten less outgoing members of the zodiac. Some Ariens are quite aggressive, and even those who appear to be mild have an aggressive or demanding streak hidden away somewhere. One friend of mine who had divorced an apparently meek and gentle Arien on the grounds of unreasonable behaviour told me that the whole weight of Arien aggression, determination and overriding need to have his own way at all costs, showed itself in the bedroom.

One thing which I have invariably found is that Ariens love words and language. They read extensively and usually have a large vocabulary. Their spelling is excellent and they have a precise way of writing and expressing themselves. They are conscious that they can express themselves well and often use this as a weapon against less able people. Ariens have a very quick sense of humour and can range from enjoying a good joke and being very funny themselves to being unpleasantly cutting and sarcastic. Other factors on each individual chart will determine how considerate the Arien may be towards other people's feelings, because the pure Arien type is self-centred, selfish and apparently uncaring. This is the sign of the military leader who needs to 'get the job done' without regard to the finer details such as who gets hurt or what gets destroyed. However, no sign is absolutely black and white, and Ariens are saved from inhumanity by their ability to empathise with the feelings of others and by their desire to help. There must be a few Arien wimps around somewhere although I, personally, haven't yet met any.

What Does The Arien Look Like?

The typical Arien is short to middling in height, skinny when young but square or rounded in appearance later in life. Ariens who belong to white races have very pale skin and blonde, light brown or red hair, while even those who belong to oriental, medium-coloured or mixed races tend to have a fairer skin than their counterparts. Arien hands and feet are small and blunt. Some Ariens comment when buying new shoes that the boxes they are stored in fit better than the shoes themselves. They also have a prominent 'seat'. Aries subjects move and walk quickly and often finish a job of work before others have even got around to starting.

There is another quite distinct Aries type. This one is tall and thin, with bony features and heavily rounded 'George Robey' eyebrows. This type of Aries subject seems to have a stronger and more awkward type of personality than the small, square ones.

Health

Astrology can be a valuable tool for both the diagnosis and treatment of ailments but this involves the use of a full birth chart for each patient. The position of the Sun alone is not enough. However, here are the traditional areas of weakness associated with Aries.

Weak spots are the head, eyes, the upper jaw and upper teeth; all Ariens seem to get headaches when they are stressed. Ariens are a pretty healthy lot on the whole but they can go down with sudden feverish ailments and they are also prone to accidents, cuts and burns due to haste or carelessness.

Ariens have little patience with illness either in themselves or those around them and they prefer to ignore it wherever possible.

Careers and Hobbies

The typical Arien likes to work among people in a large organisation which helps the public in some way. Many can, therefore, be found in the police, civil service, teaching and hospital administration. These subjects make good, if sometimes rather impatient, administrators and can organise others without putting their backs up. Their cheerfulness and lack of jealousy towards others makes them good working colleagues but their tendency to say or do things without thinking first can land them in trouble. Ariens are drawn to the military and paramilitary fields either as a career or as a part-time involvement. Oddly enough, many Ariens are attracted to religious or philosophical groups and can work for the public in those areas too. Many find work in what were once considered to be the masculine worlds of engineering and technical drawing as well as mining and ship-building. A quick round-up of some Arien acquaintances offers one who is a head in a large college of adult education, a policeman, an insurance administrator, an engineer-draftsman, the manager of a communications business, an executive of an electricity generating organisation and a gifted medium who is the secretary of the British Astrological and Psychic Society. One of these is also a part-time soldier, while another is involved with the Salvation Army. If the Arien has planets in nearby Taurus, he could work in the building trade or as an architect, and he will also be keen on music and the arts.

Aries hobbies include quasi-military interests such as serving in the territorial army and various other forms of 'dad's' army, navy or air force. They can also be found in the scout movement and similar organisations. Many Ariens love music or the arts and they may collect artistic goods of one kind or another. Most of them are energetic people who need to be out of doors at least once a week and who, therefore, may take up a sporting activity, or boating or gardening as a hobby. Ariens are impulsive and adventurous people who will take off at a moment's notice when offered an opportunity of having fun.

Money, Shopping and Acquisitions

Ariens seem to have a strange attitude to money because, while they love the stuff to death, they seem to find it hard to deal with. Some Ariens feel so uncomfortable with budgetary matters that they leave these entirely to their spouses. Others prefer to take this out of their spouse's hands altogether and deal with the whole of the family's finances on their own. Most Ariens work hard and actually manage to make good money but they may then lose a good deal of this to mendacious relatives or ex-spouses. Others are incredibly mean and penny-pinching; there seem to be no half-measures here. Anyone who finds themselves married to an Arien should either not think too much about money, or keep their finances completely separate.

All Ariens love to shop and will buy any amount of goods for their homes, their hobbies and themselves. They love new clothes and they often have wardrobes bulging with every kind of fashion. This is not helped by the fact that they hate to throw anything away or to waste time organising their wardrobes. I have one Arien friend who is a devotee of garage sales, boot sales, jumble sales and second-hand shops and he has thus cleverly managed to fit his house out in the 'contemporary' style of the 1950s which is now highly chic. Some Ariens are more interested in cars than houses and they may own more than one vehicle.

There are some Ariens who buy every kind of sports equipment known to man – and then never use any of it. Others spend a fortune on gadgets, equipping themselves with food processors, personal stereos, mobile telephones, novelties for the car, yoghurt makers and every other kind of new gismo which comes on the market. Musical Ariens buy the best sound systems that they can afford for their homes and cars while many spend a good deal of time and money on creating gardens and growing indoor plants. Most Ariens are practical and capable when it comes to do-it-yourself jobs, dressmaking and the like and they won't hesitate to tackle quite large tasks, even if these really are rather beyond their capabilities.

Living with Aries

Ariens are relaters who would rather be part of a family than on their own. However, a good many of them do seem to live alone, either because they have difficulty in finding or keeping a partner or because they have been hurt in the past and are worried about getting hurt again in the future. The vast majority of Ariens are surrounded by their families and will take care of their parents, children, in-laws and anyone else towards whom they feel a responsibility. However, these subjects are saved from being latter-day saints by their tiresome, impatient natures. Ariens are energetic and restless, always looking for something to do when they are at home which means that on any reasonable weekend, they can be found tearing down walls, building boats in the front garden, scattering tools around and stamping about in fits of rage. An Aries man will use his wife's best vegetable knife and newest tea towel when servicing the car and, for an encore, take the dishwasher to pieces half an hour before dinner guests arrive. Many Ariens are desperately untidy but, of course, there are many exceptions to this rule.

Aries women cannot help running the lives of everyone around them, giving orders like an army general and expecting everyone around to jump to their commands. Even ex-husbands and wives are 'looked after' in this way. Ariens love to sit down a visiting friend in a comfortable chair with a nice cup of coffee and a biscuit in hand, start an interesting conversation and *then walk out of the room* leaving their visitor talking to himself.

Ariens have strong allegiances to their chosen political views, often being strongly left- or right-wing. Some have violent racial or religious prejudices, while others genuinely love people of all creeds, colours and classes. Their strong political feelings probably account for the large number of Ariens who do actually go into politics and subsequently reach high office. When these subjects take up some specific kind of belief, philosophy or ideology, they embrace it wholeheartedly without being able to see the weaknesses or drawbacks in it. They may become so deeply involved in such interests that it becomes impossible to have any kind of discussion with them, without their chosen point of view being dragged into it. This is fine if their partner shares their views, or if he/she can go deaf whenever these subjects creep into the conversation, but if the partner cannot cope with this, the relationship hasn't much of a chance. It is not a good idea to live with an Arien if one cannot drive and does not own a car, because Aries subjects either drive like maniacs, shouting insults at other drivers, or sit resolutely in the middle lane travelling at a steady 30 mph.

Ariens are honest, straightforward and somewhat naive, their motto is 'Goodness, I hadn't thought of that!'. However, their partners always know where they stand, because the Arien is incapable of deviousness or manipulative behaviour. To some extent, what you see is what you get. It is not a good idea to compete with an Arien and it is better for their partners to be in a different line of work from them. Aries partners need quite a bit of support themselves because, despite their pomposity, they don't have much confidence in their own abilities.

Sexuality

Anyone reading this, who is contemplating taking up with an Arien, had better give a bit of thought to the subject of sex. If your personal pattern runs to a quick fumble on birthdays and anniversaries interspersed with late night bible readings and a cup of hot cocoa at bedtime, you had better think again. A friend of mine who had a lengthy affair with an Arien told me that she could only recall four occasions when they spent time together without actually making love. Aries women are either highly sexed or absolutely uninterested in the whole business. This is, of course, an all-or-nothing sign. Aries men, however, seem to be very ardent. Ariens can and do experience love in a purely poetic way, mooning about some dream lover from a distance, but they are more likely to put themselves in touch with their own feelings and also to express those feelings in a horizontal position!

If an Arien fancies someone, he/she will make their feelings plain and will manoeuvre the object of their desire out of their clothes as soon as possible. Bed, in the case of Ariens, is more of an image or an idea than a necessity, because they will happily make love in the car, up against a tree in the local park, in a lift which is stranded between floors or any of a thousand other unlikely places. A particularly favourite spot is the office, because there is something particularly delicious about enjoying an illicit session on such 'hallowed ground'. Sexually experimental and very oral, these subjects like nothing better than a tumble under the dining-room table. Whatever does or doesn't happen, the partner of an Aries is assured of a good laugh because, even when the lovemaking stops, Ariens have the most wonderful sense of humour. However, Ariens can be surprisingly jealous and possessive, especially if they have planets in nearby Taurus and, while they may 'play' away from home if they can get away with it, they cannot really cope with this being done to them.

Other Relationships

The Arien may be impatient with his parents or in-laws but he won't abandon them in times of trouble, and he can always be relied upon to help out financially. When the Arien becomes a parent, he puts his heart into the job. He will provide every kind of educational material for his children and will go to endless trouble and expense to see them enter the best possible schools and colleges. His competitiveness most certainly extends to his children and, if they don't or can't make the grade, he may lose all interest in them. Aries parents have little time for a timid, fussy or awkward child.

As the parent or in-law to adult children, the Arien will either leave them alone to live their lives as they wish or, more likely, will try to control them and dictate to them.

As a child, the Arien can be a demanding handful because he is full of energy and is easily bored. Some Arien children, especially girls, are studious and clever, but many of them are disinclined to study. To some extent, parents should insist on school attendance and homework being completed but if the Aries child is really not keen, then too much parental pressure will turn him off study altogether. An Aries boy may be better at coping with something practical such as construction tasks or making objects out of clay.

These children need a physical outlet such as karate, dancing, sailing or anything else which has a physical and a competitive slant to it. The Aries child needs to be encouraged to share, and to be shown that there are times and places where competitive behaviour are not appropriate. He may also need to be kept under control and prevented from being ill-mannered and selfish. However, these children are not too difficult to raise because they are usually happy, healthy and self-sufficient. Honest and decent by nature whilst also being very loving, Aries children make friends easily and need the love and approval of parents, teachers and friends.

The Arien youngster may find it hard to get along with his siblings. In some cases, the Aries child may get on with one sibling but be contemptuous of another. There is no point in making him try to like the other child; if he can't, he can't, and that's that! He is far too straightforward to be nice to the sibling in front of others and spiteful behind his back.

Elton John

Elton John's music is loved the world over and he has been in the limelight for many years. He is known for his crazy outfits, even crazier spectacles and his wonderful songs. It is widely known that Elton John trained as a classical pianist but turned to popular music in his teens. I was surprised to find that Elton is an Arien because he has always struck me as being typically Taurean. However, as you can see from his chart, the sign of Taurus and the house of Venus, the planet associated with this sign, are quite strongly emphasised. Elton John's Sun is in Aries in the eighth house; a charismatic combination which would indicate a glittering military career rather than a musical one but, if he has an interest in military matters beyond wearing flamboyant uniforms, I have no knowledge of this. I've always suspected that Elton is a hard worker who does things thor-

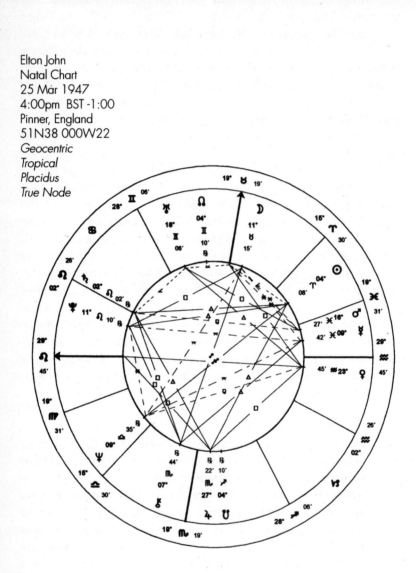

Elton John
Natal Chart
25 Mar 1947
4:00pm BST -1:00
Pinner, England
51N38 000W22
Geocentric
Tropical
Placidus
True Node

oughly and his eighth house Sun sign confirms this. Elton's Moon is in the musical sign of Taurus in the ninth house, close to the midheaven. This placement denotes world-wide success through creative endeavours, while his second house Neptune denotes earnings from the fruits of his imagination. Jupiter in the fourth house in Scorpio suggests that Elton's parents probably pushed him at school, in addition to ensuring that he had the right training for a successful musical career. Elton's Mars and Mercury in Pisces denote an artistic nature and the fact that these planets are not comfortably aspected suggests that he has the strength of character to cope with setbacks and difficulties in life. Saturn in Leo in the twelfth house suggests that his father wanted him to succeed but also that Elton might have found the father/son relationship hard to handle. This Saturn placement points to a glamorous outer image but a shy and tense inner personality, especially during childhood.

Elton's heavily aspected Venus, in the detached sign of Aquarius, tell us that he needs relationships but hates being smothered. Venus in the sixth house points to a musical career and also tells us that he has a sensitive throat. Some years ago Elton did indeed have to stop singing for a year or so after a period of treatment for a throat ailment. This chart is so full of difficult aspects that I suspect Elton's life is harder than anyone realises and that he has probably relieved many of his feelings by pouring his heart into his songs This chart is well balanced, with three planets each in fire, water and air signs, but his single planet in earth denotes a lack of caution and practicality at times. However, the emphasis on fixed signs compensates for this.

Severiano Ballesteros

Seve Ballesteros is one of the world's most famous golfers. This handsome Spaniard has, as one would expect, his Moon in the glamorous sign of Leo and most of his first house in Leo as well.

His rising sign is Cancer, which suggests that he had a happy childhood with plenty of opportunity to pursue his talents. Jupiter in Virgo is well aspected by Mercury in Taurus. These two 'sporting' planets in earth signs endow him with the ability to concentrate and to finish what he starts. It is interesting to note that golf is played *on the earth*. Pluto in the second house in Leo suggests great wealth as a result of what he does. This Pluto is well aspected by Neptune which suggests that he would earn money by travelling over water. Saturn in the sixth house in Sagittarius, opposite Mars in the eleventh house in Gemini, denotes something which worries him greatly. Seve could fear the kind of injury which would curtail

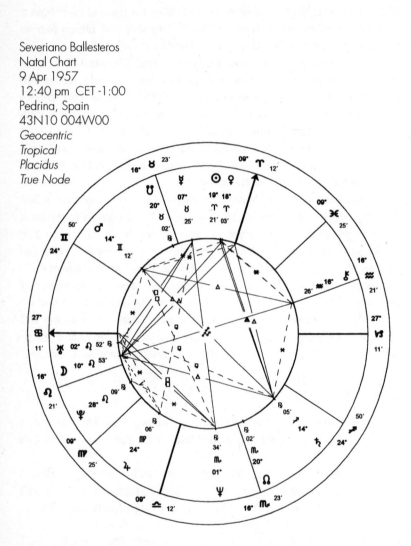

Severiano Ballesteros
Natal Chart
9 Apr 1957
12:40 pm CET -1:00
Pedrina, Spain
43N10 004W00
Geocentric
Tropical
Placidus
True Node

his career. This opposition could also suggest that it is hard for him to maintain a close contact with friends and family due to his job. The opposition of Mercury in Taurus and Neptune in Scorpio tells us that Seve has a rich inner life and a strong imagination. He could be a writer if he put his mind to it, but he may just as easily explore sexual fantasies when he is in the mood. We shall never know!

Seve's Sun is well placed for a sportsman, being in Aries and the tenth house and bracketed by Mercury and Venus. Venus in this career area of his chart tells us that his good looks and undoubtedly pleasant manner have endeared him to all who have to co-operate with him. Natural good manners and excellent public relations skills do more for a public figure in the long run than any amount of tantrums. Seve has six planets in the sporty, energetic and enthusiastic fire signs, while the remaining planets are spread round the other elements. His five fixed planets give him the determination, self-discipline and sheer grit that his life calls for and the six angular planets suggest strong leadership skills and a determination to make something of himself and his life.

2

Taurus

On Richmond Hill there lived a lass,
More sweet than May-day morn,
Whose charms all other maids surpass,
A rose without a thorn.
This lass so neat,
With smile so sweet,
Has won my right good will,
I'd crown resign
To call her mine;
Sweet lass of Richmond Hill!

The Lass of Richmond Hill by James Hook

The themes of love, the countryside and a May-day morn suit Taurus well.

Sign: The Bull

The bull in ancient times was admired for its strength. In less developed areas oxen are still used to pull ploughs and farm carts. A good bull is prized for its ability to sire numbers of good quality cattle and is, therefore, valued for its sexuality. Zeus, the King of the Gods, disguised himself as a bull in order to carry off and rape Europa.

Left alone, a bull will stand about, quietly munching grass and doing no harm to anybody, while a bull which is disturbed and frightened will charge at its adversary using great strength and a surprising turn of speed, destroy it. Taureans, therefore, have a reputation for peaceful behaviour if left to their own devices; if not, they can display a quite frightening level of temper. Taureans protect their land, property and families and will work hard to see that these are kept in good order. Like their animal counterpart, they don't enjoy change but prefer a stable and traditional way of life.

Ruling Planet: Venus

Venus is traditionally associated with love but is also linked to harmonious relationships of all kinds. This planet rules personal possessions such as land and property, goods and the money in one's bank account. Venus is concerned with pleasure in all its forms, such as the enjoyment of music and dancing, the arts, food and drink and good company. By being associated with open relationships, it tells us something about marriage (and similar relationships), close friendships and even rivals and enemies.

Gender: Feminine

Feminine subjects are more likely to wait and worry when trouble strikes, rather than to act for action's sake. Feminine sign subjects are quiet and retiring, they are likely to be unsure of themselves and are conditioned to nurture and protect rather than to rush in and destroy.

Element: Earth

Earth sign people are careful, sensible, tenacious, reliable and conventional. They hate to give up anything and may be too materialistic. These people are mature in outlook but they may be fussy and slow when tackling tasks and they may also be greedy and selfish.

Quality: Fixed

Fixed people like to stay put, remaining in the same house, the same job and the same relationship for years. They find it hard to think on their feet or adapt to changing circumstances. Most fixed sign people will see things through to the end and they find it difficult to make any kind of fresh start. Their opinions may also be fixed.

Some General Characteristics

This is the second sign of the zodiac and it is concerned with growth and protection in the same way that the first tender shoots of a plant need to be protected. Taureans worry about money. They seem to be haunted by the fear that they will shortly be sleeping under the arches, with only a cardboard box for shelter. Perhaps they lived under those circumstances in a previous life! Needless to say, they don't live beyond their means and they are never out of work for long. Some Taureans become very rich while others keep themselves and their families going in a very modest manner. These subjects can be jealous of richer or more successful people but they may miss out on reaching such dizzy heights for themselves because they tend to be lazy.

Taureans are sensualists. Many people confuse this word with sexuality and, while a sensualist often does include sex among his list of pleasures, it is not the only one. All earth sign people have well-developed senses, especially that of touch, but Taureans are the most sensual of all the signs, enjoying anything which appeals to any of their senses. These subjects are good with their hands, have excellent hand/eye co-ordination and rarely drop or break anything. I know one Taurean who is a very creative builder and decorator, another who is a really inspired cook, yet another who has created a wonderful garden and one who is the art editor of a magazine who loves to visit gardens on his day off. Notice how often the word 'creative' crops up in connection with this sign. These people may not be the most inventive members of the zodiac, but they love to create beauty in all its forms and they are often naturally artistic. Taureans are thorough and painstaking in all that they do. They are true craftsmen and women who can infuriate others by their fussiness.

It is interesting to note that such a sedentary sign includes dancers, such as Fred Astaire and Margot Fonteyn. Taureans love to dance and are often quick and light on their feet even when they are overweight.

The average Taurean subject personifies middle-class values. He wants a reasonably spacious home with a fair bit of land around it but he wants to achieve this on a very small mortgage. He needs a family, a couple of animals, a few good friends and a steady job. He may not have much imagination but he pays his bills, washes behind his ears and avoids astrologers like the plague. These subjects are private people with all the usual reserve of a feminine sign. They don't wear their hearts on their sleeves and would be embarrassed at having their problems aired in front of others. Taureans are extremely thorough in all that they do and almost totally reliable in all their undertakings. They project an image of respectability and hate to look feckless or silly. This is a fixed sign, which means that these subjects prefer to stick to a job, a home or a relationship. The families of Taureans always know just where they are and can be fairly sure that they will not be abandoned or let down in any way. There is a quality of certainty about these people which makes a nice change in these days of fly-by-night relationships.

Taureans are the plodders of the zodiac. They will make a good job of whatever they are given to do; they work at their own pace and are very thorough and painstaking. They cannot be hassled or rushed; it upsets them. In relationships, they are very loving and kind but may be inflexible and opinionated. Their outlook is traditional and they hate being crossed or undermined in any way. If a Taurean found a relationship or a situation too uncomfortable, he would simply leave it, and having done so he would rarely look back. These subjects need an uncomplicated life with a few luxuries and pleasures thrown in. They tend to attract jealousy without having or doing anything particularly obvious to cause it. It is simply that after an invariably bumpy start, their lives become so pleasant and orderly, that other people envy them. With their gentle sense of humour, lack of spite and good intentions, routinely good manners and pleasantly ordinary appearance, Taureans help to make the world a nicer place.

What Does the Taurean Look Like?

The typical Taurus is medium in height and sturdy in build. Many, but by no means all, Taureans have difficulty in keeping their weight down. Their hands and feet are small and neat and their movements are surprisingly brisk. Their movements are graceful and many of them are surprisingly good dancers. Facially they can range from being absolutely lovely to rather Churchillian, with that characteristically strong chin and jutting lower lip. Their best features are their eyes which, in nordic races, are pale grey and rather large. In all races, the eyes are attractive and the gaze steady and unafraid. One particularly Taurean trait is the lack of a bottom. Just as the Aries has, in tailoring terms, a 'prom-seat', Taureans may have hardly any 'seat' at all. Many Taureans prefer to hide their faces behind beards, heavy-framed spectacles, makeup and elaborate hair-styles while others are extremely stylish dressers. Taurean people always look good, whatever personal style they affect, because this sign is most concerned with images and appearances.

Health

Astrology can be a valuable tool for both the diagnosis and treatment of ailments but this involves the use of a full birth chart for each patient. The position of the Sun alone is not enough. However, here are the traditional areas of weakness associated with Taurus.

Weak spots are the throat, lower jaw and lower teeth, the voice, tonsils and the thyroid gland. Diabetes is a possibility through the connection with the planet Venus, as are cystitis and kidney problems. Over-indulgence can lead to obesity for these subjects but this could be mitigated by planets in nearby Gemini. Taureans don't worry overmuch about their health but they do take it seriously when they have to.

Work and Hobbies

Taureans are very good with their hands and have a wonderful eye for line, design and colour. They like to build, preserve and conserve whatever they can for the next generation to enjoy, which is why many of them can be found in the worlds of farming, building, gardening and architecture. The beauty trade attracts these people, as does the fashion industry, and many Taureans love to cook for themselves and their friends either professionally or as a hobby.

There is an attraction to the world of money and they may, therefore, be found working in banks, as accountants, book-keepers and also in the field of insurance. Another area which attracts Taureans is that of enter-tainment. Many Taurus people love to sing and dance and will make a career for themselves in opera or dancing on the stage, either as amateur or professional entertainers. The Taurean gifts of common sense and relia-bility, coupled with thoroughness and a real love of their chosen work make them excellent employees. Their natural kindness and sympathy make them wonderful employers too but they can be very tough and canny negotiators. Their flair for making money may make them extremely successful but they sometimes become too bogged down in minor money matters to see the wood for the trees. Being very visual, images in all their forms appeal to these people and this could lead to such esoteric interests as heraldry. The Taurean gift of creating images and things which look good may take them into the world of marketing.

A quick round-up of Taureans of my acquaintance reveals a builder, a roofer, a couple of dancers, a top chef and an artist, a couple of make-up artists, a dressmaker and a book-keeper. My Taurean cousin, Shirley, has always done clerical work, but she is a truly gifted amateur cook and a good dancer. Other Taureans of my acquaintance love to sing and dance, while a few actually enjoy sports. Many Taureans seem to spend a good deal of their lives dreaming of success as artists, sportsmen or performers but not all of them can summon up the energy or the courage which would be needed to succeed in these fields. Having said all this, there is an odd breed of Taurean who seems to be able to thrive in the world of fashion, art or music and even live quite an eccentric and bohemian kind of life. Some Taureans relate well to other people and, therefore, work as advisors, particularly in the financial field. However, many of them seem only to need others in order to bounce their own ideas off them.

Money, Shopping and Acquisitions

Taureans love money and spend a lifetime trying to find it. A good deal of their wealth is acquired by working but many of them seem to inherit quite large sums of money too. These subjects are wonderful managers of money and may play the stock-market to great advantage, but most are really rather cautious and prefer to keep their cash safely on deposit. Taureans don't like to admit to having anything and, given the choice, would go to their graves with their Swiss bank account numbers engraved on their hearts! Those Taureans who don't have access to large funds still manage to save for a rainy day and strive to pay off their mortgages.

Taureans need comfort but would rather wait until they can afford good things before buying anything. Many are gifted amateur builders and gardeners who make their homes as attractive and comfortable as possible, without spending money unnecessarily. Taureans are not keen on second-hand goods, except those which they inherit from their own families. Taurus subjects look after their homes and their possessions painstakingly. They think carefully and prefer to survey the market before spending anything. Taureans are not particularly dressy but what they wear is always suitable for the occasion. They only buy quality clothing for special occasions, preferring ordinary chain-store goods for everyday wear. Some Taureans like collecting valuable possessions and most will make sure that they have a good sound system both in their homes and in their cars. Taureans enjoy travelling but will only do so in great comfort and only when they can well afford to do so. These subjects look after their families but will not be taken advantage of by lazy or greedy relatives, even if these happen to be their own children.

Living with Taurus

Taurus, being an earth sign which is fixed in quality, is the most steady, reliable and sensible sign of the zodiac. Their partners are in no danger of being let down or faced with fluctuating moods and unexpected events. Taureans take their time about everything and will think long and hard before making any kind of decision. Whether they discuss potential decisions with their partners or keep their thoughts to themselves depends on other factors on their charts. Taureans are terribly stubborn and will obstinately cling to a point of view. They aren't adaptable and will stick to the same way of doing things throughout their lives. Anyone who wants a home-loving partner who will work hard to bring money into the home and not waste anything unnecessarily, should look no further than this sign. These subjects are careful with money but usually generous and thoughtful towards their families and close friends. There is a type of Taurean who doesn't want to work or take any kind of responsibility but who wants to be looked after and paid for all along the line but such types are, thankfully, quite rare. There is, however, another, far more common Taurus type who will work quite hard without ever really seeming to get anywhere in life, but as long as their partners don't mind this, they do at least offer emotional security, and there is a lot to be said for that.

Socially speaking, some Taureans are wonderful conversationalists while others seem to be completely tongue-tied and need to be persuaded to open up and chat. Often the only way to open them up is to get them to chat about their particular interests. For many Taureans, the subject which is closest to their hearts is money and they will chat away about money-making schemes for hours. Taureans are good home-makers who can cook, build, make a wonderful garden, look after pets or do anything else which requires dexterity and practicality. They need a good, comfortable and safe home life and they prefer to spend money on their homes, in areas where they can see what they have bought, rather than on such ephemeral experiences as travel or entertainments. Some Taureans will take their families away on holiday, once all possible household bills have been covered, of course! Taurus subjects need security in a relationship and will offer the same to their partners, only leaving when a situation becomes utterly untenable. They can refuse to leave a marriage which is obviously defunct.

These people don't seem to have many irritating habits. They are calm, tidy and reasonable. They do things thoroughly but at their own pace and simply cannot be rushed. They can be quite domineering and may turn into bullies if allowed to do so and some Taureans seem to have little patience for their partners when they are ill or unhappy. This is not an intuitive sign but a practical one and people of a psychic or sensitive nature may find Taureans difficult to relate to. These subjects are traditional in their outlook and they usually follow the kind of religious, philosophical or political practices with which they grew up. They can be relied upon not to behave in an embarrassing manner and, in the words of a friend of mine, 'you can take them anywhere and rely on them not to do anything stupid'. Some Taureans are very ambitious, needing a career which comes before their friends and family. This may make the partner feel like a second-class citizen, but it can't be any harder than living with the kind of Taurean who doesn't really want to work at all. Taurus subjects are, at best, keen to have enough time to rest, enjoy themselves and provide a good *quality* of life as well as quantity of life. At worst, they can be a good-looking but expensive luxury.

Taureans are possessive and jealous by nature and they can irritate their spouses by following them about or demanding to know why they are back later than usual from the shops. They are unlikely to be unfaithful unless they feel that their relationship is truly at an end. They are normally honest and straightforward and they want the same kind of treatment from their partners. They may be calm and pleasant most of the time but they do have a terrible temper which can be very destructive if they feel that they have been hurt. These people are conventional, home-loving and serious about life. They may be too authoritarian and demanding at times.

Sexuality

Taureans are extremely sensual, enjoying everything in life which looks, tastes, sounds and feels good. They do everything slowly and thoroughly which, where sex is concerned, can only be a good thing. They may be somewhat fussy about their partner's looks, but they are not too demanding and they are aware of their own imperfections. These subjects don't rush into anything and may become good friends with a potential lover long before committing themselves to anything more. They take their time getting into and out of relationships and shyness can hold them back. Taureans don't necessarily become confident or skilled as lovers until they have lived a bit. Perhaps this is why they are keen on being made love to, rather than expecting to make all the moves themselves. Taurus subjects are not kinky or peculiar in bed and they don't need or want a partner who has a repertoire of strange tricks. All they ask for is a willing and responsive partner who will make love when they want to and won't demand too much sex when their minds are on other things.

Taureans do best with an experienced and reasonably uninhibited lover who can help them to overcome their modesty and to let themselves go. Once they have overcome any inhibitions, these subjects become excellent lovers whose sensuality and kindness make the process of love-making a luxury and a pleasure for both themselves and their partners.

Other Relationships

Taureans are good to their relatives and friends and won't turn out an old granny or make life difficult for a daughter-in-law if they can help it. The problem is that they can be tiresome and even a little boring, especially when they get older. They may demand that the whole family shares their values and does everything in the same routine manner which suits them so well. This can be infuriating to other, livelier relatives. Taurean women of the type who have never exercised their brains can become unbearable in old age and elderly Taurean men may have nothing left to them except their obstinacy and their loud repetitive conversation. However, these subjects are not destructive or deliberately hurtful, although they can be extremely mean and greedy as they get older. It is best to keep older Taureans occupied, perhaps encouraging them to take up an artistic or musical hobby in order to stop them 'switching off' from life.

As relatives and friends, however, they are kind and pleasant, and while they will not rush to help others and may have little ability to sympathise with someone else's problems, they don't do much real harm. Some Taureans find it much easier to relate to animals than people because animals give love unconditionally and make very few demands in return.

As children, these subjects are plump, pleasant and easy-going. They should be encouraged to use their artistic talents and also to take up dancing. They should be dissuaded from eating too much sweet and stodgy stuff because they can develop weight problems quite early in life. Taurus children should by rights have a comfortable time of it in school, because they cause no trouble and are typically middle-of-the-road students. Yet, although they don't attract jealous reactions from other children and seem to make friends quite easily, these children can be quite unhappy at school, particularly at the younger, junior stages of education. Later on, they may develop an interest in something practical and then begin to enjoy life at a technical college or college of further education. Many Taurus children quite enjoy going to church and learning bible stories.

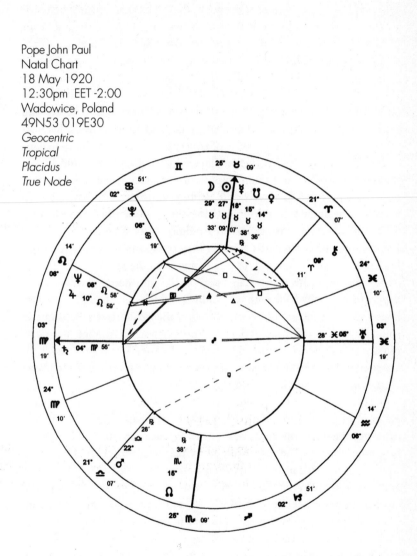

Pope John Paul
Natal Chart
18 May 1920
12:30pm EET -2:00
Wadowice, Poland
49N53 019E30
Geocentric
Tropical
Placidus
True Node

Pope John Paul II

The Sun/Moon conjunction at the top of the Pope's chart ensures that he is a man who is meant for great things. The presence of Mercury and Venus in Taurus in the ninth house tells us that Pope John Paul appreciates art. It also tells us that he has the knack of getting on with a large variety of people from very different walks of life. Mercury in the ninth suggests linguistic ability. The Pope's Saturn on his ascendant suggests that he had a hard childhood during which he spent much time alone thinking and working out his philosophy of life. Saturn in this position tells us that he is a hard worker with strong powers of concentration and an ability to cope with details. Combined with the sign of Virgo rising, he would have a strong sense of duty and of the importance of sticking to a task until it is done. The presence of Jupiter and Neptune in the twelfth house in Leo gives him pride in his position and the ability to sacrifice himself for a higher cause. His personal standards are almost impossibly high.

Although he is obviously a loving man who would have made a good husband and father, the lack of family and even the lack of a sex-life are clearly shown on his chart. Capricorn on the fifth house is traditionally supposed to signify a life without producing children, although it can also be found on the charts of people who find their children burdensome in some way. The Pope's descendant in Pisces denotes a 'strange' marriage, often with a spiritual or unworldly content. In Pope John Paul's case, he is 'married' to his spiritual life and to the church. The presence of the planet Uranus in the seventh house confirms this situation.

Taurus on the mid-heaven, even if it were not filled with the most personal of planets, would signify a strong personality with a wilful and determined nature who could be destined to reach the top of whatever tree he chose to climb. The only really nasty planet on his chart is his Mars, which is unaspected in addition to being retrograde. This can lead to illness and accidents and even the danger of assassination. In fact, someone did attempt to shoot Pope John Paul when Uranus was aspecting his difficult Mars. With five planets in earth signs and six in fixed signs, the Pope must be a very stubborn and determined man. The emphasis on angular and cadent houses balances this by giving him a purpose in life as well as the initiative and flexibility needed to carry this out.

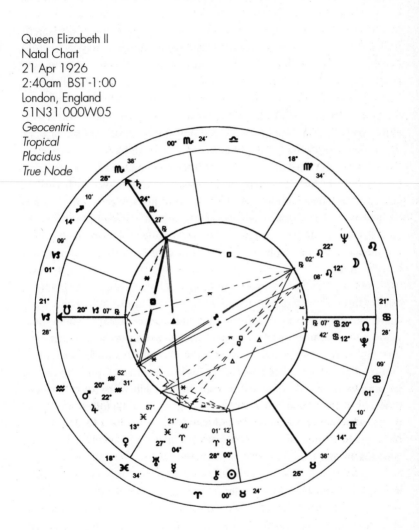

Queen Elizabeth II
Natal Chart
21 Apr 1926
2:40am BST -1:00
London, England
51N31 000W05
Geocentric
Tropical
Placidus
True Node

Queen Elizabeth II

Although the Queen's Sun is the only planet she has in the sign of Taurus, she still comes across to us as very Taurean. This is because her Sun, Mercury and Uranus are in the second house, and the second house is itself associated with the sign of Taurus. The Queen's Mercury in Aries ensures that her mind is much quicker than most people realise and also that she can be both witty and sarcastic at times. Her Moon in the 'Royal' sign of Leo gives her high personal standards and a desire to reach the top or to be the best at whatever she does. How this works out when the person is *born* at the top is hard to see, but she has certainly done an excellent job of work on our country's behalf. The presence of the cold and lonely Saturn, right at the top of her chart, denotes that she has suffered quite a bit as a result of her position in life. However, she is extremely ambitious, hard-working and keen on having and keeping the respect of her subjects. The Queen is ambitious for her children, as demonstrated by her strong Moon in Leo, and she has tried to provide the kind of upbringing which would give them the mental, moral and physical strength to cope with the lives they have been born into.

The Queen's chart ensures good health and great recuperative powers, but her throat is bound to be sensitive due to the Taurean influences on her chart. She may have a soft spot for lame ducks and a desire to help those who are weak or needy and there are occasions when she can be taken in by unscrupulous people. This is due to the presence of Neptune in her seventh house in Leo, close to her Moon. Perhaps it is just as well that she cannot become involved in business, because of this possibility. Taurus at the nadir (base) of her chart makes her very home-loving and loyal to her family. She needs to keep a part of her home and family life very private so that she can recharge her batteries in order to perform at her best in her very public workplace.

The emphasis on earth and water signs in the Queen's chart makes her sensible and tenacious while, at the same time, being intuitive and emotional. The high incidence of fixed sign planets makes her capable, reliable and unlikely to change her way of life easily. Her five angular planets enable her to take the lead and to organise her life and her work sensibly.

3

Gemini

For his bride a soldier sought her,
And a winning tongue had he,
On the banks of Allan Water,
None so gay as she.

The Banks of Allan Water,
a Scottish air

'… a winning tongue' seemed suitably Geminian!

Sign: The Twins

The twins in this case are the celestial twins of Castor and Pollux, and it is this pair of heavenly bodies who are responsible for Gemini's reputation for having a split personality. However, Gemini subjects are no more likely to have splits in their personality than any other sign because discrepancies in personality are brought about by a variety of factors on a horoscope rather than one rather misunderstood Sun sign. The twins represent different ways of looking at life. For example, one twin could be on the material plane, while the other is on the spiritual plane and the poor Gemini subject has to develop awareness to such a point that he can bring the two halves together and live a material life with the ultimate of spiritual awareness. Some Geminis manage to achieve this, thus reaching a point of contentment.

Ruling Planet: Mercury

This planet is traditionally associated with the idea of communication. The god, Mercury, was Apollo's 'gofor' who was blamed for a great deal of Apollo's dirty work. Mercury is also credited with the rulership of health, medicine and magic. All of these concepts, even in the ancient world, represented specialised knowledge and the ability to study, sift ideas and to analyse.

Gender: Masculine

Masculine subjects are more likely to tackle a problem themselves than to hand it over to someone else to deal with. Masculine sign subjects say what they mean and don't hesitate to push themselves or their children to the forefront.

Element: Air

This is the least emotional of all the elements, relying on knowledge and logic to work things out. Air subjects are intellectual, interested in everything and able to pick up and pass on knowledge as a result of being 'in the swim' and among people. Too much emotion exhausts them and too much routine bores them.

Quality: Mutable

This word may seem strange to you but if you think of transmute, commute or mutate, you will see that it concerns moving something from one place to another or one state to another. Mutable people are, therefore, flexible in their attitude, disliking too much routine and welcoming a change. They may take up too many interests, finding it difficult to concentrate deeply on any one of them. However, they are able to fit into most situations and to make themselves comfortable even when consistently on the move.

Some General Characteristics

Geminis have a reputation for being friendly, clever but not able to stick to anything or anyone for long, although in reality this is not so at all. Many Geminians have a bad start in life, often because their families drift apart, so when it comes to forming a family of their own, they make a great effort to keep the household together. They will put up with a difficult relationship for longer than most and will always keep in touch with their children, even if this is from a distance. They tend to stick to their main job although they may have subsidiary interests which bring in money, but all their jobs must offer them a variety of tasks and an opportunity to meet new people. Geminis usually have the sense to choose the kind of work which does not require deep thought or long periods of slog. They make great telephonists for example because they can cope with a busy switchboard and they are rarely phased by machinery.

One genuine Gemini fault is obsessiveness. I have never seen this mentioned in any other astrology book but I have known a number of Geminis in my time and have seen this kind of behaviour quite regularly. When something sets off this behaviour, they can become amazingly unbalanced. One example is my old school friend Sherry, whose husband left her and her daughter for another woman when she was thirty-seven years old. Sherry wept and wailed, became hysterical and stayed like it for a couple of years. Even when she later began to make a new and more interesting life for herself, she never forgot or forgave her ex-husband's treachery.

Geminis take an interest in many things but there is always one subject, one job, one interest (maybe in the background) which they tend to know thoroughly. Explaining anything to a Gemini can be frustrating because they only want to deal with the overview and they become impatient with details or logical processes. For example, if you are teaching a Geminian how to use a computer, don't bother to go through all the steps in detail, just give them an overview and stay around so that they can ask for help when they need more information. It is sometimes hard to talk to a Gemini because they ask questions and then don't bother to listen to the answer. These subjects are not interested in the moods, needs and behaviour of other people because they are so totally involved with themselves. They are restless and uncertain about life because they feel that the grass is always greener somewhere else and are often mentally on their way out of the field which they are in and looking for the next piece of grass.

Geminians are witty and they often have a very funny sense of humour which helps them get through difficult situations. Their ability to move on quickly to a new interest or a new person also helps them overcome bad times. These subjects are noted for being excellent communicators but they may be better at connecting people with each other in the sense of an agent or a broadcaster than actually talking (and listening) to people themselves. In a social setting, a Gemini will chat away nineteen to the dozen whilst at the same time their eyes roam around the room, taking in everything that is going on and analysing it with some other part of their brain.

I have to admit to being a little wary of Gemini men. They can be quite bossy and may treat the other members of their family and, indeed, women as a whole, as some kind of inferior species. They are so clever and persuasive in an argument that they become used to getting their own way and can be terribly surprised and hurt when someone potentially slower and softer gets the better of them. There may be an unfeeling or thoughtless side to these people which allows them to use others or to 'con' people into giving them what they want. This mental arrogance can lead some Geminis into criminality. Others utilise these talents to turn themselves into excellent salesmen who, by means of a mixture of cheek and persistence, manage to close deal after deal.

I recently read an excellent book about people working in the stock market, where the combination of a fast and active brain, courage, a talent for selling and the ability to work at great speed strikes me as being a place in which many Geminis would feel at home. A Gemini friend of mine who works for a merchant bank told me recently that nine out of their eleven accountants are Sun in Gemini subjects. Bankers and dealers need to be hard-hearted and this type of unfeeling Gemini is ideal for the job.

As parents, Geminians will go to great lengths to provide their children with an education. They genuinely want them to succeed but they may find it hard to express affection towards them. Geminis are not terribly keen on touching. Their sensitive nerves seem to reach out into their auras and they may feel uncomfortable cuddling a child, just as they dislike being grabbed or rubbed against by casual acquaintances. These nervy people can be quite difficult to live with or to understand but their sense of humour, quick minds and their interest in everything makes them excellent company. Another great plus is their non-hostile approach and their genuinely non-judgemental attitude to other people's foibles and failings.

What Does the Geminian Look Like?

Whatever their age, Geminis are always in vogue and they are often real trendsetters where fashion is concerned. Their trim figures help them to look good, whatever style they choose to follow.

The typical Gemini is small and thin with a slightly sallow skin colour and mousy hair. Non-white Geminis are also small and neat but will obviously vary in colouring. Some Geminis put on a lot of weight as they get older and begin to resemble that famous Gemini, Queen Victoria. All the female Geminis whom I have come across sensibly use tints to make their hair a more interesting colour, often preferring to make themselves either very blond or jet black. Both sexes are fussy about their clothes and their appearance and usually look very good indeed, preferring rather formal clothes to the casual look. Many smoke quite heavily in a rather nervous and 'twitchy' manner. Even if they are sitting down and reading a paper, they always look as if they are on the point of getting up and rushing away somewhere.

Health

Astrology can be a valuable tool for both the diagnosis and treatment of ailments but this requires the use of a full birth chart for each patient. The position of the Sun alone is not enough. However, here are the traditional areas of weakness associated with Gemini.

Weak spots are the hands, arms, shoulders and the upper respiratory tract. Some Geminis have considerable problems with bones, while others never seem to get ill at all. Asthma is a possibility, as is a whole range of auto-immune diseases such as eczema, psoriasis, migraine, rheumatism and colitis. Nerves play a large part in the health of this sign and this may underlie of most of their ailments. A number of Geminis suffer from arythmia (a fast or uneven heartbeat) whilst being otherwise healthy.

Work and Hobbies

Geminis are the communicators of the zodiac and can be found working in the media, in information technology (computers, etc.), as sales representatives and as teachers. They make excellent secretaries, telephonists and technical writers, and some of them write books for a living. Quite a number of Geminis enjoy working in hospitals, but they are usually more interested in the clerical aspects of such work than the purely medical area. Others are interested in the way other people think, which draws them towards psychology and astrology. Sport interests Geminis, especially the more prestigious kinds of sport such as tennis and golf. Paradoxically, one type of work which is rarely mentioned in connection with this sign is accountancy because Geminis are traditionally supposed to be at home with words rather than figures. I've met quite a number of Gemini broadcasters who excel at chat show interviewing.

Gemini hobbies include reading, writing, talking on the phone, organising young people in sporting or outdoor activities and driving for pleasure. These people enjoy games such as chess, Trivial Pursuit or cards and many have the kind of creative hobby which allows them to use their hands. Light engineering or carpentry interest Geminis and many spend hours solving problems associated with craftwork or model-making.

Money, Shopping and Acquisitions

Geminis are not notably money-minded but they like it for the freedom it brings. These subjects don't enjoy being beholden to anyone and will strive to gain financial independence, even under the most difficult of circumstances. Gemini women seem to attach themselves to wealthy men or to encourage their husbands to become wealthy, after which they help them to spend their money on classy and elegant goods. Geminis rarely have large sums of money put by but they are never broke either. If financial trouble strikes, they will take two or even three jobs at once in order to solve the problem.

Geminis love shopping and usually have large and very up-to-date wardrobes. The vogue for smart sportswear is right up their street. They usually look and dress younger than their actual age and can get away with quite outrageous fashions well into their old age. Their homes are kept nicely, but not usually by them! They prefer to employ someone else to clean for them and, if this is not possible, they will either do what they have to do or ignore the whole business altogether. As far as decor and furniture is concerned, Geminis will buy the best that they can afford and then live with it for years afterwards. All the Geminis I have ever come across would far rather lay out in the garden soaking up the sun or snuggle into a comfy armchair in front of the television than do housework. Many Geminis love animals and have at least a couple of dogs around the place. This mercurial sign loves to be on the move, therefore a fast and efficient vehicle is a must for them. Geminis prefer small, sporty cars but won't say no to a large and luxurious vehicle if the opportunity to own one comes their way. If all they can afford is an ancient rust-bucket, then this would be far preferable than being reduced to using public transport. Geminis love holidays in sunny, fashionable places where they can laze about in comfort.

Living with Gemini

Geminis are relaters rather than loners who will go halfway to meet a partner wherever possible. Relationship problems arise from their moodiness and restlessness. They can be dissatisfied with their lot even when it is very good, because they have an implicit belief that the grass must be a good deal greener elsewhere. To be honest, most Geminis are fairly stable and, as long as their relationship is not boring, they will put up with quite a lot. Geminis are quite mercenary and will stay in a relationship if it gives them the standard of living that they require. These subjects need to live in style but they are prepared to work hard and earn the necessary money to pay for this themselves. However, they cannot be persuaded to hand over all their hard-earned cash to the rest of the family while they, themselves, go without. Geminis can only function comfortably by being well-dressed, well-fed and in the process of looking forward to an entertaining outing of some kind. This sign has a reputation for unfaithfulness but I don't think that Geminis are any more likely to cheat on a partner than any other sign.

Geminis are never boring; they love to chat but not all of them are good listeners. They are bright and intelligent and usually well informed. Some are intellectual while others have street credibility, but none are fools, except to themselves at times. Neither sex is very domesticated and, knowing this, Geminis usually make the kind of arrangements which allow their homes to run smoothly without their having to do much themselves. They equip their homes with every kind of labour-saving gadgetry and also hire someone to come in and do some, if not all of the cleaning. Many Gemini women marry domesticated men who happily swap roles. Neither sex is particularly demanding in a relationship. These subjects won't complain if a meal is not up to scratch and they don't need a perfectly-run household. What they do need, however, is a bit of peace and quiet. Gemini nerves are sensitive and they can become extremely upset by hostility or anger, so if they have had a bad day at work, they need to come back to a peaceful atmosphere. There are a few rogue Geminis who seem to thrive in an argumentative atmosphere but these are rare. These subjects need love and affection but they cannot take smothering, jealousy or tyranny and too much emotion in a partner unnerves them. If badly treated, they will slip away and find themselves a nicer partner, probably as a result of getting to know someone at work.

Gemini faults are supposed to be flirtatiousness, restlessness and an inability to stay put in a home or a relationship. Geminis *are* flirtatious, but only in circumstances where this is both allowable and appropriate. They may start off by flirting with a new face at a party, but if the person they are chatting up turns out to be interesting, they soon forget all about flirting and get into a serious conversation. Geminis can be critical and sarcastic but usually only when they have been hurt. In some cases, their wit can be a little too cutting for comfort but is meant to amuse rather than to hurt.

Gemini people are much warmer and more considerate than they are given credit for and, although young Geminis can be a bit thoughtless, they are usually quite reasonable when they have gained a bit more experience of life.

Geminians need to keep their minds active and can become so absorbed in a hobby or interest that they begin to neglect their partners, although this is usually quite unintentional. One lady who filled in one of my questionnaires said that her Gemini husband sometimes put his computer before her. One nice thing about Geminis is that they will try to be accommodating to others in the family and they even make good step-parents. However, they can be very self-absorbed, vain and inclined to nag and worry about unimportant or transient matters. Geminis find decisions hard to cope with and can dither and even panic when faced with a problem; although they soon get over this and set their clever minds to solving the problem.

Another trait which may or may not endear them to their loved-ones is their absolute cleanliness and fussiness about their clothes and appearance. Geminis also have an irritating habit of concentrating on something which interests them for hours on end and then never touching it again. They appear to lack sympathy with people who are ill, which is due to the fact that they are unnerved by illness and don't know what to do for the best. This is balanced by an ability to ignore or to shake off their own ailments, and they hardly ever take time off from work when sick. Geminians can go on and on about little things and they do try to cross bridges before they come to them. However, as long as they are not forced to live with a person who is a wet blanket or an absolute bore and as long as they are offered enough stimulation, they are not unreasonable partners.

Sexuality

Geminis are quite highly sexed. This may seem a surprising remark, because many astrologers traditionally comment on their need for mental rather than physical stimulation and their coolness where it comes to such matters. They may not be the most affectionate of signs, partly because they were rarely, if ever, cuddled as children. However, if they find them-selves with a loving and affectionate partner, they blossom into very cuddly and loving partners themselves.

Geminis are extremely curious and not overly embarrassed by unusual sexual situations, as long as these occur in private. Being analytical, Geminians can distance themselves from their feelings and enjoy sex in the same way that others enjoy good music or a good book. Geminis like to experiment and they love variety which, added to their changing moods, makes them excellent lovers. If a Sun in Gemini subject has the planet Venus in the neighbouring sign of Taurus, sensuality is added to their need for mental stimulation. While if the Geminian has planets in nearby Cancer, he may be surprisingly shy. In a loving relationship where the Geminian can relax and allow his tensions to drain away, he or she can make a very rewarding life-long partner. If an affair is on the agenda, then the Gemini would make the most amusing and, possibly slightly kinky, lover.

Other Relationships

Geminis are friendly but not always terribly close to those who are around them. They make good in-laws and step-relatives because they don't interfere. However, if a relative takes it upon himself to dictate to the Geminian, he will be given very short shrift. Friendly but distant is the way the Geminian likes to be. He will not abandon elderly parents or other relatives and he will do all he can to see that they are comfortable and well cared for but he cannot live with cantankerous, sick or needy relatives and will not allow himself to be pushed into such a situation. Geminis are reasonably good parents but they may find it hard to cuddle their children because they themselves were not cuddled enough when young. They will do all they possibly can to ensure that their children have the very best education and they will surround youngsters with every kind of educational toy or aid. They may be a bit too pushy because they are competitive and they want their children to compete as well. A Gemini parent will not hesitate in sending a child away to school if he thinks that it is for the best. Indeed, he finds his children much easier to deal with if they are at a distance to him for part of the year.

As a child, the Gemini may be unhappy and very anxious to grow up and leave behind the misery of childhood. This is strange when one considers the Geminian's evergreen youthfulness when he eventually becomes an adult. Gemini children either do very well at school or drop out altogether. They are quick and clever and they enjoy and appreciate any toy which occupies their minds and keeps boredom at bay. Some Gemini children are excellent at sports while others have wonderful mechanical ability; all of them learn early and very quickly but they become bored with the routine of school work and homework and out of tune with the kind of teamwork and petty discipline of school life. If either a relative or a teacher takes the time to show a little approval to these children, they really blossom.

Unfortunately, this rarely happens and they have to do their blossoming much later in life.

Prince Rogers Nelson

If this guy's name is unfamiliar to you, forget the Rogers and the Nelson and see what you have left! The artist formerly known as Prince and now known as a squiggle has secretive Scorpio on the ascendant, his Moon in the shy sign of Pisces and diffident Saturn is rising, so maybe it isn't surprising that he doesn't want anybody to know who he is. All of which is fair enough except for the fact that he is an *entertainer*!

Fighting against Prince's desire for privacy is the fact that most of his first house is in Sagittarius, a particularly outgoing sign which is so often prominent in the charts of entertainers. His Sun in Gemini, Moon in Pisces and such a strong Saturn gives him more than a passing resemblance to that other incomprehensible character, Michael Jackson. However, leaving aside this man's obvious peculiarities and concentrating on what makes him such an enduring success as a singer, what is there on his chart that makes him so special? Firstly, Saturn rising concentrates Prince's mind and makes him a hard worker who has patience with boring chores and detailed work. I am sure that when he is in the recording studio he stays there until he is totally satisfied with his work. His Sun in Gemini and Moon in the third house in artistic Pisces, in addition to so much Sagittarius on his first house tells us that Prince *must* communicate – shyness notwithstanding – and music is his chosen medium. Scorpio and Pisces are both extremely musical signs and this combination suggests that he has always seen music as a means of self expression and also emotional escape. I am willing to bet that Prince enjoys many different kinds of music including classical and religious music.

Prince's childhood was probably no picnic; the Sun and Moon in Gemini and Pisces indicate a lonely childhood where he was forced to turn inwards and to live inside imagination. Saturn rising confirms this. Prince would have been subject to bullying and brutality either at home, at school or both. This is a slightly built, sensitive man who would see relationships as frightening and emotional security hard to find. Financial security will always be there as he knows that he needs money to fall back on. He is not particularly generous and he will always save and invest pretty wisely, despite the fact that managers, financial advisors and other father figures may have ripped him off when he was young and inexperienced.

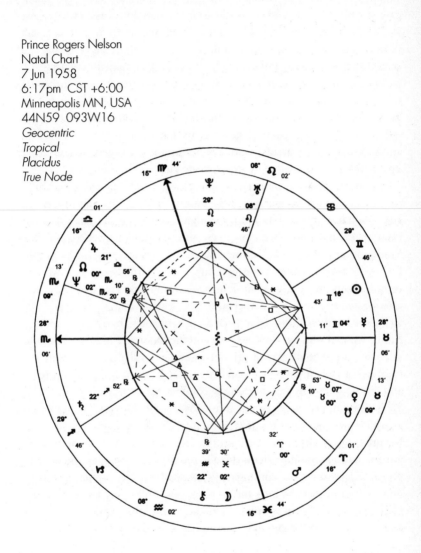

Prince Rogers Nelson
Natal Chart
7 Jun 1958
6:17pm CST +6:00
Minneapolis MN, USA
44N59 093W16
Geocentric
Tropical
Placidus
True Node

Cilla Black

Cilla Black is the only woman who emerged from the Liverpool talent machine of the 1960s, and she is still around entertaining us all when most of those charismatic Liverpool lads have long since been forgotten. Cilla's Gemini Sun is in a wide conjunction with Saturn which suggests that she enjoys working and can put in long hours and attend patiently to details. A strong Saturn is the common denominator in the charts of many successful people and it prevents their success from being short lived. Mercury in Taurus gives Cilla common sense and the ability to keep her feet on the ground. Cilla's rising sign of Cancer tells us that she must have had the love and support of her parents, especially her mother, when she was growing up and the chances are that her mum made sacrifices for her.

Venus rising in Cancer makes Cilla a pleasant and reasonable person to work with and it gives her a slightly 'mumsy' appeal. The Sun in Gemini and Moon in Pisces add humour. Having the Sun in Gemini and Moon in Pisces, there must have been loneliness and isolation somewhere in Cilla's childhood and maybe that strong Saturn gives us a clue as to its origin. Perhaps she was shy as a youngster or maybe she learned early to be wary of certain adults, especially father figures who would exploit her rather than care for her. Fortunately, Cilla seems to have a stable marriage and any suffering she has gone through has been done in private. This is to be expected from a woman who has Cancer rising and the Moon in Pisces as she would not make a public display of grief or grievances. Cilla may have suffered from being a plain young woman but money brought her plastic surgery and this undoubtedly gave her a bit of confidence.

This is not the chart of a real music lover, although Venus rising would give pleasure from all forms of art or beauty. Cilla's singing voice was never her greatest asset as it was stuck somewhere down the back of her throat. Singing and the 60s for Cilla was really the means to opening the door to her ambitious and hard working tenth house Moon. Her Jupiter in the second in Cancer ensures luck through business and easily earned money. Cilla is a lucky woman who has found an avenue that works well for her and her personality brightens up all our lives. Good on you, Cilla!

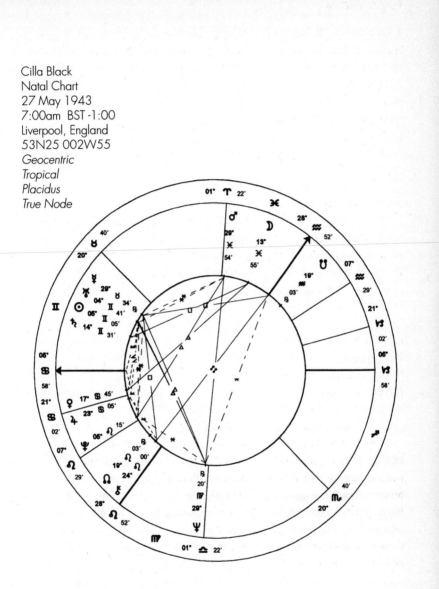

Cilla Black
Natal Chart
27 May 1943
7:00am BST -1:00
Liverpool, England
53N25 002W55
Geocentric
Tropical
Placidus
True Node

4

Cancer

A North Country maid up to London had stray'd
Although with her nature it did not agree.
She wept and she sigh'd, and she bitterly cried,
'I wish once again in the North I could be'.

The Oak and the Ash, English air

Cancerians are very attached to their homes.

Sign: The Crab

The crab lives half in water and half on land eating tasty meals of silt and the remains of dead fish accompanied, these days, by a piquant effluent sauce! Crabs take no interest in their families, or any other crustacean, except to administer a nasty nip while making love. This is just about the opposite of the usual astrological description of the Cancerian nature, except for the standard comment that these subjects have a soft nature hidden under a hard shell or that they go about things in a sideways manner. Cancerians can be cold and unpleasant at times but only with good reason.

Planet: The Moon

The Moon is not, of course, a planet but a satellite of the Earth. Astrologers call everything in the Solar system a planet just for the sake of convenience!

The Moon is extremely important, because it has such an impact on the Earth itself and upon everything which lives. If you are interested in finding out more about the Moon's influence on our personalities, I suggest you read my book, *Moon Signs*. In the case of the sign of Cancer, it emphasises the passive, reactive side of the personality and makes it hard for us to believe that Cancer is actually a cardinal sign. The Moon is associated with emotion, and Cancer is a more emotional sign than most Cancerians would have you believe. It adds a touch of femininity to any personality and it brings intuitive abilities, particularly in connection with anything which might pose a threat.

Gender: Feminine

Feminine subjects are more likely to wait and worry when trouble strikes, rather than to act for action's sake. These subjects are quiet, retiring and likely to be unsure of themselves. They are conditioned to nurture and protect rather than to rush in and destroy.

Element: Water

The water element makes for sensitivity. Therefore, water people are likely to be irritated by loud or discordant noises and upset by pain and illness. They are sensitive to atmospheres and very wary of anything which could constitute a threat. They are kind and helpful, because they are sensitive to the suffering and pain of others. However, many of them are actually more tuned in to the needs of animals than humans. Water people move and react slowly and may seem rather stupid to other quicker types, but this is a mistaken assumption because they are extremely shrewd and usually well aware of everything that is going on around them.

Quality: Cardinal

If you see in cardinality an 'act first, think later' attitude to life, then Cancer does not seem to fit the bill. The fact is, however, that Cancerians will not put up with too much without finding a way out of the problem or even wandering off in search of a new way of life. They are not as self-sacrificing as they would like us to believe and they have considerable courage in the face of troubles.

Some General Characteristics

Some Cancerians are over-responsible worriers who spend their entire time trying to cross bridges which they have yet to reach and fussing over their families. Some are hypochondriacs who drive themselves and their families crazy. Others are amazingly irresponsible types who lurch from one failed business venture to another searching for that elusive winning streak. Fortunately, by far the majority of Cancerians are sensible, responsible, hardworking and perfectly reasonable. Traditional astrology states that Cancer subjects are close to their families and inclined to cling to their children. Some of these subjects can be clinging but most are not. However, if their children are ever in need of help they only have to ask and it will be given. Cancerians are good to their parents, in-laws and even the children of second marriages. They make loyal and steadfast marriage partners as long as they are loved in return. Most Cancerians love doing things with their families.

In business, if the Cancerian can team up with a strong partner who harnesses his talent and refuses to allow him to destroy his own handiwork, he can be very successful. Librans have a reputation for needing partnerships but I think that Cancerians actually need them much more and will often form these with members of their own family. They are very good at dealing with people, either in the field of polities or through helping the public in some way and they can even cope with people who are angry or upset. Cancerians cannot cope with extremes of emotion among those closest to them because this can affect them strongly and even make them ill but they can handle tension and emotion when it does not involve them personally. Cancerians are attracted to the past, enjoying history, antiques or studying their family tree. These people are often armchair generals, great students of strategy and tactics or amateur experts on military hardware. Another Cancerian interest is travelling but they need to do so in comfort because their sensitive systems become easily upset if things are not just right. A Cancerian on a bad trip or holiday can make life hell for any fellow traveller.

Cancerian faults include moodiness and secretiveness. The problem is that they may not know why they are upset and, therefore, cannot always explain it. They can also use the tactic of moodiness and long silences to control those around them. Older Cancerian men can be so frustrating and aggravating to their partners that they finish up being dumped in favour of someone altogether more reasonable. On the other hand, Cancer people are loyal and caring towards their friends and inclined to help strangers where and when possible. Many Cancerians find work in the caring professions such as nursing or looking after animals or small children. Others make wonderful teachers, helping the next generation to better themselves.

Cancerians, both male and female, are usually talented cooks and excellent homemakers, but they don't make a fuss about a bit of mess and untidiness. Cancerians love to travel and may choose to work in a job which allows them to do so but they also need a base, a place of their own – preferably with the mortgage completely paid up.

What Does the Cancerian Look Like?

There seems to be two types of Cancerian. The first type is medium in height, rather overweight, with small hands and feet. Cancerian skin and eyes are attractive and these people often have thick, lustrous hair. This type is far happier sitting in front of the television with a bag of fruit and a packet of biscuits nearby than taking any form of exercise. In white races, the skin is fair and the hair can be any colour but is often very dark brown. Another very typical Cancerian is small and slim or even extremely thin, with red hair and lively blue eyes. This nervy, lively subject appears at first glance far more like a Gemini than a Cancer type but when you get to know them, you will find that they are pure Cancerian in nature.

Some Cancerians spend their time worrying about everything, especially money. These people can be chronically tight-fisted and their long, lined faces and downturned mouths reflect their miserable, negative outlook on life.

Health

Astrology can be a valuable tool for both the diagnosis and treatment of ailments but this involves the use of a full birth chart for each patient. The position of the Sun alone is not enough. However, here are the traditional areas of weakness associated with Cancer.

Weak spots are the chest, lungs, the breasts and the digestive system. Cancerians are prone to stomach ulcers and bowel problems and they also suffer from imbalances in the fluid content of the body. Although this is not an especially unhealthy sign, illness affects Cancerians badly because they seem to be very conscious of imbalances within the body. Cancerian children complain more than most when they are ill or when they hurt themselves.

Work and Hobbies

Anything which involves dealing with the public must be pretty high on the Cancerian list of preferred Iobs, because these people have patience and can even turn irate customers into pussycats. Their patience also makes them excellent counsellors and advisors. Many Cancerians are drawn to child-minding, looking after the elderly, teaching children or adults, nursing and the insurance business. They see this as a means of helping people to take care of themselves. Cancerians love to own their own business or to run a shop. A quick round-up of the Cancerian small-business people whom I know reveals a pet shop owner, a bed and bedding shop owner, a greengrocer, an owner of an antiques shop, a guy who runs psychic and mystic fairs all over the country, an insurance broker and a lady who runs a play-school. Their advantages are their patience and forbearance, their common sense and ability to deal with money matters, as well as their preparedness to work long and flexible hours and to take responsibility. Their faults are a tendency to cling to the past and to dislike using modern equipment or methods, which means that they may be in danger of being left behind in these days of high technology. Cancerians can also be moody and difficult to deal with. Their customers are unlikely to be affected by their moods but colleagues and employees most definitely will.

Many Cancerians are interested in the past and may read everything that they can get their hands on about some particular aspect of history. This is often an interest in naval or military history which can lead some Cancerians to take up a career in the services, especially the navy, while others take up some kind of part-time or spare-time military or para-military interest. The Cancerian love of the past and of tradition can lead to either a hobby or a career in heraldry, antiques, collecting rare books or coins, etc. Many Cancerians cannot be parted from their own old household junk, possibly because it holds some kind of sentimental attachment for them. Many Cancerians are attracted to water, so they enjoy sailing, swimming and fishing, while others seek to preserve the countryside or care for animals.

Money, Shopping and Acquisitions

In common with the other two water signs and all the other feminine signs, Cancerians are careful with money. They don't like to waste anything and they are excellent recyclers of goods. Cancerians scour the shops and supermarket shelves for bargains and keep any extra pennies in a variety of small savings accounts. They may not be high earners but they go to great lengths to conserve all that they have. In business as well as in personal life, they look for the most efficient and cost-effective option and can be very shrewd buyers and sellers.

Nothing is thrown out if there is even half a chance that it may come in handy in future and they don t worry about keeping up with fashion, the neighbours or current business trends. To some extent this can be a major drawback, because their offices and workplaces are more attuned to quill pens and roll-top desks than to the latest in information technology. Living with these people is easy as long as their partners have the same outlook but it can be a real test of love if they don't. When Cancerians do decide to lash out they look for quality goods which will last. Cancerians enjoy collecting and may make a money-spinning hobby out of antique items of one kind or another. One area where Cancerians *do* enjoy speculating is in property and many of them own more than one place. They hate paying rent and will even buy business property wherever possible. Cancerians may own more than one vehicle – one being used to carry goods and another for family and personal use.

Cancerians spend a good deal of money on clothing because they know the value of looking and feeling good about themselves. They may spend out on sports and hobbies but their major outlay is often related to travel. These people love to get away once or twice a year and will travel long distances to quite exotic locations. Camping and roughing it is not normally their style but they will put up with this if they have young families or their incomes are temporarily low. Many Cancerians own pets but these are not normally of the large or expensive type.

Living with Cancer

Cancerians are traditionally supposed to be homeloving, family-minded, caring and easy to live with. Cancerians are relaters but they may want to relate a bit too much for some people! They don't much like their own company, so they stick closely to their partners. Although both sexes are supposed to be motherly, they can be childish and demanding. Cancer subjects don't have many interests of their own but prefer to do things with the family. These subjects may work at or from their homes, running a small business of some kind with their spouses closely involved alongside them. This can make for a marvellous relationship with a partner who doesn't need much privacy or doesn't suffer from emotional claustrophobia. Cancerians are excellent listeners but they can also wallow in unhappiness or worry needlessly about minor matters. One of their favourite worries is about real or assumed shortages of money and their meanness over small things can be infuriating. Both sexes are happy to have their bills paid by a partner, even when they themselves are the major earners in the family. This is because they are convinced that they are permanently on the edge of penury.

Cancerians are highly domesticated and well able to run a home smoothly under a variety of circumstances. I come from a family of men who have Cancer strongly marked on their charts and, if the women are ill or busy working, the men step in and take over as efficiently as any Victorian housekeeper. All they ask is that we women be *around*, not necessarily doing anything domestic, but just around so that they don't feel abandoned. When illness prevents a Cancerian housewife from coping with the housework, the household may simply grind to a halt.

Cancerian women are not just pretty faces because most of them work and many of them run thriving businesses. The two favourite careers for Cancerian women seem to be antique dealing or property development, and they often make more money than a whole row of men put together. Cancerian men are excellent handymen who can save thousands of pounds on their homes by their skill and patience but their do-it-yourselfing usually involves the help of their partners and families. I have yet to work out what astrological feature makes Cancer women such high earners and Cancer men such awful losers in business. I guess that the femininity of this sign works well in the case of a woman's psyche but throws the males off-centre in some way, leading them to gamble in silly ways on large and messy ventures.

Cancerians are wonderful when anybody in the family is ill. They have endless patience and can put up with a really cantankerous partner, just as long as there is a good reason for such behaviour. Nobody can defuse a highly agitated or hysterical partner like a Cancerian and they don't take anything which is said under these circumstances too personally. In a genuine argument, however, they can be extremely nasty and they remember a partner's transgressions for years afterwards. Cancer subjects can be tied to the past in other ways too, either by clinging to their parents or by endless reminiscence about their children's babyhood and looking at old photograph albums. They love to surround themselves with souvenirs of holidays and mementos of events of long ago. Anyone choosing to live with a Cancerian will have to share the home with the junk of ages and may end up building an extension rather than throwing any of this precious stuff away. These subjects love to travel and every journey brings another shelf full of junk into the house.

Before anyone gets the idea that these subjects are saints, it is worth pointing out that they can be crabby and demanding. They are very moody, often with no apparent reason for their anger or depression. When they are ill, they grizzle. They don't take time off work but they will drive everyone crazy with their moaning. When hurt emotionally, Cancerians can become extremely spiteful. The same thing occurs if they have the sneaking feeling that they are unworthy in some way or if they think they have an inferior position in life. Cancerians are just as proud as Leos but they don't show this in quite the same way. I remember many years ago working in a company where one of the bosses was extremely nasty, throwing his weight about and making the secretaries' lives pretty unbearable at times. I later discovered that the guy was going through a messy divorce, had lost his previous job and had then been taken on by his friend, the Company Chairman, who was sorry for him. Today, after nearly twenty years of counselling work, I would be able to spot the problem and also know how to deal with it, but in those days I was afraid of him and I kept out of his way.

One really peculiar piece of typically Cancerian behaviour is their ability to live through someone else. This is the sign of the 'dancing mother' who puts her daughter on stage and bends all her psychic energy towards making her a success. Cancerians would die of fright if someone shoved *them* into the limelight but they get a great deal of pleasure from being on the edge of the fun, enjoying it at second hand without having to experience the pain of actually living the part. Some Cancerians behave like babies, expecting their partners and even their children to give them parenting. These people are very romantic and loving. They never forget an anniversary and they can be very sentimental. This is, nevertheless, a cardinal sign, so Cancerians are usually the boss of a relationship, even if this is only really noticeable to those who live with them.

Sexuality

Cancer subjects vary in their level and type of sexuality. Some are very cautious and possibly even frightened of sex. Some wait until well into their thirties before mustering the courage to experiment. These Cancerians are best suited to a warm and caring partner who is not overly sexual but who gives them the love and affection they need without making undue demands or asking for anything more than the basic act of love. These subjects worry about AIDS, sexually-related diseases, hurting themselves or losing valuable bits of their anatomy, all of which stops them relaxing and enjoying sex. If they have planets in the accompanying sign of Gemini, they may take an intellectual approach to the whole thing, preferring to read about it rather than to get in there and live it. This seems to reinforce the Cancerian need to experience life at one step removed. Films and television were invented for these people because they offer sanitised sex without any emotional or physical involvement.

There is another kind of Cancerian who gets off the ground early where sex is concerned and becomes a very good lover as life goes on. This type is happier in a steady relationship than playing the field but can be a little promiscuous if very unhappy. I have been told by various people who live with this type of Cancerian that they make very good lovers. Their sensuality, coupled with their caring nature ensures that they don't hurry the event and also that they please their partners as much as they please themselves. Cancerians are wonderful people to have an affair with because they are so sympathetic.

Other Relationships

Cancerians don't ever detach from anyone they love. Therefore, they will bring their parents, grandparents and cousins three-times-removed, into a relationship. If you love a Cancerian, you must also love his retinue, but he will happily take on someone else's family if needs be. If any form of competitiveness or a real or assumed lowering of the Cancerian's status creeps into a situation, the Cancer subject can become extremely unpleasant. The root of all this is a misplaced feeling of worthlessness, and it takes a good deal of careful handling to deal with such a situation. This complex, moody person can be extremely kind and thoughtful.

As a child the Cancerian is shy, cautious and a non-achiever. During his teenage years, he suddenly wakes up and may do quite well at school but he is haunted by shyness and feelings of inadequacy. Cancer subjects take a long time to grow up and need endless supplies of unqualified love in order to reach any kind of potential. They may return to school as adults when they gain confidence or become interested enough to make the effort. Shyness and fear attach them to their families longer than most, although if they become really unhappy at home, they rush into marriage in order to set up their own family as soon as possible. As parents, Cancerians are superb; but they may be too inclined to cling to their children and reluctant to let them grow up or reluctant to let them be children for long. Cancerians always worry about their children, even when they are grown up, and they love to bring them into their businesses.

Prince William

If we thought Princess Diana was shy, her son's suffering is ten times worse! He not only has the Sun in the introverted sign of Cancer (like Diana) but also the Moon. Although his ascendant is in the outgoing sign of Sagittarius, it is almost at the end of the sign, putting self-conscious Capricorn in pride of place in most of his first house. The Royal line is clearly shown in Prince William's chart by the Sagittarian ascendant and Jupiter in conjunction with his midheaven, plus a busy ninth house, but that other 'Royalty' sign of Leo is absent. Prince William may not relish the thought of being a Royal but he will do a good job of it.

The heavy Jupitarian and Sagittarian feel to this chart suggests that William is an idealist who won't have his feet totally on the ground and while he will do what he must, he will also seek to escape the world he is forced to live in by falling back on his strong imagination. Neptune conjunct his ascendant gives him imagination and a creative, artistic nature. Mars in Libra in the ninth house will make Prince William a natural peacemaker but he may not be quite as soft as he looks. Libra is a cardinal sign and he has Mars, Saturn and powerful Pluto placed there, which suggests that there is a side to him that will always want his own way.

With his Sun, Moon and north node in the seventh house he could find his feet as a result of marriage. A good marriage with a strong partner, perhaps along the lines of that of George the VI and Queen Elizabeth, would be the making and the saving of him. Venus and Mercury in the fifth house add to William's creativity and they also give him a love of children, so a family of his own would bring him joy, just as he and his brother did to his poor mother. The Sun and Moon in the seventh house could make him idolise the memory of his mother and he may always be somewhat in love with her. However, this in addition to Venus in the fifth, may have the effect of making him value and love women in the gentlest possible way. Alternatively, he may find it hard to relate to a well balanced woman and he may attract a dysfunctional one. We will have to wait and see.

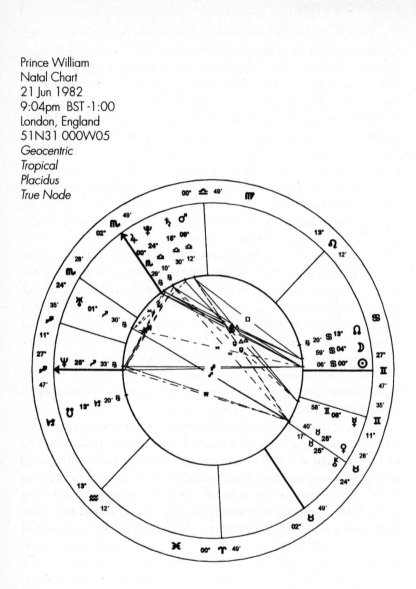

Prince William
Natal Chart
21 Jun 1982
9:04pm BST -1:00
London, England
51N31 000W05
Geocentric
Tropical
Placidus
True Node

Richard Branson

Whenever I see this terrific self-publicist on the television I try to look beyond his big smile, the goatee beard and the thick wavy hair to the real person within those surprisingly small and shrewd eyes. I think this is a classic case of the projection of a personality that may have something very different hidden behind the facade. Richard's Leo ascendant is right out front with his smile, hair and cheerful outgoing exterior but behind this is a twelfth house Cancer Sun that suggests a shrewd business mind that in combination with the twelfth house Mercury in Leo gives him the ability to think strategically. Pluto is rising in Leo just in the first house, suggesting a strong, powerful, ruthless and controlling personality with a desire to make his mark on the world.

With such a large personality and his strong connections to the travel trade (aeroplanes and balloons), we should expect to see the sign of Sagittarius or the ninth house strong in Richard's chart but this is not so. Jupiter is in his eighth house, opposed to his sensitive Moon rising behind Pluto in Virgo. So what do we make out of that? Perhaps the work and the fun it brings (let alone the money), takes Richard's mind off his insecurities and his sensitive nature. A Virgo Moon suggests that he might have had a mother who was both critical and also a bit of a neurotic and that he himself has a fussy and neurotic side to his character. Saturn is also not especially strong in his chart. It is in the second house, making him concentrate on ownership, money and possessions and the only strong aspect Saturn makes is a square to Chiron.

The only real clue to Richard's motivation for fame and acclaim is his well aspected Mars in the third house in Libra. He wants to be known by many people and to encourage others to join in his enterprises. Mars being conjunct Neptune means that he has the will and the drive to make his dreams come true and to make even the hot air of a balloon do his bidding (maybe). Finally, Mars is the ruler of his selfish and ambitious Aries midheaven, so his public face is a happy one (Mars in Libra denoting a pleasant manner). A square from this midheaven to his hidden, shy and secretive twelfth house Cancerian Sun tells us that privately, he may not be as easy and comfortable inside his self-creation of a persona as he would like us to believe.

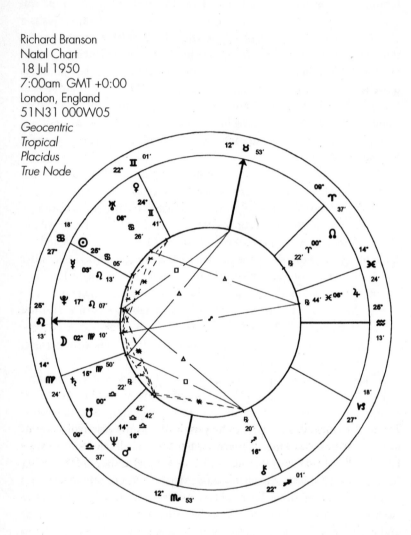

Richard Branson
Natal Chart
18 Jul 1950
7:00am GMT +0:00
London, England
51N31 000W05
Geocentric
Tropical
Placidus
True Node

5

Leo

Land of my fathers, how fair is thy fame,
Entwin'd are proud mem'ries about thy dear name
The lays of thy minstrels, thy warriors' renown
Give honour and grace to thy crown.

Land of my Fathers by James James

Leos are very attached to their traditional backgrounds and Leo is, in some traditions, the sign of the father.

Sign: The Lion

The lion is a magnificent animal who prowls the veldt in search of prey but he isn't above pinching someone else's when he can get it! He looks after his family well but isn't above giving one of his females a nasty cuff or killing a particularly tiresome infant. When he is not feeding or attending to his domestic duties, he sleeps in the shade, grooms his magnificent body and occasionally plays with some of the older males but will chase them out of the group if they become too stroppy. So how does the animal match up to the person? In this case fairly neatly. Leos will work hard for their living, look after their families and enjoy their leisure time. They have a regal reputation but they are not above the odd sneaky or unworthy act, although they don't like to admit to it.

Planet: The Sun

The Sun is not a planet. It is a minor star among a universe of stars. Astrologers call everything in the Solar system a planet for the sake of convenience. The Sun is associated with the ego, the centre of a person's being. It is also linked to royalty and many members of the Royal family have the Sun, Moon or ascendant in Leo. The Sun is associated with success, authority figures, business matters, creativity, children and young people. It is also connected with leisure activities, including games, sports, entertainments, holidays, flirtation and love affairs. In addition, the sun is associated with music through its connection with the god, Apollo.

Gender: Masculine

Masculine subjects are more likely to tackle a problem themselves than to hand it over to someone else to deal with. Masculine sign subjects say what they mean and don't hesitate to push themselves or their children to the forefront.

Element: Fire

Fire sign people are optimists who have faith in the future. They are intuitive, often appearing to jump to conclusions. They are friendly, generous and youthful but can be quick-tempered and irritable. All fire-sign people have the ability to begin large enterprises but may be less able to finish what they start or to handle details.

Quality: Fixed

Fixed sign people like to stay put and remain in the same house, the same job and the same relationship for years. Most fixed sign people will see things through to the end and they find it difficult to make any kind of fresh start. Their opinions may also be fixed.

Some General Characteristics

Most Leonine people are good-hearted, generous, helpful, good to their families, absolutely reliable and dead honest, but a minority are not. I have come across one or two really cold-hearted confidence tricksters born under this sign. These are the sort of people who couldn't be trusted to cross from one side of a room to another without causing someone heartache. To be honest, these types are few and far between and if a Leo does let you down, it will normally be due to either laziness or the simple fact that his circumstances have changed.

Leos are proud people who, except for the rogue type which I mentioned before, have great integrity. To accuse a Leo of stealing or of taking advantage of another is to risk having your head removed from your body. Leos can be irritable and very bad-tempered, but their bad temper usually evaporates quickly. Fatigue and hunger have a bad effect on the Leo temper and Leonine women become extremely irritable and depressed when premenstrual. Leos can panic when under pressure but after the initial dramatics, their brains engage and they cope marvellously. The natural Leonine state is a cheerful, charming youthful one. Leos are realists but they take a view of life which leans towards optimism, so they bounce back from problems and they can always find something good to look forward to. These subjects have very high standards and will often work harder and be far more successful than their colleagues. This earns them a good deal of jealousy and spite from less successful types. Leos instinctively understand that the harder they work, the luckier they are and that a pleasant and co-operative manner will advance their cause better than a sour or hostile one. Leonine people can be awkward, arrogant, insufferable, unco-operative and idle, but they usually reserve this kind of behaviour for people towards whom they feel contemptuous, or occasionally for their own families.

Leos usually make excellent parents, neither smothering their children nor neglecting them. They respect the innate dignity of children and will try to keep the lines of communication open whatever the circumstances. Some Leo fathers can be too loud, bossy and disciplinarian, but they usually mean well and, unless the child is exceptionally timid, he understands this. One fault which I can see in myself is that I try to protect my children from pain and find it almost impossible to step back and watch them experience unpleasant circumstances at first hand.

Leos have a strange work pattern, interspersing periods of frenetic activity with times of utter idleness. Many people watching their Leo spouse or offspring spending three days in a row stretched out on the sofa begin to wonder if there is something seriously wrong with them but as soon as the planets shift around a bit and the Leo's energy level is replenished, he gets up and gets going again.

This is a fixed sign which means that Leos don't like change, preferring to stick to a job or a relationship until it becomes clear that it really has no future for them. One way to shift them is to treat them unfairly over money and to make them repeatedly ask for what is due to them, while another way is to continually change the rules and blame them for the ensuing muddle, or to treat them with contempt. There is no way the Leo will stay in a job if he is not properly paid and if agreements are not met. The surest way to shift a Leo wife is to force her to be dependent, then pay her irregularly and insufficiently whilst, at the same time, being vaguely angry and totally uncommunicative. These methods are, of course, last resorts!

What Does the Leo Look Like?

The typical Leo may be tall or short but is usually good looking and on the plump side. A Leo can be a determined dieter but is never really well or happy when he loses weight. Leo men sweep their hair back from their foreheads while Leonine ladies have lots of thick hair which sweeps and swirls around their faces. Many Leos have a strangely forward facing and direct gaze which can make them look a bit like a chimpanzee, while others have chubby cheeks and twinkling eyes. Leo colouring can range from fair, through red to very dark but the skin is usually pale or sallow and looks far better with a suntan. Some Leos have a characteristically regal stance, walking slowly and in a very erect manner as if they were balancing a crown on their heads, while others prowl like restless lions. Most astrology books accuse Leos of being extravagant, always buying and wearing wonderful clothes. This is simply not so. Leos wear whatever is necessary for their work and then come home, rip the lot off and sit around in an old track suit. Neither do they have the kind of patience which allows them to fiddle with their appearance. They may spend money on a weight-loss pro-gramme once in a while but that's about all. On the other hand, Leos hate buying or wearing rubbish and would rather have a couple of good quality outfits which they wear to death.

Health

Astrology can be a valuable tool for both the diagnosis and treatment of ailments but this involves the use of a full birth chart for each patient. The position of the Sun alone is not enough. However, here are the traditional areas of weakness associated with Leo.

The traditional areas of weakness for Leos are the spine and the heart. Leos like to eat and drink well which leads to obesity and too much choles-terol in the arteries which, coupled with their rather tense nature, can be dangerous for the heart. The way to deal with all this is as obvious as it is boring, because it means that Leos should strive to keep a moderate life-style without too much stress, while following a 'good' diet and taking regular exercise. Unfortunately, few manage to achieve this.

Work and Hobbies

Leos must enjoy their work or they simply won t stick at it, and they need to be among pleasant and cheerful companions. Leos are well organised and they enjoy taking responsibility and have no fear of handling large and costly projects. They can be excellent salespeople if their heart is in their product, but some Leos have to beware of bordering on becoming 'pressure salesmen' or confidence tricksters. Many Leos are drawn to the world of entertainment and can happily use their talents on the stage, in films or on television, while others are happier to work behind the scenes as camera, sound or lighting engineers. Leos can be found working as theatrical agents or happily demonstrating computers at specialist exhibitions. These subjects love to be where it is all happening and to be part of the creative process, but they may not be quite as dramatic and showy as most astrology books seem to imply. Many Leos work on the land, in industry and in education but, although there is no specifically Leonine career, they all need to be clean, comfortable and to feel as if their contribution counts. Many Leos choose to work in glamorous and up-market industries which give them status. Some Leos allow themselves to become bossy and arrogant which does not endear them to their colleagues, while others can be lazy and indifferent. Traditional astrology suggests making or selling jewellery as a Leo career but I haven't really surveyed this one. A quick round-up of my own Leo acquaintances reveals a secretarial administrator, an airline reservations agent, an insurance salesman, the editor of a small publication, one absolute crook, various show-business personalities and an oil and gas engineer. Some Leos are workaholics who pressurise themselves into ever-increasing successes, due to an underlying fear of failure.

Leo hobbies can include almost anything but they would probably be unusual, expensive, glamorous and not involving too many other people. The real 'biggy' here is travel. Some Leos work in the travel or overseas property fields partly in order to take advantage of the opportunities for cheap travel which these jobs provide. Other Leonine pursuits include sports and games of all kinds, some gambling within limits and, of course, love affairs.

Many Leos enjoy working to raise money for charity or, more directly, by helping less fortunate people in some way. For example, when a Leo gets rid of his children's outgrown clothes, he usually tries to ensure that these are utilised by other, less well-off children. The Leo would, however, rather die than dress himself or his children in other people's cast-offs. This may look as if the Leo has a double standard in the way he sees his own needs and the needs of other people. As a fully paid-up member of the Leo tribe, I have to admit that it is just that; a double standard. It is not surprising, therefore, that many young Leonine mothers are excellent dressmakers.

There seems to be a need for change and adventure which can lead Leos to seek out stressful or dangerous hobbies and most of them are instantly at home with computers.

Money, Shopping and Acquisitions

Leos buy everything that their incomes will allow, and often as much as the finance companies will let them borrow too! Many Leos are high earners who will take an extra job or two to cover expenses if their main job is not bringing in enough money. If a Leo is careful with money, one can be sure that there are other factors on his birth chart which keep him in check. These subjects need a spacious and attractive home. They may not keep their homes in the latest style because, like Cancerians, they develop sentimental attachments to their belongings and surroundings.

For much the same reason they prefer to buy a house and then stay in it for many years, even when their families have flown the coop and left them with more space than they really need. If the Leo can acquire land, further property, a holiday apartment, a boat or two and even an aeroplane, they'll do so. Everything which enhances their life and makes for fun, as well as supreme comfort, is of interest to them. Leos believe that money is meant to circulate, to be spent and to be enjoyed. There is no Leo on the face of the earth who will put up with cramped conditions, cold or discomfort for one moment longer than is absolutely necessary. The typical Leo's home is well-proportioned and comfortable but not necessarily filled with the latest goods or gadgets. Leos don't set out to impress their neighbours with their wealth or their possessions but, if the neighbours happen to be impressed, the Leo won't mind one bit.

A nice car is a must for most Leos. Some of them prefer a sporty high-performance vehicle, while others prefer a large, expensive and well-appointed saloon. Whatever car the Leo chooses, you can bet that it is impressive and definitely beyond his means. Leo snobbery ensures that their children attend the best possible schools and that everything they do or have is the best that is available. As far as holidays are concerned, the Leo would rather not travel than to do so in discomfort. Leos are not particularly materialistic in the sense of deriving security from money and possessions but they must have good music, good food, a good home and a good life.

Living with Leo

Leos are relaters so they rarely live alone and are very attached to all members of their families and also to any pets. Leos grow up needing a lot of love, understanding and approval. They need to feel that they count, both out in the world and in their homes. On the whole, these people are not that hard to live with, although they do have some peculiarities which can irritate others. Leos are fussy and they have high personal standards which they may seek to impose on others. They are also snobs. My Leo daughter won't shop in certain areas because she doesn't like the class of clientele who frequent the shops! This behaviour doesn't seem a bit strange to a Leo. Their homes must be well-run and very comfortable but they are not excessively tidy, as they prefer a home to be a home rather than a shop window. One rather odd fact that I have come across is that all Leos have a place where they leave notes telling themselves what they need to do over the next few days. When entertaining, they will do so lavishly and in style. Leos can be very ambitious, both for themselves and their families, and therefore they expect their partners to get on in life. These subjects are fairly hard workers, especially when they have their minds set on some special ambition. They like their jobs, homes, families and children to have a status and standing in the community and they derive great pride from this. Leonine subjects expect their partners and, indeed, other members of their families to put their backs into work too.

Leos are loyal and very warm-hearted, sociable, good to their friends and very supportive of all members of their families. They will bend over backwards to help a partner and their children are never short-changed when it comes to love, help and advice. Being members of a fixed sign, Leos don't chop and change readily. They will stay in a relationship even when it isn't working and divorce is really a last resort. If there is any chance that they might lose their children as a result of a divorce, they simply won't go through with it. Leonine subjects can be very irritable at times; they take things to heart and blame themselves when things go wrong. They may also blame others but they really do feel that they have let *themselves* down when mistakes occur. Leos don't sulk or brood as a rule and, if they are angry or unhappy, they prefer to talk things over or even have a row, rather than cope with their problems silently or inwardly. Some psychic sense tells them that their sensitive cardiac systems cannot cope with a lot of inward fuming. These subjects can be very self-absorbed and self-centred, becoming totally involved with their own lives and their own problems and this sometimes makes their partners feel like observers of the scene rather than full participants in the relationship. They take life, and themselves, very seriously and they can be very bitter and unforgiving of those who use or hurt them. Leo loyalty makes them rush to the defence of those whom they love but they must be able to respect their partners or they can sink into sarcastic and contemptuous behaviour towards them.

Male Leos can be very demanding, expecting their wives to be superwoman but, on the whole, as long as they can run their homes smoothly, with the addition of paid help if necessary, they won't grumble too much. It is possible to talk to these subjects and get them to see reason, so most problems can be worked out. Leos don't play games in relationships, they are honest and they usually mean what they say. These subjects can be somewhat eccentric and they do appear to march down their own road, even if this is completely different from everyone else's. They are more concerned about their own measurement of their worth than other people's opinions. Like all fire signs, Leos need freedom. They don't appreciate being told what time they should be home and they won't stand for being given the third degree if they arrive late. It is unlikely that they are up to anything wrong anyway because they usually get held up by people who buttonhole them in order to talk to them. Leos are fairly careful with money, hating to be in debt but they are never mean to others. They won't sponge off others and they are embarrassed by those who see sponging as a legitimate practice. Pride can be a Leo's downfall and, although they can be teased a little, they won't be ridiculed. If they find themselves with a competitive partner, the kind who loves to have conversations in front of others about whose job is more important, they will just walk away. Leo dignity is sacrosanct and they never forget a hurt or an insult. As a Leo myself, I can absolutely guarantee that nobody outside of my immediate family is ever likely to see me cry, and the chances are that the family won't see much of this phenomenon either. Leo women don't make a sound when giving birth but they scream the hospital down after the event if they find themselves and their infant are not being properly treated by the staff! Some Leos are quite lazy, preferring to watch TV than to do anything useful but most are good steady workers if for no other reason than because they like a good lifestyle. Some Leo men and even a few women can become so immersed in their work that they neglect their partners and lose them as a result.

Sexuality

Like all fire signs, Leos are strongly sexed but they are also fussy about sex, and prefer to do without altogether than to get tied up with the wrong person or to feel in any way uncomfortable about it. Most Leos are very clean and tidy and cannot stand the idea of making love with a dirty person or in dirty surroundings. They are not particularly excited by the idea of making love in strange places or anywhere they are likely to be discovered or compromised. It is the famous Leo need for dignity which is at work here because they hate the thought of looking foolish. They are able to stay in a marriage which doesn't work on a sexual level but this can make them vulnerable and prone to extra-marital affairs. Most of all, Leos need to play in an affectionate and loving manner. These subjects are very sensual, they love to play with their partner's hair and to touch and be touched in a non-sexual manner. Even a good tickling session is part of the game to them. However, they love the feelings which surround the sex act as much as the sex itself. Leos, almost as much as Taureans and Librans, can extend sex play for as long as it amuses them and their partners, both before and after completing the sexual act as such.

Other Relationships

Leos will try to keep on good terms with the more distant members of their families and they make strenuous efforts to get on with in-laws, cousins and neighbours. They don't like family rows and they usually take a fairly responsible attitude to everyone around them. If, however, a family member persists in insulting them or harping on about their faults, they will drop them completely and forever. They won't even turn up to the offending relative's funeral. Leos are sociable and friendly and they tend to keep their friends for many years, valuing their friendship almost as much as they value their relationships. Even ex-lovers and previous marriage partners are often kept as friends wherever possible. Many Leos are good letter-writers, keeping in touch with distant friends and relatives over the years, visiting them whenever possible.

Most of all Leos love and value their children. They treat them with dignity and allow them their independence but even when their children are grown up with families of their own, they try to keep a close relationship with them. While their children are small, Leos try to give them all that they need but they may be too pushy and demanding, expecting them to live up to standards which are hard to meet. If their children show any kind of talent, the Leo parent will do everything in his power to foster this and he is never jealous of a successful child.

As children, Leos can be disappointing to their parents. This is because they seem to fall short of their parents' educational expectations and are more inclined to play than to study hard. Leos often make up for this later in life by going back into education or working hard at climbing the promotional ladder. Leonine children are affectionate and loving and even quite generous towards their siblings, although they can be fierce rivals in the race for their parents' love and for status both within and outside the family. If a school teacher ridicules a Leo child, the child will switch off and do as little as possible for that teacher. This can be a tragedy because the child can miss out on a particular school subject as a result. In all things, and at all ages and stages of life, Leos need to be treated with fairness and respect. Don't take a Leo child to a zoo; he can't bear to see animals in a prison!

Madonna

Madonna is an internationally acclaimed singer, dancer and film star who is known for her outrageous clothes and her overtly sexual image. I think that 'image' is the operative word in this case because her chart suggests that, in reality, she is nothing like her public persona. It is interesting to note that her rising sign is shy, modest and hard-working Virgo because this is the polar opposite of the image she portrays. There are many occasions when Astrology throws up a polar opposite and this is one of them. My guess is that Madonna is well-organised, extremely hard-working, totally professional and rather calculating in all that she does and that her solid, reliable and sensible behaviour has as much to do with her success as her talent. Madonna has the Sun, Uranus and Venus in the glamorous sign of Leo but the Sun and Uranus are in the twelfth house of mystery and illusion. This suggests that she uses her in-built imaginative talents to create an illusion. Her Neptune, which is the planet associated with illusion generally and film and music specifically, is in the strongly sexual sign of Scorpio and the third house of communications. This placement also helps her to act out and to project a sexy image. Venus on the cusp of Cancer and Leo in the eleventh house denote powerful and influential friends who can help her in her career aspirations, while Mars in Taurus gives her a capacity for hard work and the ability to finish whatever she starts, however difficult this may be.

The square aspect between Mars in Taurus and the Sun in Leo endow Madonna with courage and maybe even a touch of recklessness. Saturn in

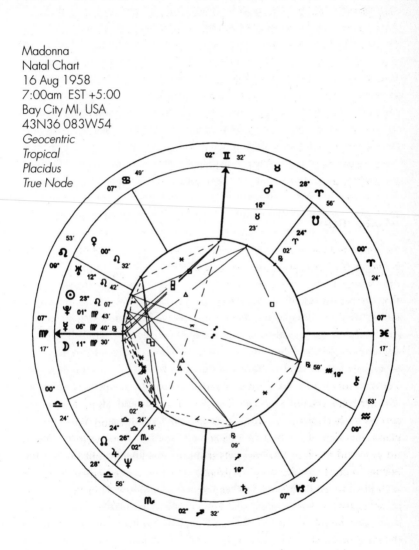

Madonna
Natal Chart
16 Aug 1958
7:00am EST +5:00
Bay City MI, USA
43N36 083W54
Geocentric
Tropical
Placidus
True Node

outgoing Sagittarius is in excellent aspect to her Leo planets and this gives her the kind of self-discipline needed for such a physically demanding life. Madonna's personal life may not be easy for her to get right. This is partly because her seventh house is in Pisces, making it hard for her to pick the right partner. Madonna must beware of being used by others. Virgo rising and Saturn in the fourth suggest a very difficult childhood and a lack of confidence in her own value as a person. Indeed a good deal of her success may be due to an endless search for self-esteem and confidence. This set-up also signifies very demanding parents and, with Neptune in the third, the probability of peculiar and manipulative siblings. The Moon being close to the ascendant, however, suggests that she will always have the love and respect of the public and will do much to influence the ideas and the fashion concepts of the younger generation. The emphasis on fire and earth signs in Madonna's chart gives her the talent and enthusiasm to be a performer, coupled with her self-discipline and her determination to cope. Five planets in fixed signs give her the endurance and resilience to carry on, while six planets in cadent houses allow her to act out any part she cares to play.

Robert Redford

Robert Redford is a fabulously successful actor who has steered his career with great care through the rapids of the crazy Hollywood system. Robert is a dedicated sportsman who went through college on a baseball scholarship. Robert Redford's Sun in Leo in the sixth house suggests that he pays a great deal of attention to details and does everything very thoroughly. This is emphasised by the presence of four planets in Virgo which are all in the sixth house along with his Leo Sun. Robert's Sun and Mars in Leo give him his wonderful charismatic film personality and his good looks but, in reality, his chart is far more Virgoan than Leonine. Robert's ascendant is Pisces which, on the one hand, gives him his imaginative flair but, on the other hand, signifies his need for privacy. The presence of Saturn in Pisces close to the ascendant suggests that Robert's childhood was far from easy. He must have felt very lonely at times and also distrustful of those upon whom he should have been able to rely. This Saturn placement denotes great concentration and the ability to cope with craftwork of a detailed and disciplined type as is often found in the horoscopes of writers and other creative people.

So what about his acting career? Well, Virgo is a sign which is very much associated with acting, denoting the kind of self-control which allows someone to project whatever image they want, even if it is completely at odds

Robert Redford
Natal Chart
18 Aug 1936
20:02am PST +8:00
Santa Monica, CA
34N01 118W29
Geocentric
Tropical
Placidus
True Node

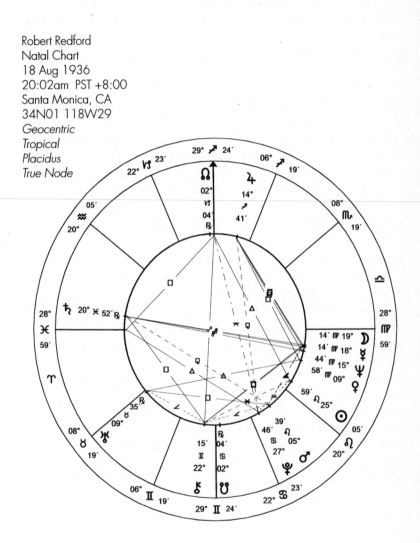

with what they are feeling inside. His Piscean ascendant also helps him to produce an image or play a part, and the presence of Mars in Leo and Pluto in Cancer, both in the glamorous, ritzy, artistic fifth house give him the looks and intensity to really shine on the screen.

Robert Redford's sporting ability is shown by Jupiter high up in his chart in its own sign of Sagittarius and its own house, the ninth. This Jupiter placement denotes a broad-minded, international outlook and a strong inner philosophy of life. This, along with his Piscean ascendant and the Virgoan Stellium, suggests that Robert is interested in maintaining the health of this planet and the plants and animals which inhabit it. Uranus in the second house suggests great ups and downs in connection with finances and possessions, in addition to the opportunity to earn money in original and unusual ways. Robert's chart has five planets in earth signs, three in fire, two in water but none in air signs. This suggests that he is most comfortable communicating to others through indirect methods, such as his ability to play sports or to act. As a person, he is probably very shy and may be tense, fussy, faddy and nervous, although he is probably helped by having an excellent sense of humour.

This sense of tension could manifest itself in health problems such as eczema or a 'funny' tummy, or fears and phobias of many kinds. Indeed, it is well-known that Robert suffers from claustrophobia. Robert's emphasis on the cadent houses emphasises his great talent and the number of planets in fixed signs suggests that he has the determination and tenacity to make it work for him.

6

Virgo

Flow gently, sweet Afton, among thy green braes;
Flow gently, I'll sing thee a song in thy praise;
My Mary's asleep by thy murmuring stream,
Flow gently, sweet Afton, disturb not her dream.

Flow Gently, Sweet Afton
by James Spilman with words by Robert Burns

A suitably rural song for gentle Virgo.

Sign: The Virgin

The virgin is, to some, a young, innocent, untouched girl, and a failed or unfulfilled woman to others. To the religious, she is the mother of Jesus and to the materialistic, a handsome profit. In medieval folklore the signs of the zodiac were closely linked to the seasons, therefore Virgo is associated with the all-important harvest. Virgoan people are sensitive, hard-working and rather cool and, as far as I can discern, quite unconnected to many of the ideas which are traditionally associated with the sign.

Planet: Mercury

Virgo's planet is Mercury which rules communications of all kinds, in addition to health, medicine and magic. All of these concepts, even in the ancient world, represented specialised knowledge and the ability to study, sift ideas and to analyse.

Gender: Feminine

Feminine subjects are more likely to wait and worry when trouble strikes, rather than to act for action's sake. Feminine sign subjects are quiet and retiring, they are more likely to be unsure of themselves and are conditioned to nurture and protect rather than to rush in and destroy.

Element: Earth

Earth sign people are careful, sensible, tenacious, reliable and conventional. They hate to give up on anything, and may be materialistic. These people are mature in outlook but may be fussy and slow when tackling tasks and they can be selfish.

Quality: Mutable

This word may seem strange to you but if you think of transmute, commute or mutate you will see that it concerns moving something from one place to another or one state to another. Mutable people, therefore, are flexible in their attitude, disliking too much routine and needing a change. They may take up too many interests, finding it difficult to finish any of them. However, they are able to fit into most situations and to make themselves comfortable even when permanently on the move.

Some General Characteristics

Virgoans are not usually good at dealing with strangers. They are shy, suspicious and unsure of how to act or react. They convey this discomfort to others and may, therefore, present a hostile or even surly front upon first acquaintance. Some Virgoans learn how to present themselves in a pleasant and welcoming manner but the coolness and suspicion are still there just below the surface, hidden from the masses, but easily detectable to those with sensitive antennae. Once they have established that the stranger is not going to borrow money from them, laugh at them or bore them to tears, Virgos can become excellent and very animated company.

Virgoans are very kind and can be a soft touch to less scrupulous types. They want to be liked and, even more importantly, to be respected. They are very sensitive, easily hurt and easily defeated or turned from their purpose. This tendency is, thankfully, often modified by the presence of planets in stronger, more determined signs. They are the specialists of the zodiac, possessing a great deal of knowledge about their own particular subject but are fascinated by all forms of knowledge and they take an interest in everything around them. Virgoans are modest and retiring, so they don't care to blow their own trumpets or to push themselves to the forefront. However, they won't tolerate being made to look foolish. Being clever and articulate, they can react in a very spiteful manner when their feelings are hurt. Many Virgoans have a great deal in common with Geminians because the planet Mercury rules both of these signs. Virgos can be as adept in the business of communicating information as Geminis, but the difference is that Virgos will usually keep within their own subject when doing so. Therefore, Virgos make excellent teachers, specialist broadcasters and sports, business or fashion reporters. These people like to help others and love to feel that their contribution to the betterment of the lives of others really makes a difference, thus many Virgoans choose to work in the field of medicine, social work or politics.

The chances are that the Virgoan's childhood was nothing to write home about. It seems that whenever this sign is prominent in a chart, the parents probably went through the motions of caring for the child but really didn't love him or imbue him with much self-confidence or self-respect. The parents may have been repressive or over-disciplinarian, with far too much emphasis on keeping up at school, keeping clothes and shoes clean and being seen and not heard. Virgoan children don't need much discipline because they respond very quickly to love and also to reasoned argument and they want their parents to love them and to approve of them. Unfortunately, they find themselves spending too much time staring at their shoes in shame while being berated for some totally unimportant minor infringement of parental rules. In childhood at least, this sign seems to have an extremely difficult karma.

Virgoans are modest and retiring and they don't like to make a display of themselves in front of others, so they are easily embarrassed. They frequently have specialised knowledge and skills which are highly developed because they concentrate on their chosen subjects and take a deeply professional and responsible attitude to all that they do. It sometimes takes a while before this knowledge and ability becomes apparent to others because they tend to hide their light under a bushel. Work is important to Virgoans and they need a measure of status within their job and also need to be acknowledged as experts within their field. If they have this status and they feel secure in their work, then they are happy and comfortable, but when uncertainty strikes or when they have to fight for their rights they lose confidence and become dejected. Whatever task a Virgoan tackles, he does it in the best way possible and likes to think that he is fulfilling his duties to the best of his abilities. He is quick, intelligent and thorough and deserves to have his efforts recognised by his superiors. The fact is that the opposite often happens and he is made use of, taken for granted and not accorded the respect which he deserves. This can turn him very sour and make him extremely tetchy and difficult, as we shall see later.

It is all too easy for Virgos to be sarcastic and hurtful to others and to undervalue their efforts in much the same way as they feel that their own efforts have been undervalued. Indeed, many Virgos have quite hard exteriors but the prevailing Virgoan nature is to be kindly and thoughtful to others and to have impeccable manners.

What Does the Virgoan Look Like?

Virgos often have quite good hair and, in common with the other earth signs of Taurus and Capricorn, males tend to keep most of it until well into old age. Virgoans look old for their age when young but they seem to stop ageing somewhere in their mid-forties and remain much the same for the next thirty years or so. Most astrology books talk about a protruding tummy and, although usually slim, they often do have a slightly bulging stomach.

Virgos have an intelligent and lively look about them which becomes very animated when they are talking on their favourite subjects. The two most common Virgo features are a strong jaw bone with a rather protruding chin and also a widow's peak. Some Virgos suffer from acne when young but most have excellent skin and a very good bone structure which makes them highly photogenic.

Health

Astrology can be a valuable tool for both the diagnosis and treatment of ailments, but this involves the use of a full birth chart for each patient. The position of the Sun alone is not enough. However, here are the traditional areas of weakness associated with Virgo.

Weak spots are the nervous system, bowels and skin. Virgos can suffer from allergies such as hay fever, eczema, asthma and stomach ailments such as colitis and ulcers. These subjects are usually very health-conscious and strive to look after themselves. However, Virgos should try not to over-analyse their problems and they should treat themselves to some gentle but regular exercise.

Work and Hobbies

Virgos like to be of service, both to the community in general and to their superiors at work, but they need to be appreciated and approved of in order to be happy in their work. They are probably better off as part of a team than as the boss of any organisation. As a boss, they can be pernickity and demanding towards those under them. Virgos have an aptitude for any kind of communications work and, therefore, can be found in the media, as secretaries, telephonists and drivers. These subjects like to help humanity and they also love to teach, so many of them take up teaching either as a main career or as a hobby. Anything which involves sorting or analysing is right up most Virgoans' street, therefore accountancy, systems analysis, computing or record keeping and even marketing jobs will suit them. Many Virgoans are attracted to the world of medicine in all its forms and thus can be found working in hospitals, as alternative health practitioners or therapists of all kinds. Their sympathy, kindness and ability to listen carefully make them excellent counsellors and advisors. Many Virgoans like to follow an unchanging routine in an organisation which has a well-defined structure.

Other Virgos are attracted to jobs which give them a bit of variety and a chance to express themselves. The sign of Virgo is associated with the harvest, so the idea of growing and preparing food, especially nutritious food, appeals to them. Virgos like travelling and will often turn their experiences to good advantage by writing both about their travels and the people they meet along the way. One profession which is peculiarly Virgoan is that of acting. It seems that Virgos can shake off their shyness and inhibitions as soon as they don the mask of another character, and they seem to have a real knack of making their portrayals realistic.

There is a fairly large segment of the Virgo community who seem to defy the usual interpretations of this sign's nature. For one thing, these people can be extremely untidy in some or all areas of their lives. Some are tidy at home but keep their papers in a muddle, while others do the reverse. Some *appear* to live in apple-pie order but shove all the mess into cupboards where it cannot be seen. Others are simply completely disorganised. The reason for this phenomenon is the theory of 'polarity' in which the very characteristic for which a sign is known is polarised so that the person displays completely opposite traits and habits.

Another Virgoan polarisation is laziness. There are many Virgos who, while having very active minds, don't actually get down to doing much of anything. Yet another anomaly is the type of Virgo who is attracted to big business and who may be a tough, heartless go-getter who neglects his family and makes everyone else's life a misery. In fact, this last one is not such an anomaly because obsessional workaholism is a very Virgo trait, although it is unusual for a Virgoan to have the confidence or the strength of character to become a mogul or a tycoon. The motivation behind the go-getter Virgo is a sneaking feeling of worthlessness or a fear of losing what they have gained.

Typical spare-time activities might include helping out in a café, making cakes for pleasure, running a small library or acting as secretary to a committee. Many Virgoans are keen on sports, either as a spectator or as a participant, and they will follow their team's progress with great dedication. A quick round-up of those Virgoans whom I know reveals Pete Murray, the famous broadcaster who was once an actor, a top chef, an accountant, a teacher and a vet.

Money, Shopping and Acquisitions

Virgos are fairly careful types who don't like spending money unnecessarily. They are quite fussy, however, and don t care to live in dirty, cramped or run-down circumstances. Virgoans are very clever at making and mending and will repair or renovate whenever they can. These subjects don't seek an ostentatious or glamorous lifestyle, but they may be more interested in the quality of life than the quantity of it. Being neither high earners nor big spenders, Virgos are thrifty, modest in their requirements and sensible. Being an earth sign, they often enjoy having a bit of land or a garden to work in and they will grow good things to eat whenever possible. Many Virgos work from home, either on a part-time basis or as part of their normal job, so a study or room where they can think is much appreciated. Virgos are sensible with money, making sure that they have enough behind them for times of trouble or to help their families out if they need it. They don't throw money around and, although charitable, don't give it away unnecessarily either.

Virgo is a mercurial sign which suggests that they can be restless and that they need a decent and reliable vehicle at hand. Many Virgos own subsidiary vehicles such as a small van or a bicycle in addition to a car. Some Virgos enjoy travelling, especially when this offers an opportunity to gain new knowledge. Virgos spend money on books, magazines, newspapers, computers, television and radio equipment and then more books. Some Virgoans are keen on gadgetry and many collect the kind of tools and equipment associated with craft work or even office work. They enjoy visiting the cinema and theatre, the ballet or opera or local sporting events. Some are avid followers of sports, while others are involved with local dramatics and dancing or exercise classes. Some Virgos spend a good deal of money on special kinds of foodstuffs or alternative remedies.

Living with Virgo

Virgos can be good family members but they can also be very difficult to live with. The two main problems are their lack of confidence and their fussiness. Unless the Virgo can find a partner who is prepared to help them get over their doubts and fears and who can also go along with their 'fiddle-faddling', they may end up out on their ear. My friend, Marion, is an expert on Virgos. She likes them, really relates to them and has had a number of Virgo man-friends in her life. Marion herself is a Pisces, but she is very, very houseproud, a good cook and a wonderful friend. These are all very Virgoan traits, so it's no wonder that she feels comfortable with these types. Virgoans are very responsible family members, taking care of their partners and their children even if the relationship breaks up. Many Virgos marry more than once, possibly because it takes the experience of a couple of serious relationships before they can relax enough to become livable with. Many Virgoans make better friends than marriage partners because they cannot take too much of the day-in, day-out demands of a serious and committed relationship, and they can be far too critical.

Virgos are kind and this kindness seems to lead them to attract a fairly demanding type of partner. Their constant attempts to fulfil these demands can wear them out in the same way that a sparrow can be worn out by an adopted cuckoo. These subjects are quite easily bored by those with whom they have to live and, in many respects, are happier when working than when trying to deal with relationship matters. Most Virgos are hard workers who define themselves by what they do rather than what they are. Some of these subjects duck out of family or relationship problems by trying to make themselves indispensable at work. Many Virgoans are so genuinely devoted to their work that this puts an unbearable strain on their relationships. Some Virgos can be intellectual snobs, choosing their friends from among those who reflect their cultural or intellectual status. Others may choose to 'marry beneath them' so that they can look down contemptuously on their partners. Virgoans don't leave jobs half done and they are not sloppy in their approach, so their partners can be sure of good meals and a well-kept home and garden. Some Virgoans are highly intellectual and fairly incompetent at 'hands-on' household jobs while others are highly dexterous, incredibly practical and capable around the home and far less tense, intellectual and difficult to live with.

Virgos can be surprisingly untidy and they may not like their own particular corner of the house or their personal papers to be cleared up or disturbed. A Virgoan household may be filled with interesting friends and relatives, because they love nothing better than to chat. Virgoans are wizard at helping others or giving excellent advice, however they don't like people to overstay their welcome. These subjects are not vain or especially demanding but they like to have things just so and can make a terrible fuss about trivial matters. Virgoans can be quite irritable, partly because they find it difficult to stand up to people. This means that they may bring their work problems home and thus become quite tetchy to live with. They can be perfectionists who expect too much of themselves and far too much of everyone around them too.

Virgo is an earth sign which gives them common sense, practicality and a love of the good things of life. Although fairly careful with money, they are not mean and they will do all that they can for their families. Virgo men are very supportive of working wives and they are often happy to occupy themselves with some of the housework. This is partly due to a reasonable attitude and partly due to their hatred of sitting still and doing nothing. These subjects can be seen at their best when one of their loved ones is ill because they make excellent nurses. However, when they themselves are ill, they can be quite demanding and some Virgoans are permanent hypochondriacs. Not all Virgoans bother with relationships: after experiencing an early failure, many of them go on to live alone and look after themselves.

Sexuality

Virgos are surprisingly strongly sexed, probably because this is an earth sign. They are also curious and may get into sexual experimentation fairly early in life. If they miss out on this, they are likely to go in for 'adventures' later in life, either after a longstanding partnership breaks up or even while it is still in operation. Virgoans of both sexes quite like to be shown what to do in bed because they sometimes find it difficult to take responsibility for their own sexuality. The rulership of their sign by the Planet Mercury suggests that they are willing to live out their fantasies and, being kind and fair-minded, they will help their lovers to live out their fantasies too. Virgos don't like making love with unwashed people or in dirty places, because their sensuality demands a certain amount of comfort. They have an almost theatrical sense of 'scene' which suggests that they enjoy lovemaking in a pleasant, perhaps even specially arranged and decorated area. Virgoans are fussy about their partner's looks and don't much care for someone who is obese or who doesn't look after him or herself. Virgos find sex easy but affectionate behaviour quite difficult, probably due to the lack of cuddling or play in their own childhood.

Other Relationships

Being very dutiful, Virgos will try their best to do the right thing by a whole variety of family members. However, they can't take too much of a good thing and, therefore, prefer to keep their visits to or from relatives very short. However, these subjects love to entertain and will happily Provide food and drink on a special occasion, and then more happily say goodbye to them at the end of the visit. Virgoans will help out their sisters and brothers when necessary and will strive to keep in touch with them over the long periods of time and over great distances. They also tend to keep in touch with friends, even those who move out of the country. Their favourite relationships are probably the ones which they can conduct on the telephone but, surprisingly enough, they are not good letter writers.

As children, Virgos are shy and diffident and easily hurt. They are easily shamed and seem to carry the burden of the guilt of the whole world on their shoulders. They may suffer quite a bit at school and can be bullied by other pupils or teachers, or both. They seem to make a very bad karmic choice of parents, having fathers whom they love but who are distant and rather demanding. Their mothers may be far more interested in keeping up appearances and fussing about silly things than loving and caring for the Virgo child. Some Virgoans have mothers who are so incapable of looking after their children that they find ways of opting out of motherhood altogether. These children are expected to excel, but their fears, phobias and lack of self-esteem makes it hard for them to do so, while other children and even the parents of other children may be jealous of their obvious intelligence. Many Virgoan children grow up with a sense of abandonment.

As parents, Virgoans try not to recreate the mistakes of their own childhood. However, because they were not shown much real affection themselves, they find it hard to relate properly to their own children and may, therefore, pass on the silly demands for scholastic performance and perfect behaviour which made their own childhood so intolerable. If the

Virgoan finds his children difficult to understand or to deal with, or if his marriage breaks up, he may physically distance himself from them.

Prince Harry

At the time of writing this piece, we hear from the press that Prince Harry is reputed to be fun-loving and outgoing and far more suited to the rough and tumble of being a modern Royal than his brother, William. Well, as an astrologer it is hard to see where all this cheeky, outgoing behaviour is coming from. Harry has his Sun and Mercury in Virgo and true enough, this endows him with a terrific sense of humour but it can also make him feel put upon and victimised by the world that he lives in. With Capricorn rising, one would assume that this is a very serious young man who is shy and easily embarrassed. However, there are a few other factors to be taken into account.

Harry has only one planet below the horizon and that is the Moon in Taurus. Chiron is also below the horizon in the fifth house but Chiron is a Centaur (a kind of oversized asteroid). Such a dearth of planets below the horizon and a corresponding glut of them at the top of the chart suggest a public rather than a private lifestyle. Harry's Saturn is close to his midheaven in Scorpio and Pluto is close by in the ninth house also in Scorpio. This placement endows a feeling of destiny and a desire to leave the world a better place for his having been part of it. With the Sun, Venus and Mercury in the eighth, this whole chart suggests that Harry will be a person who thinks things through. His feelings will run very deeply indeed. The Scorpionic nature of the chart suggests that he will take his mother's death very badly and this will colour his attitude to life for many years to come. Mars and Uranus in the eleventh house in Sagittarius suggest that sports, friendships and group activities of all kinds will attract Prince Harry. The service life that many of his relatives have enjoyed will appeal to him and he could make a great success of himself and have a very happy life if he enters the Navy.

Jupiter in Capricorn and Neptune in Sagittarius the twelfth house suggest that he will develop a mystical streak and an interest in alternative and spiritual matters later in life. This is not surprising, as both Prince Charles and Princess Diana were interested in such things and the whole of the Royal family are keen on homeopathy. Prince Harry's Moon in the fourth house in Taurus show that he will love beautiful and sensual things such as flowers, music and good food. He will strive to make a comfortable and stable home for himself and his future family.

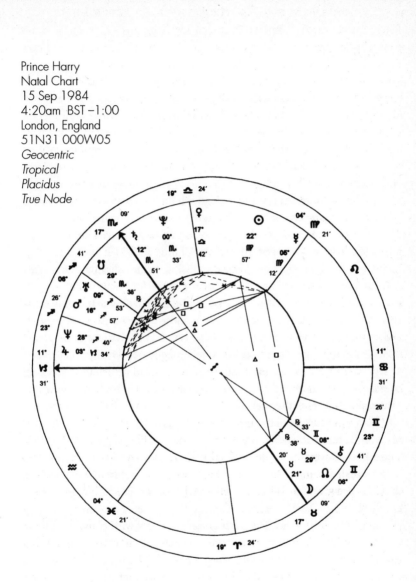

Prince Harry
Natal Chart
15 Sep 1984
4:20am BST −1:00
London, England
51N31 000W05
Geocentric
Tropical
Placidus
True Node

Peter Sellers

Peter Sellers was well known and well-loved for his Goon Show radio programmes, his films and even his records. Which Londoner could ever forget 'Balham, Gateway to the South'? We also marvelled at his wonderful portrayals of different types of people, sometimes as many as half a dozen all in the same film. Less well known, perhaps, was the fact that Peter was also a knowledgeable astrologer. Peter's Sun was in a close conjunction with Mars in the first house in Virgo, close to his Virgo ascendant. I have read that Peter Sellers didn't give a damn for anyone else's opinion of him or of his actions. I have met a number of other people with Sun/Mars conjunctions and they didn't give a 'monkey's' for anyone else's opinion either. This conjunction is explosive enough on its own but, being opposed by Uranus, it is positively electric. Virgoans are clever at the best of times and the heavy emphasis on this sign denotes a fast and tricky mind and a talent for writing. The opposition from Uranus adds brilliance and originality, but it might also have been responsible for his slightly unbalanced attitude to life. Mercury and Neptune in the twelfth house in Leo suggest immense creativity and these planets are also aspected by that highly artistic Uranus in Pisces. The Moon in Taurus, close to the midheaven, suggests a love of music and a creative career. Michel Gauquelin's theories suggested that the Moon in the ninth house denoted imaginative writing ability. Peter Sellers could have been a successful novelist instead of being a successful comic actor. However, Virgoans do like to act, possibly because they are so ill at ease when being themselves. They are often also excellent mimics.

Saturn in Scorpio, in the third house, tells us that Peter worked hard at his craft. Peter's Saturn is rather well aspected by Pluto and Jupiter, which suggests that every time he made the effort, the rewards rolled in. The opposition of Jupiter and Pluto, in Cancer and Capricorn, sometimes shows insensitivity in close personal relationships. Peter's seventh house Uranus is indicative of a person who searches for new experiences through relationships with others. His chart is well balanced with planets in all the elements although, oddly enough, the element of air is the weakest and earth the strongest. One would have expected this to be the other way round. Four planets in fixed signs, along with all that earth, gave him a stubborn determination to work and to make his work pay, while the four planets in cadent houses gave him the motivation to make it happen.

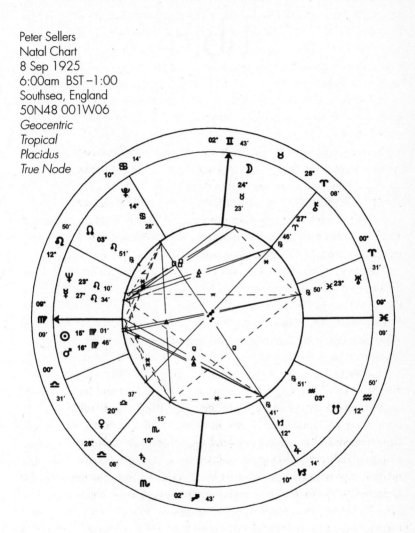

Peter Sellers
Natal Chart
8 Sep 1925
6:00am BST −1:00
Southsea, England
50N48 001W06
Geocentric
Tropical
Placidus
True Node

7

Libra

Then I will stay with you for ever,
If you will not be unkind.
Madam, I have vowed to love you;
Would you have me change my mind?
O No John! No John! No John! No!

O No John!, a Somerset folk song,
collected and arranged by Cecil J. Sharp

A suitably charming and indecisive song for Libra.

Sign: The Scales

This is the only sign which has an inanimate object as its symbol. Scales are impartial, judgemental, logical and lacking in human or animal emotion. So how do Librans measure up – or down – to this cool image? Old-fashioned scales used to have two dishes hung on a yoke, whereas modern ones may either work on the same principle or may have only one dish and a means of measuring what is placed on it. Either way, the scales have two inseparable parts. Do Librans therefore spend their lives searching for their other halves? The fact is that Librans are not the most emotional of people, depending far more upon logic than feelings. This doesn't rob them of intuition, however, and their interest in people gives them at least some understanding of the human condition.

Planet: Venus

Venus is traditionally associated with love but it is also linked to harmonious relationships of all kinds. This planet rules personal possessions such as land, property, goods and the money in one's bank account. Venus is concerned with pleasure in all its forms, such as the enjoyment of music and dancing, the arts, food and drink and good company. By being associated with open relationships, it tells us something about marriage (or similar open relationships), close friendships and even rivals and enemies.

Gender: Masculine

Masculine subjects are more likely to tackle a problem themselves than to hand it over to someone else to deal with. Masculine sign subjects say what they mean and don't hesitate to push themselves or their children to the forefront.

Element: Air

This is the least emotional of all the elements, relying on knowledge and logic to work things out. Air subjects are intelligent, interested in everything and able to pick up and pass on knowledge as a result of being in the swim and among people. Too much emotion exhausts them and too much routine bores them.

Quality: Cardinal

If you see cardinality as a forceful attitude to life, then Libra does not seem to fit the bill. The truth is that Librans will not endure much without finding a way out of the problem or even wandering off in search of a new way of life. They are not as self-sacrificing or as interested in the happiness of others as they would like to have us believe.

Some General Characteristics

Librans are pleasant. They are good company at a party, fun to be with and great to chat to. They appear to have an open, non-hostile, unsuspicious manner and make each person to whom they talk feel special. Unfortunately, if you run into these attractive people again at a later date or in another place they will probably have completely forgotten you. All the air signs tend to forget the many people they chat with but Librans are the most forgetful of all. Librans look soft, but this is a cardinal sign, which means that they are fundamentally tough and resilient.

Libran males usually grow up in the kind of reasonable family atmosphere which allows them to develop a fairly healthy level of self-esteem. The father may be an unimportant or even an absent figure which means that male Librans have nothing to resent, fear or live up to. Females seem to miss out on the father-daughter relationship either because the father is absent or because he is uninterested in them. In some cases, the father has a domineering and discouraging influence on the child. This means that, although both sexes of Librans are charming, the male is usually tougher, far more confident and more detached than the female.

There are exceptions to this rule of course, and one such example is my friend, Fay. Fay lived 'in sin' with a guy at a time when this just wasn't done. When their relationship came to an end, she shared flats with women, men or lived alone. Fay has had a few offers of marriage but prefers to stay single. Her relationships all fell apart because she couldn't help bullying any man to see if he could stand up to her. If he could, she rejected him on the grounds of his toughness and if he couldn't, she rejected him as a wimp. She probably doesn't like sharing much either. How different this is from the standard book definition of a Libran as someone who is only happy when married! As we will see later, in the relating section of this chapter, Fay is not the only Libran loner and neither is she the only strong one around. The majority of female Librans are not like Fay, they are much softer and more inclined to lean on their man or to be dominated by him.

Librans like to work. They are efficient and capable in all that they do but they vary in the amount of their ambition. The true Libran type is happy to fulfil a comfortable and undemanding role but, if there is a touch of something more fiery in the chart, the Libran's natural affinity with business comes to the fore and he can reach an executive position. Librans have a really marketable personality and ought to deal with people as part of their jobs. Many Librans have an eye for beauty which takes them into creative careers. I once commented to two attractive young makeup artists that the signs associated with their job were Libra and Taurus. They surprised me by telling me that indeed, one of them was a Libran and the other a Taurean! Librans are very clean and rather fussy in their habits and most need to live and to work in a neat and tidy environment.

As with all astrological rules, this theory can throw up a polar opposite, thus accounting for the occasional really filthy Libran.

I am not convinced about the famed Libran indecisiveness. I have met the occasional indecisive Libran but most are very good at making up their minds. It is true that they like to deliberate on a decision, taking their time over it, but once they have chosen, they do not change their minds. They prefer not to take the needs of others into consideration when making decisions, and concentrate on what best suits them. Years ago, I learned a very useful lesson from a Libran boss. This was: never be rushed into giving an answer to a serious question – always ask the other person to wait at least twenty-four hours for an answer. This wonderful ploy prevents one from making decisions under pressure or at the behest of one's emotions rather than one's reasoning powers. Having said all this, there are some truly indecisive Librans around who need their partners to make all the decisions for them. Some Librans are very self-absorbed with only one topic of conversation – themselves! They are never lonely but they may feel the lack of an audience on occasion.

What does the Libran Look Like?

Librans have a softly rounded appearance which is slightly deceptive, because they are often tallish and of medium weight. The hair, in white races, is fair or fairish and the eyes are pale grey or blue. Librans of all races have lovely eyes. Libran men may go a little thin on top later in life but they don't usually go completely bald. Librans of both sexes must watch their weight as they get older. These people are very attractive, often truly beautiful; they are also graceful and elegant and know how to dress and move. Even overweight Librans have such wonderful eyes and skin and such grace of movement and style that they are still lovely. These subjects are fussy about their appearance and will weigh up the relative merits of one item against the other before purchasing it. Despite the time and trouble taken over this, the Libran is conventional and unadventurous in his dress and appearance and rarely changes his style once he becomes an adult. One Libran Peculiarity, which I have noticed many times, is a habit of holding one shoulder higher than the other, as if a telephone was being clutched between shoulder and ear.

Health

Astrology can be a valuable tool for both the diagnosis and treatment of ailments but this involves the use of a full birth chart for each patient. The position of the Sun alone is not enough. However, here are the traditional areas of weakness associated with Libra.

The bladder and kidneys are Libra's weakest areas, but the pancreas can also be ineffective, possibly leading to diabetes later in life. Librans are usually quite healthy but they can be over-indulgent and, therefore, overweight, so a sensible diet with a limited amount of sweet stuff and plenty of liquids is recommended.

Work and Hobbies

Librans are great arbitrators, agents, advisors and arrangers. However, they are far more ambitious than most people realise and more capable than they look. Their strong sense of justice draws many Librans into the legal field. Librans like to work among other people either as part of a team or in a partnership because they find decision-making rather difficult. Some Librans are very decisive but even these people take their time over decisions and can't really cope with a swiftly-changing situation. These subjects are far more shrewd and street-wise than others realise and they usually know just how to get the best out of people or situations. However, they can lose touch with reality and make quite disastrous mistakes as a result. The Libran's worst drawbacks are his laziness and restlessness. Some Librans work exceptionally hard or stay in the same job for years, but the typical Libran will drift from place to place looking for the best or the easiest option. Librans are extremely easy to talk to and they are also a treat to listen to because they have an ability to think laterally and often come up with ingenious solutions to problems. Most Librans have a wonderful sense of judgement which some of them utilise by entering the legal profession. Others take this further by venturing into politics, but this all depends upon the amount of energy they can draw upon from other areas of their horoscope.

Libran hobbies can encompass almost anything. These subjects have a great love of beauty and need to work and to live in comfortable and pleasant surroundings. Some express themselves by going in for some truly imaginative do-it-yourself work around the house while others can create beautiful gardens. Some are keen on the world of fashion, either as a hobby or a job, while others can be found working in the cosmetic industry or as make-up artists. Many Librans cook for a hobby and the food they turn out not only tastes good but looks good too. Librans have excellent taste and judgement in many areas of life. A quick round-up of my Libran acquaintances reveals executives in the recruitment field, advertising agents and designers, engineers, computer specialists and people who work in the areas of make-up and fashion design.

Money, Shopping and Acquisitions

Librans love money and know just how to spend it, although they are not especially generous. They will pick up the bill in a restaurant when this gesture is guaranteed to make them look good but otherwise they prefer to keep their wallets in their pockets. Librans either live very well indeed or in squalid circumstances. The good-livers prefer a spacious apartment in a nice part of town or a lovely cottage surrounded by land rather than a boring suburban home. They equip their homes with good quality furniture and an excellent kitchen. Librans are noted for their taste, sense of colour and ability to create a harmonious and peaceful environment. They don't care to live close to a railway or a noisy road system. The squalid Libran type will live in any kind of dump as long as it is cheap or, better still, if someone else is paying for it. This is the sign of the scales and, in some cases, there seems to be only one dish in operation!

The Libran spender frequents sophisticated restaurants, nightclubs, the best shows and cultural activities of all kinds, while the other type will make do with, for example, second-hand books. Most Librans enjoy driving and will obtain the best vehicle they can, preferably a company car which comes with the job. Those who enjoy travel prefer to stay in a large hotel in an up-market holiday centre where they can enjoy the company of people who speak their language and have a similar lifestyle. Some Librans enjoy luxury cruising. Others travel as a result of being involved with an organisation such as the Territorial Army or a church-based group. About the only people on whom they lavish anything are their children and families, especially in connection with their education.

Living with Libra

There seem to be a number of distinct types of Libran and living with each type presents a different experience. There are a few Librans who don't seem able to cope with life at all in the usual sense of the word. These rogue Librans are dirty and scruffy both in their personal appearance and in the way that they keep their homes. These incredibly lazy people don't bother to work or to cook proper meals or look after their families, and yet they can be pretty demanding where it comes to their own requirements. They also tend to blame everyone around them for their lack of progress in life.

The second category of Librans are clean, tidy, well-organised and, for the most part, easy to live with. These kind, co-operative people are as good with their families as they are to work with. Their pleasant sense of humour is never hurtful or sarcastic but even these sainted types do have a temper and can also get themselves into a terrible state of nerves when under pressure. These lovely people support rather than dominate their partners and try to fit in with whatever the other half wants, as long as it is reasonable. Librans have a strong sense of justice and they will try to ensure that fair-play is enjoyed by all who are involved with them. They try to solve problems by discussion rather than by fighting. One Libran lady who filled in one of my pre-book questionnaires said that her Virgoan partner's greatest fault was making her behave like a servant when he was with his friends which she found unfair and unreasonable. She, being a Libran, would never have the bad manners to behave in such a manner. Librans are chivalrous and romantic in the old-fashioned way, remembering birthdays and anniversaries and filling the house with flowers. These pleasant, optimistic people are easy to live with and devoted to their partners, as long as they are treated fairly. All but the rogue variety of Librans have a sense of style and an eye for colour, and their homes are calm and happy places to visit or to live in. Both sexes are usually quite handy about the home.

Librans are good workers and are fair to their families where money is concerned. They have a reputation for being spendthrifts, but I don't think this is justified: they are usually fairly sensible where money is concerned and they don't let their credit cards run away with them. They are always youthful and optimistic in outlook and like to keep themselves up-to-date in every way.

These Librans are not afraid of new technology, new ideas or new terminology and they never become fossilised in their thinking. The very best thing about these people is that they like to do everything in conjunction with their partners and they don't abandon their other halves in favour of their own interests. Their worst fault is their need for everyone and everything around them to look good and they worry about what the neighbours might think. Their inability to make a decision is quite frustrating to live with because they often miss opportunities as a result of shilly-shallying.

There is a third type of Libran who is usually, but not always, male, and who is pretty much impossible to live with. These Librans are highly ambitious and their jobs frequently come well before their relationships. So, for that matter, do their entertainments, holidays, cars and other lovers. When caught out by a furious partner, these fascinating Librans turn on the charm and behave like the proverbial two-year old who knows that he has been naughty but now wants to be forgiven. Acquisitive, greedy and selfish, these subjects are very successful in their chosen fields and their families will enjoy a good deal of wealth and status. Most Librans have considerable charm but this type uses it to manipulate everybody in order to get his own way. These subjects can argue the hind leg off a donkey and will break up a relationship altogether rather than concede a point. These Librans talk *at* people rather than with them and they need a sycophantic audience. Many of these subjects are bare-faced liars who are chronically unfaithful. They seem to need a stream of admiring females in their lives in order to prove to themselves that their charming, suave, fascinating image is in proper working order. Vain, domineering, jealous, demanding and selfish, these Librans live a double, triple or multiple life, doing everything to excess and moving between jobs, debts, lovers and ex-spouses with the speed of light. These Librans, after trying a relationship or two, end up happily living alone. They never feel lonely because they have many interests and can make friends so easily.

All Librans seem to have a problem dealing with reality. It is as if the material world is too much to cope with and a measure of self-delusion is necessary in order for them to handle it. If they decide that black is white, they will be able to convince themselves of this despite all the evidence to the contrary!

Sexuality

The dirty, lazy negative Libran doesn't connect with anyone long enough to get into bed in the first place but all the others make the most wonderful lovers. It is probably this talent which allows them to get away with so much and encourages their partners to forgive their excesses. Being ruled by Venus, Librans are sensual and very generous lovers. They take their time over love-making and they go to a lot of trouble to ensure that their partner's requirements are met. These subjects are experimental, possibly even somewhat clinical in their approach at times but they are unlikely to demand behaviour which their partner would find embarrassing or unacceptable. Librans can be critical of a partner who gains weight or who allows his or her looks to deteriorate, and they can quite easily leave a lover on these grounds. Some Libran men confuse love with sex and can only cuddle or express love in a sexual way.

Other Relationships

Being pleasant, sociable and eager for the good opinion of others, Librans usually get on well with other members of the family. They will flirt with father- or mother-in-law, listen to aunty's grumbles, laugh at uncle's jokes and play, for a little while at least, with grandson. Some Librans genuinely like their relatives while others are simply accommodating. Most of these subjects welcome visitors and like visiting but their nerves are quite delicate and they can't take unpleasantness. If a family member insists on being offensive or difficult, the Libran will either give them an unexpectedly hard time or will simply escape from the situation until the offending relative has left. These subjects are very sociable and love to chat and to listen to others but they tend to dominate a conversation.

As children, they get away with a good deal due to their charm and good looks and they are both clever enough and wise enough to achieve the required standard. These children make sure that they have the latest in clothing and equipment and are happily accepted as part of the 'in crowd'. They don't stand out in any way and they don't cause trouble, but they can usually stand up for themselves if the need arises. Librans are either well-understood and well-loved by their parents, or at something of a distance from them. The father is often a rather detached or distant figure while the mother may be somewhat ineffective, stupid or snobbish. If they don't like their families, they manage to slide away from them by becoming involved with school friends and outside interests. As parents, Librans are kind, cool and considerate but not always terribly involved with their children. They may not be able to relate to their children on a deep and understanding level. Libran parents really need to employ a good nanny who will deal with the reality of small children, leaving them free to stroll round the shops picking up a pretty outfit and a classy bottle of wine for their next dinner party.

The Duchess of York

Sarah is a strong personality who would never fit into the formality of any Royal household. Her outgoing Sun in Libra, conjunct Mars in the eleventh house suggest that she is a true maverick who will always go her own way. She is opinionated and she may have a hot temper and she could be very argumentative and confrontational. With Scorpio rising, the chances of more than one marriage are very strong indeed. Taurus on the descendant never indicates a settled and lasting married life, at least not until later in life. Jupiter rising in Sagittarius will always bring Sarah luck and whatever scrapes she gets into, she will always find someone to help her get out of them.

With no planets in the seventh or eighth houses, it looks as though Sarah's marriage to Prince Andrew was a non-event. Right from the start of the marriage, he preferred the company of his ship-mates to hers and he was very rarely at home. The fact that the two of them are reputed to be

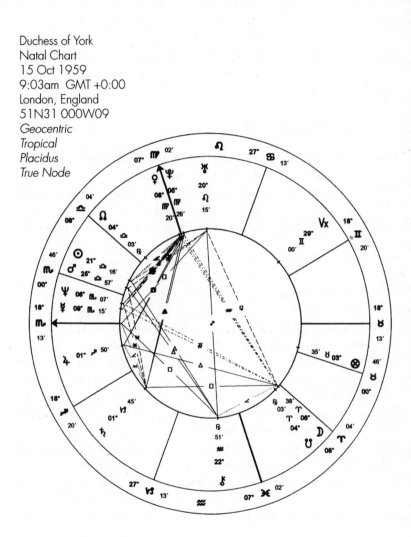

Duchess of York
Natal Chart
15 Oct 1959
9:03am GMT +0:00
London, England
51N31 000W09
Geocentric
Tropical
Placidus
True Node

very good friends is not surprising, as the Sun and Mars in the eleventh suggest that Sarah is lucky in friendship, if not in love. Sarah's Mercury and Neptune in conjunction in Scorpio in the twelfth house suggest that she has some really deep and dark secrets to keep and it may be many years before we, the public, ever hear about these.

Venus close to the midheaven suggests that Sarah will always be around powerful and influential people and that she could eventually find love through a work situation. We haven't heard the last of this lady, I'm sure of that. I can't help liking her.

Michael Douglas

Michael Douglas grew up in the world of film acting and has followed his famous father, Kirk, into the family business. A couple of his brothers have done some acting and they still work in the film business. Apart from his acting, Michael is famous for having attended a kind of clinic for sex-addicts! Well, if one is going to be addicted to something, there are worse things than sex, I guess!

Michael is a Libran and this is a notoriously flirtatious sign and with his Sun in close conjunction to Neptune, fantasy and imagination must play a large part in his life. This is a great placement for an actor and this conjunction, accompanied by Jupiter, Mercury and Chiron are all in the ambitious tenth house of career. Even if Michael were not an actor, he would be creative and artistic and I am willing to bet that he is also musical or able to paint or make beautiful things. Michael could have been a terrific fashion designer if he wanted. Mars and Venus in the eleventh house suggest that he is really far better at friendship than being a lover and his Scorpio ascendant confirms this. Those who have Scorpio rising and therefore, Taurus on the descendant often go in for multiple relationships. Uranus in the seventh house in Gemini adds to his instability in love and this suggests that he will always be looking for his next lover, even when he is happy with the one he's got.

Michael's Moon in the second house in Capricorn suggests that he is an excellent businessman. All those planets in the tenth house suggest that Michael is happy and relaxed when he is working and that he will never be able to sit around for long. Mercury in Virgo gives him a quick mind and as it is in conjunction with Jupiter, he must have a delightful sense of humour. My guess is that he would be an excellent mimic. He does have a serious and even a sad side to him and his own feelings run deeply. This man is a real character, impossible to live with but wonderfully entertaining to watch – and a really sexy treat for lady cinema-goers.

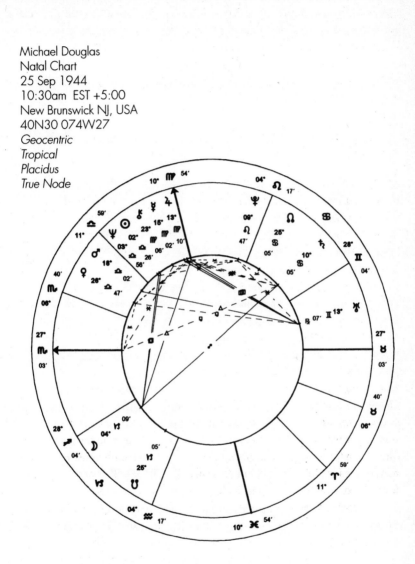

Michael Douglas
Natal Chart
25 Sep 1944
10:30am EST +5:00
New Brunswick NJ, USA
40N30 074W27
Geocentric
Tropical
Placidus
True Node

8

Scorpio

In a cavern, by a canyon,
Excavating for a mine,
Dwelt a miner, forty-niner,
And his daughter, Clementine.
Chorus: Oh, my darling, oh, my darling,
Oh, my darling, Clementine,
Thou art lost and gone for ever,
Dreadful sorry, Clementine.

Clementine

Scorpio is associated with mining, in addition to the ideas of loss and death, and all of these themes are contained in this song.

Sign: The Scorpion

The scorpion is a tiny, crusty animal which is found in hot regions of the world. Not all scorpions sting and not all scorpion stings are fatal or even dangerous but some, of course, are. In ancient astrology, the sign for Scorpio was the eagle or the phoenix and many early astrologers suggested Scorpios can be marvellous creatures who soar like the eagle, regenerate themselves like the phoenix, or nasty, grubby, dangerous ones like the scorpion. In my opinion, the scorpion's nature is very indicative of these people's behaviour because they can be silent and co-operative, hidden from view, unexpectedly meek or absolutely deadly.

Planets: Pluto and Mars

The reason for the dual rulership of Scorpio is simple. In the days before tele-scopes, astronomers could only see five planets, these being Mercury, Venus, Mars, Jupiter and Saturn. Each of these planets ruled two signs, while the Sun and Moon ruled one each. Since the discovery of Uranus, Neptune and Pluto, the signs of Aquarius, Pisces and Scorpio have been re-assigned to them.

Mars was the Roman god of war and he is associated with courage, strength, action and sexual activity, while Pluto was the god of the under-world. Pluto was extremely wealthy and disinclined to part with anything which he owned. How, in Greek mythology, Demeter persuaded him to take turns with her in having the company of her daughter, Persephone, goodness knows! Pluto is associated with things which are hidden from view, such as coal, oil, diamonds and anything else which has to be mined. He is also associated with joint finances and the legal aspect of financial affairs such as corporate matters, taxes, alimony, wills, legacies, joint accounts or any dealings with money on the behalf of others. He knows how to keep secrets both for himself and on behalf of others. He likes to search for anything that is hidden from view, so he could be drawn to detection, butchery or pathology. Pluto also rules major turning points, beginnings and endings, birth, death and sex.

Gender: Feminine

Surprisingly, Scorpio is a feminine sign, although this may simply be because the signs alternate between masculine and feminine. Scorpio is a strong sign but it is passive in nature rather than active. Maybe the best description of Scorpio would be to call it bi-sexual!

Element: Water

The water element makes for sensitivity. Therefore, water people are likely to be irritated by loud or discordant noises and upset by pain and illness. They are sensitive to atmospheres and very wary of anything which could constitute a threat. They are kind and helpful because they are sensitive to the suffering and pain of others. However, many of them are more tuned in to the needs of animals than humans. Water people move and react slowly and may seem rather stupid to other, quicker types but this is a mis-taken assumption because they are extremely shrewd and well aware of everything that is going on.

Quality: Fixed

Fixed sign people like to stay put and remain in the same house, the same job and the same relationship for years. Most fixed sign people will see things through to the end and they find it difficult to make any kind of fresh start. Their opinions may also be fixed.

Some General Characteristics

Astrology books give poor old Scorpio a very bad press. We are told that Scorpios are drunken, over-sexed, obsessive, untrustworthy, bullying rogues. This is simply not fair, although many Scorpions are not the easiest of people to live with or to work for. They respect strength and independence and really cannot cope with anyone who either needs to be treated with kid gloves or who relies upon them financially. Being members of a fixed sign, Scorpios don't appreciate change. This is not meant to imply that they are not ready to try a new hobby, meet new people or to visit an area which is new to them, but it does mean that Scorpios are reliable as friends, neighbours, relatives and employees. Once a Scorpio has made a commitment, he puts his whole heart into it and makes it work. If the enterprise turns out to be absolutely unworkable, he will still give it his best shot before abandoning it. In some ways, I consider that the sign for Scorpio should be the bulldog or the bloodhound, because they hate giving up on anything. The world is full of women who are looking for men willing to make a commitment to a relationship and stick to it, and when they ask me which zodiac signs to choose for reliability, my answer in all cases is either Scorpio or Taurus.

Scorpios have a strong sense of duty and they are the world's best keepers of secrets. They are not casual in their attitudes. If a Scorpio lends you money, you must be prepared to pay it back by the due date. If you lend a Scorpio money, he will pay you back even though this may not actually be necessary. When I was an infant, I apparently inherited some shares in an engineering company. I had no knowledge of this until I was in my mid-thirties. At this time, the company was wound up and I was sent £500 by the relative who had been charged with the administration of this matter. The relative was, of course, a Scorpio and it is characteristic that, not only did she fulfil her obligations to me to the letter, even though I didn't even know about them, but that she had never felt any obligation to tell me about this legacy until that moment. If a Scorpio finds himself the guardian of a cranky older relative, a small child or even an animal, he will take this obligation very seriously and make every effort to see the job through. He may have absolutely no affection for the unfortunate orphan but he will do what needs to be done. As far as his own family is concerned, he usually loves them all unreservedly but he can make life very difficult for anyone who he considers weak or unworthy. These subjects are not dabblers, they prefer to have specialised knowledge in a small number of fields and to shut out anything which doesn't fall into those categories.

Scorpio faults occur due to the emotional nature of the sign. Remember, this is a *water* sign which is intuitive, sensitive and inclined to make decisions on an emotional basis. A big problem for these people is their inclination to over-react and to jump into or out of something due to either excitement or anger. Scorpios are normally excellent judges of character, often being able to see below the surface, but there are occasions when they seem to turn off this faculty and enter into some scheme with a person of dubious morals because they want to believe that everything will work out well. They can just as easily cut themselves off from whole sections of their family if one member speaks to them in a disrespectful manner and, unfortunately, it is not difficult to mortally offend a Scorpio. Forgetting and forgiving is not in the Scorpio nature and they make implacable enemies. They find it extremely difficult to apologise and can dig themselves into a hole out of which they then find it impossible to climb. Scorpios hate confrontations and they know that they have a dangerously hot temper. They will back off and back down if confronted directly by a quietly assertive person. It is difficult to talk openly to these people because it is all too easy to cross some invisible line and cause them unintentional offence. They also pick up on the anger and frustration of those around them and can become unsettled and angry as a result. Like Pisceans, Scorpios can act as psychic sponges where strong feelings are concerned.

Scorpio defensiveness may manifest itself in spiteful remarks. If a Scorpio decides that one particular set of people have let him down badly, he will either loathe the whole lot of them, regardless of whether they deserve this or not, or he will choose one particular member of the group on whom he will pour out his hatred. One elderly Scorpio lady believed that none of her family had ever appreciated her or returned her good deeds, and this disappointment finally corroded into detestation of her nephew who was the last remaining relative. Even if you love or are loved by a Scorpio, don't expect to be left anything in his will; these people are notorious for getting in the last spiteful move, deserved or otherwise, by leaving their worldly goods to the nearest cats' home! There are Scorpios who are violent, oversexed, alcoholic, drug-addicted and/or obsessed by death or involved in black magic. There are others who use violent, manipulative or sexual tactics to control others. Most aim simply to live quietly and control nobody but themselves.

What Does the Scorpio Look Like?

Some Scorpios are sturdily built while others are small and wiry. The bone structure is strong and prominent and they often have a bony and angular appearance. Some of the most beautiful people on earth are born under this sign while others may have arresting looks or can even be downright ugly. A typical Scorpio has thick wavy hair which, in men, may thin out just a little in later years. Most astrology books talk about magnetic eyes but I think this is less due to the eyes themselves as the Scorpionic habit of looking directly at people. These subjects don't smile easily and may scowl with concentration when listening. Many Scorpios stay slim all their lives and have a contemptuous attitude to those who put on weight. This is because they, themselves, don't appreciate their genetic luck and they tend to consider fatness to be solely the result of weakness and over-indulgence. Fat Scorpios tend to ignore their own obesity but still don't hesitate to criticise others. Scorpios hate to throw anything out and will wear a favourite garment until it falls apart. Even when they are forced to admit that they really cannot wear that particular outfit again, they will hang on to it, just in case.

Health

Astrology can be a valuable tool for both the diagnosis and treatment of ailments but this involves the use of a full birth chart for each patient. The position of the Sun alone is not enough. However, here are the traditional areas of weakness associated with Scorpio.

Traditionally speaking, the reproductive organs are supposed to be weak in Scorpios but I think that the lower spine is much more likely to cause problems. If a Scorpio does get ill, or if he has an accident, it is usually very dramatic, but Scorpios have the most amazing powers of recovery and often manage to live a very long and, on the whole, healthy life.

Work and Hobbies

There are a number of jobs which are specifically associated with the sign of Scorpio and all of these involve investigating or looking for something which cannot be immediately seen. Many Scorpios work in the field of medicine, either as surgeons, diagnosticians or osteopaths, while others are drawn to psychiatry and hypnotherapy. This gives the Scorpio the satisfaction of both finding out what is wrong and also of putting it right.

Mining for coal or precious metals is supposed to be a Scorpio trade, but the only miner I know is Arthur Scargill – and he is a Capricorn! Another typically Scorpio interest is police work, and many Scorpios do indeed have a career in some branch of investigative or forensic work. Rather like Ariens, Scorpios can be drawn to the kind of job which was once considered to be masculine, such as engineering. The military world, and also that of armaments, appeals to Scorpios and they may even become caught up in this without making a conscious effort to do so. The urge to investigate makes many Scorpios look into psychic and mediumistic matters.

Scorpios are very physical and energetic and they don't seem to worry about getting hurt. Typical interests would be wrestling, boxing, rugby football or American football, as well as sailing, competitive tennis and hang-gliding. Many Scorpios like to dance and most love to listen to good music. This is a sensual sign, therefore it is no surprise that Scorpios love to use their bodies to their fullest extent, whether this be by going on a military exercise, indulging in physical and competitive sport or by making love! Whatever a Scorpio sets his mind to, he will do it thoroughly and to the best of his ability. Typical Scorpio sayings are, 'If you are going to do something, then do it properly!', or 'If you start something, then for goodness' sake finish it!', or even 'You only fit double-glazing once, so you might as well fit the best.'

Money, Shopping and Acquisitions

This is a most peculiar sign as far as attitudes to money are concerned, because Scorpios can vacillate between extreme parsimony and being 'the last of the big spenders'. Scorpios will spare no expense on an exciting project but shopping for boring everyday goods does absolutely nothing for them. The exception to this is food, because Scorpios like what they like and won't do without their favourite foods. All the feminine signs, especially the water signs, like to hang on to money and they seem to get as much pleasure from saving as they do from spending. These subjects retain a sentimental attachment to their homes, businesses and possessions and they prefer old favourites to novelties. Some Scorpios are wizard at hanging on to old paper bags, elastic bands and kitchen tools, while others have a wonderful ability to recycle their own junk.

If a member of a Scorpio's family is in dire financial straits, the Scorpio will help them out unstintingly and without expecting to be paid back. However, if their nearest and dearest just want a few little things to make life a bit more pleasant, they should go about getting these for themselves.

Scorpio houses are adequate but they may be scruffy because, as long as they have enough to eat and drink, many Scorpios don't actually need many possessions, although they will spend money like water on their own particular interests such as travel or the raising, breeding and keeping of animals. Having said this, there are some Scorpios who are very generous and free-spending in every way. This is a sign of extremes and, therefore, extreme meanness, extreme profligacy or extreme generosity are all possible. As far as possessions are concerned, they like books and music, tools for their trade or hobby and sporting goods. Scorpios also like to own a large and comfortable car. They enjoy owning items which have some kind of sentimental attachment for them, but the best new possession by far is a ticket for a good holiday. In short, possessions themselves mean little to Scorpios but anything which offers them the opportunity to explore and to experience life to the full is much appreciated.

Living with Scorpio

Scorpios are given a bad press in most astrology books and, while it is true that they can be hard to live with, they also have some very good points. Scorpios are not loners, they like to be in a relationship and will make great efforts to keep it going through thick and thin. These subjects are loyal and they stick to those whom they love even when this is difficult. Scorpios take marriage vows very seriously and they don't leave a partner when he or she gets ill or if the money runs out. They are definitely not fair-weather friends. These types are possessive and the very thought of divorce makes their blood run cold. They hate to lose anything, whether it be money, a battle, a business or a spouse and they will hang in there until the bitter end.

These subjects have high standards and they may try to impose these standards upon the rest of their families. They respect courage and strength and lose patience with those who whine or who cannot cope with life. When they themselves are faced with a problem, they worry intensely about it and may even do a fair bit of complaining themselves but they don't give in and they try to find a solution one way or another. I have been surrounded by Scorpio types all my life and have seen them go through terrible times when their health has let them down or their businesses have collapsed under them and in every case, these misfortunes have brought out the best in them. In a way, it is easier to live with Scorpios when they are in trouble because it is only then that they allow anyone to help. In good times they can be so independent that the relationship makes one feel like a spectator rather than a participant in their lives.

A Scorpio home is not a palace because they are not especially tidy and they don't set out to impress others. Like Cancerians, Scorpios tend to hang on to everything which comes into their homes and every cupboard is stuffed with the junk of ages; they have a sentimental love of the past and hate to part with anything. On a number of occasions I have tried suggesting to my Scorpio husband that we get rid of our old-fashioned wardrobes in favour of fitted units but he won't hear of it. Those wardrobes have twenty-seven years of memories sunk into the grain of their wood and it would be too much of a wrench for him to be parted from them! Most Scorpios are practical and will find a way of doing what needs to be done around the house. Being restless, they prefer to keep busy than simply sit about. Both sexes will handle any kind of job, and they don't feel that anything is beneath them. They need to have quite an active social life but they are easily tired by people. The answer seems to be for Scorpios and their partners to take up some sport or interest which they can do together and also in the company of others. If this allows the Scorpio to compete with others, then it serves as an outlet for some of his pent-up energies and occasional rages.

Scorpios are very emotional but they don't all express this in the same way. Some are self-pitying, especially when ill or unhappy, while others brood and get into long-term spells of free-floating bad temper. They take their work seriously and, if something goes wrong in their jobs, they can become extremely difficult to live with. The worst aspect of this is that their poor partner doesn't know why he/she is being subjected to such extreme unpleasantness, and it may be a long time after the event that the reason comes to light. The poor benighted partner knows very well that it would be far better if the Scorpio actually *told* them what was going on, but pride or the habit of silence seems to prevent this and any probing or questioning is seen by the Scorpio as being intrusive. On the other hand, Scorpios are very inquisitive and will even go through a partner's private papers if they think that something is being kept from them. Some Scorpios escape from their problems by drinking too much.

Scorpios have a reputation for wanting to be top dog in a relationship but this is not necessarily so, although mutual respect is a necessity to them. Scorpios need to be consulted about decisions and they hate being presented with a *fait accompli*, especially if it is likely to cost them money. These subjects are not easily influenced but they will listen and take note when presented with a reasoned argument and a common-sense approach. Scorpios are not good at sharing and they can use money or resources in order to control others. They either withhold money from their families or bestow it upon them as and when they think fit. The partner of a Scorpio is strongly advised to have an income and a bank account of his/her own. Oddly enough, Scorpios who behave in this way see money as a form of self-protection and they feel that, if they relinquish financial control, they will allow other people to walk all over them. They are not alone in feeling like this; Leos and Capricorns feel much the same way. These subjects see the world in black and white, either loving or hating with few feelings in between, and if anyone insults them or even mildly criticises them, they can take their hate to the point of murder. They may give their families a hard time but their love is as strong and genuine as their hatred and they will feel things deeply. They respect and understand their partner's loves and hates and will do all they can to help a partner succeed in what he or she wants to do. It is worth remembering that this is a fixed sign and these subjects cannot be influenced or moulded into something other than what they are. There are some Scorpios who are so self-absorbed that they cannot relate to anyone. Many Scorpios don't care what others think of them and therefore won't compromise or meet anyone halfway.

Sexuality

Scorpios have a reputation for sexuality which I think is probably quite wrong. They love to shock others and will come out with statements which makes people think that they are very liberated in their behaviour. For example, 'I used to go there on dirty weekends', or 'you actually *like* the missionary position?' might be typical remarks but, in my opinion, Scorpios are actually rather prudish where it comes to sex. They are not libertines and, unless there is a great deal of Libra on their charts, they cannot bounce lightly from one relationship to another without their feelings being engaged. Scorpios have a great deal of charm and are probably the greatest flirts in the world but this form of dicing with danger is rarely carried through into a true sexual adventure. They worry far too much about AIDS, other sexual diseases, the risk of pregnancy and even the possibility of falling in love to let themselves go.

Scorpios like to be desired and wanted because this gives them a feeling of power over others and they can wilt if they are not the centre of attention. At a party, a Scorpio will work the room, using conversation and his expressive face in order to entertain and draw attention but this is really just an act. Scorpios are super-cautious where their feelings are concerned and will think twice and three times before getting into anything real. When in a relationship, they can be quite demanding but they are also shy, afraid of looking foolish and nervous of trying anything new. They need a partner who will encourage and reassure them or they can become stuck in a rather boring sexual routine. Some Scorpios have a variety of sex partners but don't allow themselves to fall in love, thus avoiding potential pain.

Other Relationships

Scorpios have many acquaintances but very few friends and there are very few people who really know them well. They don't much care for the kind of cosy tête-à-tête where confidences are exchanged. They won't admit to foolish behaviour or indiscretions of their own and they are not sufficiently interested in other people to want to hear about theirs. They can be quite competitive as friends. Once a friend lets them down in any way, that is the end of the friendship and there is nothing that can be done to regain the trust which was lost. Scorpios try to get on with their relatives, but they don't lose any sleep if this doesn't work out.

As parents, Scorpios can be absolutely terrible. One astrologer describes the experience of being the child of a Scorpio as 'Rocking backwards and forwards in horror on the stairs as the Scorpio parent screams the marriage to an end and wondering what I had done to cause this.' Scorpios don't control their anger or their feelings for the sake of peace and they are capable of destroying a marriage or their children's sanity through pride coupled with the inability to ever admit that they can be wrong. On the other hand, many Scorpios are very loving parents who somehow manage to control their wilder side and give their children the security they need. All Scorpio parents have a tendency to use their children in order to compete with others and they are happiest with children who can and do cope with this pressure. Many Scorpio parents seem to be blessed with talented, successful Leo children. However, some Scorpio parents can actually become jealous of their offspring's success, even while claiming that they had a hand in bringing it about.

Scorpio children don't get on well with their siblings. They are far too competitive, too self-centred and they simply don't consider that the other children's demands and requirements are in any way as important as their own. Scorpio children find sharing very difficult and, rightly or wrongly, they feel that they are being deprived of their share of their parents' love. Scorpio Jimmy Savile was the youngest of seven children. When his mother died, he kept her body with him for five days. He says these were the happiest days of his life because he had her all to himself!

These children have high personal standards which means that they either make a great success of school or sports and of childhood in general, or they see too many obstacles in their path and opt out altogether and become anti-social. Most Scorpio' children benefit from an active, sporty outlet and they also enjoy being involved with organisations such as the girl guides, military cadet organisations or para-medical ones.

Hillary Clinton

Hillary Clinton is a clever lawyer who stands by her man. Hillary has the Sun, Chiron, Venus, Mercury and the south node of the Moon in Scorpio. Anyone with Scorpio strongly marked has a need for a loving and close marriage because there seems to be an unconscious memory of loss and abandonment lurking in their psyche. Sometimes Plutonic folk suffer betrayal and loss in their childhood while others may carry with them the memory of terrible events from previous lives. For this reason and maybe also for sheer Scorpio obstinacy, such people stick to their marriages and keep in close touch with many of their relatives through thick and thin. At the time of writing, we don't know whether Hillary Clinton is actually a wronged wife or not but the chances are that even if she is, it will take a great deal for her to be shaken loose from the man she chose to marry and to have a child by.

Hillary Clinton is definitely not a shrinking violet who lives through her husband. Her Sun, accompanied by Neptune and Venus in the fifth house tell us that she wants to be recognised for her own achievements. Hillary's tenth house Moon in Pisces suggests that she is ambitious and that she wants to do something with her life that makes the world a better place. This Moon placement also makes her sensitive and vulnerable. Her heart is in the right place and it is far softer than her chilly exterior suggests and I am willing to bet that she can be childlike and playful at times. Hillary's Gemini ascendant makes her a communicator but most of caring Cancer covers her first house. Mars, Pluto and Saturn in the third house in

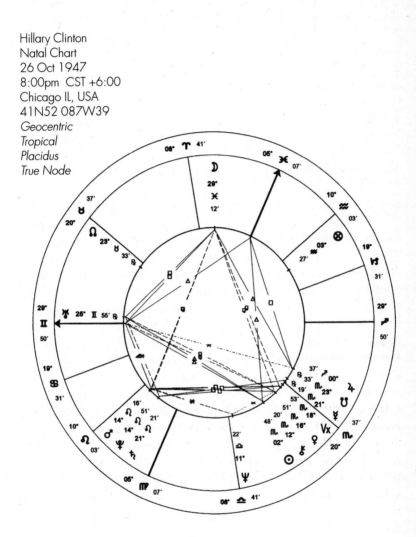

Hillary Clinton
Natal Chart
26 Oct 1947
8:00pm CST +6:00
Chicago IL, USA
41N52 087W39
Geocentric
Tropical
Placidus
True Node

Leo add to her communication skills in addition to endowing her with intelligence and diligence. This looks like a very intelligent and a very nice lady but she may be manipulative and given to emotional blackmail.

Mars often denotes the man in a woman's chart, or at least the kind of man a woman would be attracted to and in Hillary's case, Mars is in Leo. Bill Clinton has his Sun in Leo so this looks just about right. Hillary's Mars is in close conjunction with her Pluto suggesting a relationship with an exceedingly powerful man. The marriage may not be an easy one and she has probably had to adapt herself considerably to the needs of Bill Clinton's job. My guess is that when Uranus seriously opposes this Mars Pluto conjunction (in 1999), the marriage may actually break up! I hope I'm wrong but if it does, Hillary will survive because she is a strong and capable lady.

Jamie Lee Curtis

Jamie is a wonderful actress and, of course, the daughter of actor, Tony Curtis. Jamie Lee's three planets in Scorpio in addition to her Moon in Taurus are highly stabilising factors in an otherwise very exciting chart. This very stabilising factor also points to considerable problems during her childhood in which she learned to be watchful and to keep her thoughts to herself. Jamie Lee's Sagittarian ascendant gives her the adaptability to cope with changing circumstances and also the kind of brilliance which makes her stand out in a crowd. This ascendant also suggests that she has a wonderful sense of humour and the ability to generate some very bright ideas. Saturn on the ascendant points to quite a bit of hardship in her childhood and also a fight for recognition in her own right. Jamie Lee is highly disciplined and fairly cautious in her business life but her Aries Moon suggests that she is somewhat more adventurous in her personal life. Her Scorpio planets and Aries Moon suggest that she needs to feel as though she is in control of her own destiny, and the trine between the Moon and the Mercury/Saturn conjunction in Sagittarius ensures that she achieves this. The uncomfortable aspects between Pluto in her eighth house in Virgo and her Sun, Venus and Moon, suggest that she can be manipulated by unscrupulous people, especially over money. Jamie Lee must be careful when working closely with others. Her Mars, which is badly aspected, could bring losses through relationships; this Mars also suggests that she might put off having children in favour of her career. It is more than likely that Jamie Lee would be hurt from time to time by the men in her life. Neptune in her tenth house in Scorpio suggests that Jamie Lee has great creative talent that she taps into in order to enhance her work. I feel that

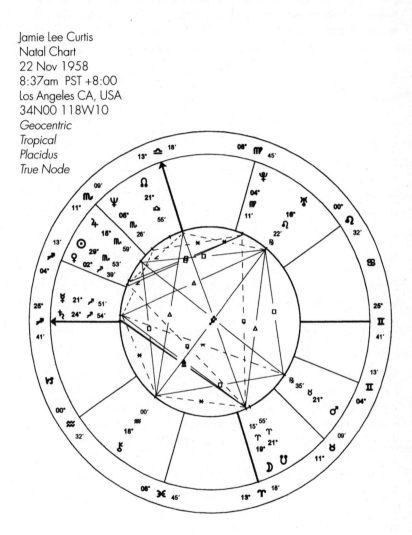

Jamie Lee Curtis
Natal Chart
22 Nov 1958
8:37am PST +8:00
Los Angeles CA, USA
34N00 118W10
Geocentric
Tropical
Placidus
True Node

she could be very musical in addition to her acting talents. With five planets in fire signs but none in air, she is more apt to jump to conclusions and make decisions intuitively rather than to rely upon pure logic. Her five planets in fixed signs and six in succeedent houses suggest that she has the self-discipline, tenacity and common sense which is required for her to succeed in her chosen career.

9

Sagittarius

O who will o'er the downs so free,
O who will with me ride,
O who will up and follow me,
To win a blooming bride
Her father he has locked the door,
Her mother keeps the key;
but neither door nor bolt shall part
My own true love from me!

O Who Will O'er The Downs So Free
by R.L. de Pearsall

Riding away to freedom and letting nothing stand in his way; who else could this be but Sagittarius.

Sign: The Archer or the Centaur

The Centaur is a mythical animal which is half-horse and half-man and it is often depicted with a bow and arrow in its hands. The Archer speaks for itself. Both these archetypes suggest travel and projectiles, but although these are strong images, there is nothing menacing about them. Sagittarians move about a great deal, they have many interests and they prefer to be in company rather than alone except perhaps when exploring and finding their way about in strange places.

Planet: Jupiter

Jupiter is associated with travel, philosophy, teaching, the law and gambling. All these images involve pushing back boundaries which may be physical, mental, legal, financial or educational. In traditional astrology, Jupiter is considered to be a 'benefic'; a lucky planet which bestows blessings on all it touches. In practical astrological terms, the effects of Jupiter on a chart may not feel all that lucky at times, but Jupiterian energy always forces one to push one's life outward in order to overcome problems. Jupiter makes us leave the safety of the nest.

Gender: Masculine

Masculine subjects are more likely to tackle a problem themselves than to hand it over to someone else to deal with. Masculine sign subjects say what they mean and don't hesitate to push themselves or their children to the forefront.

Element: Fire

Fire sign people are optimists who have faith in the future. They are intuitive and they appear to jump to conclusions. They are friendly, generous and youthful in spirit but they can sometimes be quick tempered and irritable. All fire-sign people have the ability to begin large enterprises but may be less able to finish what they start or to handle the details which may be involved.

Quality: Mutable

This word may seem strange to you but if you think of transmute, commute or mutate, you will see that it concerns moving something from one place to another or from one state to another. Mutable people are flexible in their attitude, they dislike too much routine and need variety in their work and their lives. They may take up too many interests and then find it difficult to finish any of them. They are able to fit into most situations and to make themselves comfortable even when permanently on the move.

Some General Characteristics

Sagittarians are hard to categorise or to define, because there seem to be so many different personality types within the sign. Some Sagittarians are reserved, suburban and rather 'establishment' in outlook, while others are anarchists or even iconoclasts who live a totally alternative lifestyle. Some Sagittarians appear larger than anyone else, either because they are actually tall and heavy or because they seem to fill the available space with their personality. They like dealing with a variety of people and they have a cheerful and non-hostile manner which makes them popular. These people love to travel, to explore new or unknown regions and to be outdoors.

The daughter of a friend of mine is an excellent example of this type. As a small child, Vicky was happy, playful, easygoing and ready to fit in with anything which was going on. As she got older she became sporty, fond of animals (especially horses), popular and good-looking in a tall, outdoorsy way. The moment her homework or other chores were done, she shot out of the house either to see her friends or to visit the nearby riding school. Her parents wanted their children to be college graduates and regarded Vicky in a far less favourable light than her nervy, highly intelligent older brother. After leaving school with the bare minimum of qualifications, Vicky drifted around in and out of work and then began to travel. She took a variety of strange jobs in some very strange places, such as fish-canning in Iceland and tomato picking in Spain. When she had a job to do, Vicky worked hard and saved her money but, as soon as she was able, moved on to another country and spent her savings exploring it. She has had a variety of 'relationships' with men, apparently oblivious to being labelled or losing her 'reputation' by such behaviour. The world is too exciting and time is too short for Vicky to worry about such small-minded suburban concerns.

Even the more settled and less eccentric Sagittarian types love to work in situations where they deal with large numbers of people and their kindly nature, cheerful optimistic outlook and quick wit counteract their tendency to lose their temper or to be tactless. These people are cheerful and optimistic with a positive attitude to life and more than their fair share of good luck.

There is another type of Sagittarian whom I like very much and understand very well. This one takes on the world's problems and allows himself to be imposed upon by unscrupulous personalities. Part of the problem is that the Sagittarian's value system is spiritual rather than materialistic. He loves to help others and genuinely feels that consideration to others is a reward in itself. Some people consider this type of subject to be truly saintly while others consider him to be a dope. Even fairly normal Sagittarians have homes which are full of animals and relatives, all living together in a cheerful clutter. Those few Sagittarians who prefer to live alone are rarely home except when expecting visitors. All love to be out and about doing something and none are inclined to sit in front of the television if they can help it.

There is a strain of bookish Sagittarian who studies and absorbs esoteric information. This type may be interested in religious or philosophical ideas and may choose to work, either full- or part-time in those fields. Even these people don't necessarily hide themselves away while thinking or working because they have the ability to concentrate and to blot out disturbances. Sagittarians have a strong sense of justice which leads some of them into the legal profession.

Sagittarians are surprisingly practical, being able to cook and look after themselves and also to take on quite daunting do-it-yourself tasks. Perhaps it is their 'do it first and worry about it afterwards' attitude which makes this possible.

What Does the Sagittarian Look Like?

There is no single typical Sagittarian appearance but there are a number of possibilities. The stereotypical Sagittarian is tall, large-boned, possibly with a lantern jaw and a very lively and active manner. Others are skinny and wiry with a characteristically long bony 'V-shaped' face. Others have a top-heavy shape with large, well-covered shoulders and chest. In white races, most have a pale complexion and they may range from very blond to dark haired with a sallowish skin.

Health

Astrology can be a valuable tool for both the diagnosis and treatment of ailments but this involves the use of a full birth chart for each patient. The position of the Sun alone is not enough. However, here are the traditional areas of weakness associated with Sagittarius.

The hips and thighs are the traditional Sagittarian weak points but the femoral arteries can also give trouble. Many Sagittaflans enjoy outdoor activities or are keen on vigorous exercise, therefore accidents are a possibility. On the whole this is a healthy sign, probably due to the fact that most of these subjects tend to eat a varied and reasonable diet and enjoy physical activities.

Work and Hobbies

I come across more than the average number of Sagittarians in broadcasting and in show-business generally. There are many very funny Sagittarian comedians whose quick wit and cheerful manner endear them to the public. Anything which reaches out a long way suits Sagittarians, so publishing, presenting radio programmes and journalism are attractive careers to them. Traditionally speaking, Sagittarians are supposed to be attracted to the law, higher education, publishing and religious or philosophical careers in addition to finding work in the travel trade. This list of 'traditional' Sagittarian trades seems to work quite well when put against Sagittarian reality. These subjects do work in the field of higher education but they also work in lower and middle forms of education as well. They may work as sports coaches, flying instructors and dancing teachers. Sagittarians have the brain and the wit to argue a point intelligently and thoroughly and they tend to look at all sides of any question as a matter of course. Sagittarians have an urge to explore the world around them and this takes many of them into the travel trades.

These subjects' values are rarely materialistic and their careers are chosen for what they offer in the way of exploration and fascination rather than money. There are many Sagittarians working as spiritual healers, mediums, ghost-busters and astrologers because this enables them to help others whilst simultaneously providing opportunities for exploring the unknown and unseen.

Sagittarian hobbies are often an extension of their work but those of them who do have a specific separate hobby or interest may be involved with sport, gambling or large animals. The horse is the traditional Sagittarian animal and it is true that many of these adventurous subjects do ride in their spare time. One place where a Sagittarian is unlikely to choose to work is in a zoo, because he is sickened by the sight of animals in cages. They are not alone in this – Leos and Aquarians hate zoos too.

Sagittarians who live mundane lives tend to have interesting hobbies. A quick round-up of my Sagittarian acquaintances reveals travel agents, airline workers, ministers of the church, mediums, healers, astrologers, people who work with horses, entertainers, broadcasters and a guy who is writing a book about mountain climbing.

Money, Shopping and Acquisitions

Sagittarians need stability and, therefore, will work hard to make a nice home for themselves. Many Sagittarians are very footloose when young, but as they reach maturity they develop the need for a good and stable household. They may share their home with others by opening a tea shop in part of it or even turning it into a hotel but they still need this sense of owning something worthwhile as a base. These people have excellent taste and will save and work hard to fill their homes with good quality furniture and fittings. They like to keep their homes tidy and well-maintained. Sagittarians are not especially money-minded but, because they love to live well and to be free of restriction or obligation, they usually work hard to be financially independent. These subjects are extremely generous, even over-generous at times and they love nothing better than to treat others to a good meal or a great evening out. Money for its own sake means nothing to them but they need plenty to spend on books, travel and their children's education. Some Sagittarians can live on next to nothing as long as their inner, spiritual lives are well nourished. However, most make sure that they have a high income often by doing two jobs at once, because they feel that life isn't worth living if they can't enjoy it and live it to the full. A nice car is an obvious must and Sagittarians prefer something sporty and *fast*! However, the assets they value most are books, and the feeling of freedom and independence.

Living with Sagittarius

A Sagittarian partner may use the home and the family in the same way that a racing driver uses a pit-stop, calling in for food, fuel, a change of clothes, a new cheque book and then off again. It also seems to take a Sagittarian quite a while to work out whether he actually wants a relation-ship or not. When he decides that he does want one, he then has to work out which of the many candidates for his attention will actually claim him. Sagittarians vary quite a bit in their attitudes. Some are relaters who want nothing better than to be in the middle of a happy family unit, while others are really better off alone, travelling lightly across the world, making new friends and acquaintances everywhere. Many Sagittarians live alone most of the time, floating backwards and forwards between their parents, friends, assorted lovers, sometimes spouses and pets.

These free-spirited folks need to be able to take off in a fishing boat for days at a time, to spend the evening drinking and gambling with friends or to crash out on a beach somewhere. My daughter's Sagittarian friends send her cheerful, optimistic, jokey letters and postcards from all over the world. Many of those who do settle down with a partner choose one from some far-off, exotic location where the family background and lifestyle is very different. Many Sagittarians seem to spend their lives on the brink of trav-elling to their spiritual home which is located, as far as I can ascertain, somewhere in the middle of Australia!

The more settled types of Sagittarian are easy-going, pleasant and helpful. These subjects may not be strong personalities but they are very loving and extremely kind. Sagittarians hate to see an injustice and will try to intervene in family quarrels in order to put things right. However, they can be too ineffectual to do much to change things. These people need a strong and reliable partner who will appreciate their cheerful and good-natured company. They love to talk and they need a partner who has a lively brain and a mind of his/her own. Sagittarians won't make many demands upon a partner and will not grumble too much if left at home while the other half travels or pursues a career. So long as there is give and take and trust in the relationship, these subjects can survive most things. Sagittarians can't always deal confidently and efficiently with severe problems but they do their best to help and they won't walk away just because the going gets hard. If they love someone, these generous people will give the partner everything they own and they will work hard to make the home a happy and comfortable place in which to live. However, if a Sagittarian finds himself in an increasingly difficult situation, he may be so powerless to change things that his only means of coping with it is to escape. One wonderful story which was told to me by a friend typifies the behaviour of this sign. Apparently my friend's mother had not had a pleasant marriage and, therefore, when the time came for the youngest child to start working, she arranged to go abroad and work as a contract nurse. The family came home that night to find a note on the kitchen table which announced, 'Dinner in oven. Gone to Bermuda. Back in three years.'

Sagittarians can be very eccentric. Their values are spiritual rather than material and they don't stop to worry about what the neighbours might think. I have known more than one Sagittarian who, when asked out to dinner, takes her own food and even her own saucepan and spoon! These people can be very disconcerting to those who are not used to their kind of behaviour. They follow a peculiar kind of logic and try to go through life without putting other people to any kind of trouble. They can be too outspoken for many people's taste because they don't hide their feelings. However, their honest and direct approach ensures that they are never two-faced.

Sexuality

Sagittarius is a fire sign which means that these subjects are quite strongly sexed. They are also adventurous and experimental in all areas of life, and this carries over into their sex lives as well. Sagittarians are not afraid of sexual adventures and they love to try anything new. They hate to think that they may miss out on anything and they are prevented from feeling foolish or getting hurt by their ability to put everything down to experience. Sagittarians may be unfaithful when young, although this is not done in order to punish or humiliate their partners, this simply reflects the fact that they don't take material or bodily matters very seriously. The thing which counts most for them is friendship along with the *experience* of love and sex. Later on, some of these footloose people settle down and make quite reasonable partners. By then they will have experimented enough sexually to know what works best for them and the whole business gets relegated to the background of their lives while they get on with other experiences which they find more interesting.

Even later in life, they can do without sex altogether, taking up something like archaeology, religion or growing rare orchids instead. One thing which is worth pointing out is their sense of amazed loss and their genuine grief when *someone else* makes use of *them* and subsequently moves on, leaving them behind.

Other Relationships

Sagittarians can take or leave wider relationships. These subjects are friendly and good-natured and would far prefer to get on well with in-laws, aunties and a new partner's children than live in an atmosphere of rancour. However, if it doesn't work, the Sagittarian doesn't blame himself; he simply writes this off as one of those things and steers clear of awkward relatives. Sagittarians are very broad-minded and absolutely non-racial, so relatives who are mixed in colour, race or religion are viewed as a blessing rather than a curse. The only ones they really can't stand are those who are stupid or gratuitously unpleasant.

As children, Sagittarians cause their parents very little trouble. They are out of the house almost as soon as they can walk, visiting friends, relatives or getting involved with school activities. They escape most of their parent's wrath by simply not being there, and many Sagittarian children have what amounts to a second family somewhere else in the neighbourhood. Sagittarius children are not particularly clever or remarkable, but they may do well if they are allowed to look after animals. Quite a number of Sagittarian children show an early talent for entertaining others or for sports. They have very enquiring minds and will want to travel away from home as soon as they can.

As parents, Sagittarian subjects are kind, loving and interesting; they will do all they can to teach their children and they will not leave questions unanswered. There is a danger that their children may have to take on the role of parents at a rather early stage in life, especially if there are severe difficulties to be coped with. Many Sagittarian parents can't cope with the reality of life with children and, therefore, do best if they can afford to send them off to school as weekly boarders or share the chore of bringing them up with other relatives.

Uri Geller

This strangely gifted Israeli amazed the world during the 1970s with his paranormal stunts. I have never heard a word of doubt expressed on the subject of his abilities, probably because he has allowed himself to be tested almost to destruction! As one who knows a thing or two about psychic phenomena myself, I understand that he is a 'physical' medium with a great deal of kinetic energy. In everyday language, Uri Geller can move, bend and otherwise affect everyday objects by the energy of his mind and his aura. He is also telepathic, and he probably has other psychic gifts as well. In addition to all this, he is a dedicated athlete and sportsman who now lives and works with his family in relative obscurity in Israel.

It almost goes without saying that Uri Geller has his Sun in Sagittarius, because this sign is so often associated with unusual people. The worldwide fame, travel and the sheer energy of the man is very Sagittarian, as are his interests in exercise, sports and the outdoor life. Uri's rising sign is Libra, but it is very late in the sign so that most of the first house is actually Scorpio. I have known a number of people with this kind of ascendant, all of whom have been so involved with the occult that they have become quite obsessed by it. Uri Geller's Moon, Venus and Jupiter in the first house in Scorpio suggest that he is in danger of defining himself by what he does, and also that he could make a good deal of money if he wanted to. However, the Sun in Sagittarius and a strong Jupiter don't make for a money-minded attitude, so I doubt whether Uri has actually become rich as a result of his talents. Pluto in the tenth house in Leo does suggest a desire to help the public in some way and also to be in the public eye. Saturn is in Uri's tenth house, also in Leo, and this is a common placement on the charts of famous people. Neptune in the twelfth house denotes an intuitive and psychic person, whilst its position in Libra could account for his ability to exchange energies with people and things. Mercury in Sagittarius in the second house and conjunct the south node suggests an ability to connect with others, possibly through the help of people from the past or who have been associated with a past life of some kind. Uri Geller's

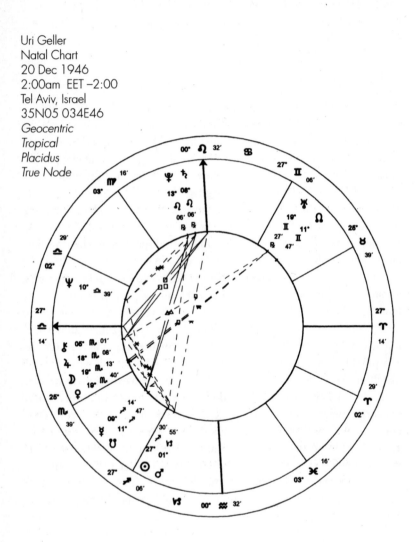

Uri Geller
Natal Chart
20 Dec 1946
2:00am EET −2:00
Tel Aviv, Israel
35N05 034E46
Geocentric
Tropical
Placidus
True Node

chart has a slight emphasis on the fire signs, and also a strongly fixed quality. This suggests enthusiasm, tempered with common sense. The five planets in angular houses make him happier to rely on himself than to follow anyone's lead. This is definitely an unusual chart which belongs to a very unusual man.

Steven Spielberg

One would expect Steven Spielberg to have an imaginative and creative chart that also shows executive ability and a measure of luck, so let us take a look at it now. Steven's Sun in Sagittarius gives him vision and the combination of the Sun, Mercury, Mars and the south node of the Moon in the sixth house tell us that he is happy when he is at work because he needs a project to get his teeth into. Uranus in Gemini in the twelfth denotes a clever and intuitive imagination. Neptune, being well aspected to the nodes in the fourth house in Libra, suggests that he needs time alone to ponder and to concentrate on making his imaginary dreams come true. Venus, Jupiter and the Moon in Scorpio denote deep feelings and an intense nature but all this being in the fifth house incline him to want to use his feelings and imagination to entertain others. My guess is that unless he is excited by an idea, he can't make himself work on it.

Planets in the fifth do give a childlike quality to any nature and in Steven's case he brings his comic book eye to life for the entertainment and education of children all around the world. Steven's Cancer ascendant and Pisces midheaven suggest that he is a caring person who loves his family and he extends this rather innocent form of love to children of all ages the world over. Cancer is a shrewd sign and Pisces is also not as daft as many are led to believe so this, coupled with his strong sixth house, suggests that he brings a good business head to what he does. Saturn and Pluto in the second mean that after a lot of hard work, he would make very large sums of money and that he would have the sense to invest this wisely.

A square aspect between the Moon and Saturn tell us that Steven's own childhood was not that comfortable and that his parents may have been at odds with each other. He would be loyal to them because these parental indicators are both in fixed signs but perhaps childhood damage or loneliness led him into the world of his own creativity and imagination, ultimately for all our benefit.

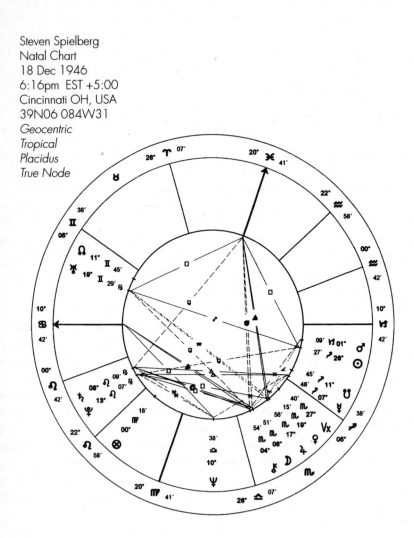

Steven Spielberg
Natal Chart
18 Dec 1946
6:16pm EST +5:00
Cincinnati OH, USA
39N06 084W31
Geocentric
Tropical
Placidus
True Node

10

Capricorn

Early one morning, just as the sun was rising,
I heard a maid sing in the valley below.
O! don't deceive me, O! never leave me,
How could you use a poor maiden so?

Early One Morning English air

Capricorns are constant, but they can be misused by less faithful types.

Sign: The Goat

Goats are attractive creatures which became very popular during the hippy era when self-sufficiency and goat products such as goat's milk and yogurt were suddenly all the rage. In other countries, they are a valuable source of food and are often looked after by the younger members of the family. Goats can live on the sides of impossibly steep mountains and can survive practically any kind of weather conditions. They eat anything and are, with help from their human keepers, partly responsible for the spreading of deserts across the face of the world. Capricorns do resemble goats in that they reach for the top wherever possible and can make a living under practically any conditions. Like goats, they are pleasant and popular and appear to be very co-operative and easy going. However, just as the goat loses its temper and butts others out of its way, so occasionally does the Capricorn.

Planet: Saturn

Saturn is considered to be the teacher of the Zodiac because it makes us struggle with life and learn from our experiences. It is traditionally associated with old age, restrictions, limitations, illness and trouble, which is why it is so feared by those who know just a little about astrology. However, Saturn has some very redeeming features because it is also associated with practicality, craftsmanship, attention to detail and the kind of self-discipline which gets things done. It is also connected with the increase in status when a job is completed correctly and the increase in income which follows increased status.

Gender: Feminine

Feminine subjects are more likely to wait and worry when trouble strikes, rather than to act for action's sake. Feminine sign subjects are quiet, retiring and much more likely to be unsure of themselves and conditioned to nurture and protect rather than to rush in and destroy.

Element: Earth

Earth sign people are careful, sensible, tenacious, reliable and conventional. They hate to give up on anything and may be materialistic. These people are mature in outlook but may be fussy and slow when tackling tasks, and they can be selfish.

Quality: Cardinal

Cardinal people like to take their own decisions and can be quite stubborn and determined. They are ambitious, either for themselves or their families, and are not easily pushed around. Some are very powerful and competitive personalities. Many, especially those with their Sun in Aries or Capricorn, reach executive positions and are also very adroit politically. However, they can also be manipulative if it helps them to gain their objectives.

Some General Characteristics

Capricorns are sensible and capable people who can vary from being surprisingly lighthearted and humorous to positively dour. Most Capricorns are naturally competent in business, although they can have problems due to mean and petty behaviour. These subjects usually have a sure touch with people and can do well in any field which requires tact and sensitivity. One area of people management at which they don't excel is dealing with the kind of coarse or vulgar person whom they see as belonging to the lower orders. When challenged, Capricorns can become stiff and formal in order to hide their embarrassment and unease with the situation. Capricorns need to have their efforts appreciated and their abilities respected because they tend to have a low level of self-esteem and need others to help them to learn to become comfortable with themselves. Capricornian ambition stems from this uneasy feeling of not quite measuring up, and they seem to grow into their skins and become far more comfortable when they have achieved a good position, got a few years of life and experience under their belt and acquired the responsibilities of a home and family. These subjects are born middle-aged and only really begin to feel at home when past forty.

Capricorns tend to feel threatened, insecure and unsure of their future. Even when they do well and get some money behind themselves, they are haunted by dreams of poverty and dependence. The roots of this feeling may stem from a difficult childhood, from listening to stories of their parent's early hardships, or it may even be a hangover from the experience of a previous life. This, of course, makes them great savers.

Shyness is a problem for younger Capricorns and even older or more confident subjects can sometimes cringe with embarrassment. Nevertheless, these people have a great deal of charm and a wonderfully dry sense of humour and they can be flirtatious in a delicately imaginative manner.

Perhaps it is their understanding of feelings of insecurity which makes Capricorns such good family members. Capricorns take good care of their parents, grandparents and even their in-laws throughout their lives. Obviously this works best when there is affection and goodwill on all sides, but even when this becomes a chore and a bore, the Capricorn will not renege on what he sees as his duty. As a parent, Capricorns can be a little out of touch because their old-fashioned and rather strict outlook can be seen as repressive by the child. However, if the child is reasonable by nature, the genuine love and care bestowed by the Capricorn parent is very much appreciated. I myself have a Capricorn stepfather and, according to all the laws of nature, this relationship should have been a very uncomfortable one. I was fourteen when my widowed mother met Sam and sixteen when they married. Being an only child, I was close to my mother and I should have resented the intrusion of a man in her life. As it happened, Sam and I got off on the right foot from day one, there was never a sour or a doubtful moment between us and we are still firm friends all these years later. Without his care and love, my teenage years would have been much harder than they were. My mother's life would naturally have been very difficult if this relationship had gone wrong. Capricorn men tend to put women on a pedestal and treat them with gentle chivalry.

There are faults to be found under this sign, of course. One of them is needless penny-pinching. They also have their own way of doing things and cannot be persuaded to work in any other way. Capricorns are slow and methodical in their approach and, although often very ambitious, they can lack imagination and the kind of flexibility which make for success. Although they reach executive positions, they can miss the top rung of the ladder through their rather fixed and negative attitudes. Some Capricorns worry about trifles and can bore everyone to death as a result. I remember one Capricorn client who went to the trouble and expense of having a horoscope cast because she needed to know the most propitious day for having blonde highlights put into her hair.

What Does the Capricornian Look Like?

Capricorns are rather good-looking in a kind of stately, formal, old-fashioned manner. One can imagine the male of the species dressed in old-style Dickensian clothes, running a counting house somewhere in the City of London. The men are often spare with sallow skin and dark straight hair. Some Capricorn women are also small and spare, whereas others tend to be rather bulky with large busts and shoulders. The women's hair often owes much to the art of their hairdressers (hence the worry over the highlights), because it is straight, mousy or dark and rather nondescript. In all races and both sexes the features are strong and the nose can be long and prominent. Many Capricorns smile with the ends of their mouths turned downwards rather than upwards! The hands and feet are small and, whatever they are wearing or whatever they are doing, they always look very clean and neat. Older Capricorn men are so smart and neat that they are often described as 'dapper'.

Health

Astrology can be a valuable tool for both the diagnosis and treatment of ailments but this involves the use of a full birth chart for each patient. The position of the Sun alone is not enough. However, here are the traditional areas of weakness associated with Capricorn.

The skeleton, the knees, the bones of the ear and the skin are typical Capricorn trouble spots but asthma is also a possibility. Many Capricorns are sickly youngsters who subsequently grow up into strong and healthy adults who live to a ripe old age.

Work and Hobbies

According to astrological theory, Capricorns are ambitious, conscientious, and so addicted to work that they seem to live for it. Is this true? To some extent, I think it is because a Capricorn without any work to do really is at a loose end. Even when these subjects retire from work, they look around for something else to do or they strive to make a success of a hobby. The idea of making an effort and making a success of what they do is important to them because they need to feel as if they are progressing. Capricorns are attracted to big business and also to money matters and are most comfortable when in an executive position in these firms.

Many of them can be found in the publishing business and in banking and accountancy, but they are also often self-employed in a variety of professional capacities. The sign of Capricorn is associated with the Earth itself, so many of them are drawn to green issues, either as part of a job or as an outside interest. This desire to make the world a better place can lead them into politics, teaching or running a humanitarian organisation. Capricorns have a formal approach to others and are not normally tactless or inappropriate in their behaviour. However, once one gets to know them, one discovers a wonderful sense of humour and a gentle form of flirta- tiousness. The main thing to bear in mind is that these polite, gentle, tactful, co-operative people are highly ambitious. They use their excellent education and training to get themselves into a large organisation of some kind and then through a combination of hard work and eye-on-the-main- chance, they move slowly but surely upwards. A quick round-up of a few Capricorn acquaintances reveals a shopkeeper, a singer, executives in the fields of building, books, shipping and banking.

Capricorn hobbies can be totally different from their work and surpris- ingly physical in content. They may be avid followers of their local football team, specialists in karate, ballroom dancing, tennis, cycling or a hundred other sports. They enjoy sports and ballroom dancing because these hobbies offer an opportunity to compete with others in a friendly fashion and also to take some exercise.

Money, Shopping and Acquisitions

Capricorns love money and will work hard to gain as much of it as they can. Once they have money they like to hang on to it, but some Capricorns have a strange tendency to gamble on dotty business schemes. If they lose their wealth, they soon build it up again and then think more carefully about such things in the future. This is an ambitious sign filled with people who do well and enjoy a successful lifestyle. These subjects are generous with their time and their money towards those whom they love and they will often take on financial responsibility for other members of their family. Capricorns need a secure base and money in the bank. They seem to come from the kind of background where poverty and hunger were prevalent and they spend their lives making sure that this doesn't happen to them or their dependents again. Some Capricorns are idealistic and will work for a better world so that other people can also enjoy a good quality of life, but most of them leave this kind of idealism to their Aquarian friends.

A Capricorn home is comfortable and well-maintained with as much surrounding land as the owner can afford. Capricorn is an earth sign, therefore these people like to have some elbow room and also a place to grow good things for the home. These subjects enjoy owning large and comfortable cars and although they don't go in for status symbols as such, they ensure that their possessions are as good quality and *value* as they can afford. Capricorns are very careful with money, having a reputation for materialism, and some of them are positively mean. There can hardly be a Capricorn in the developed world who doesn't have a bank account, a building society or Savings and Loan account and a post office savings book as well! However, Capricorns can and do spend out on travel, hobbies and their families, but they always ensure that they get value for money.

Living with Capricorn

Capricorns can live alone if they have to, but they prefer to be in a relationship and, better still, part of a family. Their shyness and awkwardness when young may make it difficult for them to get into the dating game but if they find someone quiet and reasonable, they may marry when quite young. However, it is not uncommon for these subjects to delay marriage until around their fortieth birthday, possibly having one or two fairly unsatisfactory affairs along the way. I'm not sure that Capricorns are ever really young in any case. These subjects are quite reasonable to live with. They will try to co-operate with the dreams and schemes of a partner and they will strive to make almost any situation work. One possible area of difficulty which may arise is their keen interest in their careers. In some cases their ambitions come before any thought of relationships, whilst in others, their drive for success keeps them away from home so much of the time that their marriages fall apart. This type of Capricorn can be very calculating, even to the point of marrying for money or status. Fortunately, this variety of Capricorn is rare, as most are too much in need of love and understanding to use a personal relationship that coldly.

Capricorns have an aloof outer manner, but once one gets close to them they are humorous, kindly, very loving to their families and slightly flirtatious in social situations. Capricorn men really like women. They don't merely fancy them or want to run off with them and they definitely don't want to dominate them, they simply like being with them. Capricorns are careful with money and have a reputation for being tight-fisted towards their partners. To be honest, most of the Capricorns whom I have come across are very generous to their families, and would rather go without nice things themselves than see a partner or child suffer. These subjects are practical and responsible people who are unlikely to gamble away the contents of the house or run off with the milkman; however they can be terribly pessimistic and unwilling to take any kind of chance. Like Virgos, these subjects can be too fussy for comfort, seeking perfection in all that they do, being quick to criticise other members of the family. Some of these subjects are dogmatic, opinionated and inflexible, which makes them very hard to live with, while others can be too self-absorbed to be true relaters. This self-absorption and attention to detail may be very hard to live with. Some Capricorns are quite arrogant and some land their families in trouble through crooked business deals but this is not the way that most Capricorns behave. These people have a gentle manner but a tough centre. They can compromise but they usually end up getting their own way.

As homemakers, Capricorns are really rather good. They like to invest their money in bricks and mortar and they won't allow a property to fall into disrepair. Being an earth sign, they need a bit of land around them and they can be quite keen gardeners, with an especial penchant for growing food. Capricornian homes are comfortable and well-equipped but not necessarily with the latest gadgetry. They don't actually spend much time at home because their work and their many interests keep them on the go, but they do like something comfortable and pleasant to come back to. Earth sign people are usually quite dexterous and many of them are good cooks. For example, in our family it is my Capricorn step-father who bakes the cakes!

Some Capricorns are very shy and awkward with new people and this tends to lead some of them to choose a partner who is more outgoing than themselves. In such cases, they don't feel upstaged when their partner is chatting away merrily while they sit quietly in the background. Other Capricorns need to shine in their own right and choose partners who will complement them rather than outshine them. Most of all these subjects need a partner who can offer them emotional security. Capricorns somehow seem to miss out on their share of love when young and they need to be able to rely upon this when they get into a relationship. Capricorns are easily embarrassed and their dignity is as important to them as it would be to a Leo. This means that they cannot bear the thought of living with a stupid partner who opens his/her mouth without thinking and a drunken partner is absolutely out of the question. Capricorns are quite intuitive, generally knowing when something is wrong with their loved ones, and they soon learn to trust their intuition. Generally speaking, as long as they are not hell-bent on a life in politics or a grand position in industry, Capricorns make rather good partners.

Sexuality

Most Capricorns are shy, slow to get off the ground with the opposite sex and definitely not overtly sexual. This doesn't mean that they don't care for sex; remember, this is an earth sign and all earth signs are sensual. Capricorns are not particularly experimental as far as sex is concerned, possibly because they suffer from rather old-fashioned feelings of guilt, and partly because some of them actually fear sex. Others are quite happy to make love as long as they are in charge of the proceedings and are in no danger of being faced with something surprising or, worse still, embarrassing. Some Capricorns prefer to remain virgins until well into their thirties, while others give up the whole messy business as soon as they can. Having said this, most Capricorns are quite happy to make love while they are in a safe, wholesome relationship with someone whom they can love and trust. Some astrology books give these subjects a reputation for lechery but this doesn't seem to be born out by reality. There are some very flirtatious Capricorns who may well have a soft spot for the opposite sex, but I get the distinct feeling that they use flirtation in order to either gain attention or control the people whom they meet socially. Having said all that, there are some really sexy goats around.

Other Relationships

Capricorns are ideal family people because, although they get on well enough with colleagues and acquaintances, they reserve their real affection for their families, which includes parents and grandparents as well as their partners and children. Anyone marrying a Capricorn will have to take their fondness for other members of their family into consideration. Capricorns need an atmosphere of harmony and they hate bad feeling or family feuds. Capricorns don't have many friends but they do have quite a number of acquaintances. It is not easy to get to know these people because they don't share confidences with people whom they know casually.

As parents these subjects are very loving and a trifle old-fashioned. They are ambitious on behalf of their children and they will make every effort to see that they have all the things that they need. Capricorns respect authority and will try to teach their children to respect their teachers, youth leaders and so on. These parents are very keen on education, perceiving it as the way forward for their children.

As a child, the Capricorn is shy, retiring and lacking in confidence, but he is sensible, studious and mature for his age. The Capricorn child can be quite ambitious, with his goat's feet in the valley and his eyes on the distant hills. Such a child is unlikely to be a problem to his parents but he can be obstinate and distant.

Cynthia Payne

Cynthia Payne's Sun is in Capricorn and she has Capricorn on the ascendant. This combination shrieks of a hard childhood with poverty and neglect as constant companions. She was probably close to her mother but she could have seen her as a woman who had to be tough to survive. Alternatively, Cynthia herself has had to put on a very tough front in order to get anywhere in life. The Moon in Scorpio shows that her feelings are deep and intense and that she has taken any early disappointments in life very much to heart. The Moon close to her Scorpio midheaven, coupled with all that Capricorn suggests ambition and a desire for money, status and security. Cynthia's Scorpio Moon and midheaven, coupled with Jupiter, Mars and Neptune in the eighth house in Virgo show that she chose sex as her career option (or maybe sex chose her)!

Three planets in Virgo denote a hard worker and the Sun and ascendant in Capricorn confirm this, and if this were not enough, Cynthia's rising planet is hard-working Saturn. My guess is that she was probably a

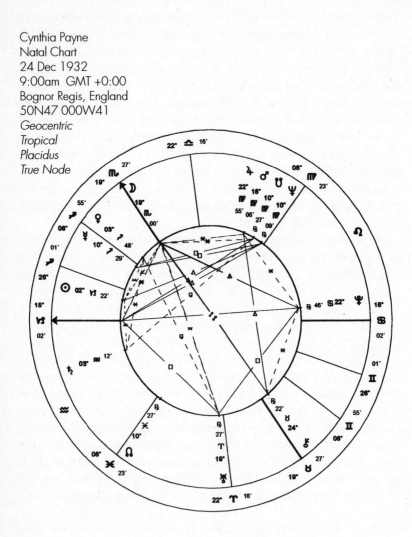

Cynthia Payne
Natal Chart
24 Dec 1932
9:00am GMT +0:00
Bognor Regis, England
50N47 000W41
Geocentric
Tropical
Placidus
True Node

bit shy and self-conscious as a youngster. The Sun in the twelfth house, the Moon in the ninth and Venus in the tenth in Sagittarius denote that Cynthia has tried to provide a real service for the men who used her brothels and for the women who earned their living there. She was not just in it for the money, she is genuinely interested in people and as long as their needs accommodate her own financial needs and didn't encroach on her privacy, she would help where she could.

Cynthia's Moon is nicely aspected to her strong Pluto which is in her seventh house in Cancer and this shows a motherly streak which also seems to have been accommodated by her strange career. She once mentioned in an interview that she spent a lot of time in the kitchen making sandwiches and drinks for clients and workers alike and this doesn't surprise me. A tough lady maybe, but a bright and entertaining one who has tried to make people happy.

David Bowie

David Bowie is a talented pop singer whose music has always been just that little bit different. He is known for his sense of style and also his bi-sexual image. There doesn't seem to be any indication of sexual problems on David's chart, so whatever he chooses to do seems to suit him very well. My guess is that this bi-sexual thing is all part of his image because, like many show-business personalities, it is the image which we see rather than the real person. David's Sun sign is in cool, calm, hard-working Capricorn, close to his Mars and Mercury. This suggests a very quick, if slightly inflexible mind and a hot temper. People who have Sun/Mars conjunctions always seem to march to their own drumbeat, and they also have the courage of their convictions. David's rising sign is Libra. This sign endows him with a pleasant outer manner and youthful good looks throughout his life. Libra is a sign which is closely associated with image and looks and is very suited to his stage persona. The planet Neptune is in an exact conjunction to the ascendant which strengthens the idea of illusion and imagery even more. David is probably very artistic in addition to being creative. One certainty is that he loves his home and would feel very threatened if he had to live without a place of his own for any length of time. This is due to the group of planets clustered around the nadir of his chart. Jupiter in the second house in Scorpio suggests that David is both lucky and clever with money and also that he thinks deeply about his values and priorities and has a strongly idealistic streak.

Friends are very important to David Bowie as shown by three planets in Leo in the eleventh house of friendship. The Moon, which is well

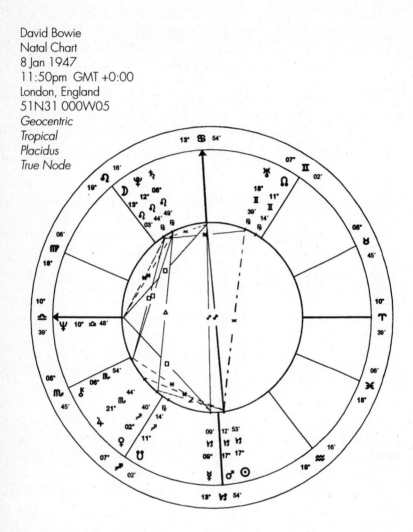

David Bowie
Natal Chart
8 Jan 1947
11:50pm GMT +0:00
London, England
51N31 000W05
Geocentric
Tropical
Placidus
True Node

aspected in the glamorous sign of Leo, gives him both his affinity with the razzle-dazzle of show-business and his love of music. This Moon position also suggests a determination to work to the highest standards and to pay attention to detail. David can be quite stubborn. Venus in Sagittarius suggests that his female friends and lovers must be independent, intelligent and interesting while Mars, strongly bracketed by the Sun and Mercury in Capricorn suggests that his male friends (and, maybe, his lovers) would be strong, sensible and clever. Incidentally, a tightly bracketed Mars can indicate unusual sexual preferences.

The way David Bowie's chart is arranged shows an up-front 'me-first' attitude to life. He has an emphasis on the energetic fire signs and also a strong set of planets in cardinal and fixed signs. Six planets in angular houses suggests that he has an ambitious, decisive personality.

11

Aquarius

Believe me, if all those endearing young charms,
Which I gaze on so fondly today,
Were to change by tomorrow, and fleet in my arms.
Like fairy gifts, fading away,
Thou wouldst still be ador'd as this moment thou art,
Let thy loveliness fade as it will;
And around the dear ruin, each wish of my heart
Would entwine itself verdantly still!

Believe Me, If All Those Endearing Young Charms
Irish air

Constant, unaffected by appearances and slightly insulting, this could only be Aquarius.

Sign: The Water Carrier

The symbol of the man pouring water from a large jug or pot looks rather like an escapee from a pack of Tarot cards. It is a peaceful symbol which conjures up images of watering crops, cleansing and purifying or even washing someone's feet. Is the mysteriousness of this sign reflected in the nature of the average Aquarian? Well perhaps, because Aquarians, while being very friendly, are actually quite hard to get to know and some of them are so strange that it is difficult to work out what they are doing and why.

Planets: Uranus and Saturn

In the past astronomers could only see five planets with the naked eye (Mercury, Venus, Mars, Jupiter and Saturn), so they ascribed two of the signs of the zodiac to each of these, and one each to the Sun and the Moon. Following the invention of really effective telescopes the three outer planets of Uranus, Neptune and Pluto were discovered and these have now been given the rulerships of Aquarius, Pisces and Scorpio. Therefore, Saturn is the old ruler of Aquarius as well as being the ruler of Capricorn, and Uranus is the modern ruler of Aquarius.

Uranus is associated with revolution, change, eccentricity and an outlook which is original and different. This planet concerns the world of ideas and ideals, the rights of man and a humanitarian outlook. Saturn is concerned with limitations and restrictions as well as the ability to work thoroughly and in a scientific manner. These two ideas are encompassed within the Aquarian Personality.

Gender: Masculine

Masculine subjects are more likely to tackle a problem themselves than to hand it over to someone else to deal with. Masculine sign subjects say what they mean and don't hesitate to push themselves or their children to the forefront.

Element: Air

This is the least emotional of all the elements, relying upon knowledge and logic to work things out. Air subjects are intellectual, interested in everything and able to pick up and pass on knowledge as a result of being in the swim and among people. Too much emotion exhausts them and too much routine bores them.

Quality: Fixed

Fixed people like to stay put and remain in the same house, the same job and the same relationship for years. Most fixed sign people will see things through to the end and they may find it difficult to make any kind of fresh start. Their opinions may also be fixed.

Some General Characteristics

An Aquarian friend of mine who unusually, perhaps, is *not* interested in astrology pointed out that both he and his wife are Aquarians, as are seven other members of their family. He told me that, as all these people were very different from each other and this proved to him that there couldn't be anything in astrology. I laughed and told him that *all* Aquarians are different from everybody else, including fellow members of their own sign and of their own family. Each one is an individual who marches to his own drumbeat and doesn't follow any kind of collective thinking. Each Aquarian must live by his own rules and needs to do his own thing most of the time.

Intelligent, logical and blessed with the ability to think not only laterally, but also around corners, these subjects are possibly the most exciting in the zodiac. They can also be infuriating because they choose to cling to their odd way of life and their ideas with great tenacity. Parents with Aquarian offspring frequently write them off because they cannot be made to conform to the family pattern. Aquarians make the most wonderful friends, but anyone who tries to cling to them or expects their friendship to be exclusive will be very disappointed. Anyone who needs encouragement can be sure of receiving it from an Aquarian friend, but they are quite competitive and won't appreciate being overtaken in their own chosen field.

Aquarius is a fixed sign which ensures that these subjects stick to jobs and relationships through thick and thin. If they decide that they need to make a break, they do this in an almost clinical manner and, although they may feel guilty about leaving, they still go ahead with it. If possible they try to remain on friendly terms with the person or group of people even after they detach themselves from them. Aquarians can be loners who feel stifled by too much closeness. They don't like to be closely questioned about their intentions, or even their whereabouts the previous night! But they appreciate a non-clinging relationship. Aquarians do need to relate to others on a deep and loving level, but it may take them some time before they can relax and trust others to love them or to be loved by them.

Aquarians can be stubborn and determined and also inflexible in their attitudes and they may have an attitude of superiority. They genuinely believe that they are special and may patronise those whom they see as unfit or unable to come up to their exacting standards. Most Aquarians have fields of specialist knowledge, often in offbeat and interesting areas, and they are happy to teach anyone who shows an interest in their particular subject. Some become involved in politics or causes of one kind or another and are often way ahead of the crowd. My friend Denise, who has Aquarius rising, recently told me that she had campaigned for lead-free petrol way back in the 1960s. Their very stubbornness makes them the most loyal and wonderful friends; the kind who can be called up in the middle of the night and asked for help.

Most Aquarians love to teach and have a real talent for the job, and many of them work in the field of education, while others are happy to coach others in a more casual manner. These subjects derive a real sense of achievement from improving the lives of others, either on an individual basis or by educating the world in general. I have noticed that most Aquarians are strangely blind to the pain and anguish of those who are around them. They can deal with problems on a distant level, for instance, by campaigning for political change but, when it comes to their own families, they cannot. Some of these subjects genuinely cannot see that a child or a partner is suffering, while others can see the pain but are irritated by it. One Aquarian friend tells me that, if anyone in his family is ill, he gets out of the house because he knows that he will lose patience with them if he hangs around. To be honest, most Aquarians are extremely helpful and sympathetic but none of them can stand moaners or the type of person who has a negative attitude to life. They will, therefore, help out immediately when faced with a practical problem but they become distant or angry when faced with someone whose emotions are out of control. They respect strength of character and have very little time for what they see as weakness or failure – even when this is their own failure. Aquarians need to see themselves as competent, clever and successful in their chosen field. They need to stand out from the crowd and to be respected for their knowledge. There is a tendency for Aquarians to be tactless and some can be bullies. This is because they are devastatingly honest about other people's faults and failings and also because they sometimes fail to understand how their own behaviour affects others. In some ways, these people are easy to respect but hard to love.

What Does the Aquarian Look Like?

The typical Aquarian is tall and slim, while some are positively skinny. Many have a strong bony frame. In white races, the complexion is pale and the hair blond or mousy. Many Aquarians have wispy and lifeless hair and many Aquarian men go bald. If the Aquarian is blessed with good hair, then it is very good indeed, being thick, straight and dark. Their hands and feet are long and elegant but they sometimes look as if they belong on a much older person. Many Aquarians have a strong jaw and a large, toothy smile and light coloured or very bright eyes which look at others with a very direct and interested gaze. Their choice of clothes is totally individualistic and often downright peculiar! Aquarians adored the fancy dress which was fashionable in the late 1960s and early 1970s because they could indulge their personal fantasies to the hilt. Even now in the staid and conventional 1990s, Aquarians can be seen in jodhpurs, flowing kaftans, strangely patterned denims and top-of-the-range designer model clothes.

Health

Astrology can be a valuable tool for both the diagnosis and treatment of ailments but this involves the use of a full birth chart for each patient. The position of the Sun alone is not enough. However, here are the traditional areas of weakness associated with Aquarius.

The ankles are the traditional Aquarian weak spot, which suggests that breaks and sprains are likely. Phlebitis, thrombosis and leg ulcers are possible. Quite a number of Aquarians have sensitive lungs so they may suffer from asthma and they may be uncomfortable when among smokers.

Work and Hobbies

Aquarians are so varied in their nature that they can do almost any kind of work. However, self-employment and owning a small business appeals to many of them. Some years ago, my friend Denise had to hire a fairly large gang of workmen at her place of work and she commented to me that out of the twelve workmen whom she was dealing with, eleven of them were Aquarians! It's not surprising that Aquarians find their way into building and other practical crafts because they are the world's best problem solvers and they are also very independent. This is the sign of the journeyman, craftsman and the computer whizz-kid. Many Aquarians take up astrology, so much so that it would be a very strange group of astrologers that didn't include at least one Aquarian. Many are drawn to the world of teaching because they have a real gift for this. All Aquarians have extremely enquiring minds and often have a great depth of knowledge in a variety of areas. Many are excellent advisors, counsellors and listeners, which leads them into either paid or voluntary counselling work. Aquarians are attracted to committee activities and to politics, and many of them find work in those areas where their sense of commitment, logical minds and humanitarianism can be put to good use. To be honest, Aquarians can be found in almost any kind of job, but they usually gravitate to something which has a humanitarian edge to it. Among my Aquarian friends I can count a bank clerk, the head of the central sterilising department of a large hospital, a designer of surgical instruments, the head of a large mail-order firm, the owner of a small publishing firm, shopkeepers, craftsmen and craftswomen of all kinds, computer experts and astrologers by the dozen.

If an Aquarian cannot help people, use his intelligence or specialise in his work, he will use these skills in his hobbies. Aquarians take their sparetime activities very seriously. These subjects may look after animals, work for the preservation of our planet or make ships in bottles but they don't simply come home and sit in an armchair in front of the television. Perhaps the greatest Aquarian hobby is friendship, because they love to chat and learn about ways of life which are different from their own. Oddly enough, very few of them seem to be keen on travel, and some become very ill at ease when away from their usual surroundings.

Money, Shopping and Acquisitions

Aquarians have a reputation for being non-materialistic, humanitarian and eccentric. These subjects are supposed to be elevated to an exalted level where all is love and light and money is unnecessary. Poppycock! Aquarians like money as much as the next sign, and more than many. Some Aquarians like money so much that they are prepared to work hard for it. Others are content to fiddle and dream their lives away while their spouses, relatives and friends pay their bills. Many Aquarians work at jobs which are far beneath their levels of ability, possibly so that they can expend their energies on more interesting pursuits. However, those who do pursue a career enjoy being well paid. Aquarians are so different from each other that few generalisations can be made. Some, for instance live in pristine cleanliness in ultra-modern apartments while others live in rambling old houses which are filled with children, animals, visitors, lodgers and filth. Many Aquarians work close to home by running farms or smallholdings and others have offices or even schools within their homes. This suggests that their homes are not viewed as a possession but as part of their general lifestyle.

There are Aquarians who have a multitude of fascinating and wonderful possessions, ranging from the latest in computers to mobile games, ornaments and even, perhaps, a spaceship in the garden. Others collect antiques, junk or animals. All Aquarians seem to collect books and bits of paper. Some Aquarians spend their money on experiences rather than things. My son, Stuart, who has Aquarius rising, asked for – and was given

– an hour's lesson in a helicopter for his birthday this year! Aquarians can be found riding horses, learning to paint, hunting for ley lines or attending astrology groups. However much friendships and experiences are valued, the Aquarian also values a comfortable home, a good fast car and whatever eclectic status symbol appeals most to him.

Living with Aquarius

Aquarians need friends but they don't all necessarily need lovers, partners, spouses or families. Their needs can change from one phase of their lives to another, so the Aquarian who starts out as a loner may end up happily surrounded by family and friends or vice-versa. These subjects are so unusual that they need partners who can understand their peculiarities and can put up with them. The best relationship for these people is usually with a partner who shares their interests and wants the same kind of lifestyle. It is not uncommon for Aquarians to live with other Aquarians or to choose partners who have a strong Aquarian cast to their charts. Hot favourites are Capricorns or Pisceans who have neighbouring planets in Aquarius. Anyone living with an Aquarian will have the benefit of his/her excellent mind, while another benefit is that boredom is unlikely to set in. Aquarians are not really homemakers in the old-fashioned sense of the word, but they do like to live in a pleasant area with enough space both indoors and out for them to be able to breathe. Some Aquarians are exceptionally neat and tidy in their habits, keeping a really well-run home, but many others seem to prefer living in a mess, complete with children, animals and neighbours wandering in and out. These homes, albeit untidy, are wonderful to visit, because the caller is always sure of a cup of tea, something to eat and an hour or two of wonderful conversation. Mess or no mess, most Aquarians are very good cooks who try to ensure that they and their families eat a healthy diet.

Aquarians are not as easygoing as they first appear, because this is a fixed sign which denotes a stubborn and determined attitude to life. Aquarians tend to do exactly what they want to do, usually just when they want to do it, and it is no good trying to get them to behave in any other way. These subjects seem to have an agenda all of their own, together with a hidden set of rules by which everyone around them is supposed to live. They frequently have strong political views, or they may be 'into' some belief or peculiar way of life. Even the most ordinary, unassuming and 'normal' Aquarian chooses the kind of career which will help humanity in some way. Sometimes their beliefs take over the whole of their lives. Being highly intelligent, these subjects are sure that they can see themselves clear-ly and that they understand others just as well. However, they actually have quite a few blind spots which can make them difficult to live with. Aquarians can be unrealistic and impractical in some ways, while being very sensible and capable in others. This all depends upon the frame of mind they happen to be in at the time.

Aquarian women need a job or interest of their own. They may choose to do something unusual but, whatever they do, they will be wholehearted about it and will find it hard to be clockwatchers. This means that their families will have to learn to cope by themselves from time to time.

Some Aquarians are amazingly mean, being unable to see that others have any kind of claim on their income. Other Aquarians are amazingly generous because their values are mental and spiritual rather than materi-alistic and they rarely worry about money or security. All Aquarians are incredibly independent people who are very hard to Influence, but if they respect their partner's views and find them logical, they can usually be brought round to a different way of thinking. Most of these subjects lead very busy lives and they would rather do almost anything in preference to sitting slumped in an armchair, staring at the television. Aquarians are frequently late for appointments because they try to pack too much into each day and they leave too much to the last minute. Aquarians enjoy going out with their families and take an interest in their partner's hobbies or pastimes, although they may not want to join in on a permanent basis. These subjects need mental and physical space and they are also prepared to give this to a partner. About the only thing they cannot stand is being probed and investigated because they seem to need to keep a little part of themselves private. Aquarians can be rude, bad-tempered and arrogant, but if their partner can laugh off these foibles and concentrate on the Aquarian's virtues, the relationship will succeed. One thing Aquarians cannot cope with is an over-emotional partner because too much emotion upsets their equilibrium and may make them ill. Oddly enough, many Aquarians are worriers and this tension can translate itself into ailments such as asthma or eczema. All Aquarians can be kind, caring and loving if given half a chance, although I usually find that female Aquarians are nicer, softer and more genuinely caring than the males of this sign.

The vast majority of Aquarians are loyal and faithful lovers who won't break up a relationship without good reason. These subjects are not comfortable with duplicity, so if they meet someone they like whilst they are still in a relationship, they are likely to break up the first relationship before becoming involved in the second. Aquarians need freedom in a relationship and a jealous or suspicious partner is absolutely no use to them at all. They find it hard to give reassurance when none is needed. The vast majority of Aquarians are perfectly reasonable people who like nothing better than to find a soul-mate and spend their lives with them. Unusually, in this age of short-lived relationships, Aquarians tend to get married when young and then stay with the same partner throughout. They love to talk to just about everyone, but they don't usually allow emotional or sexual curiosity to get them into triangle situations.

The saving grace of all Aquarians in all situations is their wonderful sense of humour.

Sexuality

Aquarians vary so much from one another that it is not surprising that they vary in their sexuality. Many of these friendly, outgoing people are very attractive, but whether they will actually take up all the romantic offers they receive depends upon other factors on their charts. Some Aquarians prefer to be on their own, without any kind of involvement other than that of friendship, while others only really enjoy sex when in a safe, comfortable partnership. These subjects have many friends but are cautious when it comes to deeper relationships and they prefer not to flirt or play dangerous games with other people's partners. Once they are in a happy relationship, they enjoy making love and can achieve a greater sense of closeness through sex than they can in practically any other way. Aquarians like a bit of variety in their sex lives and will take pleasure in a partner who dresses well and wears attractive underwear. They themselves are usually slim, elegant and good looking people who can be quite vain about their appearance. They are either well-dressed, appreciating the pleasure that this gives their partners, or they dress in an eccentric manner which pleases nobody but themselves. Aquarians can be fussy about their partner's appearance and they appreciate a lover who keeps in shape and looks good. These subjects especially enjoy the sight and the feel of good underwear and they can have fun by dressing up specially for love-making. If the sexual side of a relationship diminishes, they will remain friends but they may not continue to feel as deeply about the other person.

Other Relationships

Aquarians usually have many friends and acquaintances and they are quite happy to have company or to go on holiday in a group. As far as the family is concerned, they try to remain on good terms with everyone but they may avoid too much closeness. Aquarians see themselves as equal to other people, therefore if a member of the family demands to be treated with deference, the Aquarian will not accede to this demand. If any member of their family or of their partner's family needs help, the Aquarian will do whatever he can but will not be bullied or dictated to by anyone.

Aquarians are good parents, especially if their children are reasonable and intelligent but they will switch off if a child becomes awkward and demanding. They will try to do everything in their power to help a child succeed but they are not good at handling a child's emotional problems and they may not even notice when a child is unhappy.

Aquarian children are not difficult to deal with, as long as their parents respect their dignity and realise that they have strong opinions of their own. These children are usually keen on school and fond of a variety of outside interests. They have many friends and adjust fairly well to whatever circumstances they find themselves in. Despite their logical and somewhat unemotional natures, they need to feel secure and to be understood in addition to needing space and freedom.

Paul Newman

Paul Newman is a wonderful actor whose career has encompassed many years and many different kinds of film. His sense of humour shines through his work and his self-discipline is evident. This self-discipline is shown by the presence of Capricorn on his ascendant, and the placing of three planets in that sign. Mercury being right on the ascendant denotes an excellent communicator and, in this case, it is bracketed by charming Venus on one side and fair-minded, balanced Jupiter on the other. I remember seeing a television interview once in which Paul was asked what he would have liked to have been had he not been an actor. He replied that, if he had had to choose an alternative career, it would have been as a lawyer. These three planets wrapped around the ascendant certainly give him the ability to work with the law and Saturn near the midheaven, in the tenth house, would give him the tenacity and the intellect to cope with this. Saturn in Scorpio might have led him into criminal law. This kind of interesting digression shows how a chart can reveal untapped potential.

As we have said, Paul Newman is an excellent communicator who, in this case, uses the medium of acting. His Moon in Pisces makes him vulnerable by nature and also able to absorb and then act out the feelings of others. This Moon position is a good one for any kind of creative work

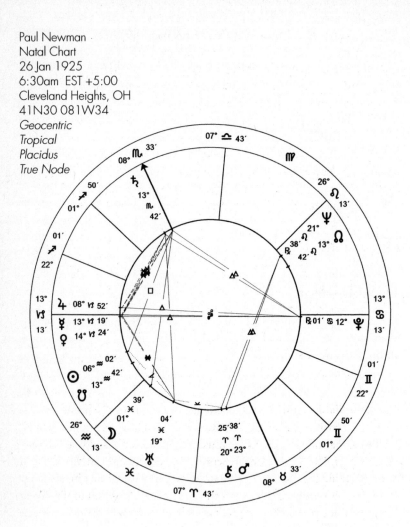

Paul Newman
Natal Chart
26 Jan 1925
6:30am EST +5:00
Cleveland Heights, OH
41N30 081W34
Geocentric
Tropical
Placidus
True Node

and, as this Moon and also Paul's Uranus are in the second house, he can earn money by creative endeavours. Mars in Aries gives him energy which is expressed by communication, due to it being in the third house and also being well aspected by Neptune in Leo. The Sun in the first house in Aquarius suggests that Paul marches to his own drumbeat and won't be pushed around. The placement of Pluto in Cancer right on the descendant and opposite the Capricorn stellium suggests that his marriage to Joanne Woodward has been a strong influence on him and that she has given him the stability he needed to pursue his career so forcefully.

Paul has a good balance between the elements of earth, fire and water but is a little short of air planets. This is surprising for such a communicator, but perhaps it suggests that he communicates best through the medium of emotion, as shown by the emphasis on water signs. Five planets in cardinal signs and five in angular houses suggest that Paul Newman is a self-starter who makes his own decisions and leads whatever team he finds himself in.

Phil Collins

The three things that stand out in my mind are Phil's music, his obvious love of his children and his utter contempt and lack of interest in his ex-wife – and that when he was apparently happily married to her! An out-wardly wonderful man maybe but perhaps with a cold and unfeeling heart. Phil's Sun is in the unusual and inventive sign of Aquarius and it is conjunct his IC in the fourth house. Also in the fourth house are Venus in Aquarius and Mars and Jupiter in Pisces so Phil's home and private life are very important to him. My guess is that he is close to his mother. Phil's Libra ascendant with the sensitive Moon and imaginative Neptune close to it suggest a creative and artistic nature and he could well be multi-talented. We know that in addition to his musical abilities, Phil is also an accom-plished actor. The Moon rising in Scorpio suggests that he can hide his own feelings behind the character of whatever part he plays or that he can pour them into his music. His emotions run deep but the position of the Moon in the first house means that he is far more interested in his own feelings than those of anyone else.

Phil probably has very strong views about the way the world should be run. Aquarians are often ethical people who have strong opinions on such matters as education, ecology and so forth and the Rising Moon in Scorpio would emphasise this. Phil's Sun in the fourth should make him very fami-ly minded and a great home lover but perhaps that only extends to those members of his family who he feels deserve his love and attention.

Phil Collins
Natal Chart
30 Jan 1951
0:05am GMT +0:00
London, England
51N31 000W05
Geocentric
Tropical
Placidus
True Node

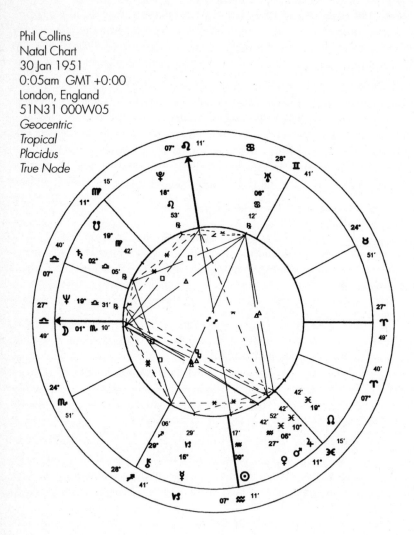

Saturn in the eleventh house in Libra, afflicted by squares from Chiron and Uranus suggest that Phil's father may have been a distant, detached figure who possibly gave him a hard time. If so, this might have given Phil little information on the way a man should be and how he should behave to others. There are no planets in the seventh or eighth houses on Phil's chart suggesting little real need for close, loving relationships. Mars, the ruler of his descendant is in artistic Pisces and it is wonderfully aspected with a grand trine. Men, music and art are lucky for him and it is amongst men and the abstract ideas of film, music and art that Phil is most comfortable. Phil Collins seems to be a talented and friendly man who likes his own company and who, mercifully, seems to love his children.

12

Pisces

Drink to me only with thine eyes,
And I will pledge with mine,
Or leave a kiss within the cup,
and I'll not ask for wine,
The thirst that from the soul doth rise
Doth ask a drink divine.
But might I of Jove's nectar sip
I would not change for thine.

Drink To Me Only With Thine Eyes
an old English air with words by
Ben Johnson

A very suitable song for Pisces with its theme of love and wine, and also the reference to Jove (Jupiter), who was the ancient ruler of the Sign of Pisces.

Sign: The Two Fish

The two fish in the sign of Pisces are tied together and are attempting to swim in two different directions at once, one upstream and the other downstream. Presumably the fish end up swimming round and round each other in the same bit of river. This image suggests confusion, an inability to get anywhere at all and a great deal of energy which is expended on futile enterprises. The two fish also represent duality in the same way as the

Scales for Libra or the Twins for Gemini. So, are Pisceans multi-faceted, sometimes confused, able to be in touch with both heaven and earth, the spiritual and the material world and also able to understand all the subtleties of thinking and feeling? The answer is maybe!

Planets: Neptune and Jupiter

In the days before telescopes were available, only five planets in the Solar system could be seen from the Earth. These were Mercury, Venus, Mars, Jupiter and Saturn. Astrologers ascribed two signs of the zodiac to each of these planets and one each to the Sun and the Moon. Since the discovery of the more distant planets of Uranus, Neptune and Pluto, these have been assigned to Aquarius, Pisces and Scorpio. The ancient ruler of Pisces was Jupiter, but nowadays the ruler is considered to be Neptune.

Neptune is associated with dreams and muddles, clouded thinking and looking at the world through rose-coloured spectacles. The Roman god, Neptune, was the ruler of the sea and also of those things which are found in it such as fish or sea-monsters. Liquids such as oil and also nebulous, cloudy, powerful substances such as gas and chemicals are also associated with Neptune. Illusion in the form of photography, film and the emotional effect of music could also be assigned to Neptune. The Neptunian list is as endless as it is hard to define but if you link it with either a shifting mass of liquidity or something which is imaginative or illusory, you will have grasped the idea.

Jupiter is associated with expansion of horizons in all manner of ways. Therefore expanding boundaries by travelling to new or inaccessible places or expanding mental boundaries by knowledge are very much a part of Jupiter's realm. Jupiter rules the higher realms of intellectuality, experimental ideas such as one would find in higher education, the legal system and also any kind of religious or philosophical thought. It is also associated with good luck and opportunity.

Gender: Feminine

Feminine subjects are more likely to wait and worry when trouble strikes rather than to act for action's sake. Feminine sign subjects are quiet and retiring, more likely to be unsure of themselves and conditioned to nurture and protect rather than to rush in and destroy.

Element: Water

The water element makes for sensitivity. Therefore, water people are likely to be irritated by loud or discordant noises and upset by pain and illness. They are sensitive to atmospheres and very wary of anything which could constitute a threat. They are kind and helpful, because they are sensitive to the suffering and pain of others. However, many of them are actually more attuned to the needs of animals than of humans. Water people move and react slowly and may seem rather stupid to quicker types but this is a mistaken assumption because they are extremely shrewd and well aware of everything that is going on.

Quality: Mutable

This word may seem strange to you but if you think of transmute, commute or mutate, you will see that it concerns moving something from one place to another or from one state to another. Mutable people, therefore, are flexible in their attitudes, dislike too much routine and have the need for a changeable lifestyle. They may take up too many interests and find it difficult to finish any of them. However, they are able to fit into most situations and can make themselves comfortable even when permanently on the move.

Some General Characteristics

Pisceans are rather unworldly people who have their heads in the clouds and their feet just about anywhere from the ground upwards! Many Pisceans are gentle creatures who want to make the world a better place than it is now but who may lack the energy or the mental co-ordination to do so. These subjects invariably choose to work in some kind of caring field which could take them into anything from politics to animal welfare. They loathe the idea of vivisection, prison, restriction and punishment of any kind and it is probably this which leads so many of them to find work as nurses, prison visitors or psychiatrists. I have a good deal of Pisces on my own chart and have spent short spells of time working in a prison, a mental hospital and, of course, a very long spell as an astrological counsellor.

It seems that Pisceans grow to adulthood with painful memories which are either left over from their own childhood or possibly from a previous life. This makes them especially sensitive to the pain of others. In most cases they respond to this by wanting to heal the world and to put right all the wrongs which they come across. Having said this, some Pisceans respond to the pain of others by lashing out and hurting the one who is suffering, presumably in order to push their own pain away in an attempt to relegate it to some far off corner. This kind of syndrome may lead a Piscean man to hit his unhappy wife and then rush out to drown his own painful emotions in the nearest pub. Others have such a need for security that they become desperately mean and penny-pinching or they collect so much junk for a rainy day that they can hardly move around their homes.

Pisceans are idealistic and, in some cases, unrealistic. They can become very excited by an idea and set off on a course of action without really thinking it through, but their superb intuition leads them safely and surely in the right direction. In both working circumstances and in their personal life, Pisceans benefit by having a steady, practical partner who keeps them from going off at a tangent or from falling into despair. Pisceans can become helpless, out-of-control and terribly depressed at times. However, these subjects have a piquant sense of humour which probably does more to save them from themselves than anything else. They also have amazing powers of recovery and can bounce back from physical or emotional problems very quickly when they want to.

Pisceans are highly creative and often very artistic, with a strongly visual imagination. This ability to visualise, added to strongly intuitive capabilities, leads many Pisceans to encounter clairvoyant experiences which means that many of them develop an interest in mystical and mediumistic subjects. Others can be found in all areas of creative or artistic work such as music, painting, film video recording, the creative side of the media and fashion design. If a Piscean finds a job he really likes or decides to go into business for himself, his stubborn determination to succeed will take his friends and relatives by surprise. These subjects also have the happy knack of making influential friends who can and do help them to get where they want to be in life.

Pisceans are not easy to live with because, although very loving and very lovable, their moodiness makes them difficult to understand. These subjects respond to everything in a mystical and sensual manner, so if something in the atmosphere is not right, they will feel it keenly. The Piscean may be uneasy because a storm is on the way, because a neighbour or friend is sick or unhappy, because one of his children have been nasty to him or because he senses changes coming in his place of work. He may not know what it is that is actually making him depressed, simply because the problem may not yet have occurred and may only be apparent in the form of a presentiment. Pisceans can be made to suffer by bullies or unscrupulous people but they do have some forms of defence. They can be surprisingly sarcastic and can, of course, see straight through to other people's underlying faults and failings regardless of how carefully hidden these may be.

In many ways, these people never grow up but retain the innocence of a child or animal and, indeed, many of them are happier in the company of children and animals than with adults. Pisceans can be surprisingly resourceful and can also manage to live on surprisingly little. In the majority of cases, their values are spiritual rather than material, but they like to eat well and to live in comfort. Most of all, they value freedom and hate to feel that they cannot come and go as they like. Some feel uncomfortable when surrounded by the trappings of material goods but most actually need a nice home and a nice garden, both as a form of security and also as a place to which they can retreat. Many are good cooks and homemakers and most are very loving parents but this can go vaguely wrong for strange reasons.

This is such an indefinable sign that it encompasses such varied characters as Paddy Ashdown, the ex-Royal Marine Commando leader of the Liberal Democrat party, top surgeons, head-teachers and down-and-outs who live in cardboard boxes, underneath the arches of a railway line.

What Does the Piscean Look Like?

Pisceans are generally medium in height and either slim or slightly rounded in appearance. Many of these subjects have to watch their weight later in life. In white races, the complexion is fair with a good colour, the nose is quite prominent, the eyes are pale and prominent and the mouth is generous with a large and happy smile. Some have fly-away hair which is hard to handle, while others have a good head of thick straight hair. Most Pisceans seem to wear glasses and many need to wear sun-glasses in the summer because their pale eyes let in too much light. Piscean women are often very photogenic due to their strong bones and large features. Pisceans are quite fussy about their appearance and they may spend quite a lot on clothing. They prefer to buy good quality clothes which will last and they always spend a good deal on comfortable shoes. Some Pisceans go for the sporty look with up-market tracksuits and training shoes while others are 'country-casual' in style.

Health

Astrology can be a valuable tool for both the diagnosis and treatment of ailments but this involves the use of a full birth chart for each patient. The position of the Sun alone is not enough. However, here are the traditional areas of weakness associated with Pisces.

The traditional Piscean area of weakness is the feet and Pisceans do have either very good or very bad feet. Pisceans seem to be'creaking gates' who lurch from one strange ailment to another but who still manage to live long and relatively healthy lives. Pisceans are very sensitive to changes both in the environment and inside their own bodies and they respond to this by admitting that something is wrong rather than ignoring any symptoms. These subjects are very health-conscious and may dose themselves with all kinds of alternative medicines or seek out treatment from a variety of alternative practitioners. Some Pisceans drink too much.

Work and Hobbies

Pisceans work in a variety of fields and can be very successful if they are excited by their jobs. However, a great many of them only work because they must and are content to take jobs which are well below their ability level. Pisceans are not particularly ambitious or materialistic in outlook, and they may save the bulk of their energies for their many and varied pastimes. Having said this, if a Piscean gets the bit between his teeth, he can be extremely successful. My Piscean friend Barbara Ellen recently opened a holistic health centre in Wales and, through a mixture of faith and determination, is turning this unusual venture into a great success. Pisceans can be found working for themselves as craftsmen or as builders, gardeners and small farmers. Traditionally, Pisceans are supposed to be attracted to work on the sea, fishing, shoe-making and chiropody (through the sign's association with feet). I can't say that I have actually noticed Pisceans being attracted to these trades, whereas the world of art and entertainment is full of them. Other traditional areas are connected to the oil and gas industry and also film and photography. A number of Pisceans are attracted to medical or veterinary work while still others teach. Pisceans love sports, dancing and movement and may be found teaching these subjects. They are restless and may therefore find work in the travel trade. Philosophy, religion and mysticism attract Pisceans, to the point where many of them find work in these fields. Among my Piscean acquaintances I know a musician, a builder, a swimming instructor, a flying instructor, a lecturer in history, an executive in an oil and energy company who sells gas; many astrologers, palmists and clairvoyants, healers, medical workers and one prostitute. Most of the people I have worked with in the psychic field (as opposed to the astrological field) have either their Sun or their Moon in Pisces.

Pisceans can be extremely determined people who will not be deflected from their chosen pathway. Their choice of occupation or road to success may be an unusual one but this is followed with more tenacity than most other members of the Zodiac put together. If a Piscean decided to open a sheep farm in the middle of Piccadilly Circus, he would end up either achieving this aim or dying in the attempt.

Money, Shopping and Acquisitions

Some Pisceans are penny-pinching but these subjects are often as miserly to themselves as they are towards others. Other Pisceans will spend freely on food and drink for themselves and others and happily forget all financial constraints if there is any chance of holding a party or festivity of some kind. Under everyday circumstances, Pisceans can be very frugal, saving paper bags, bits of string and slivers of soap for re-use. All water signs are excellent recyclers but Pisceans make an art of this. Many Pisceans are poor in a peculiarly romantic style. One example is Sarah, an acquaintance of mine who lives in a garret working as a china restorer, while another has turned her hobby of gardening into a livelihood. This type of Piscean will live for his art or craft rather than do an ordinary job which brings in real money. Despite this, Pisceans worry constantly about money and could really do with a nice fat legacy behind them. There is another kind of Piscean who actually does quite well financially but still lives on next to nothing and feels just as insecure as his genuinely impecunious cousins. There are yet more Pisceans who live quite normal lives. This is one of those signs which, like its neighbouring sign of Aquarius, is hard to categorise.

Piscean possessions can range from an ocean-going yacht to a few eating utensils and a cat. Many Pisceans don't drive, and those who do usually own beloved old bangers from which they can't bear to be parted. Some Pisceans are very independent where money is concerned and yet others may be (almost) generous.

Living with Pisces

Pisceans quite like their own company and can live happily alone. However, they don't spend all their time in isolation because they usually have many friends. Most Pisceans seem to drift in and out of relationships, perhaps being married for a time, and then slipping away to live with someone else. These subjects may share their homes with friends for a while, or they may choose to live temporarily with a friend in between one set of circumstances and the next (a situation common to Pisceans). There are Pisceans who marry when young and stay with the same partner throughout their lives, but many don't. Pisceans appear soft and malleable but they are actually rather determined people. They choose a way of life which suits them and, whether this is practical or not in financial terms, they stick with their dreams, which means that their partners have to learn to adapt and to live with their special interests. This also means that the Piscean may not earn much money, so they are probably best suited to a partner who can keep them in a reasonable style. Most Pisceans are very proud of their skills and talents and need a partner who acknowledges this and respects their particular art. If a Piscean's partner ridicules what they do, the relationship hasn't much chance of surviving. A Pisces friend of mine who is an excellent psychic medium was married for quite a few years to a guy who detested what she did. He eventually told her that she must give up her work and get a job in a shop if she wanted to stay with him and this spelled the end of the relationship. Life is never dull with these subjects because they seem to go through a fresh drama every third week. Some partners of Pisceans find this emotional see-saw too much to handle.

A Pisces home can be anything from a squat to a palace. Most Pisceans, after drifting for a while, do try to maintain a place of their own even if they are not always there. This is partly because they are not adaptable enough to live in someone else's space for any length of time and partly because they see property as a form of security. Most Pisceans do keep their homes nicely and their gardens are often really beautiful. These subjects are usually good cooks and they may also be good at making and mending things around the home but they get bored if they spend too much time indoors and they have many outside interests. Most Pisceans need to get away to the sea from time to time.

Pisceans are very sociable and are also keen on short breaks of all kinds, so they need a partner who is as restless as themselves or who doesn't object to them being out of the house a good deal of the time. Some Pisceans are great travellers who work away from home much of the time and only see their families on flying visits, when on leave or between jobs.

Pisces people can be moody and irritable and occasionally self-pitying and angry which can make them pretty difficult to live with. Female Pisceans can be draining, demanding and boring, while males can spend much of their time drowning some unexpressed sorrow in the nearest pub.

The thought of a party, a meal out or a holiday by the sea cheers them up immensely. These subjects can be mean in small ways, saving scraps of soap, little pieces of string and paper bags with all the enthusiasm of a refugee but they can be generous in big ways, good to their friends and families and always ready to spend out on food and drink. Some Pisceans are loyal and faithful lovers while others seem to need a change of bed-partner from time to time. If a Piscean's partner decides to take his/her love elsewhere for a while, the Piscean will be aware of it almost immediately, but whether he decides that he can live with this situation or not depends upon his mood and his circumstances. It is no use lying to these people, because they have excellent intuition.

Some Pisceans are very fussy and old-womanish, demanding that everything be done in a certain way and infuriating their partners by creep-ing round the house double-checking that the doors are locked and that there is enough salt in the cooking. Most Pisceans are very capable in an emergency. Their calmness at such times makes a stark contrast to their usual state of near panic. These subjects make wonderful nurses but they become bored if a sick partner complains too much. Pisces subjects cannot take too much discord and they don't enjoy a good row in the way that some other people do. When verbally attacked, they can be surprisingly hurtful because their intuition tells them exactly where their partner's weakest spot is likely to be. Pisceans seem to go out of their way to find difficult people to live with but they survive these experiences, learning a lot from them and becoming independent and strongly-centred later in life. Pisceans who are devoted to their partners will do all they can to help when problems occur and can be quite dazzlingly courageous in the face of fierce difficulties. The problem with these people is their unpredictability and their claustrophobic need to escape even from a very good relationship from time to time.

Sexuality

Pisceans are heavily into fantasy, but whether they just live these fantasies out in their mind or act them out in the bedroom depends upon the indi-vidual. Some Pisceans are happy to live with little or no sex, saving their energy and their imagination for work or for creative hobbies, while others are very keen lovers who take every opportunity to experiment. Many fluctuate between periods of intense sexual activity and nothing at all, depending upon their mood and their circumstances. If they find them-selves with a cooperative partner, there may be no holds barred. Some Pisceans enjoy making love In strange places while others like to in, near or under water. Most find the bathroom an exciting playground. There are Pisceans who enjoy dressing up and acting out a part and many like to shock their partners or encourage them to be more abandoned than they might otherwise be. Pisceans are quite comfortable with sex in any form, from playing affectionately to reaching for new heights of passion and they love to instruct or entertain a lover with new love-making experiences. Many Pisceans are total romantics who love Valentine's day, red roses and candle-lit dinners and consider this as much a part of love making as the sex act itself.

Other Relationships

Pisceans are rather good at relating to friends and relatives and will keep on good terms with their families and even ex-spouses, wherever possible. These subjects are good listeners and great gossips who can be relied upon to keep their friends and relatives entertained. Pisceans love both feeding people and being taken out for trips and meals and they enjoy sharing their interests with those around them. They can be quite unpleasant to anyone who sets out to hurt them but they will do anything to help someone they care for.

As parents, Pisceans can be rather lax and absent-minded. The children of a Piscean woman may spend a good part of their lives being brought up by someone else, whilst Piscean men may drift away from their children as a result of a divorce. When all goes well, they are very caring parents but they must have a life of their own and cannot sacrifice all their time and energy for the sake of their offspring. Pisces parents try to introduce their children to the gentler aspects of life, such as art, music and 'New Age' interests and they hate arguments and discord.

As children, Pisceans can be dreamy and somewhat ineffectual, needing a strongly caring set of parents to shield them from harsh reality. They may be good at artistic subjects and, oddly enough, mathematics and engineering, because they have a good sense of colour, line and balance. These children are not competitive or ambitious and they may suffer at the hands of bullying children or teachers. It takes a Piscean a long time to find himself and childhood is far too early for him to begin to mould his life into any kind of shape. Nevertheless, the Pisces child may get a lot out of his interests and activities and will make a few good friends among the more adult and tolerant of his schoolfellows along the way.

Mikhail Gorbachev

At the time of writing Mikhail Gorbachev is the Soviet Premier but the planets seem to indicate that he may not hold this job quite as long as some of his predecessors. I don't think anyone is completely sure of Gorbachev's correct time of birth, but there is some agreement in the astrological world on 12 noon, so this is the time which Fred Baker, my astrological researcher has chosen to use.

Mikhail Gorbachev is a Piscean which, on the face of it, seems an odd sign for someone in such a powerful situation. However, the Sun is the only planet he has in Pisces and there are other factors on his chart which endow him with the strength needed for such a position. Gorbachev has three planets in the cardinal sign of Cancer and two in the cardinal sign of Capricorn. He has the 'royal' rising sign of Leo, with the Moon in close conjunction to the ascendant. This would indicate a powerful but pleasant outer manner with a strong inner urge to make his mark on the world. A strong Moon can indicate a desire to do something for the public good and, in Mikhail Gorbachev's case, the Moon is an excellent trine aspect to the revolutionary planet, Uranus, and also to the north node. This suggests that he has a karmic or fated role, to play in orchestrating a new and very different kind of Russian revolution.

As a private person, I would imagine that Mikhail Gorbachev is kind, gentle and highly intuitive. He would make an excellent psychic medium or spiritual healer. His Aquarian seventh house suggests an unusually strong marriage and the placements of Mercury in the seventh house and the Sun in the eighth house lead us to believe that he and Raisa have a good relationship with plenty of dialogue. Jupiter in the eleventh house makes him an idealist who wants to help others wherever he can, while Venus and Saturn in Capricorn in the sixth suggest that he is a very hard worker. Mercury on the Aquarius/Pisces cusp in the seventh suggests an excellent manner when dealing with others and also a witty and sharp sense of humour. This planetary position, which is also opposed by Neptune, denotes that he would not be clever in business and could lose out or be tricked over money. It also presupposes a strong imagination and the ability to write wonderful stories or to communicate visionary ideas. This guy could be a top novelist, a wonderfully charismatic showbiz type, an artist, a psychic, a teacher or anything else he wanted to be. The strongest element in Mikhail Gorbachev's chart is water, which suggests that many of his decisions are prompted by an emotional feeling that he is doing the right thing. Six planets in cardinal signs denote a strong personality with

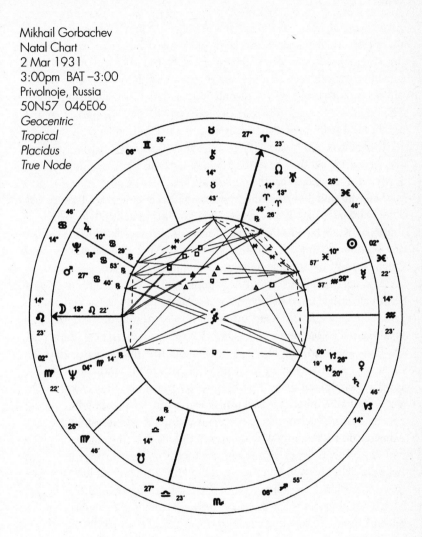

Mikhail Gorbachev
Natal Chart
2 Mar 1931
3:00pm BAT −3:00
Privolnoje, Russia
50N57 046E06
Geocentric
Tropical
Placidus
True Node

tremendous executive ability, whilst the five cadent house planets show that he can bring a situation to a close or steer it through a transformation.

Michael Caine

An actor is only as intelligent and interesting as the part he is playing and in many cases when one sees actors being interviewed they come across as boring, stupid or self-absorbed and big-headed. Not so Michael Caine. When I saw him being thrown random questions by a studio audience he turned out to be a witty and amusing raconteur with the ability to laugh at himself. The quick wit and easy repartee comes from Michael's Gemini ascendant and he has a stellium of planets in the clever and amusing sign of Virgo. The really big interest in Michael's life is his family as shown by Mars, Neptune, Jupiter and the south node of the Moon in the fourth house of domesticity. It is a well-known fact that the minute Michael's day's work is over, he doesn't hang around boozing and chatting with his colleagues, but rushes straight home to his wife and children. Virgo is associated with food and the fourth house, being like the sign of Cancer, is also associated with cooking and housework and it is also well-known that Michael loves to cook and that he owns two or three restaurants in London.

Michael came from a poor background and it wasn't until his Saturn return at the age of 30 that he made a breakthrough in the acting profession. Saturn in this case is in the ninth house, close to the midheaven, a position that is common with hard working and successful people. Michael has Pluto in the second house in Cancer and that means that he has the capacity to earn very good money. His autobiography shows that he has spent a great deal on the various homes that he and his family have bought and that makes a great deal of sense in the light of such a home-loving person. Michael's Venus is in the tenth house in Pisces signifying that women have helped him in his career aspirations. His appearance on celluloid has certainly brought him a large number of female fans – including me! Michael's Moon in Libra in the fifth house gives him an inner urge to be an entertainer who has style and panache. Michael's Sun in Pisces, Mercury in the quick-witted sign of Aries and Uranus in Aries are all in the eleventh house, suggesting an inventive mind and an independent and unusual personality. Michael Caine doesn't follow the herd, he lives his life the way he wants to. Michael is a self-confessed gourmet and also a drinker which can be seen in his Sun and Venus in Pisces.

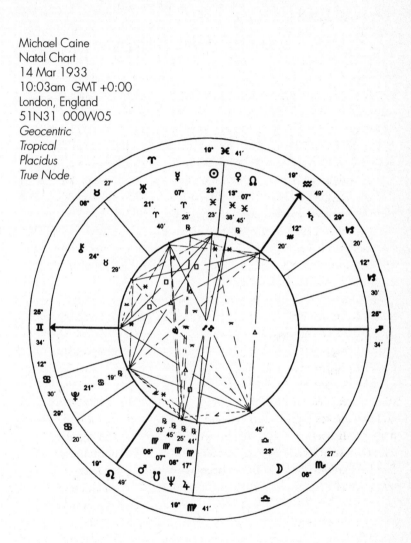

Michael Caine
Natal Chart
14 Mar 1933
10:03am GMT +0:00
London, England
51N31 000W05
Geocentric
Tropical
Placidus
True Node

How to find the true beginning and end of each sign

The dates below are taken from the astrology column in *Woman's Own* magazine and are typical of the usual kind of approximation which all magazines and papers use. Any list of dates given in a magazine or news-paper is likely to be inaccurate for some people because the Sun does not enter each of the signs at the same time or even on the same day in each year. If you need to find exactly which sign you or someone close to you was born under, then please consult the chart on the following page.

♈	Aries	21 March to 20 April
♉	Taurus	21 April to 21 May
♊	Gemini	22 May to 21 June
♋	Cancer	22 June to 23 July
♌	Leo	24 July to 23 August
♍	Virgo	24 August to 23 September
♎	Libra	24 September to 23 October
♏	Scorpio	24 October to 22 November
♐	Sagittarius	23 November to 21 December
♑	Capricorn	22 December to 20 January
♒	Aquarius	21 January to 19 February
♓	Pisces	20 February to 20 March

Sun Sign Changes

This table shows the time and day in each month when the Sun changes signs. The year is given in the left hand column, and the months are written across the top. For each month the day is given on the left and the time that the Sun is entering the sign is on the right. The time is given in GMT. For example, in January 1960 the Sun entered Aquarius on the 21st day of the month at 1.10 hours (1.10 a.m.)

YEAR	JAN ♒	FEB ♓	MAR ♈	APR ♉	MAY ♊	JUN ♋	JUL ♌	AUG ♍	SEP ♎	OCT ♏	NOV ♐	DEC ♑
1930	20 18.33	19 9.00	21 8.30	20 20.06	21 19.42	22 3.53	23 14.42	23 21.26	23 18.36	24 3.26	23 0.34	22 13.39
1931	21 0.17	19 14.40	21 14.06	21 1.40	22 1.15	22 9.28	23 20.21	24 3.10	24 0.23	24 9.15	23 6.25	22 19.30
1932	21 6.07	19 20.28	20 19.54	20 7.28	21 7.07	21 15.23	23 2.18	23 9.06	23 6.16	23 15.04	22 12.10	22 1.14
1933	20 11.53	19 2.16	21 1.43	20 13.18	21 12.57	21 21.12	23 8.05	23 14.52	23 12.01	23 20.48	22 17.53	22 6.57
1934	20 17.37	19 8.02	21 7.28	20 19.00	21 18.35	22 2.48	23 13.42	23 20.32	23 17.45	24 2.36	22 23.44	22 12.49
1935	20 23.28	19 13.52	21 13.18	21 0.50	22 0.25	22 8.38	23 19.33	24 2.24	23 23.38	24 8.29	23 5.35	22 18.37
1936	21 5.12	19 19.33	20 18.58	20 6.31	21 6.07	21 14.22	23 1.18	23 8.10	23 5.26	23 14.18	22 11.25	22 0.27
1937	20 11.01	19 1.21	21 0.45	20 12.19	21 11.57	21 20.12	23 7.07	23 13.58	23 11.13	23 20.06	22 17.16	22 6.22
1938	20 16.59	19 7.20	21 6.43	20 18.15	21 17.50	22 2.04	23 12.57	23 19.46	23 16.59	24 1.54	22 23.06	22 12.13
1939	20 22.51	19 13.09	21 12.28	20 23.55	21 23.27	22 7.39	23 18.37	24 1.31	23 22.49	24 7.46	23 4.58	22 18.06
1940	21 4.44	19 19.04	20 18.24	20 5.51	21 5.23	21 13.36	23 0.34	23 7.26	23 4.46	23 13.39	22 10.49	21 23.55
1941	20 10.34	19 0.56	21 0.20	20 11.50	21 11.23	21 19.33	23 6.26	23 13.17	23 10.33	23 19.27	22 16.38	22 5.44
1942	20 16.23	19 6.47	21 6.11	20 17.39	21 17.09	22 1.16	23 12.07	23 18.58	23 16.16	24 1.15	22 22.30	22 11.40
1943	20 22.19	19 12.40	21 12.03	20 23.31	21 23.03	22 7.12	23 18.04	24 0.55	23 22.12	24 7.06	23 4.21	22 17.29
1944	21 4.07	19 18.27	20 17.49	20 5.18	21 4.51	21 13.02	22 23.58	23 6.46	23 4.02	23 12.56	22 10.08	21 23.15
1945	20 9.54	19 0.15	20 23.37	20 11.07	21 10.40	21 18.52	23 5.45	23 12.35	23 9.50	23 18.44	22 15.55	22 5.04
1946	20 15.45	19 6.09	21 5.33	20 17.02	21 16.34	22 0.44	23 11.37	23 18.26	23 15.41	24 0.35	22 21.46	22 10.53
1947	21 21.32	19 11.52	21 11.13	20 22.39	21 22.09	22 6.19	23 17.14	24 0.09	23 21.29	24 6.26	23 3.38	22 16.43
1948	21 3.18	19 17.37	20 16.57	20 4.25	21 3.58	21 12.11	22 23.06	23 6.03	23 3.22	23 12.18	22 9.29	21 22.33
1949	20 9.09	18 23.37	20 22.48	20 10.17	21 9.51	21 18.03	23 4.57	23 11.48	23 9.06	23 18.03	22 15.16	22 4.23
1950	20 15.00	19 5.18	21 4.35	20 15.59	21 15.27	21 23.36	23 10.30	23 17.23	23 14.44	23 23.45	22 21.03	22 10.13
1951	20 20.52	19 11.10	21 10.26	21 21.48	21 21.15	22 5.25	23 16.21	23 23.16	23 20.37	24 5.36	23 2.51	22 16.00
1952	21 2.28	19 16.57	20 16.14	20 3.37	21 3.04	21 11.13	22 22.07	23 5.03	23 2.24	23 11.22	22 8.36	21 21.43
1953	20 8.21	19 22.41	20 22.01	20 9.25	21 8.53	21 17.00	23 3.52	23 10.45	23 8.06	23 17.06	22 14.22	22 3.31
1954	20 14.11	19 4.32	21 3.53	20 15.20	21 14.47	21 22.54	23 9.45	23 16.36	23 13.55	23 22.56	22 20.14	22 9.24
1955	20 20.02	19 10.19	21 9.35	20 20.58	21 20.24	22 4.31	23 15.25	23 22.19	23 19.41	24 4.43	23 2.01	22 15.11
1956	21 1.48	19 16.05	20 15.20	20 2.43	21 2.13	21 10.24	22 21.20	23 4.15	23 1.35	23 10.34	22 7.50	21 21.00
1957	21 7.39	18 21.58	20 21.17	20 8.41	21 8.10	21 16.21	23 3.15	23 10.08	23 7.26	23 16.24	22 13.39	22 2.49
1958	20 13.29	19 3.49	21 3.06	20 14.27	21 13.51	21 21.57	23 8.51	23 15.46	23 13.09	23 22.11	22 19.29	22 8.40

YEAR	JAN ♒	FEB ♓	MAR ♈	APR ♉	MAY ♊	JUN ♋	JUL ♌	AUG ♍	SEP ♎	OCT ♏	NOV ♐	DEC ♑
1959	20 19.19	19 9.38	21 8.55	20 20.17	21 19.42	22 3.50	23 14.48	23 21.44	23 19.09	24 4.11	23 1.27	22 14.34
1960	21 1.10	19 15.26	20 14.43	20 2.06	21 1.34	21 9.42	22 20.28	23 3.34	23 0.59	23 10.02	22 7.18	21 20.26
1961	20 7.01	18 21.27	20 20.32	20 7.55	21 7.22	21 15.30	23 2.24	23 9.19	23 6.43	23 15.47	22 13.06	22 2.20
1962	20 12.58	19 3.15	21 2.30	20 13.51	21 13.17	21 21.24	23 8.18	23 15.13	23 12.35	23 21.40	22 19.02	22 8.15
1963	20 18.54	19 9.09	21 8.20	20 19.36	21 18.58	22 3.04	23 13.59	23 20.58	23 18.24	23 3.29	23 0.49	22 14.02
1964	21 0.41	19 14.57	20 14.10	20 1.27	21 0.50	21 8.57	22 19.53	23 2.51	23 0.17	23 9.21	22 6.39	21 19.50
1965	20 6.29	18 20.48	20 20.05	20 7.26	21 6.50	21 14.56	23 1.48	23 8.43	23 6.06	23 15.10	22 12.29	22 1.41
1966	20 12.20	19 2.38	21 1.53	20 13.12	21 12.32	21 20.34	23 7.23	23 14.18	23 11.43	23 20.51	22 18.14	22 7.28
1967	20 18.08	19 8.24	21 7.37	20 18.55	21 18.18	21 2.23	23 13.16	23 20.13	23 17.38	23 2.44	23 0.05	22 13.16
1968	20 23.54	19 14.09	20 13.22	20 0.41	21 0.06	21 8.13	22 19.06	23 2.03	22 23.26	23 8.30	22 5.49	21 19.00
1969	20 5.38	18 19.55	20 19.06	20 6.27	21 5.50	21 13.55	23 0.48	23 7.44	23 5.07	23 14.11	22 11.31	22 0.44
1970	20 11.24	19 1.42	21 0.57	20 12.15	21 11.38	21 19.43	23 6.37	23 13.34	23 10.59	23 20.04	22 17.35	22 6.36
1971	20 17.13	19 7.27	21 6.38	20 17.54	21 17.15	22 1.20	23 12.15	23 19.15	23 16.45	24 1.53	22 23.14	22 12.24
1972	20 22.59	19 13.12	20 12.22	19 23.38	21 23.00	21 7.06	22 18.03	23 1.03	22 22.33	23 7.42	22 5.03	22 18.13
1973	20 4.48	18 19.01	20 18.13	20 5.31	21 4.54	21 13.01	23 23.56	23 6.54	23 4.21	23 13.30	22 10.54	22 0.06
1974	20 10.46	19 0.59	21 0.07	20 11.19	21 10.36	21 18.38	23 5.30	23 12.29	23 9.59	23 19.11	22 16.39	22 5.56
1975	20 16.37	19 6.50	21 5.57	20 17.06	21 16.24	22 0.27	23 11.22	23 18.24	23 15.55	24 1.06	22 22.31	22 11.46
1976	20 22.25	19 12.40	20 11.50	19 23.03	20 22.21	21 6.25	22 17.19	23 0.19	22 21.48	23 6.58	22 4.22	21 17.35
1977	20 4.15	18 18.31	20 17.43	20 4.58	21 4.15	21 12.14	23 23.04	23 6.01	23 3.30	23 12.41	22 10.07	21 23.23
1978	20 10.04	19 0.21	20 23.34	20 10.50	21 10.09	21 18.10	23 5.01	23 11.57	23 9.26	23 18.37	22 16.05	22 5.21
1979	20 16.00	19 6.14	21 5.22	20 16.36	21 15.54	21 23.57	23 10.49	23 17.47	23 15.17	24 0.28	22 21.54	22 11.10
1980	20 21.49	19 12.02	20 11.10	19 22.23	21 21.42	21 5.47	22 16.42	22 23.41	22 21.09	23 6.18	22 3.42	21 16.56
1981	20 3.36	18 17.52	20 17.03	20 4.19	21 3.40	21 11.45	22 22.40	23 5.39	23 3.06	23 12.13	22 9.36	21 22.51
1982	20 9.31	18 23.47	20 22.56	20 10.08	21 9.23	21 17.23	23 4.16	23 11.16	23 8.47	23 17.58	22 15.24	22 4.39
1983	20 15.17	19 5.31	21 4.39	20 15.51	21 15.07	21 23.09	23 10.05	23 17.08	23 14.42	23 23.55	22 21.19	22 10.30
1984	20 21.05	19 11.17	20 10.25	19 21.39	20 20.58	21 5.03	22 15.59	23 23.01	22 20.33	23 5.46	22 3.11	21 16.23
1985	20 2.58	18 17.08	20 16.14	20 3.26	21 2.43	21 10.45	22 21.37	23 4.36	23 2.06	23 11.22	22 8.51	21 22.08
1986	20 8.47	18 22.58	20 22.03	20 9.13	21 8.28	21 16.30	23 3.25	23 10.26	23 7.59	23 17.15	22 14.45	22 4.03
1987	20 14.41	19 4.50	21 3.52	20 14.58	21 14.10	21 22.11	23 9.06	23 16.10	23 13.46	23 23.01	22 20.30	22 9.46

YEAR	JAN ≋	FEB ♓	MAR ♈	APR ♉	MAY ♊	JUN ♋	JUL ♌	AUG ♍	SEP ♎	OCT ♏	NOV ♐	DEC ♑
1988	20 20.25	19 10.36	20 9.39	19 20.45	20 19.57	21 3.57	22 14.52	22 21.54	22 19.29	23 4.45	22 2.12	21 15.28
1989	20 2.07	18 16.21	20 15.29	20 2.39	21 1.54	21 9.53	22 20.46	23 3.47	23 1.20	23 10.36	22 8.05	21 21.22
1990	20 8.02	18 22.14	20 21.20	20 8.27	21 7.38	21 15.33	23 2.22	23 9.21	23 6.56	23 16.14	22 13.47	22 3.07
1991	20 13.48	19 3.6	21 3.03	20 14.1	21 13.22	21 21.2	23 8.13	23 15.15	23 12.5	23 22.07	22 19.38	22 8.55
1992	20 19.34	19 9.45	20 8.5	19 19.59	20 19.14	21 3.16	22 14.11	22 21.12	22 18.45	23 3.59	22 1.28	21 14.45
1993	20 1.25	18 15.37	20 14.43	20 1.51	21 1.04	21 9.02	22 19.53	23 2.52	23 0.24	23 9.39	22 7.09	21 20.28
1994	20 7.09	18 21.24	20 20.3	20 7.38	21 6.51	21 14.5	23 1.43	23 8.46	23 5.21	23 15.38	22 13.08	22 2.25
1995	20 13.03	19 3.13	21 2.16	20 13.24	21 12.36	21 20.36	23 7.31	23 14.37	23 12.15	23 21.33	22 19.03	22 8.19
1996	20 18.55	19 9.03	20 8.05	19 19.12	20 18.25	21 2.26	22 13.21	22 20.25	22 18.02	23 3.2	22 0.51	21 14.08
1997	20 0.45	18 14.54	20 13.57	20 1.05	21 0.2	21 5.22	22 19.17	23 2.21	22 23.57	23 9.16	22 6.49	21 20.09
1998	20 6.48	18 20.57	20 19.57	20 6.59	21 6.06	21 14.05	23 0.58	23 8.01	23 5.39	23 15.01	22 12.36	22 1.58
1999	20 12.39	19 2.49	21 1.48	20 12.48	21 11.55	21 19.51	23 6.46	23 13.53	23 11.33	23 20.54	22 18.27	22 7.46
2000	20 18.25	19 8.35	20 7.37	19 18.41	20 17.51	21 1.5	22 12.45	22 19.5	22 17.3	23 2.49	22 0.21	21 13.4

British Summer Time in Great Britain

As British Summer Time has had a somewhat irregular schedule over the years, here is a table of the time conversions to date. In some years, you will see that there was a *Double* Summer Time, when there was an additional one hour's difference from GMT (i.e. a total of two hour's difference). In these years, 'Summer' Time actually lasted all year!

All changes are at 2 a.m.

In 1968, 1969, 1970 and 1971 the government experimented with British Standard Time, but abandoned it from 1972.

1916	21 MAY – 1 OCT	1933	9 APR – 8 OCT
1917	8 APR – 17 SEPT	1934	22 APR – 7 OCT
1918	24 MAR – 30 SEPT	1935	14 APR – 6 OCT
1919	30 MAR – 29 SEPT	1936	19 APR – 4 OCT
1920	28 MAR – 25 OCT	1937	18 APR – 3 OCT
1921	3 APR – 3 OCT	1938	10 APR – 2 OCT
1922	26 MAR – 8 OCT	1939	16 APR – 19 NOV
1923	22 APR – 16 SEPT	1940	25 FEB – 31 DEC
1924	13 APR – 21 SEPT	1941	1 JAN – 31 DEC
1925	19 APR – 4 OCT	DST	4 MAY – 10 AUG
1926	18 APR – 3 OCT	1942	1 JAN – 31 DEC
1927	10 APR – 2 OCT	DST	5 APR – 9 AUG
1928	22 APR – 7 OCT	1943	1 JAN – 31 DEC
1929	21 APR – 6 OCT	DST	4 APR – 15 AUG
1930	13 APR – 5 OCT	1944	1 JAN – 31 DEC
1931	19 APR – 4 OCT	DST	2 APR – 17 SEPT
1932	17 APR – 2 OCT	1945	1 JAN – 7 OCT

DST	2 APR – 15 JUL	1984	25 MAR – 28 OCT
1946	14 APR – 6 OCT	1985	31 MAR – 27 OCT
1947	16 MAR – 2 NOV	1986	30 MAR – 26 OCT
DST	13 APR – 10 AUG	1987	29 MAR – 25 OCT
1948	14 MAR – 31 OCT	1988	27 MAR – 23 OCT
1949	3 APR – 30 OCT	1989	26 MAR – 29 OCT
1950	16 APR – 22 OCT	1990	25 MAR – 28 OCT
1951	15 APR – 21 OCT	1991	31 MAR – 27 OCT
1952	20 APR – 26 OCT	1992	29 MAR – 25 OCT
1953	19 APR – 4 OCT	1993	28 MAR – 24 OCT
1954	11 APR – 3 OCT	1994	27 MAR – 23 OCT
1955	17 APR – 2 OCT	1995	26 MAR – 29 OCT
1956	22 APR – 7 OCT	1996	31 MAR – 27 OCT
1957	14 APR – 6 OCT	1997	30 MAR – 26 OCT
1958	20 APR – 5 OCT	1998	29 MAR – 25 OCT
1959	19 APR – 4 OCT	1999	28 MAR – 24 OCT
1960	10 APR – 2 OCT	2000	26 MAR – 29 OCT
1961	26 MAR – 29 OCT		
1962	25 MAR – 28 OCT		
1963	31 MAR – 27 OCT		
1964	22 MAR – 25 OCT		
1965	21 MAR – 24 OCT		
1966	20 MAR – 23 OCT		
1967	19 MAR – 29 OCT		
1968	18 FEB – 31 DEC		
1969	1 JAN – 31 DEC		
1970	1 JAN – 31 DEC		
1971	1 JAN – 31 OCT		
1972	19 MAR – 29 OCT		
1973	18 MAR – 28 OCT		
1974	17 MAR – 27 OCT		
1975	16 MAR – 26 OCT		
1976	21 MAR – 24 OCT		
1977	20 MAR – 23 OCT		
1978	19 MAR – 29 OCT		
1979	18 MAR – 28 OCT		
1980	16 MAR – 26 OCT		
1981	29 MAR – 25 OCT		
1982	28 MAR – 24 OCT		
1983	27 MAR – 23 OCT		

2

Moon signs

Moon Data

Astronomical Data

The Moon's mean distance from the Earth, surface to surface is 376,284 kilometres, or about a quarter of a million miles. It takes 27.32 days for the Moon to travel round the Earth and also 27.32 days for it to rotate on its axis, therefore it always has the same 'face' pointing towards the Earth. Its diameter is 3475.6 kilometres and its temperature varies between plus 101° centigrade and minus 153° centigrade. The interior of the Moon is still hot enough to be made of molten rock and there are about 3000 moonquakes per year. The surface of the Moon is fatter on the side which faces towards the Earth, it is also warmer on the Earth side.

The Moon and the Earth were both formed when the solar system came into being. The Moon became attracted to the Earth's gravitational field and formed a double or binary planet system. Double planets spin round each other rather like children swinging round each other on a rope; in this case, the relative sizes of the Earth and the Moon mean that the Moon does most (not all) of the swinging. The first Moon landing was at 2.56 GMT on the 20 July 1969 by Armstrong, Aldrin and Collins in Apollo 11.

The Moon is about a quarter of the size of the Earth and its surface area is about the size of Asia, nevertheless its mountains reach 8000 metres which is higher than any on earth. There is no atmosphere on the Moon, therefore meteorites fall on to it without being burned up by friction on their way down.

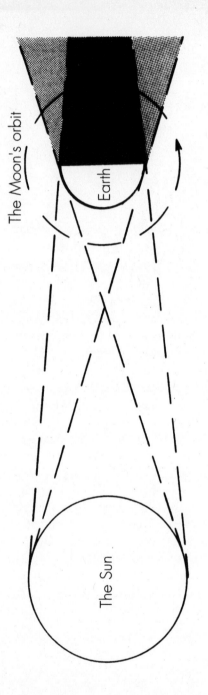

Fig 1.1
ECLIPSE OF THE MOON

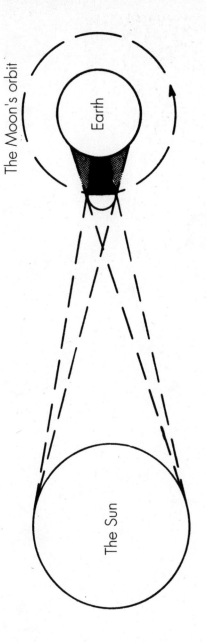

The Moon's orbit

Earth

The Sun

Fig 1.2
ECLIPSE OF THE SUN

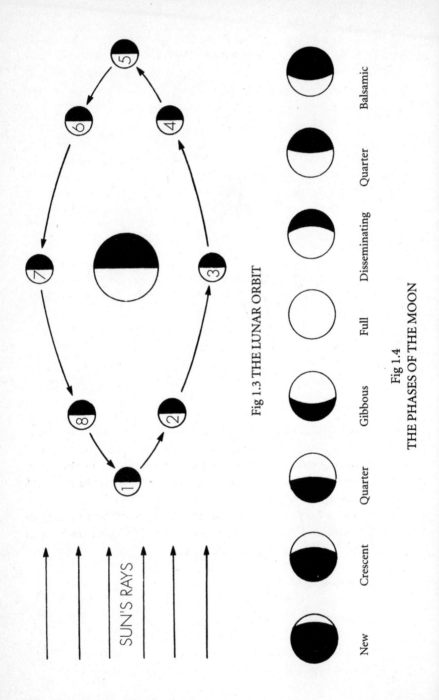

Fig 1.3 THE LUNAR ORBIT

SUN'S RAYS

New · Crescent · Quarter · Gibbous · Full · Disseminating · Quarter · Balsamic

Fig 1.4
THE PHASES OF THE MOON

Eclipses

Eclipses of the Moon occur when the Earth is between it and the Sun and only when the Moon is full. There are roughly three to four eclipses each year, most of these are partial eclipses. Total eclipses last for a few minutes but a partial eclipse can last for an hour or so.

Tides

There are two high tides a day and the areas of high tide revolve around the Earth in line with the Moon. At the time of the new Moon and the full Moon, when the Sun, Moon and Earth are in line the tides are higher.

Phases of the Moon

The Moon does not shed any light of its own, only the light reflected by the Sun. The phases of the Moon depend upon its position between the Earth and the Sun.

Adjustments to the Moon Sign Tables

The tables in this book show the times when the Moon enters a new sign *at Greenwich*. If you were born anywhere in Great Britain the times mentioned in this book will apply to you. It is unlikely that you will have to make any adjustment if you were born in Europe but if you were born further afield, for instance in the USA or India, you will have to adjust the time of your birth back to GMT.

If you were born in New York for instance you will have to add five hours to your birth time to bring it up to GMT; if you were born in Calcutta, you will have to subtract five hours.

The following list should help those born in the USA.

GMT (used throughout this book)	0° Longitude
Eastern Standard Time: 75° West	add 5 hrs.
Central Standard Time: 90° West	add 6 hrs.
Mountain Standard Time: 105° West	add 7 hrs.

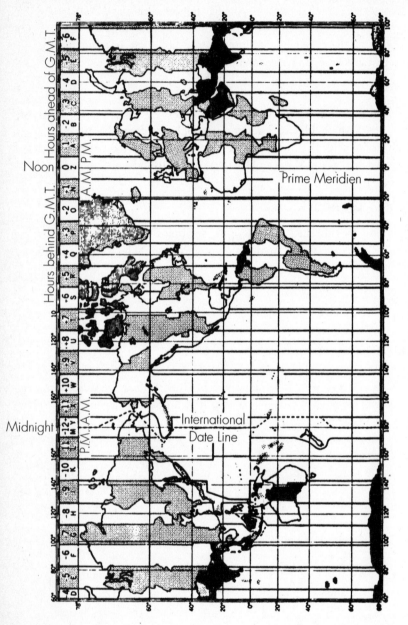

Fig 1.5 TIME ZONES AROUND THE WORLD

Pacific Standard Time: 120, West   add 7 hrs.
Yukon Standard Time: 135° West   add 9 hrs.
Alaska/Hawaii Standard Time: 150° West   add 10 hrs.
Bering Time: 165° West   add 11 hrs.

The time zone map on page 176 will help for most birthplaces but please do find out if there was daylight saving at the time of your birth. If there was, then subtract one hour.

2

Lunar Lore

Lunar Gardening

If you with flowers stick the pregnant earth
Mark well the Moon propitious to their birth
For earth the silent midnight queen obeys
And waits her course, who clad in silver rays
The eternal round of time and seasons guides

from *The English Gardener*
(seventeenth century)

If you wish to make the best use of the position of the Moon in your garden, then you must take into account both the phases of the Moon and the signs that it travels through. When the Moon is growing from new to full it is called a waxing Moon, when it goes from the full to new it is called a waning Moon. It is considered best to plant crops which produce their crops above the ground by a waxing Moon and those plants which produce crops below the ground by a waning Moon. However, those plants which spend the winter in the ground (biennials and perennials) are better off planted when the Moon is waxing.

It is well known, of course, that rain usually follows the full or new Moon but there have been recent studies on the effect of the Moon on crops and animals.

Some studies on potatoes which, when grown in laboratory conditions at a constant rate of heat and light, still respond to lunar rhythms.

A scientist called Frank A. Brown took some oysters from the Atlantic coast of America to artificial oyster beds in inland Illinois. By the time two weeks had passed, the oysters had adapted their opening and closing times from the Atlantic tidal times to suit the times of the supposed 'tides' of Illinois.

Gardening by the phases of the Moon

First quarter: Leafy plants such as cabbage, celery, endive, spinach and lettuce, also cucumber.

Second quarter: Beans, peas, peppers, courgettes, tomatoes, melon, garlic, hay, cereals and grains in either the first or the second quarter.

Third quarter: Biennials and perennials, also root crops, onions, winter wheat, trees and shrubs.

Fourth quarter: Don't plant anything, do the weeding instead.

Gardening by the signs of the Zodiac

Aries: Seeds will be quick to germinate and quick to go to seed but could be used to get an early crop.

Taurus: Advantageous for most plants especially root growth, transplanting and many flowers.

Gemini: Not particularly good except for plants grown in wet conditions such as celery.

Cancer: A very productive time to plant, promotes the growth of foliage stalks. Vines will produce sturdy plants which can survive bad weather.

Leo: This is not a productive time to plant or to transplant.

Virgo: Planting now will result in tough, woody, useless plants.

Libra: A fruitful time to plant but there might be too much bloom and not enough seed.

Scorpio: Good time for transplanting and pruning, also for plants which have to survive the winter.

Sagittarius: Plant fruit trees, hay and onions, otherwise not a good time to plant.

Capricorn: Good time for grafting and pruning wood, also for planting ornamental tree and shrubs.

| Aquarius: | Only onions and pine trees should be planted now. |
| Pisces: | This is supposed to be a good time to plant anything which the exception of potatoes which will sprout at the eye. |

Some more lunar gardening tips

Start a compost heap when the Moon is in the fourth quarter, especially in Scorpio.

Cultivate and plough the ground when the Moon is in the fourth quarter in Aries, Gemini, Leo, Virgo or Aquarius.

Dry crops in the third quarter of a fire sign.

Fertilize when the Moon is in Cancer, Scorpio or Pisces; Taurus or Capricorn will do less well. If using an organic fertilizer, do so while the Moon is waning.

Graft during Capricorn, Cancer or Scorpio on a waxing Moon.

Harvest during the third and fourth quarters in Aries, Leo, Sagittarius, Gemini or Aquarius. Harvest roots intended for seed at the full Moon, grain which is to be stored just after the full Moon in a fire or air sign. Harvest on a waning moon during an air or fire sign.

Irrigate when the Moon is in Cancer, Scorpio or Pisces.

Mow the lawn in the first or second quarters to increase growth, during the third or fourth quarters to decrease growth.

Pick mushrooms at the full Moon.

Prune during a decreasing Moon.

Spray, weed and destroy pests during the fourth quarter in a fire sign.

Plant potatoes during the 'dark of the Moon' (i.e. new Moon). One suggestion that I have come across is to plant them on Good Friday when the holy powers are at their strongest! Peas should be planted in the 'light of the Moon' (full Moon.)

(My husband tried mowing the lawn this year according to these ancient instructions in order to decrease its growth. The lawn grew like the clappers and my name was mud all summer long!)

3

The Goddess of the Moon

The Myriad Faces of the Goddess of the Moon

The Moon in mythology and in many religions represents the female force which reflects the male force of the Sun. In Hebrew she is known as Levanah, in Roman mythology Diana and in the Greek tradition as Persephone and also Aphrodite. In the Egyptian tradition she is Isis the female member of the powerful trinity of Osiris, Isis and Horus.

To the followers of the ancient traditions of witchcraft, she is Brid, Maiden-Goddess of the waxing Moon; Diana, Mother-Goddess of the full Moon and Morrigan, Crone-Goddess of the waning Moon. The following lines are an extract from a ritual associated with the Moon Goddess.

Behold the Three-Formed Goddess;
She who is ever Three – Maid, Mother and Crone.
Yet she is ever One;
She in all women, and they all in her.
Behold her, remember her,
Forget not one of her faces;

If you would like the goddess to grant you a wish, then take a piece of paper in the planetary colour of the person (or object) that your wish concerns; then light the candle and wait for it to burn down: as it does so, the spell will be working. Here is the invocation which will help the spell to work.

Upon this candle will I write
What I request of thee this night.
Grant what I wish you to do;
I dedicate this rite to you.
I trust that you will grant this boon
O lovely Goddess of the Moon.

Early man's initial concern was to survive. In some parts of the world even now where life is primitive, survival is still not guaranteed. For such people, the business of growing food and rearing animals went alongside the development of the calendar and also the development of religion and superstition. If an offering to a particular diety would help the crops grow, then obviously, that was the right thing to do. Even now, many good people like to say grace before or after a meal to thank God for feeding them. Even a total heathen such as I simply cannot eat the first fruits and vegetables of the season without offering up a Hebrew blessing.

Most religions take some account of the Moon's position in their festival calendar; for instance, in the Christian tradition, Easter and Whitsun still 'float' according the Moon's orbit. It is interesting to note that Easter was a Greco-Roman festival associated with Aphrodite and Diana, and before that a festival associate with Ishtarte, the predecessor of Aphrodite/ Diana. These goddesses, like the beginning of the spring season itself, speak of fertility and growth and the renewal of life. If you can take a trip to the re-discovered city of Ephesus in Turkey, just at the bottom of the hill on the left-hand side you will find the Temple of Diana which is close by the even more ancient site of the Temple of Aphrodite/Ishtarte. Ishtarte is the many-breasted Goddess of Fertility who was sometimes shown hung about with eggs – Easter eggs perhaps?

In the Jewish tradition, special prayers are said when festivals fall at the time of the New Moon (Boruha Levanah), prayers for each new Moon are said at the beginning of the lunar month (Rosh Hadesh). Astrologers watch the Moon carefully and there are some who will not even discuss a new project on a 'void of course Moon' which is when the Moon makes no major aspects to other planets. It is my guess that in all traditions and beliefs the Sun and Moon were, are and always will be the light which makes us turn our heads to the sky and our thoughts heavenwards.

The image of the Moon as the supreme female, the complete mother, is strongly represented in the Egyptian goddess, Isis, who presided over herbal remedies and Lunar magic. If you wish to invoke the goddess Isis, draw a circle late at night, concentrate your thoughts and visualize an image of the goddess while asking for what you want. Above all, ask for the love and strength to be able to cope with your troubles and live a kindly and decent life. Here is a tiny extract from The Worship of Isis rituals.

> And over these tides the Great Goddess presides under her aspect of the Moon. As she passeth from her rising to her setting, so answer these tides unto her. She riseth from the sea as the evening Star, and the waters of the earth rise in flood. She sinketh as Luna in the western ocean, and the waters flow back into the inner Earth and are still in that great lake of darkness wherein are the Moon and Stars reflected. Whoso is still as the dark underworld lake of Persephone shall see the tides of the Unseen moving therein and shall know all things. Therefore is Luna also called giver of visions.

In the Kabbalistic tradition, the Moon, this time known as Levanah, is associated with the section of the Tree of Life which is called Yesod. Yesod, the Foundation, is situated towards the base of the Tree just above Malkuth. Yesod is the ninth path of pure intelligence and it purifies the emanations. Yesod contains two totally different images; the watery Moon of Levanah under the presidency of the water element archangel, Gabriel, and also the magical image of a beautiful naked young man who is known for his strength alongside the powerful God name of Shaddai el Chai, the Almighty living God. Nothing in the Kabbalah is easy to understand, but the idea behind Yesod is that the universe was a vaporous and watery chaos which was gathered into order by the strength and power of God. Genesis – Boraishis. Here is a Greco/Hebrew version of the Isis worship ritual.

> Our Lady is also the Moon, called of some Selene, of others Luna, but by the wise Levanah, for therein is contained the number of her name. She is the ruler of the tides of flux and reflux. The waters of the Great Sea answer unto her, likewise the tides of all earthly seas, and she ruleth the nature of women.

Whilst reading through the proofs of this section I decided to look a little more closely into the phrase 'for therein is contained the number of her name'. This led me into a fascinating line of research where I discovered that the 'alphabet number' Hebrew letters for the names Levanah and Luna were the same, e.g. lamed, vov, nun and hey. The numerology was, of course the same: 30, 6, 50, 5, making a total of 91*. 1 haven't had a chance yet to find an ancient Greek alphabet, but my guess is that when I do Selene will turn out to have the same numeric value. This led me further into Hebrew Kabbalistic numerology, which had been a speciality of my grandfather's during his lifetime. This type of esoteric thinking is obviously beyond the scope of this book. But it just goes to show how much knowledge is wrapped up in these old sayings.

In Kabbalistic divination, Yesod rules the instincts, habit patterns, food, home environment, sex and sexual organs. This is also the wife in a male reading, and the ninth month of pregnancy.

Before we leave the world of religion and magical belief I would like to advise you to perform all ritual and psychic work during daylight (except for the Isis invocation), even if you are only trying out ideas for size. This is because one's resistance is low after dark, and low-level entities may be drawn in due to the unbalanced forces of the Moon and your tired mind. If you are at all tuned in to your own lunar phases, then avoid doing any psychic work at those times when you know you will be at a low ebb. I know, for example, that I tend to feel tired, ratty and off-colour just after the new Moon each month, probably because I was born a couple of days after a full Moon.

Good luck with your magic, may the Goddess of the Moon guide your instincts towards greater understanding and the ability to help others along their paths towards enlightenment.

---

* True Hebrew numerology is like Roman numerology with some letters representing hundreds and thousands etc.

4

Elements and Triplicities

The Elements

You will notice as you read on through this book that I use the ancient ideas of earth, air, fire and water plus the astrological triplicities of cardinal, fixed and mutable signs, also the ideas of masculine, feminine, negative and positive signs. This ancient form of shorthand gives an invaluable clue to the basic character of each sign. The following should help you to understand the thinking behind these principles.

Earth

This is concerned with security, structure, slow growth, conventional behaviour and concrete results. People whose charts contain a heavy concentration of planets and features in earth are sensible, possibly rather plodding and very practical in outlook. They do things thoroughly and carefully, they are unlikely to be extravagant and are very caring towards their family and close friends. They hold on to their possessions and may be a little too money-minded at times. They hate to give up anything and will always try to finish any job that they start. There is a sense of maturity with these people but perhaps a lack of spontaneity. Their virtue is their reliability, their vices are fussiness and an eye-on-the-main-chance attitude.

Air

This is concerned with communications, networks of all kinds, education, theoretical ideas, finding answers to questions and all-round enlightenment; also the network of one's nervous system. These subjects may be serious-minded, highly involved with the education system or the media or chirpy happy-go-lucky types who pick up their streetwise knowledge from the tabloid papers and the local pub. They will be found expounding on some pet idea or arguing a point over anything from a literary reference to a sporting event. They make good journalists and shopkeepers, teachers and travellers because they are always up to date. Although kind-hearted, they tend to forget their many friends when they are out of sight.

Fire

The key ideas here are of scintillating enthusiasm, initiative, intuition, optimism and faith in the future. People who have a strong fire stellium on their birthcharts never quite relinquish their childhood and, therefore, are very much in tune with young people and young ideas. These entertaining people display considerable egotism but also spontaneous generosity. They are concerned to get things started, to create action and pace but may leave the details to others to cope with later on. Fire sign people are quick to grasp an idea, and being on the ball, they approach life with a degree of sportsmanship as if it were a kind of game. These people find it impossible to save money but invariably earn their way out of disaster.

Water

This is concerned with the emotions and feelings, the beginnings, endings and major transformations of life and also one's moods and inner urges. Watery people respond slowly when asked a question and may appear to be slow when grasping a new concept. They are slow to change, preferring to stay on tried and tested paths. Their chief need is to be near the family, also to have financial security. Faithful, loyal and often quite tense, these people have an intuitive feeling for what is going to be right for themselves and their families. They are sensible and reliable but can fall into depression and illness if life doesn't go their way. There is a corresponding understanding of the needs of others but sometimes an unwillingness to make the effort to do something about these needs. Most watery people have an artistic streak in them, they are particularly fond of music.

The Triplicities

Cardinal

This implies action, initiative. People with a strong cardinal element in their charts cannot be held down under anyone's thumb, they initiate ideas, especially those connected with business. There is an inner sense of determination and an irrepressible desire to succeed. Another way of looking at cardinality is to see it as a beginning because it provides the energy and initiative to get things off the ground.

Fixed

These people like to stay put; in the same house and the same job for as long as possible. They have the strength and endurance to see things through and to uphold the status quo. There is always a measure of stability here, even if it is just the following through of mental exercises and ideas. This can be viewed as a form of continuation as it implies the steady effort of working things through.

Mutable

These people can also hang on to outworn lifestyles, either because they fear change or because they want to keep the peace. They will try to adapt to the behaviour of others and to supply the needs of others. They have the ability to adapt their style of work to whatever situation is prevailing at the time and can steer projects through all their necessary modifications without too much difficulty. Their thinking is wider and more lateral than the other two types but they may prefer to sit in a stew and moan about it than to grit their teeth and either bear it (fixed) or make a new start (cardinal). A further way of viewing mutability is to see it as a transforming element which can either change a situation or bring it to a conclusion.

Masculine and Positive

Outgoing, social, assertive, *apparently* confident, *apparently* courageous.

Feminine and Negative

Introspective, shy, moody, unassertive, *apparently* weak, *apparently* fearful, receptive.

NB: Remember, all that is apparent, ain't necessarily so!

5

Your Natal Moon Sign

Moon in Aries
♈ (Ruled by Mars) ♂

The sun shall not smite thee by day, nor the moon by night.

Psalm 121

The sign of Aries is masculine, positive, fiery and cardinal whilst the Moon, through its association with the sign of Cancer, is feminine, negative, watery and cardinal. This Moon position gives its owner an underlying need for power and a desire for leadership. This may lead you to reach for the top in your career or to become the leader of whichever group you find yourself in. Women with this Moon placement face emotional conflict within their personality due to their highly assertive inner nature and they frequently resolve this by choosing weak partners so that they can reverse the traditional man/woman roles. One such woman is Bernadette.

Bernadette is a hard working and successful businesswoman who travels far and wide to earn the money which her family needs. Her sensitive and artistic husband has a rather humdrum job in a local garage and is super-supportive and caring towards the children. 'I didn't choose this way of life,' says Bernadette, 'it just seems to work out better this way. David cannot take too much hassle and he is really much better with the children than I am.'

Some choose single life and a demanding career in preference to housework and motherhood. Carol is now in her late thirties and is running a successful public relations business of her own. She has had long-term lovers but has never married. 'Some years ago I debated whether to have a child and bring it up on my own because I knew by then that marriage was not for me. In the end, I decided to stay as I am, but I'm not always sure that I took the right decision even now.'

Both sexes have an inner power pack of energy, forcefulness and courage: the cardinality of this sign means that you rarely allow the grass to grow beneath your feet. If faced with a problem you would rather sort it out immediately. You may actually get others to do this for you but help is appreciated when it is given. Your mind is highly original and, given other encouraging factors on your birthchart, you may be able to turn your ideas into money-making projects which could give you the means to get yourself up the ladder of success. However you may be so idealistic and enthusiastic as to be unrealistic. You have a tendency to do things on too large a scale sometimes, over-optimism can cloud your brain and make you unrealistic in your expectations You need to have an element of risk in your life which may be reflected in the lob you do or in your personal life.

Being quickly responsive to any situation, you can be relied on in a crisis; you're not embarrassed by the sight of people who are in trouble, indeed you will do what you can to help them. Your emotional reactions are fast and instinctive, your behaviour can be over-impulsive but time and experience of life may soften some of the rough edges. Care should be taken not to be critical and impatient with those who see and do things differently from you, as this can lead you into a narrow-minded and bigoted stance. You quickly become irritated and may have difficulty in keeping your temper due to the combined blanketing effect of the watery moon and the fiery impulsiveness of the sign of Aries. This tension may be released in sudden outbursts of temper and biting sarcastic remarks. Your energy, if there are some Aquarian traits on your chart, could make you an energetic social reformer. You prefer other people to be forthright and honest in their dealings with you and unless there is a very good reason for secrecy, you prefer to be direct and honest yourself. Your excellent sense of humour gets you out of a lot of trouble and you have the ability to take a joke against yourself.

Your ability to put ideas into action can be an inspiration to others, also you can motivate people by your optimistic outlook and your faith in the future. You know instinctively how to raise the spirits of others. However, you can go 'over the top' on occasion and plunge into action without weighing the consequences and therefore you need to cultivate a sense of proportion. When being carried away on a cloud of enthusiasm be careful not to override the feelings of others; however, it is never your intention to hurt anyone. You have little patience with people who withdraw into their shell, sulk and won't tell you what's the matter with them, your own hot temper can make you insensitive at times but you don't hold a grudge. The lunar Arian heart is warm and you are the first to help and comfort those who are in trouble. You respect the beliefs of others and are happy to preserve their independence; your broad mind makes you able to relate to people of all classes and colours. You really cannot stand neurotic people who whine for nothing. You will help anyone who has practical problems but have little patience with emotional doubts and worries and you tend to avoid having them yourself.

You are more of a city person than a country type but you like to get away into the fresh air and love being in the sun. It is a fact that many lunar Arians are excellent sportsmen and sportswomen. The fiery quality of Aries indicates a need for excitement and change, a monotonous job may pay the bills but won't satisfy you for long. This need for excitement can also make steady relationships appear unappealing and this may even lead you to choose unreliable partners. Some of you, on the other hand, seek to steady your own inner nature by marrying a much more placid and reliable personality than yourself; a few of you may possibly destroy a relationship simply because it has become boring. I have a theory that Moon in Aries subjects of both sexes prefer a younger partner, this suggests that you would enjoy moulding them to your own design. Many of you choose a partner who is careful with money because you don't seem to be able to trust yourself not to overspend. You enjoy the pursuit of love and fall in love fairly easily but the flame can burn out quickly. A relationship based on friendship is more likely to be enduring than a swift passion but there must be excitement, sex and warmth or it will not work at all. Women with the Moon in Aries have a touch of masculinity at their core; that is not to say that they are all budding lesbians, just that there is dissatisfaction with the traditional feminine role. Whatever your gender, if you have this Moon placement, you may be hard to live with at times, because you can fall into the habit of being picky and fault-finding due to unreasonable fears based on imagined threats to your independence.

You can be quite a good homemaker as long as you have time and money to spare, but if you are short of both, you will ignore your surroundings. You enjoy buying gadgets for the home and you can put up with noisy or messy major alterations better than most people can.

You are a caring parent but unfortunately you could belittle any child whom you considered weak and silly. You do your best to see that your children have all that they require and will move heaven and earth to get them a good education. You may not actually wish to spend too much time with your children, the relationship works better if you have a fulfilling job and can, therefore, direct most of your energies away from the home situation. You will never hesitate to spend money on your family's appearance as you consider that good clothes give a good impression.

Sexually your attitude should be straightforward but you may wish to dominate your partner and control him or her. Talk of sex excites you but background music during love-making may put you off! You enjoy fun and laughter while making love but, above all, you need friendship with your partner as much as you need sex.

Many of you love the arts, especially music and dancing, some of you will find your way into an artistic career, certainly you need a measure of creativity in your work. Many subjects with the Sun, Moon or Ascendant in Aries have a lifelong *desire* to study music or art but somehow never quite get around to it, perhaps the fear of failure is too great.

ATTITUDE TO CAREER

The position of the Moon on a birthchart rarely determines one's actual career but can show inner motivations. You are happiest in a job where you can make your own decisions and may prefer to be self-employed. If not too impatient, you can rise to an executive position in a large and well structured organization. You enjoy wielding power and should make a sensible and benevolent manager or employer, you have the ability to delegate tasks to others and then leave them to get on with the job. Taking orders from someone you don't respect is impossible for you and you would respond very angrily to anyone who tried to bully you; however you, in turn, must try not to bully or to laugh at others.

You need to be able to use your initiative, you would find it impossible to work for a wet blanket type. Work in the military or paramilitary field might appeal to you as might engineering, electronics or work which influences the public. You may enjoy working in the media and being in the public eye so that you can receive open adulation. Marketing, promoting and thinking up new ideas comes easily to you. Your Achilles' heel may be that you are susceptible to flattery. If there are other indications on your birthchart, you could make quite a good teacher. Your love of mechanics and vehicles makes you a good driver, and even a good pilot. The modern technologies of computers and telecommunications would come fairly easily to you. You could make a living from sport or dancing, possibly as a teacher.

PARENTS AND BACKGROUND

This Moon position shows a difficult relationship with the father, you may have loved him and hated him at the same time and also tried to emulate him. Whilst growing up, you probably found yourself in a number of nose-to-nose shouting matches with him. There is a fight for emotional supremacy in this relationship with the father seeing the child as being unrealistic and the child seeing the parent as being overly restrictive or unhelpful. Sometimes the father actually shows contempt towards the child. Your mother may have been cold towards you or just too busy to take much notice of you. The family itself may be attached to a large and very structured organization such as the armed forces or the civil service. The Aries Moon child may follow his parents into the same organization but would only be happy in that environment if he quickly gained a position of rank and decision-making.

Your parents encouraged you to stand on your own feet at an early age. They would have applauded and encouraged any physical activity (sports, swimming, dancing) and wanted you to do well at school. You don't have much attachment to the past or even to your own family, this is especially true if you feel that they don't appreciate you.

Your mother might have had to face some kind of circumstances where she was forced to leave you to cope alone. This was probably due to problems at that time; however it is possible that she was vain, selfish and all too easily bored by the tasks of motherhood. The Moon sign sometimes jumps back a generation, therefore, some of the circumstances given here for *your* childhood could actually apply to *your mother's experience* when young. There may even have been jealousy and bitterness between you and your brothers and sisters.

HEALTH

In so far as the Moon sometimes reflects continuous or chronic health conditions, any trouble in this case would be in the area of the head, eyes, nose, ears (upper) teeth and throat. Your impetuosity may lead you to have silly accidents such as cuts, burns and possibly bruises as a result of dropping things on your feet.

Moon in Taurus
♉ (Ruled by Venus) ♀

Ah, Moon of my Delight who know'st no wane,
The Moon of Heaven is rising once again:
How oft hereafter rising shall she look
Through this same Garden after me – in vain!

from *The Rubaiyat* of Omar Khayyam.

The sign of Taurus is feminine, negative, earth and fixed, while the Moon, through its connections with the sign of Cancer is feminine, negative, water and cardinal. The Moon, therefore is fairly comfortable in Taurus adding a measure of stability to the personality and bestowing an uncomplicated response to sensual pleasures. You enjoy eating, drinking, making love and listening to music. The feminine aspect of this placement prevents you from being much of an initiator, indeed you prefer to spend your life sailing along on a steady course than for it to be full of storms and disruption. The fixity of Taurus stabilizes the natural restlessness of the Moon and makes you very purposeful and determined, particularly when it comes to getting what you want or hanging on to what you have. You try at all times to maintain the status quo, you may find that the circumstances of your life force you into this position. You might even find yourself putting up with a long-term lifestyle which is not of your choosing. The Moon is said to be 'exalted' in the sign of Taurus which gives an inner sense of strength and resilience. Lunar Taureans, therefore, are noted for their generally robust health and their ability to obtain practical results in all that they undertake.

People who have the Moon in an earth sign love the natural world which means that you make a hobby out of botany or animal biology. You could become involved with some scheme that seeks to preserve the countryside (this is even more likely if there is any Aquarius on your birthchart). Even if you are not actively involved with these pursuits, you will love getting out into the fresh air and into your garden. Many lunar Taureans choose to work as representatives or even milkmen, so that they can be out and about and keep in tune with the seasons. You have a strong need to build for the future and create things which will be useful and long-lasting, this could be reflected in your choice of a career. You like the sea but not with the same intensity as the solar or lunar Cancerian, you wouldn't have any great urge to run off and join the navy. Your affinity with nature could lead you to take an interest in the old religions of earth magic and the 'craft'.

You don't enter into relationships lightly, the fixity of Taurus plus your inner urge to build and preserve leads you to take any form of emotional commitment very seriously. Most astrology books tell us that this Moon position leads to possessiveness and jealousy and, to some extent, this is true. Possessiveness is more of a problem than envy or jealousy but this is a rather subtle concept to grasp. You don't envy the things that other people have or the relationships that they enjoy but if *your* partner were to leave you for another, you would be very jealous indeed. If the object of your love promised to leave his or her partner for you, you would believe him, if you then find him (or her) dragging his feet, you would become very upset indeed and would remain that way for years. It is not easy for you to give in gracefully and accept defeat, especially in the face of what you see as a form of betrayal. This tenacity and endurance are both the strengths and the weaknesses of this particular Moon Sign placement.

Your senses are strong, especially touch and smell; you love the scent of flowers and the feel of velvet. Your musical taste is well developed; one Moon in Taurus lady told me that she hates the sound of a 'murdered song' but loves the sound of laughter. Obviously this sensuality leads to a love of sex with all its scents, textures and passions, however, relating is more important to you than sex for its own sake. You love to be cuddled and stroked in both a sexual and an affectionate manner and ideally for you all this snuggling should take place within marriage.

You are, under normal circumstances, reliable and steady in relationships. You prefer to be faithful to your partner, but if for some reason you find this impossible, then you would try hard to wait for your children to grow up before actually leaving the family home; you try to do your duty for however long it takes. Oddly enough you are quite a flirt but this is 'social' flirting which is not intended to be taken seriously. You don't flirt in order to make your partner jealous, you do it just for the fun of it. You can appear to be intrusive or possessive to those who are close to you ('Where are you going and when do you intend to be back?'). This is not intended to irritate them or to show any lack of trust on your part, you just need to make sure that your family is safe. My Moon in Taurus husband, Tony, likes me to be around. He isn't afraid that I will run off with someone else, he just worries about me. When a friend commented to him about this he told them, 'If Sasha is not home at the time she says that she will be, I start to think that she has had an accident. I have to get up early for my work and if

I am kept awake worrying about her, then I get annoyed.' There is no way of changing this person's nature, one just has to be grateful that they care – there are plenty who don't.

You take naturally to parenthood, you love your own children and have patience with those of others. If you marry someone who already has a family, you cope with this very well. You take a responsible attitude towards those who depend upon you, both older and younger members of the family, even pets, without making heavy weather of this. You are very loving and caring and really enjoy looking after, even waiting upon, those you love but you become understandably resentful if this care is taken for granted and not appreciated. You are good with sick people as long as there is not too much mess to clear up, the one thing you really hate is the sight of blood (especially your own). Sometimes this practical type of caring is not enough and you may miss some essential element in your partner's make-up and fail to give him or her the understanding that he needs. Bethany, a really sensitive and intelligent friend of mine summed this up by telling me that 'I just couldn't figure out what it was that my ex-husband really wanted from me half the time. I obviously missed something but, even now, I'm not sure that I can see what it was.'

You yourself strongly need the closeness of a family around you, your sense of loyalty makes you jump to the defence of any member of your family who is criticized by an outsider. However, you yourself are convinced that you have every right to criticize them! Your own deep attachment to your family, occasional misplaced pride in them and desire for them to have the best, be the best, can make you over-critical and even tyrannical at times (especially when you are in a bad mood). A strange fault of yours is that you seem unable to cope with people who lack confidence in themselves. You could even squash the little that they have, you need a certain amount of standing up to, you could actually belittle a partner, even belittle your own children if you suspected too much weakness. You respect strength, possibly because you need to 'tap into' the strength of the other person. You are not necessarily competitive though, and would help a partner or workmate to get ahead. Above all you need a stimulating partner who has similar interests to yourself. You are emotionally habit-forming, not keen on too much change or excitement, you must beware that monotony does not seep into your sexual behaviour.

You are attracted to beauty and people who have cheerful, pleasant natures. Your pet hates are fatness, ugliness and people who wear dirty, tatty clothing. Both the people around you and your own surroundings must be clean and attractive.

You have the quality of basic common sense (rare sense perhaps?). You like your bills to be paid on time, are careful with money and like to have some savings to fall back on but despite this, you are not unduly lucky with money and *can* be taken in by a confidence trickster. There are times when your judgement deserts you. Occasionally your patience deserts you and this can be an interesting experience for those around you as your temper is really fearful when it is unleashed; it can overwhelm you and cause you to cut your nose off to spite your face.

You control your feelings very well and are adept at hiding them from others, probably due to childhood training; being a feminine and emotional sign this repression can lead to moodiness. You may break out in a sudden angry response; if someone were to push in front of you in a queue for instance, you may react differently from one day to another. Being naturally rather cautious, you prefer to allow new acquaintances to do the talking, it is only when you know people better that you can relax and open up. You are not above a bit of manipulation in social circumstances but will generally use it in the form of humour to defuse a tense situation. You usually guard your tongue well and rarely run off at the mouth. Once you have formed an opinion it is hard for you to alter it. You can have the rather unfortunate habit of laying the law down to others.

ATTITUDE TO CAREER

I use the word 'attitude' because the Moon position alone would not suggest any specific career, however one spends so much time at work that it helps to understand one's inner motivations.

You are undoubtedly ambitious, both for yourself and your family. Women with this placement seem to be given the message by their parents that they should stick to the old-fashioned idea of the feminine role and, therefore, often start out as secretaries, nurses or children's nannies. All the lunar Taurean women whom I have spoken to tell me that they resented this bitterly, and also resented the associated implication that they were not as bright or as important as their brothers. They have all subsequently drifted towards less overtly feminine forms of work.

In common with the other earth signs of Capricorn and Virgo, Taureans of both sexes have to put aside their dreams and ambitions for the sake of practicalities: later on in life they may not bother to revive those dreams which I think is rather a shame. One lady told me that she always dreamed of carrying the Olympic torch. Many of you dream about being a musician, dancer or singer but with a bit of luck from elsewhere on your birthchart, you may just be able to make it into showbusiness. Your practical side leads you to supply people with the things that they need, therefore you may deal in food, furniture, household objects or even the things which help people make themselves and their homes attractive. Other typical Taurean trades are building, architecture, farming, market gardening, make-up artist, musician, artist and dancer. Because it is the Moon that we are dealing with here, you will not necessarily follow a Taurean trade at all: however the need to be useful, get out and about and help to create something which is both durable and pleasing to the eye is a strong motivating force. You are not drawn to speculative ventures which is lust as well as you are neither a lucky gambler nor particularly good at handling business crises. You are not keen on sending memos or making up office reports – for one thing, you hate anything to be too cut and dried; however, if you have to produce these, you will do so thoroughly.

A couple of final comments on attitude to work. You prefer to find a steady job and stick to it. You finish practically everything that you start and although not terrifically analytical, you can deal with details without becoming bored. Your persistence makes you good in the field of sales, your flair for beauty could lead to a career in marketing (especially luxury products). A lot of this depends upon the rest of the chart as a touch of Pisces, Aquarius or Sagittarius for instance would add the ingredient of imagination. You hate to be rushed, you can cope with anything when left to work at your own pace.

PARENTS AND BACKGROUND

According to most astrology books you should have good parents and have enjoyed a happy and peaceful childhood. My experience as an astrologer tells me that this is just not so. Whenever the Moon is in a fixed sign there is at least one parent who has a bullying or intransigent attitude towards the subject. This may be due to the fact that the parent has had a hard life him or herself and has subsequently developed a hard and unsympathetic outlook. A high proportion of lunar Taureans have at least one parent born under the sign of Aquarius which leads to total lack of understanding and communication. All this leads to an almost Scorpionic ability to keep your thoughts and feelings away from your parents. This is fair enough as a survival mechanism but the danger is that this behaviour will be carried over into other relationships or later dealings with 'authority' figures.

It seems that one of your parents grew up in some kind of deprived circumstances: this is more likely to have been poverty, a lack of opportunity and a lack of material security than lack of love (although that could apply too). This parent, therefore, is left with the feeling that *things* are safer than people and that one must obtain goods and money in order to survive: there seems to be little space in the parent's head for love, understanding and sensitivity to the child. You may have come from a comfortable home where your practical needs were taken care of but there will have been some lack of understanding. One of your parents may have been ill, a hypochondriac or just weak-willed, you probably harbour feelings of contempt for this parent, these are very well hidden – even from yourself. You may feel that the weaker parent could have done more for you, and more for themselves as well.

Most women with this Moon placement marry quite young and have children early. Lunar Taurean judgement being what it is, the first marriage might well turn out to be a mistake. It appears that you are attracted to exciting types who in your eyes complement your own stodginess. These types are *too* exciting to be good family men, therefore the disappointments are a kind of double blow. The result of this can push female Taureans into exciting careers as a result of the need for financial survival.

HEALTH

In so far as the Moon influences health on a birthchart, an afflicted Moon in Taurus would bring problems in the area of the lower jaw, ears, throat, voice and tonsils. There may be thyroid problems and even, just possibly diabetes. You may have that famous Taurean tendency to gain weight, but this will be mitigated if there is a lot of air on your chart.

Moon in Gemini
♊ (Ruled by Mercury) ☿

When they got there, the West Wind asked him if he could tell her the way to the castle that lay *East of the Sun and West of the Moon*, for it was she who ought to have had the *Prince* who lived there.

(from a book of old Norse legends which I read and re-read, scribbled on and nearly wore out when I was very young.)

The sign of Gemini is masculine, positive, airy and mutable; the Moon, through its association with Cancer, is feminine, negative, watery and cardinal. The Moon, therefore, is not really comfortable in this sign and this may lead to some conflict within the personality. The instability of Gemini plus the fluctuating nature of the Moon could make your emotions a little too changeable and your nerves jumpy. If you have something steady such as Leo or Taurus on your Sun or Ascendant, then the Gemini nervousness would just be confined to bouts of irritability. You are impatient with demanding people and cannot cope with those who are chronically ill. Your own health is not all that good but you try to ignore bouts of illness and hardly ever take time off work to recover or recuperate.

The mutability of this sign gives you a fascination for new and interesting people and places and this leads you into the kind of job where you continually come across new people and get around from place to place. You like to be in the swing of things and hate to miss anything that is going on. Your private life is probably less changeable but you certainly have many friends and can usually be found on the end of a phone somewhere.

Women with the Moon in Gemini need to be out at work. This is even stronger with the lunar type than in women who have the Sun in Gemini because the underlying nature is highly ambitious and rather calculating. Both sexes like the home to be clean and orderly but are not interested in doing much housework themselves. Both sexes like to look nice and tend to feel confident if they go out knowing that they are well dressed. Your mind is very active and you may be intellectual; even with very little formal education; you would be a deep reader and a self-educator. Your mind (unless Mercury is badly placed) is very quick and acute and you have a fine, fast sense of humour and a gift for making amusing and witty comments. The reverse of this coin is that you may become sarcastic if irritated. Lunar Geminians think fairly deeply and are less likely to be content with surface knowledge than are Sun in Gemini subjects. However, in addition to this depth of thought, you also have a dustbin-like mind full of rag-tag bits of knowledge. Although chatty and friendly to every new face on your scene, you do have strong relationships with your family and you will keep your most personal friends for years. Your moods change quickly but you don't sulk and you have no patience with those who do. Your attention span is strange; people who moan about their problems or go on at length about their pet subject bore you, but an interesting book or TV programme will hold you riveted for ages. Your thought processes are logical and you learn in an orderly fashion but you can blend this logical approach with instinctive or even psychic awareness if there is help from other areas of your birthchart.

There is a kind of Peter Pan aspect to this Moon position which I think may also apply to the other air signs of Libra and Aquarius. Somehow you never see yourself as quite grown up and can continue to display quite babyish behaviour when away from the outside world. The reverse side of this coin is that you do seem to keep your youthful looks and a young outlook on life far longer than most. You have creative and artistic ability and may paint, make ornaments or interesting clothes, you may be interested in model-making or computer techniques. You have strong dress sense and a good eye for matching up an outfit.

If given the opportunity, you learn to drive a car while you are in your teens, explore your own neighbourhood and then travel the world as soon as you are able to. Cities appeal to you more than the countryside and you particularly enjoy visiting foreign cities. You are resourceful and can usually find a way to solve practical problems; you are probably quite good with your hands.

Although not a social reformer, you hate racism and ill treatment towards those who can't stand up for themselves such as children or animals. As a parent you would make quite sure that your own children were being well treated but would not want to spend all your time looking after them. Your worst fault is a certain inner coldness, you really cannot take to people who wish to lean upon you, and may give the appearance of having very little depth of concern for others. You can give practical help when it is needed but you may find people's emotional problems hard to cope with. Being logical by nature, you cannot see how or why they fell into their particular emotional mess in the first place. Care must be taken to watch that your witty tongue does not spill over into sarcasm.

Oddly enough you can suffer from depression at times and can become so down-hearted that you feel life to be a total waste of time. One case of these feelings might be exhaustion because you have few reserves of energy to call on and you have the habit of going beyond your limit if there is work to be done.

Some of you may delay marriage or parenthood until you feel that you are sufficiently grown up to cope with it, but when you do take the plunge, you are quite serious in your attitude. You make a delightful parent because you never quite grow up yourself; therefore you relate easily to children. You will break the bank to provide them with a good education and your children will never be short of books, materials or any other kind of mental stimulation. You will try to remain close to your grandchildren as you value family life.

You can have a real problem in the realm of relationships, leading a very busy life which leaves you too tired and over-stretched for much relating. To some extent this is a mechanism which helps you to avoid the reality of responsible relating. This 'busy-busy' business could hide a deep well of unspoken unhappiness You may avoid emotional commitment, Preferring to keep your contacts with the opposite sex on a somewhat shallow level. You could attract (or choose) a rather weak dependent type of partner who would be drawn to your inner strength – remember Gemini is a *positive* sign, but you are better off with one who can stand on his or her own feet. Helen, a young Moon in Gemini travel agent tells me 'I'm not so much afraid of commitment as bored by it. I still feel at my age (early twenties) that I want to play the field. I have to admit that to some extent I dread the thought of being tied down.' Perhaps you need to get in touch with your own feelings before being able to handle those of others. You could be a theorizer and, as far as emotions are concerned, you may prefer to read about emotional matters and to rationalize them than to feel the reality of them. To some extent this derives from a mistrust of the opposite sex and possibly a lack of sexual self-confidence. You don't like to be emotionally fenced in. Malcolm, a highly successful Sales Manager for a vehicle hire firm, told me recently that he had lust fallen in love for the first time at the age of forty-eight. 'Why?' I asked him, 'why now?' 'Well', he replied, 'I suppose I was always nervous of being vulnerable or of committing myself totally. I did go through some really stupid escapades with a number of totally mindless women at one time – escaping reality, I suppose.'

You don't suffer from jealousy if you see other people making a success of themselves and, like most of the lunar masculine signs, you measure your own successes against *your own* achievements. Not being jealous or possessive yourself you strongly resent being on the receiving end of this behaviour by others. You are proud of your achievements however, and also proud of your family; you could push your children educationally, and will make sacrifices in order to help your family.

Sex has to start in your mind and, if you are not careful, it can stay there too; like lunar Pisceans you may be happier fantasizing about sex than actually indulging in it. If you find a compatible partner who encourages you to relax you can bring all that sexuality down from your mind to reach the parts that the other beers cannot reach, then you could become the lover you always wanted to be. You are easily put off by coarseness. Your nerves are sensitive, therefore a quiet atmosphere, an amusing lover and a couple of drinks will work wonders. You may possibly experiment with bisexuality and may privately enjoy rude books and even blue films! Oddly enough both solar and lunar Geminians are tactile. They enjoy hugging, touching and being touched as long as they are not smothered or held too close. Before leaving the fascinating subject of sex, it is worth noting that anyone with Gemini strongly marked on his chart can do two things at once!

ATTITUDE TO CAREER

The position of the Moon will not indicate any specific career but will show your inner motivations. People, mental activity, words and travel are essential ingredients for your working life. You may work in sales, telephone or telex communications or marketing. Writing, especially journalism may appeal, also all forms of teaching. Your own education may have been of almost any quality but many of you do teach yourself, then others, possibly in the realms of sports or dancing. You are generally respected by others both for what you know and for your pleasant way of handling people.

Your mind should be orderly (unless there are other indications on your birthchart) and you can organize both yourself and others. Travel appeals to you, especially air travel, and many lunar Geminians work in the airforce or the travel industry. You all seem to love driving and may be able to pilot a plane as well. You have a quick grasp of new ideas and can communicate them well to others, you are very good at handling people and make a wonderful manager. You can be canny and crafty in business; you love wheeling and dealing and you may not always be a hundred per cent honest. You are at your best when teamed up with a practical partner. As this sign rules the hands and arms, you could be a super craftsman, printer, manicurist or even a palmist.

Oddly enough, religion and mysticism may interest you but only on a surface level. You may enjoy the social side of a religious group rather more than the deeper elements of its philosophy.

PARENTS AND BACKGROUND

The chances are that you had one parent, probably your father, who tended to lay down the law to you, this gave you an awareness of the need to be obedient and to conform with the parent's ideas of behaviour. Your childhood home was probably filled with books and educational aids and your parents will have been quite happy for you to have tuition in practically anything. There would have been good conversation and interesting visitors in your home. You should have been born fairly easily and may have been the youngest child in a small family or the only one of one sex among a family of the opposite one. There is some evidence of deep unhappiness in childhood and a sense of not fitting in somewhere, this may have been within the family or at school. You may have been on the receiving end of racial or religious prejudice! You may have been compared to other brothers and sisters, a dead child or even one of your parents and found wanting. It is possible that you fancied working in the services or in a hospital but somehow this either doesn't happen or just doesn't work for you when you try it.

An unusual mother is indicated for you. She may be a career woman, highly intellectual or just plain eccentric! Your mother would have shown you, either by direct reference or by example, that women must be able to stand on their own two feet in life.

This will influence you, if you are female, to become a career woman; if male, to choose a career woman for your partner.

The problems associated with this placement could jump back one generation and apply more closely to one of your parent's experiences of childhood.

HEALTH

This is not a healthy placement for the Moon especially if it is also badly aspected by other planets. Your lungs may be weak also there could be problems with your hands and arms. Some lunar Geminians suffer really horrendous accidents which affect their arms, hands, teeth and faces. This lunar position can lead to bones and features having to be rebuilt! You can suffer allergies and may have one or two ailments from among the range of nervous or auto-immune diseases. This could be asthma, eczema, rheumatism, migraine, psoriasis, ulcers, colitis, etc. Your nerves may be your worst enemy. You need to find an outlet for your nervous energy; sports, fresh air pursuits or even sex could help!

Moon in Cancer
♋ (Ruled by the Moon) ☽

'It was the lovely moon – she lifted
Slowly her white brow among
Bronze cloud-waves that ebbed and drifted
Faintly, faintlier afar.'

It was the lovely Moon,
by John Freeman (1880–1929)

The sign of Cancer is feminine, negative, watery and cardinal. The Moon is the planet which rules this sign, therefore it is quite at home here. The Moon rules the inner person, therefore like those who have the Sun in Cancer, your reactions to people and places are very strong and this will be automatically taken into account in any decisions which you make. Your feelings are very sensitive, which means that you link in very quickly to other people's feelings to the point where you can feel whether they are unhappy or in pain. You can sense a 'funny' atmosphere as soon as you walk into a room. Unless there are very conflicting forces on your chart, you should have the usual Cancerian ability to listen sympathetically. In business, you would have an instinctive feel about a deal which was about to go wrong – or go right!

The negative side of this coin is over-sensitivity. Like the other feminine water signs of Pisces and Scorpio you can take things too personally, brood, sulk and shut yourself off from others. They say that Cancerians' moods change with each tide but this is an exaggeration. Women with the Moon in any of the water signs will be very susceptible to period problems and hormone-related mood swings. The very worst aspect of this placement is that you may indulge in emotional blackmail by shutting off from others and sending out disapproving vibes. On a very bad day, you might be beset by feelings of paranoia or the kind of envy which would make you behave in a thoroughly resentful manner. You can also be over-critical and fault-finding on occasions. This kind of behaviour is rare because you are much too kind and thoughtful a person, far too receptive to the needs of others to be this unpleasant for long.

You have the ability to adjust yourself to your surroundings and fit in fairly well with other people (water signs find their own level). You may complain about the situation you find yourself in but you will make the best of it and will often find a way of changing and manipulating the circumstances to suit yourself. Remember Cancer is a *cardinal* sign and the Moon represents one's instincts. *Your* instinctive reaction is to put things right and create a better atmosphere. Some people are starters and others are runners; the ability to initiate projects and/or to see them through would depend upon a variety of factors in your birthchart, but your instinctive reaction is to set things in motion and then encourage others (or find someone else) to see them through. If you are really stuck for an answer to your problems you can always look a bit pathetic in the hope that someone will take pity on you and help you solve them.

You are considerate towards others, especially your family, it would be almost impossible for you to desert them; you would only do so under extreme duress. I think that you would try several times to put things right before giving up on them. You have patience with children and young people and are probably very fond of animals. You are not entirely selfless, it is only when *you* are settled and satisfied that you can relax and give sustenance to others. Your greatest requirements are for *emotional* security, e.g. a partner you can rely upon, harmony in the home and friends who help build up your confidence. Lack of confidence in your own abilities and feelings of relative worthlessness are your worst enemy and it's these that can make you feel jealous and resentful towards others, often quite without justification.

You like children and enjoy having them around you, not only being good to your own children but kind to other people's as well. However, you greatly resent having other people's children being dumped on you. Your gentle inner nature responds to the vulnerability and honesty of children. You may remain a bit too close to your own children after they have grown up or you may want them to be independent but find that you can't get rid of them! Alternatively, your own mother may continue to smother *you* long after *you* have grown up! It may be quite difficult for you to forget your own childhood as you have a slight tendency to live in the past.

You react to any difficult situation by worrying. You genuinely worry about your family; also money, health, the state of the nation and the imminence of nuclear war. There is a tendency for you to attract parasitical people who hang themselves on to you and make demands upon you. This is most evident among those of you who have your Sun or ascendant in a steady earth sign or an enthusiastic fire sign. Fortunately for you, you are astute enough to be able to spot these types coming and to off-load them far more easily than, for instance, a soft-hearted Moon in Pisces person could. When you care for someone you are very good to them if they are ill; being kind and sympathetic, you can become worked up on their behalf if you think that they are being hurt by someone else. Unfortunately, unless there is a lot of strength elsewhere on the chart, you won't actually *do* anything practical to help.

You might be sensual but you are not greedy. You don't have a large appetite for food, you prefer small amounts that are very well cooked and presented. Your sensitive stomach may reject spicy foods. (One Moon in Cancer friend tells me that he cannot eat raw onions.) You probably enjoy good wines but there is no evidence of this Moon placement leading to overindulgence. You could be a good cook yourself but this will depend upon other factors in your birthchart, also your lifestyle. You hate scenes and rows and are easily upset by harsh discordant noises. You can put up with any amount of chaos around you at work but you need peace and harmony in the home. You may have the Cancerian trait of collecting things, ranging from valuable antiques to junk. You don't like losing anything – or anyone.

Your senses are all strong, especially that of hearing, you really hate discordant noises. The senses of smell, touch and taste are well developed and you could be long-sighted. Sexually, you absolutely come into your own. The whole concept of an experience which involves all the senses plus love and affection is just too much for you to miss. Being basically kind and thoughtful, you should be a considerate – even a practised – lover. The fact that you are the faithful type possibly mitigates against much variety in sexual experiences. Two of my friends who happen to be married to Moon in Cancer subjects tell me that their partners are good lovers.

You enjoy the company of new people and visiting new places but also you have an attachment to old ones. You enjoy gossiping almost as much as your Gemini cousins do. You have a habit of observing the behaviour of others as a form of self-protection. Being emotionally cautious, you are slow to fall in love and open yourself to the prospect of hurt and rejection. Others may fall in love with you because you have an immediate understanding of their problems. You seem to *know* others psychically. If the one who falls for your sympathetic attitude expects you to go on and solve their problems they may be disappointed. This rather depends on your Sun and rising signs.

Being cautious, you may react in a slightly hostile manner towards new people. If you have something very outgoing, such as Sagittarius, on your Ascendant, there will be an open, confident attitude, however the caution will still be there hidden away underneath. You are basically honest both with money and in most other senses; you can be trusted in any kind of confidential situation and with any information. However, one less pleasant attribute is that you can occasionally display a touch of smarminess, flattering those whom you wish to get round or make capital out of. This is a successful ploy in most cases, but it won't wash when dealing with people who are particularly perceptive.

You can be slightly mean in small matters. This peculiarity also applies to the Moon in Pisces and Scorpio. My friend Linda tells me that she gets annoyed when her children waste toothpaste and she saves the last bits of used bars of soap and jams them together so that they can be completely finished off! I have the Moon in Pisces and have to admit to the same small economy measures. Both solar and lunar Cancerians find it hard to get rid of anything. Once in a while you decide to turn out the cupboards only to put almost everything back again. There is too much sentiment attached to your junk for you to be able to throw it out. You need a base to operate from, therefore, not only your home but also your office are important to you and you don't want these to be disturbed or 'cleaned-up' too much. Unless there is a strong dose of Libra or Virgo on your birthchart, you are not over-fussy about the appearance of your home; you could make a home anywhere.

Your likes and dislikes are strong; remember Cancer is a cardinal sign, you also have courage in odd places where others lack it. For instance, you are adept at asking questions, probing, finding out what makes people tick and keeping up to date with the local gossip. You are not above giving a gentle form of 'third degree'.

Lunar Cancerians have a long memory, therefore, you can hold a grudge if you are hurt, but you also remember those who have helped you. Being rather sentimental, you like to remember birthdays and anniversaries and you feel peeved if yours are forgotten. Your intuition is very strong and this may just be a helpful tool in everyday life or you can actually be drawn towards psychic work of some kind. Quite a few lunar Cancerians have paranormal or psychic hobbies. Because you can be trusted with secrets, you could work as a psychic consultant of some kind where you have to listen to people's confidences. You like the countryside and really love the sea. If a Cancerian Moon is *very* prominent in your birthchart, you could choose a job on or near the sea. Another of your interests is the past. You may study history or collect things which have been around for a long time such as antiquities.

In relationships you play the part of parent and may take an over-responsible attitude to others and try to organize them too much or dictate to them too much or play the child hoping to be forgiven for bad behaviour just one more time. This too may jump back one generation and you may be on the receiving end of this behaviour rather than dishing it out yourself. It is natural for you to worry about those whom you care about. If backed up by other planetary factors, you could be a blamer and complainer in a relationship – this would be especially true if there was a strong Pisces factor somewhere on your chart.

ATTITUDE TO CAREER

The Moon will show how you approach the *idea* of work rather than give specific career guidance. Unless there are other factors on the chart, such as an emphasis on the sign of Libra, you will be a hard and conscientious worker. Your inner nature leads you towards the kind of job where you can be helpful. Many lunar Cancerians work in hospitals, schools and with the elderly; others are attracted to the world of business. Some of you are drawn towards the field of antiques, rare coins, stately homes or genealogy. Insurance may attract you because of its 'protective' image. Many of you retrain later in life if your original career ceases to be viable or if you find that you lack certain qualifications which would help you to get up the career ladder. Many solar and lunar Cancerians run small businesses, shops and small agencies. Being good with your hands, you could work as a plumber, carpenter etc. Lunar Cancerians make excellent teachers too.

You will not stand in the way of a partner who wants a career, in most cases you are only too willing to see them get on and you will help if you can. Your sensitivity means that you could make a good salesman or business executive, personnel manager or counsellor. Politics may appeal, as could accountancy. Most of you have a theatrical side to your nature and might be drawn to the world of entertainment or sports. The drawback to this is the irregularity of work and the general uncertainty of this field; being a worrier, you would probably be happier in a secure job while singing and dancing during your time off. You would be a good partner for a very go-ahead person but you haven't really got the stomach for high risk or slightly criminal ventures.

PARENTS AND BACKGROUND

The Moon in this position suggests that your mother gave birth to you easily. Your parents' home will have been comfortable and the relationships there will have been pleasant. The chances are that you are the eldest in your family (although this is much more likely if the Ascendant were in Cancer). The background and history of your family is important to you and you may try to trace your family tree. The family may travel a bit, taking you with them, but there is no evidence that you moved home a lot. Mother may have been traditional and ordinary but possibly overprotective towards you.

HEALTH

This Moon position suggests strong health with good recovery from illness and operations. The weak areas associated with the Moon in Cancer would be chest, breasts and stomach, but the Moon is not the most obvious indicator of health in a chart.

You are very much in tune with your body, therefore, you would feel pain almost before something began to go wrong! Unless the Moon is very afflicted and there are other very important factors on the birthchart, there is no reason to suppose that you are any more susceptible to the dreaded disease of cancer itself than any other sign.

Moon in Leo
♌ (Ruled by the Sun) ☉

Or when the moon was overhead,
Came two young lovers lately wed;
'I am half sick of shadows,' said
The lady of Shalott.

by Alfred Lord Tennyson

The sign of Leo is masculine, positive, fiery and fixed, while the Moon, through its associations with the sign of Cancer, is feminine, negative, watery and cardinal. At first sight it doesn't look as if the Moon would be very comfortable in Leo but in many ways it is. For the sake of convenience, astrologers call *all* the bodies in the Solar system 'planets'. The Sun is, of course, a small star whilst the Moon is a satellite of the Earth. These two objects dominate man's view of the sky and their movements dominate the lives of every being on the face of the Earth.

The main differences between the Sun and the Moon from an astrologer's point of view are in the attitudes which they lend to relationships, especially inter-generation relationships. The power of the Sun seems to dominate the Moon, permeating the deepest layers of the personality with Leonine characteristics which then bubble their way up to the surface. If you have this Moon placement you are basically kind, generous and honourable with an instinctive need to encourage others. There is a real touch of Leo nobility deep down inside of you. It is worth remembering that many members of the royal family have the Moon in Leo. Being naturally dignified, honest and trustworthy, you would find it hard to behave in a callous or a crafty manner and you are far too proud to scrounge off others. Your need to *appear* honest and honourable may not reflect reality; but if you are caught out in a cowardly or underhanded act or if it becomes obvious that you harbour jealous feelings, you can react in an angry and aggressive manner. You can get on your high horse if your dignity is pricked.

The fixity of the sign gives you the determination to see things through and to finish everything that you start. It is possible that you may dig your heels in too much and try to lay the law down to others. You could be stubborn and unbending at times.

You sometimes appear to behave in a distant and superior manner, this is your shield for those times when you are in unfamiliar situations. When hurt, you retreat into something which you see as dignified silence and others see as the sulks; however, under normal circumstances you are cheerful, friendly and open. You occasionally have doubts about your own self-worth, also occasional feelings of intense superiority. The emotions are always held under control when the Moon is in a fixed sign and therefore they may break out strongly from time to time. You could become quite aggressive if pushed, or are on the receiving end of aggression from others. If hurt enough you would become jealous, full of hate, revengeful.

Lunar Leos can be surprisingly self-sacrificing towards loved ones but heaven help them if the loved one doesn't appreciate the sacrifices. You place the objects of your love on a pedestal and feel hurt when you discover that they are only human. Your intense feelings give you a longing for excitement, drama, romance and passion; with a bit of luck you will find this within a steady relationship; if not, then you will look for romance, passion etc. outside of marriage. You may even create tension within a relationship to keep it alive. For the same reason you must have an exciting career, you can put up with an insecure one but not a boring one. Too much contentment bores you.

Your mind is broad and you are unlikely to follow any of the more fanatical religious or political beliefs. You may have a religious and philosophical outlook which is different from that of your parents but this should not be a big problem in your life. Although not in any way bigoted, you may find it hard to change your mind once it is made up and you can have rather entrenched views.

The Moon is associated with the home, therefore, yours will be attractive with an interesting sort of decor. You are very fussy about your own appearance and may even be vain (men with this Moon placement are actually worse than women). The one thing which is the bane of your life is your hair. You may consider this to be too thick, thin, wiry, curly or even if male, too bald! You may be vain about your body and even your sexual performance. One lady who is married to a very nice Moon in Leo guy tells me that he doles out sex as if it were a treat! As a lover you could, like Sun in Leo, be bossy and demanding but also comfortable, relaxed and kind. It would be most unusual to find an out and out pervert with this Moon placement. Being romantic, you enjoy dining out, giving and receiving presents and remembering birthdays. You are fussy about your choice of partner, nothing less than the best will do for you. You have a strong sex drive but couldn't cope for long with a relationship based on sex alone. You need romance, passion and you need above all to be loved. Even so you would find it difficult to live without the comfort and release of sex; life without love, in all its applications would be too cold to contemplate. You don't mind taking the lead sexually and can encourage a partner who is less experienced than you. Your senses are strong, therefore everything about sex appeals to you as long as you can perform with a certain amount of decorum. The back seat of a car in a rainy car park is just not for you (except maybe a Rolls Royce!).

You may feel a need to attach yourself to some source of power. You may work with powerful and successful people, with large and powerful animals; alternatively, you might be fascinated by the power of magic and the spiritual world. This would enable you to enjoy risk-taking at second hand which is a lunar trait. Your courage, fire and enthusiasm could lead you to learn from the powerful people around you and put their lessons into action for yourself which is, of course, a solar trait.

You will do anything for those whom you love but you need your generosity of spirit to be appreciated. Being a fixed sign, you resist change and would find it hard to admit defeat in any situation, therefore, you would find it difficult to cut your losses and start again. You can put up with the wrong job for far too long and also hang on to a rotten relationship long after the time has come to end it. You are possibly a little too good at maintaining the status quo, especially in emotional situations. You may be self-centred emotionally and possibly inclined to hang on to those you love – this applies to your children as well. Laura, a gentle and skilled palmist now in her mid-forties, recently left her paranoid and violent husband after many years of abuse; but still feels that she is unable to make the final break and divorce him. 'It's too final,' she says.

Unless there are very different characteristics in your Sun and Ascendant you are sociable and enjoy being entertained but, being much shyer than the solar Leo type of personality, you can only entertain others in a quiet way. Sports and the company of young people appeal to you. You might become involved in some organization like the Boy Scouts, Girl Guides, the Territorial Army or the Red Cross. There is no need for you to be the centre of attraction in the world outside, but you do like to be in the centre of things within your own home. If you did find yourself in the spotlight, you could cope with it but you don't seek it consciously in the way that Sun in Leo would. You like to know where the various members of your family are and to make sure that they are all right, you have an inner need to organize them and keep them on the right lines.

Your inner nature, unless you are feeling hurt, is playful, sunny and friendly which makes you popular in a quiet kind of way. You appreciate beauty, creativity and art and have an instinctive sense of style. You are proud of your loved ones and even of your friends, you prefer not to be surrounded by dirty down-at-heel types. You never forget a hurt but your strong loyalty means that you remember those who have helped you too. You need to belong somewhere and may be attached to a particular set of bricks and mortar or to an area of the country with which you feel a particular affinity. Needing space, you hate cramped surroundings, you love to get away into the countryside and to take your holidays in a warm and pleasant place. You need holidays and breaks because you tend to put a lot of effort into your job and into life itself. Your vitality is never drained for long as you have inner reserves of strength.

You make an excellent parent, often treating your children as young adults and always preserving their dignity. You don't seek to hang on to them when they grow up. You are able to teach and encourage them through play, but you may not be too patient with them at times; you can be relied on to give them a cuddle whenever they are down-hearted or ill.

ATTITUDE TO CAREER

The position of the Moon does not indicate any specific career but will show your inner leanings and drives. Both solar and lunar Leo subjects learn more easily after leaving school than before. You may take a quite demanding course when already busy with a career, home and family; this may be in order to get yourself a better job or just to fulfil yourself. You lack confidence in your abilities, therefore any achievement that you make will help you to go on to further successes. Even if you do not have much formal education, you understand people and learn well from life. You have an inner need to be in an executive position, and if your circumstances mitigate against this you could be self-employed, the king of your own field, although you might need someone else around to help you cope with the details.

You make a good employer, with an understanding of the need to preserve the dignity of others.

You are career-minded and with your good concentration and good organizational skills, can climb the career ladder in a steady manner. You need to gain a reputation in some kind of creative field and may strive hard to perfect something which will bring you a quiet kind of renown. Your ability to make the right impression could lead you to the fields of marketing, personnel work, the display of works of art or antiques. The biggest problem is that you could have big dreams but may be too lazy to make them come true. You want to come out on top of your field but are strangely uncompetitive, being too self-centred to worry about others, your own high standards would give you enough to compete against. You are good at calming people down and dealing with touchy situations, therefore some kind of social work with troubled people, especially troubled youngsters might appeal. Your attraction to glamour might interest you in some form of show business. There is a creative side to you which means that you would take to dancing, singing or artistic work of some kind. Being drawn towards children and young people, you could be a teacher, (especially if there is Gemini, Aquarius or Sagittarius on your chart). You might prefer to be a nursery nurse or probation officer. Your love of the good things in life could make you a good restaurateur or hotelier but you might be best employed out in the front. You would be all right behind the scenes organizing others, but under no circumstances would you want to be the one to do the cleaning and cooking.

You are competent and capable as long as you are allowed to work at your own pace but you detest being hussled and put under pressure.

PARENTS AND BACKGROUND

There is probably something wrong here. The chances are that your father was autocratic, authoritarian or just unable to relate to children. You probably got on much better with your mother. You yourself might be too ready to push your own children but this may reflect back one generation, meaning that *you* were pushed by your parents and that they expected more from you than you were able to produce at that time. The background may have been traditional, even religious in some way involving rituals and certain kinds of behaviour. At the worst end of this spectrum you may have been afraid of your father or made to feel that you couldn't live up to some impossible image of perfection. He may have been a very successful man himself or he may have achieved a great deal while he was still young. Lunar Leos are far more likely to succeed later in life. You need parental love, encouragement and appreciation and if you get this from at least one parent plus brothers and sisters, fine, if not you could become something of an emotional cripple. The last thing you need is a cool intellectual air sign for a parent.

The Moon is not the only indicator of health problems on a chart but it might point out any underlying chronic condition. You need to keep your intake of food and drink down and to take exercise and lead a moderate life because your heart may be weak. There could be spinal trouble; this is particularly prone to occur when you are unhappy or worried.

Moon in Virgo
♍ (Ruled by Mercury) ☿

Pale moon doth rain, red moon doth blow,
White moon doth neither rain nor snow.

(Proverb)

The sign of Virgo is feminine, negative, earthy and mutable; the Moon, through its association with Cancer, is feminine, negative, watery and cardinal. This means that there is an uneasy alliance between the sign of Virgo and the energy of the Moon. You may find it very difficult to shape your world the way that you would like, it seems that the cardinality of the Moon (cardinality implies action) is halted in mutable, negative Virgo. If you cannot make your job work for you, create the right kind of environment or find the right partner, you could retreat into fiddling about and fidgeting. You may never quite finish decorating your home, you may try out one partner after another or you could become your own worst enemy at work. If thwarted, you will develop a tendency to meddle, criticize, ruin, lose or destroy the very things which you most need. You could over-analyse yourself and everything around you then hide your fears and phobias under a layer of fussiness. Be careful not to fall prey to a psychological need to organize every detail, prepare for every eventuality so that you programme out not only life's unexpected problems and but also its pleasant surprises.

Virgo is a difficult sign to understand and the Moon in this placement adds to the complications. I shall now borrow a bit of logic from my own planet of Mercury, which is placed in its own sign of Virgo, in order to analyse the problems. Virgo being an earth sign suggests an inner need to serve people in a practical way, therefore you will prefer to work in a field where you can be useful to others. You feel more comfortable in the workplace than in a social setting, especially if your talents are being used to the limit. Being dutiful and caring towards your family, you show your love for them by helping them in a practical way or by giving them material things, rather than by open displays of affection or of verbal love. You are especially helpful and understanding if they are ill. You are reliable, businesslike, tidy and efficient in all that you do; being loyal and trustworthy, you would never betray a confidence. Most lunar Virgoans are early risers and seem to be more alert in the morning than in the evening. Your mind is very clear and logical, your thinking is usually along realistic lines and you prefer to think before acting. You could be quite imaginative if there were something like Pisces or Leo on your birthchart, but the imagination would be harnessed to some kind of structure – writing poetry, making a garden or computer programming for example. You enjoy debating when you are among people with whom you can relax, you never swallow what you are told without verification. Be careful not to spend too much energy on details and miss the main point, also try not to let problems revolve round in your head growing out of all proportion. Some lunar Virgoans are vigorous social reformers, especially if there is any Aquarius on the birthchart or if the Sun or the Ascendant are in fairly confident outgoing signs. You can take practical decisions almost instantly and will go anywhere at the drop of a hat; when decisions have an emotional content, this is not so easy. Oddly enough, although the mind is quick, your bodily movements may be slow. Female lunar Virgoans are good homemakers, often loving their homes, but they need an intellectual outlet and the chance to work and earn money of their own. Although your thought processes are particularly logical, you can be very psychic. There is an acceptable logic to psychic matters which you seem to grasp more easily than many other people. Religion may not interest you overmuch, and blind faith is never acceptable to you.

Virgo being a mutable sign suggests that you can fit yourself in to almost any type of company. You are unlikely to be prejudiced about race, religion etc. because all people interest you. Lunar Virgoans rarely manipulate others for their own ends. You are shy at first but very sociable when you feel that you can relax. Although hardly likely to be the life and soul of the party, and even less likely to get drunk and make a fool of yourself, you do enjoy socializing, especially in the company of witty and interesting people. Despite being shy, you like to welcome new people but will sit back and analyse them later on.

I very much doubt whether you see money in terms of the power it may give you, and you have little desire to waste your hard-earned pennies on flashy things; you prefer to pay your bills on time and then have a bit left over for treats. A favourite treat for you would be a trip out into the country and a nice meal out. You like the fresh air and the seaside, you enjoy physical exercise of a fairly gentle nature, e.g. walking, dancing, badminton. Being an earth sign, gardening appeals to you, especially growing your own fruit and vegetables plus filling the house and garden with sweet-smelling flowers. Your senses of taste and smell (and your stomach) are easily upset, therefore good home-grown produce is a favourite with you. Reading and listening to music provide you with a passive form of escapism. One active form of escapism which is very popular among both solar and lunar Virgoans is acting, here you can forget yourself for a while and take on a completely different personality. This gives you the opportunity of behaving foolishly or even outrageously without having to risk being taken seriously.

Relationships can be a minefield for you; you tend to make yourself useful to your partner and then wonder why you are being used. In a way the most successful relationship for you would be with a partner who has an important and interesting career of his or her own where you could help to smooth their path for them. There must be a mental rapport between you and your partner, shared interests or work in common will help. You are prepared to make an effort in a relationship. Some of you attach your-selves to a glamorous glittering personality and enjoy being a part of their life. Any relationship based solely on sex alone wouldn't hold you for long. Many astrology books suggest that solar and lunar Virgoans are sexless. *This is just not true*, however there can be some really vicious problems associated with sex and sexual relationships. I think that the trouble stems from two sources; the first being that you are easily embarrassed by the apparent ludicrousness of the sex act, you find it hard to relinquish your dignity and make the necessary adjustment which would enable you to surrender to your feelings. The second problem is that you may be ashamed of your own capacity for passion, possibly due to early childhood influences and incidents. Anyone who has *any* of the personal planets (Sun, Moon, Mercury, Venus and Mars) placed in Virgo will immediately freeze up if criticized for their performance.

You may fill up your time with work in order to avoid dealing with the whole relating and sexual scene. Shyness doesn't help here, but most of this can be overcome if you find yourself a kind encouraging partner. One thing which does help is your ability to adapt; all mutable signs will try to fit in with other people's requirements, therefore, given a chance and much tender loving care, you could realize your sexual potential, especially with the 'right' lover. Coarseness puts you off immediately. Criticism will squash you, not only sexually but in every other way. You have intensely critical feelings towards others but being the lunar, inner, side of your nature, you probably keep your remarks to yourself – unless you become very angry when it all bursts out.

If a relationship goes wrong you can become desperate, even suicidally depressed. You have to beware of self-fulfilling prophecies where you tell yourself that you are going to be let down and then you allow yourself to become so; lack of confidence and too little faith in the future can actually bring this about. You may go too far the other way, keeping your emotions on such a tight rein that you never allow yourself the luxury of love and romance; this is a shame because you do need a partner and also a family.

You may find it hard to relate to your own children and may pay too much attention to their practical and educational needs and not enough to their need for love and affection. On the other hand, children may be the ideal outlet for your bottled up love, giving you the opportunity to give and receive affection unreservedly. You may be able to romp, roll around and act out parts for their amusement in a way which you could never do with adults. Teaching comes naturally to you, therefore you enjoy opening your children's minds to the world of books, museums, nature. Given a secure and loving partnership you will gain confidence and really begin to blossom.

You have an acute sense of humour which so often is able to save you from much of the unhappiness associated with this sign, if you can find an intelligent partner to laugh with, then you are really made. Being loyal yourself and having very high standards of behaviour, you may expect others to be the same with regard to you. If your partner makes a habit of wandering off and leaving you alone whenever you go to a party, you would be most put out. You need to be hugged and comforted especially if things are not going well for you and, most of all, you require a feeling of solidarity in your relationships, a feeling that your family circle will stick together and stick up for each other against the world.

ATTITUDE TO CAREER

As a rule the Position of the Moon does not indicate any specific career, only one's internal motivations. However, in this case, the sign of Virgo will dominate the personality in such a way that you identify yourself far more by what you *do* than what you *are*. There are enough wasters and losers in this world already, perhaps we could do with a few more lunar Virgoans to prevent us from losing and wasting what is left of our planet. You learn quickly and like to keep your mind and body occupied, even your leisure pursuits are healthy or useful ones such as gentle sports or working for a charity or political organization. You have a creative side which can be expressed in sewing, carpentry, cooking or writing because you like problem-solving and the bringing together of separate parts in order to make a whole.

Skills such as typing, driving and accounting come easily to you. You make an exemplary office worker, being neat, efficient, quiet, clean, practical and helpful. Given that your Sun and Ascendant are placed in an outgoing sign, you may enjoy a life in a skilled branch of the armed forces. Learning and coming to grips with highly technical matters would hold no terrors for you.

The whole field of health comes naturally to you; lunar Virgoans make good nurses, doctors and dieticians. Although unlikely to make much display of your own feelings, you are able to understand the pain of others. Your interest in health is not just in the field of caring and healing but of preventing disease from taking root in the first place, therefore, you advocate diet, exercise and moderate living. You yourself could be a hypochondriac or could genuinely suffer from a series of minor but irritating ailments and nervous disorders. Having a clear, logical and analytical mind you would be a natural for computing, accounting, systems analysing and electronic weighing and measuring. Research, especially in the medical field, would please you. Teaching might appeal, either teaching infants or older students who are highly intelligent, quiet and ready to learn. Maths and scientific subjects would suit you, but languages may be a problem. You could learn the grammar all right, it is the speaking that would get you down unless you had something fairly uninhibited like Sagittarius on your Ascendant.

It may be difficult for you to manage others because delegating requires confidence both in one's own leadership qualities plus confidence in the ability of others to do a good job on your behalf. You tend to become angry when faced with an attitude of uncaring inefficiency. You may not be overly ambitious, but you like to do things well and to be appreciated for it. The success of others doesn't upset you.

PARENTS AND BACKGROUND

At best your childhood would have been a fairly cool affair, at worst it may have had nightmarish qualities. 'Nightmarish is just about right,' said Anne, an elegant, divorced systems analyst. 'I used to study my father to judge which rules I should be playing by and just when I got the hang of the game, he changed the rules. I could never win, my place was always in the wrong'.

To start with, being born wasn't all that easy, therefore the relationship between you and your mother probably started badly. There was a great deal of discipline in your childhood, an emphasis on being on time for meals, washing behind your ears and doing your homework. You may have been compared to other children and told that you were not as good, clever, pretty, tall, etc. as them. If you were a diligent child, naturally tidy, quiet, organized and clever at school, you would have pleased your parents and would therefore have had an easier time of it. You may have only been able to win their approval by success in exams or winning medals at sports, dancing, etc. Some of your self-esteem and lack of confidence results from having been nervous or even afraid of your parents; you found them hard to please. It is even possible that you were a naturally timid child with rather boisterous parents, or one of your parents might have been particularly hard to get on with.

If your parents were born under the signs of Aries, Scorpio or Sagittarius, they would have been far too impatient, lacking in understanding and quick to criticize. This lack of praise and encouragement caused you to feel resentful, worthless, lonely and repressed. You may have been shoved aside for other reasons, e.g. family problems, a handicapped sibling or lack of money. You may have learned how to hate early in life. Your hatred of being accused of laziness is a hangover from childhood. Your shyness and repression may have been the result of severe and prolonged illness in childhood rather than awful parents.

There is always, the possibility that the Moon's position reflects the mother's experience of life, so the interpretation could be an indication that your mother had a hard time while young.

HEALTH

Both solar and lunar Virgoans are strong and healthy but the nervous system is delicate. Ailments include migraine and asthma, allergies, skin conditions and stomach ulcers. Tension and overwork is your enemy and you must take exercise in order to relax. Severe Virgoan health problems which sometimes arise are appendicitis, typhoid, peritonitis and anaemia. Tall subjects may have back problems.

Moon in Libra
♎ (Ruled by Venus) ♀

'Fly me to the Moon
Let me play among the stars
Let me see what Spring is like on Jupiter and Mars
In other words, hold my hand
In other words, darling kiss me.'

Sung by Frank Sinatra

The sign of Libra is masculine, positive, airy and cardinal. The Moon, through its association with the sign of Cancer is feminine, negative, watery and also cardinal. The cardinality is the most important factor here because, even if the Moon is not really at home in such a strong sign as Libra, its cardinality will give you the inner dynamism to put things into action, albeit *slowly*. Being an air sign, your thought processes are logical and, provided you have a fairly active Sun sign, you could achieve a high position in life. You are both ambitious and lazy at the same time but you should be able to motivate yourself enough to get things done. You never lose sight of your objectives, you never give up on a goal. Your mind is fair and balanced and you hate any form of injustice, some of you will take up a cause which champions the underdog. You object strongly to any form of racism. When others argue, you seek to be the peacemaker but you can argue like a Jesuit when the mood takes you. You're always open to new ideas but will not swallow what others tell you without proof. A surprisingly large number of people who have the Moon in Libra also have Aquarius strongly represented on their charts thereby emphasizing the need to be independent.

You seem to need a touch of glamour in your life and could be drawn to work in some kind of glamorous or luxurious trade. You make sure that both your home and your working environment are comfortable and attractive with a pleasant peaceful atmosphere. You have no patience with ugliness in any form, especially ugly or dirty people. Being fussy about your personal appearance you are also rather inclined to be vain about your own good looks. Indeed, while you are young, your partners may be chosen for their looks rather than their personality.

Whenever the Moon is in a masculine sign, the native is naturally competitive and a high climber but is only really impressed by his *own* measurements of success. With the Moon in Libra, you could have a similar 'what right do they think they have to tell me what to do!' attitude as you would expect from Moon in Aries. Although charming most of the time, you can be extremely sarcastic and hurtful when provoked, showing a grasp of vocabulary worthy of any solar Gemini!

Your nerves can sometimes let you down, therefore you need peace in the home environment. Both sexes of this Moon placement are good home-makers and are attached to their own plots of land and their property. You enjoy do-it-yourself jobs, cooking, mending and gardening, however, a life made up purely of housework would stifle you. Your good taste will ensure that your surroundings are always comfortable and elegant. Some subjects may have artistic talent, especially in the field of music. You could have a nice deepish speaking and singing voice too. You certainly enjoy listening to music and hate discordant noises. All your senses are strong but sight could probably be the strongest; if something doesn't *look* right, you couldn't live with it.

Being an air sign, you need the stimulation of meeting new people and are usually welcoming towards newcomers. Travel is liked, as long as you can do it in comfort, you feel perfectly at home in the world's nicest hotels and watering places. Although you enjoy your own company from time to time, you really cannot live or work alone for long. There is a need to keep in touch with the world and to keep your mind stimulated with new people and up-to-date experiences. You enjoy being part of a group and seem to need the approval of your peers but you wouldn't necessarily wish to lead the group. Given the chance, you prefer to be fairly near the top so that you could delegate the more distasteful chores to others!

You are excellent in a crisis but unable to give sustained help because you quickly become bored with problems. You have no patience with fools although you can hide your irritation under a layer of urbanity. Your mental responses are surprisingly fast and you can be quite calculating when necessary.

Your pet hates are loud discordant noises and, according to my lunar Libra friends, being travel sick! Perhaps this has something to do with your need to control your own environment or maybe it is because you have del-icate eyesight and hearing (through the reflected association with Aries). You like the sea and the countryside but are really a city person at heart, in amongst it all, where it's all going on.

Relationships are really where you come into your own; not that you are easy to live with. You can be critical, fussy, demanding and occasionally downright childish. However, you need to love and be loved, you also need friendship with people of both sexes. You can be capable of using, even of manipulating others but you need to be needed, therefore you also allow yourself to be used by those whom you love. As a young person you can be inconsistent in emotional relationships wanting the challenge and excitement of new faces practically each week. You enjoy the opening phase of a romance more than the later stage of commitment, because you don't like to be emotionally fenced in. Later on, your need for the security of a family and the love of children will encourage you to settle down into domesticity. Even then you will always be a flirt! Apart from the need for an attractive partner, you need one you can take anywhere. A classy type who can be relied upon to be the genial host or gracious hostess who will help out with the social side of your career. You need someone with a gentle and witty sense of humour as you hate coarseness or hurtful remarks. I have actually seen Moon in Libra subjects become ill because they were unhappy at work or home. Men with the Moon in Libra have a curious split in their personality which, on the one hand, gives them a somewhat 'macho' image, while at the same time endowing them with an almost feminine gentleness.

Lunar Librans are very clever with intricate machinery, and like the other air signs, they all seem to have a love affair with vehicles and speed. Another facet of this complex placement is that you are careful and gentle when around small children and weak people. There is no evidence to my mind of you being an animal lover, but you couldn't hurt an animal or see one hurt by others. Your gentle manner with those who are weaker than you adds to the attractiveness of your personality. You respect the dignity of others and treat them with tact and charm. Those of you who have a strong Sun sign may hide strong feelings and opinions under this charming exterior, but those who have an unassertive Sun sign may need to develop your own point of view and learn how to make a stand.

Sexually speaking you could turn out to be one of the best lovers in the Zodiac! This, of course, depends upon other factors in your birthchart. However, given a fair crack of the whip, leather underwear, luminous suspenders and an exuberant and co-operative partner, you could live out your fantasies to the full. Your sensual nature cannot be denied, and with a bit of luck you will find fulfilment within marriage. If this is not so, you will still seek fulfilment even if it is at the expense of your marriage. You could actually relate well to a difficult partner who keeps you on your toes. Someone unpredictable enough to give you a few lively arguments and passionate enough to satisfy your strong sexual needs.

Knowing instinctively when your partner is ill or unhappy, you rise to the occasion and do all that you can to make them feel better; you don't really like to see anyone down-hearted. You are good at providing little treats but cannot always be relied on to remember anniversaries etc. this is because your giving is spontaneous rather than organized. Lunar Librans need to give and to receive affection, tenderness and sympathy, also to alternate at being the 'parent' or the 'child' in a relationship. If you have the Sun or ascendant in fire signs, you could be a little too dependent on the approval of others. Some lunar Librans can be easily influenced and swayed by others but most of you have a mature outlook and can make up your own mind about life, most of you try to keep your emotions under the control of your mind.

ATTITUDE TO CAREER

The position of the Moon alone is unlikely to suggest any specific type of career but it can show one's inner motivations. Firstly you will want a job which gives you scope to express your creativity; this may be in an artistic or semi-artistic world such as architecture or fashion. You are persuasive enough to make a good salesman but unless there are strong factors elsewhere on the birthchart, you would not have the kind of sustained energy which selling requires. Public relations and marketing would be better.

The world of catering might appeal, certainly glamorous hotels and restaurants are your natural habitat. Being good at calming others and even better in a crisis, you could make a good negotiator. You have a talent for arbitration and your quick mind and sense of humour can be used to defuse potentially dangerous situations therefore you might succeed as a union negotiator or as a particularly urbane politician. Personnel and recruitment are also possible career ideas. You can appear to be lackadaisical while working furiously behind the scenes. I call this the 'duck' syndrome because a duck looks as if it is gliding along the surface of the water while it is actually paddling like fury underneath. You are a good listener, so long as the person who is doing the talking doesn't go on too long.

You enjoy money for what it brings but can have something of a 'convenient' memory when owing money to others; this memory is far less 'convenient' when money is owed to you. You don't need to have power but you do need a largish income to really enjoy life, therefore you will aim for the top anyway. The only thing you really cannot do is rough and dirty work among coarse people.

You get on well with workmates and colleagues. With your logical mind, you would make a good engineer. Driving and even flying come easily to you. Finally, you could earn a few pennies as a spare-time musician.

PARENTS AND BACKGROUND

There is some evidence from this Moon position that you were born easily. You may have had a father who pushed you educationally and possibly a rather peculiar mother! This does not mean to say that you were unhappy as a child, you seem to have been loved and understood by your parents and even overindulged a little. Your charm, even as a baby, will have got you everywhere. Your mother was probably ambitious, clever or even eccentric, she may have forgotten to feed you or wash you on occasion but she never forgot to love you. The home was a stimulating place full of books, conversation and interesting visitors. This means you grew up without having to develop a suspicious attitude or a strong shell to hide behind. Nevertheless you are happier to be an adult; this could be because your schooldays were not a very happy time for you. It is possible that you found exams troublesome because *they* test what you *know* rather than the power of your personality!

HEALTH

You are generally strong but may develop diabetes, cystitis or skin problems. You need to take exercise and keep your weight down (and not smoke) or you could develop both chest problems and arterial or arthritic problems. Hay fever and farmer's lung are other possibilities.

Moon in Scorpio
♏ (Ruled by Pluto and Mars) ♂

She's got some cruelty,
See it in the dark of the Moon,
Brother take her cruelty, face it
with her beauty and show it.

Pagan Easter
by Seldiy Bate
by kind permission of Temple Music

The sign of Scorpio is feminine, negative, watery and fixed whilst the Moon, through its association with the sign of Cancer, is feminine, negative, watery and cardinal. This would suggest that the Moon is comfortable in Scorpio but it must be remembered that this is the sign of the Moon's 'fall' and therefore, projects some of the most difficult aspects of both the sign and the planet. Scorpio's influence on the Moon adds intensity to the nature, also tenacity, capability and strong resistance to disease. It endows its natives with a strong instinct for survival plus an attraction to the more dangerous aspects of life. If this is your Moon placement, you have a tremendous ability to bounce back from illness, disappointment and even the door of death itself.

There are two quite separate needs within your personality and, bearing in mind that these needs are lying underneath the more outward and obvious aspects of your nature (as depicted by your Sun and Ascendant signs), this can make you very hard for others to understand. You seem to require challenge and excitement on one hand plus constancy and security on the other. Like all fixed signs, Scorpio Moon people want to maintain the status quo. You prefer to stay in a job with which you are familiar, occupy the same house for years and remain with the same partner even when the partnership is no longer viable. The other side of you cries out for the brink, the edge, the place where you can test your strength. Some lunar Scorpions become involved with risky or even illegal business interests while others involve themselves in risky romances or strange sexual encounters. You seem to have the feeling that you are invincible, 'bomb-proof': and you are probably right! A constructive way of dealing with this might be to build into your life an interesting and risky hobby or some kind of part-time attachment to a paramedical or paramilitary organization. You may find yourself up against difficult situations without actually going out and looking for trouble. One lunar Scorpio friend of mine has a daughter who, after twice becoming involved with the shady side of the law, turned up at her house eight and half months pregnant!

Emotionally speaking, you are even more peculiar because you have the ability to go at two speeds at once. When you meet a new attraction, you are cautious, watchful and apt to sit back and see what transpires; despite the fact that you are perfectly able to psychically sum up anyone who is likely to become important to you within minutes of meeting them. You can be manipulative towards others but often only for their own benefit. You are as caring towards your family and friends as any solar Cancerian. Like all Moon in water people, you can occasionally be emotionally wearing but you hate others being emotionally demanding towards you. You are perfectly willing to come to the aid of someone who is in a state of crisis, but if they continue to demand help and support after the immediate problem is solved, you become bored with the whole thing.

You have a built-in detector for monitoring out lonely people and those types who seek to lean on you and draw from your inner strength. Moon in Scorpio subjects all have a built-in bullshit detector and therefore are quicker than most at spotting a phoney. Sometimes the emotional sufferings of others make you feel helpless and powerless. Your worst fault emotionally is a tendency to become jealous and possessive towards others; however, secure people who have the Moon in Scorpio are able to go through life without most of these unpleasant feelings.

Your home must be peaceful, clean and attractive. Your taste runs towards the antique rather than the modern and you will spend a considerable amount of time and money on furniture and fitments. You probably spend even more time and money on your garden because your love of beauty and strong sensuality draws you towards the beauty and scent of flowers. You enjoy the countryside and outdoor pursuits. The sea is attractive to you and you love to feel both its power and its peace. You are probably a very good swimmer.

You keep a tight grip on your own emotions and tend to bottle up anger and allow your feelings to seep inwards. This can result in angry outbursts which may affect your health. On those occasions when you do become ill or suffer from some set-back in life, your first reaction is anger, then if you cannot do some thing immediate and practical about the problem, you become silent, withdrawn and depressed. An athletic hobby would make a good outlet for your considerable energies, and some of you will turn to the occasional highly-charged sexual encounter. You can usually spot the feelings and motives of others quickly; you are able to find their weak spots and then, depending on circumstances, use this information to help and encourage them or in order to wind them up and throw them off balance. You are able to get at the truth and to face up to it but you tend to conceal your feelings from others so that *they* don't get a chance to make use of you.

Neither solar nor lunar Scorpios like officialdom but you seem to have an uncanny knack of 'working the system' when you need to. You are persistent in pursuit of a goal and faced with opposition you will either find a way around it or, as a last resort, will force your way through assertively. You rarely consider asking others for help, seeing that as an admission of weakness.

You enjoy family life and make a reliable parent as long as you can step back a little from your children and let them be themselves. Many of you seem to have difficult or sickly children but you cope with these problems better than most. You must be careful neither to smother your children nor try to mould them too forcefully; you should make an effort to allow them to develop their own individual personalities. Some of you may be fussy about food; this may be due to a weight problem or just faddiness. Many lunar Scorpios are vegetarians partly through personal preference and partly due to a love of animals.

You are a hard tenacious worker and you try to finish everything which you start, disliking being interrupted. Preferring to work slowly and thoroughly you hate being rushed or placed under a lot of pressure. If there is a little help from the rest of the birthchart, you can be surprisingly artistic. Both solar and lunar Scorpios have a strong sense of structure, an eye for detail and a well developed sense of touch. This leads to a natural ability to handle materials in a creative manner. You could make an excellent sculptor, potter, design engineer or design dressmaker. Other structured interests such as dancing and sport appeal to you and being competitive, you would always strive to be better than the next person.

Your sexual feelings are intense and, if not fully gratified, you can become extremely irritable; you might even engineer arguments in order to 'rev-up' the sexual excitement. Your deepest need is for a stable relationship with a reliable person who has a high and interesting sexual drive! If you do not find satisfaction within your marriage, you will look for it on the outside. You may fancy the occasional perversion! In this aspect of your life, as in all others, you cannot seem to compromise. You must not try to reform your partners but should try to learn to accept them as they are. It would be better if you could pour your energies and reforming drive into the outside world in order to bring about beneficial changes. The ability to do this would depend upon other political or reforming factors on your birthchart. Your compelling nature makes you a pretty exciting lover but you are also sensitive enough to 'tune in' to the needs of your partner and give as much pleasure as you yourself would like to receive. Depending upon your mood at the time, you can be extremely receptive to the needs of those around you or surprisingly (maybe conveniently) dense. This depends upon your mood and the state of your health at any one time.

There is some evidence of homosexuality and bisexuality being associated with this Moon sign. You may even marry someone who is attracted to their own sex.

You have strong intuitive and even psychic gifts and may be drawn to discover more about these aspects of life. Being mediumistic and clairvoyant, you may take a further interest by studying the occult in all its forms. You seek deeper meanings in everyday events and may consider them to be omens of some kind. Many of you feel that other people block your progress or even cause you to have bad luck instead of accepting that things do go wrong from time to time. You may be superstitious and inwardly fearful when faced with new circumstances and unknown factors in your life. Many of you are drawn to the arts of witchcraft and magic which give you the opportunity of linking into group energies and earth energies. The Kabbala is another potential interest. The healing and caring aspect of psychic work would immediately attract you and, particularly later in life, you could pour your considerable mental, physical and psychic energies into the philosophy of healing and the positive use of psychic powers. You have the potential to change the world, by politics, science or even by means of war but this would depend upon a strange combination of planets in your chart. Could you be the next and last person to use Mr Oppenheimer's little toy?

ATTITUDE TO CAREER

The position of the Moon in a birthchart does not show one's actual career but the inner motivations which may affect one's choice of job. You are a slow, methodical worker preferring to stick to a job that you are accustomed to. You have an exceptionally pleasant voice and manner which makes you a natural for dealing with people, your enjoyment of new and interesting people both at work and in a social setting, gives you the potential to be a good salesman or woman. You can inspire others to get things moving, are competitive and ambitious but may give up on your ambitions for the sake of safety and practicality later on in life. You *should* make a point of striving for success as you could be jealous and resentful of others if you don't. You can learn from others and can, in your turn encourage them and guide them but you don't have enough patience with *people* to make a good teacher.

Medical matters appeal to you and you are not easily upset by the sight of blood, your patience with things (as opposed to people) would make you a fine surgeon; psychiatry would also come naturally to you. Any work which brings you to the heart of matters will appeal to you and, therefore, you could find yourself involved in the legal, forensic or political field. In business you can make spectacular gains and even more spectacular losses on occasion.

Many lunar Scorpios love the sea and can make their living on it as sailors, fishermen or swimming and diving experts and also, of course, in the navy. A life in the armed services appeals to many of you as it requires the kind of skills and dedication which come so easily to you.

There is evidence that your birth brought a problem to your parents. Many lunar Scorpios are born into some kind of 'inconvenient' situation and are adopted soon after birth. On the other hand, some of you are born to families who already have a number of children and don't really want any more. There is no doubt that you are on a different wavelength (possibly even a different planet) to that of your parents and you will have been constantly misunderstood as a child. Your experience may have been poor because you were not really the type of child that they were hoping for or that you were compared unfavourably to another child in the family. 'My parents always seemed to have much more time for my brother than they did for me', says Lorna, an attractive and active lady whom I meet regularly at the swimming baths. 'Being male gave him a head start, of course, but then he was also considered to be the "clever one". You know, looking back over our lives now, I think that I have done just as well in the long run even without academic qualifications or the unqualified love of my parents. No, I don't feel bitter; not now.'

You could, at the worst end of the spectrum, have been bullied by your parents, subjected to violence, sexual abuse or just made to feel thoroughly inadequate. You may have been told, or have been given the silent implication that you could never live up to their exalted standards. Negative attitudes die hard in fixed signs and you could, if not careful, go through life never shaking off the hatred and anger of your childhood. You may still feel yourself to be a nuisance to others and wonder why they put up with you. Nevertheless many lunar Scorpios do love their somewhat inadequate parents very much and take a really caring if rather dutiful attitude to them later in their lives.

One peculiarity associated with either the Sun or the Moon in Scorpio is there could be a death in the family at the time of your birth or soon after.

You may have been either very good or very bad at school. Sports and artistic subjects come easily to you but you could have had difficulty coping with the pace and imposed discipline of normal school lessons. Some of you will have worked hard when reaching your teens in order to overcome childhood shortages of one kind or another. Some of you will marry in order to improve your position in life.

HEALTH

Although usually very fit you can be a worrier over your health. Your weak spots are your arteries and veins and you could suffer from high blood-pressure later in life. You may suffer from headaches and migraine also other forms of allergies such as hay fever. The main problem seems to be in the reproductive organs; many women with this placement have terrible periods and may have to have a hysterectomy in the end just to stop the endless outpouring of blood.

Moon in Sagittarius
♐ (Ruled by Jupiter) ♃

Underneath your dreamlit eyes
Shades of sleep have driven you away
The moon is pale outside
And you are far from home.

from *When Tomorrow Comes*
sung by the Eurythmics

The sign of Sagittarius is masculine, positive, fiery and mutable, whilst the Moon, through its association with the sign of Cancer, is feminine, negative, watery and cardinal. Neither the planet nor the sign have anything in common with one another, therefore each will work against the other in some way. Problems which result from this will be felt in the area of your emotions and in your relationships with others. If this is your Moon sign, you probably didn't receive much physical affection from your parents. Maybe they weren't the kind who went in for touching and cuddling, or you yourself may have pushed them away. There are some children who hate being kissed and smothered by adults, although most children *do* enjoy receiving comfort and affection from their own family. It's possible that your parents had to work hard and didn't have much time to spare for you; all this could lead you, later in life, to separate the feelings of love from those of sex. I have found this to be a greater problem for male lunar Sagittarians than for females. You may shrink back from being touched by others in normal daily life, or you might find it difficult to caress and stroke your partner when making love! If this seems to be all too true, then don't despair, because you, above all the signs of the Zodiac, have the brains and the courage to face up to your problems, seek help and eventually sort yourself out. Those of you who don't have this problem are so cuddlesome that they actually prefer to choose a chubby partner for themselves!

Any physical problems which you may experience are more than made up for by the excellence of your mind. Everything interests you but you accept nothing at face value. You enjoy reading and, on the rare occasions when you watch the TV, you enjoy programmes which have something to say. Some of you are deeply philosophic in your manner of thinking. You may have been brought up in a religious family, rejected their ideas and later on found others which suited you better. There are many solar and lunar Sagittarians in the spiritualist movement and also in the psychic world, all trying to make life that bit more meaningful for others. You are intuitive, exceptionally clairvoyant and probably a good healer as well although you may not yet have discovered that you have these gifts.

You need personal freedom and independence, needing especially to be in charge of your own life rather than being under someone else's thumb. You must be able to come and go as you please, you cannot be cooped up anywhere, indeed, you may even suffer from claustrophobia when travelling in a lift or in the back seat of a two-door car. New faces fascinate you and you need plenty of friends because you become bored if you have to spend every day in the same company. Sagittarius being a mutable sign, you can adapt to most situations and enjoy all kinds of people; you are broad-minded and never racist or bigoted. Like most mutable sign subjects, you do need to get away on your own from time to time in order to think and to recharge your emotional batteries. You have exceptionally clear vision and can see to the heart of a problem when others can only see muddle; you are resourceful enough to solve most problems both for yourself and for others although you do appreciate a helping hand when it is offered. You will help anybody who is in trouble and in a crisis. Being sure of your own abilities at times of trouble, you may push others out of the way so that you can get on with sorting the problems out by yourself. This behaviour is not always appreciated by those whom you are pushing!

Solar Sagittarians are sociable and outgoing but lunar ones are shyer. This depends upon the kind of Sun and Ascendant you have on your birthchart but nevertheless, you will have some of the typically Sagittarian characteristics. You may be a good actor, certainly you have the ability to interest others, fill them with enthusiasm and motivate them. The traditional Sagittarian careers of the church, the law and teaching may not apply directly to you but you often find yourself teaching others in some way or another and your own codes of honour and ethics will be high. You may have the traditional Sagittarian tactlessness as well, but the Moon being sensitive to the feelings of others makes this less likely. You are sensitive to atmospheres, for instance, you are aware as soon as you go into a room if there has been an argument going on in there. You may over-react to people who show hostility towards you. Your temper is explosive and your tongue sharp and articulate, therefore you could make an unpleasant, if not actually dangerous adversary. However, like most fire signs, you don't hold a grudge and prefer to forget bad feelings and look towards the future with optimism.

The Moon is associated with the home and Sagittarius is a dextrous sign, therefore you should be good at do-it-yourself jobs, also cooking. This might at first seem a peculiar thing to say as the vast majority of you will spend as much time away from the home as you can and would *hate* to spend your life decorating or cooking. However, I have noticed that all lunar Sagittarians are absolutely inspired when it comes to cooking for guests and, even if you don't actually do the decorating yourself, your taste and choices in materials and decor would be perfect. If there is some Cancer on your chart, you would definitely go in for home carpentry work. Whatever you do, you will always clear up afterwards; you don't like mess and dirt and cannot stand living in chaotic surroundings. You need peace and calm in the home as you expend a lot of energy in your career and need to refresh yourself in a peaceful loving atmosphere at home in order to rest your delicate nervous system.

You enjoy sports and may be a good swimmer, you are too active to spend your spare time sitting about so any form of sports or dancing would appeal to you; this also brings out your competitive spirit. Although you may be a little on the shy side, you enjoy singing, music or artistic hobbies but probably would prefer to be among a group rather than out on your own as the solar Sagittarian would. Your active nature would make you choose a job where you have the chance to move around and meet people and also where you are up on your feet rather than sitting about. Your pattern of working may alternate between manic activity and apparent laziness. This is because you are not good at keeping to a steady routine but will go at something hammer and tongs while you are inspired and then recoup your energies, probably whilst planning for the next burst of activity.

If you have to leave your home for any reason, you would set about making another attractive place for yourself as soon as possible. Being attractive and rather vain about your appearance, you enjoy buying nice clothes and may tend to spoil yourself while conveniently forgetting that there are bills to be paid. Your appearance and your body are very important to you as activity is so much a part of your nature.

There is, like most of the mutable signs, a strange duality about you. You want something passionately and then go off it once you have got it. You need security at the same time as you need freedom; this can make you appear irresponsible to others but somehow you always find an answer and seem to be able to pull the irons out of the fire when things go wrong. You are no stranger to debts but hate to be in debt. You can soon put other people's problems in perspective for them but you may be hopeless at sorting out your own muddles. A friend of mine who is just about typical of this lunation, is responding to the fact that her husband has left her by giving up her job and spending money on clothes and nice things when it is the last thing she ought to be doing. This is an almost Piscean reaction in refusing to face reality – because reality right now is too much to face! The last split is in your attitude to personal relationships; you need and want to love and be loved but you may find it hard to be faithful because there are so many interesting people out there who will be equally fascinated by your looks and your charisma. You need a really understanding partner. Another oddity is that you *really* prefer friendship to affairs anyway, so you could appear to promise much and not really deliver anything at all! Very strange. You couldn't cope with someone who lays the law down to you; under those circumstances, you would assert your independence.

You can be a bit dual in the world of work too. You are highly ambitious but not necessarily money-minded. You need money to pay the bills and to make life fun but not for power or to impress others. Women of this lunation like to control their own finances. You need to work at something which you enjoy and which keeps you in touch with people. You can appear lazy to others because you have a habit of preparing your work at home either before or after your normal working hours, thus hiding the actual amount of effort which you put into your work. Metaphorically speaking, this gives you the appearance of a duck which as we all know, glides effortlessly over the surface of the water, but is actually paddling away like mad under the surface! However much you love your job, you also need to relax and socialize and are not as a rule a workaholic. You are, in all but shape, a well rounded person. Women of this particular sign can become wrapped up in causes and will be found saving the whale and banning the bomb. This could cause problems on the domestic front as there will sometimes be too little time left for the family. Being slightly bossy, a woman with the Moon in Sagittarius would need a very understanding husband, but she is wise enough to find the right one for herself, and if she doesn't do so the first time, she will have another go. Both sexes love children, but spending your days looking after small children wouldn't stimulate you enough mentally. Many of you are brilliant with older children and may involve yourself with the scout or guide movement or something similar. Lunar Sagittarians make excellent teachers.

Your sense of adventure means that you could take up anything from hang-gliding to mountain climbing; you enjoy every experience that comes along. This is the sign of the traveller, and the Moon being associated with travel, especially travel over water means that you take every opportunity to travel anywhere at the drop of a hat. You are fascinated by desert and mountainous areas where you can stand tall and see for miles.

Anyone choosing to live with you would find you a happy and optimistic partner as long as you have the freedom to do your own thing. You cannot stand people who try to dominate you or control your actions, neither could you live with a partner who whines and nags. The worst type for you to have to cope with, either at work or in your personal life, is someone who is critical of you whilst considering him or herself to be perfect. Your intense need for freedom and independence means that you spend time away from the home possibly travelling around in connection with your work. You would be happy to be married to someone rather like yourself as you wouldn't seek to tie *them* down either. If you have an ambitious partner, you help them to get ahead in their career. If you are allowed freedom and trust, you will probably choose to remain faithful but if restricted, you will show your resentment by straying from the straight and narrow. Your unpredictability can make you hard to live with.

You don't give up on a relationship at the first hurdle, you try to do all that you can to make it work. You will adapt your own nature and your own needs to that of the partner as far as you can in order to make the relationship work. There is a possibility that you could find yourself stuck with a partner who suffers from some kind of mental illness. I discovered while researching this book that lunar Sagittarians have many connections with mental illness, either through senile parents, a schizophrenic child or a depressive spouse. There are times when you are so busy trying to adapt to *their* unrealistic behaviour that you begin to wonder just *who* is the dotty one!

You may choose a partner who is out of the traditional mould, for instance someone older or younger than yourself or of a different racial or religious background. You may strongly attract people of a type which you really cannot stand or you may find yourself attracted to someone who pleases you ill one way and repels you in another. It is hard to find someone who is right for you in every way, that is mentally, physically and spiritually.

As a parent you are proud of your offspring and will do all you can to help them get on in life. You respect their need for space and a separate identity and also their need for dignity. There is a possibility that you could live apart from them for some part of their childhood, either due to work which takes you away from home or as a result of a divorce.

Many of you will have parents who were born in a different country from the one in which you live. This is actually more often the case when the Ascendant is in Sagittarius but also applies to the Moon quite often. There may be Irish connections or Jewish ones – emigration or just living away from home are all possible. This may, to some extent, explain some of the splits in your personality if, for example, you were educated in a different manner from those around you, brought up in a religion which is anachronistic in your present country or even speaking a different language when with your parents. I asked my friend Susan about her childhood which was spent in a variety of different countries and she told me that it was hard always to be the child who spoke the wrong language or who had the wrong accent.

ATTITUDE TO CAREER

The position of the Moon on a birthchart does not show which career you choose but it can show your inner motivation. In the case of Sagittarius, your greatest need is for freedom of action and the ability to communicate with others, possibly on a rather large scale. You are a natural teacher and if you don't work directly in education you would still enjoy helping and guiding others and passing on the knowledge which you have accumulated over the years. Most of you are surprisingly modest about your work and your achievements and tend not to promote yourselves very well, therefore, it is only when one gets to know you better that we learn just how knowledgeable you actually are.

You would enjoy a job in broadcasting or publishing or even as an entertainer. Many of you are good actors and singers but, unless you have a fair dose of Leo or Aries on your chart, you may be too shy to push yourself forward in this way. You are adaptable enough to get on with anyone and to work anywhere but you have high standards and a strong sense of your surroundings, therefore you couldn't do anything which was really downmarket, under-handed or which involved working in dirty, messy surroundings. You are stubborn enough to finish what you start but you may start too many projects and then become worn out from trying to do them all at once.

The travel trade would attract you as you love to expand your horizons in a practical sense as well as in a mental one. Some of you can work on dicey projects which involve intuition and the ability to guess right. This could be something like the futures market on the stock exchange or any other business connected with gambling. Being over-optimistic at times, this could occasionally run you into trouble. Whatever you do, and even if your own confidence deserts you at the wrong moment in your career, your pixilated sense of humour will always see you through. Lunar Sagittarians are excellent salespeople as long as they believe in the product they are handling.

PARENTS AND BACKGROUND

Your relationship with your parents was good but distant in some way, possibly because they were busy or because they didn't encourage closeness. 'I just couldn't keep my parents' attention', says Joe, a salesman for an electronics company, 'my father led a busy life which took him travelling, rather like I do I suppose. My mother was always preoccupied with her church cronies.' Joe's story is typical even down to the fact that the Lunar Sagittarian's experience of parenthood could turn out to be similar to his own parents' experiences.

Your parents may have come from a different country with a different culture from the one which you are now living in; possibly just a different part of the country and with a different outlook on life or a different religion.

You did well at school, if not in academic studies, then in something else such as art, dancing, music or sports. The greatest and most important part of your education will come later in life. Your pleasant appearance and friendly, open attitude make you popular at school.

HEALTH

You could suffer from some of the Sagittarian ailments of leg and hip problems, varicose veins, phlebitis, rheumatism and blood disorders. Women of this lunation may have period problems followed by a hysterectomy.

Moon in Capricorn
♑ (Ruled by Saturn) ♄

The first time ever I saw your face,
The Sun rose in your eyes,
The Moon and Stars were the gifts you gave.

Sung by Roberta Flack

The sign of Capricorn is feminine, negative, earthy and cardinal while the Moon, through its association with the sign of Cancer, is feminine, negative, watery and cardinal. Therefore the planet and the sign are quite compatible, however, the Moon is said to be in its detriment in Capricorn because the sign is opposite the sign of Cancer, the Moon's natural home. This means that the emotional side of your life could be a little suppressed.

Whatever you appear to be on the outside, inwardly you are sensitive, vulnerable and shy, especially where your personal feelings are concerned. The earthiness of Capricorn makes you practical and sensible, therefore if you find that an idea works for you you will use it, otherwise you will reject it. Even if you have an extroverted sign on your Ascendant, you will be shy when you are young but later in life you will cover this up with a layer of polish. Nevertheless, inwardly you are rather deep and unfathomable. You resist serious illness and have, in addition to bodily strength, considerable strength of character. These strengths enable you to survive almost anything plus giving you the kind of tenacity and determination which allows you to finish whatever you start. You rarely take time off from work, even when you *are* ill.

Many of you go into business for yourselves thereby giving yourself the opportunity to create something of your own which will stand the test of time. You learn self-discipline early in life and feel inwardly that life is a serious business. You have the feeling that you should work to build up your finances while you are young so that you can relax and enjoy the result later on. As you will probably live to a ripe old age, you are right to think like this. Another reason for self-employment is the fact that you enjoy being in a position of responsibility and you carry authority well without throwing your weight around.

You need security, your idea of hell would be to be dependent upon others because you hate to be a burden or to suffer the embarrassment of having to ask for help. You are resourceful and hard working but could be a little scheming and just a dash dishonest when chasing a goal (remember, tricky Dicky Nixon had the Moon in Capricorn). Your serious nature is relieved by a delightfully dry and witty sense of humour. You don't make hurtful jokes about others but just see the world in an off-beat way which those who share your sense of humour, will find very funny. You enjoy the company of humorous people too.

You learn well and may be academic, but practical subjects really suit you best. You can think and plan on a large scale and in a structured manner, rules and methods come easily to you, whether they be mathematical, engineering, or the pattern made by a series of dance steps. You prefer not to gamble on life but to plan your course, moving forward and then consolidating your position for a while.

Although your values are material rather than spiritual, the most important aspect of your life is probably your relationship with your family. You are very caring and you take your responsibilities towards them very seriously. You are dependable and faithful in marriage and will try to make almost any kind of situation work. Your work may occasionally come between you and your family but if they are ill, they get all of your attention immediately. Oddly enough you really enjoy hearing all the local gossip, not just family gossip either. You can really get your teeth into a nice juicy piece of scandal but you yourself would hate to be in the middle of any scandal.

Lunar Capricorns can find it difficult to form relationships due to shyness, but the intensity of this problem would depend on the type of Ascendant and Sun sign which you have; nevertheless, you are easily hurt and embarrassed. Being cautious, you take care to find yourself the right type of partner. As a parent you are gentle and caring, and although you would be unlikely to join in rough games with your children, you will do your best to teach them about the world we live in and to open their eyes to the possibilities which life has to offer. You may be a little old-fashioned in your approach when they reach their teens but you will try to see things from their point of view. At least you would always be aware of your children's need to be treated with dignity.

You exert considerable control over your own inner nature, sometimes too much so, in order to prevent your feelings from getting the better of you. Your somewhat formal manner protects your vulnerability, it would be impossible to imagine you getting drunk and making an ass of yourself. Like the other earth signs, it takes a lot to make you lose your temper, but when you do so, it is over-poweringly destructive. Making friends is a slow process with you and the few friends whom you do have, you keep for years. You adapt better to *new places* than to new people and can fit in almost anywhere. Your pet hate is to be embarrassed and humiliated, a spell in a hospital which is staffed by insensitive people would be dreadful for you. Another pet hate is coarseness or vulgarity of any kind. You are kindly and helpful towards other people, especially in a work situation and you would make a good financial adviser or a good teacher on a small group basis. You need a strong and independent partner who can, to some extent, protect you. Your hidden sensitivity can give you nervous ailments such as skin problems, asthma, rheumatism or a tendency to have colds. You listen to any advice which is offered to you but in the end you prefer to make up your own mind.

You have a love of beauty and grace in all things and a hatred of any kind of ugliness, from an ugly appearance to ugly behaviour. Being reserved, you don't readily reach out to touch people but you love to be held and touched by your partner and your children. Earth signs are sensuous and this could show up in your case as a love of flowers, music or the seasons of the year. If you are insulted or pushed aside in a queue you would, as one lunar Capricorn friend told me, 'fume inwardly' but you are too polite to say much.

Where sex is concerned you improve with age, and also with the overcoming of your shyness and inhibitions. You are fastidious and very particular both in your choice of partner and in your behaviour. One night stands are *definitely* not for you! The feeling of closeness while making love is as important to you as the act itself. You may choose to marry someone who is older than yourself but whoever you choose, whatever their age or appearance, you will feel protective and caring to them. You even like to work together so that you can share the same problems.

Most lunar Capricornians are great holiday-makers, you need to get away from work from time to time and you really enjoy a break. You are not too experimental with foods as you are a sparing eater but you enjoy good surroundings with well cooked and presented foods. Comfort is a necessity for you when travelling; you are not likely to be found on a camping site.

PARENTS AND BACKGROUND

There is something strange here. You begin by being very close to your mother and then losing your idealized picture of her. There may even be tragic circumstances involving death of a family member or a spell in a home due to illness or divorce in the family. As you grow up you may realize that your mother is a loving woman who did her best under the circumstances. Peter explained the situation to me, 'My parents were very caring towards me but there was just too much for them to cope with. My father never got over being shot up in the war and mother had to work hard during those years. The love was there but they were elderly and up against it. I felt it would be wrong to make too much noise or to bring other noisier youngsters into the house. I doubt whether they would have stopped me but I would have felt bad about it, that's all.'

There could have been some conflict and aggression between you and your father which accounts for your slight air of watchfulness when around new people. This Moon position suggests difficulties during childhood through poverty, too many other children in the family or a loss of some kind. Oddly enough this may jump back one generation and be, not your experience of childhood, but your *mother's* experience. Your parents loved you and were kind-hearted but they could have been slightly insensitive and critical of your school work. A conflict could have arisen if they wanted you to work in the same line as themselves and were disappointed when you chose not to. They, possibly due to their upbringing, taught you to be careful with money and highly realistic in your dreams; you would have learned to value (possibly over-value) material security and possessions.

Being a quiet and obedient child you did well at school and gave the teachers no problems, but you would have found sports difficult, possibly due to poor health and short-sightedness. Many of you go on to further education, especially of a practical nature.

ATTITUDE TO CAREER

The position of the Moon on a birthchart does not necessarily indicate your choice of career but it can show your inner motivations. Lunar Capricorns prefer to do something useful, this could be anything from structural engineering to making medical supplies. You could be drawn to accountancy, the law, also politics, especially if there are other political indications, such as the sign of Cancer or Libra somewhere on your birthchart. Being interested in business, the world of insurance might appeal to you, or some kind of work in a government department You prefer being in a position of management.

Travel and transport or a chain of shops are possibilities too. Being slow, thorough and efficient in all that you do, you become annoyed by petty inefficiencies in others; for instance buses being late or paperwork which has not been properly done. I have noticed that most people with the Sun, Moon or Ascendant in an earth sign are early risers. You are highly ambitious and will climb slowly towards the top of your career.

HEALTH

Your weak spots are supposed to be the bones, especially the knees, therefore you could have rheumatism later in life. Hearing problems are a possibility, especially tinnitus. You may have skin problems, even alopecia and could be short-sighted. Generally speaking you should live a long and healthy, if rather hard-working life.

Moon in Aquarius
♒ (Ruled by Uranus and Saturn) ♅ ♄

When the moon is in the seventh house
And Jupiter aligns with Mars,
Then peace will be around us
And love is in the stars.
    This is the dawning of the age of Aquarius.

from the musical Hair

The sign of Aquarius is masculine, positive, airy and fixed, while the Moon, through its association with the sign of Cancer is feminine, negative, watery and cardinal. The power of the Moon is rather muted in this sign, the greatest effect being to reduce the *feeling* element from the emotions. Inwardly you are detached, independent and rather cool. Although controlled and possibly a little bottled up at times you like others around you to show that *they* need and want you. When meeting people for the first time socially, you are pleasant and affable if a little shy; meanwhile you are weighing them up in a slightly watchful manner. You have a strong inner sense of self which would lead you to take a calculated risk in a career or even in a relationship. Although sensible, you are not over-cautious, therefore you would accept most of life's challenges whether they put your finances at risk or your feelings. This ability to inwardly weigh and measure could be confusing to those who fall in love with you because, although you can discuss feelings in an articulate manner, one wonders just how much you are actually able to feel yourself!

Your inner nature is off-beat, you could find yourself travelling in a different direction to everyone else. Like your solar Aquarian cousins, you are educationally minded and will choose a career where you can stretch your mind and also broaden the minds of others. You are kind, helpful and humanitarian but this may be directed more towards the world in general than to those who are closest to you. Although helpful in practical ways, there could be an element of embarrassment and helplessness when faced by the sight of other people's emotional pain. You are afraid that if you allow weak people to latch themselves on to you that they will drain your energies or, worse still, bore the daylights out of you! Your general outlook is balanced, optimistic and cheerful; to all except the most neurotic you would be a good friend.

Your mind is excellent and it doesn't matter whether you are educated and academic or shrewd and streetwise, either way your thinking processes are fast and your intuition is strong. You possess a dry and intelligent sense of humour. Your ideas are often excellent and you have the ability to put them into practice.

Being strongly independent, you prefer to cope alone with your own problems, however harrowing they may be. One Moon in Aquarius friend of mind wouldn't allow anyone to go with him when he went into hospital for a major heart operation. You could reject outside help in case accepting it makes you appear weak and incapable, you may even view help as a form of interference. You're not at all keen on people who try to own you or to manipulate you although you can be adept at manipulating others. Another pet dislike is of being falsely accused – you are willing to admit to your own errors but will not carry the can for others. Your attitudes can sometimes cause others to stay at a distance to you, which can consequently cause misunderstandings both at work and at home.

Your friendliness is universal and you would not reject anyone due to colour, age, race or religion. Many lunar Aquarians belong to clubs and societies of one kind or another, you enjoy committing yourself to group activities. Most of your hobbies involve people and ideas which are sociable and charitable such as Masonry, or something directly helpful, such as youth work. There is one hobby which many of you enjoy entirely alone, although the results of this involve other people, and that is cooking. I have met some truly inspired solar and lunar Aquarian amateur chefs.

You can take any amount of chaos going on around you at work but you need peace in your home, where you can be in control of your own environment (creating a little bit of chaos for others maybe). You enjoy visitors but don't appreciate people who dump themselves upon you. Many of you are clever handymen (and women), enjoying the challenge of working on your home and garden and often finding imaginative and original ways of solving practical do it yourself problems.

Your memory is also rather original and may be strangely selective, easily recalling things you find interesting but 'tuning out' irrelevant details. However, you don't duck really important issues as you have high standards of honesty and integrity. You don't as a rule go in for petty jealousies, neither do you make mountains out of molehills. If your pride is hurt, you can be quite spiteful and very sarcastic. You really do need a creative or useful outlet or you can become bored, gossipy or aloof.

Some of you are lazy and too easygoing, especially if there are planets in the sign of Libra on your birthchart; yet others can be truly very eccentric, especially if there are other planets in the sign of Aquarius. For the most part, criticism brushes off you, you have a strong ego and feel that everyone is entitled to their own opinion, even their opinion of you. You are not likely to change your ways in the face of criticism anyway.

In close personal relationships you are kind, pleasant, thoughtful and passionate; you could even be rather romantic. Aquarius being a fixed sign suggests that you don't easily walk away from situations. You may stay in the same house, the same job or the same relationship long after the time when you should move on. However, if the day comes when you *do* move on, you seem to be able to do so in a decisive manner, looking mentally forward rather than backward. If necessary, you can wait years for the right person to come along, if this paragon does not appear, you spend years of your life alone. If you become bored with your permanent partner, you may look outside the relationship for change and excitement. If you fall in love with someone while you are still married, and especially if you have children, then you will be terribly torn between the need to be loyal and the need to be with the one you want. However, your famous Aquarian detachment may come to your aid here and allow you to work out logically what would be for the best. There is no doubt that you need an interesting and stimulating partner, another very important ingredient would be shared interests and mutual respect. Without shared interests, you would gravitate towards interests of your own and this would begin the process of allowing the marriage to drift into failure and loss. There is just a suspicion that lunar Aquarian males might find a very successful career-girl type of wife too much of a good thing, there could be just a tinge of jealousy creeping in here. You can be strangely blind to both the needs and feelings of those you love. You may never really get to know them on a deep level.

Women of this lunation must have some kind of interesting work outside the home. Neither sex seems keen to have a large family but the relationship between lunar Aquarian parents and their children is usually very good. There is a natural sensitivity to the needs of children and young people and you would offer help without making undue demands upon your children or smothering them. It is just possible that you could expect too much of a very timid child but for the most part you make a successful parent. You are always ready to stump up cash for education or hobbies but you might be a little absent-minded about some of the practical details, such as making sure that they have a clean shirt for school.

Both sexes with this Moon sign are attractive rather than beautiful, in fact your features are more likely to be rugged and bony than soft and sweet. None of this matters much because your friendliness, charm, sex-appeal and humour are far more effective with the opposite sex than any amount of sterile beauty would be. Being rather shy, you might have a little difficulty in breaking the ice but your interest in people soon helps you to overcome this. Anyway, you always have the option of meeting people through mutual interests such as your work or social activities rather than, for instance, at a disco. People with fixed Moon signs can cope with a lot, it would take a great deal for you to break up a relationship, but when you do, there isn't a backward glance. In relationships, as in all things, you need freedom and independence and may demonstrate this by being deliberately forgetful, erratic and hard to pin down with regard to mutual arrangements. You seek an intelligent and independent partner and often are happiest with one who is much younger than yourself, so that to some extent you can advise or mould them. Be careful that when your good advice is taken and your pupil begins to blossom that *you* don't then become resentful. If your partner started laying the law down to you and restricting your movements, your first impulse would be to get out of the relationship.

Sex for you is a by-product of love, you *can* indulge in sex for its own sake but are much happier when love is the main motivating force. This may surprise many readers but this lunation produces amazingly sexy people! Your special combination of action, imagination and stamina seems to bring something special to the act of love. Friends who are married to lunar Aquarians have told me … well, let's draw a veil over that! It's strange how the supposedly non-tactile air sign people seem to become so good at touching and cuddling when there's the chance of a bit of sexual activity.

Your temper can be a problem when you are young but later you learn to sit back and control it; however if hurt, you retain the ability to wound verbally. There may be a lack of adaptability in your attitude to others, you will only go so far in order to fit in with their wishes, you are inclined to consider that other people ought to take or leave you just as you are. Your partners are chosen to some extent because they have the right appearance. Fatness turns you right off, as does dirt and mess. A lively person who has many outside interests would attract you; if they have a sense of humour and also look nice, better still. Lunar Aquarians of both sexes prefer an equal partnership and will do all they can to promote the interests and job of the other, even trying to help the partner to enjoy his or her hobbies. There is evidence that you wouldn't be so happy if the hobby was a particularly noisy one because you hate loud discordant noises.

Needing a pleasant home and a nice garden, you have no special preference for the town or the country. I think you would make the best of it wherever you were, as long as you are not isolated from people or fenced into a very small space.

ATTITUDE TO CAREER

The position of the Moon on a birthchart rarely determines one's actual career but can show one s inner motivations. You take work seriously and don't like chopping and changing jobs, preferring to find a career which you can settle into. You are interested in ideas and willing to learn, therefore you do well at school and continue to learn later on. Certainly your parents encouraged you to progress, but like all lunar masculine signs you are inwardly quite goal-orientated You enjoy work which is useful to the community and you also like making things which are needed. You can pursue a goal persistently, therefore, you can *close* a deal if someone else will open the door for you.

Working with children might appeal to you, either directly in education or in something tough such as the probation service, because you have patience even for the awkward ones. You take well to challenges and can ride out most problems without falling apart, therefore the armed services or police may appeal. Your incisive mind may lead you into the legal sphere, medicine, psychiatry or even astrology. Being impatient with fools, you could find delegating difficult. You usually learn from your *own* mistakes and are fairly forgiving towards others for theirs, as long as the mistakes do not occur too frequently or are not too obviously stupid. You solve problems in an original way, but must learn to keep lists and use your memory rather than your forgettery.

You seem to be happiest when working in large enterprises; you may wind up in the civil service, a large commercial firm, the teaching profession or government. You have, in common with the other fixed signs of Scorpio, Leo and Taurus, the determination to finish what you start. You don't like being pressurized by others, preferring to work things out in your own way and to do things slowly and thoroughly. Some of you enjoy being attached to some kind of glamorous or powerful enterprise where your own dynamism can come to the fore. There is a reverse side to this coin in that you can run a *small* enterprise of your own as long as you have total control. Although ambitious while young, you are prepared to settle for something comfortable later in life.

You are clever with electronics, computers, radar and other modernistic ideas and may even dream of being a spaceman. You are capable and inventive and will give the whole of your attention to the task in hand, therefore you can create some highly original and very workable methods of production.

Most solar and lunar Aquarians have a need to do something worthwhile, to put something back into life. One lunar Aquarian friend of mine raises money for handicapped children; he does this very quietly despite being one of the most prominent members of this country's civil service; another is in the scouting movement. There is an inner desire to bring a sense of love to all people.

One occasionally runs across the type of Moon in Aquarius subject who is languid and arty, unambitious and lacking in self-discipline. There are a few others who may be theorizers, never quite able to put their theories into action and too eccentric to fulfil any ordinary kind of role. Most of you, however, enjoy a challenge and will get a kick of making something succeed. Some of you are drawn to the arts of the world of drama and, if there are other encouraging factors on your birthchart, writing may come naturally to you.

PARENTS AND BACKGROUND

On the face of it you had a good childhood, certainly your practical needs were attended to. If you came from a background where there was little money to spare, your parents would have made sure that you had enough to eat and were dressed and equipped in a clean and decent manner.

Your mother may have been a busy career woman or may have poured her energies into some personal interest. One lunar Aquarian friend of mine had parents who were actively involved in the Salvation Army. Some of you will have had the kind of mother who did very little outside the home, the results of which had the reverse effect of making you feel that families are definitely better off when the mother *has* outside interests. Another Moon in Aquarius peculiarity is that you may have had religion rammed down your throat in childhood which put you completely off the idea of formal religion later in life.

It is possible that you loved your father but inwardly considered him to be weak. He may have had poor health, oddly enough, many Moon in Aquarius subjects seem to have fathers who suffered from stomach ulcers. Mother would have been the more organized and capable parent, especially as far as money is concerned. You probably come from an average family of two or three children and would have been the older and/or more capable one of the group or of a different sex to the other children. You were taught not to make scenes or allow your emotions to become a nuisance to others. It is possible that you were never really able to feel very close to your parents, it is even possible that this is a circumstance of your own making. People who have the Moon in air signs do tend to be rather emotionally self-contained and you may just have been born that way.

Your parents took a reasonable view of your educational needs, they encouraged you to learn but didn't push you unduly. They may not have been so accommodating in respect of any hobbies you wished to pursue, which may have been due to shortage of money or conflict with their moral or religious views, for instance if the activity involved participation on the sabbath.

HEALTH

You are basically very strong. Blood-pressure could be a problem especially for women during pregnancy. Allergies such as hay fever, asthma, eczema, psoriasis and hives can occur, also migraine, menstrual problems in women, rheumatism and diabetes are possibilities. The weakest part of the body is the lower legs and ankles, which could involve problems with veins, phlebitis and thrombosis, also leg ulcers later in life.

Moon in Pisces
♓ (Ruled by Neptune and Jupiter) ♆♃

I am the star that rises from the sea –
   The twilight sea.
I bring men dreams that rule their destiny.
I bring the dream-tides to the souls of men

             from *The Worship of Isis*.

The sign of Pisces is feminine, negative, watery and mutable while the Moon, through its association with the sign of Cancer, is feminine, negative, watery and cardinal. This would make the Moon appear comfortable in Pisces but to some extent, the mutability of Pisces weakens the active, cardinal nature of the Moon. The Moon is associated with one's innermost feelings and underlying emotions and the sign of Pisces, being devoted to emotion, suggests that even if the subject's outer manner is confident and capable, there will be a terribly soft heart hiding deep inside.

If this is your Moon position, you will spend some part of your life searching for answers to deep and indefinable questions. You will contemplate the meaning of life and the possibility of an after-life and could even be drawn to a religious or quasi-religious way of living. Your energies to some extent will always be directed towards trying to improve the quality of life for others and to introducing people around you to a gentle and healthy understanding of their minds, bodies and spirits. Life may disappoint you as it may never match up to your idealistic dreams and indefinable yearnings. Yet, somehow, life must go on and you will probably wish to live it to the very full. Therefore a particularly Piscean form of practicality often seems to combine with your desire for perfection, and the requirements of the hereafter.

You can be surprisingly ambitious. This ambition may take the normal route of upward mobility in the working and the suburban community or it may take a totally private form. You could push yourself to improve your performance in a creative capacity. Either way, you have the long-term patience to achieve your goals. You also have the gift of creative visualization. The only real drawback to you reaching your goals is your lack of confidence and your fear of making other people angry with you for competing with them. A sarcastic remark can wound deeply and is never forgotten.

On a more mundane level, you are extremely sensitive to the needs of others. Nobody is kinder, more thoughtful and considerate; you seem to feel other people's wants even before you are aware of your own and you can soak up other people's moods and desires psychically. There is a definite need for you to assess your own feelings from time to time to make sure that they are yours and not those of the people around you. You should also note that it doesn't always do to rush in and smooth the path of others, it might do them more good if you were to allow them to solve their own problems from time to time. Not everybody will want your intervention – although, human nature being what it is, most people will take advantage of free help when given the chance. If you become a permanent listening ear for neurotic friends and relatives, you will become worn out, depressed and even physically ill. There are people who *don't* want their problems solved because this would stop them from attracting the attention and sympathy of others. You must make a special effort to avoid the truly mad, bad and sad for your own mental health's sake, even if it means abandoning some of those who call themselves friends.

Like all those who have the Sun or Moon in mutable signs, you have an inner streak of resilience and can usually find a way round your own problems. If absolutely pressed, you can stand up for yourself very well and dish out a surprisingly devastating dose of criticism. People tend to forget that just because you are so ready to sympathize and to understand their needs, that you also see their faults and inner motivations. If you are wounded you withdraw into your shell, but if the problem is too great, you can be very spiteful and destructive. Destructive behaviour does not come naturally, you prefer to take the role of counsellor, teacher and guide.

Like Moon in Cancer subjects, you can be a really monumental worrier, beginning with worries on behalf of your family and friends, your health, money, the state of the nation and the imminence of nuclear war. You could be mean in small ways, smoothing out paper bags for reuse or moaning about small expenses. In a way, you can be penny-wise and pound-foolish because you are never mean about large issues. You are always broke but usually manage to do the things you want. You will spend money on musical and recording equipment, books, dining out and trips. Most astrologers will tell you that you like to be on or near the sea, but where travelling is concerned, you don't actually mind where you go as long as you don't get too worn out in the process.

You will not tolerate injustice in any form and, if you see a child, an animal or a person of a different race or religion being badly treated you truly go bananas. You value loyalty above all things and hate to let anyone down. Friendship is terribly important to you, especially as some of you have difficult or demanding family members thus making friendship outside the family essential.

All solar and lunar Pisceans are creative, many are artistic and you need to express this creativity somewhere in your daily life. You work at your own rather strange pace, often like a dervish for a month at a time and then switching off for a week in order to recharge your batteries. Most of you enjoy some kind of sport; swimming is probably high on your list, also dancing, tennis or just walking the dog. Every lunar Piscean that I have come across is a naturally good dancer, especially ballroom dancing. Some of you can be serious athletes or dancers, but this will require strongly competitive elements elsewhere on the chart. Those of you who have a very ordinary job will probably have a creative interest on the side. Some of you will privately work in the psychic or even the magical field, often without the people at your place of work having any idea of this other interest. You see omens in everyday events and may be superstitious and fearful of unexplainable dark forces which sometimes seem to gather around you. Even the most practical among you can feel patterns in events which seem to occur.

You are not as changeable in your moods as most astrology books would suppose, oddly enough people who have the Moon in fixed signs are by far the moodiest. However, when you do become emotional or upset, the feelings go deep. You are able to hold a grudge for ever but you are equally apt to remember those who stand by you in times of trouble.

If someone hurts you gratuitously even in a minor way, you will never quite be able to trust or really like them again. Women who have the Moon in water signs can often attribute some of their mood swings to premenstrual tension – I'm not quite sure what *men* can blame their moods upon. In some ways your apparent moodiness stems from your inability to get the whole of your life together at any one time. It seems that if your work is going well, your love life will be in a state of collapse and vice versa. Even if *everything* is going well, you can be discontented due to boredom!

Your home is your haven, it is also a haven for a good many other people. Many of you work wholly or partially from home which often involves people coming in and out. The place is also permanently full of friends and neighbourhood children. Lunar and solar Pisceans are supposed to be loners, but I have yet to see any evidence of that, your phone and your doorbell are always ringing. Many of you literally don't bother to shut your door as there are so many people pounding in and out. Your home is attractive and comfortable but not over-decorated or cleaned to the point of sterility. You love warm colours, interesting textures, pictures and music, you fill your home with these plus, of course, books, books, books. You read almost anything but probably novels, books about the occult, history, psychology, health and magic will be lying about somewhere on your shelves.

You can be so adept at hiding your inner nature that your kind heart might be buried under a shield of efficiency, toughness or even sarcasm, this is mainly a self-protective shield. You are slow to reveal your own inner feelings and it takes some time for you to get to know and trust someone. Some lunar Pisceans even go through many years of marriage without their partner ever really being let into their innermost hearts. You can be a little manipulative at times, either to prevent yourself from hurt or in order to benefit those around you. When you are entirely comfortable with someone you can be surprisingly bossy in a rather mother-hen way but you do it for their own good.

Both solar and lunar Pisceans have an all or nothing relationship with vehicles, either being fabulous drivers or hating the whole business of learning to drive and not bothering with it. Some actually do learn and then avoid driving whenever possible. Very strange.

In marriage you are so supportive that you can spend more energy on your partner's behalf than on your own and you really have to beware of becoming a martyr or a doormat. You tend to moan a bit about your partner, especially when you are feeling tired or depressed but this is almost an expression of affection and often doesn't mean much. You certainly need love and approval and although you *can* live alone, you far prefer to have someone to love and be loved by. Not receiving the love and understanding which you need in childhood, you actively chase after it in adulthood. Some of you are so shy and repressed that you *never* get the love you want and then you may retreat into a life of daydreams and illusions which would make a Walter Mitty appear down to earth. Your powerful imagination is both your most valuable asset and the point of your greatest weakness. If you can channel this into creative pursuits, spiritual development or work in the counselling field, you could overcome most of this.

You make an excellent parent because you understand the needs of children and are happy to spend time playing with them. I'm not sure about this but I think it's probable that you don't relate to babies as much as slightly older children who can talk and play. Certainly you find no difficulty in playing 'let's pretend', you are probably way ahead of them on that one anyway. Your children are encouraged to respect adults but not to be afraid of them, you respect the dignity of children. You could be so busy teaching them about the universe, the world around them and giving them all the love that they need that you overlook their need for clean shirts and breakfast cereal. Don't worry, they will survive and will love you all the more for it.

Your greatest fault is of over-sensitivity to criticism. Nobody likes to be criticized but you really do seem to suffer. Your self-esteem is low enough to begin with, you don't need to have someone else giving it a further battering.

Although you are friendly and non-hostile in your approach to new people, if you really fancy someone, your first reaction may be to run in the opposite direction. You fear rejection, ridicule and loss. You are afraid to become close to someone, in case you learn to rely on them and then lose them again for some reason or other. Love relationships make you nervous because you are aware of your great need for emotional sustenance and of your vulnerability. Adolescent relating can be very painful; later on you learn some protective techniques but these may be ultimately manipulative in that you may not allow yourself to take a chance on expressing your genuine feelings, this again is due to your fear of rejection. Do try, if you can, to be *yourself* in a love relationship and not the pseudo person whom you think your lover wants you to be. In most cases, it is better for you to connect with someone whom you know on a friendly basis rather than to jump deeply into a new relationship. Being incredibly romantic, you appreciate little presents, birthday cards, candle-lit dinners and shared memories. You have a stock of romantic melodies and catch-phrases which you link to your lover.

An important ingredient in the lunar Piscean's nature is curiosity of all kinds. Sexual and emotional curiosity strike early. I can't really find any way of putting this delicately but the fact is that you love making love. The act of sex is a great outlet for you because it combines all your favourite feelings and sensations. Your senses are terrifically strong, especially your psychic sense; love-making gives expression to every one of them, including your powerful imagination. It may be a cold-blooded thought, but your nerves are delicate and often over-stretched, and therefore sex gives you a tremendous release of tension. A pal of mine tells me that he is 'horribly romantic' and couldn't enjoy sex without love. I think that goes for all the other lunar Pisceans too, there must be affection and fondness, if not outright adoration, for you to be able to really relax and enjoy yourself. My friend Nina says that she likes to have poetry read to her while she is in bed – I like poetry anywhere!

You might try too hard to please your partner both sexually and in other ways, remember the relationship stands more of a chance of lasting if *both* of your needs are being satisfied. Another difficulty for you is that you don't like being possessed. You yourself can be possessive, especially when in the early stages of a romance; possessive, hungry for love and desperate to be reassured. There may not be enough touch, comfort or words of love in the world for you, but you can in your turn fill your partner with love and reassurance until the cows come home. You need affection even more than you need sex, you need to be cuddled. You need to play a little and to have fun with your partner. (Welcome to the pleasure dome!) Oddly enough, you don't much like to be touched by strangers. You need to keep a little distance between you and 'touchers' this may be an instinctive need to protect your rather sensitive aura!

Some men are better avoided by Moon in Pisces women. The first is the self-destructive type, such as the confirmed alcoholic. You may wish to reform this person, to teach him by loving him endlessly to mend his ways. This will get you nowhere and will only deplete your small reserves of psychic energy. Another is the paternal type who appears over-protective but who is in fact threatened by the possibility of your becoming independent or taking control of your own life. The two Piscean fish can make you stupidly romantic and earthily practical both at the same time.

Here are a few more oddities from the Piscean wash-bag. You like fresh air and the countryside but not when the weather is cold; *then* you prefer sitting by an open fire. You can be too serious at times and you should let your friends encourage you to let your hair down and have some fun. You need to have good clothes and may be fussy about the type of shoes you wear.

ATTITUDE TO CAREER

The position of the Moon does not suggest any specific career but can show one's underlying motivations. You are creative, inventive and easily bored, therefore a routine job will not satisfy. Not having endless reserves of strength, you tend to work in fits and starts, therefore, you need a job where you can work at your own pace. Many of you have an urge to do something useful and find work in hospitals or even in prisons. Many solar and lunar Pisceans can be found in the world of music, acting, dancing and art. Creative work obviously appeals, floristry and cookery are typical interests. Glamorous work such as fashion interests you as does the more up-market kind of public relations work.

Many of you are skilled engineers, electricians, telephone engineers and precision sheet-metal workers. This is because the work is detailed, creative, requires problem-solving techniques and involves drawings. Obviously drawing office work appeals and many of you can be found working in aircraft factories!

I belong to an organization called the British Astrological and Psychic Society which has nine people on the committee. We all have different Sun signs and Ascendant signs but *all* nine of us have the Moon in water signs. Two of the group have the Moon in Cancer, the other seven have the Moon in Pisces. This must be significant mustn't it? Some of us work full-time in the psychic field, others work on a part-time basis. One can find among our collective skills, astrologers, palmists, tarot readers, numerologists, clairvoyants, healers, aroma-therapists, trance mediums, aura-readers, graphologists, sand-readers etc. All lunar Pisceans are natural psychics but it is surprising how many are drawn specifically to work in the field. If you have Sagittarius, Aquarius or Gemini on your birthchart, you will probably want to teach. It seems that the Pisces connection gives one the urge to give gratuitious information to the world. Healing is also a naturally Piscean gift which many of you have.

PARENTS AND BACKGROUND

You may have been born with difficulty and could have been the youngest child in the family or perhaps an only child. The general feeling is that you were not an especially wanted child and were viewed right from the start as being a nuisance. Your parents would have been up against difficulties when you were very young; these could range from severe financial problems, deaths and tragedies in the family or the kind of situation where one half of the family doesn't talk to the other. There is, actually, strong evidence that you had early experience of the shortness and fragility of life due to the death of a parent or of someone close to you. Some of you would have been born at around the time of a death in the family; wartime births probably occurred during bombing raids!

One way or another your childhood was rather lonely. Some of you felt yourself to be 'different' in some way, possibly being the only artistic and sensitive child in a household full of very rugged and practical people. Even with nothing tragic or 'out of gear' in the childhood, there was a need to withdraw into your imagination, to get away and spend time on your own. Most of you are avid readers, often attracted to stories about magic or science fiction. Finding it hard to make friends, you could have been badly bullied at school or, worse still, badly bullied in the home. You may have felt embarrassed by your appearance, i.e. too tall, short, fat, thin, etc. Somehow, you found it hard to relate to your parents and may have been afraid of them or of other people around you. There may have been an over-emphasis on a particular kind of moral or religious observance, or there is the possibility that you were or you may have been pushed at school further and faster than was comfortable. This would be a difficult situation as your natural inclination was to please your parents and teachers. A few of you were rebels at school and hated authority.

You developed a watchful approach to adults and learned how to gauge their moods and how best to please them. This could be carried into adult life making you adept at finding out just how to please people and to manipulate them to suit your own ends. More likely, you would manipulate *yourself* to suit the other person and, therefore, never *really* learn to develop honesty and a sense of reality in personal relationships.

Adolescence is likely to have been a minefield as you learned to adapt to one person after another, not learning to appraise yourself of your own realistic needs and make them plain to others. All this can be sorted out later in life with an increase of awareness and self-awareness and, to give you your due, you do go to considerable lengths to discover what's wrong and to put things right. Pisces is a sign which is associated with illusion – as you grow and learn you should learn to channel your illusions into artistic or creative work and *out* of your dealings with others, especially in the personal sense.

HEALTH

If you have this Moon placement, you may not enjoy the best of health. You could have been weak as a child and have spent a good deal of time alone because of this, later in life the legacies of your childhood have a habit of lingering on. Your energies are quickly depleted and your nerves are delicate. You can suffer from nervous ailments. The traditional problem area for Pisces is the feet, also the lungs. Heart trouble is a possibility, also skin allergies, migraine or asthmatic problems. You may retain water or have blood disorders. I have not yet come across a lunar Piscean with a drink problem, but smoking seems to have a bad effect. An old-fashioned astrology book of mine tells me that you are susceptible to social diseases! Anybody who works with people in a counselling capacity will be able to tell you that social diseases are pretty common and don't apply to any one sign of the Zodiac or any one planet.

6

Quick Clues to Your Moon Sign

Quick Clues to the Natal Signs and Houses

This is a very brief outline which you can use to jog your memory. This just gives the impact of each sign on the inner personality.

Aries (first)	Lively positive personality. Enthusiastic, self-motivated and outgoing but lacking in patience and consideration for others.
Taurus (second)	Steady type, sorts out what is valuable to him and then hangs on to it. Family person, sensual and musical. Resourceful and materialistic.
Gemini (third)	Communicator, teacher, salesman or travel agent. Usually found on the phone, needs to keep up to date. Mental activity needed, versatile and easily bored.
Cancer (fourth)	Needs a home base and a family around. Good to others but will lean on them. Moody, wants a quiet life. Enjoys travel, novelty. Needs personal security.
Leo (fifth)	Youthful and playful, loyal but dogmatic. Needs to be respected by others. Hard worker especially in a creative field. Likes children.
Virgo (sixth)	Shy inward looking type, dedicated worker, perfectionist. Likes to help others but moans about it. Businesslike, discriminating. Apparently cool emotionally, has strong, but contained, feelings.

Libra (seventh)	Ambitious, determined, also loving. Needs to be surrounded by beauty. Theorizer, may have difficulty putting ideas into practice. Needs partners and companions to complement self and achieve harmony.
Scorpio (eighth)	Steady reliable worker. Determined and independent. Strong, intense but restrained personality. Quick to anger but very caring to those who matter. Can transform self and others.
Sagittarius (ninth)	Restless, but also needing a secure base. Philosophic and broad-minded. Interested in sport, culture and all wide ideas.
Capricorn (tenth)	Ambitious, loyal and caring family person. Career important, good business head. Lacking in confidence, shy, kind. Restrained and self-motivated. Seeks position of authority.
Aquarius (eleventh)	Friendly, humanitarian, politically-minded. Needs family but cannot be confined to the home. Serious-minded, eccentric and detached.
Pisces (twelfth)	Gentle, compassionate, mystical, reclusive. Kind, but can be too self-sacrificing. Religious outlook. Sensitive, vulnerable. Artistic and creative.

7

Reflections of the Moon

The Dark Side of the Moon

The Moon has a slightly schizophrenic effect on the unconscious aspects of the personality. Just as the Moon is responsible for the ebb and flow of the tides and fluctuations in plant growth, so it seems to be related to some of our innermost inconsistencies. One obvious manifestation of this is the phenomenon of pre-menstrual syndrome in women where every month they become ill, irritable or angry and even find themselves dropping everything on the floor. This situation which is well known in our house, because neither I nor my daughter can keep anything in our hands for a couple of days before each period!

Even men can have lunar mood swings, especially those who have their natal Sun or Moon in water signs. It is well known that mentally ill 'lunatics' are more difficult at the time of the full moon. The police also know that they will have to deal with more violence or thoughtless vandalism at full Moon time than at any other time of the month. Even in the case of perfectly stable people and discounting the pre-menstruals, there is a kind of duality about the Moon in its effect. It can enhance and at the same time confuse and muddle the effects of one of the fixed signs, create an overabundance of cardinality or undermine the dynamic quality of cardinal signs and screw up the mutables until they don't know whether they are on their emotional arms or their elbows!

Reflections

In order to confuse matters further there is the convoluted astrological theory of reflections. The idea is that the Moon 'borrows' some of its nature from the sign which is directly opposite to the sign which it is in! Therefore, a Moon in Virgo would have some characteristics of the sign of Pisces. Here is a list of the opposites.

Aries/Libra
Taurus/Scorpio
Gemini/Sagittarius
Cancer/Capricorn
Leo/Aquarius
Virgo/Pisces

For example, the charming lunar Libran can display considerable Arian aggression when under pressure.

8

The Ascendant and the Houses

How to Find Your Ascendant and Houses

If you really have no idea of the degree, or even the sign which was rising at the time of your birth then I suggest that you try one of the following ideas. *Whatever you do please find out as accurately as you can the date, place and time of your birth!*

1. Find a friendly local astrologer and get him or her to work out your birthchart for you and make up a list of the planets and houses for you.
2. Send for an astrology chart to be made up, the fee for this will be very small as long as you don't ask to have the chart interpreted. There are many people offering this kind of service either by computer or manually; either way will do, it's the chart which matters. All astrology magazines will have details of people offering this kind of service.
3. Apply to: The Foundation of Holistic Consciousness, 25b South Norwood Hill, London SE25. Remember to send a stamped addressed envelope and your birth details. Also, please send £3.00 which is the fee for this service.

The Speedy do-it-yourself Ascendant Finder

This will help you to find your Ascendant and therefore, the house your Sun and Moon occupy but you will still need the help of an astrologer if you decide that you need to know the actual degree of the natal Moon.

Place your Sun in the house slot which corresponds to your time of birth and then add the sign of the Zodiac which lies on the cusp line (house division).For example if you were born at 2.30 am on the 14 April, place your Sun in the 2 am slot and put the sign of Aries on the cusp line between the 2 am slot and the 4 am slot. Then place the signs of the Zodiac on the cusp lines around the chart *in an anti-clockwise direction* and in the right order, then place your Moon in the appropriate sign. This will give you your Rising sign (Ascendant) and the house placement of both your Sun and your Moon.

The order of the signs of the Zodiac plus their glyphs

ARIES   ♈

TAURUS   ♉

GEMINI   ♊

CANCER   ♋

LEO   ♌

VIRGO   ♍

LIBRA   ♎

SCORPIO   ♏

SAGITTARIUS   ♐

CAPRICORN   ♑

AQUARIUS   ♒

PISCES   ♓

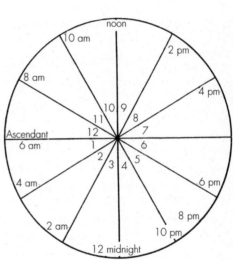

The Sun and the Ascendant in your horoscope

The Astrological Houses

THE FIRST HOUSE

Angular
Similar to Aries
Ruled by Mars

This shows how you appear to others, how you present yourself and your normal manner of expressing yourself among people who are new to you. In other words, this is your outermost personality. Obviously this shows the first impressions which you give but also the first impressions which you receive and therefore, may show what initially attracts you in other people. This house represents your childhood experiences, the parental home and the attitudes to be found in it. Early school experiences, early actions and reactions. It shows how you tackle new ventures. As this also contains information about your physical body, it might have a bearing on your appearance but other factors, especially the Sun sign, must be taken into account here. To some extent this house can show health problems. Any planets placed here are very important, especially in respect of one's early experience of life.

SECOND HOUSE

Succedent
Similar to Taurus
Ruled by Venus

This house concerns your own money, possessions and anything of value, also investments and the ability to earn money. Personal funds and personal debts. Personal and moral values can show up here, also requirements such as freedom versus security and the need for personal fulfilment. To some extent partners and relationships, especially where money and goods are involved. Matters related to property, farming, building, gardening and the land. Artistic and musical abilities or interests, if any. To some extent the way you give and receive love, also your attitude to beauty.

THIRD HOUSE

Cadent
Similar to Gemini
Ruled by Mercury

The local environment, matters under negotiation, and in some cases, papers to be signed. Messages, phone calls, correspondence of both a business and private nature. Local journeys, methods of transport. Brothers and sisters, neighbours, colleagues, sometimes nephews, nieces and friends. Business matters related to buying and selling. Education, training and retraining, foreign languages. Some sports and games. The way you think.

FOURTH HOUSE

Angular
Similar to Cancer
Ruled by the Moon

The home, property and premises of all kinds. Small businesses. Domestic life, roots and background, the basis from which you grew up into adulthood. The mother or any other person of either sex who nurtured you while you were young. The beginning and ending of life, also how you are viewed after your death. Your attitude towards family commitments. Security.

FIFTH HOUSE

Succedent
Similar to Leo
Ruled by the Sun

Children, young people and their education, even pregnancy. Fun, holidays and leisure pursuits of all kinds. Games of chance, sports, dancing, singing, writing, entertainments and any aspirations to glamour or showbusiness. Creativity and personal projects, even a business of one's own, as long as it offers the possibility of making a personal statement. Also publication, politics and social life – especially if it is influential. Traditional and religious attitudes. Most of all, this house involves *lovers and love affairs*.

SIXTH HOUSE

Cadent
Similar to Virgo
Ruled by Mercury

Duties and day to day service to others, usually related to work but includes those taking place in the home. Employers and employees, superiors and subordinates. Everything related to health, doctors, hospitals and hygiene. This could apply to the types of health problems you will encounter yourself or among your family. Your clothes and how you wear them. Details and analytical methods, meticulous work, analytical thinking and even changes in your way of thinking. Aunts and uncles. Healthy eating habits. Food and nutrition.

SEVENTH HOUSE

Angular
Similar to Libra
Ruled by Venus

Open partnerships and relationships, husband, wife, live-in lover. Open enemies. The giving and receiving of co-operation. Colleagues one is closely involved with, business partners. Work in a glamorous or attractive field. Creative and artistic endeavours which are done in partnership or a small group. Attraction to places, things and people, therefore, to some extent even sexual attitudes and exploration. The kind of person one looks for to work or live alongside who fill in the gaps in your character. To some extent documents related to partnerships are indicated here. Land, farming and gardening involving co-operation with others.

EIGHTH HOUSE

Succedent
Similar to Scorpio
Ruled by Pluto and Mars

Beginnings and endings. Birth and death. Sexual matters. Money which involves other people e.g. spouse's income, mortgages; taxes, wills, legacies, banking and insurance. Above all partner's assets or lack of them. Shared feelings, feedback of other people's feelings (especially if they are intense). Crime and investigations and the police. Surgeons and surgery, also some illnesses. Hidden assets, secrets. The occult. A sense of commitment to anything or anyone. The things we really need from other people. The ability to regenerate or recycle anything.

NINTH HOUSE

Cadent
Similar to Sagittarius
Ruled by Jupiter

Expansion of one's horizons e.g. travel, higher education, new environments. Foreigners, foreign goods and foreign dealings. Legal matters, important legal documents and court cases. Religious and mystical matters, including the philosophical and spiritual side of psychic matters. On the one hand science and on the other hand intuition, dreams and visions. The church and the clergy. Sports and games which are taken fairly seriously. Outdoor pursuits. Gambling (especially on horses). Interest in or work with large animals. Need for personal freedom. Teaching and learning of a high standard also ethics and some aspects of public and political opinion. In-laws and grandchildren.

TENTH HOUSE

Angular
Similar to Capricorn
Ruled by Saturn

Aims and aspirations, your goal in life, your professional reputation and standing in the community. This may represent one's career, but also political ambitions, creative aspirations and future success; or lack of it. The ego and its chances of being satisfied. Your employer if you work for a large organization. Authority figures of all kinds including governmental and public authorities. Achievements, fame and personal promotion. The organization of the church or any large organization. The parents, especially father, or father figures. Status, your standing in the world. Responsibilities and visible commitments. Self-promotion.

ELEVENTH HOUSE

Succedent
Similar to Aquarius
Ruled by Uranus and Saturn

Social life, friends and capacity for friendship, clubs and societies. Detached relationships but also love received, even the affection of friends. Intellectual pursuits and hobbies. Hopes, wishes, desires and goals and the chances of achieving them. Conversation, learning for pleasure. Teaching and learning of the usual kind, also instruction at work, political or philosophical training of a specialized kind. Money from one's job, especially if there has been training involved. Eccentricities, unexpected changes and circumstances. Step-children and adopted children.

Cadent
Similar to Pisces
Ruled by Neptune and Jupiter

One's inner thoughts and feelings also secrets and secret worries. Suffering, sorrows, limitations, frustration and handicaps. This house can show whether you are your own worst enemy or not, it also shows inner resources and inner weaknesses or anything which is too painful to face up to. Hidden talents, hidden thoughts, hidden love, hidden angers.

Also inhibitions, restraints, secret enemies and hidden danger. Any association with hospitals, mental institutions, prisons and other places of confinement, even exile. Any tendency to escapism, or things that we seek to hide from others. Your subconscious mind, plus karmic or spiritual debts. Self-sacrifice, love and help freely given (and possibly received). Also public charity and kindness given and received. Inspiration and insights. Illusions, meditations and daydreams. Hidden friends and enemies. Here is where one could reach the stars - or mess one's life up completely.

If you use the equal house system of chart division, the Moon, of course, will take two-and-a-half years to traverse a house. In all other methods of house division, the periods of time can vary enormously. I usually use the Placidus system, occasionally the topocentric system but if I have to 'slap' a chart together at speed, I still fall back on the equal house system.

The Moon Through the Houses

The Moon in the Astrological Houses

The houses are as interesting as the signs although their impact on a birthchart is different. The signs show *what you are* while the houses show *what you do*. In this section we will look at the Moon in each house position, look a little more closely at the areas of life which each house position represents. For the movement of the Moon through the houses, see the chapters on the progressed Moon.

Moon in the first house

You love your home and family and would not be happy to live alone. Your nature may appear quiet and introverted but you have an inner desire to be recognized as a person in your own right. You will do much to help others but you're not prepared to make too many sacrifices on their behalf. Your mother was a strong influence on you and may indeed have been an exceptional woman in *her* own right; you could even find yourself walking in her shadow. The sea calls you so strongly that you may choose to live and work on it. You may be physically restless, finding it hard to sit still, alternatively you could have a love of travel, preferably with your family along for the ride. You may be drawn to hobbies or even work in the field of food and nutrition and could be a vegetarian possibly due to your love of animals. It comes naturally to you to support the underdog wherever you can. This placement suggests a need to work for the public in some way, either before them as some kind of celebrity or, more likely in Some kind of humanitarian or welfare capacity. Being finely tuned in to your own body you usually know if you are going down with some illness. You must try not to allow your moods to dominate your personality.

Moon in the second house (accidental exaltation)

Material matters are important to you and you seem to need the security of money and possessions. There is a suggestion that these may be hard to obtain or to keep hold of in some way. Your need for security may result from a materially or emotionally deprived childhood. There is a shrewd and slightly calculating business head on your shoulders but your pleasant approach to others hides this well. Women will be involved in your personal finances in some way and you could be helped by women, possibly by inheritance or through family connections. You will probably take an interest in Taurean pursuits such as cooking, dancing, building, music, the arts, gardening and the creation of beauty.

Moon in the third house

The Moon here shows the need to communicate which could lead you towards a career in travel, the media or education. You are restless and curious but possibly lacking in concentration and easily bored. You pick up knowledge casually from others as you go through life. Your parents might be clever and bookish. Throughout life you will keep learning and then passing on information to others. You have a natural affinity to the telephone and also to vehicles which may, to others, look like an obsession.

Moon in the fourth house (accidental dignity)

This is the natural house of the Moon due to its association with the sign of Cancer which is ruled by the Moon. You prefer to work at home or at least to do your own thing, preferably in your own business. You may be nervous of the big wide world and have a habit of scuttling back home when the going gets rough. You are sympathetic towards those who are weak and helpless and are especially fond of animals. You could be strongly attached to your parents or on the other hand, separated from them by circumstances beyond your control. It is possible that you lack confidence or feel insecure as an adult due to childhood problems, you need love and affection and should try to avoid hurting yourself further by forming relationships with destructive types. The past attracts you and this might lead you to work in the field of antiques or to be a collector of old and valuable objects. You may have a strong urge to live on or near the sea.

Moon in the fifth house

You are attracted to the world of children which might draw you to work as an infant school teacher or become involved with young people's sporting activities. Your emotions are strong and you seek fulfilment on both a practical and a romantic level in relationships. You could have a number of affairs if marriage does not work out for you. You have a good deal of charm and attractive youthful appearance which is useful to you as you would take naturally to a rather public type of career such as the theatre or in marketing and public relations. Be careful not to be too clinging towards your children. A creative outlet is an emotional necessity for you. You would make a good teacher, writer or publisher.

Moon in the sixth house

You have a strong urge to serve the needs of others and may work in some kind of caring profession, especially medicine. You could be drawn to a career which involves the production of food and anything which helps the public to stay in good health. Your career will have to appeal to you on an emotional level and you could even walk out of a job if the atmosphere or the people there didn't suit you. You may be restless and better suited to having a couple of part-time jobs rather than one full-time one. You have consideration for others and would yourself be a rather maternal employer.

Moon in the seventh house

You get on with most people because you need company and companionship. Where relationships are concerned, you will bend over backwards to make them work but it may be at quite a price. There is a feeling that while young you are not quite sure who you are and you may feel the need to have your personality and even your opinions validated by others. You prefer to work in co-operation with a partner or in a small group and you may be drawn to work in some kind of caring job like personnel management. You are politically-minded and also have a good grasp of office politics. Glamour appeals to you drawing you towards the world of fashion and music and this could become part of an interesting hobby for you. Your partner may be moody and difficult, but it is possible that *you* could understand him or her where others just don't.

Moon in the eighth house

Women will be instrumental in helping you to gain money or prestige in some way. You could work in trades which cater to women's needs or work mainly among women. You have an interest in psychic matters and you will be drawn to the mediumistic and spiritual side of these things. Your clairvoyance could be prodigious but it will depend upon other factors on the chart as to how this is directed. There is a feeling that love, affection, sensuality and sex are important factors in your chart and you could have your greatest successes in life in partnership with someone who inspires you both mentally and sexually. You can be devious, hurtful and destructive, even to the point of destroying your career or your future chances of success if you feel thwarted. Strange position this, as both the Moon and the house are so involved with instinctive and reactive behaviour.

Moon in the ninth house

Religion and philosophy will be an important part of your life and you will have to go on some kind of inward journey in order to find your way forward. You think deeply and will turn to a consideration of the deeper things of life. You are a natural psychic with the ability to see and feel beyond the boundaries of this Earth. Travel will be an important part of your life as will any dealings with foreigners or foreign goods. You could be a roamer who never really touches down for long anywhere; however, you are a natural teacher and instructor of others with a clear view of how to do things. You could find yourself attached to slightly crazy people.

Moon in the tenth house (accidental detriment)

This gives you an inner urge to shine before the public in some way, or to help humanity on a grand scale. There is evidence of an emotionally impoverished childhood during which something went strangely wrong. Your parents (especially your mother) could have been super-achievers whom you seek to emulate. You will change jobs a few times until you find the right road for you. My feelings are that that road will be intensely personal leading to a good deal of acclaim – or even, if the Moon is badly aspected, public scandal and ruin. You are drawn to a career which seeks to supply the needs of women or which is traditionally carried out by women. Sales, marketing, domestic goods and women's literature are a few possibilities. Your standing in the community, especially your career standing, is of paramount importance to you and even to others who are around you. You will be known and remembered by many before your life is done. To some extent this is a compensation for feelings of insecurity deriving from your difficult childhood, and a somewhat arid personal life, but just keep telling yourself that you will one day make it and, somehow you will find the strength to carry on.

Moon in the eleventh house

You enjoy the company of others and could be heavily involved in some kind of club or society. Being extremely independent, you hate to be told what to do. Your family are sometimes left in the dark as to your plans and feelings but there is a possibility that you, yourself may find it hard to know what you really *do* feel at times. Your aims in life may change dramatically from time to time due to circumstances. Friends, especially female ones, are very helpful to you, and you have a strange kind of luck that brings them running to you in times of trouble. You are well organized and able to manage others, but you can on occasion misjudge people and be taken advantage of by more astute and crafty types.

Moon in the twelfth house

You seek to hide away from the world from time to time and to work in seclusion. Certainly you are happiest doing your own thing and working from your own home. Women will be an important part of any achievement, while men tend to interfere with your life, particularly with your career. You need to get away from time to time to recharge your batteries, too much stress will make you ill. You could be very creative as you have a rich imagination. Your instinctive need to care for others may lead you to work in the field of nursing or with animals. You may be too ready to sacrifice yourself for others. There is a secret side to your life; you may have to keep the secrets of others.

10

Introduction to the Progressed Moon

The Progressed Moon

The techniques involved in predictive astrology are complicated to learn and to apply and one really needs to have a good grasp of natal charting before embarking on this. However it is a relatively easy matter to progress the Moon and this will give you some idea of the trends during the coming year. All you have to do is work out how old you are and add as many days as there are years in your age to the date of your birth. Therefore, if you are now twenty-five years old, add twenty-five days to your date of birth. If you are forty-three years old, add forty-three days to your date of birth. Then look up the tables to find the new (progressed) Moon position.

If this looks too difficult for you to do, there are various ways around this. Firstly, if you know a friendly astrologer or someone who runs a computer chart service, you can ask them for help, it wouldn't take them more than a few moments to give you the answer. Secondly, any magazine or other publication which deals with astrology and the occult will be able to help, they might offer a chart service and certainly would have people advertising such a service to the public. As long as you only require data, the costs will be minimal. It is only when you ask for chart interpretations that the costs begin to mount.

When you have established the position of the Moon for the year in question, (that is between your last birthday and the next one) look up the progressed Moon information to see what kind of year you are going to have. If you have sufficient astrological knowledge to know what house your progressed Moon is traversing, then use the house information in conjunction with the relevant sign information. Both the house position and the sign position will apply to you in one way or another. Remember, the *sign* will show the kind of mood or circumstances surrounding you, the *house* will show how you apply yourself and to what ends. For those of you who are really deep into astrology, the progressed data can also be used for lunar transits. These only apply for two-and-a-half days at a time through each sign but can be significant when other events are gathering momentum on a birthchart. An eclipsed Moon, for example, transiting a sore spot on your natal chart can be an unbelievable experience!

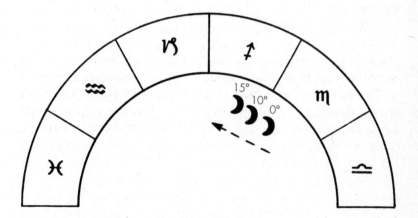

Fig 10.1
THE PROGRESSED MOON

11

Your Progressed Moon by Sign

Progressed Moon in Aries or in the First House ♈

Aries and the first house is symbolically associated with birth, therefore, with all that is new and fresh. When this progression is in operation you will find that your emotions seem to take on a life of their own, you feel more passionate in every way and even the most placid among you will become excited and enthusiastic about everyone and everything. Being more moody than usual, you could find yourself involved in a series of family arguments, in fact, your home could become something of a battle-ground which suddenly starts to resemble a nest full of egomaniacs. There will be problems with regard to your mother or other older females in the family and you will have to take extra responsibility for them in some way.

Your energy level is high and you are ready to take advantage of the new opportunities which will begin to present themselves to you now. Even without your intervention, you will find that events move themselves extremely quickly. This is the time when you could find yourself a new and more challenging job or even make a start in a business of your own. You will take chances with your money and may borrow money without thinking too deeply about how you will be able to pay it back.

The Moon in astrology often refers to the home, therefore, you may move house, relocate yourself in another part of the country, or even move right out of the country to spend a few years in another part of the world. There will be new family groupings resulting from marriage, childbirth or divorce, and if you have been sitting in a marriage which has long been worn out, this is the time you will find the courage to do something about leaving. All the familiar patterns of your life will be changing quickly now, both of their own volition and with your help.

You will be able to tackle these new beginnings with a growing confidence in yourself. If you have been assessing your potential and making plans while the Moon was in Pisces or in the twelfth house, you will put those plans into action now. You have to guard against losing your temper in the wrong place at this time. Also guard against letting all the new contacts which you are making now go to waste, or allowing your new enthusiasms to fizzle out. Short-term projects will suit you better than long-term ones but you will need to find a way of expressing yourself and of doing your 'own thing' rather than just following other people's leads.

You may realize that your moods are more changeable and your behaviour more impulsive. The Moon, of course, rules the emotional response, therefore, while it travels through Aries or the first house, the Moon's power will be at a peak. Women may be able to blame their sudden attacks of over-sensitiveness on an increase of pre-menstrual tension, men will have to look for another excuse! You may eat and drink more in order to cope with your extra energies; there is a feeling of Arian greediness for all that life has to offer.

The lunar influence could bring you into a closer connection with the sea or with work which involves liquids, there could also be an interest in mechanical and engineering projects. Women will feature in your life now and may inspire you or encourage you to reach for the stars.

Women who have spent years as housewives may go back to work under this influence; on the other hand those women who view the start of a family as a goal will choose to have their first child now. The general feeling is that you will be taking the initiative, finding new methods and forging ahead with your life. Many of you will make an effort to identify and then to satisfy your own needs rather than only those of others for a change.

Your sexual energies will increase and you may change your outlook and your requirements with regard to sex under this influence. If you meet a new love there will be a strong chemistry between you. If there is a child conceived at this time, it should by all astrological theories, be a boy. Another unproven astrological possibility is that Aries-type people may figure strongly in your life at this time.

Remember the essence of this year is to get you moving and to make a fresh start.

Progressed Moon in Taurus
or in the Second House ♉

When the Moon moves into Taurus or the second house your emotions become more settled and comfortable. The projects which were begun in a blaze of enthusiasm while the Moon was in Aries or the first house, should be well under way by now. This is a time of consolidation in all things and of steady and controlled growth.

Material matters move to the top of your priority list now, your attention will be firmly focused upon your personal income and your financial base. This would be a good time to buy a decent property especially if it has a garden as there is a need for you to be seen as a 'man of property'. If you are not buying a new property, you might refurbish the one you're living in. If you have been in the habit of living for the moment you will begin to think ahead, you will no longer allow your credit card debts to get longer and larger. You will be reluctant to lend your money to just anybody, only making loans to those whom you can trust to pay you back in a prompt and orderly manner. If you are challenged about your newly materialistic attitude you will become defensive and awkward whilst at the same time demanding a ten per cent discount! You feel instinctively that this is a good time to put personal savings schemes into operation but a bad time to risk money on nebulous or speculative ventures.

If you buy anything expensive it must be durable, the same goes for projects which are started at this time. Whenever the Moon is travelling through an earth sign, the prospects are good for long-term projects. Goods, especially luxurious or artistic ones which are bought at this time, will increase in value and business transactions will be carried out in a spirit of pragmatism rather than of overexcited speculation. You will find yourself dealing more with women now and they could become an important part of your financial or working life. There is a danger that there could be too much emphasis on materialism at the expense of other aspects of your life.

This is a good time to form durable business partnerships, especially with women. You could soon find yourself signing leases on premises or land related to your work and there will be a strong connection with people in the building trades.

Emotional partnerships may be formed now but they will not have the explosive chemistry of a meeting when the Moon is in Aries or the first house. Relationships which have been recently formed will become deeper and more reliable, new ones will be based on emotional and possibly also financial security. Your sexual drive will be strong and all your senses will be heightened as Taurus and the second house are so sensual in character. You will be far less changeable emotionally and will be possibly less inclined towards sexual experimentation now; this is a time to settle down in relationships rather than to go on voyages of exploration. Be careful not to become too set in your ways, you don't want to bore your partner to death. You will set the patterns for your future life now, certainly you will be reappraising your values and priorities. If you form a new relationship, your partner will be attractive, quiet and reliable.

You might find yourself involved with the production of food, certainly you will have to do more shopping. This will be a highly developmental time for all artistic or musical interests and you could learn to appreciate art, dancing or music for the first time. All in all, this should be a peaceful and settled period which you can relax into and enjoy.

Remember the essence of a Taurean progression is both literally and metaphorically, to build and consolidate.

Progressed Moon in Gemini
or in the third House ♊

This is going to be a very busy and rather restless year for you. You will be moving around your neighbourhood more than before and if you haven't learned to drive, this is the time to do so because you are going to need the freedom of your own transport. This will also be a year for mental exploration and you could take courses at your local college or at evening classes. The best subjects might be connected with language, communication or computer studies. All studies, whether they are taken for a specific purpose or just for fun will be successful and you shouldn't have much trouble in passing examinations now. You may need to give more attention to your children's education now or to their out-of-school hobbies and interests.

You need all your communication skills now as your work will involve you in activities such as typing, telephone and customer liaison, probably also selling and advertising. There will be more than the usual amount of meetings and discussions with colleagues and there could be some kind of brochure or catalogue to be made up. You will travel around visiting different departments at your place of work and you will deal directly with clients both at your location or at theirs. You might take a series of temporary jobs or travel around your area carrying your skills with you. This will be an especially interesting time in your life as you will be meeting new people and will begin to become known outside your immediate circle. One instance could be that of a youngster taking a job delivering newspapers or groceries on a bicycle for a local firm.

You will have more dealings with neighbours and also with local issues. Although you might want to redecorate or otherwise change the appearance of your home and your garden, this would not be a particularly good time to make major changes or to make a move of house. There will be more visitors to your home than is normal and you will also spend more time visiting friends and family. Party-plan selling with friends and neighbours is a possibility. Gossip and trivial conversations on the phone are all an important part of your life now and you might find other people affecting your thinking in some fairly profound way.

Your own thought processes are more intuitive and instinctive than is usual for you, and in some cases you could find yourself feeling more nervous and jumpy; however when you focus your mind on work or on studies your concentration level will be good. There will be letters and parcels to be sent in the post, also possible are hire-purchase agreements and other minor documents to be signed. There will be more than the usual amount of dealings with females, it is possible that products or services which cater to female requirements or capture the imagination of women could be important in some way. You will be involved with mechanical and inventive ideas and will have to learn new methods, your dexterity will increase now. If you have been away from work for some time, you will return now.

This is not a particularly romantic time but if you do become involved with someone new, you will find that conversation and greater understanding are the keynotes to the relationship. If you are experimenting socially or sexually at this time it would be best if you didn't commit yourself too firmly to one person as your heart will be a little fickle. Romance will involve outings to restaurants, theatres and other local events, even to sporting events. You should become involved in some kind of sport or hobby now and this could give you an outlet which will help you to contend with your restlessness and also heighten your tendency to over-analyse and intellectualize your feelings.

The essence of this progression is education and communication.

Progressed Moon in Cancer
or in the Fourth House ♋

The Moon rules the sign of Cancer, therefore when it travels through this sign or through the fourth house, one's lunar characteristics will make themselves strongly felt. This may on the one hand make you more moody, emotional and 'Cancerian' or it may emphasize your own natal lunar position. Regardless of your basic nature and outlook on life, you will act and react in a far more emotional manner and will become more interested in the private and personal aspects of your life.

Your home circumstances are going to play a major part in your life this year; which may include a move of house, building work to be done, decorating or buying new furniture and fittings. The definite domestic slant to this progression will temporarily anchor you firmly to your home and family. You will take on more responsibility for relatives, this could be a source of irritation or a great comfort to you depending, of course, on the prevailing circumstances. There will be more dealings with your mother, also other female friends and relatives, especially those who are older than yourself. Feelings of family loyalty will strengthen, and you might spend some time researching your family's history and background. There will be a need to identify with a specific group on the basis of family, race, religion or nationality and you will experience some kind of patriotic or group identity.

You may need to retreat from the outside world and to sink back into comfort and security, having little desire to meet new people and preferring to stay close to reliable old friends. You will want some novelty in your life, but this will come in the form of new domestic interests or learning how to use new gadgets in and around the house. You could work from home at this time or even start a small business from your own back room. The sign of Cancer is associated with shops, therefore you may take a job in one or even open a shop of your own. Whatever sex you are, you will be more concerned with day to day chores and the reason for this could range from retirement to setting up a family. Antiques are associated with the sign of Cancer, also history and genealogy, therefore you could find yourself delving into the past for a while or even searching for your roots. You will be over-sensitive, especially over family issues and you could even become unaccountably possessive towards those around you. You may feel alienated, neglected and superfluous, your moods could vacillate between wanting to be alone and fearing loneliness. Never mind, this will change soon enough when the Moon progresses into Leo or the fifth. Friends could cling to you now, or you could cling to them; old friends that you haven't seen for years could suddenly come back into your life now. Some of you could start to work with liquids. The sea could prove to be a pull, urging you to live and work on or near it. Travel on or over water will be especially pleasant at this time.

Cancerian-type people may influence you at this time and, due to the active femininity of the sign, a child conceived now should, by all accounts, be female.

This time is a time of gradual change where you spend time looking inside yourself and revising your needs and attitudes. Old habits could now be seen as being inappropriate to your present and future way of life.

The essence of this period is to set up or continue to care for a family, to keep your feelings hidden and to deal more frequently with women.

Progressed Moon in Leo or in the Fifth House ♌

During this progression you will be dealing with children and young people. This is often the time when a mother is at the height of her involvement with a growing family. Whoever you are, you will enjoy a more youthful attitude possibly joining in sporting activities and youthful pastimes. The sign of Leo (and the fifth house) is concerned with creativity, therefore you will embark upon projects which are close to your heart. You should develop the ideas and the determination at this time to make something of yourself and to create something which will stand the test of time, but you might have to wait until the Moon progresses into Virgo before you gain the ability to focus your attention and to get on with the job.

Travel will be important now but it might prove something of a trial to you as you may, for instance, have to cart restless and difficult children around with you. Another possibility is that of business travel; this is far harder and less glamorous than it sounds as it is difficult to conduct important negotiations with jet lag and the inevitable touch of Montezuma's revenge.

There might be some connection with work in a glamorous field; indeed you may join some branch of show business. You might take up attractive or amusing hobbies now, skating and dancing are possibilities, also light and interesting sports. This is a good time to give attention to your personal appearance, to keep your figure trim and be prepared to go out and knock 'em in the aisles because it is going to be important for you to look good. This may be the time when you emerge from your shell and find yourself in the limelight; it is even possible that after years of being held back you find yourself breaking out with a vengeance. You may even become the stronger partner in a relationship after years of having been kept down. This is definitely not going to be the time to keep your light under a bushel but to discover the power of your own personality and to enjoy expressing it.

Your feelings will rise to the surface and will be hard to hide and they may even be difficult to control. All your relationships and friendships will be re-evaluated and some changes may be made soon. You could become more aware of and more wrapped up with your own feelings. Sexual feelings will also be high and there might be an affair of the heart (or body) now. None of this may last too long but you will learn a lot about yourself, other people and life generally. You may sometimes appear to be wasting time and energy on frivolities, but this will all be part of the learning process.

The sign of Leo (and the fifth house) is associated with children and you will find yourself dealing with and enjoying the company of children. You might help out the local boy scouts or girl guides, become involved in the activities of the local dancing school or in some other way find yourself in charge of children. You may start your own family now or you may find yourself responsible for someone else's children. All dealings with women will be good, your mood will be generous and happy a good deal of the time and you might gamble a little, either literally or figuratively as this *can* be a time of great gains, but also there may be surprising losses.

All in all this is a time to laugh and enjoy life, also to take a few chances.

Progressed Moon in Virgo or in the Sixth House ♍

Work will be important to you now and you could find that either your normal job becomes more interesting or that you begin to do something new and highly satisfying. You will have to cope with paperwork, bookkeeping, correspondence and record-keeping; computers and word processors might become an important feature of your life now. You will perform precise and delicate tasks whilst analysing and checking your own work carefully; these jobs could include do-it-yourself work, home dress-making or gardening. You might take a course at your local evening classes. If you do take lessons, these would be in useful and practical subjects such as car maintenance or cookery. Whoever you are, you will be dealing with household chores and, if you are not skilled at these types of job, you will soon learn the ropes. If gardening becomes important now, you will con-centrate on producing fruit and vegetables.

You will fall into a sensible routine of work this year and may find yourself following a strict set of directions. This is the time to establish good work habits and you will find reliable and efficient colleagues to work alongside at this time. Women may pose problems on the one hand but they can turn out to be of great benefit as well, perhaps one group of women will give you trouble while another will help enormously. All this talk of duty and effort may seem a bit dull, but the resulting rewards will make it all worthwhile. This is not, strictly speaking, a great time for creative pursuits but writing would work out well, especially if it involves specialized research and analysis.

You may become involved with hospitals now, either because you yourself need treatment or people close to you may be sick. It is possible that you could work in a hospital at this time, but either way, you will take more notice of your own state of health and will try to improve it in any way that you can. You will concentrate on your diet and appearance and could even go a bit overboard by becoming too clean and tidy or by devel-opoing hypochondria. There will be some irritating nervous ailments to put up with which, although not dangerous, could make life difficult at times.

Your behaviour under this progression might irritate others as you will try to over-rationalize or over-analyse everything. You must guard against playing the martyr, taking on unnecessary chores and then moaning to everyone about this. Guilty feelings will plague you even though you really have nothing to feel guilty about. You must make time to rest and enjoy life because you will be ill if you don't.

This is hardly the best progression for romance but it is possible that you could meet someone special through your work. Relationships which are formed under this progression should be steady and relatively trouble free, if rather dull. On a brighter note, this is a great time to buy new clothes, perhaps this is a consolation prize result of all that hard work.

All in all this is the year where you should get the work done and attend to all those little details.

Progressed Moon in Libra
or in the Seventh House ♎

Partnerships and relationships are going to be of paramount importance to you this year. Whether you are at the dating stage or even contemplating the end of your present partnerships, new relationships made will have an air of freshness and a strangely experimental feel about them. It appears that you will be searching around for the right person rather than making a serious commitment. This doesn't mean that you *won't* settle down with your current date, just that you need to keep your options open now. Not all your relationships will be pleasant as there could be some major confrontations especially with women at this time. The seventh house (and the sign of Libra) are supposed to represent one's first marriage, but I have found this progression to be more concerned with forming and breaking relationships, *including* one's first marriage, rather than settling down for life.

Your emotions will be strong at this time which will cause you to over-react; you will find it particularly hard to be detached and objective. You may require both security and freedom at the same time, wanting your partner to be faithful while you yourself slip off the leash. Hooray for the old double standard! There will be an element of sexual exploration and experimentation too.

You should become drawn into the world of business now, and if you have no business knowledge, you will have to acquire it quickly. The communications side of business will be important, and you will need to keep in touch with current ideas and methods. Although you will not necessarily be directly responsible for the sale of goods and services, you will have to deal with the marketing aspect of sales, which means finding ways to advertise and to present your organization's image in an attractive and modern manner. There will be a good deal of interaction with other business people and also with the general public. Libra is a cardinal sign (the seventh house is a cardinal house) therefore, you will be much more decisive and dynamic now than ever before. You will have to present yourself in a stylish way in front of others, therefore your appearance and manner of dress will become more modern and interesting now.

In your career as in relationships, there will be interesting new beginnings and new working relationships with inspiring and dynamic people. You will spend far more time in cities than in the countryside but you will probably see something of the countryside as you travel through it on business. Your self-esteem will take a few knocks, mainly due to the fact that you will be working in an unfamiliar field and you will inevitably make errors.

There is some evidence that you will find yourself being manipulated in some way and this, when you discover what is going on, could lead you to react angrily or in an uncharacteristically thoughtless manner. In the areas of both your work and in your domestic life you could find that your finances and your financial decisions are inevitably wrapped up with your emotions.

The essence of this progression is that you will experiment with new people, methods and ideas which will lead to some kind of change and renewal of your partnership situation.

Progressed Moon in Scorpio or in the Eighth House ♏

This is where you will reach out and make the changes which will set the pattern of your life for many years to come. If you have been experimenting with friendships and relationships during the past couple of years, you may settle into marriage now; on the other hand, if you have been travelling towards a potential divorce, this is when you might bring it about. There will be major beginnings and endings which might include setting up a home or dismantling one. You could start a family now or, equally possibly, find yourself at the stage when your children are growing into adults in their own right. Your children may soon start their own families, or there may be births around you in other branches of your family or among your friends. Unfortunately, a time of births is also, astrologically speaking, a time of deaths and there could well be a funeral or two to attend.

You will either make a fresh commitment to your present job or make a change for one which will stand you in good stead in the future. A young woman for example, may give up work for a couple of years in order to stay at home with children. Whichever way this progression works for you it will mean transformation, rebirth and a redefinition of your goals both within and outside the home. You may become interested in conservation, especially re-cycling of used objects, certainly you will be spending money on your surroundings now.

Work changes could take you into the farming or food production industries; another possibility is some kind of professional contact with the police, private detectives or hospitals. Health or legal matters might enter your private life too. You will be more aware of the mystical and psychic elements of life and you might have some kind of psychic experience, possibly for the first time in your life. This progression will make your intuition and hunches strong and you might even go as far as to develop mediumistic qualities.

Financial matters which involve other people's money will become important now also their attitude to financial matters. This could include alimony, legacies, mortgages, taxes, joint accounts and business finances. You must guard against too great an emotional response to legal and financial matters. Joint properties and joint possessions can be sorted out at this time, but you must guard against feelings of greed and covetousness. There may be family or business wrangles, especially over property. These problems would be typical of a divorce situation, the ending of a business partnership or as a result of a death in the family. The structure of your life will be transformed in some way.

Some activities will be deeply satisfying and these could fulfil a variety of instinctual needs. These could include almost anything that makes you happy but I would have to put sex pretty high on the list plus, perhaps, settling into a happy home or a more comfortable way of life. New habits will be formed, probably resulting from a new understanding of your inner needs. Your instinctive side will overshadow your logical mind and you could experience an almost compulsive pursuit of your objectives.

There are some mighty awful problems which could emerge under this progression, the intensity of your intense feelings could spill over into jealousy and passion of a particularly lustful or obsessive kind. You could become trapped or manipulated into a situation which under normal circumstances you would avoid, or conversely, you may seek to possess or manipulate another. The abnormal over-emotional response will take some living with and could cause you to act in a manner which is totally out of character. This would be the right time to delve into the bottom of a long-standing mess and finally sort out the reasons for it, even if it means bringing a few skeletons out of the cupboard. You might feel as if you are in an emotional killing field now but you will emerge at the end of it as if reborn, salvaged from destruction.

Progressed Moon in Sagittarius
or in the Ninth House ♐

The key notion behind this progression is the expansion of your personal horizons. You might travel overseas for the first time or you could take the time to really investigate a particular part of the world which you have always fancied knowing better. Your work could take you away and you might enter into a business venture which involves overseas goods, services or property. You may have to sell to foreigners, thereby learning about them and their way of living. Your family may move to another country or there may be people entering the family who are themselves from a different cultural background and this could be the cause of some of your long distance journeys. Some of you will fall in love with a person who comes from a different country or a different cultural background now and this may cause you to review your own religious or philosophical outlook.

You may be subjected to economic or cultural changes in conditions around you which would affect your private or your business life. There is even a chance that you will have to deal with people whose views are biased or even bigoted regarding race and religion.

There might be increased dealings with institutions such as schools, colleges and churches either personally or as a matter of business. You could go back into training or just study for fun at this time. The subjects which you choose will be of a philosophical or mind-broadening type rather than of a purely practical nature; however, you may learn a foreign language as a means of meeting a larger range of interesting people or in order to progress in your career. You will find ways to overcome mental stagnation and boredom at this time. School connections may take you into teaching or training others and you may have to give lectures on a special subject. Another career possibility is in the realm of publishing; certainly you could be writing brochures or trade journals for your company and having them printed now. There is a feeling that the end of a phase in your working life is on the way now and you could finish this progression with a determination to do something quite different. This may be a high point, a culmination of all that you have worked for, alternatively, you may reach the bottom of a pit of unhappiness with regard to your work and decide to change direction for good and all.

You should be able to enjoy life and have some fun. The chances are that you will become enthusiastic about a number of new ideas, hobbies and pastimes; sports could be high on the list. There will be more chance for you to get out into the fresh air, and you may become interested in the world of large animals, especially horses. Gambling on horses is a possibility, or just taking a chance or two on life. This should be a time of increased fun and a sense of adventure. Your level of confidence will be high, maybe too high, but this might just begin to wane as the progression moves towards the cusp of the tenth house.

Sometimes there is an increase of activity concerning legal matters under this progression, but it is usually the tail end of outstanding problems rather than new ones rearing their heads. This may be a detail or two which is still hanging on from a recent divorce settlement, or some kind of family or business matter that has still to be put to rest.

Sagittarius and the ninth house is concerned with second marriages, therefore this may be the time when you meet a second partner or when you decide to marry for the second time.

To sum this progression up, this is when you can expect to expand your life (plus your waistline if you're not careful), move onwards and outwards mentally and physically, also to forget some of your cares and worries and enjoy yourself.

Progressed Moon in Capricorn or in the Tenth House ♑

This is a time of hard work but also of ultimate achievement. This progression may start with a monumental set-back in your life or just a feeling that you cannot go on any longer in the same old way. The chances are that the frustrations and the problems which are affecting your working life will spill over into your personal life as well. You will receive a great deal of useful help from others at work now. Some of those who help you may be in positions of seniority or they may be equipped with some kind of specialized knowledge which they are willing to pass on to you. If you are selling a product or a service, buyers will be more receptive now; one interesting point is that women are likely to be particularly helpful to you.

Business methods will be important even if your work is not strictly in the business world. If you are not used to working in a structured organization, you will learn how to do so; alternatively, you might go from one sort of structure to a completely different one which runs by a different set of rules. It is important that you be honest in all your dealings whether they be in your working or your private life and you should, with luck, be among people who themselves are honest. You will need to be seen as being respectable both in your public and family life as this is a time when secrets and deceptions might emerge in an uncomfortably embarrassing way.

Your work will bring you into contact with the public and you will perform services for people both individually and in large groups. You will need to dress the part of a successful and competent person as both you and your work will be highly visible at this time. Sales and promotional work will be important and you will have to make public appearances, possibly even give lectures or make speeches from time to time.

Colleagues will be more sympathetic to your aims than before and you, in turn, will be more responsive to the needs of others. It is possible that you could be temporarily short of money, maybe because you are investing fairly heavily in a project or because your job offers training and future possibilities rather than present financial rewards.

You will take a sensitive attitude towards those you work with and will be careful not to tread on their egos. There will be responsibility now attached to the work which you do and you may well also be responsible for the efforts of others. This is the time to build a team of juniors or a sensible framework of method and experience which will follow you into the future. Delays and set-backs in your career will be followed by success, good will come out of bad. Your work will need a conventional attitude and old-fashioned skills and there will be the need for a structured and practical outlook. You may find yourself reviving the spirits of a flagging company or institution, which will require you to be responsive to the moods and feelings of groups around you, possibly in the form of union negotiations. Time-keeping will be important, either in the form of working hours or of timetables of one sort or another.

Your professional and personal relationships may become a bit blurred as you could turn towards someone who you work closely with or alternatively, you could begin a work project with someone you love. This is not, truthfully speaking, a romantic time; your feelings may be dampened or you may be forced to keep them on a tight rein. However, if you do meet someone, it is likely that this will happen through your work.

In personal relationships you will be shyer than usual and also very slow to commit yourself. There may be some strangely public displays of emotion either directed towards you or coming from you. Angry scenes could take place where others can see and hear or feelings of loving and caring which you have been keeping dark might also emerge in a somewhat public manner. Domestic life will have to take a back seat now but the work which you are doing will go to make the domestic scene nicer and more comfortable later on.

The basic feeling of this progression is that this is your time for career advancement and a redefinition of aims and goals.

Progressed Moon in Aquarius or in the Eleventh House ≈≈

This is a time when friends will be extremely important to you, you will have to rely on them to help you and you will in turn, be a good friend to others. There will be an involvement with clubs and societies of one kind or another and you will definitely feel the need to become part of a group. This group identity may be political or work related. There may be spare time activities with a sports team, people who are interested in artistic pursuits, or some kind of intellectual grouping. You will make achievements as part of a group or a team. At work, you will have to work in co-operation with, and possibly in charge of, others; you cannot achieve much on your own now.

Friendships with women will be important and you will become slightly less attached to your family, finding that your time and attention is diverted from them by outside considerations. Even in the realm of friendships there will be changes as you move on to newer, more dynamic type of people. Both you and your associates could try to achieve something which would be of benefit to humanity, your attitude being highly idealistic but possibly rather impractical at times. It would be wise to guard against being drawn into specific and fixed ideologies which don't leave room for differences of opinion.

It will be necessary for you to learn new methods which could arise from your work or as a result of a change in your way of life. If, for instance, you were to move house at this time, you would have to get to grips with decorating or making a garden. You may learn to sew, drive a car or bring your work skills up to date. If you have school-aged children, you will be dealing with educational matters on their behalf and may be drawn into some of their school activities. It is possible that you could return full-time to college to complete a course; you yourself may turn or return to teaching. Retirement at this time would give you an opportunity to learn to ski, play the piano or to learn any one of a million new ideas. You may have to deal with very modern methods or ideas which are out of the ordinary.

This may include learning to use a computer or something similar; you could find yourself dealing with electronics, radio or radar, even taking up astrology.

You will redefine your personal goals and ask yourself what you want out of life in general terms. By investigating your own hopes and wishes you will change the direction of your thinking in some radical way. One instance may be a person who has thus far, never wanted children deciding that he or she wants them after all, another person who had always been lazy might suddenly become ambitious. New goals and values will replace outworn ones now.

There can be a surprisingly disruptive element in this progression which could change your outlook or your life completely. You might re-emerge soon with a new career; almost certainly with a new home, possibly even with a new set of personal relationships. This is the time when you could revolutionize your own life or find that it is being revolutionized for you by bringing a complete breakdown in your present status quo. If this is the case, you may react by becoming jealous and possessive in an attempt to hang on too tightly. It all depends upon your circumstances at the time of entering the progression and your particular nature as to how you handle these changes. Others of you who have been through difficult times during the previous progression, will find this a surprisingly good time when money comes your way, gambles come off and your dreams begin to come true. There is no doubt that this is a phase where anything could happen – and frequently does. Try to keep a strong grip on reality as events around you might become tinged with fantasy or even a subtle form of lunacy.

Remember to keep in touch with friends; whether things are good or bad, they will sustain you now.

Progressed Moon in Pisces or in the Twelfth House ♓

This will be a time of reflection, possibly even retreat from the hurly-burly of life, events seem to be in the hands of fate now and there doesn't seem to be much you can do about it. You may have to suppress your own personality for a while, possibly until your progressed Moon crosses over the Ascendant into Aries, and in addition to having to keep a good many of your feelings under wraps, there could be work projects carried on in secret. One example might be of preparing to set up a small business of your own while still carrying on at your usual job. There may, of course, be some kind of secret relationship going on; this doesn't necessarily have to be an 'eternal triangle' situation but may be something much odder, such as keeping in touch with a 'black sheep' relative that the rest of the family ignores. This progression may be a sad, even a depressing time, as you seem to be working through some kind of karmic programme. The outcome will be a change in your consciousness leading to a renewal of life and hope which will sweep you away into a completely new direction.

It is important to keep some kind of hold on reality during this progression as it would be only too easy to slip into a strange state of mental limbo. Some aspect of your life will be insecure, probably on the emotional level, and you may find it hard to face the facts which confront you. It would be easy to slide into a state of disillusion or even despair, worse still, you could try to chase illusion, exacerbating the situation by the use of drugs and drink. It would be best to keep away from opiates at this time, especially sleeping pills.

There is a much more positive side to all this and it is the opportunity for you to learn how to relax, meditate and travel on a series of inward journeys. One way or another, you will be spending much more time alone than you have before and, while you are looking inwards, you may discover talents and abilities which you never knew you possessed. I can remember when my Moon travelled through the twelfth some years ago, I was at home with small children, running a small dressmaking business, also studying foreign languages and astrology – and discovering that I had a talent for both. The benefits of this progression tend to be recognized only in retrospect. Artistic and creative abilities will come to the fore now, also you should be able to enjoy quiet pleasures like reading, listening to the radio and gardening. Photography or film-making is a strong possibility now too.

If you are naturally rather moody, this aspect of your personality will be accentuated but you may find yourself on the receiving end of someone else's moodiness at this time. Your intuitive abilities will develop and you should follow any instincts which you feel. Being more sensitive and shyer than usual, you may find others strangely difficult or even unsympathetic to your needs and wants. It is possible that psychic or mediumistic abilities will become noticeable now and you might begin to take a serious interest in these subjects. There could even be a revelation, a kind of 'gateway' which thrusts you forward into spirituality.

Typical Piscean or twelfth house circumstances would be that of a young woman finding herself at home with small children at the very time when her husband is having to make the maximum effort at his job and therefore, is being less supportive than before. Another reason might be the beginning of retirement with its inevitable change of perspective. One unfortunate reason for this situation might be a period of illness, or possibly of having to take care of somebody else who becomes ill or incapacitated. There may well be a connection with hospitals, even mental institutions or prisons at this time, either because you yourself are directly involved or through those close to you. You could even find yourself working in one of these places. You will have an uncanny ability to link with the moods of others and to give real help and understanding to those who need it.

One of the nicer possibilities is of travel. There may be a move or a drift towards water for you now and, depending upon circumstances you could buy property by the sea, rent a holiday villa on the coast or become involved in the world of boats. Some people go cruising when the Moon is in Pisces.

If you are working, you will be better off as a backroom boy now than out in front. You may find it hard to trust others either in your private or your working life. Relations with women could be particularly difficult or even peculiar now, and you may have to face a change in perspective regarding the women in your life at this time, probably due to factors which are outside your control. An easy way to grasp the idea behind this progression is to think of a seed spending the winter lying in the soil waiting to come to life in the spring.

Strange and subconscious forces affect your moods as the axis of your previous way of life subtly shifts. This is truly a time to recharge your inner forces by retreat and reflection in readiness for the 'first house breakout' which will surely, surely come.

The Moon may set but the Sun also rises.

12

Advanced Techniques of Lunar Progression

The Moon progresses forward at roughly one degree per month. It may travel eleven, twelve, thirteen, or fourteen degrees during the course of a year but most of the time, conveniently for us, it travels at a rate of twelve degrees per year. The method is simple; once you have established the exact degree of the progressed Moon on your last birthday, move it forward a degree for each month as the year goes by. As there are thirty degrees in a sign, one can see that the Moon will spend roughly two-and-a-half years in each sign. It is strange how this two-and-a-half year time scale does seem to affect the lives of many of us. As an astrologer, I am accustomed to people telling me that a particular situation, such as a relationship or a job lasted for about two-and-a-half years.

When looking at the progressed Moon, first look to see whether it has recently changed signs, if it is in the middle of a sign or if it is wending its way to the end of a sign. Sometimes it takes a few months for a new sign to make an impression on one's life but on other occasions, effects are noticeable immediately, even as the Moon draws to the end of the previous sign.

Once you have established the actual degree of the progressed Moon at the time of the reading, then simply move it forward a degree for a month to see what the year (or couple of years) ahead will bring. If the Moon crosses another planet, this will be a conjunction and, although this is going beyond the scope of this book, I have listed the lunar conjunctions here for you. In the case of positive aspects such as the trine or sextile, read the conjunction information but stress the positive sides of it. In the case of the 'hard' aspects such as the square or opposition, the more difficult reactions will probably apply but, don't forget that more can be achieved under a hard aspect than under an easy one.

Moon/Sun conjunction

There may be events concerning children, also this is a time of increased self-confidence or even of personal triumph. Fun, holidays, speculation, games, sports, will become part of your life now. You could fall in love with an exciting person and have an affair to remember. There is a possibility that you may buy yourself a holiday home, a house in the sun. There should be some good times with older relatives now. You might find yourself dealing with more than the usual number of Leo type people at this time.

Moon/Moon conjunction

Domestic matters come to the fore, there could even be a move of house or you may take out a lease on business premises. Travel is a possibility especially over or near water and you may revisit the place of your birth. There will be some special dealings with females, especially mother figures. Your emotions will be stronger now. There could be a connection with the provision of food or domestic goods. Things which have been kept secret may suddenly be revealed. You may have more dealings with Cancerian people now.

Moon/Mercury conjunction

Communications with the family characterize this progression. There may be documents to be dealt with in connection with property and premises. There could be a new vehicle for you now or you may simply change your method of daily commuting. Paperwork will be important. Any education courses which are undertaken now will go well, exams can be passed at this time, as can the driving test. There should be friendly dealings with neighbours, friends and relatives of your own generation or a bit younger. You could take up a new sporting interest in company with others. Groups of friends may begin to meet in your home. You will begin to think about diet and food values and could make plans to alter the appearance of your home. There may also be a rethink about your methods of working and improvements in the methods you use. You may begin to write for publication. You may have more than the usual amount of dealings with Gemini or Virgo people now.

Moon/Venus conjunction

Family affairs come to the fore, you will get on well with the women of the family. There could be public relations involving women, or even a business partnership with a woman. This is a good time to decorate the house or to have a celebration in the home. Food and catering, diet and appearance will occupy you now. There could be a new romance, certainly you will begin to feel more attractive and more romantic. There may be some involvement with artists and with artistic work at this time. There will be an increase in business opportunities and good new contacts. You may find yourself dealing with more than the usual number of Taurus or Libra people now.

Moon/Mars conjunction

You will experience a high level of energy and drive, and you could develop sudden enthusiasms for work projects or energetic hobbies. There will be some kind of fresh start now. There could be a working partnership with a young man and you will have a more energetic and youthful attitude to work matters. If you are in a competitive field or are playing in competitive sports you should be able to win. Your ambition level will be high and opportunities will suddenly come your way. This is not a great time for dealing with women and you will have to watch your temper now as all your feelings will run high. You may become ill, feverish or even have an accident (especially in the home). If you change vehicles now, the new one will go faster than the previous one did. Your sex drive will be high but you could also fight over emotional and sexual matters. For women, this transit is almost bound to bring a man into your life; probably young, certainly sexy and energetic. You could be dealing with more than the usual number of Aries or Scorpio people now.

Moon/Jupiter conjunction

You might rethink your religious and philosophical views now. There will be an interest in travel and dealings with foreigners, possibly in connection with work. There is a feeling of optimism and change for the better although it may not be apparent immediately. You will make new and useful contacts and could have unexpected opportunities at work. Money should become easier to find and doors will open for you. There might be an involvement with legal matters at this time and, if so, you will come out on the winning side, especially if property is involved. This is a good time to deal with women in regard to financial matters, also to invest in property. Domestic matters should go well and you will be given the opportunity to expand your horizons and even to look at yourself in a new way. You may be involved with more than the usual number of Sagittarius or Pisces people now.

Moon/Saturn conjunction

There will be problems now, these could relate to your home situation, your parents or other elderly relatives. It is possible that you could feel depressed and rather lonely now even though you might be surrounded by people. You will have extra responsibilities and very little time to rest and, apart from feeling down-hearted, you might actually be ill or just over-tired and run down. Life will feel restricted and rather boring at this time and your love life may also be depressing, it is possible that your loved one is living or working at some distance from you at the moment. Business matters will go slowly but plans which are made now will work out well in the long run. Dealings with people in positions of responsibility or with older people may be awkward but should work out well *after* the progression has passed. There could be the need to make far-reaching decisions with regard to your parents. Money may be short, especially in the home but that will also improve soon. A good time to do some long-range thinking and to chat to knowledgeable and responsible people about your plans for the future. You may meet more than the usual number of Capricorn or Aquarius people now.

Moon/Uranus conjunction

Sudden changes in mood characterize this progression. This is one of those times when you will suddenly realize that you can no longer bear the job you're in or the person you are living with. This is the kind of situation which brews up slowly possibly for years beforehand and then, *apparently* all of a sudden, changes for good. You may make an unexpected change of house or suddenly decide to tear down and rebuild some part of your home, there could be unexpected family problems or sudden changes with the home set-up. Friends will be more in evidence at this time. You could have some brilliant ideas or you may find answers to questions which have been bothering you for ages. Working life could bring unexpected changes and benefits, almost anything could happen and you will have to study the signs and the houses involved in order to work out all the possibilities. You might even take up astrology! You should have more than the usual number of dealings with Aquarian people at this time.

Moon/Neptune conjunction

If you fall in love now you will see your loved one through rose-coloured glasses. There will be a strong element of fantasy in any love affair at this time, therefore you could do most of your loving at a distance or even confine it to the inside of your own head. Old half-buried memories will come back to haunt you and you could find yourself dealing with ancient fears and phobias, possibly facing up to them at last. There will be an increase in your intuition and you could have some interesting psychic experiences. You will be re-examining your philosophical views and religious outlook and could even go so far as to change your religion. You may spend much time daydreaming or you may go in for some inspired forms of meditation. You will feel atmospheres acutely and could well develop clairvoyant and precognitive abilities. Business matters could become confusing and you might find out that you have been dealing with dishonest people. You may have some great ideas but will have to wait until the progression has passed before putting them into practice. There may be travel to the sea or over it for you, and there should be renewed contact with family and friends overseas. You may rearrange the method of water supply in your home or you may become interested in or work with fluids, gasses, oil and photography. There could be increased contacts with mystical people or those born under the sign of Pisces or who have strongly Piscean birthcharts. Love affairs could be wonderful, inspired or they could really screw you up but you will definitely be awash with emotion and hardly able to think straight. You might be involved with hospitals especially in connection with family members. There may be work in a hospital or institution for you at this time.

You may develop a taste for alcohol or develop strange allergic ailments.

Moon/Pluto conjunction

This is a transforming progression which could change the whole of your life from now on. It will certainly change your outlook on life and your view of yourself. You will be emotionally wrought up, possibly because you will be coping with some pretty monumental problems. There will be financial matters to sort out and these may stem from a previous divorce, a legacy or some kind of outstanding tax problem. There could be outstanding business finances to sort out and even liquidation is a possibility. You will want to alter a bad family situation and could clear the air with a really terrific argument or you could even walk out for good. There may be dealings with the police, the courts or hospitals at this time and the matters which are involved could be quite serious. There may be literal births and deaths around you now, certainly there will be figurative ones. There is even the possibility that your life could be affected by geological upheavals or by war! There could be a connection with mines and miners or explosives. There may be some rather strange occult and psychic experiences. Any kind of subterranean rumblings of discontent which have been going on in your life could erupt explosively now.

Moon/Ascendant conjunction

This is a time of new beginnings as the Moon moves from the twelfth house to the first. You will want to come out of the shadows and be noticed. Your personal and domestic affairs will change for the better now although it might be uncomfortable while this progression is in operation. You will probably change your appearance and your attitudes soon.

Moon/Mid-heaven conjunction

This is the culmination of a phase of your life. You should feel that you have reached as far as you can in your present job and now want to change direction. You could become more involved with the public or find that your status and public image is improving. You may achieve some long-cherished dream regarding your career. Domestic matters will go well, and if you move house, you will make money on the deal and will like your new home. Domestic matters will influence your professional life either indirectly, via changes in your home and family arrangements or directly, as a result of working in industries related to food and household goods. A woman may influence your thinking in regard to your objectives in life.

Moon/IC conjunction

This could bring you closer to your family, especially your mother, and will bring you closer to your home. You may begin to work from home now. Any lingering emotional or relationship problem in the home can be sorted out for good now.

Moon and nodes

When the Moon crosses the nodes, you may move, redecorate, have interesting visitors or possibly go on holiday to a completely different place than the one you usually visit. You make take up some special project in the home or start working from home. You could re-appraise your direction in life now. You may have some kind of *Karmic* experience at this time.

13

Personality and Phases of the Moon

Please see explanation and tables from pages 305–330 to find *your* natal moon phase.

First quarter

Whatever sign you were born under, wherever your other planets are placed, you will have an underlying sense of youthful enthusiasm, a touch of Aries at the heart of your nature. You probably prefer to take the initiative, especially in romance and you will always be ready to look for new interests in life, new people and new ideas. Your lively outlook and optimistic approach to life is an attractive feature but you have to guard against selfishness. You can see how things can be made to work and how situations can be improved. You will spur others into action but then leave them to finish the project. You could be self-employed. No-one can make you do something if you really don't want to and this may stand in the way of successful relationships. You should get off to a good start and become quite successful when young; other factors on the chart will indicate whether this early promise will be maintained throughout life. You should try not to react too fast or to take others too much by surprise.

Second quarter

You are ambitious and sociable with an underlying touch of Cancer and Leo in your nature, you are locked into your own goals and your strong need to create something which will be seen and remembered by other people. You need a place of your own where you can express your own personality; this may be your home or your workplace. Your rather charismatic personality will always draw others towards you. You try to be helpful to others but can't be called on to make sacrifices on their behalf for very long. You may use others for your own ends; this behaviour is instinctive rather than calculated. You need the status and outlet of a career but one where your face is out in front, possibly in sales or reception work. You draw attention to yourself and while you can achieve much, you may miss some of the needs of others. You should reach considerable heights of success while still young, other factors in your chart will determine whether you maintain that success. You are slow to anger but formidable when you do lose your temper. You hate to be hurried and may be slightly suspicious of methods and ideas which are presented to you as a *fait accompli*. You don't mind hurrying other people as you know that it puts them slightly off balance and tips the odds in your favour.

Third quarter

You are sensitive to the needs of others and you want them to be equally sensitive to your needs. There is an underlying watchfulness with this quarter rather reminiscent of Libra and Scorpio. You need friendships, colleagues and relationships and you relate well to individuals within a group. You like an exciting life but want others to share the excitement. You are aware of what others think of you and may not be entirely sure of yourself unless acceptably reflected in the eyes of others. You are drawn to more active, more successful people and can help them to achieve their aims; this phase of the Moon suggests that you will be a supreme achiever in your own right but you would still need the help and encouragement of others. There is a nerviness about you, a kind of coiled-spring tension which can lend you originality and wit but also a short attention span and a hungry search for new people and new experiences. In some peculiar way, sex could have a special importance to you. It may transform your life in some manner or other. It is said that people who are born just after a full Moon has passed the Mid-heaven on their birthchart will be rich and famous! Your most sucessful time of your life is in your middle years.

Fourth quarter

Whatever else there may be on your chart, there is an underlying feeling of Capricorn or Pisces here. You finish the projects which others start, you reorganize and sort out problems left by others; you may never start projects of your own. You have clairvoyant insight and may follow hunches rather than work things out logically. You are aware of all kinds of under-currents and can become upset by the demands of others. You have to try to let their feelings flow past you and always trust your basic instincts. You can be too inclined to sit back and let things happen around you. You are proba-bly at your best when helping a group to achieve something beneficial. You can blend in with a large group or work entirely alone. You are probably not too materialistic but you do need job satisfaction. You may be very slow to grow up, happy to sit back and allow things to change around you, however, you are likely to go through some kind of metamorphosis later in life and achieve success in something unusual and completely individual.

Romany tradition and the Moon's phases

A friend passed this piece of Romany wisdom on to me. I had not realized that such minute observations of human behaviour and lifestyle had been made. I tested out the ideas on my family and friends and found that they work well.

Those born between the new Moon and the first quarter.

You will have a long life.

Born in the first twenty-four hours, you will be lucky.
Born on the second day, you will be exceptionally lucky.
Born on the third day, you will have important and influential friends.
Born on the fourth day, up and down life with luck and reverses.
Fifth and sixth day, pride could be your downfall.

Seventh day, you have to hide the wishes that you want to come true.

Those born between the first quarter and the full Moon.

You will do better in life than your parents.

First day, prosperity.
Second day, easy life.
Third day, wealth through travel.
Fourth and fifth days, charm.
Sixth, easy success.
Seventh, many friends.

Those born between the full Moon and the last quarter.

You will have difficulties but will overcome them by doggedness.

First day, you will succeed in another continent.
Second day, you will do well in business.
Third day, success as a result of (and probably foreseen by) intuition.
Fourth day, bravery.
Fifth day, care must be taken with money.
Sixth and seventh, great strength.

Those born between the last quarter and the new Moon.

You will be affectionate and honest.

First and second days, you will be happy in your home.
Third day, you are dependable.
Fourth day, you are sensitive.
Fifth day, you will make ideal parents.
Sixth and seventh days, you will acquire money (or maybe non-material wealth) through loyalty.

An Eclipsed Moon

Solar Eclipse ♂ ⊕☽ – ☉

If the Moon was lying between the Earth and the Sun when you were born, your inner and outer natures would interact well. Your emotional reactions will be fast, you would act instinctively without having to stop to think in a structured and logical manner. This would enable you to avoid or get out of sticky situations admirably but it might be hard for you to make plans and carry them out.

Lunar Eclipse ☍ ⊕ ☉ – ☽

If the Sun was between the Earth and the Moon when you were born you would be restless, intense and creative. You are apt to go overboard in relationships as you take everything in life seriously. You need people and you also have a knack of drawing them close to you. You may allow your logical mind to override your instincts, thereby misjudging situations where you might have been better served by trusting your gut reaction.

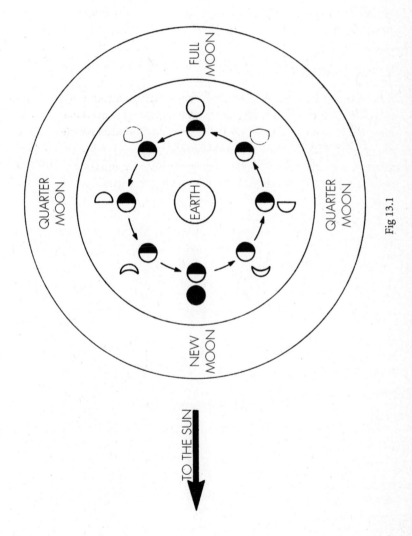

Fig 13.1

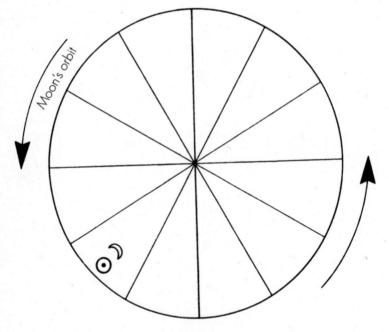

Fig 13.2

CONJUNCTION

When the Sun and Moon are in the same sign, the Moon is either at the end of
the fourth quarter or the beginning of the first quarter.

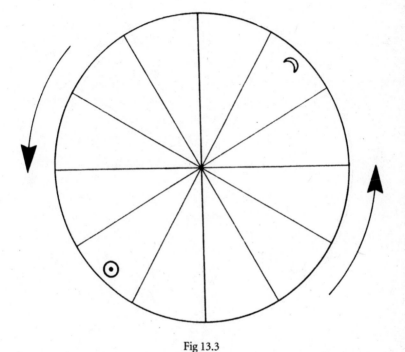

Fig 13.3
OPPOSITION
When the Sun and Moon are in opposite signs, the Moon is full (start of the
third quarter)

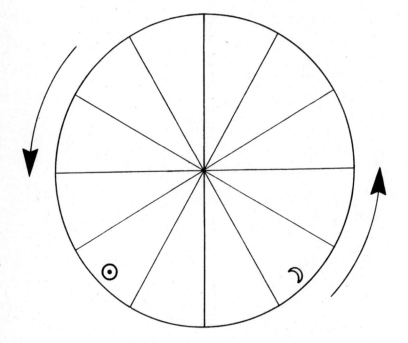

Fig 13.4
SQUARE
A 90° angle shows the Moon at the start of the second quarter.

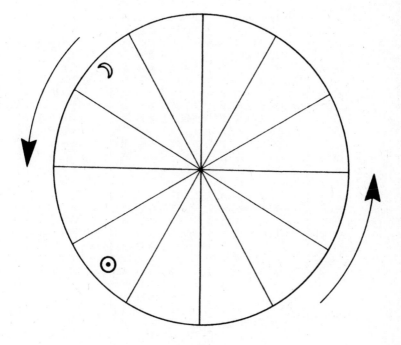

Fig 13.5
SQUARE
A 90° angle shows the Moon at the start of the fourth quarter.

1920	1921	1922	1923
Jan 5 F 9:06 P	Jan 1 ¾ 4:36 A	Jan 6 ¼ 10:25 A	Jan 3 F 2:34 A
13 ¾ 0:09 A	9 N 5:28 A	13 F 2:37 P	10 ¾ 0:55 A
21 N 5:28 A	17 ¼ 6:32 A	20 ¾ 6:01 A	17 N 2:42 A
28 ¼ 3:39 P	23 F 11:08 P	27 N 11:49 P	25 ¼ 4:00 A
Feb 4 F 8:43 A	30 ¾ 8:03 P	Feb 5 ¼ 4:53 A	Feb 1 F 3:54 P
11 ¾ 8:50 P	Feb 8 N 0:38 A	12 F 1:18 A	8 ¾ 9:17 A
19 N 9:35 P	15 ¼ 6:54 P	18 ¾ 6:19 P	15 N 7:08 P
26 ¼ 11:50 P	22 F 9:33 A	26 N 6:49 P	24 ¼ 0:07 A
Mar 4 F 9:13 P	Mar 1 ¾ 2:04 P	Mar 6 ¼ 7:22 P	Mar 3 F 3:24 A
12 ¾ 5:58 P	9 N 6:10 P	13 F 11:15 A	9 ¾ 6:32 P
20 N 10:56 A	17 ¼ 3:50 A	20 ¾ 8:44 A	17 N 0:52 P
27 ¼ 6:46 A	23 F 8:20 P	28 N 1:04 P	25 ¼ 4:42 P
Apr 3 F 10:55 A	30 ¾ 9:14 A	Apr 5 ¼ 5:46 A	Apr 1 F 1:11 P
11 ¾ 1:25 P	Apr 8 N 9:06 A	11 F 8:44 P	8 ¾ 5:23 A
18 N 9:44 P	15 ¼ 10:12 A	19 ¾ 0:55 P	16 N 6:29 A
25 ¼ 1:28 P	22 F 4:10 A	27 N 5:05 A	24 ¼ 5:21 A
May 3 F 1:48 A	30 ¾ 4:10 A	May 4 ¼ 0:56 P	30 F 9:31 P
11 ¾ 5:52 A	May 7 N 9:02 P	11 F 6:07 A	May 7 ¾ 6:19 P
18 N 6:26 A	14 ¼ 3:25 P	18 ¾ 6:18 P	15 N 10:39 P
24 ¼ 9:08 P	21 F 8:16 P	26 N 6:05 P	23 ¼ 2:26 P
Jun 1 F 5:19 P	29 ¾ 9:34 P	Jun 2 ¼ 6:10 P	30 F 5:08 A
9 ¾ 6:59 P	Jun 6 N 6:15 A	9 F 3:59 P	Jun 6 ¾ 9:20 A
16 N 1:42 P	12 ¼ 9:00 P	17 ¾ 0:04 P	14 N 0:43 P
23 ¼ 6:50 P	20 F 9:42 A	25 N 4:20 A	21 ¼ 8:47 P
Jul 1 F 8:42 A	28 ¾ 1:18 P	Jul 1 ¼ 10:53 P	28 F 1:05 P
9 ¾ 5:06 A	Jul 5 N 1:37 P	9 F 3:08 A	Jul 6 ¾ 1:57 A
15 N 8:26 P	12 ¼ 4:16 A	17 ¾ 5:12 A	14 N 0:46 P
30 ¼ 7:21 P	20 F 0:09 A	24 N 0:48 P	21 ¼ 1:33 A
30 F 11:20 P	28 ¾ 2:21 A	31 ¼ 4:22 A	27 F 10:34 P
Aug 7 ¾ 0:51 P	Aug 3 N 8:18 P	Aug 7 F 4:20 P	Aug 4 ¾ 7:23 P
14 N 3:44 A	10 ¼ 2:14 P	15 ¾ 8:47 P	12 N 11:17 A
21 ¼ 10:53 A	18 F 3:29 P	22 N 8:35 P	19 ¼ 6:08 A
29 F 1:04 P	26 ¾ 0:52 P	29 ¼ 11:56 A	26 F 10:30 A
Sep 5 ¾ 7:06 P	Sep 2 N 3:34 A	Sep 6 F 7:48 A	Sep 3 ¾ 0:48 P
12 N 0:52 P	9 ¼ 3:30 A	14 ¾ 10:21 A	10 N 8:54 P
20 ¼ 4:56 A	17 F 7:21 A	21 N 4:39 A	17 ¼ 0:05 P
28 F 1:57 A	24 ¾ 9:18 P	27 ¼ 10:41 P	25 F 1:17 A
Oct 5 ¾ 0:54 A	Oct 1 3 0:27 P	Oct 6 F 0:59 A	Oct 3 ¾ 5:30 A
12 N 0:51 A	9 N 8:13 P	13 ¾ 9:56 P	10 N 6:06 A
20 ¼ 0:30 A	17 ¼ 11:00 P	20 N 1:41 P	16 ¼ 8:54 P
27 F 2:10 P	23 F 4:32 A	27 ¼ 1:27 P	24 F 6:27 P
Nov 3 ¾ 7:36 A	30 ¾ 11:39 P	Nov 4 F 6:37 P	Nov 1 ¾ 8:50 P
10 N 4:06 P	Nov 7 ¼ 3:55 P	12 ¾ 7:53 A	8 N 3:28 P
18 ¼ 8:13 P	15 F 1:40 P	19 N 0:07 A	15 ¼ 9:42 A
26 F 1:43 A	22 ¾ 11:42 P	26 ¼ 8:16 A	23 F 0:59 P
Dec 2 ¾ 4:30 P	29 N 1:26 P	Dec 4 F 11:24 A	Dec 1 ¾ 10:10 A
10 N 10:05 A	Dec 7 ¼ 1:20 P	11 ¾ 4:41 P	8 N 1:31 A
18 ¼ 2:41 P	15 F 2:51 A	18 N 0:21 P	15 ¼ 2:39 A
25 F 0:39 P	21 ¾ 7:55 P	26 ¼ 5:54 A	23 F 7:34 A
	29 N 5:40 A		30 ¾ 9:08 P

1924	1925	1926	1927
Jan 6 N 0:49 P	Jan 1 ¼ 11:27 P	Jan 7 ¾ 7:23 A	Jan 3 N 8:29 P
13 ¼ 10:45 P	10 F 2:48 A	14 N 6:36 A	10 ¼ 2:44 P
22 F 0:58 A	17 ¾ 11:34 P	20 ¼ 10:32 P	17 F 10:28 P
29 ¾ 5:54 A	24 N 2:46 P	28 F 9:36 P	26 ¾ 2:06 A
Feb 5 N 1:39 A	31 ¼ 4:44 P	Feb 5 ¾ 11:26 P	Feb 2 N 8:55 A
12 ¼ 8:10 P	Feb 8 F 9:50 P	12 N 5:21 P	8 ¼ 11:55 P
20 F 4:08 P	16 ¾ 9:42 A	19 ¼ 0:37 P	16 F 4:19 P
27 ¾ 1:16 P	23 N 2:13 A	27 F 4:52 P	24 ¾ 8:43 P
Mar 5 N 3:59 P	Mar 2 ¼ 0:08 P	Mar 7 ¾ 11:50 A	Mar 3 N 7:26 P
13 ¼ 4:51 P	10 F 2:22 P	14 N 3:21 A	10 ¼ 11:04 A
21 F 4:31 A	17 ¾ 5:22 P	21 ¼ 5:13 A	18 F 10:25 A
27 ¾ 8:25 P	24 N 2:04 P	29 F 10:01 A	26 ¾ 11:36 A
Apr 4 N 7:18 A	Apr 1 ¼ 8:13 A	Apr 5 ¾ 8:51 P	Apr 2 N 4:25 A
12 ¼ 11:13 A	9 F 3:34 A	12 N 0:57 P	9 ¼ 0:22 A
19 F 2:12 P	15 ¾ 11:41 P	19 ¼ 11:24 P	17 F 3:36 A
26 ¾ 4:29 A	23 N 2:29 A	28 F 0:18 A	24 ¾ 10:22 P
May 3 N 11:01 P	May 1 ¼ 3:21 A	May 5 ¾ 3:14 P	May 1 N 0:41 P
12 ¼ 2:15 A	8 F 1:44 P	11 N 10:56 P	8 ¼ 3:28 P
18 F 9:53 P	15 ¾ 5:47 A	19 ¼ 5:49 P	16 F 7:04 P
25 ¾ 2:17 P	22 N 3:49 A	27 F 11:50 A	24 ¾ 5:35 A
Jun 2 N 2:35 P	30 ¼ 8:05 P	Jun 3 ¾ 8:10 P	30 N 9:07 P
10 ¼ 1:38 P	Jun 6 F 9:49 P	10 N 10:09 A	Jun 7 ¼ 7:50 A
17 F 4:42 A	13 ¾ 0:45 P	18 ¼ 11:15 A	15 F 8:20 A
24 ¾ 2:17 A	21 N 6:18 A	25 F 9:14 P	22 ¾ 10:30 A
Jul 2 N 5:36 A	29 ¼ 9:44 A	Jul 2 ¾ 1:03 P	29 N 6:33 A
9 ¼ 9:47 P	Jul 6 F 4:55 A	9 N 11:07 P	Jul 7 ¼ 0:53 A
16 F 11:50 A	12 ¾ 9:35 P	18 ¼ 2:56 A	14 F 7:23 P
23 ¾ 4:37 A	20 N 9:41 P	25 F 5:14 P	21 ¾ 2:44 P
31 N 7:43 P	28 ¼ 8:24 P	31 ¾ 7:26 P	28 N 5:37 P
Aug 8 ¼ 3:42 A	Aug 4 F 12:00 P	Aug 8 N 1:50 P	Aug 5 ¼ 6:06 P
14 F 8:20 P	11 ¾ 9:12 A	16 ¼ 4:40 P	13 F 4:38 A
22 ¾ 9:12 A	19 N 1:16 P	23 F 0:39 P	19 ¾ 7:55 P
30 N 8:38 A	27 ¼ 4:47 A	30 ¾ 4:41 A	27 N 6:47 A
Sep 6 ¼ 8:46 A	Sep 2 F 7:54 P	Sep 7 N 5:46 A	Sep 4 ¼ 10:46 A
13 F 7:01 A	10 ¾ 0:13 A	15 ¼ 4:28 A	11 F 0:55 P
21 ¾ 3:36 A	18 N 4:13 A	21 F 8:20 P	18 ¾ 3:31 A
28 N 8:17 P	25 ¼ 11:52 A	28 ¾ 5:49 P	25 N 10:12 P
Oct 5 ¼ 2:31 P	Oct 2 F 5:24 A	Oct 6 N 10:14 P	Oct 4 ¼ 2:03 A
12 F 8:22 P	9 ¾ 6:35 P	14 ¼ 2:29 P	10 F 9:16 P
20 ¾ 10:55 P	17 N 6:07 P	21 F 5:16 A	17 ¾ 2:33 P
28 N 6:58 A	24 ¼ 6:39 P	28 ¾ 10:58 A	25 N 3:39 P
Nov 3 ¼ 10:19 P	31 F 5:18 P	Nov 5 N 2:35 P	Nov 2 ¼ 3:17 P
11 F 0:32 P	Nov 8 ¾ 3:14 P	12 ¼ 11:02 P	9 F 6:37 A
19 ¾ 5:39 P	16 N 6:59 A	19 F 4:22 P	16 ¾ 5:29 A
26 N 5:17 P	23 ¼ 2:06 A	27 ¾ 7:16 P	24 N 10:10 A
Dec 3 ¼ 9:11 A	30 F 8:12 A	Dec 5 N 6:13 A	Dec 2 ¼ 2:16 A
11 F 7:05 A	Dec 8 ¾ 0:12 P	12 ¼ 6:48 A	8 F 5:33 P
19 ¾ 10:12 A	15 N 7:06 P	19 F 6:10 A	16 ¾ 0:05 A
16 N 3:46 A	22 ¼ 11:09 A	27 ¾ 5:00 A	26 N 4:14 A
	30 F 2:03 A	¼	31 ¼ 11:23 A

1928	1929	1930	1931
Jan 7 F 6:09 A	Jan 2 ¾ 6:45 P	Jan 8 ¼ 3:12 A	Jan 4 F 1:16 P
14 ¾ 9:15 P	11 N 0:29 A	14 F 10:22 P	11 ¾ 5:10 A
22 N 8:20 P	18 ¼ 3:16 P	21 ¾ 4:08 P	18 N 6:37 P
29 ¼ 7:27 P	25 F 7:10 A	29 N 7:08 P	27 ¼ 0:07 A
Feb 5 F 8:12 P	Feb 1 ¾ 2:11 P	Feb 6 ¼ 5:27 P	Feb 3 F 0:27 A
13 ¾ 7:06 P	9 N 5:56 P	13 F 8:39 A	9 ¾ 4:11 P
21 N 9:42 A	17 ¼ 0:23 A	20 ¾ 8:46 A	17 N 1:12 P
28 ¼ 3:22 A	23 F 7:00 P	28 N 1:34 P	25 ¼ 4:43 P
Mar 6 F 11:28 A	Mar 3 ¾ 11:10 A	Mar 8 ¼ 4:01 A	Mar 4 F 10:37 A
14 ¾ 3:21 P	11 N 8:38 A	14 F 6:59 P	11 ¾ 5:16 A
21 N 8:30 P	18 ¼ 7:42 A	22 ¾ 3:14 A	19 N 7:52 A
28 ¼ 11:55 A	25 F 7:47 A	30 N 5:47 A	27 ¼ 5:05 A
Apr 5 F 3:39 A	Apr 2 ¾ 7:30 A	Apr 6 ¼ 11:26 A	Apr 2 F 8:07 P
13 ¾ 8:10 A	9 N 8:34 P	13 F 5:50 A	9 ¾ 8:16 P
20 N 5:25 A	16 ¼ 2:10 P	20 ¾ 10:10 P	18 N 1:01 A
26 ¼ 9:43 P	23 F 9:49 P	28 N 7:10 P	25 ¼ 1:41 P
May 4 F 8:13 P	May 2 ¾ 1:27 A	May 5 ¼ 4:54 P	May 2 F 5:15 A
12 ¾ 8:51 P	9 N 6:08 A	12 F 5:30 P	9 ¾ 0:49 P
19 N 1:15 P	15 ¼ 8:57 P	20 ¾ 4:23 P	17 N 3:29 P
26 ¼ 9:13 A	23 F 0:51 P	28 N 5:38 A	24 ¼ 7:40 P
Jun 3 F 0:15 A	31 ¾ 4:14 P	Jun 3 ¼ 9:57 P	31 F 2:34 P
11 ¾ 5:52 A	Jun 7 N 1:57 P	11 F 6:13 A	Jun 8 ¾ 6:19 A
17 N 8:43 P	14 ¼ 5:16 A	19 ¾ 9:02 A	16 N 3:03 A
24 ¼ 10:48 P	22 F 4:16 A	26 N 1:48 P	23 ¼ 0:24 A
Jul 3 F 2:50 A	30 ¾ 3:55 A	Jul 3 ¼ 4:04 A	30 F 0:48 A
10 ¾ 0:17 P	Jul 6 N 8:48 P	10 F 8:02 A	Jul 7 ¾ 11:53 P
17 N 4:36 A	13 ¼ 4:06 A	18 ¾ 11:30 P	15 N 0:21 P
24 ¼ 2:39 P	21 F 7:22 P	25 N 8:43 A	22 ¼ 5:17 A
Aug 1 F 3:32 P	29 ¾ 0:57 P	Aug 1 ¼ 0:27 P	29 F 0:49 P
8 ¾ 5:25 P	Aug 5 N 3:41 A	9 F 10:59 A	Aug 6 ¾ 4:29 P
15 N 1:50 P	12 ¼ 6:03 A	1 ¾ 11:32 A	13 N 8:28 P
23 ¼ 8:22 A	20 F 9:43 A	24 N 3:38 A	20 ¼ 11:37 A
31 F 2:35 A	27 ¾ 8:03 P	30 ¼ 11:58 P	28 F 3:11 A
Sep 6 ¾ 10:36 P	Sep 3 N 11:48 A	Sep 8 F 2:49 A	Sep 5 ¾ 7:22 A
14 N 1:21 A	10 ¼ 10:58 A	15 ¾ 9:14 P	12 N 4:27 A
22 ¼ 2:59 A	18 F 11:17 P	22 N 11:43 A	18 ¼ 8:38 P
29 F 0:44 P	26 ¾ 2:08 A	29 ¼ 2:59 P	26 F 7:46 P
Oct 6 ¾ 5:07 A	Oct 2 N 10:20 P	Oct 7 F 6:57 P	Oct 4 ¾ 8:16 P
13 N 3:57 P	10 ¼ 6:06 A	15 ¾ 5:13 A	11 N 1:07 P
21 ¼ 9:07 P	18 F 0:07 A	21 N 9:49 P	18 ¼ 9:21 A
28 F 10:44 P	25 ¾ 8:22 A	29 ¼ 9:23 A	26 F 1:35 P
Nov 4 ¾ 2:07 P	Nov 1 N 0:02 P	Nov 6 F 10:29 A	Nov 3 ¾ 7:19 A
12 N 9:37 A	9 ¼ 2:11 P	13 ¾ 0:28 P	9 N 10:56 P
20 ¼ 1:37 P	17 F 0:15 A	20 N 10:22 A	17 ¼ 2:15 A
27 F 9:06 A	23 ¾ 4:05 P	28 ¼ 6:19 A	25 F 7:11 A
Dec 4 ¾ 2:33 A	Dec 1 N 4:50 A	Dec 6 F 0:41 A	Dec 2 ¾ 4:51 P
12 N 5:07 A	9 ¼ 9:43 A	12 ¾ 8:08 P	9 N 10:17 A
20 ¼ 3:44 A	16 F 11:39 A	20 N 1:25 A	16 ¼ 10:44 P
26 F 7:56 P	23 ¾ 2:28 A	28 ¼ 4:00 A	24 F 11:25 P
	30 N 11:43 P		

1932	1933	1934	1935
Jan 1 ¾ 1:24 A	Jan 3 ¼ 4:25 P	Jan 8 ¾ 9:37 P	Jan 5 N 5:21 A
7 N 11:30 P	11 F 8:37 P	15 N 1:38 P	11 ¼ 8:56 P
15 ¼ 8:56 P	19 ¾ 6:16 A	22 ¼ 11:51 A	19 F 3:45 P
23 F 1:45 P	25 N 11:21 P	30 F 4:33 P	27 ¾ 8:00 P
30 ¾ 9:33 A	Feb 2 ¼ 1:17 P	Feb 7 ¾ 9:23 A	Feb 3 N 4:28 P
Feb 6 N 2:46 P	10 F 1:02 P	14 N 0:44 A	10 ¼ 9:26 A
14 ¼ 6:17 P	17 ¾ 2:09 P	21 ¼ 6:06 A	18 F 11:18 A
22 F 2:08 A	24 N 0:45 P	Mar 1 F 10:27 A	26 ¾ 10:15 A
28 ¾ 6:04 P	Mar 4 ¼ 10:24 A	8 ¾ 6:07 P	Mar 5 N 2:41 A
Mar 7 N 7:45 A	12 F 2:47 A	15 N 0:09 P	12 ¼ 0:31 A
15 ¼ 0:42 P	18 ¾ 9:06 P	23 ¼ 1:46 A	20 F 5:33 A
22 F 0:38 P	26 N 3:21 A	31 F 1:16 A	27 ¾ 8:52 P
29 ¾ 3:45 A	Apr 3 ¼ 5:58 A	Apr 7 ¾ 0:50 A	Apr 3 N 0:12 P
Apr 6 N 1:22 A	10 F 1:39 P	13 N 11:58 P	10 ¼ 5:43 P
14 ¼ 3:17 A	17 ¾ 4:19 A	21 ¼ 9:22 P	18 F 9:11 P
20 F 9:28 P	24 N 6:39 P	29 F 0:47 P	26 ¾ 4:22 A
27 ¾ 3:15 P	May 2 ¼ 10:40 P	May 6 ¾ 6:42 A	May 2 N 9:37 P
May 5 N 6:13 P	9 F 10:05 A	13 N 0:31 P	10 ¼ 11:55 A
13 ¼ 2:03 P	16 ¾ 0:51 A	21 ¼ 3:21 P	18 F 9:58 A
20 F 5:09 A	24 N 10:08 A	28 F 9:42 P	25 ¾ 9:45 A
27 ¾ 4:56 A	Jun 1 ¼ 11:54 A	Jun 4 ¾ 0:54 P	Jun 1 N 7:53 P
Jun 4 N 9:17 A	8 F 5:06 A	12 N 2:13 A	9 ¼ 5:51 A
11 ¼ 9:40 P	14 ¾ 11:27 P	20 ¼ 6:38 A	16 F 8:21 P
18 F 0:39 P	23 N 1:23 A	27 F 5:09 A	23 ¾ 2:22 P
25 ¾ 8:37 P	30 ¼ 9:41 P	Jul 3 ¾ 8:29 P	30 N 7:46 P
Jul 3 N 10:21 P	Jul 7 F 11:52 A	11 N 5:07 P	Jul 8 ¼ 10:29 P
11 ¼ 3:08 A	14 ¾ 0:25 P	19 ¼ 6:54 P	16 F 5:01 A
17 F 9:07 P	22 N 4:04 P	26 F 0:10 P	22 ¾ 7:43 P
25 ¾ 1:43 P	30 ¼ 4:45 A	Aug 2 ¾ 6:28 A	30 N 9:34 A
Aug 2 N 9:43 A	Aug 5 F 7:33 P	10 N 8:47 A	Aug 7 ¼ 1:24 P
9 ¼ 7:42 A	13 ¾ 3:51 A	18 ¼ 4:34 A	14 F 0:45 A
16 F 7:43 A	21 N 5:49 A	24 F 7:38 P	21 ¾ 3:19 A
24 ¾ 7:23 A	28 ¼ 10:14 A	31 ¾ 7:41 P	29 N 1:02 A
31 N 7:56 P	Sep 4 F 5:05 A	Sep 9 N 0:21 A	Sep 6 ¼ 2:27 A
Sep 7 ¼ 0:50 P	11 ¾ 9:31 P	16 ¼ 0:27 P	12 F 8:19 P
14 F 9:07 A	19 N 6:22 P	23 F 4:20 P	19 ¾ 2:24 P
23 ¾ 0:48 A	26 ¼ 3:37 P	30 ¾ 0:30 P	27 N 5:31 P
30 N 5:31 A	Oct 3 F 5:09 P	Oct 8 N 3:06 P	Oct 5 ¼ 1:41 P
Oct 6 ¼ 8:06 P	11 ¾ 4:47 P	15 ¼ 7:40 P	12 F 4:40 A
14 F 1:19 P	19 N 5:46 A	22 F 3:02 P	19 ¾ 5:38 A
22 ¾ 5:15 P	25 ¼ 10:22 P	30 ¾ 8:23 A	27 N 10:17 A
29 N 2:57 P	Nov 2 F 8:00 A	Nov 7 N 4:45 P	Nov 3 ¼ 11:13 P
Nov 5 ¼ 6:52 A	10 ¾ 0:19 P	14 ¼ 2:40 A	10 F 2:43 P
13 F 7:29 A	17 N 4:25 P	21 F 4:27 A	18 ¾ 0:37 A
21 ¾ 7:59 A	24 ¼ 7:40 A	29 ¾ 5:40 A	26 N 2:37 A
28 N 0:44 A	Dec 2 F 1:32 A	Dec 6 N 5:26 P	Dec 3 ¼ 7:29 A
Dec 4 ¼ 9:46 P	10 ¾ 6:25 A	13 ¼ 10:53 A	10 F 3:11 A
13 F 2:22 A	17 N 2:54 A	20 F 8:55 P	17 ¾ 9:59 P
20 ¾ 8:23 P	23 ¼ 8:10 P	29 ¾ 2:09 A	25 N 5:51 P
27 N 11:23 A	31 F 8:55 P		

1936	1937	1938	1939
Jan 1 ¼ 3:16 P	Jan 4 ¾ 2:23 P	Jan 1 N 6:59 P	Jan 5 F 9:31 P
8 F 6:16 P	12 N 4:48 P	9 ¼ 2:14 P	12 ¾ 1:12 P
16 ¾ 7:42 P	19 ¼ 8:03 P	16 F 5:54 A	20 N 1:28 P
24 N 7:19 A	26 F 5:16 P	23 ¾ 8:10 A	28 ¼ 3:01 P
30 ¼ 11:37 P	Feb 3 ¾ 0:06 P	31 N 1:36 P	Feb 4 F 7:56 A
Feb 7 F 11:20 A	11 N 7:35 A	Feb 8 ¼ 0:34 A	11 ¾ 4:13 A
15 ¾ 3:47 P	18 ¼ 3:51 A	14 F 5:16 P	19 N 8:29 A
22 N 6:43 P	25 F 7:44 A	22 ¾ 4:26 A	27 ¼ 3:27 A
29 ¼ 9:29 A	Mar 5 ¾ 9:18 A	Mar 2 N 5:41 A	Mar 5 F 6:02 P
Mar 8 F 5:15 A	12 N 7:33 P	9 ¼ 8:36 A	12 ¾ 9:38 P
16 ¾ 8:36 A	19 ¼ 11:47 P	16 F 5:16 A	21 N 1:51 A
23 N 4:14 A	26 F 11:13 P	24 ¾ 1:07 A	28 ¼ 0:17 P
29 ¼ 9:23 P	Apr 4 ¾ 3:54 A	31 N 6:53 P	Apr 4 F 4:19 A
Apr 6 F 10:48 P	11 N 5:11 A	Apr 7 ¼ 3:11 P	11 ¾ 4:13 P
14 ¾ 9:22 A	17 ¼ 8:35 P	14 F 6:22 P	19 N 4:36 P
21 N 0:34 P	25 F 3:25 P	22 ¾ 8:16 P	26 ¼ 6:26 P
28 ¼ 11:17 A	May 3 ¾ 6:38 P	30 N 5:29 A	May 3 F 3:16 P
May 6 F 3:02 P	10 N 1:18 P	May 6 ¼ 9:25 P	11 ¾ 10:41 A
14 ¾ 6:13 A	17 ¼ 6:51 P	14 F 8:40 A	19 N 4:26 A
20 N 8:36 P	25 F 7:39 A	22 ¾ 0:37 P	25 ¼ 11:21 P
28 ¼ 2:47 A	Jun 2 ¾ 5:25 A	29 N 2:01 P	Jun 2 F 3:12 A
Jun 5 F 5:24 A	8 N 8:44 P	Jun 5 ¼ 4:33 A	10 ¾ 4:08 A
12 ¾ 0:06 P	15 ¼ 7:04 P	12 F 11:48 P	17 N 1:38 P
19 N 5:15 A	23 F 11:01 P	21 ¾ 1:53 A	24 ¼ 4:36 A
26 ¼ 7:24 P	Jul 1 ¾ 1:04 P	27 N 9:11 P	Jul 1 F 4:17 P
Jul 4 F 5:36 P	8 N 4:14 A	Jul 4 ¼ 1:48 A	9 ¾ 7:50 P
11 ¾ 4:29 P	15 ¼ 9:38 A	12 F 3:06 P	16 N 9:04 P
18 N 3:20 P	23 F 0:47 P	20 ¾ 0:20 A	23 ¼ 11:35 A
26 ¼ 0:37 P	30 ¾ 6:48 P	27 N 3:54 A	31 F 6:38 A
Aug 3 F 3:48 A	Aug 6 N 0:38 P	Aug 3 ¼ 2:01 A	Aug 8 ¾ 9:19 A
9 ¾ 9:00 P	14 ¼ 2:30 A	11 F 5:58 A	15 N 3:54 A
17 N 3:22 A	22 F 0:48 A	18 ¾ 8:31 P	21 ¼ 9:22 P
25 ¼ 5:50 A	28 ¾ 11:56 P	25 N 11:18 A	29 F 10:10 P
Sep 1 F 0:38 P	Sep 4 N 10:55 P	Sep 1 ¼ 5:29 P	Sep 6 ¾ 8:26 P
8 ¾ 3:15 A	12 ¼ 8:58 P	9 F 8:09 P	13 N 11:23 A
15 N 5:43 P	20 F 11:34 A	17 ¾ 3:13 A	20 ¼ 10:35 A
23 ¼ 10:14 P	27 ¾ 5:44 A	23 N 8:35 P	28 F 2:28 P
30 F 902 P	Oct 4 N 11:59 A	Oct 1 ¼ 11:46 A	Oct 6 ¾ 5:29 A
Oct 7 ¾ 0:29 P	12 ¼ 3:48 P	9 F 9:38 A	12 N 8:31 P
15 N 10:22 A	19 F 9:49 P	16 ¾ 9:25 A	20 ¼ 3:26 A
23 ¼ 0:55 P	26 ¾ 1:27 P	23 N 8:43 A	28 F 6:43 P
30 F 5:59 A	Nov 3 N 4:17 A	31 ¼ 7:46 A	Nov 4 ¾ 1:13 P
Nov 6 ¾ 1:30 A	11 ¼ 9:35 A	Nov 7 F 10:25 P	11 N 7:55 A
14 N 4:43 A	18 F 8:10 A	14 ¾ 4:21 P	18 ¼ 11:22 P
22 ¼ 1:20 A	25 ¾ 0:05 A	22 N 0:06 A	26 F 9:56 P
28 F 4:13 P	Dec 2 N 11:12 P	30 ¼ 4:01 A	Dec 3 ¾ 8:41 P
Dec 5 ¾ 6:21 P	11 ¼ 1:14 A	Dec 7 F 10:23 A	10 N 9:47 P
13 N 11:26 P	17 F 6:54 P	14 ¾ 1:18 A	18 ¼ 9:05 P
21 ¼ 11:31 A	24 ¾ 2:21 P	21 N 6:08 P	26 F 11:30 A
28 F 4:01 A		29 ¼ 10:54 P	

1940	1941	1942	1943
Jan 2 ¾ 4:57 A	Jan 5 ¼ 1:41 P	Jan 2 F 3:43 P	Jan 6 N 0:39 P
9 N 1:54 P	13 F 11:05 A	10 ¾ 6:06 A	13 ¼ 7:50 A
17 ¼ 6:22 P	20 ¾ 10:03 A	16 N 9:33 P	21 F 10:49 A
24 F 11:23 P	27 N 11:04 A	24 ¼ 6:37 A	29 ¾ 8:14 A
31 ¾ 2:48 P	Feb 4 ¼ 11:44 A	Feb 1 F 9:13 A	Feb 4 N 11:30 P
Feb 8 N 7:46 A	12 F 0:28 A	8 ¾ 2:53 P	12 ¼ 0:41 A
16 ¼ 0:57 P	18 ¾ 6:08 P	15 N 10:04 A	20 F 5:46 A
23 F 9:56 A	26 N 3:03 A	23 ¼ 3:41 A	27 ¾ 6:24 P
Mar 1 ¾ 2:36 A	Mar 6 ¼ 7:44 A	Mar 3 F 0:21 A	Mar 6 N 10:35 A
9 N 2:24 A	13 F 11:48 A	9 ¾ 10:02 P	13 ¼ 7:31 P
17 ¼ 3:26 A	20 ¾ 2:53 A	16 N 11:51 P	21 F 10:09 P
23 F 7:34 P	27 N 8:15 P	25 ¼ 0:02 A	29 ¾ 1:53 A
30 ¾ 4:21 P	Apr 5 ¼ 0:13 A	Apr 1 F 0:33 P	Apr 4 N 9:54 P
Apr 7 N 8:20 P	11 F 9:16 P	8 ¾ 4:44 A	12 ¼ 3:05 P
15 ¼ 1:47 P	18 ¾ 1:04 P	15 N 2:35 P	20 F 11:12 A
22 F 4:38 A	26 N 1:24 P	23 ¼ 6:11 P	27 ¾ 7:52 A
29 ¾ 7:50 A	May 4 ¼ 0:50 P	30 F 10:01 P	May 4 N 9:44 A
May 7 N 0:08 P	11 F 5:16 A	May 7 ¾ 0:14 P	12 ¼ 9:54 A
14 ¼ 8:52 P	18 ¾ 1:18 A	15 N 5:46 A	19 F 9:14 P
21 F 1:34 P	26 N 5:20 A	23 ¼ 9:12 A	26 ¾ 1:35 P
29 ¾ 0:42 A	Jun 2 ¼ 9:57 P	30 F 5:30 A	Jun 2 N 10:34 P
Jun 6 N 1:06 A	9 F 0:35 P	Jun 5 ¾ 9:27 P	11 ¼ 2:37 A
13 ¼ 2:00 A	16 ¾ 3:46 P	13 N 9:03 P	18 F 5:15 A
19 F 11:03 P	24 N 7:23 P	21 ¼ 8:46 P	24 ¾ 8:09 P
27 ¾ 6:14 P	Jul 2 ¼ 4:25 A	28 F 0:10 P	Jul 2 N 0:45 P
Jul 5 N 11:29 A	8 F 8:19 P	Jul 5 ¾ 8:59 A	10 ¼ 4:30 P
12 ¼ 6:36 A	16 ¾ 8:09 A	13 N 0:04 P	17 F 0:23 P
19 F 9:57 A	24 N 7:40 A	21 ¼ 5:14 A	24 ¾ 4:40 A
27 ¾ 11:31 A	31 ¼ 9:20 A	27 F 7:15 P	Aug 1 N 4:08 A
Aug 3 N 8:10 P	Aug 7 F 5:40 A	Aug 3 ¾ 11:05 P	9 ¼ 3:37 A
10 ¼ 0:01 P	15 ¾ 1:41 A	12 N 2:29 A	15 F 7:35 P
17 F 11:04 P	22 N 6:35 P	19 ¼ 11:32 A	22 ¾ 4:05 P
26 ¾ 3:34 A	29 ¼ 2:05 P	26 F 3:47 A	30 N 8:01 P
Sep 2 N 4:16 A	Sep 5 F 5:37 P	Sep 2 ¾ 3:43 P	Sep 7 ¼ 0:34 P
8 ¼ 7:33 P	13 ¾ 7:32 P	10 N 3:54 P	14 F 3:41 A
16 F 2:42 P	21 N 4:40 A	17 ¼ 4:58 P	21 ¾ 7:07 A
24 ¾ 5:48 P	27 ¼ 8:10 P	24 F 2:35 P	29 N 11:31 A
Oct 1 N 0:42 P	Oct 5 F 8:34 A	Oct 2 ¾ 10:28 A	Oct 6 ¼ 8:11 P
8 ¼ 6:19 A	10 ¾ 0:53 P	10 N 4:07 A	13 F 1:24 P
16 F 8:16 A	20 N 2:21 P	16 ¼ 10:59 P	21 ¾ 1:43 A
24 ¾ 6:05 A	27 ¼ 5:05 A	24 F 4:07 A	29 N 2:00 A
30 N 10:04 P	Nov 4 F 2:01 A	Nov 1 ¾ 6:19 A	Nov 5 ¼ 3:23 A
Nov 6 ¼ 9:09 P	12 ¾ 4:55 A	8 N 3:20 P	12 F 1:28 A
15 F 2:25 A	19 N 0:05 A	15 ¼ 6:58 A	19 ¾ 10:44 P
22 ¾ 4:37 P	25 ¼ 5:54 P	22 F 8:26 P	27 N 3:24 P
29 N 8:43 A	Dec 3 F 8:52 P	Dec 1 ¾ 1:38 A	Dec 4 ¼ 11:05 A
Dec 6 ¼ 4:02 P	11 ¾ 6:49 P	8 N 2:00 A	11 F 4:26 P
14 F 7:39 P	18 N 10:19 A	14 ¼ 5:48 P	19 ¾ 8:05 P
22 ¾ 1:46 A	25 ¼ 10:45 A	22 F 3:04 P	27 N 3:51 A
28 N 8:57 P		30 ¾ 6:38 P	

1944	1945	1946	1947
Jan 2 ¼ 8:05 P	Jan 6 ¾ 0:49 P	Jan 3 N 0:31 P	Jan 7 F 4:48 A
10 F 10:11 A	14 N 5:08 A	10 ¼ 8:28 P	14 ¾ 2:57 A
18 ¾ 3:33 P	20 ¼ 11:49 P	17 F 2:48 P	22 N 8:36 A
25 N 3:25 P	28 F 6:42 A	25 ¾ 5:01 A	30 ¼ 0:08 A
Feb 1 ¼ 7:09 A	Feb 5 ¾ 9:57 A	Feb 2 N 4:44 A	Feb 5 F 3:52 P
9 F 5:31 A	12 N 5:34 P	9 ¼ 4:29 A	12 ¾ 9:59 P
17 ¾ 7:43 A	19 ¼ 8:39 A	16 F 4:29 A	21 N 2:01 A
24 N 2:00 A	27 F 0:08 A	24 ¾ 2:38 A	28 ¼ 9:13 A
Mar 1 ¼ 8:41 P	Mar 7 ¾ 4:31 A	Mar 3 N 6:03 P	Mar 7 F 3:16 A
10 F 0:29 A	14 N 3:52 A	10 ¼ 0:04 P	14 ¾ 6:29 P
17 ¾ 8:06 P	20 ¼ 7:13 P	17 F 7:12 P	22 N 4:35 P
24 N 11:37 A	28 F 5:46 P	25 ¾ 10:39 P	29 ¼ 4:16 P
31 ¼ 0:36 P	Apr 5 ¾ 7:20 P	Apr 2 N 4:38 A	Apr 5 F 3:30 P
Apr 8 F 5:23 P	12 N 0:31 P	8 ¼ 8:05 P	13 ¾ 2:25 P
16 ¾ 5:00 A	19 ¼ 7:48 A	16 F 10:48 A	21 N 4:20 A
22 N 8:45 P	27 F 10:34 A	24 ¾ 3:20 P	27 ¼ 10:19 P
30 ¼ 6:08 A	May 5 ¾ 6:03 A	May 1 N 1:17 P	May 5 F 4:55 P
May 8 F 7:29 A	11 N 8:23 P	8 ¼ 5:15 A	13 ¾ 8:09 A
15 ¾ 11:13 A	18 ¼ 10:13 A	16 F 2:54 A	20 N 1:45 P
22 N 6:14 A	27 F 1:50 A	24 ¾ 4:03 A	27 ¼ 4:37 A
30 ¼ 0:08 A	Jun 3 ¾ 1:16 P	30 N 8:51 P	Jun 3 F 7:28 P
Jun 6 F 6:59 P	10 N 4:27 A	Jun 6 ¼ 4:08 P	11 ¾ 10:59 P
13 ¾ 3:58 P	17 ¼ 2:07 P	14 F 6:43 P	18 N 9:27 P
20 N 5:01 P	25 F 3:09 P	22 ¾ 1:13 P	25 ¼ 0:26 P
28 ¼ 5:28 P	Jul 2 ¾ 6:14 P	29 N 4:07 A	Jul 3 F 10:40 A
Jul 6 F 4:28 A	9 N 1:36 P	Jul 6 ¼ 5:17 A	11 ¾ 10:56 A
12 ¾ 8:40 P	17 ¼ 7:02 A	14 F 9:24 A	18 N 4:16 A
20 N 5:44 A	25 F 2:27 A	21 ¾ 7:53 P	24 ¼ 10:55 P
28 ¼ 9:25 A	31 ¾ 10:31 P	28 N 11:55 A	Aug 2 F 1:51 A
Aug 4 F 0:40 P	Aug 8 N 0:33 A	Aug 4 ¼ 8:57 P	9 ¾ 8:23 P
11 ¾ 2:53 A	16 ¼ 0:28 P	12 F 10:27 P	16 N 11:14 A
18 N 8:26 P	23 F 0:04 P	20 ¾ 1:18 A	23 ¼ 0:41 P
26 ¼ 11:40 P	30 ¾ 3:46 A	26 N 9:09 P	31 F 4:35 P
Sep 2 F 8:22 P	Sep 6 N 1:45 P	Sep 3 ¼ 2:50 P	Sep 8 ¾ 3:58 A
9 ¾ 0:04 P	14 ¼ 5:40 P	11 F 10:01 A	14 N 7:29 P
17 N 0:38 P	21 F 8:47 P	18 ¾ 6:46 A	22 ¼ 5:43 A
25 ¼ 0:08 P	28 ¾ 11:25 A	25 N 8:46 A	30 F 6:42 A
Oct 2 F 4:23 A	Oct 6 N 5:24 A	Oct 3 ¼ 9:55 A	Oct 7 ¾ 10:30 A
9 ¾ 1:13 A	14 ¼ 9:39 A	10 F 8:42 P	14 N 6:11 A
17 N 5:36 A	21 F 5:33 P	17 ¾ 1:29 P	22 ¼ 1:12 A
24 ¼ 10:49 P	27 ¾ 10:31 P	24 N 11:33 P	29 F 8:08 P
31 F 1:37 P	Nov 4 N 11:12 P	Nov 2 ¼ 4:42 A	Nov 5 ¾ 5:05 P
Nov 7 ¾ 6:30 P	12 ¼ 11:35 P	9 F 7:11 A	12 N 8:02 P
15 N 10:31 P	19 F 3:14 P	15 ¾ 10:36 P	20 ¼ 9:45 P
23 ¼ 7:54 A	26 ¾ 1:29 P	23 N 5:25 P	28 F 8:46 A
30 F 0:53 A	Dec 4 N 6:08 P	Dec 1 ¼ 9:49 P	Dec 5 ¾ 0:56 A
Dec 7 ¾ 2:58 P	12 ¼ 11:06 A	8 F 5:53 P	12 N 0:55 P
15 N 2:36 P	19 F 2:18 A	15 ¾ 10:58 A	20 ¼ 5:45 P
22 ¼ 3:55 P	26 ¾ 8:02 A	23 N 1:07 P	27 F 8:28 P
29 F 2:39 P		31 ¼ 0:24 P	

1948	1949	1950	1951
Jan 3 ¾ 11:14 A	Jan 7 ¼ 11:53 A	Jan 4 F 7:48 A	Jan 1 ¾ 5:12 A
11 N 7:46 A	14 F 10:01 P	11 ¾ 10:32 A	7 N 8:11 P
19 ¼ 11:33 A	21 ¾ 2:09 P	18 N 8:00 A	15 ¼ 0:23 A
26 F 7:12 A	29 N 2:44 A	26 ¼ 4:40 A	23 F 4:48 A
Feb 2 ¾ 0:33 A	Feb 6 ¼ 8:07 A	Feb 2 F 10:17 P	30 ¾ 3:14 P
10 N 3:03 A	13 F 9:09 A	9 ¾ 6:33 P	Feb 6 N 7:54 P
18 ¼ 1:56 A	20 ¾ 0:44 A	16 N 10:53 P	13 ¼ 8:56 P
24 F 5:17 P	27 N 8:56 P	25 ¼ 1:53 P	21 F 9:13 P
Mar 2 ¾ 4:37 P	Mar 8 ¼ 0:43 A	Mar 4 F 10:34 A	28 ¾ 11:00 P
10 N 9:16 P	14 F 7:04 P	11 ¾ 2:39 A	Mar 7 N 8:51 P
18 ¼ 0:28 P	21 ¾ 1:12 P	18 N 3:21 P	15 ¼ 5:40 P
25 F 3:11 A	29 N 3:12 P	26 ¼ 8:10 P	23 F 10:50 A
Apr 1 ¾ 10:26 A	Apr 6 ¼ 1:03 P	Apr 2 F 8:49 P	30 ¾ 5:35 A
9 N 1:18 A	13 F 4:09 A	9 ¾ 11:43 A	Apr 6 N 10:52 A
16 ¼ 7:43 P	20 ¾ 3:29 A	17 N 8:26 A	14 ¼ 0:56 P
23 F 1:30 P	28 N 8:04 A	25 ¼ 10:40 A	21 F 9:31 P
May 1 ¾ 4:50 A	May 5 ¼ 9:34 P	May 2 F 5:20 A	28 ¾ 0:18 P
9 N 2:31 A	12 F 0:52 P	8 ¾ 10:32 P	May 6 N 1:36 A
16 ¼ 0:56 A	19 ¾ 7:23 P	17 N 0:55 A	14 ¼ 5:32 A
23 F 0:38 A	27 N 10:25 P	24 ¼ 9:29 P	21 F 5:45 P
30 ¾ 10:44 P	Jun 4 ¼ 3:28 A	31 F 0:44 P	27 ¾ 8:17 P
Jun 7 N 0:57 P	10 F 9:47 P	Jun 7 ¾ 11:36 A	Jun 4 N 4:41 P
14 ¼ 5:41 A	18 ¾ 0:31 P	15 N 3:53 P	12 ¼ 6:52 P
21 F 0:55 P	26 N 10:03 A	23 ¼ 5:13 A	19 F 0:37 P
29 ¾ 3:24 P	Jul 3 ¼ 8:09 A	29 F 7:59 P	26 ¾ 6:22 A
Jul 6 N 9:10 P	10 F 7:42 A	Jul 7 ¾ 2:54 A	Jul 4 N 7:49 A
13 ¼ 11:31 A	18 ¾ 6:03 A	15 N 5:06 A	12 ¼ 4:57 A
21 F 2:32 A	25 N 7:34 P	22 ¼ 10:51 A	18 F 7:18 A
29 ¾ 6:13 A	Aug 1 ¼ 0:59 P	29 F 4:18 A	25 ¾ 7:00 P
Aug 5 N 4:14 A	8 F 7:35 P	Aug 5 ¾ 7:56 P	Aug 2 N 10:40 P
11 ¼ 7:41 P	16 ¾ 11:00 P	13 N 4:49 P	10 ¼ 0:23 P
19 F 5:33 P	24 N 4:00 A	20 ¼ 3:36 P	17 F 3:00 A
27 ¾ 6:47 P	30 ¼ 7:18 P	27 F 2:52 P	24 ¾ 10:21 A
Sep 3 N 11:22 A	Sep 7 F 10:01 A	Sep 4 ¾ 1:54 P	Sep 1 N 0:50 P
10 ¼ 7:06 A	15 ¾ 2:30 P	12 N 3:29 A	8 ¼ 6:17 P
18 F 9:44 A	22 N 0:22 P	18 ¼ 8:55 P	15 F 0:39 P
26 ¾ 5:08 A	29 ¼ 4:20 A	26 F 4:22 A	23 ¾ 4:14 A
Oct 2 N 7:43 P	Oct 7 F 2:54 A	Oct 4 ¾ 7:54 A	Oct 1 N 1:57 A
9 ¼ 10:12 P	15 ¾ 4:07 A	11 N 1:34 P	8 ¼ 0:01 P
18 F 2:25 A	21 N 9:24 P	18 ¼ 4:18 A	15 F 0:52 P
25 ¾ 1:43 P	28 ¼ 5:06 P	25 F 8:47 P	22 ¾ 11:56 P
Nov 1 N 6:04 A	Nov 5 F 9:10 P	Nov 3 ¾ 1:01 A	30 N 1:55 P
8 ¼ 4:48 P	13 ¾ 3:49 P	9 N 11:26 P	Nov 6 ¼ 6:59 A
16 F 6:33 P	20 N 7:30 A	16 ¼ 3:07 P	13 F 3:53 P
23 ¾ 9:23 P	27 ¼ 10:03 A	24 F 3:15 P	21 ¾ 8:02 P
30 N 6:46 P	Dec 5 F 3:15 P	Dec 2 ¾ 4:22 P	29 N 1:01 A
Dec 8 ¼ 1:59 P	13 ¾ 1:49 A	9 N 9:29 P	Dec 5 ¼ 4:21 P
16 F 9:12 A	19 N 6:57 P	16 ¼ 5:57 A	13 F 9:31 A
23 ¾ 5:13 A	27 ¼ 6:33 A	24 F 10:24 A	21 ¾ 2:38 P
30 N 9:46 A			28 N 11:44 A

1952	1953	1954	1955
Jan 4 ¼ 4:43 A	Jan 8 ¾ 10:10 A	Jan 5 N 2:22 A	Jan 1 ¼ 8:29 P
12 F 4:56 A	15 N 2:09 P	12 ¼ 0:22 A	8 F 0:45 P
20 ¾ 6:10 A	22 ¼ 5:43 A	19 F 2:37 A	15 ¾ 10:14 P
26 N 10:27 P	29 F 11:45 P	27 ¾ 3:29 A	24 N 10:7 A
Feb 2 ¼ 8:02 P	Feb 7 ¾ 4:10 A	Feb 3 N 3:56 P	31 ¼ 5:06 A
11 F 0:29 A	14 N 1:11 A	10 ¼ 8:30 A	Feb 7 F 1:43 A
18 ¾ 6:02 A	20 ¼ 5:45 A	17 F 7:18 P	14 ¾ 7:40 A
25 N 9:16 A	28 F 6:59 P	25 ¾ 11:30 P	22 N 3:55 P
Mar 3 ¼ 1:44 P	Mar 8 ¾ 6:27 P	Mar 5 N 3:12 A	Mar 1 v 0:41 P
11 F 6:15 P	15 N 11:05 A	11 ¼ 5:52 P	8 F 3:42 P
19 ¾ 2:40 A	22 ¼ 8:11 A	19 F 0:43 P	16 ¾ 4:37 P
25 N 8:13 P	30 F 0:55 P	27 ¾ 4:14 P	24 N 3:43 P
Apr 2 ¼ 8:49 A	Apr 7 ¾ 4:59 A	Apr 3 N 0:25 P	30 ¼ 8:10 P
10 F 8:54 A	13 N 8:10 P	10 ¼ 5:06 A	Apr 7 F 6:36 A
17 ¾ 9:08 A	21 ¼ 0:41 A	18 F 5:49 A	15 ¾ 11:01 A
24 N 7:28 A	29 F 4:21 A	26 ¾ 4:58 A	22 N 1:07 P
May 2 ¼ 3:58 A	May 6 ¾ 0:21 P	May 2 N 8:23 P	29 ¼ 4:24 A
9 F 8:16 P	13 N 5:06 A	9 ¼ 6:18 P	May 6 F 10:15 P
16 ¾ 2:40 P	20 ¼ 6:21 P	17 F 9:48 P	15 ¾ 1:43 A
23 N 7:28 P	28 F 5:04 P	25 ¾ 1:50 P	21 N 8:59 P
31 ¼ 9:47 P	Jun 4 ¾ 5:36 P	Jun 1 N 4:03 A	28 ¼ 2:02 P
Jun 8 F 5:07 A	11 N 2:55 P	8 ¼ 9:14 A	Jun 5 F 2:09 P
14 ¾ 8:28 P	19 ¼ 0:02 P	16 F 0:06 P	13 ¾ 0:38 P
22 N 8:46 P	27 F 3:30 A	23 ¾ 7:46 P	20 N 4:12 A
30 ¼ 1:12 P	Jul 3 ¾ 10:04 A	30 N 0:26 P	27 ¼ 1:45 A
Jul 7 F 0:34 P	11 N 2:29 A	Jul 8 ¼ 1:34 A	Jul 5 F 5:219 A
14 ¾ 3:43 A	19 ¼ 4:48 A	16 F 0:30 A	12 ¾ 8:31 P
21 N 11:31 P	26 F 0:21 P	23 ¾ 0:14 A	19 N 11:35 A
30 ¼ 1:52 A	Aug 2 ¾ 3:17 A	29 N 10:20 P	26 ¼ 4:00 P
Aug 5 F 7:41 P	9 N 4:11 P	Aug 6 ¼ 6:51 A	Aug 3 F 7:31 P
12 ¾ 1:28 P	17 ¼ 8:09 P	14 F 11:04 P	11 ¾ 2:33 A
20 N 3:21 P	24 F 8:21 P	23 ¾ 4:52 A	17 N 7:59 P
28 ¼ 0:04 P	31 ¾ 10:47 A	28 N 10:21 P	25 ¼ 8:52 A
Sep 4 F 3:20 A	Sep 8 N 7:49 A	Sep 5 ¼ 0:29 P	Sep 2 F 8:00 A
11 ¾ 2:37 A	16 ¼ 9:50 A	12 F 8:20 P	9 ¾ 8:00 A
19 N 7:22 P	23 F 4:16 A	19 ¾ 11:12 A	16 N 6:20 A
26 ¼ 8:31 P	29 ¾ 9:52 A	27 N 0:51 A	24 ¼ 3:41 A
Oct 3 F 0:16 P	Oct 8 N 0:41 A	Oct 5 ¼ 5:32 A	Oct 1 F 7:18 P
10 ¾ 7:33 P	15 ¼ 9:45 P	12 F 5:10 A	8 ¾ 2:04 P
18 N 10:43 P	22 F 0:56 P	18 v 8:31 A	15 N 7:33 P
26 ¼ 4:05 A	29 ¾ 1:10 P	26 N 5:48 P	23 ¼ 11:05 P
Nov 1 F 11:10 P	Nov 6 N 5:58 P	Nov 3 ¼ 8:55 P	31 F 6:04 A
9 ¾ 3:44 P	14 ¼ 7:53 A	10 F 2:30 P	Nov 6 ¾ 9:57 P
17 N 0:56 P	20 F 11:13 P	17 ¾ 9:33 A	14 N 0:02 P
24 ¼ 11:35 A	28 ¾ 8:17 A	25 N 0:31 P	22 ¼ 5:30 P
Dec 1 F 0:42 P	Dec 6 N 10:49 A	Dec 3 ¼ 9:57 A	29 F 4:51 P
9 ¾ 1:22 P	13 ¼ 4:31 P	10 F 0:57 P	Dec 6 ¾ 8:36 A
17 N 2:03 A	20 F 11:44 A	17 ¾ 2:22 A	14 N 7:08 A
23 ¼ 7:52 P	28 ¾ 5:44 A	25 N 7:34 A	22 ¼ 9:40 A
31 F 5:06 A			29 F 3:44 A

1956				1957				1958				1959			
Jan	4	¾	10:42 P	Jan	1	N	2:14 A	Jan	5	F	8:09 P	Jan	2	¾	10:51 A
	13	N	3:02 A		9	¼	7:07 A		12	¾	2:02 P		9	N	5:34 A
	20	¼	10:59 P		16	F	6:22 A		19	N	10:09 P		16	¼	9:27 P
	27	F	2:41 P		22	¾	9:48 P		28	¼	2:17 A		24	F	7:33 P
Feb	3	¾	4:09 P		30	N	9:26 P	Feb	4	F	8:06 A		31	¾	7:07 P
	11	N	9:38 P	Feb	7	¼	11:24 P		10	¾	11:34 P	Feb	7	N	7:23 P
	19	¼	9:22 A		14	F	4:39 P		18	N	3:39 P		15	¼	7:21 P
	26	F	1:42 A		21	¾	0:19 P		26	¼	8:52 P		23	F	8:54 A
Mar	4	¾	11:54 A	Mar	1	N	4:13 P	Mar	5	F	6:29 P	Mar	2	¾	2:55 A
	12	N	1:37 P		9	¼	11:51 A		12	¾	10:48 A		9	N	10:52 A
	19	¼	5:14 P		16	F	2:22 A		20	N	9:51 P		17	¼	3:11 P
	26	F	1:12 P		23	¾	5:05 A		28	¼	11:19 P		24	F	8:03 P
Apr	3	¾	8:07 A		31	N	9:20 A	Apr	4	F	3:45 A		31	¾	11:07 A
	11	N	2:39 A	Apr	7	¼	8:33 P		10	¾	11:51 P	Apr	8	N	3:30 A
	17	¼	11:29 P		14	F	0:10 P		19	N	3:24 A		16	¼	7:33 A
	25	F	1:41 A		21	¾	11:01 P		26	¼	9:36 P		23	F	5:14 A
May	3	¾	2:56 A		29	N	11:54 P	May	3	F	0:24 P		29	¾	8:39 P
	10	N	1:05 P	May	7	¼	2:30 A		10	¾	2:38 P	May	7	N	8:12 P
	17	¼	5:16 A		13	F	10:35 P		18	N	7:01 P		15	¼	8:10 P
	24	F	3:27 P		21	¾	5:04 P		26	¼	4:39 A		22	F	0:57 P
Jun	1	¾	7:14 P		29	N	11:40 A	Jun	1	F	8:56 P		29	¾	8:14 A
	8	N	9:30 P	Jun	5	¼	7:10 A		9	¾	7:00 A	Jun	6	N	11:54 A
	15	¼	11:57 A		12	F	10:03 A		17	N	8:00 A		14	¼	5:23 A
	23	F	6:14 A		20	¾	10:23 A		24	¼	9:45 A		20	F	8:00 P
Jul	1	¾	8:41 A		27	N	8:54 P	Jul	1	F	605 A		27	¾	10:13 P
	8	N	4:38 A	Jul	4	¼	0:10 P		9	¾	0:22 A	Jul	6	N	2:01 A
	14	¼	8:47 P		11	F	10:50 P		16	N	6:34 P		13	¼	0:02 P
	22	F	9:30 P		20	¾	2:18 A		23	¼	2:20 P		20	F	3:34 A
	30	¾	7:32 P		27	N	4:29 A		30	F	4:48 P		27	¾	2:23 P
Aug	6	N	11:25 A	Aug	2	¼	6:56 P	Aug	7	¾	5:50 P	Aug	4	N	2:34 P
	13	¼	8:46 A		10	F	1:09 P		15	N	3:34 A		11	¼	5:10 A
	21	F	0:38 P		18	¾	4:17 P		21	¼	7:45 P		18	F	0:51 P
	29	¾	4:13 A		25	N	11:33 P		29	F	5:54 P		26	¾	8:04 A
Sep	4	N	6:58 P	Sep	1	¼	4:35 A	Sep	6	¾	10:25 A	Sep	3	N	1:56 A
	12	¼	0:14 A		9	F	4:56 A		13	N	0:03 P		9	¼	10:08 P
	20	F	3:20 A		17	¾	4:03 A		20	¼	3:18 A		17	F	0:52 A
	27	¾	11:26 A		23	N	7:19 P		27	F	9:45 P		25	¾	2:23 A
Oct	4	N	4:25 A		30	¼	5:50 P	Oct	6	¾	1:21 A	Oct	3	N	0:31 P
	11	¼	6:45 P	Oct	8	F	9:43 P		12	N	8:53 P		9	¼	4:23 A
	19	F	5:25 P		16	¾	1:45 P		19	¼	2:08 P		16	F	3:59 A
	26	¾	6:03 P		23	N	4:44 A		27	F	3:41 P		24	¾	8:22 P
Nov	2	N	4:44 P		30	¼	10:49 A	Nov	4	¾	2:20 P		31	N	10:42 P
	10	¼	3:10 P	Nov	7	F	2:33 P		11	N	6:34 A	Nov	7	¼	1:24 P
	18	F	6:45 A		14	¾	10:00 P		18	¼	5:00 A		15	F	9:42 A
	25	¾	1:13 A		21	N	4:20 P		26	F	10:18 P		23	¾	1:04 P
Dec	2	N	8:13 A		29	¼	6:58 P	Dec	4	3	1:25 A		30	N	8:46 A
	10	¼	11:52 A	Dec	7	F	6:16 A		10	N	5:24 P	Dec	7	¼	2:12 A
	17	F	7:07 P		14	¾	5:46 A		17	¼	11:53 P		15	F	4:50 A
	24	¾	10:10 A		21	N	6:12 A		26	F	3:55 A		23	¾	3:29 A
					29	¼	4:53 A						29	N	7:10 P

1960

Jan 5 ¼ 6:54 P
13 F 11:51 P
21 ¾ 3:01 P
28 N 6:16 A
Feb 4 ¼ 2:27 P
12 F 5:25 P
19 ¾ 11:48 P
26 N 6:24 P
Mar 5 ¼ 11:06 A
13 F 8:26 A
20 ¾ 6:41 A
27 N 7:38 A
Apr 4 ¼ 7:05 A
11 F 8:28 A
18 ¾ 0:57 P
25 N 9:45 P
May 4 ¼ 1:01 A
11 F 5:43 A
17 ¾ 7:55 P
25 N 0:27 P
Jun 2 ¼ 4:02 P
9 F 1:02 P
16 ¾ 4:36 A
24 N 3:28 A
Jul 2 ¼ 3:49 A
8 F 7:37 P
15 ¾ 3:43 P
23 N 6:31 P
31 ¼ 0:39 P
Aug 7 F 2:41 A
14 ¾ 5:37 A
22 N 9:16 A
29 ¼ 7:23 P
Sep 5 F 11:19 A
12 ¾ 10:20 P
20 N 11:13 P
28 ¼ 1:13 A
Oct 4 F 10:17 P
12 ¾ 5:26 P
20 N 0:03 P
27 ¼ 7:34 A
Nov 3 F 11:58 A
11 ¾ 1:48 P
18 N 11:47 P
25 ¼ 3:42 P
Dec 3 F 4:25 A
11 ¾ 9:39 A
18 N 10:47 A
25 ¼ 2:30 A

1961

Jan 1 F 11:07 P
10 ¾ 3:03 A
16 N 9:31 P
23 ¼ 4:14 P
31 F 6:47 P
Feb 8 ¾ 4:50 P
15 N 8:11 A
22 ¼ 8:35 A
Mar 2 F 1:35 P
10 ¾ 2:58 A
16 N 6:51 P
24 ¼ 2:49 A
Apr 1 F 5:48 A
8 ¾ 10:16 A
15 N 5:38 A
22 ¼ 9:50 P
30 F 6:41 P
May 7 ¾ 3:58 P
14 N 4:55 P
22 ¼ 4:19 P
30 F 4:38 A
Jun 5 ¾ 9:19 P
13 N 5:17 A
21 ¼ 9:02 A
28 F 0:38 P
Jul 5 ¾ 3:33 A
12 N 7:12 P
20 ¼ 11:14 P
27 F 7:51 P
Aug 3 ¾ 11:48 A
11 N 10:37 A
19 ¼ 10:52 A
26 F 3:14 A
Sep 1 ¾ 11:06 P
10 N 2:50 A
17 ¼ 8:24 P
24 F 11:34 A
Oct 1 ¾ 2:11 P
9 N 6:53 P
17 ¼ 4:35 A
23 F 9:31 P
31 ¾ 8:59 A
Nov 8 N 9:59 A
15 ¼ 0:13 A
22 F 9:44 A
30 ¾ 6:19 A
Dec 7 N 11:52 P
14 ¼ 8:06 P
22 F 0:43 P
30 ¾ 3:58 A

1962

Jan 6 N 0:36 P
13 ¼ 5:02 A
20 F 6:17 P
28 ¾ 11:37 P
Feb 5 N 0:11 A
11 ¼ 3:43 P
19 F 1:19 P
27 ¾ 3:50 A
Mar 6 N 10:31 A
13 ¼ 4:39 A
21 F 7:56 A
29 ¾ 4:12 A
Apr 4 N 7:46 P
11 ¼ 7:51 P
20 F 0:34 A
27 ¾ 1:00 P
May 4 N 4:25 A
11 ¼ 0:45 P
19 F 2:33 P
26 ¾ 7:06 P
Jun 2 N 1:27 P
10 ¼ 6:22 A
18 F 2:03 P
24 ¾ 11:43 P
Jul 1 N 11:53 P
9 ¼ 11:40 P
17 F 11:41 A
24 ¾ 4:19 A
31 N 0:24 P
Aug 8 ¼ 3:56 P
15 F 8:10 P
22 ¾ 10:27 A
30 N 3:10 A
Sep 7 ¼ 6:45 A
14 F 4:12 A
20 ¾ 7:36 P
28 N 7:40 P
Oct 6 ¼ 7:55 P
13 F 0:34 P
20 ¾ 8:48 A
28 N 1:06 P
Nov 5 ¼ 7:15 A
11 F 10:04 P
19 ¾ 2:10 A
27 N 6:30 A
Dec 4 ¼ 4:49 P
11 F 9:28 P
18 ¾ 10:43 P
26 N 11:00 P

1963

Jan 3 ¼ 1:02 A
9 F 11:09 P
17 ¾ 8:35 P
25 N 1:43 P
Feb 1 ¼ 8:51 A
8 F 2:52 P
16 ¾ 5:39 P
24 N 2:06 A
Mar 2 ¼ 5:18 P
10 F 7:49 A
18 ¾ 0:08 P
25 N 0:10 P
Apr 1 ¼ 3:15 A
9 F 0:58 A
17 ¾ 2:53 A
23 N 8:29 P
30 ¼ 3:08 P
May 8 F 5:24 P
16 ¾ 1:37 P
23 N 4:00 P
30 ¼ 4:56 A
Jun 7 F 8:31 A
14 ¾ 8:54 P
21 N 11:46 A
28 ¼ 8:24 P
Jul 6 F 9:56 P
14 ¾ 1:58 A
20 N 8:43 P
28 ¼ 1:14 P
Aug 5 F 9:31 A
12 ¾ 6:22 P
19 N 7:35 A
27 ¼ 6:55 P
Sep 3 F 7:34 P
10 ¾ 11:43 P
17 N 8:51 P
26 ¼ 0:39 A
Oct 3 F 4:44 A
9 ¾ 7:28 P
17 N 0:43 P
25 ¼ 5:21 P
Nov 1 F 1:56 P
8 ¾ 6:37 A
16 N 6:51 P
24 ¼ 7:56 P
30 F 11:55 P
Dec 7 ¾ 9:35 P
16 N 2:07 A
23 ¼ 7:55 P
30 F 11:04 A

1964	1965	1966	1967
Jan 6 ¾ 3:59 P	Jan 2 N 9:07 P	Jan 7 F 5:17 A	Jan 3 ¾ 2:20 P
14 N 8:44 P	10 ¼ 9:00 P	13 ¾ 8:00 P	10 N 6:07 P
22 ¼ 5:29 A	17 F 1:38 P	21 N 3:47 P	18 ¼ 7:42 P
28 F 11:23 P	24 ¾ 11:08 A	29 ¼ 7:49 P	26 D 6:41 A
Feb 5 ¾ 0:43 P	Feb 2 N 4:36 P	Feb 5 F 3:59 P	Feb 1 ¾ 11:04 P
13 N 1:02 P	9 ¼ 8:53 A	12 ¾ 8:53 A	9 N 10:45 A
20 ¼ 1:25 P	16 F 0:27 A	20 N 10:49 A	17 ¼ 3:57 P
27 F 0:40 P	23 ¾ 5:40 A	28 ¼ 10:16 A	24 F 5:44 P
Mar 6 ¾ 10:01 A	Mar 3 N 9:56 A	Mar 7 F 1:46 A	Mar 3 ¾ 9:11 A
14 N 2:14 A	10 ¼ 5:53 P	14 ¾ 0:20 A	11 N 4:30 A
20 ¼ 8:40 P	17 F 11:24 A	22 N 4:47 A	19 ¼ 8:32 A
28 F 2:49 A	25 ¾ 1:37 A	29 ¼ 8:44 P	26 F 3:21 A
Apr 5 ¾ 5:46 A	Apr 2 N 0:21 A	Apr 5 F 11:14 A	Apr 1 ¾ 8:59 P
12 N 0:38 P	9 ¼ 0:40 A	12 ¾ 5:29 P	9 N 10:21 P
19 ¼ 4:10 A	15 F 11:03 P	20 N 8:36 P	17 ¼ 8:48 P
26 F 5:50 P	23 ¾ 9:07 P	28 ¼ 3:50 A	24 F 0:04 P
May 4 ¾ 10:20 P	May 1 N 11:56 A	May 4 F 9:01 P	May 1 ¾ 10:33 A
11 N 9:02 P	8 ¼ 6:20 A	12 ¾ 11:20 A	9 N 2:56 P
18 ¼ 0:43 P	15 F 11:53 A	20 N 9:43 A	17 ¼ 5:18 A
26 F 9:30 A	23 ¾ 2:41 P	27 ¼ 8:51 A	23 F 8:23 P
Jun 3 ¾ 11:08 A	30 N 9:13 P	Jun 3 F 7:41 A	31 ¾ 1:53 A
10 N 4:23 A	Jun 6 ¼ 0:12 P	11 ¾ 4:59 A	Jun 8 N 5:14 A
16 ¼ 11:02 P	14 F 2:00 A	18 N 8:09 P	15 ¼ 11:12 P
25 F 1:09 A	22 ¾ 5:37 A	25 ¼ 1:23 P	22 F 4:58 A
Jul 2 ¾ 8:31 P	29 N 4:53 A	Jul 2 F 7:37 P	29 ¾ 6:40 P
9 N 11:31 A	Jul 5 ¼ 7:37 P	10 ¾ 9:43 P	Jul 7 N 5:01 P
16 ¼ 11:48 A	13 F 5:03 P	18 N 4:31 A	14 ¼ 3:54 P
24 F 3:59 P	21 ¾ 5:54 A	24 ¼ 7:00 P	21 F 2:40 P
Aug 1 ¾ 3:30 A	28 N 11:45 A	Aug 1 F 9:06 A	29 ¾ 0:15 P
7 N 7:17 P	Aug 4 ¼ 5:48 A	9 ¾ 0:56 A	Aug 6 N 2:49 A
15 ¼ 3:20 A	12 F 8:23 A	16 N 11:48 A	12 ¼ 8:45 P
23 F 5:26 A	20 ¾ 3:51 A	23 ¼ 3:02 A	20 F 2:27 P
30 ¾ 9:16 A	26 N 6:51 P	31 F 0:15 A	28 ¾ 5:36 A
Sep 6 N 4:34 A	Sep 2 ¼ 7:28 P	Sep 8 ¾ 2:08 A	Sep 4 N 11:38 A
13 ¼ 9:24 P	10 F 11:33 P	14 N 7:14 P	11 ¼ 3:06 A
21 F 5:31 P	18 ¾ 11:59 A	21 ¼ 2:25 P	18 F 5:00 P
28 ¾ 3:02 P	25 N 3:18 A	29 F 4:48 P	26 ¾ 9:44 P
Oct 5 N 4:20 P	Oct 2 ¼ 0:38 P	Oct 7 ¾ 1:09 P	Oct 3 N 8:25 P
13 ¼ 4:57 P	10 F 2:14 P	14 N 3:52 A	10 ¼ 0:12 P
21 F 4:46 A	17 ¾ 7:00 P	21 ¼ 5:35 A	18 F 10:12 A
27 ¾ 9:59 P	24 N 2:12 P	29 F 10:01 A	26 ¾ 0:04 P
Nov 4 N 7:17 A	NOV1 ¼ 8:27 A	Nov 5 ¾ 10:19 P	Nov 2 N 5:49 A
12 ¼ 0:21 P	9 F 4:16 A	12 N 2:27 P	9 ¼ 1:00 A
19 F 3:44 P	16 ¾ 1:54 A	20 ¼ 0:21 A	17 F 4:53 A
26 ¾ 7:11 A	23 N 4:11 A	28 F 2:41 A	25 ¾ 0:24 A
Dec 4 N 11:19 A	Dec 1 ¼ 5:25 A	Dec 5 ¾ 6:23 A	Dec 1 N 4:10 P
12 ¼ 6:02 A	8 F 5:22 P	12 N 3:14 A	8 ¼ 5:58 P
19 F 2:42 A	15 ¾ 9:52 A	19 ¼ 9:42 P	16 F 11:22 P
25 ¾ 7:28 P	22 N 9:04 P	27 F 5:44 P	24 ¾ 10:49 A
	31 ¼ 1:47 A		31 N 3:39 A

1968	1969	1970	1971
Jan 7 ¼ 2:23 P	Jan 3 F 6:28 P	Jan 7 N 8:36 P	Jan 4 ¼ 4:56 A
15 F 4:12 P	11 ¾ 2:01 P	14 ¼ 1:19 P	11 F 1:21 P
22 ¾ 7:39 P	18 N 4:59 A	22 F 0:57 P	19 ¾ 6:09 P
29 N 4:30 P	25 ¼ 8:24 A	30 ¾ 2:39 P	26 N 10:56 P
Feb 6 ¼ 0:21 P	Feb 2 F 0:57 P	Feb 6 N 7:13 A	Feb 2 ¼ 2:31 P
14 F 6:44 A	10 ¾ 0:09 P	13 ¼ 4:11 A	10 F 7:42 A
21 ¾ 3:28 A	16 N 4:26 A	21 F 8:20 A	18 ¾ 0:14 P
28 N 6:56 A	24 ¼ 4:31 A	Mar 1 ¾ 2:34 A	25 N 9:49 A
Mar 7 ¼ 9:21 A	Mar 4 F 5:18 A	7 N 5:43 P	Mar 4 ¼ 2:02 A
14 F 6:53 P	11 ¾ 7:45 A	14 ¼ 9:16 P	12 F 2:34 A
21 ¾ 11:08 A	18 N 4:52 A	23 F 1:53 A	20 ¾ 2:31 A
28 N 10:49 P	26 ¼ 0:49 A	30 ¾ 11:05 A	26 N 7:24 P
Apr 6 ¼ 3:28 A	Apr 2 F 6:46 A	Apr 6 N 4:10 A	Apr 2 ¼ 3:47 P
13 F 4:52 A	9 ¾ 1:59 P	13 ¼ 3:44 P	10 F 8:11 P
19 ¾ 7:36 P	16 N 6:17 P	21 F 4:22 P	18 ¾ 0:59 P
27 N 3:22 P	24 ¼ 7:45 P	28 ¾ 5:19 P	25 N 4:02 A
May 5 ¼ 5:55 P	May 2 F 5:14 A	May 5 N 2:52 P	May 2 ¼ 7:35 A
12 F 1:05 P	8 ¾ 8:12 P	13 ¼ 10:26 A	10 F 11:24 A
19 ¾ 5:45 A	16 N 8:27 A	21 F 3:38 A	17 ¾ 8:16 P
27 N 7:30 A	24 ¼ 0:16 P	27 ¾ 10:32 P	24 N 0:33 P
Jun 4 ¼ 4:47 A	31 F 1:19 P	Jun 4 N 2:22 A	Jun 1 ¼ 0:43 A
10 F 8:14 P	Jun 7 ¾ 3:40 A	12 1 4:07 A	9 F 0:04 P
17 ¾ 6:14 P	14 N 11:09 P	19 F 0:28 P	16 ¾ 1:25 A
25 N 10:25 P	23 ¼ 1:45 A	26 ¾ 4:02 A	22 N 9:58 P
Jul 3 ¼ 0:42 P	29 F 8:04 P	Jul 3 N 3:19 P	30 ¼ 6:11 P
10 F 3:18 A	Jul 6 ¾ 1:18 P	11 ¼ 7:44 P	Jul 8 F 10:37 A
17 ¾ 9:12 A	14 N 2:12 P	18 F 7:59 P	15 ¾ 5:47 A
25 N 11:50 A	22 ¼ 0:10 P	25 ¾ 11:00 A	22 N 9:16 A
Aug 1 ¼ 6:35 P	29 F 2:46 A	Aug 2 N 5:59 A	30 ¼ 11:08 A
8 F 11:33 A	Aug 5 ¾ 1:39 A	10 ¼ 8:51 A	Aug 6 F 7:43 P
16 ¾ 2:14 A	13 N 5:17 A	17 F 3:16 A	13 ¾ 10:56 A
23 N 11:57 P	20 ¼ 8:04 P	23 ¾ 8:35 P	20 N 10:54 P
30 ¼ 11:35 P	27 F 10:33 A	31 N 10:02 P	29 ¼ 2:57 A
Sep 6 F 10:08 P	Sep 3 ¾ 4:59 P	Sep 8 ¼ 7:39 P	Sep 5 F 4:03 A
14 ¾ 8:32 P	11 N 7:57 P	15 F 11:10 A	11 ¾ 6:24 P
22 N 11:09 A	19 ¼ 2:25 A	22 ¾ 9:43 A	19 N 2:43 P
29 ¼ 5:07 A	25 F 8:22 P	30 N 2:32 P	27 ¼ 5:18 P
Oct 6 F 11:47 A	Oct 3 ¾ 11:06 A	Oct 8 ¼ 4:44 A	Oct 4 F 0:20 P
14 ¾ 3:06 P	11 N 9:40 A	14 F 8:22 P	11 ¾ 5:30 A
21 N 9:45 P	18 ¼ 8:32 A	22 ¾ 2:48 A	19 N 8:00 A
28 ¼ 0:40 P	25 F 8:45 A	30 N 6:29 A	27 ¼ 5:55 A
Nov 5 F 4:26 A	Nov 2 ¾ 7:15 A	Nov 6 ¼ 0:48 P	Nov 2 F 9:20 P
13 ¾ 8:54 A	9 N 10:12 P	13 D 7:29 A	9 ¾ 8:52 P
20 N 8:02 A	16 ¼ 3:46 P	20 ¾ 11:14 P	18 N 1:47 A
26 ¼ 11:31 P	23 F 11:55 P	26 N 9:15 P	25 ¼ 4:38 P
Dec 4 F 11:08 P	Dec 2 ¾ 3:51 A	Dec 5 ¼ 8:36 P	Dec 2 F 7:49 A
13 ¾ 0:50 A	9 N 9:43 A	12 F 9:04 P	9 ¾ 4:03 P
19 N 6:19 P	16 ¼ 1:10 P	20 ¾ 9:10 P	17 N 7:04 P
26 ¼ 2:15 P	23 F 5:36 P	28 N 10:43 A	25 ¼ 1:36 A
	31 ¾ 10:53 P		31 F 8:20 P

1972	1973	1974	1975
Jan 8 ¾ 1:32 P	Jan 4 N 3:43 P	Jan 1 ¼ 6:07 P	Jan 4 ¾ 7:05 P
16 N 10:53 A	12 ¼ 5:28 A	8 F 0:37 P	12 N 10:21 A
23 ¼ 9:30 A	18 F 9:29 P	15 ¾ 7:05 A	20 ¼ 3:15 P
30 F 10:59 A	26 ¾ 6:06 A	23 N 11:03 A	27 F 3:10 P
Feb 7 ¾ 11:12 A	Feb 3 N 9:24 A	31 ¼ 7:40 A	Feb 3 ¾ 6:24 A
15 N 0:30 A	10 ¼ 2:06 P	Feb 6 F 11:25 P	11 N 5:18 A
21 ¼ 5:21 P	17 F 10:08 A	14 ¾ 0:05 A	19 ¼ 7:40 A
29 F 3:13 A	25 ¾ 3:12 A	22 N 5:35 A	26 F 1:15 A
Mar 8 ¾ 7:06 A	Mar 5 N 0:08 A	Mar 1 ¼ 6:03 P	Mar 5 ¾ 8:21 P
15 N 11:35 A	11 ¼ 9:26 P	8 F 10:04 A	12 N 11:48 P
22 ¼ 2:13 A	18 F 11:34 P	15 ¾ 7:16 P	20 ¼ 8:05 P
29 F 8:06 P	26 ¾ 11:47 P	23 N 9:25 P	27 F 10:37 A
Apr 6 ¾ 11:45 P	Apr 3 N 11:46 A	31 ¼ 1:45 A	Apr 3 ¾ 0:26 P
13 N 8:32 P	10 ¼ 4:29 A	Apr 6 F 9:01 P	11 N 4:40 P
20 ¼ 0:46 P	17 F 1:52 P	14 ¾ 2:59 P	19 ¼ 4:42 A
28 F 0:45 P	25 ¾ 6:00 P	22 N 10:17 A	25 F 7:56 P
May 6 ¾ 0:27 P	May 2 N 8:56 P	29 ¼ 7:40 A	May 3 ¾ 5:45 A
13 N 4:09 A	9 ¼ 0:07 P	May 6 F 8:55 A	11 N 7:06 A
20 ¼ 1:17 A	17 F 4:59 A	14 ¾ 9:30 A	18 ¼ 10:30 A
28 F 4:28 A	25 ¾ 8:41 A	21 N 8:35 P	25 F 5:51 A
Jun 4 ¾ 9:22 P	Jun 1 N 4:35 A	28 ¼ 1:04 P	Jun 1 ¾ 11:24 P
11 N 11:31 A	7 ¼ 9:12 P	Jun 4 F 10:11 P	9 N 6:50 P
18 ¼ 3:42 P	15 F 8:36 P	13 ¾ 1:46 A	16 ¼ 2:59 P
26 F 6:47 P	23 ¾ 7:46 P	20 N 4:56 A	23 F 4:55 P
Jul 4 ¾ 3:26 A	30 N 11:39 A	26 ¼ 7:21 P	Jul 1 ¾ 4:38 P
10 N 7:40 P	Jul 7 ¼ 8:27 A	Jul 4 F 0:41 P	9 N 4:11 A
18 ¼ 7:47 A	15 F 11:57 A	12 ¾ 3:29 P	15 ¼ 7:48 P
26 F 7:24 A	23 ¾ 3:58 A	19 N 0:07 P	23 F 5:29 A
Aug 2 ¾ 8:03 A	29 N 7:00 P	26 ¼ 3:52 A	31 ¾ 8:49 A
9 N 5:27 A	Aug 5 ¼ 10:28 P	Aug 3 F 3:58 A	Aug 7 N 11:58 A
17 ¼ 1:10 A	14 F 2:17 A	11 ¾ 2:47 A	14 ¼ 2:24 A
24 F 6:23 P	21 ¾ 10:23 A	17 N 7:02 P	21 F 7:49 P
31 ¾ 0:49 P	28 N 3:26 A	24 ¼ 3:39 P	29 ¾ 11:20 P
Sep 7 N 5:29 P	Sep 4 ¼ 3:23 P	Sep 1 F 7:26 A	Sep 5 N 7:20 P
15 ¼ 7:14 P	12 F 3:17 P	9 ¾ 0:02 P	12 ¼ 0:00 P
23 F 4:08 A	19 ¾ 4:11 P	16 N 2:46 A	20 F 11:51 A
29 ¾ 7:17 P	26 N 1:55 P	23 ¼ 7:09 A	28 ¾ 11:47 A
Oct 7 N 8:09 A	Oct 4 ¼ 10:33 A	Oct 1 F 10:39 A	Oct 5 N 3:24 A
15 ¼ 0:56 P	12 F 3:10 A	8 ¾ 7:46 P	12 ¼ 1:16 A
22 F 1:26 P	18 ¾ 10:33 P	15 N 0:26 P	20 F 5:07 A
29 ¾ 4:42 A	26 N 3:17 A	23 ¼ 1:54 A	27 ¾ 10:08 P
Nov 6 N 1:22 A	Nov 3 ¼ 6:30 A	31 F 1:20 A	Nov 3 N 1:06 P
14 ¼ 5:02	10 F 2:28 P	Nov 7 ¾ 2:48 A	10 ¼ 6:22 P
20 F 11:07 P	17 ¾ 6:35 A	14 N 0:54 A	18 F 10:29 P
27 ¾ 5:45 P	24 N 7:56 P	21 ¼ 10:40 P	26 ¾ 6:53 A
Dec 5 N 8:25 P	Dec 3 ¼ 1:30 A	29 F 3:11 P	Dec 3 N 0:51 A
13 ¼ 6:36 P	10 F 1:35 A	Dec 6 ¾ 10:11 A	10 ¼ 2:40 P
20 F 9:46 A	16 ¾ 5:13 P	13 N 4:26 P	18 F 2:40 P
27 ¾ 10:28 A	24 N 3:08 P	21 ¼ 7:44 P	25 ¾ 2:63 P
		29 F 3:52 A	

1976	1977	1978	1979
Jan 1 N 2:41 P	Jan 5 F 0:11 P	Jan 2 ¾ 0:08 P	Jan 5 ¼ 11:16 A
9 ¼ 0:40 P	12 ¾ 7:56 P	9 N 4:00 A	13 F 7:10 A
17 F 4:48 A	19 N 2:12 P	16 ¼ 3:04 A	21 ¾ 11:24 A
23 ¾ 11:05 P	27 ¼ 5:13 A	24 F 7:57 A	28 N 6:20 A
31 N 6:21 A	Feb 4 F 3:57 A	31 ¾ 11:52 P	Feb 4 ¼ 0:37 A
Feb 8 ¼ 10:06 A	11 ¾ 4:08 A	Feb 7 N 2:55 P	12 F 2:40 A
15 F 4:44 P	18 N 3:38 A	14 ¼ 10:12 P	20 ¾ 1:18 A
22 ¾ 8:17 A	26 ¼ 2:51 A	23 F 1:27 A	26 N 4:46 P
29 N 11:26 P	Mar 5 F 5:14 P	Mar 2 ¾ 8:35 A	Mar 5 ¼ 4:24 P
Mar 9 ¼ 4:39 A	12 ¾ 11:36 A	9 N 2:37 A	13 F 9:15 P
16 F 2:53 A	19 N 6:34 P	16 ¼ 6:22 P	21 ¾ 11:23 A
22 ¾ 6:55 P	27 ¼ 10:27 P	24 F 4:21 P	28 N 3:00 A
30 N 5:09 P	Apr 4 F 4:10 A	31 ¾ 3:12 P	Apr 4 ¼ 9:58 A
Apr 7 ¼ 7:03 P	10 ¾ 7:15 P	Apr 7 N 3:16 P	12 F 1:16 P
14 F 11:50 A	18 N 10:36 A	15 ¼ 1:57 P	19 ¾ 6:31 P
21 ¾ 7:15 A	26 ¼ 2:43 P	23 F 4:12 A	26 N 1:16 P
29 N 10:20 A	May 3 F 1:04 P	29 ¾ 9:03 P	May 4 ¼ 4:27 P
May 7 ¼ 5:18 A	10 ¾ 4:09 A	May 7 N 4:48 A	12 F 2:02 A
13 F 8:05 P	18 N 2:52 A	15 ¼ 7:41 A	18 ¾ 11:58 P
20 ¾ 9:23 P	26 ¼ 3:21 A	22 F 1:18 P	26 N 0:01 A
29 N 1:48 A	Jun 1 F 8:32 P	29 ¾ 3:31 A	Jun 2 ¼ 10:38 P
Jun 5 ¼ 0:21 P	8 ¾ 3:08 P	Jun 5 N 7:02 P	10 F 11:56 A
12 F 4:16 A	16 N 6:24 P	13 ¼ 10:45 P	17 ¾ 5:02 A
19 ¾ 1:16 P	24 ¼ 0:45 P	20 F 8:32 P	24 N 11:59 A
27 N 2:51 P	Jul 1 F 3:25 A	27 ¾ 11:45 A	Jul 2 ¼ 3:25 P
Jul 4 ¼ 5:29 P	8 ¾ 4:40 A	Jul 5 N 9:52 A	9 F 8:00 P
11 F 1:10 P	16 N 8:37 A	13 ¼ 10:50 A	16 ¾ 11:00 A
19 ¾ 6:30 A	23 ¼ 7:39 P	20 F 3:06 A	24 N 1:42 A
27 N 1:39 A	30 F 10:53 A	26 ¾ 10:32 P	Aug 1 ¼ 5:58 A
Aug 2 ¼ 10:07 P	Aug 6 ¾ 8:41 P	Aug 4 N 1:02 A	8 F 3:22 A
9 F 11:44 P	14 N 9:32 P	11 ¼ 8:07 P	14 ¾ 7:03 P
18 ¾ 0:14 A	22 ¼ 1:05 A	18 F 10:15 A	22 N 5:11 P
25 N 11:01 A	28 F 8:11 P	25 ¾ 0:19 P	30 ¼ 6:10 P
Sep 1 ¼ 3:36 A	Sep 5 ¾ 2:34 P	Sep 2 N 4:10 P	Sep 6 F 10:59 A
8 F 0:53 P	13 N 9:24 A	10 ¼ 3:21 A	13 ¾ 6:16 A
16 ¾ 5:21 P	20 ¼ 6:19 A	16 F 7:02 P	21 N 9:48 A
23 N 7:56 P	27 F 8:18 A	24 ¾ 5:09 A	29 ¼ 4:21 A
30 ¼ 11:13 A	Oct 5 ¾ 9:22 A	Oct 2 N 6:42 A	Oct 5 F 7:36 P
Oct 8 F 4:56 A	12 N 8:32 P	9 ¼ 9:39 A	12 ¾ 9:25 P
16 ¾ 9:00 A	19 ¼ 0:47 P	16 F 6:10 A	21 N 2:24 A
23 N 5:10 A	26 F 11:36 P	24 ¾ 0:35 A	28 ¼ 1:07 P
29 ¼ 10:06 P	Nov 4 ¾ 3:59 A	31 N 8:07 P	Nov 4 F 5:48 A
Nov 6 F 11:16 P	11 N 7:10 A	Nov 7 ¼ 4:19 P	11 ¾ 4:25 P
14 ¾-10:40 P	17 ¼ 9:53 P	14 F 8:01 P	19 N 6:05 P
21 N 3:12 P	25 F 5:32 P	22 ¾ 9:25 P	26 ¼ 9:09 P
28 ¼ 1:00 P	Dec 3 ¾ 9:17 P	30 N 8:20 A	Dec 3 F 6:09 P
Dec 6 F 6:16 P	10 N 5:34 P	Dec 7 ¼ 0:35 A	11 ¾ 2:00 P
14 ¾ 10:15 A	17 ¼ 10:38 A	14 F 0:32 P	19 N 8:24 A
21 N 2:09 A	25 F 0:50 P	22 ¾ 5:42 P	26 ¼ 5:12 A
28 ¼ 7:49 A		29 N 7:37 P	

1980	1981	1982	1983
Jan 2 F 9:03 A	Jan 6 N 7:25 A	Jan 3 ¼ 4:47 A	Jan 6 ¾ 4:01 A
10 ¾ 11:51 A	13 ¼ 10:11 A	9 F 7:54 P	14 N 5:09 A
17 N 9:20 P	20 F 7:40 A	16 ¾ 11:59 P	22 ¼ 5:35 A
24 ¼ 1:59 P	28 ¾ 4:20 A	25 N 4:57 A	28 F 10:27 P
Feb 1 F 2:22 P	Feb 4 N 10:15 P	Feb 1 ¼ 2:29 P	Feb 4 ¾ 7:18 P
9 ¾ 7:36 A	11 ¼ 5:50 P	8 F 7:58 P	13 N 0:33 A
16 N 8:52 A	18 F 10:59 P	15 ¾ 8:22 P	20 ¼ 5:33 P
23 ¼ 0:15 A	27 ¾ 1:15 A	23 N 9:14 P	27 F 8:59 A
Mar 1 F 9:01 P	Mar 6 N 10:32 A	Mar 2 ¼ 10:16 P	Mar 6 ¾ 1:17 P
9 ¾ 11:50 P	13 ¼ 1:51 A	9 F 8:46 P	14 N 5:44 P
16 N 6:57 P	20 F 3:23 P	17 ¾ 5:16 P	22 ¼ 2:26 A
23 ¼ 0:32 P	28 ¾ 7:35 P	25 N 10:19 A	28 F 7:28 P
Apr 8 F 3:15 P	Apr 4 N 8:20 P	Apr 1 ¼ 5:09 A	Apr 5 ¾ 8:39 A
15 ¾ 0:07 P	11 ¼ 11:11 P	8 F 10:19 A	13 N 7:59 A
22 N 3:47 A	19 F 8:00 P	16 ¾ 0:43 P	20 ¼ 8:59 A
30 ¼ 3:00 A	27 ¾ 10:16 A	23 N 8:30 P	27 F 6:32 A
May 7 F 7:36 A	May 4 N 4:20 A	30 ¼ 0:08 P	May 5 ¾ 3:44 A
14 ¾ 8:51 P	10 ¼ 10:23 P	May 8 F 0:46 A	12 N 7:26 P
21 N 0:01 P	19 F 0:04 A	16 ¾ 5:12 A	19 ¼ 2:18 P
29 ¼ 7:17 P	26 ¾ 9:01 P	23 N 4:41 A	26 F 6:49 P
Jun 6 F 9:29 P	Jun 2 N 11:32 A	29 ¼ 8:07 P	Jun 3 ¾ 9:08 P
12 ¾ 2:54 A	9 ¼ 11:34 A	Jun 6 F 4:00 P	11 N 4:38 P
20 N 8:39 P	17 F 3:05 P	14 ¾ 6:07 P	17 ¼ 7:47 P
28 ¼ 0:33 P	25 ¾ 4:26 A	21 N 11:53 A	25 F 8:33 A
Jul 5 F 9:03 A	Jul 1 N 7:04 P	28 ¼ 5:57 A	Jul 3 ¾ 0:13 P
12 ¾ 7:28 A	9 ¼ 2:40 A	Jul 6 F 7:33 P	10 N 0:19 P
20 N 6:47 A	17 F 4:40 A	14 ¾ 3:48 A	17 ¼ 2:51 A
27 ¼ 5:52 A	24 ¾ 9:41 A	20 N 6:58 P	24 F 11:28 P
Aug 3 F 6:55 P	31 N 3:53 A	27 ¼ 6:23 P	Aug 2 ¾ 0:53 A
10 ¾ 0:01 P	Aug 7 ¼ 7:27 P	Aug 4 F 10:35 P	8 N 7:19 P
18 N 7:10 P	15 F 4:38 P	12 ¾ 11:09 A	15 ¼ 0:48 P
26 ¼ 10:29 P	22 ¾ 2:17 P	19 N 2:46 A	23 F 3:00 P
Sep 1 F 3:43 A	29 N 2:45 P	26 ¼ 9:51 A	31 ¾ 11:23 A
9 ¾ 6:08 P	Sep 6 ¼ 1:27 P	Sep 3 F 0:29 P	Sep 7 N 2:36 P
17 N 10:01 A	14 F 3:10 A	10 ¾ 5:20 P	14 ¼ 2:25 A
24 ¼ 1:55 P	20 ¾ 7:48 P	17 N 0:10 P	22 F 6:37 A
Oct 1 F 0:09 P	28 N 4:08 A	25 ¼ 4:08 A	29 ¾ 8:06 P
9 ¾ 3:19 A	Oct 6 ¼ 7:46 A	Oct 3 F 1:09 A	Oct 6 N 11:17 A
17 N 2:51 A	13 F 0:50 P	9 ¾ 11:27 P	13 ¼ 7:43 P
23 ¼ 3:48 A	20 ¾ 3:42 A	17 N 0:05 A	21 F 9:54 P
30 F 8:53 P	27 N 8:15 P	25 v 0:09 A	29 ¾ 3:38 P
Nov 7 ¾ 4:34 P	Nov 5 ¼ 1:10 P	Nov 1 F 0:58 P	Nov 4 N 10:22 P
15 N 8:44 P	11 F 10:28 P	8 ¾ 6:39 A	12 ¼ 3:50 P
22 ¼ 3:48 P	18 ¾ 2:55 P	15 N 3:11 P	20 F 0:30 P
29 F 6:40 A	26 N 2:40 P	23 ¼ 8:07 P	27 ¾ 10:51 A
Dec 7 ¾ 10:00 A	Dec 4 ¼ 4:23 P	Dec 1 F 0:22 A	Dec 4 N 0:27 P
15 N 2:36 P	11 F 8:42 A	7 ¾ 3:54 P	12 ¼ 1:10 P
21 ¼ 1:48 A	18 ¾ 5:48 A	15 N 9:19 A	20 F 2:01 A
29 F 6:09 P	26 N 10:11 A	23 ¼ 2:18 P	26 ¾ 6:53 P
¾ 6:33 A		30 F 11:34 A	

1984	1985	1986	1987
Jan 3 N 5:17 A	Jan 7 F 2:17 A	Jan 3 ¾ 7:48 P	Jan 6 ¼ 10:36 P
11 ¼ 9:49 A	13 ¾ 11:28 P	10 N 0:23 P	15 F 2:32 A
18 F 2:06 P	21 N 2:29 A	17 ¼ 10:14 P	22 ¾ 10:46 P
25 ¾ 4:49 A	29 ¼ 3:30 A	26 F 0:32 A	29 N 1:46 P
Feb 1 N 11:47 P	Feb 5 F 3:20 P	Feb 2 ¾ 4:42 A	Feb 5 ¼ 4:22 P
10 ¼ 4:01 A	12 ¾ 7:58 A	9 N 0:56 A	13 F 8:59 P
17 F 0:42 A	19 N 6:44 P	16 ¼ 7:56 P	21 ¾ 8:57 A
23 ¾ 5:13 P	27 ¼ 11:42 P	24 F 3:03 P	28 N 0:52 A
Mar 2 N 6:32 P	Mar 7 F 2:14 A	Mar 3 ¾ 0:18 P	Mar 7 ¼ 11:59 A
10 ¼ 6:28 P	13 ¾ 5:35 P	10 N 2:53 P	15 F 1:14 P
17 F 10:11 A	21 N 0:00 P	18 ¼ 4:40 P	22 ¾ 4:23 P
24 ¾ 7:59 A	29 ¼ 4:12 P	26 F 3:03 A	29 N 0:47 P
Apr 1 N 0:11 P	Apr 5 F 11:33 A	Apr 1 ¾ 7:31 P	Apr 6 ¼ 7:49 A
9 ¼ 4:52 A	12 ¾ 4:43 A	9 N 6:09 A	14 F 2:32 A
15 F 7:12 P	20 N 5:23 A	17 ¼ 10:36 A	20 ¾ 10:16 P
23 ¾ 0:27 A	28 ¼ 4:26 A	24 F 0:47 P	28 N 1:35 A
May 1 N 3:47 A	May 4 F 7:54 P	May 1 ¾ 3:23 A	May 6 ¼ 2:27 A
8 ¼ 11:51 A	11 ¾ 5:35 P	8 N 10:11 P	13 F 0:51 P
15 F 4:30 A	19 N 9:42 P	17 ¼ 1:01 A	20 ¾ 4:03 A
22 ¾ 5:46 P	27 ¼ 0:57 P	23 F 8:46 P	27 N 3:15 P
30 N 4:49 P	Jun 3 F 3:51 A	30 ¾ 0:56 P	Jun 4 ¼ 6:54 P
Jun 6 ¼ 4:42 P	10 ¾ 8:20 A	Jun 7 N 2:01 P	11 F 8:50 P
13 F 2:43 P	18 N 11:59 A	15 ¼ 0:01 P	18 ¾ 11:04 A
21 ¾ 11:11 A	25 ¼ 6:54 P	22 F 3:43 A	26 N 5:38 A
29 N 3:19 A	Jul 2 F 0:09 P	29 ¾ 0:54 A	Jul 4 ¼ 8:35 A
Jul 5 ¼ 9:05 P	10 ¾ 0:51 A	Jul 7 N 4:56 A	11 F 3:34 A
13 F 2:21 A	17 N 11:57 P	14 ¼ 8:11 P	17 ¾ 8:18 P
21 ¾ 4:02 A	24 ¼ 11:40 P	21 F 10:41 P	25 N 8:39 P
28 N 11:52 A	31 F 9:42 P	28 ¾ 3:35 P	Aug 2 ¼ 7:25 P
Aug 4 ¼ 2:34 A	Aug 8 ¾ 6:29 P	Aug 5 N 6:37 P	9 F 10:18 A
11 F 3:44 P	16 N 10:07 A	13 ¼ 2:22 A	16 ¾ 8:26 A
19 ¾ 7:42 P	23 ¼ 4:37 A	19 F 6:55 A	24 N 0:00 P
26 N 7:27 P	30 F 9:28 A	27 ¾ 8:40 A	Sep 1 ¼ 3:49 A
Sep 2 ¼ 10:31 A	Sep 7 ¾ 0:17 P	Sep 4 N 7:11 A	7 F 6:14 P
10 F 7:02 A	14 N 7:21 P	11 ¼ 7:42 A	14 ¾ 11:46 P
18 ¾ 9:32 A	21 ¼ 11:04 A	18 F 5:35 A	23 N 3:09 A
25 N 3:12 A	29 F 0:10 A	26 ¾ 3:19 A	30 ¼ 10:40 A
Oct 1 ¼ 9:53 P	Oct 7 ¾ 5:05 A	Oct 3 N 6:56 P	Oct 7 F 4:13 A
9 F 11:59 P	14 N 4:34 A	10 ¼ 1:29 P	14 ¾ 6:07 P
17 ¾ 9:15 P	20 ¼ 8:14 P	17 F 7:23 P	22 N 5:29 P
24 N 0:09 P	28 F 5:39 P	25 ¾ 10:27 P	29 ¼ 5:11 P
31 ¼ 1:09 P	Nov 5 ¾ 8:07 P	Nov 2 N 6:03 A	Nov 5 F 4:47 P
Nov 8 F 5:44 P	12 N 2:21 P	8 ¼ 9:12 P	13 ¾ 2:39 P
16 ¾ 7:00 A	19 ¼ 9:05 A	16 F 0:13 P	21 N 6:34 A
22 N 10:58 P	27 F 0:43 P	24 ¾ 4:51 P	28 ¼ 0:38 A
30 ¼ 8:02 A	Dec 5 ¾ 9:02 A	Dec 1 N 4:44 P	Dec 5 F 8:02 A
Dec 8 F 10:54 A	12 N 0:55 A	8 ¼ 8:03 A	13 ¾ 11:42 A
15 ¾ 3:26 P	19 ¼ 1:59 A	16 F 7:06 A	20 N 6:26 A
22 N 11:48 A	27 F 7:31 A	24 ¾ 9:18 A	27 ¼ 10:02 A
30 ¼ 5:29 A		31 N 3:11 A	

1988

Jan 4 F 1:42 A
12 ¾ 7:05 A
19 N 5:26 A
25 ¼ 9:54 P
Feb 2 F 8:53 P
10 ¾ 11:02 P
17 N 3:55 P
24 ¼ 0:16 P
Mar 3 F 4:02 P
11 ¾ 10:57 A
18 N 2:03 A
25 ¼ 4:43 A
Apr 2 F 9:22 A
9 ¾ 7:22 P
16 N 0:01 P
23 ¼ 10:33 P
May 1 F 11:42 P
9 ¾ 1:24 A
15 N 10:12 P
23 ¼ 4:50 P
31 F 10:54 A
Jun 7 ¾ 6:23 A
14 N 9:15 A
22 ¼ 10:24 A
29 F 7:47 P
Jul 6 ¾ 11:37 A
13 N 9:54 P
22 ¼ 2:15 A
29 F 3:26 A
Aug 4 ¾ 6:23 P
12 N 0:32 P
20 ¼ 3:53 P
27 F 10:57 A
Sep 3 ¾ 3:51 A
11 N 4:50 A
19 ¼ 3:19 A
25 F 7:08 A
Oct 2 ¾ 4:59 P
10 N 9:50 P
18 ¼ 1:02 P
25 F 4:36 A
Nov 1 ¾ 10:13 A
9 N 2:21 P
16 ¼ 9:36 P
23 F 3:54 P
Dec 1 ¾ 6:51 A
9 N 5:37 A
16 ¼ 5:41 A
23 F 5:30 A
31 ¾ 4:58 A

1989

Jan 7 N 7:23 P
14 ¼ 1:59 P
21 F 9:35 P
30 ¾ 2:03 A
Feb 6 N 7:38 A
12 ¼ 11:16 P
20 F 3:33 P
28 ¾ 8:09 P
Mar 7 N 6:20 P
14 ¼ 10:12 A
22 F 9:59 A
30 ¾ 10:23 A
Apr 6 N 3:33 A
12 ¼ 11:14 P
21 F 3:14 P
28 ¾ 8:47 P
May 5 N 11:47 A
12 ¼ 2:21 P
20 F 6:17 P
28 ¾ 4:02 A
Jun 3 N 7:54 P
11 ¼ 7:00 A
19 F 6:58 A
26 ¾ 9:10 A
Jul 3 N 5:00 A
11 ¼ 0:20 A
18 F 5:43 P
25 ¾ 1:32 P
Aug 1 N 4:07 P
9 ¼ 5:30 P
17 F 3:08 A
23 ¾ 6:41 P
31 N 5:46 A
Sep 8 ¼ 9:50 A
15 F 11:52 A
22 ¾ 2:11 A
29 N 9:48 P
Oct 8 ¼ 0:53 A
14 F 8:33 P
21 ¾ 1:20 P
29 N 3:28 P
Nov 6 ¼ 2:12 P
13 F 5:52 A
20 ¾ 4:45 A
28 N 9:42 A
Dec 6 ¼ 1:27 A
12 F 4:31 P
19 ¾ 11:56 P
28 N 3:21 A

1990

Jan 4 ¼ 10:41 A
11 F 4:58 A
18 ¾ 9:18 P
26 N 7:21 P
Feb 2 ¼ 6:33 P
9 F 7:17 P
17 ¾ 6:49 P
25 N 8:55 A
Mar 4 ¼ 2:06 A
11 F 11:00 A
19 ¾ 2:32 P
26 N 7:49 P
Apr 2 ¼ 10:25 A
10 F 3:20 A
18 ¾ 7:04 A
25 N 4:28 A
May 1 ¼ 8:19 P
9 F 7:32 P
17 ¾ 7:46 P
24 N 11:48 A
31 ¼ 8:12 A
Jun 8 F 11:02 A
16 ¾ 4:49 A
22 N 6:56 P
29 ¼ 10:09 P
Jul 8 F 1:25 A
15 ¾ 11:05 A
22 N 2:55 A
29 ¼ 2:03 P
Aug 6 F 2:21 P
13 ¾ 3:55 A
20 N 0:40 P
28 ¼ 7:35 A
Sep 5 F 1:47 A
11 ¾ 8:54 P
19 N 0:47 A
27 ¼ 2:07 A
Oct 4 F 0:03 P
11 ¾ 3:32 A
18 N 3:38 P
26 ¼ 8:28 P
Nov 2 F 9:49 P
9 ¾ 1:03 P
17 N 9:06 A
25 ¼ 1:13 P
Dec 2 F 7:50 A
9 ¾ 2:05 A
17 N 4:23 A
25 ¼ 3:17 A
31 F 6:36 P

1991

Jan 7 ¾ 6:36 P
15 N 11:51 P
23 ¼ 2:23 P
30 F 6:11 A
Feb 6 ¾ 1:53 P
14 N 5:33 P
21 ¼ 10:59 P
28 F 6:26 P
Mar 8 ¾ 10:33 A
16 N 8:12 A
23 ¼ 6:04 A
30 F 7:18 A
Apr 7 ¾ 6:47 A
14 N 7:39 P
21 ¼ 0:40 P
28 F 9:00 P
May 7 ¾ 0:47 A
14 N 4:37 A
20 ¼ 7:47 P
28 F 11:38 A
Jun 5 ¾ 3:31 A
12 N 0:07 P
19 ¼ 4:20 A
27 F 3:00 A
Jul 5 ¾ 2:51 A
11 N 7:07 P
18 ¼ 3:12 P
26 F 6:26 P
Aug 3 ¾ 11:27 A
10 N 2:29 A
17 ¼ 5:02 A
25 F 9:08 A
Sep 1 ¼ 6:18 A
8 N 11:02 A
15 ¼ 10:03 P
23 F 10:41 P
Oct 1 ¾ 0:31 A
7 N 9:40 P
15 ¼ 5:34 P
23 F 11:09 A
30 ¾ 7:12 A
Nov 6 N 11:12 A
14 ¼ 2:03 P
21 F 10:57 P
28 ¾ 3:22 P
Dec 6 N 3:57 A
14 ¼ 9:33 A
21 F 10:24 A
28 ¾ 1:56 A

1992	1993	1994	1995
Jan 4 N 11:11 P	Jan 1 ¼ 3:40 A	Jan 5 ¾ 0:02 A	Jan 1 N 10:57 A
13 ¼ 2:33 A	8 F 0:38 P	11 N 11:11 P	8 ¼ 3:47 P
19 F 9:29 P	15 ¾ 4:02 A	19 ¼ 8:28 P	16 F 8:28 P
26 ¾ 3:28 P	22 N 6:28 P	27 F 1:24 P	24 ¾ 4:59 A
Feb 3 N 7:01 P	30 ¼ 11:21 P	Feb 3 ¾ 8:07 A	30 N 10:49 P
11 ¼ 4:16 P	Feb 6 F 11:56 P	10 N 2:31 P	Feb 7 ¼ 0:55 P
18 F 8:05 A	13 ¾ 2:58 P	18 ¼ 5:48 P	15 F 0:17 P
25 ¾ 7:57 A	21 N 1:06 N	26 F 1:16 A	22 ¾ 1:05 P
Mar 4 N 1:23 P	Mar 1 ¼ 3:47 P	Mar 4 ¾ 4:54 P	Mar 1 N 11:49 A
12 ¼ 2:37 A	8 F 9:47 A	12 N 7:06 A	9 ¼ 10:15 A
18 F 6:19 P	15 ¾ 4:18 A	20 ¼ 0:15 P	17 F 1:27 A
26 ¾ 2:31 A	23 N 7:16 A	27 F 11:10 A	23 ¾ 8:11 P
Apr 3 N 5:02 A	31 ¼ 4:11 A	Apr 3 ¾ 2:56 A	31 N 2:10 A
10 ¼ 10:07 A	Apr 6 F 6:44 P	11 N 0:18 A	Apr 8 ¼ 5:36 P
17 F 4:43 A	13 ¾ 7:40 P	19 ¼ 2:35 A	15 F 0:09 P
24 ¾ 9:41 P	21 N 11:50 P	25 F 7:46 P	22 ¾ 3:19 A
May 2 N 5:46 P	29 ¼ 0:42 P	May 2 ¾ 2:34 P	29 N 5:38 P
9 ¼ 3:45 P	May 6 F 3:35 A	10 N 5:08 P	May 7 ¼ 9:45 P
16 F 4:04 P	13 ¾ 0:21 P	18 ¼ 0:51 P	14 F 8:49 P
24 ¾ 3:54 P	21 N 2:08 P	25 F 3:40 P	21 ¾ 11:37 A
Jun 1 N 3:58 A	28 ¼ 6:22 P	Jun 1 ¾ 4:04 A	29 N 9:29 A
7 ¼ 8:48 A	Jun 4 F 1:03 P	9 N 8:28 A	Jun 6 ¼ 10:27 A
15 F 4:51 A	12 ¾ 5:37 A	16 ¼ 7:58 P	13 F 4:04 A
23 ¾ 8:12 A	20 N 1:54 A	23 F 11:34 A	19 ¾ 10:02 A
30 N 0:19 P	26 ¼ 10:44 P	30 ¾ 7:32 P	28 N 0:51 A
Jul 7 ¼ 2:45 A	Jul 3 F 11:46 P	Jul 8 N 9:39 P	Jul 5 ¼ 8:04 P
14 F 7:07 P	11 ¾ 10:50 P	16 ¼ 1:13 A	12 F 10:50 A
22 ¾ 10:13 P	19 N 11:25 A	22 F 8:17 P	19 ¾ 11:11 A
29 N 7:36 P	26 ¼ 3:26 A	30 ¾ 0:41 P	27 N 3:14 P
Aug 5 ¼ 11:00 A	Aug 2 F 0:11 P	Aug 7 N 8:46 A	Aug 4 ¼ 3:17 A
13 F 10:28 A	10 ¾ 3:21 P	14 ¼ 5:58 A	10 F 6:17 P
21 ¾ 10:02 A	17 N 7:29 P	21 F 6:48 A	18 ¾ 3:05 A
28 N 2:43 A	24 ¼ 9:59 A	29 ¾ 6:42 A	26 N 4:32 A
Sep 3 ¼ 10:40 P	Sep 1 F 2:34 A	Sep 5 N 6:34 P	Sep 2 ¼ 9:04 A
12 F 2:18 A	9 ¾ 6:28 A	12 ¼ 11:35 A	9 F 3:38 A
19 ¾ 7:54 A	16 N 3:11 A	19 F 8:02 P	16 ¾ 9:11 P
26 N 10:41 A	22 ¼ 7:33 P	28 ¾ 0:25 A	24 N 4:56 P
Oct 3 ¼ 2:13 P	30 F 6:55 P	Oct 5 N 3:56 A	Oct 1 ¼ 2:37 P
11 F 6:04 P	Oct 8 ¾ 7:36 P	11 ¼ 7:18 P	8 F 3:53 P
19 ¾ 4:13 A	15 N 11:37 A	19 F 0:19 P	16 ¾ 4:27 P
25 N 8:35 P	22 ¼ 8:53 A	27 ¾ 4:45 A	24 N 4:37 A
Nov 2 ¼ 9:12 A	30 F 0:39 P	Nov 3 N 1:37 P	30 ¼ 9:18 P
10 F 9:21 A	Nov 7 ¾ 6:37 A	10 ¼ 6:15 A	Nov 7 F 7:22 A
17 ¾ 11:40 A	13 N 9:35 P	18 F 6:58 A	15 ¾ 11:41 A
24 N 9:12 A	21 ¼ 2:05 A	26 ¾ 7:05 A	22 N 3:44 P
Dec 2 ¼ 6:18 A	29 F 6:32 A	Dec 2 N 11:55 P	29 ¼ 6:29 A
9 F 11:42 P	Dec 6 ¾ 3:50 P	9 ¼ 9:07 P	Dec 7 F 1:28 A
16 ¾ 7:14 P	13 N 9:28 A	18 F 2:18 A	15 ¾ 5:32 A
24 N 0:44 A	20 ¼ 10:27 P	25 ¾ 7:07 P	22 N 2:23 A
	28 F 11:06 P		28 ¼ 7:08 P

1996	1997	1998	1999
Jan 5 F 8:52 P	Jan 2 ¾ 1:46 A	Jan 5 ¼ 2:19 P	Jan 2 F 2:51 A
13 ¾ 8:46 P	9 N 4:27 A	12 F 5:25 P	9 ¾ 2:23 P
20 N 0:52 P	15 ¼ 8:03 P	20 ¾ 7:41 P	17 N 3:47 P
27 ¼ 11:15 A	23 F 3:12 P	28 N 6:02 A	24 ¼ 7:16 P
Feb 4 F 3:59 P	31 ¾ 7:41 P	Feb 3 ¼ 10:55 P	31 F 4:08 P
12 ¾ 8:38 A	Feb 7 N 3:07 P	11 F 10:24 A	Feb 8 ¾ 11:59 A
18 N 11:31 P	14 ¼ 8:59 A	19 ¾ 3:28 P	16 N 6:40 A
26 ¼ 5:54 A	22 F 10:28 A	26 N 5:27 P	23 ¼ 2:44 A
Mar 5 F 9:24 A	Mar 2 ¾ 9:39 A	Mar 5 ¼ 8:42 A	Mar 2 F 7:00 A
12 ¾ 5:16 P	9 N 1:16 A	13 F 4:36 A	10 ¾ 8:42 A
19 N 10:46 A	16 ¼ 0:07 A	21 ¾ 7:39 A	17 N 6:49 P
27 ¼ 1:32 A	24 F 4:47 A	28 N 3:15 A	24 ¼ 10:19 A
Apr 4 F 0:08 A	31 ¾ 7:39 P	Apr 3 ¼ 8:20 P	31 F 10:50 P
10 ¾ 11:37 P	Apr 7 N 11:03 A	11 F 10:25 P	Apr 9 ¾ 2:52 A
17 N 10:50 P	14 ¼ 5:01 P	19 ¾ 7:54 P	16 N 4:23 A
25 ¼ 8:41 P	22 F 8:35 P	26 N 11:42 P	22 ¼ 7:03 P
May 3 F 11:49 A	30 ¾ 2:38 A	May 3 ¼ 10:05 A	30 F 2:56 P
10 ¾ 5:05 A	May 6 N 8:48 P	11 F 2:31 P	May 8 ¾ 5:30 A
17 N 11:47 P	14 ¼ 10:56 A	19 ¾ 4:37 A	15 N 0:06 P
25 ¼ 2:14 P	22 F 9:15 A	25 N 7:33 P	22 ¼ 5:35 A
Jun 1 F 8:48 P	29 ¾ 7:53 A	Jun 2 ¼ 1:46 A	30 F 6:41 A
8 ¾ 11:07 A	Jun 5 N 7:05 A	10 F 4:20 A	Jun 7 ¾ 4:21 A
16 n 1:37 A	13 ¼ 4:53 A	17 ¾ 10:39 A	13 N 7:04 P
24 ¼ 5:25 A	20 F 7:10 P	24 N 3:51 A	20 ¼ 6:14 P
Jul 1 F 3:59 A	27 ¾ 0:43 P	Jul 1 ¼ 6:44 P	28 F 9:39 P
7 ¾ 6:56 P	Jul 4 N 6:41 P	9 F 4:02 P	Jul 6 ¾ 11:58 A
14 N 4:16 P	12 ¼ 9:45 P	16 ¾ 3:15 P	13 N 2:25 P
23 ¼ 5:50 P	20 F 3:21 A	23 N 1:45 P	20 ¼ 9:01 A
30 F 10:36 A	26 ¾ 6:29 P	31 ¼ 0:06 P	28 F 11:26 A
Aug 6 ¾ 5:26 A	Aug 3 N 8:15 A	Aug 8 F 2:11 A	Aug 4 ¾ 5:26 P
14 N 7:35 A	11 ¼ 0:44 P	14 ¾ 7:50 A	11 N 11:10 A
22 ¼ 3:38 A	18 F 10:56 A	22 N 2:04 A	19 ¼ 1:48 A
28 F 5:53 P	25 ¾ 2:25 A	30 ¼ 5:08 A	26 F 11:49 P
Sep 4 ¾ 7:07 P	Sep 1 N 11:53 P	Sep 6 F 11:22 A	Sep 2 ¾ 10:18 P
12 N 11:08 P	10 ¼ 1:32	13 ¾ 1:59 A	9 N 10:04 P
20 ¼ 11:24 A	16 F 6:51 P	20 N 5:03 P	17 ¼ 8:07 P
27 F 2:52 A	23 ¾ 1:36 P	28 ¼ 9:12 P	25 F 10:52 A
Oct 4 ¾ 0:05 P	Oct 1 N 4:53 P	Oct 5 F 8:13 P	Oct 2 ¾ 4:03 A
12 N 2:16 P	9 ¼ 0:23 P	12 ¾ 11:12 A	9 N 11:36 A
19 ¼ 6:10 P	16 F 3:47 A	20 N 10:11 P	17 ¼ 3:01 P
26 F 2:12 P	23 ¾ 4:50 A	28 ¼ 11:47 A	24 F 9:04 P
Nov 3 ¾ 7:52 A	31 N 10:02 A	Nov 4 F 5:19 A	31 ¾ 0:05 P
11 N 4:17 A	Nov 7 ¼ 9:45 P	11 ¾ 0:29 A	Nov 8 N 3:54 A
18 ¼ 1:10 A	14 F 2:13 A	19 N 4:28 A	16 ¼ 9:04 A
25 F 4:11 A	21 ¾ 11:59 P	27 ¼ 0:24 A	23 F 7:05 A
Dec 3 ¾ 5:07 A	30 N 2:15 A	Dec 3 F 3:20 P	29 ¾ 11:20 P
10 N 4:57 P	Dec 7 ¼ 6:10 A	10 ¾ 5:55 P	Dec 7 N 10:33 P
17 ¼ 9:32 A	14 F 2:38 A	18 N 10:44 P	16 ¼ 0:51 A
24 F 8:42 P	21 ¾ 9:44 P	26 ¼ 10:47 A	22 F 5:33 P
	29 N 4:58 P		29 ¾ 2:06 P

14

A Brief Introduction to Chart Synthesis

1. When you have discovered the degree and sign of your Ascendant, place it on the left-hand side of the chart.
2. Place the other eleven glyphs round the chart in an *anti-clockwise* direction.
3. Place the Sun and the Moon in their respective positions.
4. Look at the chart and work out how many masculine and feminine features there are. If all three Sun, Moon and Ascendant are in masculine/positive signs, the personality will be extrovert, confident, possibly sporty and energetic. If all three are in feminine signs, the subject will be introverted, domestically inclined, gentle and possibly a little shy with strangers.
5. Give the same treatment to the elements and triplicities. There is no need to make heavy weather of this, just make a note of the elements to see whether there is some kind of imbalance e.g. two features in fire signs or none in cardinal signs. This will give you a quick clue to the character of the subject.
6. Now look to see what signs the Sun and Moon occupy, this will really reveal the subject's character for you.
7. Finally, and most importantly take a look at the houses the Sun and Moon occupy to see *where* the subject's energies are directed, what he does and what he is trying to achieve.

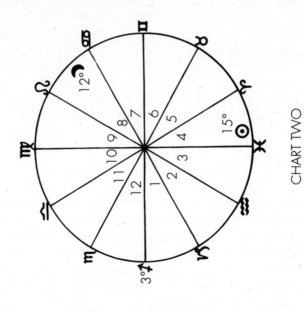

CHART ONE

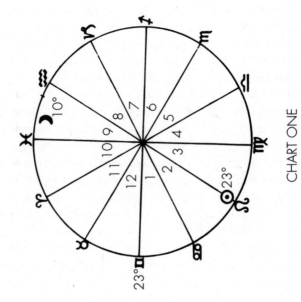

CHART TWO

Fig 14.1

15

Compatibility between the Sun and the Moon

When the Sun and Moon are in compatible signs there is a sense of inner harmony, one's normal daily behaviour and one's instinctive inner responses would be of a similar nature. If these two planets are in incompatible signs, there will be a split in the personality making the inner and instinctive reactions very different from the outer manner. This is further complicated by the fact that most of us actually project the Ascendant out to the world. I have to make a confession here, and that is that I hate people asking me the question, 'can you guess what sign I am?' because, as an astrologer I know that I am far more likely to 'pick up' their Ascendant than their Sun sign. It is pointless trying to explain this to the uninitiated.

If the first impression that one gives to the world is normally represented by the Ascendant or a combination of the Sun and the Ascendant, you might find yourself sending out a strong solar/Ascendant message saying 'I'm personality type AA', thereby drawing a response from others appropriate for type 'AA' while deep inside, you may be hiding a 'BB' type personality which requires quite a different kind of response!

Where close emotional relationships are concerned most people probably project the lunar or inner image anyway, therefore obtaining the correct type of response from the other person (doubtless the other person's lunar response). Placements which are *apparently* inharmonious to each other are actually not such a bad thing to have because they make for a more rounded personality. The thinking which lies behind this concept can be explained by a mixture of astrology and psychology or from pure astrological theory.

Elements, Triplicities and Aspects

If we look at this purely from the astrological view, it is a matter of breaking each sign down into its elements and triplicities plus the astrological aspects. Therefore planets which are in the same element (air, fire, earth or water) have something in common; planets in the same triplicity (cardinal, fixed, mutable) also have something in common. The only time two planets are in complete harmony is when they are in the same sign, otherwise there are mixtures of harmony and inharmony in most planetary aspects. This concept is very advanced and very complicated but I have broken it down in order to explain it for you.

1. Planets in the same element have something in common.
   Sun in Aries   –fire
   Moon in Leo   –fire
   These planets are in TRINE aspect.

2. Planets in the same triplicity have something in common.
   Sun in Aries   – cardinal
   Moon in Cancer   – cardinal
   These planets are in SQUARE aspect.
   Sun in Aries   – cardinal
   Moon in Libra   – cardinal
   These planets are in OPPOSITION to each other.

3. Planets of the same gender have something in common.
   Sun in Aries   – masculine
   Moon in Gemini   – masculine
   These planets are in SEXTILE aspect.

4. Generally speaking, air and fire get on fairly well together as do earth and water, but air plus water/earth are different in nature as are fire plus earth/water etc. The really awkward aspects are the semi-sextile and the inconjunct because, in both cases, neither the elements nor the triplicities are harmonious. In the case of the semi-sextile, at least the signs are adjacent to one another and adjacent signs *do* have a little in common with each other but planets which are inconjunct to each other have nothing at all in common.
   Sun in Aries   – fire, cardinal
   Moon in Taurus   – earth, fixed
   This is a SEMI-SEXTILE aspect.

Sun in Aries   – fire, cardinal
Moon in Virgo   – earth, mutable
This is an INCONJUNCT aspect.

Standard astrological theory tells us that conjunctions (planets in the same sign) are a strong force for good or ill, sextiles and trines are easy placements while squares and oppositions cause tension. Semi-sextiles don't usually have much effect either way but inconjuncts can be a real pain. Figure 15.2 shows the geometric shape of these aspects.

Psychologically speaking, the apparently super-harmonious situation of Sun plus Moon in the same sign may be a *little too much* of a good thing. The effect of having one's most important planets in the same sign may make the personality too one-sided. An interesting exercise for an absolute beginner would be to combine the effects of the Sun and Moon in your own personality and see how they blend. First look at Figure 15.1 to see how they blend astrologically and then look up the list to see how they work together in practice.

SUN/MOON COMPATIBILITY CHART

LOCATE YOUR SUN POSITION ALONG HERE

	Ar	Ta	Ge	Cn	Le	Vi	Li	Sc	Sg	Cp	Aq	Pi
Ar	*	0	=	=	=	0	=	0	=	=	=	0
Ta	0	*	0	-	-	-	0	-	0	=	=	=
Ge	=	0	*	0	=	=	=	0	=	0	=	=
Cn	=	=	0	*	0	=	=	=	0	=	0	=
Le	=	=	=	0	*	0	=	=	=	0	=	0
Vi	0	=	=	=	0	*	0	=	=	=	0	=
Li	=	0	=	=	=	0	*	0	=	=	=	0
Sc	0	=	0	=	=	=	0	*	0	=	=	=
Sg	=	0	=	0	=	=	=	0	*	0	=	=
Cp	=	=	0	=	0	=	=	=	0	*	0	=
Aq	=	=	=	0	=	0	=	=	=	0	*	0
Pi	0	=	=	=	0	=	0	=	=	=	0	*

(Left margin, reading downward: LOCATE YOUR MOON POSITION HERE)

* Harmonious
0 Inharmonius
= Reasonable

Figure 15.1

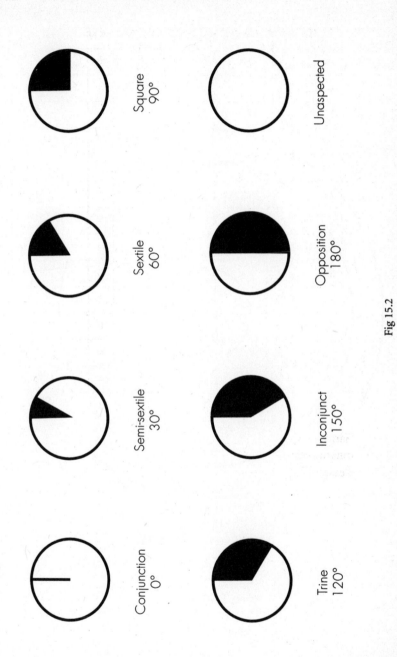

Square
90°

Unaspected

Sextile
60°

Opposition
180°

Semi-sextile
30°

Inconjunct
150°

Conjunction
0°

Trine
120°

Fig 15.2

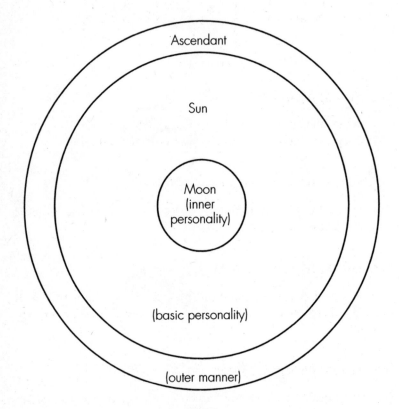

Fig 15.3
LAYERS OF PERSONALITY

Sun/Moon Combinations

Sun Aries, Moon Aries ☉ ♈ ☽ ♈

An extrovert and self-starter with an endless supply of enthusiasm, quick to think and act. You lack patience and may be too self-centred.

Sun Aries, Moon Taurus ☉ ♈ ☽ ♉

Confident, enthusiastic and lovable, good builder, architect or gardener with an artistic eye. Could be dogmatic.

Sun Aries, Moon Gemini ☉ ♈ ☽ ♊

Dextrous, good engineer or draftsman, full of bright ideas. Clever with words but sharp and sarcastic at times. You may leave tasks for others to finish off.

Sun Aries, Moon Cancer ☉ ♈ ☽ ♋

Very determined, a good business head on your shoulders and a pleasant manner. Home life is very important to you. Sensitive but you hide it from others.

Sun Aries, Moon Leo ☉ ♈ ☽ ♌

A real go-getter, you need the limelight. Enthusiastic and optimistic you may be bossy and domineering. Very creative, but blind to underlying influences at times.

Sun Aries, Moon Virgo ☉ ♈ ☽ ♍

Probing, analytical and clever. Very efficient and clever worker, shy in personal matters. Good writer, harsh critic, may be too fond of nit-picking details.

Sun Aries, Moon Libra ☉ ♈ ☽ ♎

Outwardly confident and ebullient, inwardly calmer. Sensitive to others also loving and passionate. Good business sense but may be overambitious.

Sun Aries, Moon Scorpio ☉ ♈ ☽ ♏

An excellent soldier or surgeon, good concentration level. Single-minded, intense and passionate about everything; you may be too much for anyone to handle for long. Try to relax and let others do the same.

Sun Aries, Moon Sagittarius ☉ ♈ ☽ ♐

Restless and energetic, you are a born explorer on both the physical and mental level. You can fill others with a zest for life and idealism. Tactless and sarcastic.

Sun Aries, Moon Capricorn ☉ ♈ ☽ ♑

Determined, unstoppable, must reach the top but this could be at the expense of your personal life. You seek to dominate others by force of your personality.

Sun Aries, Moon Aquarius ☉ ♈ ☽ ♒

Humanitarian and enthusiastic, you would make a wonderful sports coach or teacher, but you must be careful not to hurt others by thoughtlessly sarcastic remarks.

Sun Aries, Moon Pisces ☉ ♈ ☽ ♓

Outwardly enthusiastic, inwardly shy and lacking in confidence. Kind and well-meaning but could be apt to preach. You need to get away from others from time to time.

Sun Taurus, Moon Aries ☉ ♉ ☽ ♈

Outwardly calm, inwardly ambitious and determined. Could be very creative in a practical way. You may be too fond of your own opinions. Good engineer and builder, artistic too.

Sun Taurus, Moon Taurus ☉ ♉ ☽ ♉

Stubborn, fixed in your views and materialistic but also creative and artistic with a love of music. You will make things that stand the test of time. Loyal in love.

Sun Taurus, Moon Gemini ☉ ♉ ☽ ♊

Artistic and perceptive, a good media worker or marketing expert. Home-loving but occasional outbursts of restlessness. Affectionate but not too sensual.

Sun Taurus, Moon Cancer ☉ ♉ ☽ ♋

A real homemaker and family person. You can motivate others to achieve a great deal but you hold back from the limelight. Your imagination can be successfully harnessed.

Sun Taurus, Moon Leo ☉ ♉ ☽ ♌

Very fixed opinions and a definite personality, you find it hard to adapt to change. You love children and are intensely loyal to others. You could be a good singer or dancer.

Sun Taurus, Moon Virgo ☉ ♉ ☽ ♍

A careful worker who can combine detail and artistry. Good family person, can learn and teach wordy or musical skills. Don't be too critical or pessimistic. A strong interest in nutrition.

Sun Taurus, Moon Libra ☉ ♉ ☽ ♎

Very sensual and also artistic with a good business head. Maybe too lazy to achieve much but when motivated can reach the top. Lovable and kind but selfish too.

Sun Taurus, Moon Scorpio ☉ ♉ ☽ ♏

Artistic and sensual, you can achieve much. Your opinions are fixed and your nature stubborn. Very loyal and persistent, could be a good sales person, also strongly independent.

Sun Taurus, Moon Sagittarius ☉ ♉ ☽ ♐

Outwardly steady, inwardly restless. Could be an armchair traveller. Traditional religion interests you, don't be too old-fashioned or quick to judge others.

Sun Taurus, Moon Capricorn ☉ ♉ ☽ ♑

Determined and ambitious with a strong need for security. A shrewd and practical business head but inwardly shy and nervous in personal situations. Very loyal and loving.

Sun Taurus, Moon Aquarius ☉ ♉ ☽ ♒

Innovative and artistic you are good company and a hard worker. You need freedom but will insist on others toeing the line. Good concentration and high level of confidence.

Sun Taurus, Moon Pisces ☉ ♉ ☽ ♓

Dreamy and patient, highly artistic you may have difficulty in getting projects off the ground. Your sympathy may land you with the care of lame ducks. Sensual and loving.

Sun Gemini, Moon Aries ☉ ♊ ☽ ♈

Very sharp mind and a great deal of enthusiasm which can carry you away. Good media type, interesting friend but a touch too sarcastic for comfort.

Sun Gemini, Moon Taurus ☉ ♊ ☽ ♉

You have good ideas and the patience to finish what you start. A good homemaker and parent. You need communication and comfort in a relationship and work in a mentally artistic field.

Sun Gemini, Moon Gemini ☉ ♊ ☽ ♊

You have dozens of bright ideas but difficulty in completing anything. Very clever and dextrous but could be a bit unfeeling. Tension is your problem, try to relax and feel.

Sun Gemini, Moon Cancer ☉ ♊ ☽ ♋

Friendly and chatty, usually on the phone. You love travel and novelty plus family life. Don't be put upon by stronger characters. You can make a happy home for others, your memory is good.

Sun Gemini, Moon Leo ☉ ♊ ☽ ♌

Lively, friendly and good looking you will always be popular. You need to express your ideas creatively. Good with children as you will never quite grow up yourself.

Sun Gemini, Moon Virgo ☉ ♊ ☽ ♍

Inventive, versatile and full of ideas but lacking in confidence. Your nerves sometimes get the better of you. Good researcher, writer, secretary.

Sun Gemini, Moon Libra ☉ ♊ ☽ ♎

You are full of ideas which may not always get off the ground. Diplomatic and fun you can be a bit too restless. Flirtatious and fun but inclined to be long-winded.

Sun Gemini, Moon Scorpio ☉ ♊ ☽ ♏

Brilliant and perceptive mind. Outwardly a cool-hearted loner but burning with secret passions also emotionally vulnerable. Very creative writer, musician, doctor or spy. Clever with words, sarcastic.

Sun Gemini, Moon Sagittarius ☉ ♊ ☽ ♐

Restless, good sportsman or adventurous traveller. Good scholar and teacher. Might need to get in touch with your own feelings and those of others.

Sun Gemini, Moon Capricorn ☉ ♊ ☽ ♑

Clever and ambitious, literate, would succeed in the media. Relationships may bring suffering, you must try to be warmer to others. Capable and businesslike.

Sun Gemini, Moon Aquarius ☉ ♊ ☽ ♒

Broad-minded, good scholar and teacher. Wide-ranging ideas, perceptive. May fear emotional display or even own feelings. Detachment sought, good journalist or traveller.

Sun Gemini, Moon Pisces ☉ ♊ ☽ ♓

Hidden depths to personality, good with children, also sports and dancing. Imaginative writer but too ready to explain all to others. Bubbly personality but lacking in confidence, nervous and incapable if under severe stress.

Sun Cancer, Moon Aries ☉ ♋ ☽ ♈

Capable and competitive type with a good business head and the ability to understand others. Would need a good home but easily bored if spending too much time on it. A strange mixture of caring and impatience.

Sun Cancer, Moon Taurus ☉ ♋ ☽ ♉

Kind, caring and cuddly. You love your home and family, you also have a good head for business. Artistic, musical and rather lazy, inclined to brood.

Sun Cancer, Moon Gemini ☉ ♋ ☽ ♊

Clever and businesslike, pleasant and successful. You appear slow but can be quick and cunning. Good politician, terrific traveller. Could have sporting abilities.

Sun Cancer, Moon Cancer ☉ ♋ ☽ ♋

Strong emotions, strong attachment to family. You tend to be moody and to cut off from other people. Kind-hearted, aware of the needs of others. Attached to the past, good historian.

Sun Cancer, Moon Leo ☉ ♋ ☽ ♌

Caring and compassionate, very loving towards your family and friends. Emotionally vulnerable. You have high standards and can cut off your nose to spite your face.

Sun Cancer, Moon Virgo ☉ ♋ ☽ ♍

Good placement for a nurse or doctor, caring in a practical way. Good with details, excellent memory. Will cut off from others when hurt. Good business head, rather dogged, good salesperson. A worrier.

Sun Cancer, Moon Libra ☉ ♋ ☽ ♎

Good business head on your shoulders. Ambitious for self and your family. Love of beauty and harmony, probably artistic. May have difficulty in putting ideas into practice.

Sun Cancer, Moon Scorpio ☉ ♋ ☽ ♏

Strongly intuitive and probably very moody. You would be difficult to ignore. Try to keep a positive outlook on life and avoid being too pessimistic.

Sun Cancer, Moon Sagittarius ☉ ♋ ☽ ♐

This combination makes you a family person who needs emotional freedom. You are idealistic and lovable but you may ask more from life than you could reasonably expect to obtain.

Sun Cancer, Moon Capricorn ☉ ♋ ☽ ♑

You have a very good head for business, you are shrewd and intuitive. You can succeed as long as you don't try to cut corners or to save money in silly ways.

Sun Cancer, Moon Aquarius ☉ ♋ ☽ ♒

A clever politician with a quirky mind which operates behind a placid façade. You can put your point of view across well. You keep your eye firmly fixed on the main chance.

Sun Cancer, Moon Pisces ☉ ♋ ☽ ♓

Very sensitive and intuitive, you are so tuned in to others that you can forget your own needs. You may prefer to work in a field where you can care for less fortunate people (or animals).

Sun Leo, Moon Aries ☉ ♌ ☽ ♈

You have courage, verve and enthusiasm but you must learn not to ride roughshod over others. If you can see beyond your own needs, you can go far.

Sun Leo, Moon Taurus ☉ ♌ ☽ ♉

You are kind, reliable, dedicated to your family and highly practical but you may be too obstinate for your own good. Traditional outlook on life.

Sun Leo, Moon Gemini ☉ ♌ ☽ ♊

You like to be busy and your mind works overtime. You are independent, creative and clever with good leadership qualities but your sarcasm might be a bit too much for some people.

Sun Leo, Moon Cancer ☉ ♌ ☽ ♋

A real family person with strong need to mother people. Your emotions may overtake you at times. You like the past and tradition. Very caring and kind.

Sun Leo, Moon Leo ☉ ♌ ☽ ♌

Dramatic and outgoing, you need to dazzle others. You are funny and entertaining but might be a bit too self-centred for comfort. Try to cope with details rather than ignore them.

Sun Leo, Moon Virgo ☉ ♌ ☽ ♍

You could be an excellent employer as you can delegate and also work in a logical manner. Your sharp tongue might be a bit hard to live with. You are very honest and basically kind natured.

Sun Leo, Moon Libra ☉ ♌ ☽ ♎

Very affectionate and probably very sexy, you have a great sense of style. You also have a good head for business but you may be too fond of having things your own way.

Sun Leo, Moon Scorpio ☉ ♌ ☽ ♏

Very intense and strong personality, possibly too dramatic. You are very loyal and may be rather possessive but your colleagues will respect you for your honesty and your capacity for work.

Sun Leo, Moon Sagittarius ☉ ♌ ☽ ♐

Very adventurous, you cannot be tied down. You are loyal, proud and kind-hearted. You have high personal standards but will have to curb your sarcasm and also think before committing yourself.

Sun Leo, Moon Capricorn ☉ ♌ ☽ ♑

Very organized and ambitious, you are destined to succeed in some traditional field of work. Don't ride roughshod over others or cover up your softness too much.

Sun Leo, Moon Aquarius ☉ ♌ ☽ ♒

You have strong opinions and can throw yourself into a cause. You are loyal, faithful and have a well developed sense of fair play. Try to develop practicality and a flexible outlook.

Sun Leo, Moon Pisces ☉ ♌ ☽ ♓

A dreamer and mystic who can bring dreams to life. It is hard for you to turn away from those who need your help and strength. Don't become down-hearted if all your plans don't work out. Creative and kind-hearted.

Sun Virgo, Moon Aries ☉ ♍ ☽ ♈

Your mind is sharp and so is your tongue. Being quick and clever you can succeed at many jobs. Self-expression in the form of writing is essential for you.

Sun Virgo, Moon Taurus ☉ ♍ ☽ ♉

Interested in the growing and preparing of food, creative in a structured way and kind. You may lack the confidence to get things off the ground. Sensible, helpful and practical outlook.

Sun Virgo, Moon Gemini ☉ ♍ ☽ ♊

You are very quick and clever, your mind and tongue are rarely still. You can gather and analyse information but your intellect may prevent you from getting in touch with your own and other people's feelings.

Sun Virgo, Moon Cancer ☉ ♍ ☽ ♋

Very canny, interested in food and nutrition. Could be a good business person in a small way. You worry about your family and can be a bit too fussy and moody for comfort.

Sun Virgo, Moon Leo ☉ ♍ ☽ ♌

Caring, conscientious and organized, you can be relied upon to get things done. You may work with children. Your personal standards are very high but you lack confidence.

Sun Virgo, Moon Virgo ☉ ♍ ☽ ♍

Lack of confidence partly due to an unhappy childhood. You may pay too much attention to details and worry too much about small matters. Honest and kind, you always try to help others and do your duty in every way.

Sun Virgo, Moon Libra ☉ ♍ ☽ ♎

You are neat and tidy, you enjoy organizing. Could be a good mediator or co-operative worker. Good thinker but slow to make decisions. A good cook.

Sun Virgo, Moon Scorpio ☉ ♍ ☽ ♏

Clever and critical, you would make a very good doctor or nurse. You need to get to the bottom of things but may be too cool for comfort towards others.

Sun Virgo, Moon Sagittarius ☉ ♍ ☽ ♐

Humanitarian and thoughtful, you are interested in education. Warm and friendly and sometimes impulsive, you can also attend to details. Could make a good teacher but an even better travel agent.

Sun Virgo, Moon Capricorn ☉ ♍ ☽ ♑

Good in business but possibly too self-disciplined and serious. You are capable, conscientious and clever but you need to cultivate a sense of fun and give some attention to the needs of others. Very reliable family member.

Sun Virgo, Moon Aquarius ☉ ♍ ☽ ♒

You could be a wonderful teacher. Deep thinker, very helpful to those in need. Don't let your need for independence deprive you of family life or keep you separated from your feelings.

Sun Virgo, Moon Pisces ☉ ♍ ☽ ♓

You live to serve the needs of others and then wonder why your own needs are not being met. Your mind is good when projected outwardly towards intellectual pursuits. Intuitive, interested in medicine and nutrition.

Sun Libra, Moon Aries ☉ ♎ ☽ ♈

You are a good initiator but might find it difficult to finish what you start. Others may help you to do this. You are clever and intuitive but can be selfish and impatient. Good in a crisis.

Sun Libra, Moon Taurus ☉ ♎ ☽ ♉

You are attractive to look at and have excellent taste. You love music and art but may be too lazy to become skilled yourself. Good homemaker and family person with practical business mind.

Sun Libra, Moon Gemini ☉ ♎ ☽ ♊

A theorizer with a good mind, you can be superficial. Dextrous and clever you have the ability to put techniques into practice as long as you have help from others. Keep in touch with your feelings and those of others.

Sun Libra, Moon Cancer ☉ ♎ ☽ ♋

Kind and pleasant, you make a nice home and are a good caring family member. Good personnel manager or accountant. You need to close off from others from time to time to do your own thing.

Sun Libra, Moon Leo ☉ ♎ ☽ ♌

You are in love with love half the time with a romantic and dramatic attitude to life. Clever and creative but could become easily bored. Very clever in business or politics.

Sun Libra, Moon Virgo ☉ ♎ ☽ ♍

Pleasant, charming and sensible, you can do most things as long as they are not messy or dirty. Loyal to friends. Good at detailed work. Literate and musical.

Sun Libra, Moon Libra ☉ ♎ ☽ ♎

You are very attractive both in looks and as a personality but you may be in a bit of a dream half the time. You may need to be more decisive and more energetic.

Sun Libra, Moon Scorpio ☉ ♎ ☽ ♏

Strongly sexed and intense, you would be a handful for anyone who comes close to you. You are determined and businesslike but must watch a tendency to dominate others.

Sun Libra, Moon Sagittarius ☉ ♎ ☽ ♐

You will probably travel quite a bit on business and should be great at dealing with and negotiating with foreigners. The legal profession would draw you as you have a good sense of judgement.

Sun Libra, Moon Capricorn ☉ ♎ ☽ ♑

You are very purposeful and a harder worker than Librans usually are. You could be very successful as your judgement of people is pretty acute.

Sun Libra, Moon Aquarius ☉ ♎ ☽ ♒

Very independent and also quite clever. You have good judgement and are able to lead others strongly but calmly. Your imagination is strong and could be used to make your living.

Sun Libra, Moon Pisces ☉ ♎ ☽ ♓

Very artistic and musical, you can be a dreamy romantic. Both your appearance and your nature are attractive. You have a deep level of intuition but may be a bit slow to put things into action.

Sun Scorpio, Moon Aries ☉ ♏ ☽ ♈

You have a strong character but might be *too* ready to fight everything and everyone. Your feelings are intense and your temper rather short but you have deep reserves of courage and can achieve a great deal.

Sun Scorpio, Moon Taurus ☉ ♏ ☽ ♉

Sensual and musical you might have great talent for something attractive like horticulture. You may be too obstinate or too practical. A very reliable type.

Sun Scorpio, Moon Gemini ☉ ♏ ☽ ♊

This combination shows a difficult childhood and an early sense of loss. Don't continue to view the world with too much suspicion. Very clever and intuitive about people.

Sun Scorpio, Moon Cancer ☉ ♏ ☽ ♋

Attractive to look at and talk to, you are deeply intuitive but may be able to relate more easily to animals than to people. Your moodiness will be your weak point.

Sun Scorpio, Moon Leo ☉ ♏ ☽ ♌

Very fixed opinions it is hard for you to adapt. Loyal to your family especially your children. You can finish what you start. Guard against overdramatizing everything.

Sun Scorpio, Moon Virgo ☉ ♏ ☽ ♍

This shows a difficult childhood with feelings of alienation. Try to develop trust in others. Clever and dutiful, you could be drawn to a career in the medical profession.

Sun Scorpio, Moon Libra ☉ ♏ ☽ ♎

You are attractive and clever, this combination gives diplomacy and determination, you would make a good politician. You may either swamp your family with your personality or ignore them while pursuing your career.

Sun Scorpio, Moon Scorpio ☉ ♏ ☽ ♏

You have a powerful personality and often feel passionate about everything. Try not to dominate others. You can achieve almost anything you set your mind to.

Sun Scorpio, Moon Sagittarius ☉ ♏ ☽ ♐

Clever and clairvoyant, you would make a good lawyer or businessman but also a good detective. Your sense of humour helps you to keep everything in perspective.

Sun Scorpio, Moon Capricorn ☉ ♏ ☽ ♑

You could be a rather serious and determined person. You would reach the top in any field you set your heart on but could miss out on the personal side of life until your later years.

Sun Scorpio, Moon Aquarius ☉ ♏ ☽ ♒

You are independent and clever with a strong intuitive streak. You are decisive and instinctive but might be something of an intolerant tough guy.

Sun Scorpio, Moon Pisces ☉ ♏, ☽ ♓

Intuitive and artistic, probably musical. You have a strong drive to help others, probably in the field of health. You can withdraw into injured silence or spitefulness if you feel threatened.

Sun Sagittarius, Moon Aries ☉ ♐ ☽ ♈

You are open and honest but may be too quick to jump into exciting new schemes. Your restlessness might take you around the world but also may make it difficult for you to hang on to relationships.

Sun Sagittarius, Moon Taurus ☉ ♐ ☽ ♉

You are kind and good-hearted with great enthusiasm for the good things of life. You could be an inspired cook or artist and have the ability to combine practicality with imagination.

Sun Sagittarius, Moon Gemini ☉ ♐ ☽ ♊

You are always busy and restless. You could be a very good sportsman or entertainer. Clever and articulate, you could make a good writer.

Sun Sagittarius, Moon Cancer ☉ ♐ ☽ ♋

You are intuitive and creative and would make a good medium. There is a split between your need for home comforts and your need for freedom. Childish at times.

Sun Sagittarius, Moon Leo ☉ ♐ ☽ ♌

Dramatic and outgoing, you would do well on the stage. Try to tune in a bit more to the needs of others. Youthful and active, you are great fun to be with.

Sun Sagittarius, Moon Virgo ☉ ♐ ☽ ♍

You have the ability to think both deeply and in an organized manner. You would make a wonderful teacher. Don't lay the law down to others.

Sun Sagittarius, Moon Libra ☉ ♐ ☽ ♎

You would make a fabulous barrister as you have a gift for all things legal. Don't be too hard on others who are not as bright or as successful as you.

Sun Sagittarius, Moon Scorpio ☉ ♐ ☽ ♏

You could make a good detective as you have both investigative ability and a legal mind. Don't be too hard on those who either don't share your interests or are not as capable as you.

Sun Sagittarius, Moon Sagittarius ☉ ♐ ☽ ♐

You would make a terrific explorer as you love travel and are too restless to sit still for long. Try to tune into ordinary people as not everyone will understand the breadth of your mind.

Sun Sagittarius, Moon Capricorn ☉ ♐ ☽ ♑

Clever and determined, honest and entertaining, you could go far in life. You should travel and be involved with business but you must have some patience with less capable people.

Sun Sagittarius, Moon Aquarius ☉ ♐ ☽ ♒

Your mind is broad and you can teach others. You tend to live in a world of your own which is out of step with most of the rest of the world. Could be an eccentric genius.

Sun Sagittarius, Moon Pisces ☉ ♐ ☽ ♓

You are intuitive, kind and spiritual and would make a good teacher. You are artistic and imaginative and have much to give others but you may be a bit vague and impractical at times.

Sun Capricorn, Moon Aries ☉ ♑ ☽ ♈

You have a great deal of determination and may be very clever as well. Once you have set your mind on something, you will get there for sure but you may tread on a few toes while doing it.

Sun Capricorn, Moon Taurus ☉ ♑ ☽ ♉

Practical and sensible, you can achieve much both in the artistic and the business world. Guard against stubbornness and try to see the other person's point of view.

Sun Capricorn, Moon Gemini ☉ ♑ ☽ ♊

Clever but organized. Could make a good writer, salesman, business person with the ability to put good ideas into practice and finish what you start.

Sun Capricorn, Moon Cancer ☉ ♑ ☽ ♋

Home-loving family person, very loyal, decent, also extremely business-like. Can have a tendency to withdraw into your shell. You worry about everything. A good teacher or counsellor.

Sun Capricorn, Moon Leo ☉ ♑ ☽ ♌

Good in positions of authority. A caring boss. Decent, reliable, but also very determined, may be apt to ride over people who are weaker.

Sun Capricorn, Moon Virgo ☉ ♑ ☽ ♍

Very stable, reliable, family person. Probably a very good cook. Very good head for business. Could be a bit too lacking in humour or too pedantic.

Sun Capricorn, Moon Libra ☉ ♑ ☽ ♎

A good mixture of stability plus business ability. Can get on with people and also achieve a great deal, but may be a bit over enthusiastic when it comes to money-making ideas.

Sun Capricorn, Moon Scorpio ☉ ♑ ☽ ♏

Great strength of character. Clear idea of where you are going and what you want out of life. Very dependable, loyal, kind, but you have no time for fools. You hate to show your feelings.

Sun Capricorn, Moon Sagittarius ☉ ♑ ☽ ♐

Great stability and ability plus a broad sweeping mind. Could work Sin the travel industry or teaching, legal or church work. Good in any sort of concentrated work where you deal with people in authority.

Sun Capricorn, Moon Capricorn ☉ ♑ ☽ ♑

Very shy and withdrawn. Very hard worker, good with the elderly. Could find life very difficult until later on. A creative hobby or outlet would be very beneficial to you.

Sun Capricorn, Moon Aquarius ☉ ♑ ☽ ♒

Good organizer. Able to do things on a big scale. Can be a bit hard on yourself and on other people, but very determined and capable.

Sun Capricorn, Moon Pisces ☉ ♑ ☽ ♓

Deep, kindly, intuitive, very good in a caring profession, particularly dealing with the old, but could be a bit too shy and too easily hurt. Rather serious.

Sun Aquarius, Moon Aries ☉ ♒ ☽ ♈

A very broad-ranging mind. Good teacher, engineer, very clever, but might be difficult to live with. Don't judge other people too harshly. Good sense of humour.

Sun Aquarius, Moon Taurus ☉ ♒ ☽ ♉

You can cope with a lot and achieve a lot. You are very steady, determined and reliable, but could be too stubborn. You may be interested in music, art or beauty products.

Sun Aquarius, Moon Gemini ☉ ♒ ☽ ♊

A natural student or teacher, very clever. A bit inclined to flip from one idea to another and also need to develop stability in relationships with other people.

Sun Aquarius, Moon Cancer ☉ ≈ ☽ ♋

A good family person, good with small children and animals. Can teach, a good companion but can be a bit inclined to withdraw into a shell.

Sun Aquarius, Moon Leo ☉ ≈ ☽ ♌

Very lively personality, always busy doing a lot of things at once. Loyal, a bit stubborn, determined, but can be independent and awkward.

Sun Aquarius, Moon Virgo ☉ ≈ ☽ ♍

Clever, studious, able to put ideas into practice in a very detailed way. Probably very good in research but could be a bit eccentric and nit-picking, difficult to live with.

Sun Aquarius, Moon Libra ☉ ≈ ☽ ♎

Great fun, easy-going, great friend to everybody, but a bit unreliable in close relationships. Good in almost any field that doesn't require too much steady effort.

Sun Aquarius, Moon Scorpio ☉ ≈ ☽ ♏

Full of self confidence. The ability to be a leader. Can be too inclined to ride roughshod over other people. A very original thinker. Easily irritated with fools.

Sun Aquarius, Moon Sagittarius ☉ ≈ ☽ ♐

Very independent, outspoken, a bit tactless, interested in any kind of novel idea. Intelligent, a good teacher. You have a tendency to rush into things without thinking.

Sun Aquarius, Moon Capricorn ☉ ≈ ☽ ♑

A mixture of seriousness and spontaneity. Responsible, capable, a good family person, a good business person. Original ideas and a lot of determination.

Sun Aquarius, Moon Aquarius ☉ ♒ ☽ ♒

Very eccentric, very freedom-loving, independent, great fun. Original ideas and an original lifestyle, but not really a family person. Don't judge others too harshly.

Sun Aquarius, Moon Pisces ☉ ♒ ☽ ♓

Very imaginative, intuitive, with the ability to blend common sense and mysticism. Kindly, intelligent, a bit apt to wander off on your own and go into flights of fancy.

Sun Pisces, Moon Aries ☉ ♓ ☽ ♈

Intuitive, quick and clever, quite determined, great fun and good friend, but not a very reliable family person. You may fluctuate between selfishness and consideration for others.

Sun Pisces, Moon Taurus ☉ ♓ ☽ ♉

Sociable and pleasant, artistic, kind and musical. It's difficult for you to start things but once started you will finish them. You are good looking and graceful. Inclined to be lazy.

Sun Pisces, Moon Gemini ☉ ♓ ☽ ♊

Nervous, talkative, clever, a worrier. You need a stable partner. You're good fun, good looking and interesting, but you never really grow up. Your nerves let you down from time to time.

Sun Pisces, Moon Cancer ☉ ♓ ☽ ♋

Sensitive, kind, thoughtful, very moody, but also kind and caring. You would make a good nurse, doctor or teacher. You may be interested in diets and cooking. Understanding but somewhat impractical.

Sun Pisces, Moon Leo ☉ ♓ ☽ ♌

Generous, imaginative, creative and kindly. You need to be out and about. You like stimulation of new people but your confidence goes very quickly and you can be susceptible to flattery.

Sun Pisces, Moon Virgo ☉ ♓ ☽ ♍

Nervous, thoughtful, deep, intuitive, could work very well on your own in a creative way. Can be too fussy, too worrying, would need a strong partner. Interested in food and diets.

Sun Pisces, Moon Libra ☉ ♓ ☽ ♎

You will need to keep in touch with reality. Your ideas are good. You could achieve a lot if allied to somebody with strength and practicality. You need other people to encourage you.

Sun Pisces, Moon Scorpio ☉ ♓ ☽ ♏

Perceptive, intuitive, deep, attracted to medicine, police and forensic work. Deep insight into people, can manipulate others. Moody but also caring and kind. Can be self-absorbed and difficult to live with.

Sun Pisces, Moon Sagittarius ☉ ♓ ☽ ♐

Great traveller with a deep and thoughtful mind. Could work in the religious field or as a conservationist. Unreliable as a family person as your mind is elsewhere most of the time.

Sun Pisces, Moon Capricorn ☉ ♓ ☽ ♑

Creativity, intuition and practicality mixed together here, so you can make achievements on the work front and also be a good family person. The only problem is lack of confidence.

Sun Pisces, Moon Aquarius ☉ ♓ ☽ ♒

Friendly, could start projects and then lose interest. Mystical, a good teacher and a caring person but you need a stable and practical partner as you don't often have your feet on the ground.

Sun Pisces, Moon Pisces ☉ ♓ ☽ ♓

Very active imagination. You see omens and meanings in things. You prefer to work from home by yourself: You find people tend to wear you out, you soak up other people's problems and do find family life hard sometimes.

Conclusion

For those of you who have never delved deeper into astrology than to read about your Sun sign or to read the horoscopes in magazines and newspapers, I hope that this book will whet your appetite and encourage you to look deeper now. For those of you who are already interested in the subject, to the point of erecting charts and pursuing your own research, I hope that this book adds to your knowledge and understanding of how just *one* of the planets works through our lives.

I have learned a great deal about the Moon during the course of researching this book. I never realized that there was so much to be found in one tiny satellite. I dread to think of erecting charts for births on other planets such as Saturn which has around a dozen moons or more! I think I will leave the next generation of astrologers to grapple with that one.

Astrology is a living and growing subject, an intuitive science which will be taken more seriously as the age of Aquarius rolls in. I hope you now progress alongside your planets, learn and enjoy a totally fascinating subject.

The Ephemeris

How to use the Ephemeris

The Ephemeris shows the position of the Moon at midnight on every other day. To find *your* Moon position:

1. Find the year of your birth.
2. Find the month of your birth.
3. Find the date of your birthday, or the date immediately preceding your birthday.
4. Unless you were born on or just after midnight on the date as shown you will have to make an adjustment by *counting forward half a degree per hour.*
   Midnight on birthday – position as shown in the Ephemeris

6 am	same day	add	3°
12 noon	same day	add	6°
6 pm	same day	add	9°
Midnight	next day	add	12°
6 am	next day	add	15°
12 noon	next day	add	18°
6 pm	next day	add	21°

If you counting takes you to more than 29° of any sign, the Moon will move to the *next sign.*

Remember if you were born in New York – in addition to the above *add* a further five hours (2½°). If you were born in Bombay, subtract five hours (or 2½°). See page 175.

If you are now completely flummoxed, phone a friendly astrologer and ask for help.

1930

	Jan	Feb	Mar	Apr	May	Jun	Jul	Aug	Sep	Oct	Nov	Dec
1	20Cp	5Pi	14Pi	1Ta	7Ge	0Le	10Vi	1Sc	19Sg	22Cp	6Pi	8Ar
3	14Aq	19Pi	9Ar	27Ta	5Cn	29Le	8Li	27Sc	13Cp	16Aq	0Ar	2Ta
5	8Pi	24Ar	4Ta	25Ge	4Le	27Vi	4Sc	22Sg	7Aq	10Pi	24Ar	29Ta
7	2Ar	20Ta	0Ge	23Cn	2Vi	24Li	0Sg	16Cp	1Pi	4Ar	20Ta	26Ge
9	28Ar	18Ge	28Ge	22Le	0Li	20Sc	25Sg	10Aq	25Pi	28Ar	17Ge	25Cn
11	25Ta	18Cn	27Cn	20Vi	28Li	16Sg	19Cp	4Pi	19Ar	24Ta	14Cn	24Le
13	24Ge	18Le	18Le	19Li	24Sc	11Cp	13Aq	28Pi	14Ta	20Ge	13Le	22Vi
15	25Cn	18Vi	18Vi	16Sc	20Sg	5Aq	7Pi	22Ar	10Ge	18Cn	11Vi	20Li
17	25Le	17Li	17Li	12Sg	14Cp	28Aq	1Ar	17Ta	7Cn	16Le	9Li	17Sc
19	24Vi	13Sc	21Sc	7Cp	8Aq	22Pi	25Ar	14Ge	6Le	15Vi	7Sc	13Sg
21	22Li	8Sg	16Sg	1Aq	2Pi	17Ar	21Ta	12Cn	6Vi	14Li	5Sg	9Cp
23	17Sc	2Cp	11Cp	24Aq	26Pi	13Ta	19Ge	12Le	6Li	13Sc	1Cp	4Aq
25	12Sg	26Cp	4Aq	19Pi	22Ar	11Ge	19Cn	13Vi	5Sc	10Sg	26Cp	28Aq
27	6Cp	20Aq	28Aq	14Ar	18Ta	10Cn	19Le	12Li	2Sg	6Cp	20Aq	21Pi
29	29Cp		23Pi	10Ta	17Ge	10Le	19Vi	10Sc	28Sg	0Aq	14Pi	15Ar
31	23Aq		18Ar		16Cn		18Li	6Sg		24Aq		10Ta

1931

	Jan	Feb	Mar	Apr	May	Jun	Jul	Aug	Sep	Oct	Nov	Dec
1	23Ta	13Cn	21Cn	14Vi	23Li	14Sg	19Cp	5Pi	19Ar	22Ta	9Cn	16Le
3	20Ge	12Le	20Le	14Li	22Sc	11Cp	15Aq	29Pi	13Ta	16Ge	5Le	13Vi
5	19Cn	13Vi	21Vi	14Sc	20Sg	8Aq	9Pi	23Ar	7Ge	12Cn	3Vi	12Li
7	19Le	12Li	21Li	12Sg	16Cp	1Pi	3Ar	17Ta	3Cn	9Le	2Li	11Sc
9	18Vi	10Sc	20Sc	8Cp	11Aq	25Pi	26Ar	12Ge	1Le	8Vi	2Sc	10Sg
11	17Li	7Sg	16Sg	3Aq	5Pi	18Ar	21Ta	9Cn	0Vi	8Li	2Sg	8Cp
13	14Sc	2Cp	12Cp	27Aq	29Pi	13Ta	17Ge	7Le	0Li	9Sc	0Cp	5Aq
15	10Sg	27Cp	6Aq	20Pi	22Ar	9Ge	14Cn	7Vi	0Sc	8Sg	27Cp	0Pi
17	5Cp	21Aq	0Pi	14Ar	17Ta	5Cn	13Le	6Li	29Sc	5Cp	22Aq	24Pi
19	0Aq	15Pi	23Pi	8Ta	13Ge	3Le	12Vi	5Sc	26Sg	1Aq	16Pi	18Ar
21	24Aq	8Ar	17Ar	3Ge	9Cn	2Vi	11Li	3Sg	22Cp	26Aq	10Ar	12Ta
23	18Pi	2Ta	11Ta	29Ge	7Le	0Li	9Sc	0Cp	17Aq	20Pi	4Ta	6Ge
25	11Ar	27Ta	6Ge	26Cn	5Vi	28Li	6Sg	25Cp	11Pi	13Ar	28Ta	2Cn
27	6Ta	23Ge	2Cn	24Le	3Li	26Sc	3Cp	20Aq	4Ar	7Ta	23Ge	29Cn
29	1Ge		0Le	23Vi	2Sc	23Sg	28Cp	14Pi	28Ar	1Ge	19Cn	26Le
31	28Ge		29Le		0Sg		23Aq	7Ar		26Ge		24Vi

1932

	Jan	Feb	Mar	Apr	May	Jun	Jul	Aug	Sep	Oct	Nov	Dec
1	8Li	1Sg	26Sg	15Aq	18Pi	2Ta	5Ge	21Cn	10Vi	18Li	12Sg	20Cp
3	6Sc	29Sg	22Cp	9Pi	12Ar	26Ta	29Ge	17Le	9Li	18Sc	11Cp	17Aq
5	5Sg	25Cp	17Aq	3Ar	6Ta	21Ge	25Cn	15Vi	8Sc	17Sg	8Aq	13Pi
7	3Cp	21Aq	12Pi	27Ar	29Ta	16Ge	21Le	13Li	7Sg	15Cp	4Pi	8Ar
9	0Aq	16Pi	6Ar	20Ta	24Ge	11Le	18Vi	11Sc	5Cp	12Aq	29Pi	2Ta
11	25Aq	10Ar	0Ta	14Ge	18Cn	8Vi	16Li	10Sg	2Aq	7Pi	23Ar	25Ta
13	20Pi	3Ta	24Ta	9Cn	14Le	6Li	15Sc	8Cp	28Aq	2Ar	17Ta	19Ge
15	14Ar	27Ta	18Ge	5Le	11Vi	4Sc	14Sg	5Aq	23Pi	26Ar	10Ge	13Cn
17	7Ta	22Ge	13Cn	2Vi	10Li	4Sg	12Cp	2Pi	17Ar	20Ta	4Cn	8Le
19	2Ge	18Cn	10Le	1Li	10Sc	3Cp	10Aq	27Pi	11Ta	13Ge	29Cn	4Vi
21	27Ge	16Le	8Vi	2Sc	10Sg	2Aq	6Pi	21Ar	5Ge	7Cn	23Le	0Li
23	24Cn	15Vi	8Li	2Sg	10Cp	28Aq	1Ar	15Ta	29Ge	2Le	21Vi	28Li
25	22Le	15Li	9Sc	1Cp	7Aq	23Pi	25Ar	9Ge	24Cn	28Le	19Li	28Sc
27	20Vi	14Sc	8Sg	28Cp	3Pi	17Ar	19Ta	3Cn	20Le	26Vi	19Sc	28Sg
29	19Li	12Sg	6Cp	24Aq	27Pi	11Ta	13Ge	29Cn	18Vi	26Li	20Sg	27Cp
31	17Sc		2Aq		21Ar		8Cn	26Le		27Sc		25Aq

1933

	Jan	Feb	Mar	Apr	May	Jun	Jul	Aug	Sep	Oct	Nov	Dec
1	9Pi	24Ar	2Ta	16Ge	18Cn	4Vi	9Li	2Sg	25Cp	3Pi	22Ar	26Ta
3	4Ar	18Ta	26Ta	10Cn	12Le	0Li	7Sc	1Cp	24Aq	0Ar	17Ta	20Ge
5	28Ar	12Ge	20Ge	4Le	8Vi	28Li	7Sg	1Aq	22Pi	26Ar	12Ge	14Cn
7	22Ta	6Cn	14Cn	0Vi	5Li	28Sc	7Cp	29Aq	18Ar	21Ta	5Cn	7Le
9	16Ge	1Le	9Le	27Vi	4Sc	29Sg	7Aq	27Pi	13Ar	15Ge	29Cn	2Vi
11	10Cn	27Le	5Vi	26Li	5Sg	28Cp	5Pi	23Ar	8Ge	9Cn	23Le	27Vi
13	5Le	24Vi	3Li	26Sc	5Cp	27Aq	2Ar	18Ta	1Cn	3Le	18Vi	23Li
15	1Vi	21Li	2Sc	25Sg	4Aq	23Pi	27Ar	11Ge	25Cn	28Le	15Li	22Sc
17	27Vi	20Sc	1Sg	24Cp	1Pi	18Ar	21Ta	5Cn	20Le	24Vi	14Sc	22Sg
19	25Li	18Sg	29Sg	21Aq	27Pi	12Ta	15Ge	29Cn	16Vi	21Li	14Sg	23Cp
21	23Sc	16Cp	27Cp	17Pi	21Ar	6Ge	9Cn	24Le	13Li	20Sc	14Cp	22Aq
23	22Sg	14Aq	24Aq	12Ar	15Ta	0Cn	3Le	20Vi	11Sc	20Sg	13Aq	20Pi
25	21Cp	11Pi	20Pi	6Ta	9Ge	24Cn	28Le	17Li	9Sg	18Cp	10Pi	16Ar
27	19Aq	7Ar	15Ar	0Ge	3Cn	18Le	23Vi	14Sc	8Cp	16Aq	6Ar	11Ta
29	16Pi		10Ta	24Ge	27Cn	13Vi	20Li	12Sg	6Aq	13Pi	2Ta	5Ge
31	12Ar		4Ge		21Le		17Sc	11Cp		9Ar		29Ge

1934

	Jan	Feb	Mar	Apr	May	Jun	Jul	Aug	Sep	Oct	Nov	Dec
1	11Cn	25Le	4Vi	22Li	29Sc	22Cp	1Pi	22Ar	9Ge	12Cn	25Le	27Vi
3	4Le	20Vi	29Vi	19Sc	28Sg	21Aq	29Pi	18Ta	4Cn	6Le	19Vi	22Li
5	28Le	16Li	26Li	17Sg	26Cp	19Pi	26Ar	13Ge	27Cn	29Le	14Li	19Sc
7	23Vi	12Sc	23Sc	16Cp	25Aq	16Ar	21Ta	7Cn	21Le	24Vi	11Sc	17Sg
9	19Li	10Sg	20Sg	14Aq	22Pi	12Ta	16Ge	0Le	15Vi	19Li	8Sg	16Cp
11	16Sc	9Cp	19Cp	12Pi	19Ar	7Ge	10Cn	24Le	10Li	15Sc	7Cp	15Aq
13	15Sg	9Aq	18Aq	9Ar	15Ta	1Cn	3Le	18Vi	5Sc	12Sg	5Aq	14Pi
15	16Cp	8Pi	17Pi	6Ta	10Ge	25CN	27Le	13Li	2Sg	10Cp	3Pi	12Ar
17	16Aq	7Ar	14Ar	2Ge	4Cn	18Le	21Vi	8Sc	29Sg	8Aq	1Ar	8Ta
19	15Pi	3Ta	11Ta	26Ge	28Cn	12Vi	16Li	5Sg	28Cp	7Pi	29Ar	4Ge
21	12Ar	28Ta	6Ge	20Cn	22Le	7Li	12Sc	3Cp	27Aq	5Ar	25Ta	29Ge
23	8Ta	22Ge	0Cn	14Le	16Vi	3Sc	10Sg	3Aq	26Pi	3Ta	21Ge	24Cn
25	2Ge	16Cn	24Cn	8Vi	12Li	1Sg	9Cp	3Pi	25Ar	0Ge	16Cn	17Le
27	26Ge	10Le	18Le	4Li	9Sc	1Cp	10Aq	3Ar	22Ta	26Ge	9Le	11Vi
29	20Cn		13Vi	1Sc	8Sg	1Aq	10Pi	1Ta	18Ge	20Cn	3Vi	5Li
31	13Le		8Li		7Cp		8Ar	27Ta		13Le		0Sc

1935

	Jan	Feb	Mar	Apr	May	Jun	Jul	Aug	Sep	Oct	Nov	Dec
1	13Sc	3Cp	12Cp	5Pi	14Ar	5Ge	10Cn	25Le	9Li	13Sc	0Cp	7Aq
3	11Sg	3Aq	11Aq	5Ar	12Ta	1Cn	4Le	19Vi	3Sc	8Sg	27Cp	5Pi
5	10Cp	3Pi	11Pi	4Ta	10Ge	26Cn	28Le	12Li	28Sc	3Cp	25Aq	4Ar
7	10Aq	3Ar	12Ar	2Ge	6Cn	20Le	22Vi	7Sc	24Sg	0Aq	23Pi	2Ta
9	10Pi	2Ta	10Ta	28Ge	1Le	14Vi	16Li	2Sg	21Cp	29Aq	23Ar	1Ge
11	8Ar	28Ta	7Ge	23Cn	24Le	8Li	11Sc	29Sg	21Aq	20Pi	22Ta	28Ge
13	5Ta	23Ge	2Cn	16Le	18Vi	3Sc	7Sg	27Cp	21Pi	0Ta	21Ge	25Cn
15	1Ge	17Cn	26Cn	10Vi	12Li	29Sc	5Cp	27Aq	21Ar	29Ta	17Cn	20Le
17	26Ge	11Le	20Le	4Li	8Sc	26Sg	4Aq	28Pi	20Ta	26Ge	12Le	14Vi
19	20Cn	5Vi	13Vi	29Li	4Sg	25Cp	4Pi	27Ar	17Ge	22Cn	6Vi	7Li
21	14Le	28Vi	8Li	25Sc	1Cp	24Aq	3Ar	25Ta	13Cn	16Le	0Li	2Sc
23	8Vi	23Li	2Sc	21Sg	29Cp	22Pi	1Ta	21Ge	7Le	9Vi	24Li	26Sc
25	2Li	18Sc	28Sc	18Cp	27Aq	20Ar	28Ta	16Cn	1Vi	3Li	18Sc	23Sg
27	26Li	14Sg	24Sg	16Aq	25Pi	18Ta	24Ge	10Le	25Vi	27Li	14Sg	20Cp
29	22Sc		21Cp	15Pi	24Ar	14Ge	19Cn	4Vi	18Li	22Sc	10Cp	18Aq
31	19Sg		20Aq		21Ta		13Le	27Vi		17Sg		16Pi

1936

	Jan	Feb	Mar	Apr	May	Jun	Jul	Aug	Sep	Oct	Nov	Dec
1	1Ar	23Ta	17Ge	5Le	8Vi	22Li	25Sc	11Cp	1Pi	9Ar	3Ge	10Cn
3	29Ar	20Ge	13Cn	29Le	2Li	16Sc	20Sg	8Aq	0Ar	9Ta	2Cn	8Le
5	27Ta	16Cn	8Le	23Vi	26Li	11Sg	16Cp	6Pi	0Ta	9Ge	29Cn	3Vi
7	24Ge	11Le	2Vi	17Li	20Sc	6Cp	13Aq	5Ar	29Ta	7Cn	25Le	28Vi
9	20Cn	6Vi	26Vi	11Sc	14Sg	3Aq	11Pi	4Ta	27Ge	3Le	19Vi	22Li
11	15Le	0Li	20Li	5Sg	10Cp	0Pi	9Ar	2Ge	23Cn	28Le	13Li	16Sc
13	10Vi	23Li	14Sc	0Cp	6Aq	28Pi	7Ta	0Cn	18Le	22Vi	7Sc	9Sg
15	3Li	17Sc	8Sg	26Cp	3Pi	27Ar	6Ge	26Cn	13Vi	16Li	1Sg	4Cp
17	27Li	12Sg	3Cp	23Aq	2Ar	26Ta	3Cn	22Le	7Li	10Sc	25Sg	29Cp
19	22Sc	8Cp	0Aq	22Pi	2Ta	24Ge	0Le	17Vi	1Sc	4Sg	19Cp	25Aq
21	17Sg	6Aq	29Aq	23Ar	1Ge	22Cn	26Le	11Li	25Sc	28Sg	15Aq	22Pi
23	14Cp	6Pi	29Pi	23Ta	0Cn	18Le	21Vi	5Sc	19Sg	23Cp	12Pi	20Ar
25	13Aq	6Ar	0Ta	22Ge	27Cn	13Vi	15Li	28Sc	14Cp	19Aq	11Ar	19Ta
27	12Pi	6Ta	29Ta	19Cn	22Le	7Li	8Sc	23Sg	10Aq	17Pi	10Ta	19Ge
29	11Ar	4Ge	27Ge	14Le	17Vi	1Sc	3Sg	19Cp	9Pi	17Ar	11Ge	18Cn
31	10Ta		23Cn		11Li		28Sg	16Aq		18Ta		15Le

1937

	Jan	Feb	Mar	Apr	May	Jun	Jul	Aug	Sep	Oct	Nov	Dec
1	29Le	14Li	22Li	6Sg	8Cp	25Aq	1Ar	24Ta	17Cn	25Le	13Li	17Sc
3	24Vi	8Sc	16Sc	29Sg	3Aq	21Pi	29Ar	23Ge	15Le	21Vi	8Sc	10Sg
5	18Li	1Sg	9Sg	24Cp	28Aq	19Ar	28Ta	21Cn	12Vi	17Li	2Sg	4Cp
7	12Sc	26Sg	3Cp	20Aq	26Pi	19Ta	28Ge	20Le	8Li	11Sc	25Sg	28Cp
9	6Sg	21Cp	29Cp	18Pi	25Ar	19Ge	27Cn	17Vi	3Sc	5Sg	19Cp	22Aq
11	0Cp	17Aq	26Aq	17Ar	26Ta	19Cn	25Le	13Li	27Sc	29Sg	13Aq	17Pi
13	25Cp	15Pi	24Pi	17Ta	26Ge	17Le	22Vi	7Sc	21Sg	23Cp	9Pi	14Ar
15	22Aq	14Ar	23Ar	17Ge	25Cn	14Vi	17Li	1Sg	15Cp	18Aq	6Ar	13Ta
17	19Pi	12Ta	23Ta	15Cn	22Le	9Li	11Sc	25Sg	10Aq	14Pi	5Ta	13Ge
19	17Ar	10Ge	21Ge	12Le	17Vi	3Sc	5Sg	19Cp	6Pi	12Ar	5Ge	13Cn
21	15Ta	8Cn	19Cn	8Vi	12Li	26Sc	29Sg	14Ar	4Ar	12Ta	5Cn	13Le
23	14Ge	5Le	15Le	3Li	6Sc	20Sg	23Cp	11Pi	3Ta	11Ge	4Le	11Vi
25	12Cn	2Vi	11Vi	29Sc	29Sc	14Cp	18Aq	9Ar	1Ge	10Cn	2Vi	7Li
27	10Le	27Vi	6Li	23Sg	23Sg	9Aq	15Pi	7Ta	0Cn	8Le	28Vi	2Sc
29	6Vi		0Sc	17Cp	17Cp	5Pi	12Ar	5Ge	28Cn	5Vi	23Li	25Sc
31	2Li		24Sc	12Aq	12Aq		10Ta	3Cn		1Li		19Sg

1938

	Jan	Feb	Mar	Apr	May	Jun	Jul	Aug	Sep	Oct	Nov	Dec
1	1Cp	16Aq	25Aq	13Ar	20Ta	13Cn	22Le	13Li	29Sc	1Cp	15Aq	17Pi
3	25Cp	11Pi	21Pi	11Ta	19Ge	13Le	20Vi	9Sc	23Sg	25Cp	9Pi	12Ar
5	19Aq	7Ar	17Ar	9Ge	18Cn	11Vi	17Li	3Sg	17Cp	19Aq	5Ar	9Ta
7	14Pi	4Ta	15Ta	8Cn	17Le	7Li	12Sc	27Sg	11Aq	14Pi	1Ta	8Ge
9	10Ar	2Ge	13Ge	6Le	14Vi	3Sc	6Sg	20Cp	5Pi	10Ar	29Ta	8Cn
11	8Ta	0Cn	11Cn	4Vi	10Li	27Sc	0Cp	14Aq	1Ar	6Ta	28Ge	7Le
13	6Ge	0Le	9Le	1Li	6Sc	21Sg	24Cp	9Pi	27Ar	4Ge	27Cn	6Vi
15	6Cn	29Le	8Vi	27Li	0Sg	15Cp	17Aq	4Ar	24Ta	2Cn	26Le	4Li
17	6Le	27Vi	5Li	22Sc	24Sg	8Aq	12Pi	0Ta	21Ge	0Le	23Vi	0Sc
19	5Vi	23Li	1Sc	16Sg	18Cp	3Pi	7Ar	27Ta	20Cn	29Le	20Li	25Sc
21	3Li	18Sc	26Sc	10Cp	12Aq	28Pi	3Ta	25Ge	19Le	27Vi	16Sc	20Sg
23	28Li	12Sg	20Sg	3Aq	6Pi	24Ar	1Ge	24Cn	18Vi	24Li	11Sg	14Cp
25	22Sc	6Cp	14Cp	28Aq	2Ar	22Ta	0Cn	24Le	16Li	20Sc	5Cp	7Aq
27	16Sg	0Aq	8Aq	24Pi	29Ar	22Ge	1Le	23Vi	12Sc	15Sg	29Cp	1Pi
29	9Cp		3Pi	21Ar	28Ta	22Cn	1Vi	21Li	7Sg	9Cp	23Aq	25Pi
31	4Aq		29Pi		28Ge		29Vi	17Sc				20Ar

	Jan	Feb	Mar	Apr	May	Jun	Jul	Aug	Sep	Oct	Nov	Dec
1	3Ta	24Ge	3Cn	27Le	5Li	26Sc	0Cp	15Aq	0Ar	3Ta	22Ge	0Le
3	1Ge	24Cn	2Le	26Vi	3Sc	21Sg	25Cp	9Pi	24Ar	29Ta	19Cn	28Le
5	1Cn	24Le	2Vi	25Li	0Sg	16Cp	18Aq	3Ar	19Ta	25Ge	17Le	26Vi
7	1Le	24Vi	2Li	22Sc	26Sg	10Aq	12Pi	27Ar	15Ge	22Cn	16Vi	24Li
9	1Vi	23Li	1Sc	18Sg	20Cp	4Pi	6Ar	22Ta	12Cn	21Le	14Li	22Sc
11	0Li	19Sc	27Sc	12Cp	14Aq	28Pi	1Ta	19Ge	12Le	21Vi	13Sc	19Sg
13	27Li	14Sg	22Sg	6Aq	8Pi	23Ar	27Ta	18Cn	12Vi	20Li	10Sg	15Cp
15	22Sc	8Cp	16Cp	0Pi	2Ar	19Ta	25Ge	18Le	12Li	19Sc	7Cp	9Aq
17	17Sg	1Aq	10Aq	24Pi	28Ar	17Ge	25Cn	19Vi	11Sc	16Sg	2Aq	3Pi
19	11Cp	25Aq	4Pi	19Ar	24Ta	16Cn	25Le	18Li	8Sg	11Cp	26Aq	27Pi
21	4Aq	19Pi	28Pi	15Ta	22Ge	16Le	25Vi	16Sc	3Cp	6Aq	19Pi	21Ar
23	28Aq	14Ar	23Ar	12Ge	21Cn	15Vi	23Li	12Sg	27Cp	29Sq	13Ar	16Ta
25	22Pi	9Ta	19Ta	10Cn	20Le	12Li	19Sc	6Cp	21Aq	23Pi	8Ta	13Ge
27	17Ar	5Ge	16Ge	8Le	18Vi	9Sc	15Sg	0Aq	15Pi	18Ar	4Ge	11Cn
29	12Ta		13Cn	7Vi	16Li	5Sg	9Cp	24Aq	9Ar	13Ta	2Cn	10Le
31	9Ge		12Le		12Sc		3Aq	18Pi		9Ge		9Vi

1940

	Jan	Feb	Mar	Apr	May	Jun	Jul	Aug	Sep	Oct	Nov	Dec
1	23Vi	15Sc	8Sg	26Cp	29Aq	12Ar	14Ta	1Cn	22Le	0Li	23Sc	0Cp
3	21Li	12Sg	4Cp	20Aq	22Pi	6Ta	10Ge	29Cn	21Vi	0Sc	22Sg	28Cp
5	18Sc	7Cp	29Cp	14Pi	16Ar	1Ge	6Cn	28Le	21Li	0Sg	20Cp	24Aq
7	15Sg	2Aq	23Aq	7Ar	10Ta	27Ge	4Le	27Vi	20Sc	28Sg	15Aq	18Pi
9	10Cp	26Aq	17Pi	1Ta	5Ge	24Cn	3Vi	26Li	18Sg	24Cp	10Pi	12Ar
11	5Aq	20Pi	10Ar	26Ta	1Cn	22Le	1Li	24Sc	14Cp	19Aq	3Ar	5Ta
13	29Aq	13Ar	4Ta	21Ge	28Cn	20Vi	29Li	21Sg	9Aq	13Pi	27Ar	29Ta
15	23Pi	7Ta	29Ta	17Cn	25Le	19Li	27Sc	17Cp	4Pi	6Ar	21Ta	25Ge
17	17Ar	2Ge	24Ge	15Le	24Vi	17Sc	24Sg	13Aq	28Pi	0Ta	15Ge	21Cn
19	11Ta	28Ge	21Cn	14Vi	23Li*	15Sg	21Cp	7Pi	21Ar	24Ta	11Cn	17Le
21	7Ge	27Cn	20Le	14Li	22Sc	12Cp	16Aq	1Ar	15Ta	18Ge	7Le	15Vi
23	4Cn	27Le	20Vi	13Sc	20Sg	8Aq	11Pi	24Ar	9Ge	14Cn	4Vi	13Li
25	4Le	27Vi	20Li	12Sg	17Cp	3Pi	4Ar	18Ta	4Cn	10Le	2Li	11Sc
27	4Vi	27Li	20Sc	9Cp	12Aq	26Pi	28Ar	13Ge	1Le	8Vi	2Sc	10Sg
29	3Li	25Sc	17Sg	4Aq	7Pi	20Ar	22Ta	9Cn	0Vi	8Li	1Sg	8Cp
31	2Sc		13Cp		0Ar		18Ge	7Le		8Sc		6Aq

1941

	Jan	Feb	Mar	Apr	May	Jun	Jul	Aug	Sep	Oct	Nov	Dec
1	19Aq	3Ar	12Ar	25Ta	29Ge	16Le	23Vi	16Sc	9Cp	16Aq	4Ar	7Ta
3	14Pi	27Ar	5Ta	19Ge	23Cn	13Vi	21Li	14Sg	6Aq	12Pi	28Ar	0Ge
5	8Ar	21Ta	29Ta	14Cn	19Le	11Li	20Sc	13Cp	3Pi	7Ar	22Ta	24Ge
7	1Ta	15Ge	23Ge	10Le	17Vi	10Sc	19Sg	11Aq	28Pi	1Ta	15Ge	18Cn
9	25Ta	11Cn	19Cn	8Vi	16Li	10Sg	18Cp	7Pi	23Ar	25Ta	9Cn	13Le
11	20Ge	8Le	16Le	8Li	16Sc	10Cp	16Aq	2Ar	17Ta	19Ge	4Le	9Vi
13	16Cn	6Vi	15Vi	8Sc	17Sg	8Aq	12Pi	27Ar	10Ge	13Cn	29Le	5Li
15	13Le	5Li	15Li	8Sg	16Cp	4Pi	7Ar	21Ta	5Cn	8Le	26Vi	4Sc
17	11Vi	4Sc	14Sc	7Cp	13Aq	29Pi	1Ta	14Ge	0Le	4Vi	25Li	4Sg
19	9Li	3Sg	13Sg	4Aq	8Pi	23Ar	24Ta	9Cn	26Le	3Li	26Sc	4Cp
21	8Sc	0Cp	11Cp	29Aq	2Ar	16Ta	19Ge	5Le	25Vi	2Sc	26Sg	4Aq
23	6Sg	27Cp	7Aq	23Pi	26Ar	10Ge	14Cn	2Vi	24Li	3Sg	26Cp	1Pi
25	4Cp	23Aq	2Pi	17Ar	19Ta	5Cn	9Le	0Li	23Sc	2Cp	23Aq	27Pi
27	1Aq	17Pi	26Pi	11Ta	13Ge	0Le	6Vi	28Li	22Sg	0Aq	18Pi	22Ar
29	27Aq		20Ar	4Ge	8Cn	26Le	4Li	27Sc	20Cp	26Aq	13Ar	15Ta
31	21Pi		14Ta		3Le		2Sc	25Sg		22Pi		9Ge

1942

	Jan	Feb	Mar	Apr	May	Jun	Jul	Aug	Sep	Oct	Nov	Dec
1	21Ge	7Le	15Le	3Li	11Sc	5Cp	13Aq	3Ar	19Ta	21Ge	5Le	7Vi
3	15Cn	2Vi	11Vi	2Sc	11Sg	4Aq	11Pi	29Ar	13Ge	15Cn	29Le	2Li
5	10Le	29Vi	9Li	1Sg	10Cp	2Pi	7Ar	23Ta	7Cn	9Le	24Vi	29Li
7	6Vi	26Li	7Sc	0Cp	9Aq	28Pi	2Ta	17Ge	1Le	4Vi	22Li	29Sc
9	2Li	24Sc	5Sg	28Cp	6Pi	23Ar	26Ta	11Cn	26Le	0Li	20Sc	29Sg
11	29Li	23Sg	4Cp	25Aq	1Ar	17Ta	20Ge	5Le	21Vi	27Li	20Sg	29Cp
13	28Sc	21Cp	2Aq	22Pi	26Ar	11Ge	14Cn	29Le	18Li	26Sc	19Cp	28Aq
15	28Sg	20Aq	29Aq	17Ar	20Ta	5Cn	8Le	25Vi	16Sc	25Sg	18Aq	25Pi
17	27Cp	17Pi	25Pi	12Ta	14Ge	29Cn	3Vi	21Li	14Sg	23Cp	15Pi	21Ar
19	26Aq	13Ar	21Ar	6Ge	8Cn	23Le	28Vi	19Sc	12Cp	21Aq	11Ar	16Ta
21	22Pi	8Ta	15Ta	29Ge	2Le	18Vi	24Li	17Sg	10Aq	18Pi	7Ta	10Ge
23	18Ar	2Ge	9Ge	23Cn	26Le	15Li	22Sc	16Cp	8Pi	15Ar	1Ge	4Cn
25	12Ta	25Ge	3Cn	18Le	22Vi	13Sc	22Sg	15Aq	6Ar	10Ta	25Ge	28Cn
27	6Ge	20Cn	27Cn	14Vi	20Li	13Sg	22Cp	14Pi	2Ta	5Ge	19Cn	21Le
29	29Ge		23Le	11Li	19Sc	13Cp	21Aq	11Ar	27Ta	29Ge	13Le	16Vi
31	24Cn		19Vi		20Sg		19Pi	7Ta		23Cn		11Li

1943

	Jan	Feb	Mar	Apr	May	Jun	Jul	Aug	Sep	Oct	Nov	Dec
1	24Li	15Sg	25Sg	19Aq	27Pi	17Ta	21Ge	6Le	20Vi	24Li	14Sg	22Cp
3	22Sc	15Cp	24Cp	17Pi	24Ar	12Ge	15Cn	29Le	15Li	20Sc	11Cp	20Aq
5	22Sg	15Aq	23Aq	15Ar	20Ta	6Cn	9Le	23Vi	10Sc	17Sg	9Aq	18Pi
7	22Cp	15Pi	23Pi	12Ta	16Ge	0Le	2Vi	18Li	6Sg	14Cp	8Pi	16Ar
9	22Aq	13Ar	21Ar	8Ge	10Cn	24Le	26Vi	13Sc	4Cp	13Aq	6Ar	13Ta
11	21Pi	9Ta	17Ta	2Cn	4Le	18Vi	21Li	10Sg	3Aq	12Pi	4Ta	10Ge
13	18Ar	4Ge	12Ge	26Cn	27Le	13Li	18Sc	9Cp	3Pi	11Ar	1Ge	5Cn
15	13Ta	28Ge	6Cn	19Le	22Vi	9Sc	16Sg	9Aq	2Ar	9Ta	27Ge	29Cn
17	7Ge	21Cn	0Le	144Vi	18Li	8Sg	16Cp	9Pi	1Ta	6Ge	21Cn	23Le
19	1Cn	15Le	24Le	9Li	15Sc	7Cp	16Aq	9Ar	28Ta	1Cn	15Le	17Vi
21	25Cn	10Vi	18Vi	6Sc	14Sg	7Aq	16Pi	6Ta	23Ge	25Cn	9Vi	11Li
23	18Le	5Li	14Li	4Sg	13Cp	6Pi	14Ar	2Ge	17Cn	19Le	3Li	6Sc
25	13Vi	0Sc	11Sc	3Cp	12Aq	4Ar	10Ta	27Ge	11Le	13Vi	28Li	3Sg
27	7Li	27Sc	8Sg	1Aq	10Pi	1Ta	6Ge	21Cn	5Vi	8Li	25Sc	2Cp
29	3Sc		6Cp	29Aq	7Ar	26Ta	0Cn	14Le	29Vi	3Sc	23Sg	1Aq
31	1Sg		4Aq		4Ta		24Cn	8Vi		0Sg		1Pi

1944

	Jan	Feb	Mar	Apr	May	Jun	Jul	Aug	Sep	Oct	Nov	Dec
1	15Pi	7Ta	29Ta	16Cn	18Le	2Li	4Sc	21Sg	12Aq	20Pi	14Ta	21Ge
3	13Ar	3Ge	25Ge	10Le	12Vi	26Li	0Sg	19Cp	12Pi	21Ar	13Ge	18Cn
5	10Ta	28Ge	19Cn	4Vi	6Li	22Sc	27Sg	19Aq	12Ar	21Ta	10Cn	13Le
7	6Ge	22Cn	13Le	27Vi	0Sc	18Sg	25Cp	19Pi	12Ta	18Ge	5Le	7Vi
9	1Cn	16Le	7Vi	22Li	26Sc	16Cp	24Aq	18Ar	10Ge	15Cn	0Vi	1Li
11	26Cn	10Vi	1Li	17Sc	22Sg	14Aq	23Pi	16Ta	5Cn	9Le	23Vi	25Li
13	19Le	4Li	25Li	12Sg	20Cp	13Pi	22Ar	13Ge	0Le	3Vi	17Li	20Sc
15	13Vi	28Li	20Sc	9Cp	17Aq	11Ar	19Ta	8Cn	24Le	27Vi	11Sc	15Sg
17	7Li	23Sc	15Sg	7Aq	16Pi	9Ta	16Ge	3Le	18Vi	20Li	6Sg	12Cp
19	1Sc	19Sg	13Cp	5Pi	14Ar	6Ge	11Cn	27Le	11Li	15Sc	2Cp	9Aq
21	27Sc	18Cp	11Aq	5Ar	13Ta	2Cn	6Le	21Vi	5Sc	9Sg	29Cp	7Pi
23	25Sg	17Aq	11Pi	4Ta	11Ge	28Cn	0Vi	14Li	0Sg	5Cp	26Aq	5Ar
25	24Cp	18Pi	11Ar	2Ge	7Cn	22Le	24Vi	8Sc	25Sg	2Aq	24Pi	3Ta
27	25Aq	18Ar	10Ta	29Ge	2Le	16Vi	18Li	3Sg	22Cp	0Pi	23Ar	2Ge
29	24Pi	16Ta	8Ge	24Cn	26Le	10Li	12Sc	29Sg	20Aq	29Pi	22Ta	29Ge
31	23Ar		4Cn		20Vi		8Sg	27Cp		29Ar		26Cn

1945

	Jan	Feb	Mar	Apr	May	Jun	Jul	Aug	Sep	Oct	Nov	Dec
1	8Le	23Vi	2Li	16Sc	19Sg	7Aq	15Pi	9Ta	1Cn	8Le	24Vi	27Li
3	3Vi	17Li	25Li	10Sg	14Cp	4Pi	13Ar	7Ge	28Cn	3Vi	18Li	21Sc
5	27Vi	11Sc	19Sc	5Cp	10Aq	3Ar	12Ta	4Cn	23Le	27Vi	12Sc	15Sg
7	21Li	5Sg	13Sg	1Aq	8Pi	2Ta	11Ge	1Le	18Vi	21Li	6Sg	9Cp
9	15Sc	1Cp	9Cp	29Aq	7Ar	1Ge	9Cn	27Le	13Li	15Sc	0Cp	4Aq
11	10Sg	28Cp	6Aq	28Pi	7Ta	0Cn	6Le	22Vi	7Sc	9Sg	24Cp	0Pi
13	7Cp	27Aq	5Pi	29Ar	7Ge	28Cn	2Vi	16Li	0Sg	3Cp	20Aq	27Pi
15	4Aq	27Pi	6Ar	29Ta	6Cn	24Le	26Vi	10Sc	24Sg	28Cp	17Pi	26Ar
17	3Pi	26Ar	6Ta	28Ge	3Le	18Vi	20Li	4Sg	19Cp	25Aq	16Ar	25Ta
19	2Ar	25Ta	5Ge	24Cn	28Le	12Li	14Sc	29Sg	16Aq	23Pi	17Ta	25Ge
21	0Ta	22Ge	2Cn	19Le	22Vi	6Sc	8Sg	25Cp	15Pi	23Ar	17Ge	24Cn
23	28Ta	18Cn	28Cn	14Vi	16Li	0Sg	4Cp	22Aq	15Ar	24Ta	16Cn	21Le
25	25Ge	13Le	22Le	7Li	10Sc	25Sg	0Aq	21Pi	15Ta	23Ge	13Le	17Vi
27	21Cn	7Vi	16Vi	1Sc	4Sg	21Cp	27Aq	21Ar	14Ge	21Cn	9Vi	12Li
29	17Le		10Li	25Sc	29Sg	18Aq	26Pi	20Ta	12Cn	17Le	3Li	6Sc
31	11Vi		4Sc		24Cp		24Ar	18Ge		12Vi		29Sc

1946

	Jan	Feb	Mar	Apr	May	Jun	Jul	Aug	Sep	Oct	Nov	Dec
1	11Sg	27Cp	5Aq	24Pi	2Ta	25Ge	3Le	23Vi	9Sc	11Sg	24Cp	27Aq
3	6Cp	23Aq	2Pi	23Ar	2Ge	25Cn	1Vi	19Li	3Sg	4Cp	19Aq	23Pi
5	1Aq	20Pi	0Ar	23Ta	2Cn	23Le	28Vi	13Sc	26Sg	28Cp	15Pi	20Ar
7	27Aq	18Ar	29Ar	22Ge	0Le	19Vi	23Li	7Sg	20Cp	23Aq	12Ar	19Ta
9	24Pi	17Ta	28Ta	20Cn	27Le	14Li	17Sc	0Cp	15Aq	20Pi	11Ta	19Ge
11	22Ar	15Ge	26Ge	17Le	22Vi	8Sc	10Sg	25Cp	12Pi	18Ar	11Ge	20Cn
13	20Ta	13Cn	23Cn	13Vi	17Li	2Sg	4Cp	20Aq	9Ar	18Ta	11Cn	19Le
15	19Ge	10Le	20Le	8Li	11Sc	25Sg	28Cp	16Pi	8Ta	17Ge	10Le	16Vi
17	18Cn	7Vi	16Vi	2Sc	5Sc	19Cp	23Aq	13Ar	6Ge	15Cn	7Vi	12Li
19	16Le	3Li	11Li	26Sc	28Sg	14Aq	20Pi	11Ta	4Cn	13Le	3Li	7Sc
21	12Vi	27Li	5Sc	19Sg	22Cp	9Pi	16Ar	9Ge	2Le	10Vi	27Li	1Sg
23	8Li	21Sc	29Sc	13Cp	17Aq	6Ar	14Ta	8Cn	0Vi	6Li	22Sc	24Sg
25	2Sc	15Sg	23Sg	8Aq	13Pi	4Ta	13Ge	6Le	26Vi	1Sc	15Sg	18Cp
27	25Sc	9Cp	17Cp	4Pi	11Ar	4Ge	13Cn	4Vi	22Li	25Sc	9Cp	12Aq
29	19Sg		12Aq	2Ar	10Ta	4Cn	12Le	1Li	17Sc	19Sg	3Aq	6Pi
31	14Cp		10Pi		10Ge		10Vi	27Li		12Cp		2Ar

	Jan	Feb	Mar	Apr	May	Jun	Jul	Aug	Sep	Oct	Nov	Dec
1	15Ar	7Ge	17Ge	10Le	19Vi	8Sc	11Sg	26Cp	11Pi	15Ar	5Ge	13Cn
3	13Ta	6Cn	16Cn	9Vi	15Li	2Sg	5Cp	20Aq	6Ar	12Ta	3Cn	13Le
5	12Ge	6Le	15Le	6Li	11Sc	26Sg	29Cp	14Pi	2Ta	9Ge	2Le	11Vi
7	13Cn	5Vi	13Vi	2Sc	6Sg	20Cp	22Aq	9Ar	28Ta	7Cn	0Vi	8Li
9	13Le	3Li	11Li	27Sc	0Cp	14Aq	17Pi	5Ta	26Ge	5Le	28Vi	5Sc
11	11Vi	29Li	7Sc	22Sg	23Cp	8Pi	12Ar	2Ge	25Cn	4Vi	25Li	0Sg
13	8Li	24Sc	2Sg	15Cp	17Aq	3Ar	8Ta	0Cn	24Le	2Li	21Sc	25Sg
15	3Sc	18Sg	26Sg	9Aq	12Pi	0Ta	7Ge	0Le	23Vi	0Sc	16Sg	19Cp
17	28Sc	11Cp	19Cp	4Pi	8Ar	28Ta	6Cn	0Vi	22Li	26Sc	11Cp	13Aq
19	21Sg	5Aq	13Aq	0Ar	5Ta	28Ge	7Le	29Vi	18Sc	21Sg	5Aq	6Pi
21	15Cp	0Pi	9Pi	27Ar	5Ge	28Cn	7Vi	27Li	13Sg	15Cp	28Aq	1Ar
23	9Aq	26Pi	5Ar	26Ta	4Cn	28Le	5Li	23Sc	7Cp	9Aq	23Pi	26Ar
25	3Pi	22Ar	2Ta	24Ge	4Le	26Vi	1Sc	17Sg	1Aq	3Pi	18Ar	23Ta
27	29Pi	19Ar	0Ge	23Cn	2Vi	22Li	26Sc	11Cp	25Aq	28Pi	15Ta	22Ge
29	25Ar		28Ge	21Le	29Vi	17Sc	20Sg	4Aq	19Pi	24Ar	14Ge	22Cn
31	23Ta		26Cn		25Li		14Cp	28Aq		21Ta		22Le

1948

	Jan	Feb	Mar	Apr	May	Jun	Jul	Aug	Sep	Oct	Nov	Dec
1	7Vi	28Li	20Sc	6Cp	8Aq	21Pi	24Ar	11Ge	3Le	12Vi	5Sc	11Sg
3	5Li	24Sc	15Sg	0Aq	2Pi	16Ar	20Ta	10Cn	3Vi	12Li	3Sg	8Cp
5	2Sc	19Sg	10Cp	24Aq	26Pi	12Ta	17Ge	9Le	4Li	11Sc	0Cp	3Aq
7	27Sc	13Cp	3Aq	18Pi	21Ar	9Ge	16Cn	10Vi	3Sc	9Sg	25Cp	27Aq
9	22Sg	6Aq	27Aq	12Ar	16Ta	7Cn	16Le	10Li	0Sg	5Cp	19Aq	21Pi
11	16Cp	0Pi	21Pi	8Ta	14Ge	6Le	15Vi	8Sc	26Sg	29Cp	13Pi	15Ar
13	9Aq	24Pi	16Ar	4Ge	11Cn	5Vi	14Li	4Sg	20Cp	23Aq	7Ar	9Ta
15	3Pi	19Ar	11Ta	1Cn	10Le	3Li	11Sc	29Sg	14Aq	17Pi	1Ta	5Ge
17	27Pi	14Ta	7Ge	29Cn	8Vi	1Sc	7Sg	23Cp	8Pi	11Ar	27Ta	2Cn
19	22Ar	10Ge	4Cn	27Le	6Li	27Sc	2Cp	17Aq	2Ar	5Ta	23Ge	1Le
21	18Ta	8Cn	3Le	26Vi	4Sc	23Sg	26Cp	11Pi	26Ar	0Ge	21Cn	29Le
23	15Ge	8Le	2Vi	25Li	1Sg	18Cp	20Aq	5Ar	21Ta	27Ge	18Le	28Vi
25	15Cn	9Vi	2Li	23Sc	27Sg	12Aq	14Pi	29Ar	16Ge	24Cn	17Vi	26Li
27	16Le	9Li	1Sc	19Sg	22Cp	6Pi	8Ar	24Ta	13Cn	22Le	15Li	23Sc
29	16Vi	7Sc	28Sc	14Cp	16Aq	0Ar	2Ta	20Ge	12Le	21Vi	13Sc	20Sg
31	15Li		24Sg		10Pi		28Ta	18Cn		20Li		16Cp

1949

	Jan	Feb	Mar	Apr	May	Jun	Jul	Aug	Sep	Oct	Nov	Dec
1	28Cp	13Pi	22Pi	6Ta	10Ge	29Cn	7Vi	1Sc	23Sg	29Cp	15Pi	17Ar
3	23Aq	7Ar	15Ar	1Ge	6Cn	27Le	6Li	29Sc	19Cp	24Aq	9Ar	11Ta
5	17Pi	1Ta	9Ta	26Ge	2Le	25Vi	4Sc	26Sg	14Aq	18Pi	2Ta	5Ge
7	11Ar	25Ta	4Ge	22Cn	0Vi	23Li	2Sg	22Cp	9Pi	12Ar	26Ta	0Cn
9	5Ta	21Ge	29Ge	20Le	29Vi	22Sc	29Sg	18Aq	3Ar	5Ta	20Ge	25Cn
11	0Ge	19Cn	27Cn	20Vi	28Li	20Sg	26Cp	12Pi	26Ar	29Ta	16Cn	22Le
13	27Ge	18Le	26Le	20Li	28Sc	18Cp	22Aq	6Ar	20Ta	23Ge	12Le	19Vi
15	25Cn	18Vi	27Vi	20Sc	26Sg	14Aq	16Pi	0Ta	14Ge	19Cn	9Vi	17Li
17	25Le	18li	27Li	18Sg	23Cp	8Pi	10Ar	24Ta	10Cn	16Le	8Li	16Sc
19	24Vi	17Sc	26Sc	15Cp	18Aq	2Ar	4Ta	19Ge	7Le	14Vi	7Sc	16Sg
21	23Li	13Sg	23Sg	10Aq	12Pi	26Ar	28Ta	15Cn	6Vi	14Li	7Sg	14Cp
23	20Sc	9Cp	19Cp	4Pi	6Ar	20Ta	24Ge	13Le	6Li	14Sc	6Cp	12Aq
25	16Sg	4Aq	13Aq	28Pi	0Ta	15Ge	21Cn	13Vi	6Sc	14Sg	4Aq	7Pi
27	12Cp	28Aq	7Pi	21Ar	24Ta	12Cn	19Le	12Li	5Sg	12Cp	29Aq	1Ar
29	7Aq		1Ar	15Ta	19Ge	9Le	18Vi	11Sc	3Cp	8Aq	23Pi	25Ar
31	1Pi		24Ar		16Cn		17Li	9Sg		3Pi		19Ta

382 How to Read Your Star Signs

1950

	Jan	Feb	Mar	Apr	May	Jun	Jul	Aug	Sep	Oct	Nov	Dec
1	1Ge	17Cn	25Cn	14Vi	22Li	16Sg	24Cp	13Pi	28Ar	0Ge	14Cn	18Le
3	26Ge	14Le	22Le	14Li	23Sc	16Cp	22Aq	8Ar	22Ta	24Ge	9Le	14Vi
5	22Cn	12Vi	21Vi	14Sc	23Sg	14Aq	18Pi	2Ta	16Ge	18Cn	5Vi	11Li
7	19Le	11Li	20Li	14Sg	21Cp	10Pi	12Ar	26Ta	10Cn	14Le	2Li	10Sc
9	16Vi	9Sc	20Sc	12Cp	18Aq	4Ar	6Ar	20Ge	6Le	10Vi	2Sc	10Sg
11	14Li	7Sg	18Sg	9Aq	13Pi	28Ar	0Ge	15Cn	2Vi	9Li	2Sg	11Cp
13	12Sc	5Cp	15Cp	4Pi	7Ar	22Ta	24Ge	11Le	0Li	9Sc	2Cp	10Aq
15	11Sg	2Aq	11Aq	28Pi	1Ta	15Ge	19Cn	7Vi	29Li	8Sg	1Aq	7Pi
17	9Cp	28Aq	7Pi	22Ar	25Ta	10Cn	15Le	5Li	28Sc	7Cp	28Aq	3Ar
19	6Aq	23Pi	1Ar	16Ta	19Ge	5Le	11Vi	3Sc	27Sg	5Aq	24Pi	27Ar
21	2Pi	17Ar	25Ar	9Ge	13Cn	1Vi	8Li	2Sg	24Cp	1Pi	18Ar	21Ta
23	27Pi	11Ta	19Ta	4Cn	8Le	28Vi	6Sc	0Cp	21Aq	26Pi	12Ta	14Ge
25	21Ar	4Ge	13Ge	28Cn	4Vi	26Li	5Sg	28Cp	17Pi	21Ar	6Ge	8Cn
27	15Ta	29Ge	7Cn	25Le	2Li	25Sc	4Cp	25Aq	12Ar	15Ta	29Ge	3Le
29	9Ge		3Le	23Vi	1Sc	25Sg	2Aq	21Pi	6Ta	9Ge	23Cn	28Le
31	4Cn		0Vi		1Sg		0Pi	16Ar		2Cn		23Vi

1951

	Jan	Feb	Mar	Apr	May	Jun	Jul	Aug	Sep	Oct	Nov	Dec
1	7Li	29Sc	10Sg	3Aq	10Pi	28Ar	2Ge	16Cb	1Vi	6Li	26Sc	5Cp
3	4Sc	28Sg	8Cp	0Pi	6Ar	22Ta	25Ge	10Le	27Vi	3Sc	25Sg	5Aq
5	3Sg	27Cp	6Aq	27Pi	1Ta	16Ge	19Cn	5Vi	23Li	1Sg	24Cp	3Pi
7	4Cp	26Aq	4Pi	22Ar	26Ta	10Cn	13Le	0Li	20Sc	29Sg	22Aq	0Ar
9	3Aq	23Pi	1Ar	17Ta	20Ge	4Le	7Vi	26Li	18Sg	28Cp	20Pi	26Ar
11	2Pi	19Ar	27Ar	11Ge	13Cn	28Le	3Li	23Sc	17Cp	26Aq	16Ar	21Ta
13	28Pi	13Ta	21Ta	5Cn	7Le	23Vi	29Li	22Sg	16Aq	23Pi	12Ta	15Ge
15	23Ar	7Ge	15Ge	29Cn	2Vi	20Li	28Sc	22Cp	14Pi	20Ar	7Ge	9Cn
17	17Ta	1Cn	9Cn	24Le	28Vi	19Sc	27Sg	21Aq	12Ar	16Ta	1Cn	3Le
19	11Ge	25Cn	3Le	20Vi	26Li	19Sg	28Cp	20Pi	8Ta	11Ge	24Cn	27Le
21	5Cn	21Le	29Le	18Li	25Sc	19Cp	27Aq	17Ar	3Ge	5Cn	18Le	21Vi
23	29Cn	17Vi	25Vi	17Sc	26Sg	19Aq	25Pi	12Ta	27Ge	28Cn	13Vi	16Li
25	24Le	14Li	23Li	16Sg	25Cp	17Pi	22Ar	7Ge	20Cn	22Le	8Li	14Sc
27	20Vi	11Sc	22Sc	16Cp	24Aq	13Ar	16Ta	1Cn	15Le	17Vi	6Sc	13Sg
29	17Li		21Sg	14Aq	20Pi	8Ta	10Ge	24Cn	9Vi	14Li	5Sg	13Cp
31	15Sc		19Cp		16Ar		4Cn	19Le		12Sc		14Aq

1952

	Jan	Feb	Mar	Apr	May	Jun	Jul	Aug	Sep	Oct	Nov	Dec
1	28Aq	19Ar	10Ta	26Ge	27Cn	11Vi	14Li	2Sg	24Cp	3Pi	25Ar	2Ge
3	26Pi	15Ta	5Ge	20Cn	21Le	6Li	10Sc	0Cp	24Aq	2Ar	23Ta	28Ge
5	23Ar	9Ge	0Cn	13Le	15Vi	2Sc	8Sg	0Aq	24Pi	1Ta	20Ge	23Cn
7	18Ta	3Cn	23Cn	7Vi	10Li	29Sc	7Cp	1Pi	23Ar	29Ta	15Cn	17Le
9	12Ge	27Cn	17Le	2Li	7Sc	28Sg	7Aq	0Ar	21Ta	25Ge	9Le	10Vi
11	6Cn	21Le	11Vi	28Li	5Sg	28Cp	7Pi	29Ar	16Ge	19Cn	3Vi	4Li
13	0Le	15Vi	6Li	25Sc	4Cp	27Aq	5Ar	25Ta	11Cn	13Le	26Vi	29Li
15	24Le	9Li	2Sc	23Sg	2Aq	25Pi	2Ta	20Ge	5Le	7Vi	21Li	26Sc
17	18Vi	5Sc	29Sc	21Cp	1Pi	22Ar	28Ta	14Cn	28Le	1Li	17Sc	23Sg
19	12Li	2Sg	26Sg	20Aq	28Pi	18Ta	23Ge	8Le	22Vi	26Li	15Sg	22Cp
21	9Sc	0Cp	25Cp	18Pi	25Ar	14Ge	17Cn	1Vi	17Li	22Sc	13Cp	21Aq
23	6Sg	0Aq	24Aq	16Ar	22Ta	8Cn	11Le	25Vi	12Sc	18Sg	11Aq	20Pi
25	6Cp	29Aq	23Pi	13Ta	17Ge	2Le	4Vi	20Li	8Sg	16Cp	9Pi	18Ar
27	6Aq	29Pi	21Ar	9Ge	12Cn	26Le	28Vi	15Sc	5Cp	14Aq	7Ar	15Ta
29	6Pi	27Ar	18Ta	4Cn	5Le	19Vi	23Li	11Sg	3Aq	12Pi	5Ta	11Ge
31	5Ar		13Ge		29Le		18Sc	9Cp		11Ar		6Cn

	Jan	Feb	Mar	Apr	May	Jun	Jul	Aug	Sep	Oct	Nov	Dec
1	19Cn	3Vi	12Vi	27Li	1Sg	21Cp	29Aq	23Ar	15Ge	20Cn	5Vi	7Li
3	13Le	27Vi	6Li	22Sc	27Sg	19Aq	28Pi	21Ta	10Cn	14Le	29Vi	1Sc
5	7Vi	21Li	0Sc	17Sg	24Cp	17Pi	26Ar	18Ge	5Le	8Vi	22Li	25Sc
7	0Li	15Sc	25Sc	14Cp	22Aq	15Ar	24Ta	13Cn	29Le	2Li	17Sc	21Sg
9	24Li	11Sg	20Sg	12Aq	21Pi	14Ta	21Ge	8Le	23Vi	26Li	11Sg	17Cp
11	20Sc	9Cp	18Cp	11Pi	20Ar	11Ge	17Cn	2Vi	17Li	20Sc	7Cp	14Aq
13	17Sg	9Aq	17Aq	11Ar	19Ta	8Cn	12Le	26Vi	10Sc	14Sg	3Aq	11Pi
15	16Cp	9Pi	17Pi	10Ta	17Ge	3Le	6Vi	20Li	5Sg	10Cp	1Pi	10Ar
17	16Aq	9Ar	17Ar	8Ge	13Cn	28Le	29Vi	14Sc	0Cp	7Aq	29Pi	8Ta
19	15Pi	8Ta	16Ta	5Cn	8Le	21Vi	23Li	9Sg	27Cp	5Pi	29Ar	7Ge
21	14Ar	5Ge	14Ge	0Le	2Vi	15Li	18Sc	5Cp	26Aq	5Ar	28Ta	5Cn
23	12Ta	0Cn	9Cn	24Le	25Vi	10Sc	14Sg	3Aq	27Pi	5Ta	27Ge	1Le
25	8Ge	24Cn	3Le	17Vi	19Li	6Sg	11Cp	3Pi	27Ar	5Ge	24Cn	27Le
27	3Cn	18Le	27Le	11Li	14Sc	3Cp	10Aq	3E	27Ta	3Cn	19Le	21Vi
29	27Cn		21Vi	6Sc	10Sg	1Aq	9Pi	3Ta	24Ge	29Cn	13Vi	15Li
31	21Le		15Li		7Cp		9Ar	1Ge		23Le		9Sc

1954

	Jan	Feb	Mar	Apr	May	Jun	Jul	Aug	Sep	Oct	Nov	Dec
1	21Sc	7Cp	15Cp	5Pi	13Ar	7Ge	14Cn	3Vi	18Li	20Sc	5Cp	9Aq
3	16Sg	4Aq	12Aq	5Ar	14Ta	6Cn	12Le	28Vi	12Sc	14Sg	29Cp	5Pi
5	12Cp	3Pi	12Pi	5Ta	14Ge	4Le	7Vi	22Li	6Sg	8Cp	25Aq	2Ar
7	10Aq	2Ar	12Ar	5Ge	12Cn	29Le	2Li	16Sc	0Cp	3Aq	23Pi	1Ta
9	8Pi	1Ta	11Ta	3Cn	8Le	24Vi	26Li	10Sg	25Cp	1Pi	23Ar	1Ge
11	6Ar	0Ge	10Ge	29Cn	3Vi	18Li	20Sc	5Cp	22Aq	0Ar	23Ta	1Cn
13	5Ta	27Ge	7Cn	24Le	27Vi	12Sc	14Sg	1Aq	21Pi	0Ta	23Ge	0Le
15	3Ge	23Cn	3Le	19Vi	21Li	6Sg	9Cp	28Aq	21Ar	0Ge	22Cn	27Le
17	0Cn	18Le	27Le	12Li	15Sc	1Cp	5Aq	27Pi	21Ta	29Ge	19Le	23Vi
19	27Cn	13Vi	22Vi	6Sc	9Sg	26Cp	3Pi	26Ar	19Ge	26Cn	14Vi	17Li
21	22Le	7Li	15Li	0Sg	4Cp	22Aq	1Ar	24Ta	16Cn	22Le	9Li	11Sc
23	17Vi	1Sc	9Sc	24Sg	29Cp	20Pi	29Ar	22Ge	12Le	17Vi	2Sc	5Sg
25	11Li	24Sc	3Sg	19Cp	25Aq	18Ar	27Ta	19Cn	8Vi	11Li	26Sc	29Sg
27	4Sc	19Sg	27Sg	16Aq	23Pi	17Ta	26Ge	16Le	2Li	5Sc	20Sg	23Cp
29	29Sc		23Cp	14Pi	22Ar	16Ge	23Cn	11Vi	27Li	29Sc	14Cp	19Aq
31	24Sg		20Aq		22Ta		20Le	6Li		23Sg		15Pi

1955

	Jan	Feb	Mar	Apr	May	Jun	Jul	Aug	Sep	Oct	Nov	Dec
1	28Pi	21Ta	2Ge	25Cn	2Vi	19Li	22Sc	6Cp	21Aq	26Pi	18Ta	26Ge
3	26Ar	20Ge	0Cn	22Le	27Vi	13Sc	15Sg	0Aq	17Pi	24Ar	17Ge	26Cn
5	25Ta	18Cn	28Cn	18Vi	22Li	7Sg	9Cp	25Aq	15Ar	23Ta	16Cn	24Le
7	25Ge	16Le	25Le	13Li	16Sc	0Cp	3Aq	21Pi	13Ta	22Ge	14Le	21Vi
9	24Cn	13Vi	21Vi	7Sc	10Sg	24Cp	28Aq	18Ar	11Ge	20Cn	11Vi	17Li
11	22Le	9Li	17Li	1Sg	3Cp	19Aq	24Pi	16Ta	9Cn	17Le	7Li	12Sc
13	18Vi	3Sc	11Sc	25Sg	27Cp	14Pi	21Ar	14Ge	7Le	15Vi	2Sc	6Sg
15	13Li	27Sc	5Sg	19Cp	22Aq	11Ar	19Ta	13Cn	5Vi	11Li	27Sc	29Sg
17	7Sc	21Sg	28Sg	13Aq	18Pi	10Ta	19Ge	12Le	2Li	6Sc	21Sg	23Cp
19	1Sg	15Cp	23Cp	10Pi	17Ar	10Ge	18Cn	10Vi	28Li	0Sg	14Cp	17Aq
21	25Sg	11Aq	18Aq	8Ar	16Ta	10Cn	18Le	7Li	22Sc	24Sg	8Aq	11Pi
23	20Cp	7Pi	16Pi	8Ta	17Ge	9Le	16Vi	2Sc	16Sg	18Cp	3Pi	7Ar
25	15Aq	5Ar	15Ar	8Ge	16Cn	7Vi	12Li	27Sc	10Cp	12Aq	29Pi	4Ta
27	12Pi	4Ta	14Ta	7Cn	15Le	3Li	6Sc	20Sg	4Aq	7Pi	26Ar	3Ge
29	9Ar		13Ge	5Le	11Vi	28Li	0Sg	14Cp	29Aq	4Ar	26Ta	4Cn
31	7Ta		11Cn		7Li		24Sg	9Aq		3Ta		4Le

1956

	Jan	Feb	Mar	Apr	May	Jun	Jul	Aug	Sep	Oct	Nov	Dec
1	19Le	9Li	0Sc	15Sg	17Cp	1Pi	4Ar	23Ta	15Cn	24Le	17Li	23Sc
3	17Vi	5Sc	25Sc	9Cp	11Aq	26Pi	0Ta	21Ge	15Le	23Vi	14Sc	18Sg
5	14Li	29Sc	19Sg	3Aq	5Pi	22Ar	28Ta	21Cn	15Vi	22Li	10Sg	12Cp
7	9Sc	23Sg	13Cp	27Aq	1Ar	20Ta	27Ge	21Le	14Li	19Sc	4Cp	6Aq
9	3Sg	17Cp	7Aq	23Pi	28Ar	19Ge	28Cn	21Vi	11Sc	14Sg	28Cp	0Pi
11	26Sg	11Aq	1Pi	19Ar	26Ta	19Cn	28Le	19Li	6Sg	9Cp	22Aq	24Pi
13	20Cp	5Pi	27Pi	17Ta	25Ge	19Le	27Vi	15Sc	1Cp	2Aq	16Pi	19Ar
15	14Aq	1Ar	24Ar	15Ge	24Cn	17Vi	24Li	10Sg	24Cp	26Aq	11Ar	16Ta
17	8Pi	27Ar	21Ta	14Cn	23Le	14Li	19Sc	4Cp	18Aq	21Pi	8Ta	14Ge
19	4Ar	24Ta	19Ge	12Le	20Vi	9Sc	13Sg	28Cp	12Pi	16Ar	6Ge	13Cn
21	0Ta	22Ge	17Cn	10Vi	17Li	4Sg	7Cp	22Aq	8Ar	13Ta	4Cn	13Le
23	28Ta	21Cn	15Le	7Li	13Sc	28Sg	1Aq	16Pi	3Ta	10Ge	3Le	12Vi
25	27Ge	20Le	14Vi	3Sc	7Sg	22Cp	25Aq	11Ar	0Ge	8Cn	2Vi	10Li
27	27Cn	19Vi	12Li	29Sc	1Cp	16Aq	19Pi	6Ta	27Ge	6Le	29Vi	6Sc
29	27Le	17Li	8Sc	23Sg	25Cp	10Pi	14Ar	3Ge	25Cn	5Vi	26Li	2Sg
31	26Vi		3Sg		19Aq		10Ta	1Cn		3Li		27Sg

1957

	Jan	Feb	Mar	Apr	May	Jun	Jul	Aug	Sep	Oct	Nov	Dec
1	9Cp	23Aq	2Pi	17Ar	22Ta	12Cn	21Le	15Li	5Sg	10Cp	25Aq	27Pi
3	3Aq	17Pi	26Pi	13Ta	19Ge	11Le	20Vi	13Sc	1Cp	5Aq	19Pi	20Ar
5	27Aq	11Ar	21Ar	9Ge	16Cn	10Vi	19Li	9Sg	26Cp	28Aq	12Ar	15Ta
7	20Pi	6Ta	16Ta	5Cn	14Le	8Li	16Sc	4Cp	20Aq	22Pi	7Ta	11Ge
9	15Ar	2Ge	12Ge	3Le	13Vi	5Sc	12Sg	28Cp	13Pi	16Ar	2Ge	8Cn
11	10Ta	0Cn	9Cn	2Vi	11Li	2Sg	7Cp	23Aq	7Ar	10Ta	28Ge	6Le
13	7Ge	29Cn	8Le	2Li	9Sc	28Sg	2Aq	16Pi	1Ta	5Ge	25Cn	4Vi
15	6Cn	0Vi	8Vi	1Sc	7Sg	23Cp	26Aq	10Ar	26Ta	1Cn	23Le	2Li
17	7Le	0Li	8Li	29Sc	3Cp	17Aq	20Pi	4Ta	21Ge	28Cn	21Vi	0Sc
19	7Vi	29Li	7Sc	25Sg	27Cp	11Pi	13Ar	29Ta	19Cn	27Le	20Li	28Sc
21	6Li	26Sc	4Sg	20Cp	21Aq	5Ar	8Ta	26Ge	18Le	26Vi	19Sc	25Sg
23	3Sc	21Sg	29Sg	13Aq	15Pi	0Ta	4Ge	24Cn	18Vi	26Li	17Sg	21Cp
25	29Sc	15Cp	23Cp	7Pi	9Ar	26Ta	1Cn	24Le	18Li	25Sc	13Cp	16Aq
27	24Sg	9Aq	17Aq	1Ar	4Ta	23Ge	1Le	25Vi	17Sc	23Sg	9Aq	11Pi
29	18Cp		11Pi	26Ar	1Ge	22Cn	1Vi	24Li	14Sg	18Cp	3Pi	4Ar
31	12Aq		5Ar		28Ge		1Li	22Sc		13Aq		28Ar

1958

	Jan	Feb	Mar	Apr	May	Jun	Jul	Aug	Sep	Oct	Nov	Dec
1	10Ta	27Ge	5Cn	26Le	4Li	28Sc	5Cp	23Aq	8Ar	10Ta	25Ge	0Le
3	6Ge	25Cn	3Le	26Vi	4Sc	26Sg	2Aq	18Pi	2Ta	4Ge	20Cn	27Le
5	3Cn	24Le	2Vi	26Li	4Sg	24Cp	27Aq	12Ar	25Ta	28Ge	17Le	24Vi
7	1Le	24Vi	3Li	26Sc	2Cp	19Aq	22Pi	5Ta	20Ge	24Cn	14Vi	23Li
9	0Vi	24Li	3Sc	24Sg	29Cp	14Pi	16Ar	29Ta	16Cn	21Le	14Li	22Sc
11	29Vi	21Sc	1Sg	20Cp	24Aq	8Ar	9Ta	24Ge	13Le	20Vi	14Sc	22Sg
13	27Li	18Sg	28Sg	15Aq	18Pi	1Ta	4Ge	21Cn	12Vi	21Li	14Sg	20Cp
15	25Sc	14Cp	24Cp	9Pi	11Ar	26Ta	29Ge	19Le	12Li	21Sc	13Cp	18Aq
17	21Sg	9Aq	18Aq	3Ar	5Ta	21Ge	26Cn	18Vi	12Sc	20Sg	9Aq	13Pi
19	17Cp	3Pi	12Pi	26Ar	29Ta	17Cn	24Le	18Li	11Sg	17Cp	5Pi	7Ar
21	12Aq	27Pi	6Ar	20Ta	24Ge	14Le	23Vi	16Sc	8Cp	13Aq	29Pi	1Ta
23	7Pi	21Ar	29Ar	15Ge	20Cn	12Vi	21Li	14Sg	4Aq	8Pi	22Ar	24Ta
25	0Ar	14Ta	23Ta	10Cn	17Le	10Li	19Sc	11Cp	29Aq	2Ar	16Ta	19Ge
27	24Ar	9Ge	18Ge	7Le	15Vi	9Sc	17Sg	7Aq	23Pi	26Ar	10Ge	14Cn
29	18Ta		14Cn	5Vi	14Li	7Sg	14Cp	2Pi	17Ar	19Ta	5Cn	10Le
31	14Ge		11Le		13Sc		10Aq	26Pi		13Ge		7Vi

1959

	Jan	Feb	Mar	Apr	May	Jun	Jul	Aug	Sep	Oct	Nov	Dec
1	21Vi	14Sc	24Sc	17Cp	23Aq	9Ar	12Ta	26Ge	12Le	17Vi	8Sc	17Sg
3	18Li	12Sg	23Sg	13Aq	18Pi	3Ta	5Ge	20Cn	8Vi	15Li	8Sg	17Cp
5	17Sc	10Cp	20Cp	9Pi	12Ar	27Ta	29Ge	16Le	6Li	14Sc	8Cp	16Aq
7	16Sg	7Aq	16Aq	3Ar	6Ta	21Ge	24Cn	13Vi	4Sc	14Sg	6Aq	13Pi
9	14Cp	3Pi	12Pi	27Ar	0Ge	15Cn	20Le	10Li	3Sg	12Cp	3Pi	8Ar
11	12Aq	29Pi	7Ar	21Ta	24Ge	10Le	16Vi	8Sc	1Cp	10Aq	28Pi	2Ta
13	8Pi	23Ar	1Ta	15Ge	18Cn	6Vi	13Li	6Sg	29Cp	6Pi	23Ar	26Ta
15	3Ar	16Ta	24Ta	9Cn	13Le	3Li	11Sc	5Cp	26Aq	1Ar	17Ta	20Ge
17	27Ar	10Ge	18Ge	4Le	9Vi	1Sc	10Sg	3Aq	22Pi	26Ar	11Ge	13Cn
19	20Ta	5Cn	13Cn	0Vi	7Li	1Sg	9Cp	1Pi	18Ar	20Ta	4Cn	8Le
21	15Ge	1Le	9Le	29Vi	7Sc	1Cp	8Aq	27Pi	12Ta	14Ge	28Cn	2Vi
23	10Cn	28Le	6Vi	29Li	7Sg	0Aq	6Pi	22Ar	6Ge	8Cn	23Le	28Vi
25	6Le	27Vi	5Li	29Sc	7Cp	28Aq	2Ar	16Ta	0Cn	2Le	19Vi	25Li
27	3Vi	26Li	5Sc	29Sg	6Aq	24Pi	26Ar	10Ge	24Cn	27Le	17Li	24Sc
29	1Li		5Sg	27Cp	2Pi	18Ar	20Ta	4Cn	20Le	24Vi	16Sc	25Sg
31	29Li		3Cp		27Pi		14Ge	29Cn		23Li		25Cp

1960

	Jan	Feb	Mar	Apr	May	Jun	Jul	Aug	Sep	Oct	Nov	Dec
1	10Aq	29Pi	20Ar	5Ge	7Cn	21Le	25Vi	14Sc	7Cp	16Aq	8Ar	13Ta
3	8Pi	25Ar	15Ta	29Ge	1Le	16Vi	21Li	13Sg	6Aq	15Pi	4Ta	8Ge
5	4Ar	19Ta	9Ge	22Cn	25Le	12Li	19Sc	12Cp	6Pi	12Ar	0Ge	3Cn
7	29Ar	13Ge	3Cn	17Le	20Vi	10Sc	18Sg	12Aq	4Ar	9Ta	24Ge	26Cn
9	23Ta	7Cn	27Cn	12Vi	18Li	10Sg	19Cp	12Pi	1Ta	4Ge	18Cn	20Le
11	16Ge	1Le	22Le	9Li	17Sc	10Cp	19Aq	10Ar	26Ta	28Ge	12Le	14Vi
13	10Cn	26Le	18Vi	8Sc	16Sg	10Aq	18Pi	6Ta	20Ge	22Cn	6Vi	9Li
15	5Le	22Vi	15Li	7Sg	16Cp	9Pi	14Ar	0Ge	14Cn	16Le	1Li	6Sc
17	29Le	19Li	13Sc	6Cp	15Aq	5Ar	9Ta	24Ge	8Le	11Vi	28Li	4Sg
19	25Vi	16Sc	11Sg	4Aq	12Pi	0Ta	4Ge	18Cn	3Vi	6Li	26Sc	4Cp
21	22Li	14Sg	9Cp	2Pi	8Ar	25Ta	27Ge	12Le	28Vi	3Sc	26Sg	5Aq
23	19Sc	13Cp	8Aq	28Pi	3Ta	19Ge	21Cn	6Vi	24Li	2Sg	25Cp	4Pi
25	18Sg	12Aq	5Pi	24Ar	28Ta	12Cn	15Le	2Li	22Sc	0Cp	24Aq	1Ar
27	18Cp	10Pi	2Ar	19Ta	22Ge	6Le	9Vi	28Li	20Sg	29Cp	21Pi	28Ar
29	18Aq	7Ar	28Ar	13Ge	15Cn	0Vi	5Li	25Sc	18Cp	27Aq	18Ar	23Ta
31	16Pi		23Ta		9Le		1Sc	23Sg		24Pi		17Ge

1961

	Jan	Feb	Mar	Apr	May	Jun	Jul	Aug	Sep	Oct	Nov	Dec
1	29Ge	14Le	22Le	8Li	13Sc	4Cp	13Aq	6Ar	26Ta	0Cn	15Le	16Vi
3	23Cn	8Vi	17Vi	4Sc	10Sg	3Aq	12Pi	4Ta	22Ge	25Cn	8Vi	10Li
5	17Le	2Li	11Li	0Sg	9Cp	2Pi	10Ar	0Ge	16Cn	18Le	2Li	5Sc
7	11Vi	27Li	7Sc	28Sg	7Aq	0Ar	7Ta	25Ge	10Le	12Vi	27Li	2Sg
9	5Li	23Sc	3Sg	26Cp	5Pi	27Ar	3Ge	19Cn	3Vi	6Li	23Sc	29Sg
11	1Sc	21Sg	1Cp	24Aq	3Ar	23Ta	28Ge	13Le	27Vi	1Sc	20Sg	28Cp
13	28Sc	21Cp	0Aq	23Pi	0Ta	19Ge	22Cn	6Vi	22Li	27Sc	17Cp	26Aq
15	27Sg	21Aq	29Aq	21Ar	27Ta	13Cn	16Le	0Li	17Sc	23Sg	15Aq	24Pi
17	28Cp	21Pi	29Pi	19Ta	23Ge	7Le	9Vi	24Li	13Sg	20Cp	13Pi	22Ar
19	28Aq	19Ar	27Ar	15Ge	17Cn	1Vi	3Li	20Sc	10Cp	19Aq	12Ar	20Ta
21	27Pi	16Ta	24Ta	9Cn	11Le	25Vi	28Li	17Sg	9Aq	18Pi	10Ta	16Ge
23	24Ar	11Ge	19Ge	3Le	5Vi	19Li	24Sc	15Cp	8Pi	17Ar	7Ge	12Cn
25	20Ta	5Cn	13Cn	27Le	29Vi	16Sc	22Sg	15Aq	8Ar	15Ta	4Cn	6Le
27	14Ge	29Cn	7Le	21Vi	24Li	14Sg	22Cp	15Pi	7Ta	13Ge	28Cn	0Vi
29	8Cn		1Vi	16Li	21Sc	13Cp	22Aq	15Ar	5Ge	8Cn	22Le	24Vi
31	2Le		25Vi		20Sg		22Pi	13Ta		3Le		18Li

	Jan	Feb	Mar	Apr	May	Jun	Jul	Aug	Sep	Oct	Nov	Dec
1	0Sc	17Sg	26Sg	17Aq	26Pi	19Ta	26Ge	13Le	28Vi	1Sc	16Sg	22Cp
3	26Sc	15Cp	24Cp	16Pi	25Ar	17Ge	22Cn	8Vi	22Li	25Sc	12Cp	18Aq
5	23Sg	15Aq	23Aq	17Ar	25Ta	14Cn	17Le	1Li	16Sc	19Sg	8Aq	16Pi
7	22Cp	15Pi	23Pi	16Ta	23Ge	9Le	11Vi	25Li	10Sg	15Cp	5Pi	14Ar
9	22Aq	15Ar	24Ar	14Ge	19Cn	3Vi	5Li	19Sc	6Cp	12Aq	5Ar	14Ta
11	21Pi	13Ta	22Ta	11Cn	13Le	27Vi	29Li	14Sg	3Aq	11Pi	5Ta	13Ge
13	19Ar	10Ge	19Ge	5Le	7Vi	21Li	24Sc	11Cp	3Pi	11Ar	5Ge	11Cn
15	16Ta	5Cn	14Cn	29Le	1Li	16Sc	20Sg	10Aq	3Ar	12Ta	3Cn	7Le
17	13Ge	29Cn	9Le	23Vi	25Li	11Sg	17Cp	9Pi	3Ta	11Ge	0Le	3Vi
19	8Cn	23Le	2Vi	17Li	20Sc	8Cp	16Aq	9Ar	2Ge	8Cn	25Le	27Vi
21	3Le	17Vi	26Vi	11Sc	16Sg	6Aq	15Pi	8Ta	29Ge	4Le	19Vi	20Li
23	27Le	11Li	20Li	6Sg	12Cp	4Pi	14Ar	6Ge	25Cn	28Le	12Li	14Sc
25	20Vi	5Sc	14Sc	2Cp	10Aq	3Ar	12Ta	2Cn	19Le	22Vi	6Sc	9Sg
27	14Li	0Sg	9Sg	29Cp	7Pi	1Ta	9Ge	28Cn	13Vi	16Li	1Sg	5Cp
29	8Sc		5Cp	27Aq	6Ar	29Ta	5Cn	22Le	7Li	10Sc	26Sg	1Aq
31	4Sg		3Aq		5Ta		1Le	16Vi		4Sg		29Aq

1963

	Jan	Feb	Mar	Apr	May	Jun	Jul	Aug	Sep	Oct	Nov	Dec
1	13Pi	6Ta	17Ta	8Cn	14Le	29Vi	2Sc	16Sg	1Aq	7Pi	29Ar	8Ge
3	11Ar	4Ge	15Ge	4Le	9Vi	23Li	25Sc	10Cp	29Aq	6Ar	0Ge	8Cn
5	9Ta	1Cn	12Cn	29Le	3Li	17Sc	20Sg	6Aq	27Pi	6Ta	29Ge	6Le
7	8Ge	28Cn	7Le	24Vi	26Li	11Sg	15Cp	4Pi	26Ar	6Ge	28Cn	3Vi
9	5Cn	23Le	2Vi	18Li	20Sc	6Cp	11Aq	2Ar	25Ta	4Cn	24Le	28Vi
11	2Le	18Vi	27Vi	11Sc	14Sg	1Aq	7Pi	0Ta	24Ge	1Le	19Vi	23Li
13	28Le	12Li	21Li	5Sg	9Cp	27Aq	5Ar	29Ta	21Cn	27Le	14Li	16Sc
15	22Vi	6Sc	14Sc	29Sg	4Aq	24Pi	4Ta	27Ge	17Le	22Vi	7Sc	10Sg
17	16Li	0Sg	8Sg	24Cp	0Pi	23Ar	2Ge	24Cn	13Vi	17Li	1Sg	4Cp
19	10Sc	25Sg	3Cp	21Aq	28Pi	22Ta	1Cn	21Le	8Li	11Sc	25Sg	28Cp
21	4Sg	21Cp	29Cp	19Pi	28Ar	22Ge	29Cn	17Vi	2Sc	4Sg	19Cp	23Aq
23	0Cp	19Aq	26Aq	19Ar	28Ta	20Cn	26Le	12Li	26Sc	28Sg	14Aq	20Pi
25	27Cp	18Pi	26Pi	20Ta	28Ge	18Le	21Vi	6Sc	19Sg	22Cp	10Pi	17Ar
27	24Aq	17Ar	26Ar	20Ge	26Cn	13Vi	16Li	29Sc	14Cp	18Aq	8Ar	16Ta
29	23Pi		26Ta	18Cn	22Le	8Li	10Sc	23Sg	9Aq	15Pi	7Ta	16Ge
31	22Ar		25Ge		17Vi		3Sg	18Cp		14Ar		15Cn

1964

	Jan	Feb	Mar	Apr	May	Jun	Jul	Aug	Sep	Oct	Nov	Dec
1	0Le	19Vi	10Li	25Sc	27Sg	11Aq	16Pi	6Ta	29Ge	8Le	29Vi	4Sc
3	28Le	15Li	5Sc	18Sg	20Cp	6Pi	12Ar	5Ge	28Cn	6Vi	25Li	29Sc
5	24Vi	9Sc	29Sc	12Cp	15Aq	3Ar	10Ta	4Cn	26Le	3Li	20Sc	23Sg
7	19Li	3Sg	22Sg	7Aq	11Pi	1Ta	10Ge	3Le	24Vi	29Li	14Sg	16Cp
9	13Sc	26Sg	16Cp	2Pi	8Ar	1Ge	10Cn	2Vi	21Li	24Sc	8Cp	10Aq
11	7Sg	21Cp	11Aq	0Ar	7Ta	1Cn	9Le	0Li	16Sc	18Sg	1Aq	4Pi
13	0Cp	16Aq	8Pi	29Ar	8Ge	1Le	8Vi	26Li	10Sg	12Cp	26Aq	29Pi
15	25Cp	13Pi	6Ar	29Ta	8Cn	29Le	5Li	20Sc	4Cp	5Aq	21Pi	26Ar
17	20Aq	10Ar	5Ta	28Ge	6Le	26Vi	0Sc	14Sg	28Cp	0Pi	18Ar	25Ta
19	17Pi	8Ta	3Ge	26Cn	3Vi	21Li	24Sc	8Cp	22Aq	27Pi	17Ta	25Ge
21	14Ar	7Ge	2Cn	23Le	29Vi	15Sc	17Sg	2Aq	18Pi	25Ar	17Ge	25Cn
23	12Ta	5Cn	29Cn	19Vi	24Li	9Sg	11Cp	27Aq	16Ar	23Ta	17Cn	25Le
25	10Ge	3Le	26Le	15Li	18Sc	2Cp	5Aq	23Pi	14Ta	23Ge	16Le	23Vi
27	9Cn	0Vi	23Vi	9Sc	12Sg	26Cp	0Pi	20Ar	12Ge	21Cn	13Vi	19Li
29	8Le	27Vi	18Li	3Sg	5Cp	21Aq	26Pi	17Ta	10Cn	19Le	9Li	14Sc
31	6Vi		13Sc		29Cp		23Ar	15Ge		16Vi		8Sg

	Jan	Feb	Mar	Apr	May	Jun	Jul	Aug	Sep	Oct	Nov	Dec
1	20Sg	4Aq	12Aq	28Pi	3Ta	25Ge	4Le	27Vi	17Sc	20Sg	4Aq	6Pi
3	13Cp	28Aq	7Pi	25Ar	2Ge	25Cn	4Vi	25Li	12Sg	14Cp	28Aq	0Ar
5	7Aq	23Pi	2Ar	22Ta	0Cn	24Le	2Li	21Sc	6Cp	8Aq	22Pi	25Ar
7	1Pi	18Ar	29Ar	20Ge	29Cn	22Vi	29Li	15Sg	0Aq	2Pi	17Ar	22Ta
9	26Pi	15Ta	25Ta	18Cn	27Le	19Li	24Sc	9Cp	24Aq	26Pi	14Ta	20Ge
11	22Ar	13Ge	23Ge	16Le	25Vi	14Sc	18Sg	3Aq	18Pi	22Ar	11Ge	19Cn
13	19Ta	12Cn	21Cn	15Vi	22Li	9Sg	12Cp	27Aq	13Ar	18Ta	9Cn	18Le
15	18Ge	11Le	20Le	12Li	18Sc	3Cp	6Aq	21Pi	8Ta	15Ge	7Le	17Vi
17	18Cn	11Vi	19Vi	9Sc	13Sg	27Cp	0Pi	16Ar	4Ge	13Cn	6Vi	15Li
19	18Le	10Li	17Li	4Sg	7Cp	21Aq	24Pi	11Ta	2Cn	11Le	4Li	11Sc
21	18Vi	6Sc	14Sc	29Sg	1Aq	15Pi	19Ar	8Ge	0Le	10Vi	1Sc	7Sg
23	15Li	1Sg	9Sg	23Cp	24Aq	10Ar	15Ta	6Cn	0Vi	8Li	28Sc	2Cp
25	10Sc	25Sg	3Cp	16Aq	19Pi	6Ta	13Ge	6Le	29Vi	6Sc	23Sg	26Cp
27	5Sg	19Cp	27Cp	11Pi	14Ar	4Ge	12Cn	6Vi	28Li	3Sg	18Cp	20Aq
29	28Sg		21Aq	6Ar	12Ta	4Cn	12Le	6Li	25Sc	28Sg	12Aq	14Pi
31	22Cp		15Pi		10Ge		13Vi	4Sc		22Cp		8Ar

1966

	Jan	Feb	Mar	Apr	May	Jun	Jul	Aug	Sep	Oct	Nov	Dec
1	20Ar	8Ge	17Ge	8Le	18Vi	10Sc	17Sg	4Aq	18Pi	21Ar	7Ge	13Cn
3	16Ta	6Cn	14Cn	8Vi	17Li	8Sg	12Cp	28Aq	12Ar	15Ta	3Cn	10Le
5	13Ge	6Le	14Le	8Li	15Sc	4Cp	7Aq	21Pi	6Ta	10Ge	0Le	8Vi
7	13Cn	6Vi	14Vi	7Sc	13Sg	29Cp	1Pi	15Ar	1Ge	6Cn	28Le	7Li
9	13Le	6Li	15Li	5Sg	8Cp	23Aq	25Pi	9Ta	26Ge	3Le	27Vi	5Sc
11	13Vi	5Sc	13Sc	1Cp	3Aq	17Pi	19Ar	5Ge	24Cn	2Vi	26Li	3Sg
13	11Li	1Sg	10Sg	25Cp	27Aq	11Ar	13Ta	1Cn	24Le	2Li	25Sc	1Cp
15	8Sc	26Sg	5Cp	19Aq	21Pi	6Ta	10Ge	0Le	24Vi	2Sc	23Sg	27Cp
17	4Sg	20Cp	29Cp	13Pi	15Ar	1Ge	7Cn	0Vi	24Li	1Sg	19Cp	22Aq
19	29Sg	14Aq	22Aq	7Ar	10Ta	29Ge	7Le	1Li	23Sc	28Sg	14Aq	16Pi
21	23Cp	7Pi	16Pi	2Ta	6Ge	27Cn	6Vi	0Sc	20Sg	24Cp	9Pi	10Ar
23	17Aq	1Ar	10Ar	27Ta	4Cn	26Le	6Li	27Sc	15Cp	18Aq	2Ar	4Ta
25	10Pi	25Ar	5Ta	23Ge	1Le	25Vi	4Sc	23Sg	10Aq	12Pi	26Ar	29Ta
27	4Ar	20Ta	0Ge	21Cn	0Vi	23Li	1Sg	18Cp	4Pi	6Ar	21Ta	25Ge
29	29Ar		26Ge	19Le	28Vi	20Sc	26Sg	13Aq	27Pi	0Ta	16Ge	23Cn
31	24Ta		24Cn		26Li		21Cp	7Pi		25Ta		21Le

1967

	Jan	Feb	Mar	Apr	May	Jun	Jul	Aug	Sep	Oct	Nov	Dec
1	5Vi	28Li	8Sc	29Sg	4Aq	20Pi	21Ar	5Ge	22Cn	27Le	20Li	28Sc
3	4Li	26Sc	6Sg	25Cp	29Aq	13Ar	15Ta	0Cn	19Le	27Vi	20Sc	28Sg
5	2Sc	23Sg	3Cp	20ASq	23Pi	7Ta	9Ge	27Cn	18Vi	27Li	20Sg	27Cp
7	29Sc	19Cp	28Cp	14Pi	17Ar	1Ge	5Cn	25Le	18Li	27Sc	18Cp	23Aq
9	26Sg	14Aq	23Aq	8Ar	10Ta	26Ge	2Le	24Vi	17Sc	25Sg	15Aq	19Pi
11	23Cp	8Pi	17Pi	2Ta	5Ge	22Cn	29Le	23Li	15Sg	23Cp	10Pi	13Ar
13	18Aq	2Ar	11Ar	25Ta	29Ge	19Le	28Vi	21Sc	13Cp	18Aq	4Ar	6Ta
15	12Pi	26Ar	4Ta	20Ge	25Cn	17Vi	26Li	19Sg	9Aq	13Pi	28Ar	0Ge
17	6Ar	20Ta	28Ta	15Cn	22Le	15Li	24Sc	16Cp	4Pi	7Ar	21Ta	24Ge
19	0Ta	14Ge	23Ge	12Le	20Vi	14Sc	22Sg	12Sq	28Pi	1Ta	15Ge	19Cn
21	24Ta	11Cn	19Cn	11Vi	19Li	12Sg	19Cp	7Pi	22Ar	24Ta	10Cn	15Le
23	20Ge	9Le	17Le	10Li	19Sc	11Cp	16Aq	2Ar	16Ta	18Ge	5Le	12Vi
25	17Cn	9Vi	17Vi	11Sc	18Sg	8Aq	11Pi	25Ar	9Ge	13Cn	1Vi	9Li
27	16Le	9Li	17Li	10Sg	16Cp	3Pi	5Ar	19Ta	4Cn	8Le	29Vi	8Sc
29	15Vi		17Sc	8Cp	13Aq	28Pi	29Ar	13Ge	0Le	6Vi	28Li	7Sg
31	14Li		16Sg		8Pi		23Ta	8Cn		5Li		6Cp

1968

	Jan	Feb	Mar	Apr	May	Jun	Jul	Aug	Sep	Oct	Nov	Dec
1	20Cp	9Pi	0Ar	14Ta	17Ge	2Le	7Vi	28Li	22Sg	1Aq	21Pi	25Ar
3	18Aq	4Ar	24Ar	8Ge	11Cn	27Le	4Li	26Sc	20Cp	28Aq	16Ar	19Ta
5	14Pi	28Ar	18Ta	2Cn	5Le	24Vi	2Sc	25Sg	18Aq	24Pi	10Ta	13Ge
7	9Ar	22Ta	12Ge	27Cn	1Vi	22Li	1Sg	24Cp	15Pi	19Ar	4Ge	7Cn
9	2Ta	16Ge	6Cn	23Le	29Vi	21Sc	1Cp	23Aq	11Ar	14Ta	28Ge	0Le
11	26Ta	11Cn	1Le	20Vi	28Li	22Sg	0Aq	20Pi	6Ta	8Ge	22Cn	25Le
13	20Ge	7Le	28Le	20Li	28Sc	22Cp	28Aq	15Ar	0Ge	1Cn	16Le	20Vi
15	15Cn	4Vi	27Vi	20Sc	29Sg	20Aq	25Pi	10Ta	23Ge	25Cn	11Vi	17Li
17	12Le	2Li	26Li	20Sg	28Cp	17Pi	20Ar	4Ge	17Cn	20Le	9Li	16Sc
19	8Vi	1Sc	25Sc	18Cp	25Aq	11Ar	14Ta	27Ge	12Le	17Vi	7Sc	16Sg
21	6Li	29Sc	24Sg	15Aq	20Pi	5Ta	7Ge	22Cn	9Vi	15Li	8Sg	16Cp
23	4Sc	27Sg	22Cp	11Pi	14Ar	29Ta	1Cn	17Le	7Li	14Sc	8Cp	16Aq
25	2Sg	25Cp	18Aq	5Ar	8Ta	23Ge	26Cn	14Vi	5Sc	14Sg	7Aq	14Pi
27	1Cp	21Aq	14Pi	29Ar	2Ge	17Cn	21Le	11Li	4Sg	13Cp	5Pi	10Ar
29	29Cp	17Pi	8Ar	23Ta	26Ge	12Le	18Vi	9Sc	3Cp	11Aq	0Ar	4Ta
31	26Aq		3Ta		20Cn		14Li	7Sg		8Pi		28Ta

1969

	Jan	Feb	Mar	Apr	May	Jun	Jul	Aug	Sep	Oct	Nov	Dec
1	10Ge	24Cn	2Le	18Vi	24Li	16Sg	25Cp	18Pi	7Ta	10Ge	24Cn	25Le
3	4Cn	19Le	27Le	15Li	23Sc	16Cp	25Aq	15Ar	2Ge	4Cn	18Le	20Vi
5	28Cn	14Vi	23Vi	13Sc	22Sg	16Aq	23Pi	11Ta	26Ge	28Cn	12Vi	15Li
7	22Le	10Li	20Li	12Sg	21Cp	14Pi	20Ar	5Ge	20Cn	22Le	7Li	12Sc
9	17Vi	7Sc	17Sc	11Cp	20Aq	10Ar	15Ta	0Cn	14Le	16Vi	4Sc	11Sg
11	13Li	5Sg	15Sg	9Aq	17Pi	5Ta	9Ge	23Cn	8Vi	12Li	2Sg	11Cp
13	10Sc	3Cp	14Cp	6Pi	13Ar	0Ge	3Cn	17Le	3Li	9Sc	1Cp	10Aq
15	9Sg	3Aq	12Aq	3Ar	8Ta	24Ge	26Cn	11Vi	29Li	7Sg	0Aq	9Pi
17	9Cp	2Pi	10Pi	29Ar	3Ge	17Cn	20Le	6Li	26Sc	5Cp	28Aq	6Ar
19	9Aq	0Ar	8Ar	24Ta	27Ge	11Le	14Vi	2Sc	24Sg	3Aq	26Pi	2Ta
21	8Pi	26Ar	4Ta	18Ge	21Cn	5Vi	9Li	29Sc	23Cp	2Pi	22Ar	28Ta
23	5Ar	21Ta	28Ta	12Cn	14Le	0Li	6Sc	28Sg	21Aq	29Pi	18Ta	22Ge
25	0Ta	15Ge	22Ge	6Le	9Vi	26Li	4Sg	27Cp	20Pi	26Ar	14Ge	16Cn
27	25Ta	8Cn	16Cn	1Vi	4Li	25Sc	3Cp	27Aq	18Ar	23Ta	8Cn	10Le
29	18Ge		10Le	26Vi	2Sc	25Sg	4Aq	26Pi	15Ta	18Ge	2Le	4Vi
31	12Cn		5Vi		1Sg		3Pi	24Ar	27Ta	12Cn		28Vi

1970

	Jan	Feb	Mar	Apr	May	Jun	Jul	Aug	Sep	Oct	Nov	Dec
1	10Li	28Sc	8Sg	1Aq	10Pi	2Ta	8Ge	24Cn	9Vi	11Li	28Sc	5Cp
3	6Sc	27Sg	6Cp	29Aq	8Ar	28Ta	3Cn	18Le	2Li	6Sc	25Sg	3Aq
5	4Sg	27Cp	5Aq	29Pi	6Ta	24Ge	27Cn	11Vi	26Li	1Sg	22Cp	1Pi
7	4Cp	27Aq	5Pi	27Ar	3Ge	19Cn	21Le	5Li	21Sc	28Sg	20Aq	29Pi
9	4Aq	27Pi	5Ar	25Ta	28Ge	13Le	15Vi	0Sc	18Sg	25Cp	18Pi	27Ar
11	4Pi	25Ar	3Ta	20Ge	23Cn	6Vi	9Li	25Sc	15Cp	24Aq	17Ar	25Ta
13	3Ar	21Ta	0Ge	15Cn	17Le	0Li	3Sc	22Sg	15Aq	23Pi	16Ta	22Ge
15	29Ar	16Ge	25Ge	9Le	10Vi	25Li	0Sg	21Cp	15Pi	23Ar	13Ge	17Cn
17	25Ta	10Cn	19Cn	2Vi	5Li	22Sc	28Sg	21Aq	15Ar	22Ta	9Cn	12Le
19	19Ge	4Le	12Le	27Vi	0Sc	20Sg	28Cp	22Pi	13Ta	19Ge	4Le	6Vi
21	13Cn	28Le	6Vi	22Li	27Sc	19Cp	28Aq	21Ar	11Ge	14Cn	28Le	29Vi
23	7Le	22Vi	1Li	18Sc	25Sg	18Aq	27Pi	18Ta	6Cn	8Le	22Vi	24Li
25	1Vi	16Li	26Li	15Sg	24Cp	17Pi	25Ar	14Ge	0Le	2Vi	16Li	19Sc
27	25Vi	12Sc	22Sc	13Cp	22Aq	15Ar	22Ta	9Cn	24Le	26Vi	11Sc	16Sg
29	19Li		19Sg	11Aq	21Pi	12Ta	18Ge	3Le	17Vi	20Li	7Sg	14Cp
31	15Sc		16Cp		18Ar		12Cn	27Le		15Sc		13Aq

1971

	Jan	Feb	Mar	Apr	May	Jun	Jul	Aug	Sep	Oct	Nov	Dec
1	27Aq	20Ar	0Ta	20Ge	25Cn	9Vi	11Li	25Sc	12Cp	18Aq	11Ar	19Ta
3	26Pi	18Ta	28Ta	16Cn	19Le	3Li	5Sc	20Sg	10Aq	17Pi	11Ta	19Ge
5	24Ar	15Ge	24Ge	11Le	13Vi	27Li	0Sg	17Cp	9Pi	18Ar	11Ge	17Cn
7	21Ta	10Cn	10Cn	4Vi	6Li	21Sc	26Sg	16Aq	9Ar	18Ta	9Cn	13Le
9	18Ge	5Le	14Le	28Vi	0Sc	17Sg	23Cp	15Pi	9Ta	16Ge	5Le	8Vi
11	13Cn	29Le	7Vi	22Li	25Sc	14Cp	21Aq	14Ar	7Ge	14Cn	0Vi	2Li
13	8Le	22Vi	1Li	16Sc	21Sg	11Aq	20Pi	13Ta	4Cn	9Le	24Vi	26Li
15	2Vi	16Li	25Li	11Sg	17Cp	9Pi	18Ar	11Ge	0Le	3Vi	18Li	20Sc
17	26Vi	10Sc	19Sc	7Cp	14Aq	7Ar	16Ta	7Cn	24Le	27Vi	12Sc	15Sg
19	19Li	5Sg	14Sg	4Aq	12Pi	6Ta	14Ge	3Le	18Vi	21Li	6Sg	10Cp
21	14Sc	1Cp	10Cp	2Pi	11Ar	4Ge	11Cn	27Le	12Li	15Sc	1Cp	6Aq
23	10Sg	0Aq	8Aq	1Ar	10Ta	1Cn	6Le	21Vi	6Sc	9Sg	26Cp	3Pi
25	7Cp	29Aq	8Pi	1Ta	9Ge	28Cn	1Vi	15Li	0Sg	4Cp	23Aq	1Ar
27	7Aq	0Ar	8Ar	1Ge	7Cn	23Le	25Vi	9Sc	24Sg	29Cp	21Pi	0Ta
29	6Pi		8Ta	29Ge	3Le	17Vi	19Li	3Sg	20Cp	27Aq	20Ar	29Ta
31	6Ar		7Ge		27Le		13Sc	28Sg		26Pi		27Ge

1972

	Jan	Feb	Mar	Apr	May	Jun	Jul	Aug	Sep	Oct	Nov	Dec
1	11Cn	29Le	20Vi	5Sc	7Sg	23Cp	29Aq	21Ar	14Ge	23Cn	12Vi	16Li
3	8Le	24Vi	14Li	28Sc	1Cp	19Aq	26Pi	19Ta	12Cn	19Le	6Li	10Sc
5	4Vi	18Li	8Sc	22Sg	26Cp	15Pi	24Ar	18Ge	9Le	15Vi	1Sc	3Sg
7	28Vi	12Sc	2Sg	17Cp	22Aq	14Ar	23Ta	16Cn	5Vi	10Li	24Sc	27Sg
9	22Li	6Sg	26Sg	13Aq	20Pi	13Ta	22Ge	13Le	1Li	4Sc	18Sg	21Cp
11	16Sc	1Cp	21Cp	11Pi	19Ar	13Ge	21Cn	10Vi	25Li	28Sc	12Cp	16Aq
13	10Sg	27Cp	18Aq	10Ar	19Ta	12Cn	18Le	5Li	19Sc	21Sg	6Aq	11Pi
15	6Cp	25Aq	17Pi	11Ta	20Ge	10Le	14Vi	29Li	13Sg	15Cp	2Pi	8Ar
17	2Aq	24Pi	17Ar	11Ge	18Cn	6Vi	9Li	23Sc	7Cp	10Aq	29Pi	7Ta
19	0Pi	23Ar	17Ta	9Cn	15Le	1Li	3Sc	17Sg	2Aq	7Pi	28Ar	7Ge
21	28Pi	22Ta	16Ge	6Le	10Vi	25Li	27Sc	12Cp	29Aq	5Ar	29Ta	7Cn
23	26Ar	19Ge	13Cn	1Vi	5Li	29Sc	21Sg	7Aq	27Pi	5Ta	29Ge	6Le
25	25Ta	16Cn	9Le	26Vi	29Li	13Sg	16Cp	4Pi	27Ar	6Ge	28Cn	4Vi
27	23Ge	12Le	4Vi	20Li	22Sc	7Cp	12Aq	3Ar	26Ta	5Cn	25Le	0Li
29	20Cn	7Vi	29Vi	13Sc	16Sg	3Aq	9Pi	1Ta	25Ge	3Le	21Vi	24Li
31	16Le		23Li		11Cp		7Ar	0Ge		29Le		18Sc

1973

	Jan	Feb	Mar	Apr	May	Jun	Jul	Aug	Sep	Oct	Nov	Dec
1	0Sg	14Cp	22Cp	8Pi	14Ar	7Ge	16Cn	8VI	27Li	0Sg	13Cp	15Aq
3	24Sg	9Aq	17Aq	6Ar	14Ta	7Cn	15Le	6Li	22Sc	24Sg	7Aq	9Pi
5	18Cp	5Pi	14Pi	5Ta	14Ge	7Le	14Vi	1Sc	16Sg	17Cp	1Pi	5Ar
7	13Aq	1Ar	11Ar	4Ge	13Cn	5Vi	10Li	26Sc	9Cp	11Aq	27Pi	2Ta
9	8Pi	29Ar	10Ta	3Cn	11Le	1Li	5Sc	19Sg	3Aq	6Pi	24Ar	1Ge
11	5Ar	27Ta	8Ge	1Le	8Vi	26Li	29Sc	13Cp	28Aq	3Ar	23Ta	1Cn
13	2Ta	25Ge	6Cn	28Le	4Li	20Sc	23Sg	7Aq	24Pi	0Ta	23Ge	2Le
15	1Ge	24Cn	4Le	24Vi	29Li	14Sg	16Cp	2Pi	21Ar	29Ta	22Cn	0Vi
17	0Cn	22Le	1Vi	20Li	23Sc	8Cp	10Aq	28Pi	19Ta	27Ge	20Le	28Vi
19	0Le	20Vi	28Vi	14Sc	17Sg	1Aq	5Pi	24Ar	17Ge	26Cn	18Vi	24Li
21	28Le	16Li	24Li	8Sg	11Cp	26Aq	1Ar	22Ta	15Cn	24Le	14Li	19Sc
23	25Vi	10Sc	18Sc	2Cp	4Aq	21Pi	27Ar	20Ge	13Le	21Vi	9Sc	13Sg
25	20Li	4Sg	12Sg	26Cp	29Aq	18Ar	25Ta	19Cn	11Vi	17Li	4Sg	7Cp
27	15Sc	28Sg	6Cp	20Aq	25Pi	16Ta	24Ge	18Le	9Li	13Sc	28Sg	0Aq
29	8Sg		0Aq	16Pi	23Ar	16Ge	24Cn	16Vi	5Sc	8Sg	22Cp	24Aq
31	2Cp		25Aq		22Ta		24Le	14Li		2Cp		18Pi

1974

	Jan	Feb	Mar	Apr	May	Jun	Jul	Aug	Sep	Oct	Nov	Dec
1	1Ar	20Ta	0Ge	23Cn	2Vi	23Li	29Sc	14Cp	29Aq	2Ar	19Ta	26Ge
3	27Ar	18Ge	28Ge	21Le	0Li	19Sc	23Sg	8Aq	23Pi	27Ar	16Ge	24Cn
5	25Ta	17Cn	27Cn	20Vi	27Li	14Sg	17Cp	2Pi	18Ar	23Ta	14Cn	23Le
7	24Ge	18Le	26Le	18Li	23Sc	9Cp	11Aq	26Pi	13Ta	20Ge	12Le	22Vi
9	25Cn	17Vi	25Vi	15Sc	18Sg	2Aq	5Pi	20Ar	9Ge	17Cn	11Vi	19Li
11	25Le	16Li	23Li	10Sg	12Cp	26Aq	29Pi	16Ta	7Cn	16Le	9Li	16Sc
13	24Vi	12Sc	20Sc	5Cp	6Aq	20Pi	24Ar	13Ge	6Le	15Vi	7Sc	12Sg
15	20Li	7Sg	15Sg	28Cp	0Pi	15Ar	20Ta	12Cn	6Vi	14Li	4Sg	7Cp
17	16Sc	0Cp	9Cp	22Aq	25Pi	12Ta	19Ge	12Le	5Li	12Sc	29Sg	2Aq
19	10Sg	24Cp	2Aq	17Pi	20Ar	10Ge	18Cn	12Vi	4Sc	9Sg	24Cp	25Aq
21	4Cp	18Aq	26Aq	12Ar	18Ta	10Cn	19Le	12Li	1Sg	4Cp	18Aq	19Pi
23	27Cp	12Pi	21Pi	9Ta	16Ge	10Le	19Vi	9Sc	26Sg	28Cp	11Pi	13Ar
25	21Aq	7Ar	17Ar	7Ge	15Cn	9Vi	17Li	5Sg	20Cp	22Aq	6Ar	9Ta
27	15Pi	3Ta	13Ta	5Cn	14Le	7Li	13Sc	29Sg	13Aq	16Pi	1Ta	6Ge
29	10Ar		11Ge	4Le	13Vi	3Sc	8Sg	23Cp	7Pi	10Ar	28Ta	4Cn
31	6Ta		8Cn		10Li		2Cp	17Aq		6Ta		4Le

1975

	Jan	Feb	Mar	Apr	May	Jun	Jul	Aug	Sep	Oct	Nov	Dec
1	19Le	12Li	21Li	11Sg	14Cp	29Aq	0Ar	15Ta	2Cn	9Le	2Li	11Sc
3	18Vi	10Sc	19Sc	6Cp	9Aq	23Pi	24Ar	10Ge	0Le	8Vi	2Sc	9Sg
5	16Li	6Sg	15Sg	1Aq	3Pi	17Ar	19Ta	7Cn	0Vi	9Li	1Sg	7Cp
7	13Sc	1Cp	10Cp	24Aq	26Pi	11Ta	16Ge	6Le	0Li	9Sc	29Sg	3Aq
9	9Sg	25Cp	4Aq	18Pi	21Ar	7Ge	13Cn	6Vi	0Sc	7Sg	25Cp	28Aq
11	4Cp	19Aq	28Aq	12Ar	16Ta	4Cn	12Le	6Li	29Sc	4Cp	20Aq	22Pi
13	28Cp	12Pi	21Pi	7Ta	12Ge	3Le	12Vi	5Sc	25Sg	29Cp	14Pi	16Ar
15	22Aq	6Ar	15Ar	2Ge	8Cn	1Vi	11Li	2Sg	20Cp	24Aq	8Ar	10Ta
17	16Pi	0Ta	10Ta	28Ge	6Le	0Li	8Sc	28Sg	15Aq	17Pi	2Ta	5Ge
19	9Ar	25Ta	5Ge	25Cn	4Vi	28Li	5Sg	23Cp	9Pi	11Ar	26Ta	1Cn
21	4Ta	22Ge	1Cn	24Le	3Li	25Sc	1Cp	18Aq	2Ar	5Ta	22Ge	28Cn
23	0Ge	20Cn	29Cn	23Vi	2Sc	22Sg	26Cp	12Pi	26Ar	0Ge	18Cn	26Le
25	28Ge	20Le	29Le	22Li	0Sg	18Cp	21Aq	5Ar	20Ta	25Ge	15Le	24Vi
27	27Cn	21Vi	29Vi	21Sc	26Sg	13Aq	15Pi	29Ar	15Ge	21Cn	13Vi	22Li
29	27Le		29Li	19Sg	22Cp	7Pi	9Ar	23Ta	11Cn	18Le	12Li	20Sc
31	28Vi		27Sc		17Aq		3Ta	19Ge		17Vi		18Sg

1976

	Jan	Feb	Mar	Apr	May	Jun	Jul	Aug	Sep	Oct	Nov	Dec
1	2Cp	19Aq	19Pi	25Ar	27Ta	14Cn	21Le	13Li	6Sg	14Cp	3Pi	6Ar
3	28Cp	14Pi	4Ar	18Ta	22Ge	10Le	18Vi	11Sc	4Cp	10Aq	27Pi	0Ta
5	24Aq	8Ar	28Ar	12Ge	17Cn	7Vi	16Li	9Sg	0Aq	6Pi	21Ar	23Ta
7	18Pi	1Ta	22Ta	7Cn	13Le	5Li	15Sc	7Cp	26Aq	0Ar	15Ta	17Ge
9	12Ar	25Ta	16Ge	4Le	11Vi	4Sc	13Sg	4Aq	21Pi	24Ar	8Ge	12Cn
11	5Ta	20Ge	11Cn	2Vi	10Li	4Sg	11Cp	0Pi	15Ar	18Ta	2Cn	7Le
13	0Ge	17Cn	9Le	1Li	10Sc	3Cp	9Aq	25Pi	9Ta	11Ge	27Cn	3Vi
15	26Ge	15Le	8Vi	2Sc	10Sg	0Aq	4Pi	19Ar	3Ge	5Cn	23Le	0Li
17	23Cn	15Vi	9Li	2Sg	9Cp	26Aq	29Pi	13Ta	27Ge	1Le	20Vi	28Li
19	21Le	15Li	9Sc	0Cp	6Aq	21Pi	23Ar	7Ge	22Cn	28Le	19Li	28Sc
21	20Vi	14Sc	7Sg	27Cp	1Pi	15Ar	17Ta	1Cn	19Le	26Vi	19Sc	28Sg
23	19Li	11Sg	5Cp	22Aq	25Pi	9Ta	11Ge	28Cn	18Vi	26Li	20Sg	27Cp
25	17Sc	8Cp	0Aq	16Pi	19Ar	3Ge	25Le	25Le	18Li	26Sc	19Cp	24Aq
27	14Sg	3Aq	25Aq	10Ar	12Ta	28Ge	24Vi	24Vi	18Sc	26Sg	16Aq	20Pi
29	11Cp	28Aq	19Pi	4Ta	6Ge	24Cn	23Li	23Li	17Sg	24Cp	12Pi	14Ar
31	7Aq		13Ar		1Cn		22Sc	22Sc		20Aq		8Ta

1977

	Jan	Feb	Mar	Apr	May	Jun	Jul	Aug	Sep	Oct	Nov	Dec
1	20Ta	4Cn	12Cn	29Le	5Li	28Sc	7Cp	29Aq	17Ar	19Ta	3Cn	6Le
3	14Ge	29Cn	7Le	27Vi	4Sc	28Sg	6Aq	26Pi	11Ta	13Ge	27Cn	0Vi
5	8Cn	26Le	5Vi	26Li	5Sg	28Cp	4Pi	21Ar	5Ge	7Cn	21Le	25Vi
7	4Le	23Vi	3Li	25Sc	4Cp	26Aq	1Ar	15Ta	29Ge	1Le	17Vi	23Li
9	0Vi	21Li	2Sc	25Sg	3Aq	22Pi	25Ar	9Ge	23Cn	26Le	15Li	22Sc
11	27Vi	19Sc	0Sg	23Cp	0Pi	17Ar	19Ta	3Cn	18Le	23Vi	14Sc	22Sg
13	24Li	18Sg	29Sg	20Aq	25Pi	10Ta	13Ge	27Cn	15Vi	21Li	14Sg	23Cp
15	23Sc	16Cp	26Cp	16Pi	20Ar	4Ge	7Cn	23Le	12Li	20Sc	14Cp	22Aq
17	22Sg	13Aq	23Aq	10Ar	13Ta	28Ge	1Le	19Vi	10Sc	19Sg	12Aq	19Pi
19	21Cp	10Pi	19Pi	4Ta	7Ge	22Cn	26Le	16Li	9Sg	18Cp	9Pi	15Ar
21	19Aq	6Ar	14Ar	28Ta	1Cn	17Le	22Vi	14Sc	7Cp	16Aq	5Ar	9Ta
23	15Pi	0Ta	8Ta	22Ge	25Cn	12Vi	19Li	12Sg	5Aq	12Pi	0Ta	3Ge
25	10Ar	24Ta	2Ge	16Cn	20Le	9Li	17Sc	11Cp	3Pi	8Ar	24Ta	27Ge
27	4Ta	17Ge	25Ge	11Le	16Vi	7Sc	16Sg	9Aq	29Pi	3Ta	18Ge	21Cn
29	28Ta		20Cn	7Vi	13Li	6Sg	15Cp	7Pi	25Ar	27Ta	12Cn	15Le
31	22Ge		15Le		13Sc		15Aq	4Ar		21Ge		9Vi

1978

	Jan	Feb	Mar	Apr	May	Jun	Jul	Aug	Sep	Oct	Nov	Dec
1	22Vi	11Sc	22Sc	15Cp	24Aq	15Ar	20Ta	5Cn	19Le	22Vi	10Sc	17Sg
3	18Li	10Sg	20Sg	14Aq	22Pi	10Ta	14Ge	28Cn	13Vi	18Li	8Sg	16Cp
5	16Sc	9Cp	19Cp	11Pi	18Ar	5Ge	8Cn	22Le	8Li	14Sc	6Cp	15Aq
7	15Sg	9Aq	18Aq	9Ar	13Ta	29Ge	1Le	16Vi	4Sc	12Sg	5Aq	14Pi
9	15Cp	8Pi	16Pi	5Ta	8Ge	23Cn	25Le	11Li	1Sg	10Cp	3Pi	11Ar
11	16Aq	6Ar	14Ar	0Ge	2Cn	16Le	19Vi	7Sc	29Sg	8Aq	1Ar	7Ta
13	14Pi	2Ta	9Ta	24Ge	26Cn	10Vi	14Li	4Sg	28Cp	6Pi	28Ar	3Ge
15	11Ar	26Ta	4Ge	18Cn	20Le	5Li	11Sc	3Cp	27Aq	5Ar	24Ta	28Ge
17	6Ta	20Ge	28Ge	12Le	14Vi	2Sc	9Sg	3Aq	26Pi	2Ta	19Ge	22Cn
19	0Ge	14Cn	22Cn	6Vi	10Li	1Sg	9Cp	3Pi	24Ar	28Ta	14Cn	15Le
21	24Ge	8Le	16Le	2Li	8Sc	1Cp	10Aq	2Ar	21Ta	23Ge	7Le	9Vi
23	17Cn	3Vi	11Vi	0Sc	7Sg	1Aq	10Pi	29Ar	16Ge	18Cn	1Vi	3Li
25	12Le	28Vi	7Li	28Sc	7Cp	1Pi	8Ar	25Ta	10Cn	11Le	25Vi	29Li
27	6Vi	25Li	5Sc	27Sg	7Aq	28Pi	4Ta	20Ge	3Le	5Vi	21Li	26Sc
29	2Li		3Sg	26Cp	5Pi	25Ar	29Ta	13Cn	27Le	0Li	18Sc	25Sg
31	28Li		1Cp		2Ar		23Ge	7Le		26Li		25Cp

1979

	Jan	Feb	Mar	Apr	May	Jun	Jul	Aug	Sep	Oct	Nov	Dec
1	10Aq	3Ar	11Ar	1Ge	4Cn	18Le	20Vi	5Sc	23Sg	0Aq	23Pi	2Ta
3	10Pi	1Ta	9Ta	26Ge	29Cn	12Vi	14Li	1Sg	21Cp	29Aq	23Ar	0Ge
5	8Ar	27Ta	5Ge	21Cn	22Le	6Li	9Sc	28Sg	21Aq	29Pi	22Ta	27Ge
7	4Ta	21Ge	0Cn	14Le	16Vi	1Sc	6Sg	27Cp	21Pi	29Ar	19Ge	23Cn
9	0Ge	15Cn	24Cn	8Vi	10Li	28Sc	4Cp	28Aq	21Ar	28Ta	15Cn	18Le
11	24Ge	9Le	18Le	2Li	6Sc	26Sg	4Aq	28Pi	19Ta	25Ge	10Le	12Vi
13	18Cn	3Vi	12Vi	27Li	3Sg	25Cp	4Pi	26Ar	16Ge	20Cn	4Vi	5Li
15	12Le	27Vi	6Li	23Sc	0Cp	24Aq	2Ar	24Ta	11Cn	14Le	27Vi	29Li
17	6Vi	21Li	1Sc	20Sg	29Cp	22Pi	0Ta	19Ge	5Le	7Vi	22Li	25Sc
19	0Li	16Sc	26Sc	18Cp	27Aq	20Ar	27Ta	14Cn	29Le	1Li	17Sc	22Sg
21	24Li	13Sg	23Sg	16Aq	25Pi	17Ta	22Ge	8Le	22Vi	25Li	13Sg	19Cp
23	20Sc	12Cp	21Cp	15Pi	23Ar	13Ge	17Cn	2Vi	16Li	20Sc	10Cp	18Aq
25	18Sg	11Aq	20Aq	13Ar	20Ta	8Cn	11Le	25Vi	11Sc	16Sg	7Aq	16Pi
27	18Cp	12Pi	20Pi	11Ta	17Ge	3Le	5Vi	19Li	6Sg	13Cp	5Pi	14Ar
29	18Aq		19Ar	8Ge	12Cn	26Le	28Vi	14Sc	2Cp	10Aq	3Ar	12Ta
31	18Pi		17Ta		6Le		22Li	9Sg		9Pi		9Ge

1980

	Jan	Feb	Mar	Apr	May	Jun	Jul	Aug	Sep	Oct	Nov	Dec
1	23Ge	10Le	1Vi	15Li	18Sc	5Cp	12Aq	5Ar	28Ta	6Cn	23Le	26Vi
3	19Cn	4Vi	24Vi	9Sc	13Sg	2Aq	10Pi	4Ta	26Ge	2Le	17Vi	20Li
5	14Le	28Vi	18Li	3Sg	9Cp	29Aq	9Ar	2Ge	22Cn	26Le	11Li	13Sc
7	8Vi	21Li	12Sc	29Sg	5Aq	27Pi	7Ta	29Ge	17Le	20Vi	5Sc	8Sg
9	1Li	15Sc	6Sg	25Cp	3Pi	26Ar	5Ge	25Cn	11Vi	14Li	29Sc	3Cp
11	25Li	11Sg	2Cp	23Aq	1Ar	25Ta	2Cn	20Le	5Li	8Sc	23Sg	28Cp
13	20Sc	7Cp	0Aq	22Pi	1Ta	23Ge	29Cn	15Vi	29Li	2Sg	18Cp	24Aq
15	16Sg	6Aq	29Aq	22Ar	1Ge	21Cn	24Le	9Li	23Sc	26Sg	14Aq	22Pi
17	14Cp	6Pi	29Pi	22Ta	29Ge	16Le	19Vi	2Sc	17Sg	21Cp	11Pi	20Ar
19	13Aq	6Ar	29Ar	21Ge	26Cn	11Vi	12Li	26Sc	13Cp	18Aq	10Ar	19Ta
21	12Pi	5Ta	28Ta	17Cn	21Le	4Li	6Sc	21Sg	10Aq	17Pi	10Ta	19Ge
23	11Ar	3Ge	26Ge	12Le	15Vi	28Li	1Sg	18Cp	8Pi	17Ar	10Ge	17Cn
25	9Ta	29Ge	21Cn	6Vi	8Li	23Sc	26Sg	16Aq	9Ar	17Ta	9Cn	14Le
27	6Ge	24Cn	16Le	0Li	2Sc	18Sg	23Cp	15Pi	9Ta	17Ge	6Le	10Vi
29	2Cn	19Le	9Vi	24Li	27Sc	15Cp	22Aq	15Ar	8Ge	15Cn	2Vi	4Li
31	27Cn		3Li		22Sg		21Pi	14Ta		11Le		20Li

1981

	Jan	Feb	Mar	Apr	May	Jun	Jul	Aug	Sep	Oct	Nov	Dec
1	10Sc	24Sg	2Cp	19Aq	25Pi	19Ta	28Ge	19Le	6Li	9Sc	23Sg	26Cp
3	4Sg	20Cp	27Cp	17Pi	25Ar	19Ge	27Cn	15Vi	1Sc	3Sg	17Cp	20Aq
5	29Sg	17Aq	25Aq	17Ar	26Ta	19Cn	24Le	11Li	25Sc	27Sg	11Aq	16Pi
7	24Cp	15Pi	23Pi	17Ta	26Ge	16Le	20Vi	5Sc	19Sg	21Cp	7Pi	14Ar
9	21Aq	13Ar	23Ar	17Ge	24Cn	12Vi	15Li	29Sc	13Cp	16Aq	5Ar	13Ta
11	19Pi	12Ta	22Ta	15Cn	21Le	7Li	9Sc	23Sg	8Aq	13Pi	5Ta	13Ge
13	17Ar	10Ge	21Ge	11Le	16Vi	1Sc	3Sg	17Cp	5Pi	12Ar	5Ge	13Cn
15	15Ta	8Cn	18Cn	6Vi	10Li	24Sc	27Sg	13Aq	3Ar	12Ta	5Cn	13Le
17	14Ge	4Le	14Le	1Li	4Sc	18Sg	22Cp	10Pi	2Ta	11Ge	4Le	10Vi
19	12Cn	0Vi	9Vi	25Li	27Sc	13Cp	17Aq	8Ar	1Ge	10Cn	1Vi	5Li
21	9Le	25Vi	4Li	19Sc	21Sg	8Aq	14Pi	6Ta	0Cn	8Le	26Vi	0Sc
23	5Vi	20Li	28Li	12Sg	16Cp	3Pi	11Ar	5Ge	27Cn	4Vi	21Li	24Sc
25	0Li	13Sc	22Sc	6Cp	11Aq	0Ar	9Ta	3Cn	24Le	29Vi	15Sc	17Sg
27	24Li	7Sg	15Sg	1Aq	7Pi	29Ar	8Ge	1Le	20Vi	24Li	8Sg	11Cp
29	17Sc		10Cp	27Aq	4Ar	28Ta	7Cn	28Le	15Li	18Sc	2Cp	5Aq
31	12Sg		5Aq		4Ta		5Le	24Vi		11Sg		0Pi

1982

	Jan	Feb	Mar	Apr	May	Jun	Jul	Aug	Sep	Oct	Nov	Dec
1	13Pi	4Ta	14Ta	8Cn	16Le	6Li	10Sc	25Sg	9Aq	12Pi	1Ta	8Ge
3	9Ar	2Ge	13Ge	5Le	13Vi	1Sc	4Sg	18Cp	4Pi	8Ar	29Ta	8Cn
5	7Ta	1Cn	11Cn	3Vi	9Li	25Sc	28Sg	12Aq	29Pi	6Ta	28Ge	7Le
7	6Ge	0Le	9Le	29Vi	4Sc	19Sg	22Cp	7Pi	26Ar	4Ge	27Cn	6Vi
9	6Cn	28Le	7Vi	25Li	28Sc	13Cp	15Aq	3Ar	23Ta	2Cn	25Le	3Li
11	6Le	26Vi	4Li	20Sc	22Sg	6Aq	10Pi	29Ar	21Ge	0Le	22Vi	29Li
13	4Vi	22Li	29Li	14Sg	16Cp	1Pi	6Ar	26Ta	19Cn	28Le	19Li	24Sc
15	1Li	16Sc	24Sc	8Cp	10Aq	26Pi	2Ta	25Ge	18Le	26Vi	15Sc	18Sg
17	26Li	10Sg	18Sg	1Aq	4Pi	23Ar	1Ge	24Cn	17Vi	23Li	9Sg	12Cp
19	20Sc	4Cp	11Cp	26Aq	1Ar	22Ta	0Cn	24Le	14Li	19Sc	3Cp	5Aq
21	14Sg	28Cp	6Aq	22Pi	29Ar	22Ge	0Le	22Vi	11Sc	13Sg	27Cp	29Aq
23	8Cp	23Aq	1Pi	20Ar	28Ta	22Cn	0Vi	20Li	5Sg	7Cp	21Aq	23Pi
25	2Aq	19Pi	28Pi	20Ta	28Ge	21Le	28Vi	15Sc	29Sg	1Aq	15Pi	19Ar
27	27Aq	16Ar	26Ar	19Ge	28Cn	19Vi	24Li	9Sg	23Cp	25Aq	11Ar	16Ta
29	23Pi		25Ta	18Cn	26Le	15Li	19Sc	3Cp	17Aq	20Pi	9Ta	16Ge
31	20Ar		24Ge		23Vi		13Sg	27Cp		17Ar		16Cn

1983

	Jan	Feb	Mar	Apr	May	Jun	Jul	Aug	Sep	Oct	Nov	Dec
1	1Le	24Vi	2Li	21Sc	24Sg	8Aq	10Pi	26Ar	14Ge	22Cn	15Vi	24Li
3	1Vi	21Li	0Sc	16Sg	18Cp	2Pi	4Ar	21Ta	12Cn	21Le	14Li	21Sc
5	29Vi	17Sc	26Sc	10Cp	12Aq	26Pi	29Ar	19Ge	11Le	20Vi	12Sc	18Sg
7	26Li	12Sg	20Sg	4Aq	6Pi	21Ar	26Ta	18Cn	12Vi	20Li	9Sg	13Cp
9	21Sc	6Cp	14Cp	28Aq	0Ar	18Ta	25Ge	18Le	12Li	18Sc	5Cp	7Aq
11	15Sg	29Cp	8Aq	22Pi	26Ar	16Ge	25Cn	19Vi	10Sc	15Sg	29Cp	1Pi
13	9Cp	23Aq	2Pi	18Ar	24Ta	16Cn	25Le	18Li	6Sg	9Cp	23Aq	25Pi
15	2Aq	17Pi	26Pi	15Ta	22Ge	15Le	24Vi	15Sc	1Cp	3Aq	17Pi	19Ar
17	26Aq	12Ar	22Ar	12Ge	21Cn	14Vi	22Li	10Sg	25Cp	27Aq	12Ar	15Ta
19	20Pi	8Ta	18Ta	10Cn	19Le	12Li	18Sc	5Cp	19Aq	21Pi	7Ta	12Ge
21	15Ar	5Ge	15Ge	8Le	17Vi	8Sc	13Sg	28Cp	13Pi	16Ar	4Ge	10Cn
23	11Ta	3Cn	13Cn	6Vi	15Li	4Sg	7Cp	22Aq	7Ar	11Ta	1Cn	9Le
25	9Ge	2Le	12Le	5Li	11Sc	28Sg	1Aq	16Pi	2Ta	8Ge	29Cn	9Vi
27	9Cn	2Vi	11Vi	2Sc	7Sg	23Cp	25Aq	10Ar	28Ta	5Cn	28Le	7Li
29	9Le		10Li	29Sc	2Cp	16Aq	19Pi	5Ta	24Ge	3Le	26Vi	4Sc
31	9Vi		7Sc		26Cp		13Ar	1Ge		1Vi		1Sg

1984

	Jan	Feb	Mar	Apr	May	Jun	Jul	Aug	Sep	Oct	Nov	Dec
1	14Sg	0Aq	21Aq	5Ar	9Ta	26Ge	3Le	27Vi	20Sc	27Sg	13Aq	16Pi
3	9Cp	24Aq	15Pi	0Ta	4Ge	24Cn	2Vi	26Li	17Sg	22Cp	8Pi	10Ar
5	3Aq	18Pi	8Ar	24Ta	0Cn	22Le	1Li	24Sc	13Cp	17Aq	1Ar	3Ta
7	27Aq	11Ar	2Ta	20Ge	27Cn	20Vi	29Li	20Sg	8Aq	11Pi	25Ar	28Ta
9	21Pi	6Ta	27Ta	16Cn	25Le	18Li	27Sc	16Cp	2Pi	5Ar	19Ta	23Ge
11	15Ar	1Ge	23Ge	14Le	24Vi	17Sc	23Sg	11Aq	26Pi	28Ar	14Ge	19Cn
13	10Ta	28Ge	20Cn	14Vi	23Li	14Sg	19Cp	5Pi	19Ar	22Ta	9Cn	16Le
15	6Ge	26Cn	20Le	14Li	21Sc	11Cp	14Aq	29Pi	13Ta	17Ge	6Le	14Vi
17	4Cn	27Le	20Vi	13Sc	19Sg	6Aq	8Pi	22Ar	8Ge	12Cn	4Vi	13Li
19	3Le	27Vi	20Li	11Sg	15Cp	0Pi	2Ar	16Ta	3Cn	9Le	2Li	11Sc
21	4Vi	27Li	19Sc	7Cp	10Aq	24Pi	26Ar	11Ge	0Le	8Vi	2Sc	10Sg
23	3Li	24Sc	16Sg	2Aq	4Pi	18Ar	20Ta	8Cn	29Le	8Li	1Sg	7Cp
25	1Sc	20Sg	12Cp	26Aq	28Pi	13Ta	16Ge	6Le	0Li	8Sc	29Sg	4Aq
27	28Sc	15Cp	6Aq	20Pi	22Ar	8Ge	14Cn	6Vi	0Sc	7Sg	26Cp	29Aq
29	23Sg	9Aq	0Pi	14Ar	17Ta	5Cn	13Le	6Li	29Sc	5Cp	22Aq	24Pi
31	18Cp		23Pi		13Ge		12Vi	6Sc		1Aq		17Ar

1985

	Jan	Feb	Mar	Apr	May	Jun	Jul	Aug	Sep	Oct	Nov	Dec
1	29Ar	13Ge	21Ge	9Le	16Vi	10Sc	19Sg	9Aq	27Pi	29Ar	13Ge	17Cn
3	23Ta	9Cn	17Cn	8Vi	16Li	10Sg	17Cp	6Pi	21Ar	23Ta	7Cn	12Le
5	18Ge	7Le	15Le	8Li	16Sc	9Cp	14Aq	1Ar	15Ta	16Ge	2Le	8Vi
7	15Cn	6Vi	15Vi	8Sc	16Sg	6Aq	10Pi	25Ar	8Ge	11Cn	28Le	5Li
9	13Le	6Li	15Li	8Sg	15Cp	2Pi	5Ar	18Ta	3Cn	6Le	26Vi	4Sc
11	11Vi	4Sc	14Sc	6Cp	11Aq	27Pi	29Ar	12Ge	28Cn	3Vi	25Li	4Sg
13	9Li	2Sg	13Sg	2Aq	6Pi	21Ar	22Ta	7Cn	25Le	2Li	26Sc	4Cp
15	8Sc	29Sg	9Cp	27Aq	0Ar	14Ta	17Ge	3Le	24Vi	3Sc	26Sg	3Aq
17	5Sg	25Cp	5Aq	21Pi	24Ar	8Ge	12Cn	1Vi	24Li	3Sg	25Cp	0Pi
19	3Cp	21Aq	0Pi	15Ar	18Ta	3Cn	8Le	0Li	23Sc	2Cp	22Aq	26Pi
21	29Cp	16Pi	24Pi	9Ta	12Ge	29Cn	6Vi	28Li	22Sg	29Cp	17Pi	20Ar
23	25Aq	10Ar	18Ar	2Ge	6Cn	25Le	4Li	27Sc	19Cp	25Aq	11Ar	13Ta
25	19Pi	3Ta	12Ta	27Ge	2Le	23Vi	2Sc	25Sg	15Aq	20Pi	5Ta	7Ge
27	13Ar	27Ta	5Ge	22Cn	28Le	21Li	0Sg	22Cp	11Pi	14Ar	28Ta	1Cn
29	7Ta		0Cn	18Le	26Vi	20Sc	28Sg	18Aq	5Ar	8Ta	22Ge	26Cn
31	1Ge		26Cn		25Li		26Cp	14Pi		1Ge		22Le

1986

	Jan	Feb	Mar	Apr	May	Jun	Jul	Aug	Sep	Oct	Nov	Dec
1	5Vi	26Li	7Sc	0Cp	8Aq	27Pi	1Ta	15Ge	29Cn	2Vi	21Li	28Sc
3	1Li	24Sc	5Sg	28Cp	5Pi	22Ar	24Ta	8Cn	24Le	29Vi	20Sc	29Sg
5	29Li	22Sg	3Cp	25Aq	0Ar	15Ta	18Ge	3Le	20Vi	27Li	20Sg	29Cp
7	28Sc	21Cp	1Aq	20Pi	24Ar	9Ge	12Cn	28Le	17Li	25Sc	19Cp	27Aq
9	27Sg	19Aq	28Aq	15Ar	18Ta	3Cn	6Le	24Vi	15Sc	24Sg	17Aq	24Pi
11	26Cp	16Pi	24Pi	10Ta	12Ge	27Cn	1Vi	21Li	13Sg	23Cp	14Pi	20Ar
13	25Aq	11Ar	19Ar	4Ge	6Cn	21Le	27Vi	18Sc	12Cp	20Aq	10Ar	14Ta
15	21Pi	6Ta	14Ta	27Ge	0Le	17Vi	24Li	17Sg	10Aq	17Pi	5Ta	8Ge
17	16Ar	29Ta	7Ge	21Cn	25Le	14Li	22Sc	16Cp	8Pi	13Ar	29Ta	2Cn
19	10Ta	23Ge	1Cn	16Le	21Vi	12Sc	21Sg	15Aq	5Ar	9Ta	23Ge	26Cn
21	3Ge	18Cn	25Cn	13Vi	19Li	12Sg	21Cp	13Pi	0Ta	3Ge	17Cn	20Le
23	27Ge	13Le	21Le	11Li	19Sc	13Cp	21Aq	10Ar	25Ta	27Ge	11Le	14Vi
25	22Cn	10Vi	19Vi	11Sc	19Sg	12Aq	18Pi	5Ta	19Ge	20Cn	5Vi	10Li
27	18Le	8Li	17Li	11Sg	19Cp	10Pi	14Ar	29Ta	13Cn	15Le	1Li	7Sc
29	15Vi		17Sc	10Cp	18Aq	6Ar	9Ta	23Ge	7Le	10Vi	29Li	6Sg
31	12Li		16Sg		14Pi		3Ge	17Cn		7Li		7Cp

1987

	Jan	Feb	Mar	Apr	May	Jun	Jul	Aug	Sep	Oct	Nov	Dec
1	22Cp	14Pi	22Pi	10Ta	14Ge	28Cn	0Vi	16Li	6Sg	14Cp	8Pi	16Ar
3	22Aq	12Ar	20Ar	6Ge	8Cn	22Le	24Vi	12Sc	4Cp	13Aq	5Ar	12Ta
5	20Pi	7Ta	15Ta	0Cn	1Le	16Vi	20Li	10Sg	3Aq	12Pi	3Ta	8Ge
7	16Ar	2Ge	10Ge	24Cn	25Le	11Li	16Sc	9Cp	3Pi	10Ar	29Ta	3Cn
9	11Ta	26Ge	4Cn	18Le	20Vi	8Sc	15Sg	9Aq	2Ar	8Ta	25Ge	27Cn
11	5Ge	19Cn	28Cn	12Vi	16Li	7Sg	16Cp	9Pi	0Ta	4Ge	19Cn	21Le
13	29Ge	13Le	22Le	8Li	14Sc	7Cp	16Aq	8Ar	26Ta	29Ge	13Le	15Vi
15	23Cn	8Vi	17Vi	5Sc	13Sg	7Aq	15Pi	5Ta	21Ge	23Cn	7Vi	9Li
17	17Le	3Li	13Li	4Sg	13Cp	6Pi	13Ar	1Ge	15Cn	17Le	1Li	5Sc
19	11Vi	29Li	10Sc	2Cp	12Aq	3Ar	9Ta	25Ge	9Le	11Vi	27Li	2Sg
21	6Li	27Sc	7Sg	1Aq	10Pi	20Ar	4Ge	19Cn	3Vi	6Li	24Sc	1Cp
23	3Sc	25Sg	6Cp	29Aq	6Ar	24Ta	28Ge	12Le	27Vi	2Sc	23Sg	1Aq
25	0Sg	24Cp	4Aq	26Pi	2Ta	19Ge	22Cn	6Vi	23Li	29Sc	22Cp	1Pi
27	0Cp	23Aq	3Pi	23Ar	27Ta	13Cn	15Le	1Li	19Sc	27Sg	20Aq	29Pi
29	0Aq		1Ar	19Ta	22Ge	6Le	9Vi	26Li	16Sg	25Cp	18Pi	26Ar
31	0Pi		27Ar		16Cn		4Li	22Sc		23Aq		22Ta

	Jan	Feb	Mar	Apr	May	Jun	Jul	Aug	Sep	Oct	Nov	Dec
1	5Ge	21Cn	11Le	25Vi	29Li	17Sg	25Cp	19Pi	11Ta	17Ge	4Le	5Vi
3	29Ge	14Le	5Vi	20Li	25Sc	15Cp	24Aq	18Ar	8Ge	13Cn	28Le	29Vi
5	24Cn	8Vi	29Vi	15Sc	22Sg	14Aq	23Pi	15Ta	4Cn	7Le	21Vi	23Li
7	17Le	2Li	23Li	11Sg	19Cp	12Pi	21Ar	12Ge	28Cn	1Vi	15Li	18Sc
9	11Vi	26Li	18Sc	8Cp	17Aq	11Ar	18Ta	7Cn	22Le	25Vi	9Sc	14Sg
11	5Li	21Sc	14Sg	6Aq	16Pi	8Ta	15Ge	1Le	16Vi	18Li	5Sg	11Cp
13	0Sc	19Sg	12Cp	5Pi	14Ar	5Ge	10Cn	25Le	9Li	13Sc	1Cp	9Aq
15	26Sc	17Cp	11Aq	5Ar	12Ta	1Cn	4Le	19Vi	3Sc	8Sg	28Cp	7Pi
17	24Sg	18Aq	11Pi	3Ta	9Ge	26Cn	28Le	12Li	28Sc	4Cp	26Aq	5Ar
19	24Cp	18Pi	11Ar	1Ge	5Cn	20Le	22Vi	7Sc	24Sg	1Aq	24Pi	3Ta
21	25Aq	17Ar	9Ta	27Ge	0Le	14Vi	16Li	2Sg	21Cp	0Pi	23Ar	1Ge
23	24Pi	15Ta	6Ge	22Cn	24Le	8Li	10Sc	28Sg	20Aq	29Pi	22Ta	28Ge
25	22Ar	11Ge	2Cn	16Le	18Vi	2Sc	6Sg	27Cp	20Pi	29Ar	20Ge	24Cn
27	19Ta	5Cn	26Cn	10Vi	12Li	28Sc	4Cp	27Aq	21Ar	28Ta	16Cn	19Le
29	14Ge	29Cn	20Le	4Li	7Sc	26Sg	4Aq	27Pi	20Ta	25Ge	11Le	13Vi
31	8Cn		13Vi		3Sg		4Pi	27Ar		21Cn		7Li

1989

	Jan	Feb	Mar	Apr	May	Jun	Jul	Aug	Sep	Oct	Nov	Dec
1	19Li	3Sg	12Sg	0Aq	8Pi	1Ta	10Ge	0Le	17Vi	19Li	4Sg	8Cp
3	13Sc	0Cp	8Cp	29Aq	7Ar	1Ge	8Cn	26Le	11Li	13Sc	28Sg	3Aq
5	9Sg	28Cp	6Aq	28Pi	7Ta	29Ge	5Le	20Vi	4Sc	7Sg	23Cp	29Aq
7	6Cp	27Aq	5Pi	29Ar	7Ge	27Cn	0Vi	14Li	28Sc	1Cp	19Aq	26Pi
9	4Aq	27Pi	5Ar	29Ta	5Cn	22Le	24Vi	8Sc	23Sg	27Cp	17Pi	25Ar
11	3Pi	26Ar	5Ta	27Ge	1Le	16Vi	18Li	2Sg	18Cp	24Aq	16Ar	25Ta
13	2Ar	24Ta	4Ge	23Cn	26Le	10Li	12Sc	27Sg	16Aq	23Pi	17Ta	25Ge
15	0Ta	21Ge	1Cn	18Le	20Vi	4Sc	7Sg	24Cp	15Pi	23Ar	17Ge	23Cn
17	27Ta	17Cn	26Cn	12Vi	14Li	28Sc	2Cp	22Aq	15Ar	24Ta	15Cn	20Le
19	24Ge	12Le	21Le	5Li	8Sc	24Sg	29Cp	21Pi	15Ta	23Ge	12Le	15Vi
21	20Cn	6Vi	15Vi	29Li	2Sg	20Cp	27Aq	20Ar	14Ge	20Cn	7Vi	10Li
23	15Le	29Vi	8Li	23Sc	27Sg	17Aq	26Pi	19Ta	11Cn	16Le	1Li	3Sc
25	9Vi	23Li	2Sc	18Sg	23Cp	15Pi	24Ar	17Ge	7Le	10Vi	25Li	27Sc
27	3Li	17Sc	26Sc	13Cp	20Aq	13Ar	22Ta	14Cn	1Vi	4Li	19Sc	22Sg
29	27Li		21Sg	10Aq	18Pi	12Ta	20Ge	9Le	25Vi	28Li	13Sg	17Cp
31	21Sc		17Cp		17Ar		17Cn	4Vi		22Sc		13Aq

1990

	Jan	Feb	Mar	Apr	May	Jun	Jul	Aug	Sep	Oct	Nov	Dec
1	26Aq	18Ar	28Ar	22Ge	29Cn	17Vi	21Li	4Sg	19Cp	22Aq	11Ar	19Ta
3	23Pi	16Ta	27Ta	20Cn	26Le	12Li	14Sc	28Sg	14Aq	19Pi	11Ta	20Ge
5	21Ar	15Ge	25Ge	16Le	21Vi	6Sc	8Sg	23Cp	11Pi	18Ar	11Ge	20Cn
7	20Ta	13Cn	23Cn	11Vi	15Li	0Sg	2Cp	19Aq	9Ar	17Ta	11Cn	18Le
9	19Ge	10Le	19Le	6Li	9Sc	23Sg	27Cp	15Pi	7Ta	17Ge	9Le	15Vi
11	17Cn	6Vi	14Vi	0Sc	3Sg	18Cp	22Aq	13Ar	6Ge	15Cn	6Vi	10Li
13	15Le	1Li	9Li	24Sc	26Sg	12Aq	18Pi	11Ta	4Cn	12Le	1Li	5Sc
15	11Vi	25Li	3Sc	17Sg	21Cp	8Pi	16Ar	9Ge	2Le	9Vi	26Li	29Sc
17	5Li	19Sc	27Sc	11Cp	15Aq	5Ar	14Ta	8Cn	29Le	4Li	20Sc	22Sg
19	29Li	13Sg	21Sg	6Aq	12Pi	4Ta	13Ge	6Le	25Vi	29Li	14Sg	16Cp
21	23Sc	8Cp	15Cp	3Pi	10Ar	4Ge	12Cn	3Vi	20Li	23Sc	7Cp	10Aq
23	17Sg	3Aq	11Aq	1Ar	10Ta	4Cn	11Le	29Vi	15Sc	17Sg	1Aq	5Pi
25	12Cp	1Pi	9Pi	1Ta	10Ge	3Le	8Vi	24Li	8Sg	10Cp	26Aq	1Ar
27	9Aq	29Pi	8Ar	2Ge	10Cn	0Vi	4Li	19Sc	2Cp	4Aq	22Pi	28Ar
29	6Pi		8Ta	2Cn	8Le	26Vi	29Li	12Sg	26Cp	0Pi	19Ar	27Ta
31	4Ar		8Ge		5Vi		23Sc	6Cp		27Pi		28Ge

1991

	Jan	Feb	Mar	Apr	May	Jun	Jul	Aug	Sep	Oct	Nov	Dec
1	13Cn	4Vi	12Vi	1Sc	4Sg	18Cp	20Aq	7Ar	28Ta	7Cn	0Vi	7Li
3	12Le	2Li	9Li	25Sc	28Sg	12Aq	15Pi	4Ta	26Ge	5Le	27Vi	3Sc
5	10Vi	27Li	5Sc	19Sg	21Cp	6Pi	11Ar	1Ge	25Cn	3Vi	24Li	29Sc
7	7Li	22Sc	0Sg	13Cp	15Aq	1Ar	8Ta	0Cn	24Le	1Li	20Sc	23Sg
9	2Sc	16Sg	23Sg	7Aq	10Pi	29Ar	6Ge	0Le	23Vi	28Li	15Sg	17Cp
11	26Sc	9Cp	17Cp	2Pi	7Ar	28Ta	6Cn	0Vi	20Li	24Sc	9Cp	11Aq
13	19Sg	3Aq	12Aq	28Pi	5Ta	28Ge	7Le	28Vi	16Sc	19Sg	2Aq	4Pi
15	13Cp	28Aq	7Pi	26Ar	4Ge	28Cn	6Vi	25Li	11Sg	13Cp	26Aq	29Pi
17	7Aq	24Pi	4Ar	25Ta	4Cn	27Le	4Li	21Sc	5Cp	6Aq	21Pi	25Ar
19	2Pi	21Ar	1Ta	25Ge	3Le	25Vi	0Sc	15Sg	29Cp	1Pi	17Ar	23Ta
21	28Pi	19Ta	0Ge	23Cn	1Vi	20Li	24Sc	9Cp	23Aq	26Pi	15Ta	22Ge
23	24Ar	17Ge	28Ge	21Le	28Vi	15Sc	18Sg	2Aq	18Pi	23Ar	14Ge	22Cn
25	22Ta	16Cn	26Cn	18Vi	23Li	9Sg	12Cp	26Aq	14Ar	21Ta	13Cn	22Le
27	21Ge	14Le	24Le	14Li	18Sc	3Cp	6Aq	22Pi	11Ta	19Ge	12Le	21Vi
29	21Cn		21Vi	9Sc	12Sg	27Cp	0Pi	17Ar	9Ge	18Cn	10Vi	18Li
31	20Le		18Li		6Cp		25Pi	14Ta		16Le		13Sc

1992

	Jan	Feb	Mar	Apr	May	Jun	Jul	Aug	Sep	Oct	Nov	Dec
1	26Sc	11Cp	1Aq	16Pi	19Ar	8Ge	16Cn	10Vi	2Sc	7Sg	23Cp	25Aq
3	20Sg	4Aq	25Aq	11Ar	16Ta	7Cn	16Le	9Li	29Sc	3Cp	17Aq	19Pi
5	14Cp	28Aq	19Pi	6Ta	13Ge	6Le	15Vi	7Sc	24Sg	27Cp	11Pi	13Ar
7	7Aq	22Pi	14Ar	3Ge	11Cn	5Vi	13Li	3Sg	19Cp	21Aq	5Ar	8Ta
9	1Pi	17Ar	10Ta	0Cn	9Le	3Li	10Sc	27Sg	12Aq	15Pi	0Ta	4Ge
11	25Pi	13Ta	6Ge	28Cn	8Vi	0Sc	6Sg	22Cp	6Pi	9Ar	26Ta	2Cn
13	20Ar	10Ge	4Cn	27Le	6Li	26Sc	0Cp	15Aq	0Ar	4Ta	23Ge	0Le
15	17Ta	8Cn	2Le	26Vi	3Sc	21Sg	25Cp	9Pi	24Ar	29Ta	20Cn	29Le
17	15Ge	8Le	2Vi	24Li	0Sg	16Cp	18Aq	3Ar	20Ta	26Ge	18Le	27Vi
19	15Cn	8Vi	1Li	21Sc	25Sg	10Aq	12Pi	27Ar	16Ge	23Cn	16Vi	25Li
21	15Le	8Li	0Sc	17Sg	20Cp	3Pi	6Ar	23Ta	13Cn	21Le	15Li	22Sc
23	15Vi	6Sc	27Sc	12Cp	13Aq	27Pi	1Ta	19Ge	11Le	21Vi	13Sc	19Sg
25	14Li	1Sg	22Sg	6Aq	7Pi	22Ar	27Ta	18Cn	11Vi	20Li	10Sg	14Cp
27	10Sc	26Sg	16Cp	29Aq	2Ar	19Ta	25Ge	18Le	11Li	18Sc	6Cp	9Aq
29	5Sg	19Cp	9Aq	24Pi	27Ar	16Ge	24Cn	18Vi	10Sc	15Sg	1Aq	3Pi
31	29Sg		3Pi		24Ta		24Le	18Li		11Cp		26Pi

1993

	Jan	Feb	Mar	Apr	May	Jun	Jul	Aug	Sep	Oct	Nov	Dec
1	8Ar	23Ta	2Ge	21Cn	29Le	23Li	2Sg	21Cp	7Pi	10Ar	24Ta	28Ge
3	3Ta	20Ge	28Ge	20Le	29Vi	22Sc	29Sg	16Aq	1Ar	3Ta	19Ge	24Cn
5	29Ta	18Cn	26Cn	19Vi	28Li	20Sg	25Cp	10Pi	24Ar	27Ta	14Cn	21Le
7	26Ge	18Le	26Le	20Li	27Sc	16Cp	20Aq	4Ar	18Ta	22Ge	11Le	19Vi
9	25Cn	18Vi	26Vi	19Sc	25Sg	12Aq	14Pi	28Ar	13Ge	17Cn	8Vi	17Li
11	24Le	18Li	27Li	17Sg	21Cp	6Pi	8Ar	22Ta	8Cn	15Le	8Li	16Sc
13	24Vi	16Sc	25Sc	13Cp	16Aq	0Ar	2Ta	17Ge	6Le	14Vi	8Sc	15Sg
15	22Li	12Sg	22Sg	8Aq	10Pi	24Ar	26Ta	14Cn	6Vi	14Li	7Sg	13Cp
17	19Sc	8Cp	17Cp	2Pi	4Ar	18Ta	22Ge	12Le	6Li	15Sc	6Cp	10Aq
19	15Sg	2Aq	11Aq	25Pi	28Ar	14Ge	20Cn	12Vi	6Sc	14Sg	2Aq	5Pi
21	11Cp	26Aq	5Pi	19Ar	23Ta	11Cn	18Le	12Li	5Sg	11Cp	27Aq	29Pi
23	5Aq	20Pi	29Pi	14Ta	18Ge	9Le	18Vi	11Sc	2Cp	6Aq	21Pi	23Ar
25	29Aq	13Ar	22Ar	9Ge	15Cn	7Vi	17Li	9Sg	27Cp	1Pi	15Ar	17Ta
27	23Pi	7Ta	17Ta	5Cn	12Le	6Li	15Sc	5Cp	22Aq	25Pi	9Ta	12Ge
29	17Ar		12Ge	1Le	10Vi	4Sc	12Sg	0Aq	16Pi	18Ar	3Ge	7Cn
31	11Ta		8Cn		9Li		8Cp	25Aq		12Ta		4Le

1994

	Jan	Feb	Mar	Apr	May	Jun	Jul	Aug	Sep	Oct	Nov	Dec
1	18Le	11Li	20Li	13Sg	20Cp	8Pi	11Ar	24Ta	8Cn	12Le	2Li	10Sc
3	16Vi	9Sc	20Sc	11Cp	17Aq	2Ar	4Ta	18Ge	4Le	10Vi	2Sc	10Sg
5	14Li	7Sg	17Sg	7Aq	11Pi	26Ar	28Ta	13Cn	2Vi	9Li	2Sg	10Cp
7	12Sc	4Cp	14Cp	2Pi	5Ar	20Ta	22Ge	9Le	0Li	9Sc	2Cp	9Aq
9	10Sg	0Aq	10Aq	26Pi	29Ar	14Ge	17Cn	7Vi	29Li	8Sg	0Aq	6Pi
11	8Cp	26Aq	5Pi	20Ar	23Ta	8Cn	13Le	5Li	28Sc	7Cp	27Aq	1Ar
13	5Aq	21Pi	0Ar	14Ta	17Ge	4Le	10Vi	3Sc	26Sg	4Aq	22Pi	25Ar
15	1Pi	15Ar	23Ar	8Ge	11Cn	0Vi	8Li	1Sg	24Cp	0Pi	16Ar	19Ta
17	25Pi	9Ta	17Ta	2Cn	7Le	27Vi	6Sc	29Sg	20Aq	25Pi	10Ta	12Ge
19	19Ar	2Ge	11Ge	27Cn	3Vi	26Li	5Sg	27Cp	16Pi	19Ar	4Ge	6Cn
21	13Ta	27Ge	5Cn	24Le	1Li	25Sc	3Cp	24Aq	11Ar	13Ta	27Ge	1Le
23	7Ge	23Cn	1Le	22Vi	1Sc	24Sg	1Aq	20Pi	5Ta	7Ge	22Cn	26Le
25	2Cn	21Le	29Le	22Li	1Sg	23Cp	28Aq	14Ar	28Ta	0Cn	16Le	23Vi
27	29Cn	21Vi	29Vi	23Sc	1Cp	20Aq	24Pi	8Ta	22Ge	25Cn	13Vi	20Li
29	27Le		29Li	22Sg	29Cp	16Pi	18Ar	2Ge	16Cn	20Le	10Li	19Sc
31	26Vi		29Sc		25Aq		12Ta	26Ge		18Vi		18Sg

1995

	Jan	Feb	Mar	Apr	May	Jun	Jul	Aug	Sep	Oct	Nov	Dec
1	3Cp	25Aq	3Pi	21Ar	24Ta	8Cn	11Le	29Vi	20Sc	29Sg	22Aq	29Pi
3	3Aq	22Pi	0Ar	15Ta	17Ge	2Le	6Vi	25Li	18Sg	27Cp	19Pi	24Ar
5	1Pi	17Ar	25Ar	9Ge	11Cn	26Le	2Li	23Sc	16Cp	25Aq	15Ar	19Ta
7	27Pi	11Ta	19Ta	3Cn	5Le	22Vi	29Li	22Sg	15Aq	22Pi	10Ta	13Ge
9	22Ar	5Ge	13Ge	27Cn	0Vi	19Li	27Sc	21Cp	13Pi	19Ar	5Ge	7Cn
11	15Ta	29Ge	7Cn	22Le	27Vi	18Sc	27Sg	21Aq	10Ar	14Ta	29Ge	1Le
13	9Ge	23Cn	1Le	19Vi	25Li	19Sg	27Cp	19Pi	6Ta	8Ge	22Cn	25Le
15	3Cn	19Le	27Le	17Li	25Sc	19Cp	27Aq	16Ar	1Ge	2Cn	16Le	19Vi
17	28Cn	16Vi	25Vi	17Sc	25Sg	18Aq	24Pi	11Ta	24Ge	26Cn	11Vi	15Li
19	23Le	13Li	23Li	16Sg	25Cp	16Pi	20Ar	5Ge	18Cn	21Le	7Li	13Sc
21	20Vi	11Sc	22Sc	15Cp	23Aq	11Ar	14Ta	28Ge	13Le	16Vi	5Sc	12Sg
23	17Li	9Sg	20Sg	13Aq	19 Pi	6Ta	8Ge	22Cn	8Vi	13Li	5Sg	13Cp
25	14Sc	8Cp	18Cp	9Pi	14Ar	29Ta	2Cn	17Le	5Li	11Sc	5Cp	13Aq
27	13Sg	6Aq	16Aq	5Ar	9Ta	23Ge	26Cn	12Vi	2Sc	11Sg	4Aq	12Pi
29	12Cp		13Pi	0Ta	2Ge	17Cn	21Le	9Li	0Sg	10Cp	2Pi	9Ar
31	11Aq		8Ar		26Ge		16Vi	6Sc		8Aq		4Ta

1996

	Jan	Feb	Mar	Apr	May	Jun	Jul	Aug	Sep	Oct	Nov	Dec
1	16Ta	1Cn	21Cn	6vi	9Li	28Sc	7Cp	1Pi	22Ar	27Ta	13Cn	15Le
3	10Ge	25Cn	15Le	1Li	6Sc	28Sg	7Aq	0Ar	19Ta	23Ge	7Le	8Vi
5	4Cn	19Le	10Vi	27Li	5Sg	28Cp	7Pi	28Ar	15Ge	17Cn	1Vi	2Li
7	28Cn	13Vi	5Li	25Sc	3Cp	27Aq	5Ar	23Ta	9Cn	11Le	25Vi	28Li
9	22Le	8Li	1Sc	23Sg	2Aq	25Pi	1Ta	18Ge	3Le	5Vi	20Li	24Sc
11	16Vi	4Sc	28Sc	21Cp	0Pi	21Ar	26Ta	12Cn	26Le	29Vi	16Sc	23Sg
13	11Li	1Sg	26Sg	20Aq	28Pi	17Ta	21Ge	6Le	20Vi	24Li	14Sg	22Cp
15	8Sc	0Cp	25Cp	18Pi	24Ar	12Ge	15Cn	29Le	15Li	20Sc	12Cp	21Aq
17	6Sg	0Aq	24Aq	15Ar	20Ta	6Cn	9Le	23Vi	11Sc	18Sg	11Aq	20Pi
19	6Cp	29Aq	22Pi	11Ta	15Ge	0Le	2Vi	18Li	7Sg	15Cp	9Pi	17Ar
21	6Aq	28Pi	20Ar	7Ge	9Cn	24Le	26Vi	14Sc	5Cp	14Aq	7Ar	14Ta
23	6Pi	26Ar	16Ta	1Cn	3Le	17Vi	21Li	10Sg	3Aq	12Pi	4Ta	9Ge
25	4Ar	21Ta	11Ge	25Cn	27Le	12Li	17Sc	9Cp	3Pi	11Ar	0Ge	5Cn
27	0Ta	16Ge	5Cn	19Le	21Vi	9Sc	15Sg	9Aq	2Ar	9Ta	26Ge	29Cn
29	25Ta	9Cn	29Cn	13Vi	17Li	7Sg	15Cp	9Pi	0Ta	5Ge	21Cn	23Le
31	19Ge		23Le		14Sc		16Aq	8Ar		1Cn		16Vi

1997

	Jan	Feb	Mar	Apr	May	Jun	Jul	Aug	Sep	Oct	Nov	Dec
1	28Vi	14Sc	23Sc	13Cp	22Aq	15Ar	23Ta	12Cn	27Le	0Li	15Sc	19Sg
3	23Li	10Sg	19Sg	11Aq	21Pi	13Ta	20Ge	6Le	21Vi	24Li	10Sg	16Cp
5	18Sc	9Cp	17Cp	11Pi	19Ar	10Ge	15Cn	0Vi	15Li	18Sc	6Cp	13Aq
7	16Sg	9Aq	17Aq	10Ar	18Ta	6Cn	10Le	24Vi	8Sc	13Sg	3Aq	11Pi
9	16Cp	9Pi	17Pi	9Ta	15Ge	2Le	4Vi	18Li	3Sg	9Cp	0Pi	9Ar
11	16Aq	9Ar	17Ar	7Ge	11Cn	26Le	27Vi	12Sc	29Sg	6Aq	29Pi	8Ta
13	16Pi	7Ta	16Ta	3Cn	6Le	19Vi	21Li	7Sg	27Cp	5Pi	28Ar	6Ge
15	14Ar	3Ge	12Ge	28Cn	0Vi	13Li	16Sc	4Cp	26Aq	5Ar	28Ta	4Cn
17	11Ta	28Ge	7Cn	22Le	23Vi	8Sc	12Sg	3Aq	27Pi	5Ta	26Ge	0Le
19	6Ge	23Cn	1Le	15Vi	17Li	4Sg	10Cp	3Pi	27Ar	4Ge	22Cn	25Le
21	1Cn	16Le	25Le	9Li	13Sc	2Cp	10Aq	3Ar	26Ta	1Cn	17Le	19Vi
23	26Cn	10Vi	19Vi	4Sc	9Sg	1Aq	9Pi	2Ta	23Ge	27Cn	11Vi	13Li
25	19Le	4Li	13Li	0Sg	7Cp	29Aq	8Ar	0Ge	18Cn	21Le	5Li	7Sc
27	13Vi	28Li	7Sc	26Sg	5Aq	28Pi	6Ta	26Ge	12Le	15Vi	29Li	2Sg
29	7Li		3Sg	24Cp	3Pi	26Ar	3Ge	21Cn	6Vi	8Li	23Sc	28Sg
31	1Sc		29Sg		1Ar		29Ge	15Le		2Sc		25Cp

1998

	Jan	Feb	Mar	Apr	May	Jun	Jul	Aug	Sep	Oct	Nov	Dec
1	9Aq	2Ar	12Ar	5Ge	11Cn	28Le	0Li	14Sc	28Sg	2Aq	23Pi	1Ta
3	8Pi	1Ta	11Ta	2Cn	7Le	22Vi	24Li	8Sg	24Cp	0Pi	22Ar	1Ge
5	6Ar	29Ta	9Ge	28Cn	2Vi	16Li	18Sc	3Cp	22Aq	29Pi	23Ta	1Cn
7	4Ta	26Ge	6Cn	23Le	25Vi	9Sc	12Sg	0Aq	21Pi	0Ta	23Ge	0Le
9	2Ge	22Cn	1Le	17Vi	19Li	4Sg	8Cp	28Aq	21Ar	0Ge	21Cn	26Le
11	29Ge	17Le	26Le	10Li	13Sc	29Sg	5Aq	26Pi	20Ta	28Ge	18Le	21Vi
13	25Cn	11Vi	20Vi	4Sc	7Sg	25Cp	2Pi	25Ar	18Ge	25Cn	12Vi	15Li
15	21Le	5Li	13Li	28Sc	2Cp	22Aq	0Ar	24Ta	15Cn	21Le	6Li	9Sc
17	15Vi	28Li	7Sc	23Sg	28Cp	19Pi	29Ar	22Ge	11Le	15Vi	0Sc	3Sg
19	8Li	22Sc	1Sg	18Cp	25Aq	18Ar	27Ta	19Cn	6Vi	9Li	24Sc	27Sg
21	2Sc	17Sg	26Sg	15Aq	23Pi	17Ta	25Ge	15Le	1Li	3Sc	18Sg	22Cp
23	27Sc	14Cp	22Cp	13Pi	22Ar	15Ge	22Cn	10Vi	24Li	27Sc	12Cp	18Aq
25	22Sg	12Aq	20Aq	13Ar	22Ta	14Cn	19Le	4Li	18Sc	21Sg	8Aq	14Pi
27	20Cp	12Pi	20Pi	13Ta	21Ge	10Le	14Vi	28Li	12Sg	15Cp	4Pi	12Ar
29	18Aq		20Ar	13Ge	19Cn	6Vi	8Li	22Sc	7Cp	11Aq	2Ar	10Ta
31	18Pi		20Ta		15Le		2Sc	16Sg		8Pi		10Ge

1999

	Jan	Feb	Mar	Apr	May	Jun	Jul	Aug	Sep	Oct	Nov	Dec
1	24Ge	15Le	24Le	11Li	14Sc	28Sg	2Aq	20Pi	12Ta	21Ge	14Le	20Vi
3	23Cn	12Vi	20Vi	5Sc	8Sg	23Cp	27Aq	17Ar	11Ge	20Cn	10Vi	15Vi
5	21Le	7Li	15Li	29Sc	1Cp	17Aq	23Pi	15Ta	9Cn	17Le	6Li	10Sc
7	17Vi	1Sc	9Sc	23Sg	26Cp	13Pi	20Ar	14Ge	7Le	13Vi	1Sc	4Sg
9	11Li	25Sc	3Sg	17Cp	21Aq	10Ar	19Ta	13Cn	4Vi	9Li	25Sc	27Sg
11	5Sc	19Sg	27Sg	12Aq	17Pi	10Ta	19Ge	11Le	0Li	4Sc	19Sg	21Cp
13	29Sc	13Cp	21Cp	9Pi	16Ar	10Ge	18Cn	9Vi	26Li	28Sc	12Cp	15Aq
15	23Sg	9Aq	17Aq	8Ar	16Ta	10Cn	17Le	5Li	20Sc	22Sg	6Aq	10Pi
17	18Cp	7Pi	15Pi	8Ta	17Ge	9Le	14Vi	0Sc	14Sg	16Cp	1Pi	6Ar
19	14Aq	5Ar	14Ar	8Ge	16Cn	6Vi	10Li	24Sc	8Cp	10Aq	27Pi	4Ta
21	11Pi	3Ta	14Ta	7Cn	14Le	1Li	4Sc	18Sg	2Aq	6Pi	26Ar	4Ge
23	9Ar	2Ge	13Ge	4Le	10Vi	26Li	28Sc	12Cp	28Aq	3Ar	26Ta	4Cn
25	7Ta	0Cn	11Cn	1Vi	5Li	20Sc	22Sg	7Aq	25Pi	2Ta	26Ge	4Le
27	5Ge	27Cn	8Le	26Vi	29Li	13Sg	16Cp	3Pi	24Ar	2Ge	26Cn	3Vi
29	4Cn		3Vi	20Li	23Sc	7Cp	11Aq	0Ar	23Ta	2Cn	24Le	29Vi
31	2Le		29Vi		17Sg		7Pi	28Ar		0Le		25Li

	Jan	Feb	Mar	Apr	May	Jun	Jul	Aug	Sep	Oct	Nov	Dec
1	7Sc	21Sg	11Cp	25Aq	29Pi	19Ta	28Ge	21Le	13Li	17Sc	2Cp	4Aq
3	1Sg	15Cp	5Aq	21Pi	27Ar	19Ge	28Cn	20Vi	9Sc	13Sg	26Cp	28Aq
5	24Sg	9Aq	0Pi	18Ar	26Ta	19Cn	28Le	18Li	5Sg	7Cp	20Aq	22Pi
7	18Cp	4Pi	26Pi	16Ta	25Ge	18Le	26Vi	14Sc	29Sg	0Aq	14Pi	18Ar
9	12Aq	29Pi	23Ar	15Ge	24Cn	16Vi	22Li	8Sg	22Cp	24Aq	10Ar	15Ta
11	7Pi	26Ar	20Ta	14Cn	22Le	13Li	17Sc	2Cp	16Aq	19Pi	7Ta	14Ge
13	2Ar	23Ta	18Ge	12Le	19Vi	8Sc	11Sg	26Cp	11Pi	15Ar	5Ge	13Cn
15	29Ar	22Ge	17Cn	9Vi	16Li	2Sg	5Cp	20Aq	6Ar	12Ta	4Cn	13Le
17	27Ta	21Cn	15Le	6Li	11Sc	26Sg	29Cp	14Pi	2Ta	10Ge	3Le	12Vi
19	27Ge	20Le	13Vi	2Sc	6Sg	20Cp	23Aq	9Ar	29Ta	8Cn	1Vi	9Li
21	27Cn	18Vi	10Li	27Sc	29Sg	14Aq	17Pi	5Ta	27Ge	6Le	29Vi	5Sc
23	26Le	15Li	6Sc	21Sg	23Cp	8Pi	12Ar	2Ge	25Cn	4Vi	25Li	1Sg
25	24Vi	11Sc	1Sg	15Cp	17Aq	3Ar	9Ta	1Cn	24Le	2Li	21Sc	25Sg
27	21Li	5Sg	25Sg	9Aq	11Pi	29Ar	7Ge	0Le	23Vi	29Li	16Sg	19Cp
29	15Sc	29Sg	19Cp	3Pi	7Ar	28Ta	6Cn	0Vi	21Li	25Sc	11Cp	13Aq
31	9Sg		13Aq		5Ta		6Le	29Vi		20Sg		6Pi

3

Rising Signs

Part One

Background

1

The Rising Sign

The rising sign is the sign which is passing over the horizon at the time of the subject's birth. The actual point where the zodiac sign passes upwards over the horizon is called the *ascendant*. This sign has a strong modifying effect on the personality. It frequently governs the subject's outer manner and modifies his mental outlook; it explains much of his behaviour to others, especially in impersonal situations. This sign often represents the *public face* of the subject; in other words, the image which he displays to those outside his home environment. This image may be part and parcel of his normal personality or it may be a carefully constructed mask. To some extent this side of the personality is under the subject's own control, which suggests that he can adapt it to fit different circumstances at various stages of his life. However, even the *way* he seeks to change his image is strongly influenced by the rising sign. Nothing in astrology is cut and dried, there are many people who are exceptions to these rules. In some cases there may be technical reasons for someone having an apparently weak rising sign.

The ascendant represents the moment of birth, and the sign which it occupies is associated with one's earliest experiences of life. when one looks at the old and fascinating argument of whether heredity or environment is the stronger influence on a personality, the rising sign gives valuable clues to the environmental factors, whilst the arrangement of the planets and the signs in which they are placed would fill in the bulk of the genetic information. These observations have to be weighed carefully when looking at each individual person and each individual birth-chart but even so, the rising sign will throw a great deal of light on the early programming which affects a subject's manners and behaviour in various situations.

One can argue that the ascendant represents the kind of person our parents and teachers wanted us to be, while the Sun, Moon and other planets show the true self. This would account for the fact that we tend to project the ascendant when we are unsure of ourselves. The ascendant may act as a shield which hides and protects the real personality, thereby allowing us to assess any new situation before relaxing and revealing our true feelings. The opposite point to the ascendant on a birthchart is the *descendant*, and this gives an interesting insight into the kind of person to whom we are attracted.

Appearance

The sign on the ascendant frequently modifies a subject's appearance. Some people look far more like their rising sign than their Sun sign, while others are a mixture of both. However, there are people whose appearance is strongly influenced by other factors on their birthchart. Astrologers who suggest that all those who have Aries rising automatically have round faces and red hair can run into trouble. What if the subject were a Mshona tribesman from Zimbabwe? If the tribesman had a strongly Arien chart plus an Aries ascendant, he probably would have a round face and would also be small, stocky and fierce, but what chance of red hair? Appearance is therefore relative and must be considered against the background of race and family likeness.

Several years ago I read of a survey which had been carried out with 100 subjects. About 45 per cent looked like their Sun sign and about another 40 per cent resembled their rising sign while the remainder looked like either their Moon sign or the sign in which their chart ruler⊙ was placed. I'm not sure that one survey of 100 people proves much, but it is interesting all the same. It is possible that the outward projection of the rising sign is more apparent in our mannerisms and our outward behaviour than our looks. I have noticed that whenever I or any other astrologer has been daft enough to try to guess a person's Sun sign, we invariably come up with their rising sign instead.

It is always interesting to take a look at a family group to see how the signs are distributed within it. So often one finds that the Sun sign of one person becomes the rising sign of another and the Moon sign or the

---

⊙ The planet which is associated with the rising sign. Therefore, if Aries were rising the chart ruler would be Mars whilst if Virgo were rising the chart ruler would be Mercury.

mid-heaven of yet a third. It is also interesting to note the factors on the birthcharts of people whom we choose as close associates of one kind or another to see whether they are drawn to our ascendant/descendant cusps or those of our MC/IC⊙⊙

What Is A Rising Sign?

Technically speaking, the rising sign is the sign of the zodiac which is rising over the horizon at the time of birth. Less technically speaking, let us try to imagine the break of day when the Sun and the eastern horizon (the ascendant) are at the same point. By noon the Sun will be overhead and at dusk the Sun will be on the opposite side to the eastern horizon. Remember that the Earth revolves around the Sun once every 24 hours, therefore the Sun and the corresponding 'Sun sign' will be in a different position at different times of the day.

As the Earth turns all the way round once in 24 hours, the ascendant appears to travel through each one of the 12 signs of the zodiac once in each complete 24-hour day.

The ascendant is the starting point of a birthchart. It is the point where the first house begins with the other 11 houses following on around the chart. This means that the various planets will be assigned to their own particular **houses** according to the time of birth, whilst they are assigned to their various **signs** according to the **date** of birth.

Variations in influence of the ascendant on a birthchart

The rising sign is not the only modifying force in a birthchart. A grouping of planets, usually called a *stellium*, placed in one sign or house will have a strong effect. The angles between the planets which are called *aspects* will also have an influence. However, there are a couple of other factors which may cause the ascendant to be a stronger or weaker force in the chart.

⊙⊙ The abbreviation MC stands for medium coeli which is another term for the mid-heaven, which is at the top of the chart, while the term IC refers to the immum coeli or nadir which is at the bottom of the chart.

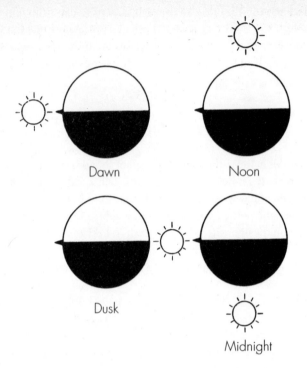

Dawn

Noon

Dusk

Midnight

Figure 1: The sun's passage in relation to the ecliptic (▲)

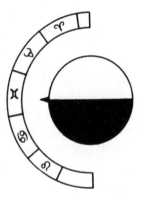

Figure 2: The signs of the zodiac rising up over the ecliptic; in this
case, the rising sign is Gemini

a) **Strong ascendants**: There are 30° in each sign, these run from 0 to 29° respectively. If the ascendant is placed towards the beginning of a sign, most of the first house will be in that same sign. If the ascendant falls late in a sign, most of the first house will fall into the next sign and thus weaken the effect of the ascendant's power.

b) **Weak Suns:** The Sun is in a weak position when it is at the bottom of the chart, near the immum coeli (also called the IC, the nadir or the cusp of the fourth house). This is because the Sun was literally far away on the other side of the Earth when the subject was born, hidden from view and weakened in influence. The seventh and twelfth houses are also somewhat weak placements for the Sun whilst an unaspected Sun would probably be overshadowed by other factors on the chart.

Signs of long and short ascension

During the course of a 24-hour day, all 12 signs of the zodiac cross the ecliptic. In the tropics they do this more or less in neat two hourly intervals but the further away one moves from the equator the more distorted this movement becomes. This means that in Great Britain, we can have up to two and three-quarter hours during which the sign of Cancer is passing upwards over the ecliptic, whereas there could be little more than half an hour for Pisces to rise. In our part of the world, it is far easier to find people who have the longer ascension signs of Cancer and Leo rising than the shorter ascension signs of Pisces or Aries. In southern hemisphere countries the situation is different but not quite the reverse. There the signs of longest ascension are Capricorn and Aquarius, while the shorter signs are Virgo and Libra.

Do we grow out of our rising sign?

There is a popular theory that many people are far more like their Moon sign or their rising sign during the first 30 years of their lives, becoming more like their Sun sign later on. Another theory is that the progression of the ascendant from one sign to the next weakens the influence and allows the subject to grow and change. These are both worthwhile theories but like everything else in astrology, they have to be looked at against the birthchart as a whole and used alongside the application of both common sense and intuition.

2

How to Find Your Ascendant

The easy way out

If you are completely turned off by the thought of any kind of chart calculation then do not despair. Most astrologers will be happy to supply you with a chart and a list of your planetary positions including your ascendant, descendant, mid-heaven and nadir. As long as you only require the figure work to be done and do not ask to have a chart interpreted as well, the fee should be minimal. Many astrologers these days use computers in order to remove the chore of calculating and they would be quite happy to run the figures off for you.

A quick way to find your ascendant for yourself

This method will work for births in the United Kingdom and for those in countries which are nearby, such as France and the Low Countries. Remember that the nearer the subject is born to Greenwich, the greater the accuracy of the method.

a) Look at Figure 3 (page 445) to see whether British Summer Time or Double Summer Time were operating when you were born.
b) Take a look at the table of figures on pages 446-449. Find your date of birth in the list on the left.
c) Look along the lines to find your exact time of birth. The zodiac sign at the top of the column will be your rising sign.

Figure 3: British Summer Times

Changing at 2 a.m., GMT

1916	21 May	–	1 Oct.	*1947	16 Mar.	–	2 Nov.
1917	8 Apr.	–	17 Sep.	1948	14 Mar.	–	31 Oct.
1918	24 Mar.	–	30 Sep.	1949	3 Apr.	–	30 Oct.
1919	30 Mar.	–	29 Sep.	1950	16 Apr.	–	22 Oct.
1920	28 Mar.	–	25 Oct.	1951	15 Apr.	–	21 Oct.
1921	3 Apr.	–	3 Oct.	1952	20 Apr.	–	26 Oct.
1922	26 Mar.	–	8 Oct.	1953	19 Apr.	–	4 Oct.
1923	22 Apr.	–	16 Sep.	1954	11 Apr.	–	3 Oct.
1924	13 Apr.	–	21 Sep.	1955	17 Apr.	–	2 Oct.
1925	19 Apr.	–	4 Oct.	1956	22 Apr.	–	7 Oct.
1926	18 Apr.	–	3 Oct.	1957	14 Apr.	–	6 Oct.
1927	10 Apr.	–	2 Oct.	1958	20 Apr.	–	5 Oct.
1928	22 Apr.	–	7 Oct.	1959	19 Apr.	–	4 Oct.
1929	21 Apr.	–	6 Oct.	1960	10 Apr.	–	2 Oct.
1930	13 Apr.	–	5 Oct.	1961	26 Mar.	–	29 Oct.
1931	19 Apr.	–	4 Oct.	1962	25 Mar.	–	28 Oct.
1932	17 Apr.	–	2 Oct.	1963	31 Mar.	–	27 Oct.
1933	9 Apr.	–	8 Oct.	1964	22 Mar.	–	25 Oct.
1934	22 Apr.	–	7 Oct.	1965	21 Mar.	–	24 Oct.
1935	14 Apr.	–	6 Oct.	1966	20 Mar.	–	23 Oct.
1936	19 Apr.	–	4 Oct.	1967	19 Mar.	–	29 Oct.
1937	18 Apr.	–	3 Oct.	1968	from 18 Feb.		
1938	10 Apr.	–	2 Oct.			to 31 Oct. 1971	
1939	16 Apr.	–	2 Oct.	1972	19 Mar.	–	29 Oct.
1940	25 Feb.	–	31 Dec.	1973	18 Mar.	–	28 Oct.
*1941	1 Jan.	–	31 Dec.	1974	17 Mar.	–	27 Oct.

*1942 1 Jan. – 31 Dec. Thereafter, from 2 a.m. GMT on
*1943 1 Jan. – 31 Dec. the day following the third
*1944 1 Jan – 31 Dec. Saturday in March until 2 a.m.
*1945 1 Jan. – 31 Dec. GMT on the day following the
1946 14 Apr. – 6 Oct. fourth Sunday in October.

* Double Summer Time

1941	5 Apr.	–	10 Aug.	1944	2 Apr.	–	17 Sept.
1942	5 Apr.	–	9 Aug.	1945	2 Apr.	–	15 Jul.
1943	4 Apr.	–	15 Aug.	1947	13 Apr.	–	10 Aug.

Figure 4: Ascendant table

Birthdate		Aries	Taurus	Gemini
ARIES	21 to 31 Mar.	5.30am to 6.29am	6.30am to 7.44am	7.45am to 9.29am
	1 to 10 Apr.	5am to 5.59am	6am to 7.14am	7.15am to 8.59am
	11 to 20 Apr.	4.15am to 5.14am	5.15am to 6.29am	6.30am to 8.14am
TAURUS	21 to 30 Apr.	3.30am to 4.29am	4.30am to 5.44am	5.45am to 7.29am
	1 to 10 May	3am to 3.59am	4am to 5.14am	5.15am to 6.59am
	11 to 21 May	2.30am to 3.29am	3.30am to 4.44am	4.45am to 6.29am
GEMINI	22 to 31 May	2am to 2.59am	3am to 4.14am	4.15am to 5.59am
	1 to 10 Jun	1.30am to 2.29am	2.30am to 3.44am	3.45am to 5.29am
	11 to 12 Jun	12.45am to 1.44am	1.45am to 2.59am	3am to 4.44am
CANCER	22 to 30 Jun.	12am to 12.59am	1am to 2.14am	2.15am to 3.59am
	1 to 11 Jul.	11.30pm to 12.29am	12.30am to 1.44am	1.45am to 3.29am
	12 to 22 Jul.	11pm to 11.59pm	12am to 1.14am	1.15am to 2.59am
LEO	23 to 31 Jul.	9.45pm to 10.44pm	10.45pm to 11.59pm	12am to 1.44am
	1 to 11 Aug.	9.15pm to 10.14pm	10.15pm to 11.29pm	11.30pm to 1.14am
	12 to 23 Aug.	8.30pm to 9.29pm	9.30pm to 10.44pm	10.45pm to 12.29am
VIRGO	24 to 31 Aug.	7.30pm to 8.29pm	8.30pm to 9.44pm	9.45pm to 11.29pm
	1 to 11 Sep.	7pm to 7.59pm	8pm to 9.14pm	9.15pm to 10.59pm
	12 to 22 Sep.	6.15pm to 7.14pm	7.15pm to 8.29pm	8.30pm to 10.14pm
LIBRA	23 to 30 Sep.	5.30pm to 6.29pm	6.30pm to 9.44pm	9.45pm to 11.29pm
	1 to 11 Oct.	5pm to 5.59pm	6pm to 7.14pm	7.15pm to 8.59pm
	12 to 23 Oct.	4.15pm to 5.14pm	5.15pm to 6.29pm	6.30pm to 8.14pm
SCORPIO	24 to 31 Oct.	3.30pm to 4.29pm	4.30pm to 5.44pm	5.45pm to 7.29pm
	1 to 11 Nov.	2.45pm to 3.44pm	3.45pm to 4.59pm	5pm to 6.44pm
	12 to 22 Nov.	2.15pm to 3.14pm	3.15pm to 4.29pm	4.30pm to 6.14pm
SAGITTARIUS	23 to 30 Nov.	1.30pm to 2.29pm	2.30pm to 3.44pm	3.45pm to 5.29pm
	1 to 11 Dec.	12.45pm to 1.44pm	1.45pm to 2.59pm	3pm to 4.44pm
	12 to 21 Dec.	12.15pm to 1.14pm	1.15pm to 2.29pm	2.30pm to 4.14pm
CAPRICORN	22 to 31 Dec.	11.15am to 12.14pm	12.15pm to 1.29pm	1.30pm to 3.14pm
	1 to 11 Jan.	10.45am to 11.44am	11.45am to 12.59pm	1pm to 2.44pm
	12 to 20 Jan.	10.15am to 11.14am	11.15am to 12.29pm	12.30pm to 2.14pm
AQUARIUS	21 to 31 Jan.	9.30am to 10.29am	10.30am to 11.44am	11.45am to 1.29pm
	1 to 10 Feb.	9am to 9.59am	10am to 11.14am	11.15am to 12.59pm
	11 to 18 Feb.	8.15am to 9.14am	9.15am to 10.29am	10.30am to 12.14pm
PISCES	19 to end Feb.	7.30am to 8.29am	8.30am to 9.44am	9.45am to 11.29am
	1 to 10 Mar.	7.15am to 8.14am	8.15am to 9.29am	9.30am to 11.14am
	11 to 20 Mar.	6.30am to 7.29am	7.30am to 8.44am	8.45am to 10.29am

Birthdate		Cancer	Leo	Virgo
ARIES	21 to 31 Mar.	9.30am to 11.59am	12pm to 2.44pm	2.45pm to 5.29pm
	1 to 10 Apr.	9am to 11.29am	11.30am to 2.14pm	2.15pm to 4.59pm
	11 to 20 Apr.	8.15am to 10.44am	10.45am to 1.29pm	1.30pm to 4.14pm
TAURUS	21 to 30 Apr.	7.30am to 9.59am	10am to 12.44pm	12.45pm to 3.29pm
	1 to 10 May	7am to 9.29am	9.30am to 12.14pm	12.15pm to 2.59pm
	11 to 21 May	6.30am to 8.59am	9am to 11.44am	11.45am to 2.29pm
GEMINI	22 to 31 May	6am to 8.29am	8.30am to 11.14am	11.15am to 1.59pm
	1 to 10 Jun	5.30am to 7.59am	8am to 10.44am	10.45am to 1.29pm
	11 to 12 Jun	4.45am to 7.14am	7.15am to 9.59am	10am to 12.44pm
CANCER	22 to 30 Jun.	4am to 6.29am	6.30am to 9.14am	9.15am to 11.59am
	1 to 11 Jul.	3.30am to 5.59am	6am to 8.44am	8.45am to 11.59am
	12 to 22 Jul.	3am to 5.29am	5.30am to 8.14am	8.15am to 10.59am
LEO	23 to 31 Jul.	1.45am to 4.14am	4.15am to 6.59am	7am to 9.44am
	1 to 11 Aug.	1.15am to 3.44am	3.45am to 6.29am	6.30am to 9.14am
	12 to 23 Aug.	12.30am to 2.59am	3am to 5.44am	5.45am to 8.29am
VIRGO	24 to 31 Aug.	11.30pm to 1.59am	2am to 4.44am	4.45am to 7.29am
	1 to 11 Sep.	11pm to 1.29am	1.30am to 4.14am	4.15am to 6.59am
	12 to 22 Sep.	10.15pm to 12.44am	12.45am to 3.29am	3.30am to 6.14am
LIBRA	23 to 30 Sep.	9.30pm to 11.59pm	12am to 2.44am	2.45pm to 5.29pm
	1 to 11 Oct.	9pm to 11.29pm	11.30pm to 2.14am	2.15pm to 4.59pm
	12 to 23 Oct.	8.15pm to 10.44pm	10.45pm to 1.29am	1.30pm to 4.14pm
SCORPIO	24 to 31 Oct.	7.30pm to 9.59pm	10pm to 12.44am	12.45am to 3.29am
	1 to 11 Nov.	6.45pm to 9.14pm	9.15pm to 11.59pm	12am to 2.44am
	12 to 22 Nov.	6.15pm to 8.44pm	8.45pm to 11.29pm	11.30pm to 2.14am
SAGITTARIUS	23 to 30 Nov.	5.30pm to 7.59pm	8pm to 10.44pm	10.45pm to 1.29am
	1 to 11 Dec.	4.45pm to 7.14pm	7.15pm to 9.59pm	10pm to 12.44am
	12 to 21 Dec.	4.15pm to 6.44pm	6.45pm to 9.29pm	9.30pm to 12.14am
CAPRICORN	22 to 31 Dec.	3.15pm to 5.44pm	5.45pm to 8.29pm	8.30pm to 11.14pm
	1 to 11 Jan.	2.45pm to 5.14pm	5.15pm to 7.59pm	8pm to 10.44pm
	12 to 20 Jan.	2.15pm to 4.44pm	4.45pm to 7.29pm	7.30pm to 10.14pm
AQUARIUS	21 to 31 Jan.	1.30pm to 3.59pm	4pm to 6.44pm	6.45pm to 9.29pm
	1 to 10 Feb.	1pm to 3.29pm	3.30pm to 6.14pm	6.15pm to 8.59pm
	11 to 18 Feb.	12.15pm to 2.44pm	2.45pm to 5.29pm	5.30pm to 8.14pm
PISCES	19 to end Feb.	11.30am to 1.59pm	2pm to 4.44pm	4.45pm to 7.29pm
	1 to 10 Mar.	11.15am to 1.44pm	1.45pm to 4.29pm	4.30pm to 7.14pm
	11 to 20 Mar.	10.30am to 12.59pm	1pm to 3.44pm	3.45pm to 6.29pm

Birthdate		Libra	Scorpio	Sagittarius
ARIES	21 to 31 Mar.	5.30pm to 8.14pm	8.15pm to 10.59pm	11pm to 1.29am
	1 to 10 Apr.	5pm to 7.44pm	7.45pm to 10.29pm	10.30pm to 12.59am
	11 to 20 Apr.	4.15pm to 6.59pm	7pm to 9.44pm	9.45pm to 12.14am
TAURUS	21 to 30 Apr.	3.30pm to 6.14pm	6.15pm to 8.59pm	9pm to 11.29pm
	1 to 10 May	3pm to 5.44pm	5.45pm to 8.290pm	8.30pm to 10.59pm
	11 to 21 May	2.30pm to 5.14pm	5.15pm to 7.59pm	8pm to 10.29pm
GEMINI	22 to 31 May	2pm to 4.44pm	4.45pm to 7.29pm	7.30pm to 9.59pm
	1 to 10 Jun	1.30pm to 4.14pm	4.15pm to 6.59pm	7pm to 9.29pm
	11 to 12 Jun	12.45pm to 3.29pm	3.30pm to 6.14pm	6.15pm to 8.44pm
CANCER	22 to 30 Jun.	12pm to 2.44pm	2.45pm to 5.29pm	5.30pm to 7.59pm
	1 to 11 Jul.	11.30am to 2.14pm	2.15pm to 4.59pm	5pm to 7.29pm
	12 to 22 Jul.	11am to 1.44pm	1.45pm to 4.29pm	4.30pm to 6.59pm
LEO	23 to 31 Jul.	9.45am to 12.29pm	12.30pm to 3.14pm	3.15pm to 5.44pm
	1 to 11 Aug.	9.15am to 11.59am	12pm to 2.44pm	2.45pm to 5.14pm
	12 to 23 Aug.	8.30am to 11.14am	11.15am to 1.59pm	2pm to 4.29pm
VIRGO	24 to 31 Aug.	7.30am to 10.14am	10.15am to 12.59pm	1pm to 3.29pm
	1 to 11 Sep.	7am to 9.44am	9.45am to 12.29pm	12.30pm to 2.59pm
	12 to 22 Sep.	6.15am to 8.59am	9am to 11.14am	11.45am to 2.14pm
LIBRA	23 to 30 Sep.	5.10am to 8.14am	8.15am to 10.59am	11am to 1.29pm
	1 to 11 Oct.	5am to 7.44am	7.45am to 10.29am	10.30am to 12.59pm
	12 to 23 Oct.	4.15am to 6.59am	7am to 9.44am	9.45am to 12.14pm
SCORPIO	24 to 31 Oct.	3.30am to 6.14am	6.15am to 8.59am	9am to 11.29am
	1 to 11 Nov.	2.45am to 5.29am	5.30am to 8.14am	8.15am to 10.44am
	12 to 22 Nov.	2.15am to 4.59am	5am to 7.44am	7.45am to 10.14am
SAGITTARIUS	23 to 30 Nov.	1.30am to 4.14am	4.15am to 6.59am	7am to 9.29am
	1 to 11 Dec.	12.45am to 3.29am	3.30am to 6.14am	6.15am to 8.44am
	12 to 21 Dec.	12.15am to 2.59am	3am to 5.44am	5.45am to 8.14am
CAPRICORN	22 to 31 Dec.	11.15pm to 1.59am	2am to 4.44am	4.45am to 7.14am
	1 to 11 Jan.	10.45pm to 1.29am	1.30am to 4.14am	4.15am to 6.44am
	12 to 20 Jan.	10.15pm to 12.59am	1am to 3.44am	5.45am to 6.14am
AQUARIUS	21 to 31 Jan.	9.30pm to 12.14am	12.15am to 2.59am	3am to 5.29am
	1 to 10 Feb.	9pm to 11.44pm	11.45pm to 2.29am	2.30am to 4.59am
	11 to 18 Feb.	8.15pm to 10.59pm	11pm to 1.44am	1.45am to 4.14am
PISCES	19 to end Feb.	7.30pm to 10.14pm	10.15pm to 12.59am	1am to 3.29am
	1 to 10 Mar.	7.15pm to 9.59pm	10pm to 12.44am	12.45am to 3.14am
	11 to 20 Mar.	6.30pm to 9.14pm	9.15pm to 11.59pm	12am to 2.29am

Birthdate			Capricorn	Aquarius	Pisces
ARIES	21 to 31 Mar.		1.30am to 3.14am	3.15am to 4.29am	4.30am to 5.29am
	1 to 10 Apr.		1am to 2.44am	2.45am to 3.59am	4am to 4.59am
	11 to 20 Apr.		12.15am to 1.59am	2am to 3.14am	3.15am to 4.14am
TAURUS	21 to 30 Apr.		11.30pm to 1.14am	1.15am to 2.29am	2.30am to 3.29am
	1 to 10 May		11pm to 12.44am	12.45am to 1.59am	2am to 2.59am
	11 to 21 May		10.30pm to 12.14am	12.15am to 1.29am	1.30am to 2.29am
GEMINI	22 to 31 May		10pm to 11.44pm	11.45pm to 12.59am	1am to 1.59am
	1 to 10 Jun		9.30pm to 11.14pm	11.15pm to 12.29am	12.30am to 1.29am
	11 to 12 Jun		8.45pm to 10.29pm	10.30pm to 11.44pm	11.45pm to 12.44am
CANCER	22 to 30 Jun.		8pm to 9.44pm	9.45pm to 10.59pm	11pm to 11.59pm
	1 to 11 Jul.		7.30pm to 9.14pm	9.15pm to 10.29pm	10.30pm to 11.29pm
	12 to 22 Jul.		7pm to 8.44pm	8.45pm to 9.59pm	10pm to 10.59pm
LEO	23 to 31 Jul.		5.45pm to 7.29pm	7.30pm to 8.44pm	8.45pm to 9.44pm
	1 to 11 Aug.		5.15pm to 6.59pm	7pm to 8.14pm	8.15pm to 9.14pm
	12 to 23 Aug.		4.30pm to 6.14pm	6.15pm to 7.29pm	7.30pm to 8.29pm
VIRGO	24 to 31 Aug.		3.30pm to 5.14pm	5.15pm to 6.29pm	6.30pm to 7.29pm
	1 to 11 Sep.		3pm to 4.44pm	4.45pm to 5.59pm	6pm to 6.59pm
	12 to 22 Sep.		2.15pm to 3.59pm	4pm to 5.14pm	5.15pm to 6.14pm
LIBRA	23 to 30 Sep.		1.30pm to 3.14pm	3.15pm to 4.29pm	4.30pm to 5.29pm
	1 to 11 Oct.		1pm to 2.44pm	2.45pm to 3.59pm	4pm to 4.59pm
	12 to 23 Oct.		12.15pm to 1.59pm	2pm to 3.14pm	3.15pm to 4.14pm
SCORPIO	24 to 31 Oct.		11.30am to 1.14pm	1.15pm to 2.29pm	2.30pm to 3.29pm
	1 to 11 Nov.		10.45am to 12.29pm	12.30pm to 1.44pm	1.45pm to 2.44pm
	12 to 22 Nov.		10.15am to 11.59am	12pm to 1.14pm	1.15pm to 2.14pm
SAGITTARIUS	23 to 30 Nov.		9.30am to 11.14am	11.15am to 12.29pm	12.30pm to 1.29pm
	1 to 11 Dec.		8.45am to 10.29am	10.30am to 11.44am	11.45am to 12.44pm
	12 to 21 Dec.		8.15am to 9.59am	10am to 11.14am	11.15am to 12.14pm
CAPRICORN	22 to 31 Dec.		7.15am to 8.59am	9am to 10.14am	10.15am to 11.14am
	1 to 11 Jan.		6.45am to 8.29am	8.30am to 9.44am	9.45am to 10.44am
	12 to 20 Jan.		6.15am to 7.59am	8am to 9.14am	9.15am to 10.14am
AQUARIUS	21 to 31 Jan.		5.30am to 7.14am	7.15am to 8.29am	8.30am to 9.29am
	1 to 10 Feb.		5am to 6.44am	6.45am to 7.59am	8am to 8.59am
	11 to 18 Feb.		4.15am to 5.59am	6am to 7.14am	7.15am to 8.14am
PISCES	19 to end Feb.		3.30am to 5.14am	5.15am to 6.29am	6.30am to 7.29am
	1 to 10 Mar.		3.15am to 4.59am	5am to 6.14am	6.15am to 7.14am
	11 to 20 Mar.		2.30am to 4.14am	4.15am to 5.29am	5.30am to 6.29am

Here is an example using this method:

Stuart Fenton was born at 8.35 p.m. BST on 31 July 1968. Deduct one hour to make the revised birth time 7.35 p.m. GMT 31 July is in the first (uppermost) section of the three Leo dates. The last but one column shows a birth time of 7.30 p.m. to 8.44 p.m. The column is headed 'Aquarius', therefore Stuart has the sign of Aquarius on the ascendant. Furthermore, we can see that he only just comes inside the limits of this birth time which gives him an early degree of Aquarius rising. An accurate computer reading which took into account the exact place of birth as well as the time of birth confirmed that Stuart's actual ascendant is 5° Aquarius.

Quick method for births elsewhere in the northern hemisphere

This quick method becomes less accurate the further away from Greenwich the birth occurs, so I do suggest that you take your data to an astrologer. However, in the meantime, you can adjust the time of birth as follows:

GMT (used throughout all astrology books)	0 hours
Eastern standard time 75° west	add 5 hours
Central standard time 90° west	add 6 hours
Mountain standard time 105° west	add 7 hours
Pacific standard time 120° west	add 8 hours
Yukon standard time 135° west	add 9 hours
Alaska/Hawaii standard time 150° west	add 10 hours
Bering time 165° west	add 11 hours

For births in the eastern hemisphere, reverse the procedure and *deduct* hours as required.

This method is too generalized for the southern hemisphere.

Home computer calculations

If you own a personal computer and don't mind spending a bit of money on an astrological programme, you can contact one of the software houses which advertise in astrological magazines. A simple programme which will give you enough information to make up natal and progressed charts will actually cost less than visiting an astrologer and having a full chart interpretation!

Calculating your ascendant by hand

It is worth noting here that astrology is a creative and interpretive skill which suits the slightly arty or linguistic type of person, therefore the person who makes a good natural astrologer is usually a poor mathematician. I am an absolute dunce where maths are concerned, yet I can calculate an ascendant, which goes to show that anyone can.

Here is an example of someone who was born in London (Great Britain) at 02.18 (2.18 a.m.) on the 21 August 1965. The subject's name is Helen. (NB: I have used a *midnight* ephemeris for these calculations.)

1. As Helen was born in London, there is no need to make any adjustment for place of birth. Astrological calculations are based on the proximity of the birth to the Greenwich meridian.

	02.18.00
	1.00.00 −
	01.18.00

2. An August birth means that British Summer Time was in operation, therefore deduct one hour making the birth time 01.18 GMT

   21.56.25

3. The sidereal time (exact star time rather than calendar time) at midnight on 21 August was 21 hours 56 minutes 25 seconds.

   21.56.25

4. Add the time of birth to the sidereal time. Remember that when adding there are 60 seconds to a minute and 60 minutes to an hour.

	1.18.00+
	23.14.25

5. Now you will have to make an extra calculation which is called 'interval time'. This means that you add 10 seconds for every hour, 5 for every half hour or 3 for every 20 minutes. If you forget this, the chart will be slightly inaccurate but not by so much that the actual rising sign will be changed.

	23.14.25
	13+
	23.14.38

6. Now look up the resulting figures in an ephemeris (book of ascendants and planetary positions).

   23.14.38

7. In Helen's case, when we look in the ephemeris, we can see that her figure of 23hrs 14mins 38secs falls between 23.12.10 which comes out as 17° 37′ of Cancer and 23.15.52 which comes out as 18° 20′ of Cancer. For most purposes the round figure of 18° of Cancer which falls between the two will be quite good enough.

	23.12.10
	=13°37′
	23.15.52
	=18°20′
	***23.14.38
	=Approx. 18°

In order to double check this I ran the co-ordinates through my computer, even taking account of the fact that Helen's actual place of birth was 11 minutes of a degree to the west of Greenwich. The computer gave an exact reading of 17° 57' of Cancer. As there are 60 minutes in every degree, the figure of 17° 57' is as near as dammit 18° Cancer.

This kind of calculation will do for births in the southern part of Great Britain. For births in the north, follow exactly the same procedure but look at the figures for Liverpool rather than for London in a table of houses or in your ephemeris.

The nit-picker's guide to a fully calculated ascendant

Example: James Smith. Born in New York City at 2.15 p.m. (14.15) on 10 January 1968.

1. Check that the date is correct because Americans sometimes reverse the day and the month so that 10.7.68 could be 7 October 1968!
2. Check for daylight saving. If you are going to do much of this kind of work, you will need a couple of books which are called *Time Changes in the World* and *Time Changes in the USA*. These can be obtained from specialist dealers.
3. Look up the map reference for New York City.

Revision section

Date: 10.7.68
Daylight saving: Yes, one hour.
Map Refs: 40°45' North, 74°0' West.

Calculations

1. Note down the birth time in hours, minutes and seconds	14.15.00
2. Deduct 1 hour for daylight saving.	14.15.00 1.00.00 − _____ 13.15.00

3. Convert the local mean time to GMT. New York uses a time zone which is 5 hours behind Greenwich, therefore add 5 hours.	13.15.00 5.00.00+ ——— 18.15.00
4. Look up the sidereal time in a midnight ephemeris for midnight (00.00) on 10.7.68	19.11.55 ———
5. Add the birth time to the sidereal time.	19.11.55 18.15.00+ ——— 37.26.55
6. Add 10 seconds for every hour which has been added, also 5 seconds for every half hour.	37.26.55 3.02+ ——— 37.29.57
7. Deduct the exact longitude from the new time. New York is 74° west of Greenwich, therefore the exact difference is 4 hours 56 minutes. This is based on 4 minutes for every degree of longitude.	37.29.57 4.56.00 – ——— 32.33.57
8. The tables of hours are based on figures from 0 to 24 hours. Our sample figure is more than 24 hours; therefore we must deduct 24 hours and look up the resulting figure in the tables.	32.33.57 24.00.00 – ——— 8.33.57
9. A book called *Raphael's Tables of Houses for Northern Latitudes* (or something which does the same thing) will be needed for this part of the calculation.	

In my Raphael's Tables, the nearest figure to our result of 8.33.57 is 8.33.35. This few seconds difference is negligible, therefore we may safely conclude that James has an ascendant of 0°20' Scorpio and a mid-heaven of 6° Leo.

Further complications

If James had been born at exactly the same map references but *south* of the equator, he would have first seen the light of day at a place in Chile called the Archipelago de los Chonos. If that were the case, we would have to work out the calculations up to the end of step 8 and then *add* 12 hours. After looking up the ascendant and mid-heaven, we would then need to *reverse* the resulting ascendant and mid-heaven to give us the new southern latitude ascendant of 28°46' Scorpio and a mid-heaven of 6° Leo.

All professional astrologers are familiar with this routine and, when exactitude is required, they will also fine tune the map references and correctly locate the planets for time of birth by means of logarithms. Computers reduce what was once a day's work calculating a chart into the work of a few minutes and they do it with perfect accuracy. But even when using a computer, remember to adjust the time differential – e.g. deduct any daylight saving and add or subtract to bring the time to GMT.

How the Signs of the Zodiac are Arranged

The signs of the zodiac are always listed in the following order.

1. Aries	7. Libra
2. Taurus	8. Scorpio
3. Gemini	9. Sagittarius
4. Cancer	10. Capricorn
5. Leo	11. Aquarius
6. Virgo	12. Pisces

The signs with odd numbers (Aries, Gemini, Leo, Libra, Sagittarius and Aquarius) are masculine/positive in character. This suggests extroversion, confidence and assertiveness, and the ability to solve problems with courage and enterprise. The even numbered signs (Taurus, Cancer, Virgo, Scorpio, Capricorn and Pisces) are feminine/negative in character. These suggest introversion, shyness and passivity, the ability to nurture, conserve and to solve problems by intuitive means.

The signs are grouped into ancient elements of fire, earth, air and water:

The fire signs are Aries, Leo and Sagittarius.
The earth signs are Taurus, Virgo and Capricorn.
The air signs are Gemini, Libra and Aquarius.
The water signs are Cancer, Scorpio and Pisces.

The signs are also grouped into the ancient qualities of cardinal, fixed and mutable:

The cardinal signs are Aries, Cancer, Libra and Capricorn. The fixed signs are Taurus, Leo, Scorpio and Aquarius.

The mutable signs are Gemini, Virgo, Sagittarius and Pisces.

The fire signs – Aries, Leo, Sagittarius

The key ideas here are of energy, enthusiasm and optimism. These people need to be in the centre of whatever is going on, thoroughly involved and even directing. Fire people take the initiative and throw their enthusiasm, intuition and faith behind any enterprise. They never quite relinquish their childhood and are therefore very much in tune with young people and young ideas.

Fire people are egotistic, headstrong and sometimes arrogant but they are also generous, warm-hearted and spontaneously kind, preferring to help others wherever possible than to take advantage of them. Fire people get things started; they create activity but need a back-up team to fill in the details for them. These people are quick to grasp an idea and tackle it with gusto, treating life like a kind of game, complete with the sportsman's sense of fair play. They find it impossible to save for a rainy day but will invariably find a way to earn money when in trouble. Oddly enough fire people are often very materialistic, measuring their self-worth by their ability to accumulate money and possessions and by having an expensive lifestyle. These people are quick to anger but rarely sulk.

Fire rising

When a fire sign is on the ascendant, the outer manner is friendly, uncritical and non-hostile which makes these people good mixers and excellent public relations executives. Aries rising gives a well-organized, slightly military bearing which makes them fit well into any kind of para-military or civil service organization. Leo rising subjects have a dignified and rather formal manner which inspires confidence, while Sagittarius risers have a cheerful, pleasant and rather witty outer manner which suits all kinds of teaching, training and public speaking situations. The typically friendly but professionally competent signals which fire rising subjects send out draws a friendly and often rather respectful response from others.

The earth signs – Taurus, Virgo, Capricorn

The key ideas here are of practicality and security. Earth is concerned with structure and slow growth and also conventional behaviour and concrete results. This element is connected with physical things which can be touched and held and which perform a function. Earth people are sensible, they take their time over everything and tend to finish every task which they start. They are shrewd and careful, usually very good at figure work and also surprisingly dexterous so they don't often drop or break anything.

Earth people hate to waste anything and they are careful with their money. However they are invariably generous to their own families. They need a secure home and a solid financial base; requirements which make them appear materialistic to others. Earthy types like to socialize among small groups of familiar people who appreciate their intelligence and dry sense of humour. They may lack spontaneity and can be too cautious and fussy at times but they are reliable and capable. It takes time to get to know these individuals as they prefer to hang back in social situations, while in business situations they behave in a rather formal manner. Earth people are suspicious of the motives of others and are extra sensitive to hurt. They are slow to fall in love but when they do, they will remain loyal and faithful to their partner in the majority of cases.

Earth rising

When an earth sign is on the ascendant the outer manner is shy, serious and cautious. Taurus risers are the most sociable of the three and are often musical or artistic. Virgo risers look for mental stimulation in others while Capricorn risers enjoy both work and social pursuits. People with these signs on the ascendant send out signals which are pleasant and tactful suggesting they they prefer to form part of a team – at least to begin with – than to push themselves immediately to the front.

The air signs – Gemini, Libra, Aquarius

The key idea here is of communication. Air people are concerned with ideas and theories of all kinds including education, networks and news. They seek answers to questions and then go on to enlighten other people. The network of their nervous system is always on the alert and sometimes over-stretched. These people may be serious-minded intellectuals who are highly involved with the education system or the media, or they may be chirpy happy-go-lucky types who pick up their street-wise knowledge from the tabloid newspapers and the local pub. They can be found arguing, exploring ideas and becoming excited by means and methods which can apply to anything from the way the universe was formed to a recent football game. They make good journalists, shopkeepers, teachers and travellers because they are always up-to-date.

Although kind hearted and genuinely concerned with humanity, they can forget their many friends when they are out of sight. They cannot deal with emotional dependency on the part of others, as this drains them, leaving them exhausted and irritable. Air rising subjects love gadgets, especially those which help them communicate or travel, such as computers, fancy telephones and a good fast car.

Air rising

When an air sign is on the ascendant the subject is friendly and sociable but also independent and somewhat detached. The Gemini riser is constantly busy, fully engaged in a kind of juggling act with at least a dozen balls being kept in the air by some kind of mental sleight of hand. The Libra riser occupies himself with business schemes which often need the aid of a more earthy partner to make them come into fruition. The Aquarian riser makes wonderful plans for himself and for others and may even carry some of them out. Air risers can sometimes appear arrogant and offensive if threatened or caught off guard but they will rush to the aid of anyone who is genuinely in need. They send out rather superior, macho or businesslike signals which command the respect of others.

The water signs – Cancer, Scorpio, Pisces

The key ideas here are of emotion, intuition and feeling. These people may spend their lives helping others or at least involving themselves in human problems. They are attached to the kind of matters which bring beginnings, endings and transformations to the lives of others. Watery people respond slowly when asked a question and may appear slow to grasp a new concept but this is deceptive because they are filtering the ideas through their layers of intuition before accepting them. Being slow to change, they prefer familiar surroundings and the closeness of family and friends.

Water people are often quite tense and can worry themselves into illness. They need a lot of understanding as their moods and emotions make them changeable and unfathomable at times. They are the kindest of friends, often giving practical and sensible help when it is needed but they cannot take too much neurotic dependence from others. These people are hypersensitive, creative and often psychic. They can appear withdrawn and distant in some cases but they desperately need stable relationships with plenty of love and affection.

Water rising

When a water sign is on the ascendant the subject will hide his true feelings. He fears the world around him and feels a strong need to protect himself and also, in some cases, to protect the helpless. What you see is definitely *not* what you get with these people. Cancerians appear chatty and helpful and they do well in any situation which requires tact. Scorpio risers use many different forms of camouflage, one of their favourites being offensiveness and an off-putting manner. It is always worth being patient with such people because there is often a reason for their difficult attitude and the reward is usually worth the effort. Pisces risers appear soft, gentle, self-sacrificing and sometimes even helpless but don't be taken in, they will fight strongly and sometimes underhandedly for what they think is right. The signals which these types give out are consciously or subconsciously chosen for their effect, making them appear fierce, friendly, peaceful or docile depending upon their choice of mask.

Cardinal

Cardinal people cannot be held under anyone's thumb, they need to take charge of their own world. Their energies may be directed towards themselves, their homes and families or to the wider world of work and politics. The cardinal signs, being on the angles of a birthchart, provide the energy and initiative to get things moving.

Fixed

Fixed people have the strength and endurance to see things through and to uphold the status quo. They rarely change their homes, careers or partnerships, preferring to live with an existing situation rather than face uncertainty. Fixed people are loyal and dependable but also very obstinate. They project an image of strength which is an effective shield for their considerable vulnerability.

Mutable

These people can adapt to the prevailing circumstances at any given time while, at the same time, managing to alter a situation to suit themselves.

Mutable people can steer projects through periods of transition as well as, when necessary, bringing things to a conclusion. Although gentle and likable, mutable people can be quite ruthless when the need arises.

Part Two

Rising Sign-by-Sign

4

Aries Rising

The whole art of war consists of getting at what is on the other side of the hill.

Arthur Wellesley, 1st Duke of Wellington

A few words of explanation

A sign on the ascendant expresses itself in a different way from a Sun sign. However, some of the characteristics, if only the childhood experiences, will apply if you have the Sun in Aries or in the first house. They may be present if you have Mars in Aries or in the first house; if your Moon is in Aries your emotions and reactions will have an Arian flavour. If the ascendant is weak (see Chapter 1), the Aries overlay will not be so noticeable. If the rest of the birthchart is very different from the rising sign, there could be a conflict in the personality. This is because the outer manner, as displayed by the signals which are given out on first meeting the subject, is different from the main character which lies underneath. However, Aries is so direct and open that this is far less likely to be the case than with some of the other ascendants. Another Possibility is that the subject rejects all that his parents, parent figures and teachers stood for, and creates a life for himself which is very different from the one which they envisaged for him, or from the one he lived through as a child.

Remember that this sign is cardinal which implies the start of anything, and also a fire sign which implies enthusiasm and impulsiveness. It is masculine/positive in its approach which suggests an outwardly extrovert nature. Aries rising is a sign of *short ascension* which means that it only applies in the northern hemisphere for a very short period of time in any day - therefore only a few British people are born each day with this sign on the ascendant.

Early experiences

If you are one of these rare creatures, the chances are that there was something missing in your childhood. Many Aries rising children are born into military families who move about from one place to another. They may also spend a part of each year at boarding school. The child experiences feelings of strangeness, dislocation and of distance from the parents. Self-reliance and some measure of self-centredness are natural for Aries risers, even if their childhood experiences don't force this upon them, and this can make it difficult for them to form successful family relationships later on.

The Aries riser may opt for a life in the services where he becomes part of a larger family-type group. Several years ago, I did a horoscope for a rather sturdy looking middle-aged lady who was coming to the end of a service career. She told me that it had been a good life full of travel and good fellowship, and that she wasn't quite sure what she was going to do with her time now that she was a civilian once more.

Aries risers who grow up in a normal, stay-at-home family often experience discord and conflict. There may be a difficult relationship between the child and his parents; this is especially true of the father/son relationship. There can't be two bosses in one family and, in this case, neither wants to concede any kind of authority to the other. It is quite usual for the two to be very different in character with little real understanding between them; it seems that neither can really approve of the other and there could be some pretty noisy disagreements.

Paul, an Aries rising guy, cut himself off from his parents as soon as he grew up and has had as little as possible to do with them ever since. Diana, another Aries rising subject, had quite a good childhood but never became close to her father. Her older sister worshipped him and couldn't see any wrong in him (at least until much later in life) whereas Diana could see him warts and all and therefore experienced a far cooler relationship with him. It is worth remembering that an Arian nature makes for a noisy, bouncy and rather bumptious child whose restless behaviour and argumentative ways can aggravate even the most saintly of parents.

In some cases, the parents are sporty and adventurous by nature encouraging a kind of gung-ho bravery in the child. This is all very well if the child is also an outdoor and- athletic type, but if he isn't the parents will write him off as an over-timid wimp. This situation is even more likely to work the other way around. One such example is Miriam who was brought up in a classically claustrophobic pre-war Jewish family where both her parents and her sister studiously avoided anything which might involve the slightest hint of danger. In addition to this, her mother coddled her younger sister. Miriam wasn't the kind to encourage coddling, being a raw-boned athletic type of child who ran up, climbed on and jumped off every-thing at the slightest opportunity. On those occasions when she found herself in real trouble, stuck up a tree, for example, her mother's reaction was to fall down in a faint. This, to Miriam's eyes, confirmed her opinion that her mother was useless and ineffective. Incidentally, Miriam is still leaping about now that she is in her eighties! Human nature being totally contrary, Miriam still feels that she was unnecessarily deprived of the love and approval of her parents.

Women who have this rising sign have a masculine outlook on life, which may lead them to experience difficulty in adapting to the traditional feminine role. This does not imply that all Aries rising women are militant feminists; on the contrary, these women get on very well with men, enjoy-ing their company and sharing their interests. Some women prefer not to marry, either living an independent life with or without boyfriends or find-ing happiness within a military career. Those who do marry and have a family need an interesting career outside the home in order to sop up their extra energy and give them something worthwhile to do. Fortunately, these days, there is plenty of scope for the extrovert, enthusiastic Aries woman to have the unrestricted independent kind of lifestyle that she needs.

It is worth remembering that the sign on the cusp of the fourth house (the IC) which is concerned with family matters is, in this case, Cancer. This makes you a surprisingly caring family member, even to the extent of being self-sacrificial in this area of your life, but more of this in the charac-teristics section later on.

When I take a look at Aries rising or even Sun in Aries subjects in reality rather than by blindly following the rules of astrology, I find a com-mon theme. Many of you come from small families who themselves have little contact with their own relatives, either because your parents moved away from the area where their own relatives lived, or because they chose to cut themselves off from them. The Arien child, therefore, doesn't have the opportunity of benefiting from a wider family group and this leaves him with only his parents' views and values to fall back on. Frequently these val-ues are distorted and lacking in common sense. Furthermore, the Arien child is often an only child, or so separated in age and type from the other siblings that he feels like an only child.

It is likely that one or both parents disliked you or saw no value in you. There was no discernible reason for this, you were simply viewed as an irritation or an inconvenience. This leads many of you to seek self-validation through marriage, often marrying young and choosing an older partner, or someone who is deemed to be wiser and more competent at the game of life. If the marriage doesn't work out, you may begin to philander. There is no guarantee that second or subsequent relationships work out either, unless you are able to go through a good deal of self-analysis and reach a stage where you can finally throw off the distorted lessons of your childhood.

Some Arians succeed in one-to-one relationships, but go on to face difficulties in relating to their children. The Arian never quite grows up enough to be able to cope with the role of parent and, therefore, either leans too far towards the position of authority and dominance, becoming a bully towards his own children, or overdoes the nurturing role by clinging to them and sacrificing on their behalf for far too long. It seems as if the 'pulling factor' at the top of the chart (Capricorn) leads to too much authority, while in other cases the 'pulling factor' at the bottom of the chart (Cancer) leads to too much clinging.

However, nothing stays the same forever; children grow up and relationships come and go. With a bit of luck you can learn from life and finally make some kind of viable relationship which brings you pleasure. Perhaps in compensation, Aries subjects often have a good friend or two, while others make a viable 'family' out of a couple of pet animals.

Basically this is neither the best nor the worst sign to have on the ascendant. There may have been loneliness in childhood but this seems to breed Arian self-reliance and doesn't usually cause you to have any difficulty in relating to others later on in life. Aries is a sociable sign and, on the whole, a cheerful and optimistic one.

Appearance

Bearing in mind racial differences, family tendencies and the influence of the rest of your birthchart, the Aries influence would suggest a shortish stature with a strong and muscular body (which may run to fat later); your arms and shoulders are strong and you can lift and carry surprisingly heavy weights for your size. Your face is broad across the eyes and maybe rounded with a rather large head for your body. Arian eyes are neither protruding nor deep set, they stare out honestly from under thick, arched eyebrows.

Aries rising women can do a lot with eye make-up as there is a rather large and flat area of eyelid to play with. The hair may be reddish in colour, quickly going grey. Men of this sign lean towards baldness – well, they do say that bald men are sexy! Women may moan about their thin and awkward hair which needs much perming and colouring in order to keep it looking good. Ariens don't, as a rule, have much body hair.

Being a palmist as well as an astrologer, I tend to notice people's hands. Arian hands are small and graceful even in those cases when they are plump. The finger-nails have a characteristic 'A' shape, being much wider at the tip than at the cuticle end. (These hands are used so elegantly that an Aries-type guy can quite mistakenly be taken as being gay!) Most Arians walk quickly and move fast, they are graceful and light on their feet which may add to their slightly feminine appearance. Don't be taken in; these guys are far from being gay – though they might be very cheerful, especially when making love to an attractive woman.

Aries women are also graceful and are often good dancers, but can have a mental outlook that is adventurously masculine. Their quick wit and ready smile, plus their somewhat childlike appearance is quite endearing to the opposite sex. To my mind, Jimmy Tarbuck has an Aries appearance, as did Mark McManus who played Taggart in the TV series of that name.

Outer manner

You present yourself in a cheerful, friendly, non-hostile manner but may find it hard to conceal your contempt for those whose minds and actions are slower than your own. Not being easily influenced, you prefer to make up your own mind about everything, and you can appear rather opinionated. Others see you as quick, clever and courageous but they may become annoyed by your tendency to push yourself to the front of every queue and to fight for the best of whatever is going. Your sense of humour and child-like appeal can help you get away with murder – especially with the opposite sex.

Aries characteristics

This section can double up as a brief guide to Aries as a Sun sign *or* as a rising sign, so it makes a handy reference if you need to check out some Sun sign characteristics as well as those for the rising sign.

If yours is a strong rising sign, you will display a fair amount of Aries behaviour. You are probably the most capable and energetic person in your family, prepared to fight for their rights, and look after their interests, against all comers. Your career is important to you, and you use your earnings in order to give the members of your family what they need. Ariens think, move and walk quickly; many enjoy speed for its own sake and cannot get by without owning a fast car. Being quick to take action and to throw your enthusiasm behind any venture, you sometimes step on the toes of slower more sensitive types. Being honest and frank, others always know where they stand with you, and on occasion you can be too honest for comfort because lies and prevarication don't come easily to you.

There is a tendency to argumentativeness; it might just be that you enjoy a stimulating debate but some of you will argue about anything. Your temper erupts quickly but usually settles down just as quickly, and thankfully, you don't sulk. Oddly enough, you prefer a rather structured life; you cannot cope with too much change except for those changes which you yourself initiate, neither can you take too much adversity. When too many pressures arise at once, your natural ebullience and confidence evaporate leaving you to fall back on other steadier members of the family for support. Some Aries rising subjects lash out when angry and either give whoever is in the way a verbal bashing or, worse still, a physical one.

There is a strange need for you to spoil yourself or to be spoiled by others. Perhaps this stems from your slightly neglected childhood. Arians love gadgetry; the current age of Japanese wizardry is just made for you. You may spend your money on expensive sports equipment which you never actually find the time or the patience to use properly. Certainly you will spend money on your hobbies whatever they may be, always making sure that you have the best equipment which can be bought. Some Arians spend money on household gadgets, abandoning them if they are found to be useless. A new car, boat, caravan or any other kind of vehicle is always an exciting buy.

You don't seek to deprive others in order to have the things you fancy, but male Arians may simply forget that their wives also need some spoiling. When you do buy something for your wife, it is something beautiful and very personal such as clothing, underwear or jewellery. Arian women love gold and jewellery, and both sexes love to have a wardrobe which is stuffed with the latest and nicest fashions.

You can be surprisingly snobbish and contemptuous of those whom you see as being inferior. You like your family to move in the right circles and for your children to become educated and accomplished in an almost Victorian manner. This seems to stem from a concealed contempt for your own background and an upwardly mobile desire to get away from all that it represented to you.

My friend and colleague, Eve Bingham, pointed out that many Ariens have a talent for self-sacrifice, especially in respect of their family. She's right. I have seen Arians running around after their elderly parents to an extent which is above and beyond the call of duty. There are others who seem to give up most of their time and money to their children. There is some method in this particular form of madness, however, because what the Arian is after is *control*. By taking charge of the situation and making himself indispensable, he keeps the people concerned in a situation where he can keep an eye upon them.

The midheaven

This section and those which follow apply *only* to Aries rising and not to Sun in Aries. The midheaven can show the subject's aims and ambitions, his attitude to work and his public standing. An Aries rising child may not show much interest in learning while he is at school but, as he reaches his teens, his desire for money and status will lead him to work hard and make achievements. He may also return to study later on in order to gain some specific qualification.

All Aries rising subjects have the sign of Capricorn on their midheaven, which suggests that you work best in a well ordered structure, perhaps in a large public service organization. Some of you prefer to run your own well-planned businesses. You are determined and capable. Your leadership qualities and common sense attitude to money can lead to great success, but this could well come rather late in life. You prefer to start something new, but if you do take over an existing position or an existing team, you soon reorganize it to reflect your own personal style. You could be drawn to the Arien careers of engineering, public service or the armed services, or to the Capricornian ones of business and banking. Red tape gets you down, and you become irritated by details. Company politics bore you, however, the world of national or local politics may be very attractive to you as a career. Your brain is excellent and, if the rest of the chart backs this up, you could find a future in the academic world.

Many Ariens seem to spend years coasting along in a job making no discernible effort to push themselves forward until circumstances demand that an effort be made. Others are far more interested in the money which the job brings in or the company politics or the social life which comes with the job, rather than taking a real interest in the job for its own sake.

Despite the fact that the MCs supposed to represent aims, ambitions etc. it can also show the type of person whom you find attractive. A Capricorn partner, or one with a strong Saturn on the chart will be in sympathy with your goals in life and could well make a very pleasant complementary person with whom to live.

The descendant

The opposite point to the ascendant is the descendant or, in other words, the cusp of the seventh house. Traditionally, this is supposed to show the kind of person to whom we are attracted. In the case of Aries rising, the descendant is in Libra and it is surprising how many people who have either Aries rising or an Arian Sun do marry Librans. If your ascendant is late in Aries, a good deal of the seventh house will lie in Scorpio, so there could be an attraction to Scorpio types too. To be honest, I don't think that either Aries/Libra or Aries/Scorpio make particularly successful matches, but the Aries/Libra mix works well in more detached areas such as business partnerships or, possibly, a short-lived affair, while Aries/Scorpio is too explosive in any kind of situation to survive for long.

In the case of Aries/Libra, the fiery enthusiastic Aries would be attracted by the calm detachment of Libra, his pleasantness, good taste and desire for harmony and balance. Librans are often good looking and stylish, which is attractive to you, but Libra's tendency to drift towards an easy and comfortable life would bore you, while your Aries energy and occasional tantrums would cause the Libran to switch off and tune out.

If the Scorpio partner were one of the sexy variety (contrary to popular opinion, many Scorpios are not especially sexy), there would be a strong initial attraction, but both are self-centred and bad tempered, and both would want to be the top dog. It is worth bearing in mind that the Aries riser himself may behave in a Libran way by trying to create a peaceful and harmonious atmosphere in a relationship.

Love, sex and relating – regardless of the descendant

Your most attractive features are generosity, honesty, spontaneous kindness and a sense of humour. To be honest, as long as your partner is humorous, intelligent and tolerant of your daft behaviour, you will be happy and so will your partner. You need an independent partner who has work and interests of his or her own, or better still someone who doesn't need to be waited on hand and foot. However, you need them within phone-shot so that you can have your needs attended to immediately! Aries risers don't require a terribly domesticated partner, but you do need help in the house and with the children as you, yourself, are not especially domesticated or tidy.

Your partner must give you space, not only for your career but also for your hobbies and interests. You need to be able to take off from time to time, either on business trips or sporting holidays with a group of mates. Your partner must understand that there is a side of you that needs this kind of freedom, and that this doesn't constitute either a lack of loyalty or a dereliction of duty.

You love your children very deeply, and want the best for them, going to great lengths to educate them. However, you should try not to dominate your children or to show impatience, especially if they seem slow, timid, introverted or clumsy. if you behave impatiently to this kind of child, he will freeze up which will make him even more awkward and withdrawn, and will subsequently deprive you of the special kind of warmth that you could derive from a loving parent/child relationship.

With your abundance of energy, sex is an obvious necessity. You don't mind taking the lead in bed, and will be quite inventive but you must guard against selfishness especially while you are young and inexperienced. An un-Arian application of patience and thoughtfulness here will pay off. However, your natural kindness and generosity in this, as in all things, should ensure that you give as much as you get,e so to speak. Remember that your partner may well enjoy the occasional sexual marathon but not necessarily every day and twice on Sundays! Arians are quite greedy where sex is concerned and can't really get enough of a good thing. Even a slightly dodgy relationship will work for you if the sexual side is good. In some ways, you suit a moody, changeable partner who varies in his or her sexual needs and responses from one day to the next so that you can avoid your pet hate – boredom.

Health

Traditionally, Aries rules the head down as far as the upper jaw. So headaches, eyes, ears, sinuses and the upper teeth are trouble spots. Some Aries rising subjects have bad skin and continue to fight off acne well into adult life. You have neither the time nor the nature to give in to illness, but sudden fevers and accidents are possibilities. You can become quite severely ill at times, but will bounce back quickly because your level of resistance is generally high. You enjoy food and may be a drinker, therefore weight gain could present a problem later in life, but if you maintain your preference for an active life, you quickly use up the extra calories.

Your sixth house is Virgo, so please also look at the Virgo section on health on page 519.

5

Taurus Rising

Shall I compare thee to a summer's day?
Thou art more lovely and more temperate:
Rough winds do shake the darling buds of May,
and summer's lease hath all too short a date.

William Shakespeare, *Sonnet*

A few words of explanation

A sign on the ascendant expresses itself in a different way from the Sun sign; however, some of the characteristics, even the childhood experiences, will apply if you have the Sun in Taurus or in the second house. Some of these characteristics will be apparent if you have Venus in Taurus or in the second house. If your Moon is in Taurus, your emotions and reactions will have a Taurean flavour. If the ascendant is weak (see Chapter 1), the Taurus overlay will not be so noticeable. If the rest of your birthchart is very different from the rising sign there could be conflict in the personality. This is because the outer manner, the signals which are given out by the Taurus rising subject on first meeting, are very different from the main character which lies underneath. Another possibility is that the subject rejects all that his parents, parent figures and teachers stood for and creates a life for himself which is very different from the one which they envisaged for him, or from the one he lived through as a child.

Remember that this is a fixed sign which implies the ability to stay with a situation and see it through. It is also an earth sign which implies practicality and a certain rootedness and it is feminine/negative which suggests introversion. This is a sign of *short ascension* which means that it only applies in our northern latitude for a short period of time in any day, therefore only a few people are born each day with this ascendant. However, it is not quite such a short ascending sign as Pisces or Aries, so there are a few more of you around than there are of them.

Early experiences

The sign of Taurus suggests comfort, and this was certainly true of your childhood. All the earth signs place an emphasis on the need for material security and, in the case of any earth sign on the ascendant, the subject's parents may accumulate money and goods in reaction to their own experiences of childhood poverty. They probably had to work very hard in order to make a home and bring up children. By the time you came along, your parents may have got over the early struggles, or may have still been trying to get it all together. Either way, the message given to the Taurus rising child is one of the need for security, comfort and better still, wealth.

The old-fashioned virtues of a steady job, money in the bank and solid family life were programmed into you but it is also possible that the 'Victorian' values of crass materialism and the devil-take-the-hindmost could also have been pushed upon you. This is fine if you have the same kind of requirements elsewhere in your birthchart, but not so good if you have a gamut of planets in a completely different type of sign, such as Aquarius. Another and far more serious problem is that, although you were taken care of materially, you may have suffered emotional deprivation.

When a rising sign is both earthy and fixed, there is a strong possibility that one or both of the parents behaved in an authoritarian manner. Approval may have been given and withheld in subtle ways making you slightly withdrawn and rather mulish in return. Another possibility is that your father was a slightly awesome figure and that you were closer to, and more comfortable with, your mother. However, there is much that is good about this rising sign, and one could do a lot worse than to be born with a Taurean ascendant.

Your parents' outlook was conservative and their behaviour expressed moderation, commonsense, practicality and kindness. You were encouraged to be kind, thoughtful and conscientious. In the unlikely event that you grew up in anything other than the nuclear family, this would have been because one of your parents died. You are unlikely to have witnessed open discord or divorce at first hand. Civilized, unexpressed discontent might have been the order of the day in your parent's household.

You may have grown up with parents who were wrapped up in one another leaving you emotionally stranded, the consequence being that you learned to demand nothing and to avoid, at all costs, bringing the familiar look of irritation to their faces. If you were lucky enough to find another relative or perhaps a person outside the family to whom you could relate, the situation would not have been quite so bad. You may have been at odds with a brother or sister, either envying them for being more successful and more acceptable to your parents than you were, or, on the other hand, despising them for being dull, incompetent and irritating. This situation would also have caused you to hide your real feelings, to become devious or to boil inwardly. Your rage, on those occasions when you could no longer control yourself, would have been towering, frightening and quite destructive. As you grew older, you managed to avoid scenes or 'tune out' unpleasantness and ignore it altogether. This could make you difficult to live with because rather than face facts you continue to conceal your feelings, either erupting in anger or retreating into a world of silent withdrawal which is incomprehensible to others.

Somewhere along the line you will have been affected by beauty in some form or another. Many Taureans love gardening, because they can enjoy both the scent and beauty of the flowers and the production of their other love, good things to eat. It is possible that your parents were farmers or landscape gardeners because there is a natural feeling for the land and all that it produces. The twin messages of conservatism and conservation would lead you, in any situation, to build rather than destroy and to continue rather than to end.

Your family may have been instrumental in introducing you to the world of music, dance or art. You have a natural appreciation of beauty and harmony which derives from your ruling planet Venus. I know one Taurus-rising lady who grew up in a 'dancing' family. Everyone in the family danced, some being professional or semi-professional ballet dancers, chorus line hoofers or ballroom dancers. Although she was a rather plump young woman, she took up ballroom dancing and reached quite a high standard.

If your home life was stable and your parents loving, united and caring, the situation at school was a little different. You were not the kind of child to cause trouble at school; disruption and disobedience is hardly your way of doing things. However, unless the rest of the chart is very different, you were probably slow to catch on, especially in the years before adolescence. Bad behaviour would have been expressed as stubbornness and a kind of switching off from the people around you. If your parents and teachers accepted you as you were, your school life would have been pleasant, if rather unproductive. However, if they didn't, then you might have been made to feel as if you were worthless and a failure in everything which was demanded of you.

Taureans are not the most sporty of children; many are plump and all of them hate to feel cold, wet and uncomfortable. Neither you nor your parents could see any value in romping around on a muddy sports field, although a Sunday afternoon tramp across the field with a dog was quite another matter. Your natural talent and interests lay in the areas of art and music. Nowadays, these interests are fostered for both sexes, but in the days when boys had to be boys and self-expression was not on the curriculum, this could have caused some suffering.

Far better for a beleaguered boy was your natural talent for making and mending things, so you probably enjoyed working with natural substances such as wood or clay. One area which attracted you was home economics, catering and dietetics. I can remember a client of mine who, while training as a dietician during her teens, had to switch to a secretarial course because her family's circumstances changed and they could no longer afford to keep her in training. She retained her interest in cooking and still makes the best cakes for miles around.

Basically, if you have a strong Taurean rising sign, your childhood would have been a better experience than for many others, although school was probably something of a trial, especially during your younger years. Many Taurus rising subjects develop an interest in reading and go on to educate themselves later in life at their own pace.

Appearance

Bearing in mind racial differences, family tendencies and the influence of the rest of your birthchart, the Taurean influence displays itself in a plump and sturdy body with a squarish head on a thick short neck. Taurean women look luscious when young but have to guard against weight gain later in life. Your complexion is clear, your eyes are marvellous and in white races your skin is rather pale and luminous. Your hands and feet are probably small. Your pleasant smile and gentle manner add to your attractive looks and take most people's minds off the fact that you might be a few pounds overweight. Oddly enough many Taurean types seem to like to hide their faces in some way. Men hide behind heavy rimmed glasses and beards, while women tend to wear plenty of make-up and have long wavy hair. It is fairly common for members of this rising sign to have a 'Churchillian' appearance.

Outer manner

Your outer manner is pleasant, slightly reserved but friendly and non-hostile. You enjoy a chat with neighbours or colleagues from the office, you probably enjoy listening to office gossip and jokes. Taureans, whether Sun sign or rising sign, have a good clean sense of humour which doesn't depend upon cruelty or sarcasm for effect. You appear slow moving to others, preferring to make your way through life at quite a gentle pace. Some Taureans give an appearance of hardness, especially in business situations but this is a form of protection and a cover-up.

Taurus characteristics

This section can double up as a brief guide to Taurus as a Sun sign *or* as a rising sign, so it makes a handy reference for you if you need to check out some Sun sign characteristics as well as the ones for the rising sign.

Conventional and sociable, you are pleasant companions and easy-going work-mates, as long as things are going your way! You don't like breaking promises, betraying a trust or leaving obligations unfulfilled. You are an exemplary employee, needing to feel as if you belong in a job, that your work is serving a useful purpose and that people are pleased with what you do. Work for work's sake doesn't excite you, but if temporarily short of cash, you'll cope with even the most boring job. You are capable and thorough, especially when left to do things at your own pace. While still on the subject of work, Taureans like concrete results, a nicely balanced set of figures or well filled shelves of stock. You can make and mend most things and can see the value of other people's work and make it useable and saleable. There will be more about career matters in the midheaven section later on in this chapter.

When coupled with someone who has a creative imagination, your ability to work with materials and make something concrete out of them is exceptional. My friend, Barry Gillam, who is a double Taurus (Sun and ascendant) lives with my pal, Kay Bielecki, a Leo. Although having very little money to play with, they bought a run-down house and gradually renovated it; they now have an attractive and comfortable home which has some intriguing and rather beautiful touches. Barry is typically Taurean in his ability to build and also to create a garden. All his work is carefully and properly prepared and finished; nothing slap-dash is good enough for him. Incidentally, most Taureans prefer to live in the country rather than in town.

You have the ability to finish all that you start and you rarely become rattled or walk away from a job if it doesn't go right straight away. You have patience with children and also with animals; indeed family life on a farm would probably suit you very well. You are in tune with nature even to the point of being interested in earth magic and the 'Craft'. (The Craft being Wicca or the ancient religion of white witchcraft.)

As a parent, you are patient and kind but you won't stand rudeness and bad behaviour. You seek a conventional education for your children and try to give them a practical and sensible upbringing. If they have any creative talent, you are happy to help them bring this out. There are times when your famous patience finally snaps and, on the odd occasion when you lose your temper, everyone around you runs for cover. Taureans are irritable when they are hungry. The worst time for your partner to tackle you on some thorny subject is the moment when you first put your foot in the front door after a hard day's work. After a meal and a rest, your temper is much improved, as is your sense of perspective.

The one characteristic which is guaranteed to be present when Taurus is the Sun sign or the rising sign, His the famous Taurean stubbornness and obstinacy. All the earth signs are happier with stability and are slow to change their minds and their lifestyles. Fixed sign people stand by their beliefs and principles and don't easily change their minds. Taurus is fixed earth, therefore the most reliable and the least flexible of all signs. I have one Taurus rising friend who appears to display very few Taurean characteristics, but when he received a tactless and somewhat insulting letter from a junior colleague, he merely compressed his mouth in a white-lipped smile. The junior's career came to a grinding halt from that time on.

Taureans traditionally are loyal, dependable and faithful in any relationship. If you became so unhappy with a partner, or so smitten with someone else that you are forced to leave, you would be just as loyal and faithful to the second partner as you had tried to be with the first. You prefer a stable relationship to courtship and you enjoy settling down to become part of a family. Many Taureans are so dedicated to relating that they put their partner even before their children. Your worst fault is a kind of emotional idleness. It is all too easy, when you are at home, to sit slumped in an armchair snoozing in front of the telly, taking your partner for granted to the point where you even forget to talk. Remember that a few outings and entertainments won't go amiss and this kind of thoughtfulness would be much appreciated by the other half! If you refuse to make any effort, you are in danger of waking up one day to find a note on the mantel-piece and a vacant space where the partner should be.

People of this sign have a totally unjustified reputation for being mean, materialistic and money-minded. It's true that you won't go out of your way to take on the problems of people outside of your immediate family, but this has something to do with your lack of spontaneity. It takes a certain kind of initiative to solve the world's problems and this is not a particularly Taurean feature. You don't throw money away if you can help it. You fear insolvency and you hate waste but you are not particularly mean, or at least, no more so than other 'careful' signs such as Cancer, Pisces or Capricorn.

The midheaven

This section and those which follow apply only to Taurus rising, *not* to Sun in Taurus. The midheaven shows the subject's aims and ambitions, his public standing and his attitude to work outside the home. In the case of births in the UK and in similar (northern) latitudes, the Taurus rising subject's midheaven is always in Capricorn. In much of the United States, people who have a late degree of Taurus on the ascendant may have Aquarius on the MC.

Taurus/Capricorn

Capricorn, like Taurus, is an earth sign but it is cardinal in nature, whereas Taurus is fixed. This cardinality on the MC may be one of the reasons why so many Taurus risers go in for running their own show, by owning their own businesses. Being an earth sign, you would tend to produce or supply goods which are practical and useful. You may run a shop, a gardening service, something in the farming or farm-supply line or a small factory. Many of you work in the building trade. Your love of beauty and your subtle sense of touch could lead you into the fields of dressmaking, cooking and craft-work. Some Taureans take up beauty therapy or become involved with the cosmetic industry, possibly as make-up artists. Many others find their way into the entertainment world, often as singers. However, life being what it is, many Taurus rising people actually work in offices and banks.

The Capricorn connection gives a fondness for big business and banking while the Taurean thoroughness ensures that errors are few.

Taurus/Aquarius

Generally speaking, Taurus rising subjects resist pressure and dislike hectic or worrying jobs but the Taurus/Aquarius combination is a little more able to cope with this. Remember that these are both fixed signs which need to do things at their own pace and in their own way. The ingenuity of Aquarius could produce a powerfully competent wheeler-dealer or someone who reaches the top in an unusual career. I guess that the combination of these two could produce a show-business impressario or the owner of a respected art auctioneering business. This combination adds determination and stubbornness.

Despite the fact that the midheaven is supposed to represent one's direction in life, it can also show the type of person who might attract you, especially if you require a partner who is in sympathy with your goals. Therefore, a partner who has a strong Capricorn or Aquarius emphasis on the chart could appeal to you.

The descendant

The opposite point to the ascendant is the descendant. This is traditionally supposed to show the type of person to whom we are initially attracted. In this case, the descendant is in Scorpio; therefore a strong, equally dependable and almost equally stubborn partner is suggested. You seem to be looking for the fireworks which accompany the Scorpion, either in the form of uncertain moods or sexual energy.

I have no evidence of a particularly high incidence of Taurus/Scorpio relationships but I guess that this combination would work quite well. Both partners need stability in relationships, both are happier in familiar surroundings than with a life of constant change, both are dutiful family members who are also orientated towards getting on in life. There is much in common, but there are times when Scorpio's moods might be hard for Taurus to take. Both signs prefer commitment to playing the field.

Love, sex and relationships – regardless of the descendant

You can cope with a financially independent partner or even one who is heavily involved with a career, just as long as the emotional security is there. You need the love which might have been missing during your childhood. You like to know where your partner is, also what they are doing; not because you distrust them but because you feel safer if there are no mysteries going on around you. You also like your partner to be around at mealtimes.

Your senses are very acute and you like to indulge them. Sex competes even with food for your attention! Taureans have a reputation for being delightful lovers and a couple of female acquaintances of mine who live with Taurus rising men, tell me that they are very well looked after in bed! You know the expression 'enough is as good as a feast', don't you? Well, there's nothing Taurus likes better than a feast. A spiteful person might suggest that the Taurean propensity for being lazy means that you enjoy nothing better than a day spent in good company wrapped in a duvet wearing nothing but a smile.

On a more serious note, what Taurus rising subject's like best and need most is cuddling. The adult Taurus rising subject may still suffer the residual effects of the childhood lack of closeness between himself and his parents. This could give him a need to make up for lost comforts by way of touch and closeness in a relationship.

Health

Taurus is a robust sign with good powers of recovery. The weak spots are the throat, thyroid gland and the lower teeth. Weight may cause problems and the connection with the planet Venus might bring ailments such as cystitis and diabetes later in life.

Your sixth house is in Libra, so please also look at the health section on page 527.

6

Gemini Rising

The flower that smiles today
Tomorrow dies:
All that we wish to stay
Tempts and then flies.
What is this world's delight?
Lightening that mocks the night.
Brief even as bright.

Percy Bysshe Shelley, *Mutability*

A few words of explanation

A sign on the ascendant expresses itself in a different way from a Sun sign. However, some of the characteristics, even the childhood experiences, will apply if you have the Sun in Gemini or in the third house. They may be present if you have Mercury in Gemini or the third house and, if you have the Moon in Gemini or in the third house, your emotions and reactions will have a Gemini flavour. If the ascendant is weak (see Chapter 1), the Gemini overlay will not be noticeable. If the rest of your birthchart is very different from the rising sign there could be a conflict in the personality. This is because the outer manner and the signals which are given out when one first meets someone new are very different from the main character which lies underneath. The subject may reject all that his parents, teachers and parent figures stood for and go on to create a lifestyle for himself which is very different from the one which they envisaged for him or the one he experienced as a child.

Remember that this sign is mutable, which implies flexibility of mind. It is an air sign, which implies an intellectual approach to everything and it is masculine/positive which suggests an outwardly extrovert nature. Gemini rising is a sign of shortish to medium ascension, therefore there are fewer Gemini rising people born each day than there are of some of the other signs.

Early experiences

If you have this rising sign, your childhood may have been unsatisfactory, emotionally deprived or even something of a horror story. There may even have been a mystery surrounding your origins. If your childhood was genuinely all sweetness and light, I suggest that you actually re-check your birth time! I call this the 'orphan's ascendant' because there is a feeling of having been left out in the cold. A surprisingly high proportion of orphans, foundlings, fostered, adopted and Dr Barnardo's children seem to be born with Gemini on the ascendant. Many people who started out with two parents in the normal manner seem to mislay one or both of them somewhere along the way!

Even if you were brought up in a normal nuclear family, there would have been feelings of isolation and of being a square peg in a round hole. All this would have been bad enough for the silent withdrawn type who is given to hiding his feelings and putting on an act of dumb acceptance, but you're not like that, are you? You're friendly, garrulous and filled with a need to explain yourself to others. You need to communicate, to connect with other people on an intellectual level and to analyse yourself and the world around you in order to put it into a sensible and meaningful kind of order.

There may have been difficulty in your dealings with brothers and sisters; it is possible that you were brought up in some kind of patched-together family with older half-brothers and sisters or even cousins who became brothers and sisters of a kind to you. It is possible that yours was a large family in which you somehow missed out in the rush to gain your parent's attention. You may be so different from your natural parents and siblings that you appear to have originated from a different planet.

Tania, for example, was brought up in a normal nuclear family of mother, father, brother and two cats. The parents were kind and caring but wrapped up in each other and they were also burdened by commitments to elderly relatives. Both of Tania's parents worked hard to make a living, therefore the children were not able to take centre stage. Tania's older brother was a quiet studious kind of lad who developed an excellent relationship with his ascetic grandfather. Tania was bouncy, noisy, demanding, talkative and a trial to her sorely pressed parents. She spent a lot of time being overtly or subtly shoved out of the way, or snapped at for being a nuisance. There were not many opportunities for her to gain approval from anyone.

Tania now has a job in one of the caring professions; she travels a good deal and has many friends of her own. She is needed, respected for her work and approved of by those whom she helps. If this all sounds more like Pisces than Gemini, remember that these signs have much in common. Both are mutable signs and both have a strange kind of duality; the two fishes of Pisces and the Geminian twins are always tied together but often seem to be trying to travel in different directions.

You were probably one of the younger children or even actually the youngest child in the family, born to parents for whom the novelty of parenthood had rather worn off. You may have been pushed around or ignored by older siblings or left with minders, while your mother went out to earn much-needed extra money. Something may have gone badly wrong early in your childhood, maybe the death of a parent or some kind of financial disaster. You may have been acutely aware that the people with whom you had been left looked after you under sufferance or for money. Even in a more normal family, there is a feeling of being the odd one out.

You may have been an academic child in a practical family, or a school failure in a family where the only things which counted were brains and the exam papers. You may have had a personal or religious outlook which was different from that of the rest of the family. The whole thing may have been such a mess that, in the light of adult experience, the only thing to do is to put it all behind you, look at yourself as you are now and begin to build from there.

If your childhood was actually quite tolerable, you will have gained from the better side of this ascendant. The benefits are exposure to books, ideas and teaching aids of one kind or another from an early age. You were encouraged to read, write and to express yourself. If self-expression in the form of too much talking was discouraged, you will have been encouraged by your teachers to write, draw and make things. Being restless and lively, you enjoyed sports or dancing and you could have achieved a high standard. It is possible that you enjoyed being involved in some kind of youth organization but probably not for long as Geminians hate to be regimented. Even as an adult, you enjoy movement and often do most of your thinking while walking or exercising in the local swimming pool.

Gemini risers have an inventive streak and are often dexterous, so you can always find something with which to occupy yourself when there is nobody else around. This sign is not especially associated with animals, but you may like small animals which can be very comforting if your life is at all lonely. You may even talk to the goldfish, which is just one manifestation of your marvellous communications skills, but more of this in the mid-heaven section.

Gemini rising subjects are surprisingly ambitious and these ambitions may have seen the first light of day through childhood dreams. There is a feeling that, if you can develop some kind of strength, power or self-esteem, you can avoid being laughed at and shoved out of the way later in life. There are some among you who don't seem to learn the first time around and have to go through a sticky marriage before the message of your *apparent* worthlessness in the eyes of close family members finally reaches your brain.

Geminis are workers; this is your salvation. You probably have two or more careers going at once, together with a couple of committee positions to boot. You need to feel important and, one day, you realize with a jolt that you *are* important and no one talks down to you any more. The Gemini clown then disappears for ever, being replaced by the Gemini ring-master.

Appearance

Bearing in mind family and racial tendencies, plus the rest of the chart, you are likely to be shortish, slim and neat in appearance. You prefer to wear your hair in a short and tidy style, partly because yours is not the easiest hair to deal with but also because you are usually too busy to fiddle around with it. You may be sharp featured, especially when young, even slightly monkey-like but with a steady forward gaze which is full of Gemini curiosity. Your hands and feet are neat, and you try to maintain a rather stylish and youthful appearance throughout life. Your chic, attractive clothes reflect your busy super-modern lifestyle. Your car is an important part of your turnout, and this too would be small, neat, sporty and fast. Joan Collins is a good example of some one who looks typically Geminian. Her large eyes, small face, difficult hair and perennially youthful appearance are strong Gemini characteristics.

Outer manner

Your outer manner is cheerful, confident and friendly, but possibly sharp and off-putting to newcomers. Personally, I am rather nervous of Gemini rising subjects, your sarcastic and unfeeling outer manner can put me on the defensive. This is stupid of me because I know that the sharp-edged cleverness is a sham, a shield which protects your vulnerability and shaky sense of self-esteem. You can appear strong, efficient and businesslike but, if you feel threatened in any way, you can be cutting and hurtful. Females with this sign on the ascendant give an appearance of capability and efficiency which doesn't seem to detract from their femininity. The Gemini rising mind is masculine and the mental processes are logical and orderly, more suited to the engineer or computer programmer than anyone's idea of a dizzy woman.

You use your hands while talking and may be emphatic when excited about something. You remain young looking throughout life. You may actually fear old age yourself, but your attitude and appearance guarantee that you remain youthful even in your old age. Your quick mind and sense of humour are delightful.

Gemini characteristics

This section can double up as a brief guide to Gemini as a sun sign *or* as a rising sign, so it provides a handy reference for you if you wish to check out someone's Sun sign as well as their rising sign.

Your movements are quick, you walk and talk quickly and appear to have little patience with those who can't keep up with you but this is misleading. Just because you think and act quickly doesn't necessarily mean that you lack patience with those who don't; on the contrary, you *expect* others to be slower than you and you take time to explain things to them in an orderly manner. You may well lack patience with people who avoid making any kind of effort or who are mentally lazy. However, your sense of humour and genuine interest in other people protects you from true hardness. Some weak people may be frightened off by your dynamism, while others are drawn towards it. At least you do take the trouble to *talk* to others.

Gemini rising subjects can be seen passing the time of day with children, the elderly and even the local pussy-cat; you even talk back to the television! You like to listen as well as to talk because you find people interesting. This ensures that you have many acquaintances. You are capable of a good deal of lateral thinking and you will listen to and take advice from those whom you respect.

Practically everything interests you; your curiosity leads you to ask about everything which is going on around you. You never stop learning and therefore pick up snippets of information on many subjects. This leads to the common accusation by astrologers that Geminians know a little about many subjects; the implication being that they know nothing in depth. I don't go along with this old saw. It's true that most Geminians have dustbin-like minds, but you are able to study in depth and may well know at least one subject thoroughly, even if is only the performance of your local football team.

You need mental stimulation and also seek to stimulate the minds of others. In social situations, you are considered to be witty, funny, friendly, clever and amusing. Usually very talkative, you may appear boastful at times, but your slight tendency to exaggerate is actually just a device which is used to entertain and amuse others or to push home a particular point. You hide behind humour, because this covers you when panic sets in or when you feel yourself to be out of your depth. Although this sign is not especially associated with actors, you can act a part to suit your circumstances, and you tend to keep your true feelings hidden. Think back to that difficult childhood where you were taught that your demands were unlikely to be met, and that your feelings were unlikely to be important to others.

You learned early how to get on with life and how to put up with emotional discomfort or to adapt yourself to the prevailing situation. However, despite your ability to adapt to difficult situations, you can't half moan about them! You must beware that you don't adopt the typically Geminian moany, whiny little voice.

There is a myth among non-astrologers that Geminians have split personalities, this remark often being accompanied by the comment that Gemini is the sign of the twins. But how about the two fish of Pisces or the two cups in Libra's weighing scales? I personally doubt that schizophrenia is especially reserved for Geminians. It is true that as a Gemini subject, you can do many different things, sometimes all at the same time, and you can often accomplish more in one day than anyone else can in a week. You can also vary your behaviour according to the company in which you find yourself, but you are not alone in that.

On the whole, Geminians are consistent even in their inconsistency and you are no less reliable than many other signs. Geminians are dextrous, you are clever when it comes to making, fixing and mending things but some Geminis go out of their way to avoid this kind of work due to the fact that they have been criticized or made to feel clumsy during childhood. I have a couple of female Gemini acquaintances who considered themselves useless when it came to practical matters because they had husbands who always 'knew better'. Eventually, a day came when they *had* to cope and, of course, they managed very well. Obviously, none of us know what we can do until we are up against it, but Geminis, when given the two-pennyworth of encouragement, are pretty capable people.

Some of you lack intellectual confidence and may consider studying to be beyond you. However, when you put your mind to a subject, you soon find that your brains are the equal of anyone else's. If you have Gemini very strongly on your chart, you could be a first-class fidget, never stopping still for long enough to accomplish anything and always moving on to something (or someone) new. If the Gemini traits are diluted by a few planets in earth and/or fixed signs, you will be able to think more deeply and achieve a balance between frenetic activity and concentrated effort. This type of Gemini subject translates his need to rise above the shortcomings of his childhood into achievement. It's worth bearing in mind that this is one of the most ambitious of all the Zodiac signs. Your worst enemies are your nerves and your fear of boredom and entrapment. A Gemini rising friend of mine pointed out that she can only cope with a job which offers variety and that doing the same thing all the time would drive her crazy.

The midheaven

This section and those which follow apply only to Gemini rising subjects. The midheaven can show the subject's aims and ambitions, his attitude to work and his public standing. Those who have an early degree of Gemini on the ascendant will have Capricorn on the midheaven, but all the rest (e.g. the majority of you) have Aquarius on the midheaven. Those of you who have Capricorn on the MC are ambitious and determined, looking for security and advancement. The majority of self-made multi-millionaires have Gemini strong in their charts, which proves the point that you often work harder than most people. You can put your mind to the job and get on with it in a way that other people can only envy. You can turn your selling and communicating skills to good account by sticking at a job and climbing slowly up the career ladder.

The earth sign quality of Capricorn suggests that you are probably attracted to work where the values are material, in business, banking and large corporations, because you feel a need to achieve something solid by your efforts. This combination could make you a highly skilled and ambitious operator. Alternatively, you could find a comfortable job and stick with it for years as long as there were plenty of new faces around for company and entertainment.

The vast majority of Gemini rising subjects, however, have Aquarius on the mid-heaven and this brings both vision and humanitarianism into the picture. There may be a measure of idealism in your choice of career and this, coupled with your need to communicate, leads you towards the whole area of teaching. Not all Gemini rising subjects train as teachers, of course, but my bet is that your job is bound to lead you into aspects of teaching or training somewhere along the way. If you follow any of the other typically Gemini careers such as sales representative, journalist, writer, broadcaster or telephonist, you will still try to help people, both on a personal day-to-day basis or by means of communicating useful or instructive ideas.

Gemini's ruling planet is Mercury. In mythology, the Roman god, Mercury, was a messenger who worked for all the gods, but especially for Apollo. Indeed he was Apollo's errand-boy and, as such, did a good deal of his boss's dirty work, often getting the blame or being 'dropped in it' by his ungrateful superior; a situation which is familiar even today! Another, more satisfying side of this god's work was healing, and this still draws Mercurial people even now. Strictly speaking, the healing attributes are often laid at the feet of the other Mercury-ruled sign of Virgo, but Geminians do their bit in their own way. The idealistic Aquarian mid-heaven coupled with the Geminian need to help can lead to a medical or nursing career, but the need to communicate often manifests itself in some kind of counselling work. Therefore, psychiatry, marriage guidance or the counselling side of astrology could appeal to you either as a full-time occupation or as a satisfying sideline.

The presence of such forward looking air signs on both the ascendant and mid-heaven gives an interest in computers, electronics, word-processing and also radar, radio, telephone communications and television, both from an engineering point of view and by working directly in the broadcasting field. The need to communicate over vast distances can even lead to an interest in the para-normal, mediumship and even more obviously, when one considers the *healing* emphasis, a talent for spiritual or 'faith' healing. Remember that Aquarius is a *fixed* sign, therefore your interests may be varied but you will stick with them throughout your life. Aquarius and Capricorn also bring a deep-seated need for status and public recognition.

The MC can throw some light on the kind of partners you choose both in business and in personal life. You may be attracted to people who reflect the values of the signs on your midheaven or who are actually born under those signs (e.g. Capricorns or Aquarians).

The descendant

The opposite point to the ascendant is the descendant or the cusp of the seventh house. Traditionally this is supposed to show the kind of person to whom we are attracted. When Gemini is rising, the descendant is in Sagittarius so, in theory, you should find yourself especially attracted to Sagittarians. In practice, you could be attracted to any one of the 12 signs – or none of them! Perhaps you look for Sagittarian values in your friends, or your approach to a prospective mate is Sagittarian in character. The Sagittarian values are intelligence, broadmindedness and a taste for adventure.

This descendant denotes a need for personal freedom in relationships. You may or may not wish to try out different partners, but you do need to be free to come in and go out without being subjected to the third degree. You need to be able to follow a career or a particular leisure interest without your partner complaining of neglect. The Gemini need for *mental* stimulation plus space, suggests that the most successful partnership would be with someone who is equally involved with a career and who also has a measure of self-reliance.

When your nerves let you down, when your confidence evaporates, when the world suddenly makes you feel like the inept, incompetent, unwanted child you once were perceived to be, then you need a partner who will be there to reassure and comfort you, perhaps in a slightly motherly way. With Sagittarius on the descendant, you might not get all the love and reassurance that you need from a partner.

If your ascendant is late in Gemini, much of your seventh house will be in Capricorn which will encourage you to seek out a reliable and responsible kind of partner, perhaps one who is on his way to a position of power and influence.

Love, sex and relating - regardless of the descendant

This is above all a sign of the intellect, therefore a stimulating partner is a necessity. You can even put up with an absolute rat more easily than you can a boring partner. It hardly needs to be stressed that the old familiar triangle of 'safe partner and thrilling but unreliable lover', could have been made for you. Even a thrilling but unreliable partner is all right, just as long as you can still enjoy your first real loves which are your work and your hobbies!

Geminians are curious, so you probably experimented with sex quite early in life. I know one Gemini rising lady who, on being told that such-and-such a young man was 'dangerous', simply had to go and find out if it was true. There is an element of the 'don't die wondering' syndrome here, the source of which is the same kind of fiddle-fingered curiosity which leads you to pick spots.

To be honest, you *can* live without sex, as long as you are creatively occupied. Under extreme circumstances, you could go without it for at least four days, however your need for comfort and company will soon draw you back to companionship. Most of you are tuned into the needs of others which, alongside your famous dexterity and penchant for doing two things at once, makes you an inventive and exciting bed partner. Your greatest need is to communicate, therefore you are unlikely to be so tuned into your own needs that you don't also take into account the needs of a partner.

Health

Gemini rules the arms, shoulders, wrists and hands, also the bronchial tubes and lungs. Therefore, asthma, bronchitis and rheumatism are all possible complaints. Strained ligaments and broken wrists are common too. Your nerves are delicate so you could expect skin eruptions, allergies, migraine and nervous bowel problems. You may have an occasional spell of hysteria due to overstretched nerves, or as a result of too much worry. If ever a sign benefited from meditation, massage and relaxation techniques, this is the one.

Your sixth house is in Scorpio, so please also look at the health section on page 543.

7

Cancer Rising

Keep the home fires burning, while
your hearts are yearning,
Though your lads are far away they
dream of home;
There's a silver lining through the dark
clouds shining,
Turn the dark cloud inside out, till the
boys come home.

Lena Guilbert Ford, *Keep the Home Fires Burning*

A few words of explanation

A sign on the ascendant expresses itself in a different way from a Sun sign. However, some of the characteristics, even the childhood experiences, will apply if you have the Sun in Cancer or in the fourth house. They may be present if you have the Moon in Cancer or the fourth house because the Moon is a strong influence on any chart and it is the natural ruler of the sign of Cancer. If the ascendant is weak (see Chapter 1), the Cancer overlay will not be so noticeable. If the rest of the birthchart is very different from the rising sign, there could be a conflict within the personality. This is because the outer manner, the signals which are given out at first meeting by the subject are very different from the main underlying character.

Another possibility is that the subject rejects all that his parents and parent figures stood for and creates a life which is very different from the one which they envisaged for him or the one which he lived through as a child.

Cancer is a feminine/negative sign which belongs to the water group but we must remember that it is a cardinal sign which implies a certain underlying decisiveness. Even though Cancer is deemed to be a gentle sign, oriented towards the feminine principles of home and family, people with this sign rising know what they want and will not be made to do without it for long. This is a sign of long ascension, therefore there are many people with this sign on the ascendant, at least in the northern hemisphere.

Early experiences

As I said in the previous paragraph, there are many people born with this sign rising which is nice because, thankfully, it represents a fairly pleasant childhood. The chances are that you were well cared for by at least one of your parents and never left for long periods with other people or badly treated. Very few people have a perfect childhood and one could argue that a completely trouble-free childhood is a poor training for adult life. It is better if a little rain *does* fall from time to time, so that one learns to use an umbrella later on! Your childhood had a few showers, so to speak, but it was far from being a deluge of misery. This sign is especially associated with the mother, mother-figure or anybody who took on the nurturing role.

Your childhood home would have been fairly comfortable with a slight emphasis on materialism, but not as much as in the case of Taurus or Libra rising where the emphasis was on *things* rather than feelings. You were a wanted child, possibly the first one born into the family and you were able to have your parent's exclusive attention for a few years at least. Maybe you were the youngest child, being allowed to stay young while the others were encouraged to grow up more quickly.

You had a responsible attitude to life and a slightly dignified manner. You didn't get into any ridiculous escapades and neither did you find it necessary to play the part of the clown. You were quiet and rather cautious, a bit inclined to cling to home and mother and reluctant to move on out into the world. This attitude tends to change later in life as the ascendant progresses from cautious Cancer into adventurous Leo.

There is some evidence of religious or spiritual messages being handed out by your parents and these are accepted or rejected later in life according to your changing views and circumstances. I personally tend to see this very much as a Jewish rising sign; just think of the traditional relationship between the Jewish mother and her children! A quick survey of my Jewish friends confirms that there is a particularly high incidence of this ascendant. In non-Jewish families, the Cancerian ascendant does seem to lead to a faint whiff of religious or moral pressure being put on the child; in short, the child is urged to conform with the parent's ideological outlook. This doesn't pose much of a problem because the Cancerian is conformist by nature.

In all probability, you had a good relationship with your father but he might have been a slightly remote figure, being wrapped up in his work or personal interests. Some Cancer rising subjects have a sneaking contempt for their fathers, considering them to be weak willed or wimpish. In some cases, the father becomes seriously ill either in a dramatic way which frightens the child, or in a lingering way which requires some kind of permanent care and attention. One Cancer rising friend of mine told me that his father had a weak and frequently ulcerated stomach which meant the father needed to eat very carefully whilst also being protected from worry. This ensured that the mother was the power in the family, so reinforcing the typical Cancerian respect for the power of the mother. Incidentally, unless there are hard aspects from the planet Saturn to your ascendant, you were probably born very easily.

Many Cancer rising subjects experience some kind of problem in connection with their schooling, especially during the secondary or college phase of their education. This stems more from peer group pressure than actual education problems. You were probably rather slow and lazy when young, being more inclined to sit and dream rather than to get down to work. However, your desire to conform and a growing awareness that the road to adult success begins with school achievement, ensures that you catch up later and leave your earlier classmates behind. This increase of academic speed may bring a jealous and spiteful response from your erstwhile and soon-to-be-left-behind friends. You don't seem to go through the same kind of rebellious phase as other teenagers, thereby further alienating yourself from your peers, for a while at least.

There is some evidence that the famed Cancerian attitude of obedience to parental wishes doesn't last forever. The evidence is that you will eventually quietly but firmly reject your parents' preferences in favour of a career or lifestyle of your own choice. A Cancer rising client of mine gave up an intended career in medicine by dropping out half-way through the course and taking a job in a shop. When asked why he had done this, he replied that he realized that medicine was his *parents'* choice and that he really needed to find out for himself how he really wanted to live and what he was really fitted for. Despite these changes of direction, you tend to remain affectionately close to your parents throughout their lives.

Appearance

Cancer rising subjects are attractive rather than beautiful, with chubby features, full cheeks and lips and a nicely shaped nose. Your chest and rib cage are large and your shoulders and arms well covered. This gives males a slightly top heavy look, while females frequently have an hourglass type of figure. In white races, the skin is pale and the hair can range from mid-brown to almost black, and it is usually strong and abundant with a will of its own. Your height is probably small to average, and you have to watch your weight later in life. Your hands and feet are small and neat. Both sexes with this ascendant like to look after their appearance and women hate to go out without make-up and nail polish. Both sexes prefer to wear conservative clothes in plain colours. Garish patterns and checks are not liked at all.

Outer manner

Women with this ascendant appear very feminine and rather cuddly. Men appear kind, gentle and equally cuddly. Both sexes are popular because they are pleasant, kindly and humorous. The strange thing is that you do not really seek friendship and are not terribly interested in people outside your immediate family. Most Cancer rising subjects get over their early shyness and become outgoing adults, often with a talent for salesmanship and the more pleasant kind of company politics. You prefer to pour oil on troubled waters than to stir up a storm. You are a bit shy, being rather modest and retiring in new company. You hate to look outrageous, to draw attention to yourself or to make a public fool of yourself. You obey the rules, and are generally very civilized in your manner. You are good to talk to because you are such a good listener but your habit of questioning others may be a bit too intrusive to some people.

Cancer characteristics

In the case of Cancer rising, the Moon assumes a greater level of importance than is usual because it is associated with the sign of Cancer and is, therefore, the chart ruler. It will be especially strong if in the sign of Cancer and/or in the first house or in the fourth house.

My questionnaire revealed that Cancerians consider that they remain *themselves* in all situations. They tell me that they don't vary their behaviour to suit the company in which they find themselves. As an outside observer, I don't entirely agree with this. You are definitely not two-faced, you don't tell one thing to one person and something else to another, neither do you go to pains to put on an act, but you do behave differently in different settings. When out at work or with friends, you are friendly, chatty, charming and apparently confident. If someone takes it upon themselves to patronize or criticize you, this results in you immediately clamming up – it is worth remembering that your memory is very good and that you rarely forgive or forget a hurt. In the home you can vary between being cheerful, loving and considerate, sulky and withdrawn, or cross and irritable.

Like your Taurean cousins, you are pretty foul to be around if you are cold and hungry and only a complete fool would try to tackle you on some contentious subject the moment you walked in the door after a hard day's work. Later on when you have had time to eat, relax and digest your meal, you can be safely approached! Your worst fault is your tendency to switch off and retreat into yourself. For instance, if something goes wrong at work, you can come home in a bad mood and stay that way for several weeks! By the time your spouse begins to suggest divorce proceedings, you have completely forgotten what put you in the mood in the first place. Another fault is your parsimony. No one is more careful with money, except for a Piscean.

You prefer to make up your own mind about everything and cannot be dictated to. This, of course, is what one would expect of a cardinal sign. You can be slow to make up your mind about people and you don't trust snap judgements, not even your own. Unless you are under intense pressure, you can be comfortable anywhere; however, you prefer classy people and clean, comfortable surroundings. Your senses are strong, especially the senses of hearing and smell, you cannot stand noisy and smelly surroundings.

You are sensible and realistic, preferring to solve problems in a practical manner than to analyse and agonize over them for any length of time. In fact, you shy away from any intense examination of feelings; you have no patience with people who insist on studying their own navels for hours on end. You fear emotional stress and become ill if you have to face too much of it. You may even appear unsympathetic to the troubles of others, but the truth is that your psychic skin is very thin, and you automatically shy away from too much drama in an effort to protect yourself.

You love having people around you, both the family and your work colleagues, but you do need to recharge your psychic batteries by spending a bit of time alone on occasion. Going for a walk, doing a few chores in the garden or having a late lay-in are all ways in which you do this. You dislike housework but can make use of it to give you space and peace from the demands of others. Another peculiarity is that you can take any amount of noise and panic at work but you do need a peaceful and tension-free atmosphere at home. If forced into an argument in any sphere of your life, you can be surprisingly blunt and hurtful. You observe more than other people realize, but you tend to keep your observations to yourself, so it is only when challenged that you show just how well you know your opponent.

Most astrology books stress the traditional Cancerian closeness to the home and the family, and this is true. You don't like living alone. You enjoy an afternoon of your own company but you really can't manage for long without some kind of companionship. You are naturally domesticated and probably quite a skilled cook. Although very attentive to the needs of your family, you also need life outside the home. You prefer a job which is both steady and secure but which also gives you a measure of authority and autonomy. Remember this is a cardinal sign which suggests that you are a good decision maker. You like to do your job properly and can be relied upon to complete a project unsupervised. You have a natural affinity to the world of business and enjoy managing or running a business of your own.

Your outlook and values tend to be traditional. The chances are that your parents were sensible and you probably find it quite easy to follow their example. You need a secure base; a home of your own with your family around - you hate to part company with any relative, however demanding or cantankerous they may become. You will drop friends and acquaintances however, if they begin to take the mickey out of you or to make jokes at your expense. Your sense of humour and tolerance of human nature disappears the minute a 'wind-up merchant' comes along to prick your dignity.

Your tastes are simple; you enjoy good food and drink, good company, books, music and the scent of flowers. Many of you are voracious readers, often sticking to one or two preferred kinds of book. History is liked and you may be quite a knowledgeable amateur historian. The collecting instinct is not so noticeable in the rising sign as it is with Sun in Cancer but you join your Cancer Sun sign cousins in hating to throw anything away. Your senses are strong – discordant sounds offend you but not nearly as much as bad smells. Oddly enough, you don't follow the current fad for complaining about the smell of other people's cigarettes. You love to travel, especially by water, but your weak stomach makes you a poor sailor. You need access to a car; if possible you want to buy your own car because you feel frustrated if you cannot get up and go whenever you feel inclined.

The midheaven

People who were born in the UK, northern Europe and Canada may have one of three midheavens, while people born in southern Europe and the USA have a choice of two. The correct placement of the MC, like everything else in astrology, demands an accurate date, time and place of birth. The most usual MC in Britain and most northerly latitudes is Pisces, whereas in the USA and southern Europe Pisces and Aries are equally possible. A very few northern births may result in an Aquarius MC.

Cancer/Aquarius

There is some conflict here because Cancer seeks security while Aquarius seeks freedom. In resolving this conflict, you may behave in one way dealing with friends and family and in another pursuing your worldly ambitions. If the signs are allowed to blend rather than conflict with one another, you could be drawn to one of the caring professions due to the fact that these are both caring signs. Counselling work is a possibility, as is medicine, veterinary work and, of course, teaching. Another talent which these signs share is the ability to buy and sell. Cancer wants to drive a hard bargain, while Aquarius wants to be friends with the world but both signs are adept at looking friendly while hiding their true thoughts and feelings. The intuitive skills of astrology, palmistry, graphology, numerology and the Tarot etc. may appeal to you, possibly enough to make a part-time or full-time living from them. Political activity is a natural for you, so you could be drawn to work in the civil service, local government or you may choose to serve on committees.

Cancer/Pisces

This mixture produces a sentimental person for whom continuity is important. You probably prefer to stay in a job where you feel yourself to be appreciated as part of a successful team. The Pisces element can bring confusion regarding your aims, so you could drift along, hoping for the best rather than reaching for a specific goal. If Neptune (the ruler of Pisces), is well aspected in the chart, career muddles will be less of a problem. The travel trade may attract you, or you may have to travel in connection with some other type of work. The combination does not usually bring any burning ambitions; you just want a happy working life and contentment at home. Some of you may not actually go out to work, preferring to work from home or spend your energies looking after children or animals.

This combination brings an interest in healing, so you may work in the medical or the alternative medical fields. Just to digress for a moment, all the Cancer/Pisces people whom I know seem to consult alternative medical practitioners either in addition to, or in place of conventional doctors. Whether personally involved or not, you find it quite easy to accept the idea of spiritual healing and psychic or mediumistic work, probably due to your own natural highly developed level of intuition. You have a natural affinity with money and budgeting, therefore finance work (which also requires intuition) and fund raising for a charity are possible interests.

Cancer/Aries

This combination brings together two cardinal signs, so you would be unlikely to blindly follow any course of action which was against your own interests. The charm of the Cancerian ascendant masks your wilfulness to some extent. You could make a good politician or diplomat because you appear to be sociable and reasonable, but you are usually able to make your point. If you want to, you can push your way to the top by sheer hard work and by keeping your goals clearly in sight, however some of you are too lazy to make the effort.

You probably prefer self-employment to being part of a team and may be interested in a mixture of the rather muscular Aries type of job and the gentler, more domestic, Cancerian type. This could lead you to run a small building concern, or to employ a group of gardening contractors or a battalion of office cleaners. Both Cancer, which is associated with patriotism and history, plus Aries which has military inclinations, lead to an interest in military matters. This could suggest a career in the services (especially the navy) or part-time involvement with a paramilitary organization. You might be interested in the Scout movement or something similar. Whatever you choose to do, you won't allow the grass to grow under your feet.

General comments

Cancerians are often good cooks, so you might work in the fields of catering or of dietetics. Your need to help others can lead to teaching or nursing, although you may not have the stomach for some kinds of medical work.

Many subjects are drawn to those who have their Sun in the subject's midheaven sign, so you could be attracted to Aquarian, Piscean or Arian types according to the position of your MC.

The descendant

The opposite point to the ascendant is the descendant, or the cusp of the seventh house. Traditionally this is supposed to show the type of person to whom we are attracted. When Cancer is rising, the descendant is Capricorn so in theory, you should find yourself attracted to Capricorn people. In practice, you could be attracted to any one of the 12 signs but you may look for friends and associates who have Capricornian attributes or you may approach others in a Capricornian manner.

This descendant denotes a need for safe and secure relationships. You are sincere in your dealings with others and you seek the same sincerity from others. You need a practical partner who can stand on his own feet and who has a sense of personal dignity. You are very caring and dutiful in your attitude to others, even when the relationship is a detached one such as a close colleague at work. You don't appreciate people whose eccentricities include a lack of personal principles, laziness or stupidity; you appreciate efficiency. You may be attracted to a partner who is ambitious or outstanding. Then having found your high-flyer, set out to curb or control them in some way.

I have not noticed any prevalence of Cancer/Capricorn marriages; however, these two signs have much in common so this could work quite well. Both signs are family minded, therefore both would understand the other's attachment to his own family. Parents, in-laws and grandparents will be looked after by both parties whenever necessary. The cautious attitude suggested by this descendant makes you slow to begin experimenting with relationships and inclined to marry later in life than usual. When you do commit yourself; however, you do so wholeheartedly.

Love, sex and relating – regardless of the descendant

Your caution and shyness means that you are slow to get off the ground in this area of life; many of you seem to wait until your thirties before marrying and having children, but when you do, your intentions are that you stay married, preferably for life. It is possible that this very sense of commitment is one reason for your hesitancy. Another peculiarity of this rising sign is that you are probably most comfortable with a partner who is quite a bit younger or older than yourself. You are protective towards your partner but you may take this a bit too far, becoming a bit of a mother hen.

This is not a notably sexy sign. Comments which came in on the questionnaires such as 'an affectionate cuddle is as important to me as sex' and 'I see sex as being part of a larger relationship rather than as an end in itself' are typical. You need to love and be loved and to have the love of a family around you, and this includes parents, siblings and children. You are potty about your own children and can also give a great deal of love and affection to other people's children. Some Cancer rising women unfortunately seem to lose their fragile sexuality as soon as the babies come along, it seems that once the goal of motherhood has been reached, they have no more real use for their sex drive. If the Cancerian lady is shrewd (and I haven't met one yet who wasn't) she will try to re-activate this side of herself in order to keep the interest of her husband and to prevent him straying. Sex at its best for you is a mixture of love, physical contact, affectionate play and a pleasurable release of energy; it is rarely an end in itself. Your strong senses lead you to enjoy music, flowers and a good meal with much the same relish as you enjoy sex. When in a loving relationship which is fairly free of money worries, you are contentedly sexy; otherwise you can do without it – for a while at least. An urge which is far more powerful than sex for you is to find a partner who shares your values, interests, and beliefs.

Health

Traditionally the areas which give you trouble are the stomach, breasts and the lower end of the lungs. Many Cancer rising subjects seem to have weak throats and also suffer from rheumatism. I can work out the reason for the rheumatism because it is a reflection from the Capricorn descendant, but I cannot see any astrological reason for your weak throats, even though they nevertheless seem to be there.

Your sixth house is in Sagittarius, so please also look at the health section on page 554.

8

Leo Rising

I suppose that means that I shall have to die beyond my means.

Oscar Wilde
– on being presented with a Doctor's fee for an operation

A few words of explanation

A sign on the ascendant expresses itself in a different way from a Sun sign; however, some of the characteristics, even the childhood experiences, might apply if you have the Sun in Leo or in the fifth house. They may be present if you have the Sun in the first house and even, to some extent, if you have the Moon in Leo, although the Moon rules the emotions and the reactions rather than one's conscious day-to-day activities. If the ascendant is weak (see Chapter 1), the Leo overlay will not be so noticeable. If the rest of the birthchart is different in character, there could be a conflict within the personality. This is because the outer manner, the signals which are given out by the subject on first meetings, are very different from the underlying personality. Another possibility is that the subject rejects all that his parents, teachers and parent figures stood for and creates a life which is very different from theirs.

Leo is a masculine, positive sign which is fixed in quality, therefore the subject will present a confident, capable and reliable image to the world. This is a sign of long ascension which implies that there are a lot of these people about but, oddly enough, we seem to run across far fewer Leo rising subjects in daily life than we do their immediate neighbours of Cancer and Virgo rising. There is no astrological reason for this discrepancy but there may be a few less obvious ones.

Firstly, Leo rising infants are not strong and don't all survive the first months of infancy. Secondly, these subjects don't seem to lead ordinary lives; they become captains of industry, sports champions or stars in the entertainment world, which suggests that they are not to be found in the local pub or at the office. Thirdly, this is a royal sign and is actually well represented as either a Sun sign, rising sign or Moon sign within the royal family. The few members of the 'nobility and gentry' whom I have come across invariably have Leo strongly placed on their charts, so once again these types are not likely to abound at one's local garage or under the dryer in the hairdressers. All in all, this sign carries a pedigree!

Early experiences

The chances are that your parents wanted you and valued your presence in their life from the day you were born, but this doesn't suggest that everything in your childhood was rosy. Your father (or anyone taking on the paternal role) would have had an old-fashioned, rather authoritarian attitude. You were encouraged to develop your talents and abilities but also to conform to rather set patterns of thought and behaviour. Your parents were traditional in outlook, probably following some kind of religious belief in a ritualistic and traditional manner. This is not because they 'saw the light' or were 'born again', but because they themselves followed their own family traditions. If you were born with this ascendant, you could have come from a family of practising Roman Catholics, Anglo-catholics, Jews, Moslems or any other respectable, traditional and rather authoritarian religion. The chances are that later in life, you questioned your parents' beliefs, finally finding some kind of philosophy or religious outlook which was better suited to your own views. You would be unlikely to live without some kind of personal belief.

Your parental home was probably comfortable and your parents fairly well off. They may not have been rich but they would have been respectable. It is most unlikely that you came from a broken home, because your parents believed in staying together and working out their problems within the family. Although home life was comfortable and, on the whole, peaceful, you do not seem to have been spoiled or over-indulged as a child because you were expected to behave in a reasonable and responsible manner.

There is usually something weird about the childhood when Leo is rising and this same quality of weirdness may also be experienced by the Sun in Leo children. As a child you would have been imbued with messages which told you that you were in some way special – you doubtless also experienced feelings of isolation. Your parents may have favoured you because you were the first child to be born to the family, the only child, or a child of one sex in a family mainly composed of the opposite one. You may have been a much-loved late addition, born when your parents had time and money to spare; therefore right from the beginning, you learned to stand slightly apart.

Leonine children are often talented; some are academic, some artistic, others are creative, sporty or even mediumistic. A talented child, especially if he comes from a non-talented family, always stands a little apart from the others and this is even more likely if his talent is consciously fostered by the parents. This slight sense of isolation is less noticeable when the rest of the birthchart inclines the child towards good relationships. Leos are warm and friendly creatures who love to give and receive affection and this suggests that you manage to overcome any slight difficulties which this sense of specialness might have given you.

Your relationship with your mother was probably very good but your father may have been an authoritarian figure. He could have been distant and even rather frightening. If you were lucky, you compensated for this by becoming close to a grandparent or a favourite uncle. It may have been difficult for you to make friends at school, especially if you were accustomed to spending your spare time with adults. There is, as with all fixed signs on the ascendant, a slightly watchful air about you, but this is nothing compared to the barriers which are associated with some of the other rising signs.

Appearance

Remember to make allowances for racial differences when looking at astrological appearances. Leo risers are quite distinctive, usually tall and well built, with a slow and regal way of moving. Both sexes are vain and will go to a lot of trouble to look good. You worry about your hair which is probably thick and abundant. Both sexes prefer to wear their hair long. Leo men are terrified they might lose their hair and may spend hours worrying about this. You like to dress fashionably, even glamorously, and to surround yourself with quality goods. A good car is an essential addition to your turnout.

Outer manner

Leos have a regal deportment, the head is often held high and the pace of movements are slow, even measured. You are genuinely interested in people and present a kindly, non-hostile personality to the world. You can appear arrogant and demanding, even unrealistic at times, but for the most part you are liked and admired. Leos have presence, graciousness and inborn public relations skills. You are a good listener and an interesting talker which makes you popular in social situations. You are quite fussy about your choice of friends, and this is where a touch of the Leo snobbery can often be seen.

Leo characteristics

This section can double up as a brief guide to Leo as a Sun sign *or* as a rising sign, so it can provide a handy reference if you want to check up on someone's Sun sign as well as their rising sign.

Leos prefer to live and work at a steady pace, often getting a lot done without rushing; indeed, you hate being rushed and hustled as this makes you irritable, even angry. Some of you are content to peg along doing your own thing, but many of you rise naturally to positions of responsibility and authority which you carry off very well. When in charge of others you rarely cause them to be resentful, but you can be bossy, arrogant and overbearing when under stress. Your attitude in the home is much the same, being loving, responsible and kind but needing to be respected by those around you. As a parent, you are sensible and responsible. You may spoil your children a little but you will not stand for rudeness or uncivilized behaviour.

You enjoy living in a grand manner and are quite prepared to work hard for the money you need. Money for its own sake doesn't interest you, but home comforts, a good holiday, a nice car and the wherewithal to provide yourself and your family with entertainment certainly does. Your home is bound to be attractive, possibly even impressive; it may not be terribly tidy but it is comfortable and structurally sound. You like space, large rooms and a bit of land around you, indeed you prefer to live in the country rather than in town. You do need to be on a good commuter route because you enjoy nipping into the city from time to time. My Leo rising friend, Malcolm, is a good example of this. He has always lived in the West Country but in his youth commuted up to London to play in a jazz band. Nowadays he travels up to town to work at the occasional psychic exhibition or on various other kinds of business.

Most Leos are fond of animals, especially cats. You are also fond of company, therefore your home is never silent or lonely. You need to be excited about life by becoming involved with either your job, hobby or sporting interests. You enjoy competition and also a good-natured dispute with your many friends. If you are a typical Leo, you will have a tendency to hold court and to treat a group of people as an audience. However, you are so entertaining that they rarely resent this.

You probably married while you were quite young. Leos on the whole have a good track record where marriage is concerned, preferring to stay with a partner and make things work rather than to flit irresponsibly from one partner to another. However, when this sign is on the ascendant, the descendant (the opposite point to the ascendant) is in the volatile sign of Aquarius, which throws a different complexion on things, but more of this later in the ascendant/descendant section. If you are forced to leave a partner, you don't go off the idea of relationships altogether but hope one day to meet someone else with whom you can live in trust and comfort. This preference for stability also extends to your working life and your friendships. You stick to people and situations and, in practical terms, you prefer to finish anything which you start. Your values could, by today's standards, be considered old-fashioned.

Leonine people love to travel, preferably in five-star comfort. Travel in connection with work is made for you because you were born to have an expense account. You are an excellent organizer, a kind of walking Filofax. You can organize your own day and also the work of others and fortunately, you make a popular if fairly demanding boss. Your enthusiasm, faith in the future and occasional headstrong leaps into impossible situations are an inspiration to others, even if a trifle wearing to your family. Your sense of humour, optimism and kindness makes you popular. You have an air of competence, even of invincibility; but your family, who see you a bit more clearly, know that you can have bouts of quite severe depression when something occurs which knocks your confidence. Nevertheless, even if you do become downhearted or angry, this won't last for long as you soon bounce back in order to get on with what you see as the game of life.

If challenged or made to feel inadequate in any way, you react by becoming pompous and putting on an air of self-importance. Try to avoid this if you can as it can have the effect of making you look even sillier. Although you have an excellent sense of humour, you are touchy. You don't appreciate having the mickey taken out of you and, if someone decides that you would make a good Aunt Sally, they soon find that they have taken on more than they have bargained for.

There are a couple of interesting observations which I would like to make before leaving this section, the first being that Leos can be mean! The sign is noted for its generosity and, true enough, some of you are the soul of generosity but many of you are quite the opposite! It is also wrong to say that Leos are over-dramatic. To be sure, you can put on a drama, especially if you are angry, but you can't compete with either Scorpio or Pisces when it comes to making a real scene. However, you are both proud and at the same time insecure, which means that you *hate* to be criticized.

The midheaven

This section and those which follow apply only to Leo rising subjects. The mid-heaven can show the subject's aims and ambitions, his attitude to work and his public standing. If Leo is rising, you could have either Aries or Taurus on the MC. The Leo/Aries combination adds sparkle to the chart as both are fire signs. The fixed/fire quality of Leo together with the cardinal/fire quality of Aries make for an ambitious, determined and capable person who attacks his goals with considerable enthusiasm. The Leo/Taurus combination shares the fact that both are fixed signs, therefore the person is less overtly ambitious but far more stubborn, determined and practical. Now let's take a deeper look at each combination on its own.

Leo/Aries

This combination inclines you towards self-employment, management positions and team leadership. In short, you're probably the boss. Being a faceless member of a team is not really your scene and therefore, even when joining an organization as a junior member, you stand out from the others and very soon begin to climb up the promotion ladder. You may not appear ambitious in the normal sense of the word, but you seem to drift towards the top, as if it were your rightful place in life. You enjoy success, status symbols and the feeling of being looked up to. The careers which may draw you are engineering, building and the driving of trains, planes and road vehicles. You could be an actor, teacher or jeweller – or a combination of these. You work at a steady pace but with periods of sheer idleness in between. Needless to say, most of the time you manage to achieve a great deal. It is possible that you will decide to 'drop out' at some later stage in your life, preferring a quiet lifestyle as a country gentleman. However, you can be relied upon to make sure that you can afford to do this beforehand.

Leo/Taurus

This makes for success just as long as you don't completely give in to your tendency for laziness. Both signs dislike change and prefer the continuity of a settled job. Both are quite ambitious even if this is not obvious. You can work at a job purely for the money it brings in or for the power and influence you might obtain from it; however you are happiest when your work contains a creative element. Both signs are creative and musical, so you could find work in the fields of fashion, art, music, engineering design, landscape gardening or catering. Your creativity could lead you to start a business of your own or, if you are not career minded, to create a lovely home of your own. If your job doesn't give you an opportunity for creativity, you will look for a creative hobby. You could grow prize plants and vegetables in your garden or you could add to your considerable popularity by being the neighbourhood's best cook.

Before leaving the career and aptitudes section of the MC, I would like to include a fact which my friend Denise has noticed. It occurred to her that people who have a strong dose of Leo on their birthchart get on very well with new technology such as word-processors, computers and computerized telex machines. Soon after Denise spotted this phenomenon, she did a head count around the offices where she works and sure enough, those people who really enjoyed using machinery all had either Sun, Moon or ascendant in Leo. After she told me this, I did my own head count and came up with the same answer. Neither of us can think of an astrological reason for this, except perhaps for the fact that Leos never really grow up and enjoy playing with toys all through their lives.

Some people are attracted to those whose Sun signs are the same as their MC sign. This would suggest that the partner is in tune with the subject's aims and ambitions. In your case, you get on well both at work and in your personal life, with Aries or Taurus people.

The descendant

When the ascendant is in Leo, the opposite point or descendant is in Aquarius. There is no evidence to suggest that Leo rising subjects are particularly inclined to marry Aquarians but you may be attracted to Aquarian qualities in a partner. These qualities are independence, humanity and an individual outlook on life. You may treat your partner in a slightly Aquarian manner, thereby giving him space and freedom to be himself. You are incredibly difficult to please because you prefer a partner who is capable, independent and intrinsically fascinating, but at the same time you cannot stand too much competition. One Leo rising friend told me that he had given up a highly exciting relationship with a young woman because she was so clever and resourceful that she made him feel inadequate by comparison. You are choosy with regard to whom you call friends, but once somebody becomes a friend your loyalty towards them is almost completely unshakeable.

This Aquarian descendant can cause problems due to the unstable and revolutionary nature of the sign. In terms of relationships, this means that you are quite likely to be married more than once, possibly to partners who are rather odd. In some cases, your partners seem to start out normal and become odd at some later date!

Love, sex and relating – regardless of the descendant

You are truly a family person, but you cannot subordinate yourself too far to the wishes of a partner because you need to be treated with respect. If you feel that your role is important, either as wage-earner or home-maker and that your decisions count for something within the home, all is well. You need to love and be loved, and the love which you seek takes every form, including the love of your children, genuine care and affection for your mate and, of course, the satisfaction of your sexual desires. Hopefully this can be accomplished with your mate, but if it doesn't work out that way you are quite able to cope with a bit of extra-marital bliss.

Sexually, you are warm, caring, gentle and at the same time, demanding. You have a well-developed sense of touch and therefore will enjoy the relaxed sensuality of love-making rather than just looking for the pleasurable relief of an orgasm. You may not be all that ambitious when it comes to sexual acrobatics, but the act of love with a few interesting variations is, in your opinion, a better way of spending a couple of hours than most. Your technique is unhurried and your habitual attitude is generous and caring towards your partner. I cannot imagine anyone having any complaints and you are unlikely to complain if you are loved, cared for and made love to by someone whom you love and respect.

Any form of ridicule on the part of your partner would spell out the death of the relationship. You cannot bear to be ridiculed or embarrassed either in public or in private in respect of your body or your sexual performance. When things work out well, you are the most generous, kind, loyal and genuine partner that anyone can have.

Health

Leo is traditionally associated with the back and the heart. The husband of a friend of mine has his Sun in Leo and has had operations for spinal problems and a couple of heart attacks along the way. These ailments are not much fun, but they are typically Leonian in being traumatic and dramatic.

Your sixth house is in Capricorn, so please also look at the health section on page 565.

9

Virgo Rising

Men of England wherefore plough
For the lords who lay ye low?
Wherefore weave with toil and care
The rich robes your tyrants wear?

Percy Bysshe Shelley, *Song to the Men of England*

A few words of explanation

A sign on the ascendant expresses itself in a different way from a Sun sign; however some of the characteristics and even the childhood experiences will apply if you have the Sun in Virgo or in the sixth house. They may also be present if you have Mercury in Virgo or in the sixth house. If your Moon is in Virgo or in the sixth house, your emotions and reactions will have a Virgoan flavour. If the ascendant is weak (see Chapter 1), the Virgo overlay will not be so noticeable.

If the rest of the birthchart is very different from the rising sign there could be a conflict within the personality. This is because the outer manner, the signals which are given out at first meeting by the subject, is very different from the main character which lies underneath. Another possibility is that the subject rejects all that his parents and teachers stood for and creates a life for himself which is very different from the one which they envisaged for him or the one which he lived through as a child.

Remember that this sign is mutable which implies flexibility of mind and is an earth sign which suggests practicality, while also being feminine/negative in nature which implies introversion. Virgo rising is a sign of long ascension, which means that there are plenty of you around.

Early experiences

One of the questions on my research questionnaire asked 'would you like to have your childhood over again?' All but one of the Virgo rising respondents replied 'No, definitely not!' The only one who gave a 'yes' answer had her rising sign on the Virgo/Libra cusp. This is such a difficult ascendant to be born with that if your childhood was abnormally *happy* I'd suggest that you re-check your birth time!

Your parental home may have been comfortable or it may have been spartan, but whether your family was rich or poor, their attitude to the spending of money was probably frugal. This is assuming that you were brought up in a normal nuclear family. It is possible that you spent time being looked after by other people. And if your parents were particularly difficult, this could have been a blessing in disguise. It is quite common for a Virgo rising subject to have quite a good relationship with his mother but a difficult one with his father. In some cases, the father takes delight in tormenting or bullying the Virgo rising child. I'm not saying that all Virgo rising children go through this kind of experience but it is not that uncommon. In some cases, the father loves the child unreservedly but the mother cannot see any good in him (or more likely her) which leads to the child growing up under a constant barrage of criticism, knowing that whatever she does, she is never going to win her mother's approval. Not every case is as extreme as this, but the chances are that if you have this sign on the ascendant, you would have been on the receiving end of totally unfair and undeserved ill-treatment at the hands of others – most probably from just the people you should have been most able to trust.

Your parents were probably quite dutiful in their attitude towards you, making sure that you had your practical needs catered for. If they did this out of a sense of obligation rather than genuine affection, you would have been aware of this and you may even have felt guilty for putting them to the trouble of looking after you! You were expected to conform to a set of rules and regulations and to be clean and tidy at all times with polished shoes and straight, unwrinkled socks. Your school may also have been over-disciplined with too much emphasis on stuffy rules. I recall one Virgo rising lady telling me that she remembered being severely punished at school for turning up with the wrong coloured ribbons in her hair – and all this at the age of seven!

Your parents expected you to do well at school, to behave perfectly and to maintain a position at the top of the class at all times. This constant pressure and the unremitting requirement for you to be perfect at everything (except maybe for those subjects they themselves felt were unnecessary) could have left you rigid with nerves and shyness and prey to all kinds of nervous ailments. On the positive side, you had access to books; educational aids and extra-curricular activities. You were encouraged to read and to learn; and if you are typical of the sign, you probably got the hang of this quite early on. Your well-behaved manner endeared you to teachers and your modesty was inoffensive to the other children. You probably didn't try hard to make or keep friends, being happiest in your own company or with your pets; neither did you take much interest in any of the contemporary fads and fancies in which the other children were involved.

You have a surprisingly stubborn and uncompromisingly selfish streak which may not be immediately obvious to others. Your survival instincts are strong, endowing you with a knack of appearing to be accommodating while actually pleasing yourself. You may have developed into an eccentric and uncompromising adult, preferring to live and work alone or among your pet animals. This may be the result of the unfair and unreasonable treatment you suffered as a child or it may be something which is purely a product of your personality. Some Virgo rising children actually resist love and affection, behaving so oddly and in such an offensive manner that nobody can really take to them.

Some Virgo rising subjects grow up in an overbearing religious atmosphere where the fear of God is added to the fear of what the neighbours might think. (This is especially so when the fourth house is in Sagittarius.) One Virgo rising friend of mine grew up in a Salvation Army family where everything was made subservient to religion.

Appearance

Virgo rising subjects are good looking as a rule, especially if they are born with a fairly late degree of the sign rising. You are probably a little taller than average with a long slim well-defined face and large pale eyes. All this has to be considered alongside racial differences and the influence of the rest of the chart. Typical subjects have a cheery smile and an intelligent sense of humour which shines out of the eyes. Your complexion is pale, even in the Summer, because you haven't the patience to waste time lolling around in the sun. You may be a little overweight or even thin with a bit of a pot-belly, but your above-average height and your good posture allows you to get away with this.

Outer manner

Your outer manner is polite, formal and a little guarded. You can hang back and be shy on first meeting, especially in new social circumstances but you soon warm up when you relax. Unless the rest of the chart is made up of pure 'pudding', your mind is very sharp and you can be surprisingly intuitive. You always *appear* confident and capable; the very image of the perfect purchasing officer, secretary or nurse. Being shy, you may also appear to be a little stand-offish on first acquaintance and you prefer to let others do the talking, while you assess the people and the situation around you. When you're at ease, of course, you can talk the hind legs off a donkey. You are usually very smartly dressed, in an up-to-date manner with stylish and slightly unconventional clothing.

Virgo characteristics

This section can double up as a brief guide to Virgo as a Sun sign as well as a rising sign, so it provides a handy reference for you if you wish to check out someone s Sun sign as well as their rising sign. Do be a bit wary in the case of Virgo rising because there are quite a few differences between the Sun in Virgo and Virgo rising.

This is a contradictory and complicated sign to describe; the repressive childhood can leave a legacy of shyness and poor self-esteem which may never be overcome. Although there are others who, perhaps because they have several planets in less inhibited signs, can achieve a good deal of worldly success later in life. The earthiness of the sign makes you practical, capable and good with your hands. You may be an excellent gardener, decorator or a terrific cook. I have come across Virgo rising subjects whose daily life is spent in high-level business negotiations but whose private pastimes are cooking and gardening. The energies of this sign are directed to both the hands and the mind, therefore you bring craftsmanship to all your tasks and the orderliness of your mind suggests that you go about things in a logical and sensible manner. Your home and your workplace may be untidy but they are probably clean and fairly systematic.

You need a stable family environment, especially if you suffered from the usual Virgoan emotional poverty during your childhood. Many Virgo rising subjects marry and bring up children while they are quite young. You cope with early responsibility of this kind very well. if you are lucky with your choice of partner you will grow in confidence, going on to lead a happy, if rather ordinary, life. You take marriage seriously, and your desire to serve the needs of others suggests that you put a lot of effort into relationships. It may be hard for you to express affection openly because you find it easier to show your love by doing things for your family rather than by any show of sloppy sentimentality. As a parent, you may be fussy and inclined to worry too much about your children's health or with their behaviour, but your love for them is genuine and very generously given. Under the best of circumstances, you can put right the wrongs of your own childhood and become a truly successful relater. If you are not so lucky in your choice of partner, you will continue to suffer the kinds of injustices which you endured in your childhood.

Having harped on rather sanctimoniously about Virgoans' undoubted worth as caring and responsible family members, I will now bring us all back to earth. You are saved from being a complete stuffed-shirt or a self-righteous bore by your habit of unfaithfulness! Even though you are an exemplary person in most ways, you can be 'slippery' in personal relationships; but more of this in the 'relating' section.

Your generosity and kindness leads you to offer help to others, either directly by working in one of the caring professions, or on a spare-time basis. Virgo rising subjects can be found in the Scout movement, in nursing, as ambulance drivers, committee members and as astrological counsellers. You are an early riser and a hard and conscientious worker; you even take your spare time duties seriously. You can be surprisingly ambitious but you might find it difficult to progress if you bog yourself down with too much detail, worry too much about what other people think of you or allow your shyness to hold you back. Once you overcome these problems you can aim very high and your success is often aided by your intuitive understanding of the motives of others and a quick grasp of the political situation in your workplace.

You are hard on yourself, being very self-critical and if you find yourself misjudging a situation or coming out with an inappropriate remark, you may punish yourself silently for days afterwards. You also worry far too much about things which just aren't worth worrying about. If there were going to be a change in management at your workplace, you would worry yourself sick. Your dreams would be filled with sackings and applications to the social security office.

Virgoans are naturally rather secretive and are also subtle thinkers, therefore you can handle sensitive and confidential matters very well. Emotionally you are withdrawn. The Virgo rising child who lowered his eyes in silent shame when being harangued by an adult may later turn into a self-contained and secretive adult. If too much pain goes inwards, it will re-emerge later in nervous ailments or old-womanish fussiness. Even if you are well-adjusted to life you will have perfectionist habits somewhere along the line. Your own personal standards are high, you expect too much of yourself and sometimes also of others.

Many Virgoans are funny about food. You may have become a vegetarian years ago, long before it was fashionable or you may follow some kind of religion which prohibits normal eating. You may simply be choosy, only liking certain kinds of food, or foods which are cooked in a particular way. One Virgo rising friend of mine will eat almost anything – as long as it is cooked and prepared to gourmet standards!

Your faults are small but irritating for others to live with; for example, you may drive yourself and others to distraction by worrying needlessly about some small problem. The feminine/ earth aspects of Virgo certainly give you practicality but the sign's ruler, Mercury, makes you quick to change your mind and your moods, thereby making it hard for other people to understand you.

You need to spend time alone, to think and to relax your taut nerves. You may take up some sport or hobby because you think it will be 'good for you', but you soon become bored with it because you enjoy mental stimulation far more than the physical kind. You can sink into pettiness and fussy old-womanish ways if you are not careful. However, this will be alleviated if you have some fire influence on your birthchart.

The midheaven

This section and those which follow apply only to Virgo rising. The midheaven can show your aims and ambitions, therefore it can throw some light on your choice of career. In the case of Virgo rising in UK latitudes, the mid-heaven covers the latter part of Taurus and a good deal of Gemini. In southern Europe and the United States, you will have a Taurus midheaven only if your ascendant is in the first couple of degrees. The vast majority of people born with Virgo rising have their midheaven in Gemini.

Virgo/Taurus

The effect of having earth signs on both the ascendant and the MC makes you practical, sensible and probably rather materialistic and this need for security leads you to find work in a safe and established trade. Both Virgo and Taurus are interested in the growth and production of food, therefore you could work as a farmer, market gardener, dietician or cook. The building trade is another possibility, as is work connected with buildings, such as fitting out, furnishing or dealing with property. The insurance business is also possible.

Your outlook is traditional and your attitude to work and money practical and sensible. Too much change, challenge and excitement would unnerve you but a steady, ordinary and reasonable job would suit you well. Virgo is concerned with health and healing but Taurus can't stand blood and mess, so the prevention of illness by diet and exercise might appeal more than dealing directly with sick people. This combination suggests a need for comfort at home and a good standard of living. Your considerable ambition would be turned towards providing this for yourself and your family. Taurus is associated with music and Virgo with words, therefore, if your birthchart has a creative slant, you could be drawn to the music or the publishing trades.

Virgo/Gemini

This is the sign of the competent secretary, media researcher, nurse or teacher. Both Virgo and Gemini are ruled by the planet Mercury, therefore you are very interested in all forms of communication; this might include teaching and studying, telephone and telex work, writing and publishing, journalism or driving. Your mind is active and you have a need to express yourself but your shyness suggests that you are happier as a backroom boy or girl than out in front of the public. The food and health connection could lead you to write on these subjects as well as to work in their fields. You might be interested in nutrition, medical research or methods of plant cultivation.

The Gemini factor could take you into journalism where your attention to detail and analytical mind would come in handy. There is a kind of intellectual detachment about you which suggests that you look deeply at whatever you are working on rather than taking anything on face value. Your strong desire to help others both directly and indirectly, could lead you into the counselling or medical fields, especially medical research. Communication in the form of travel and transport might attract you, therefore the travel trades, driving or vehicle maintenance could be good careers. Your meticulous and orderly mind could attract you to computing, systems analysis or accountancy. Other possibilities are electrical work or maintenance, electronics, radar, telecommunications or television and video engineering. Any kind of statistical work might appeal, as might research and analysis. Some Virgo rising subjects make very good historians.

The mid-heaven can sometimes denote the kind of person who attracts us or with whom we feel comfortable in day-to-day life. Therefore, you might find that you get on well, both at work and in your private life, with Taurus or Gemini types.

The descendant

The opposite point to the ascendant is the descendant or the cusp of the seventh house. Traditionally, this is supposed to show the kind of person to whom you are attracted. When Virgo is rising, the descendant is in Pisces and this nebulous sign may bring difficulties in relationships. You may attract people who are out of the ordinary or even somewhat peculiar. It seems as if this descendant is trying to compensate for your down-to-earth attitude to life by throwing a spanner in the works just where you least need one. You may find yourself attached to a partner who drinks or, worse still, is mentally unstable. To some extent it is your desire to help and to reform others which may land you in this pickle. You may fall for someone whose superficial appearance hides weakness, an inability to relate or even a cruel streak.

On the plus side, you could attract gentle, rather mystical types who want to care for and serve the needs of the family, just as you do. You seek kindness in a partner and will act kindly and charitably towards them. You can be happy with a partner who is musical, artistic and caring as long as they also pull their weight at work and at home. You can put up with a lot, just as long as your partner is basically decent and honest. You, yourself, can be decent and totally reliable in practical matters but potentially unfaithful sexually. Here we go again with those Virgoan contradictions.

Love, sex and relating – regardless of the descendant

This area of your life, as you have probably guessed, has all the appearance of a first-class minefield, especially when one looks at the contradictions in your own nature. You are shy, modest and possibly a touch fearful when it comes to sex. On the face of it, it might be better if you left this side of life until you were mature enough to cope with it – say around the age of 70; but that's not the way it happens. The chances are that your first encounter with sex came when you were in your teens – and your early teens at that! There could be any number of reasons for this. You could have been attracted, lulled or projected into a sexual relationship far too quickly. Your own desperate need for someone to provide you with some form of love and approval might have been the spur here. Some Virgoans trade sex for company, comfort and companionship. Oddly enough, considering the modesty and fastidiousness of this sign, you have a strong, needy and inventive sex-drive which, coupled with your curiosity, can lead you into all kinds of adventures. In short, despite all the repression, guilt and fear of making a fool of yourself, the enjoyment of lunch, love and lust creates a surprising metamorphosis in you.

You are experimental in bed and analytical afterwards; you may enjoy your private mental action-replays as much as you enjoyed the first-hand experience. Oddly enough, for such a responsible and family-minded sign, you are quite likely to be unfaithful in marriage. Why, I wonder? Possibly the need to experiment, compare and to analyse; the intellectual need to know what the world and the people in it are all about; or perhaps the need to keep a door open on all relationships and give yourself an impression of freedom even within a commitment. Maybe it's your way of getting back at a repressive partner or coping with a bad marriage. It seems that when you meet someone interesting you simply have to check them out; it is a form of the 'don't die wondering' syndrome! Your quiet, humorous and laid-back manner is charming and attractive to others, as is your quite genuine desire to please and, above all, to communicate.

Health

Your health is probably lousy. If it isn't, then you could suffer from hypochondria! Traditionally, your skin, bowels and nerves are weak spots but, in truth, you could have any ailment you desire. Like your Gemini-rising cousins, your nerves will let you down and can be guaranteed to plunge you into an illness whenever the going gets tough. Toothache, backache and inexplicable stomach pains are all possibilities, as are chronic ailments of all kinds. If you haven't had asthma or hay fever yet, you never know – this might be your 'lucky' year.

Here comes that contradiction again: Virgoans are *strong*, far stronger than their Leo or Libra neighbours, but they *need* a spell of bad health from time to time in order to switch off and rest.

Your sixth house is in Aquarius, so please also look sat the health section on page 575.

10

Libra Rising

We don't bother much about dress and
Manners in England, because as a
Nation we don't dress well and we've
No manners.

George Bernard Shaw, *You Never Can Tell*

A few words of explanation

A sign on the ascendant expresses itself in a different way from a Sun sign; however some of the characteristics, even the childhood experiences will apply if you have the Sun in Libra or the seventh house. If your Moon is in Libra or the seventh house, your emotions and reactions will have a Libran flavour. If the ascendant is weak (see Chapter 1), the Libra overlay will not be so noticeable. If the, rest of the birthchart is very different from the rising sign there could be a conflict within the personality. This is because the outer manner, the signals which are given out at first meeting by the subject, is very different from the main character which lies underneath. Another possibility is that the subject rejects all that his parents and teachers stood for and creates a life for himself very different from the one which he lived through as a child.

Remember that Libra is a cardinal sign which means that there is a limit to what you will put up with. It is also masculine, positive and airy in character, which suggests that you appear outgoing and enterprising and that you prefer to deal with the world from a mental or intellectual standpoint. This is a sign of long Ascension, so there are plenty of you around.

Early experiences

This sign on the ascendant denotes a good start in life. However there may be a few drawbacks even when this most pleasant sign is rising. Your parental home was probably comfortable, your parents kind and your relationship with childhood friends reasonable. As a small child, you were good looking, popular and charming and you managed to keep out of any real trouble both at home and at school. All in all, your childhood experiences were better than most, so what's the problem?

The problem is subtle, and it varies a little from one Libra rising subject to the next. Your parents may have left you to your own devices because they were busy. In some cases the father was a distant figure, he may have travelled away from home in connection with work or he may have walked away from the marriage and left the family; in many cases he actually died when the subject was very young. Sometimes the relationship with the father is quite good but the subject seems to be at odds with the mother. Whatever the actual situation may be, the feeling is one of distance and neglect. It may be that the subject and his parents don't share the same values or that they have natures which clash, although any clashing will be done quietly when this sign is rising. There are many Libra rising subjects who are lavished with guilt-induced 'goodies' by parents who neglect them.

In less difficult circumstances, you will have grown up being well cared for and well understood. Your sisters and brothers may have been less than impressed by your charm, and could have behaved in a jealous and spiteful manner towards you. You were probably a langorous child; lazy, slow-moving, quiet and well-behaved. If your parents were not too neglectful, they would have given you every opportunity to stretch your mind and encouraged you to do well at school. It is unlikely that a great deal of pressure was put on you to succeed but there was pressure to conform and not to make waves.

Being independent, even as a child, it is possible that your religious beliefs and political opinions have developed differently from those of your parents. Libra rising subjects don't usually come from a highly religious background but, oddly enough, their parents seem to have very strong political views. Belonging as you do to an independent-minded air sign, you would have listened to their opinions and then formed your own at a later stage in life. Although slow to do anything, and very slow to come to any kind of decision, you were quite able to think things out for yourself and to work out what you wanted to believe in.

You had, even as a child, a great desire to be surrounded by beauty. Your sense of taste and style is innate - it would have been hard for you to live with mess, dirt and disorder. The chances are that your parents' home was tasteful and attractive, and your own possessions clean and well cared for. You are not slovenly yourself and neither were your parents. You appreciate the arts, music and anything which is attractive and well thought out. You could have been artistically creative, especially if there are other forces on your birthchart to back this up. Librans have a natural kind of refinement. It is possible, even as a small child, that you assisted your parents in planning and working on a garden or in choosing the colour schemes for the house. This natural Libran taste can be useful to others. I usually ask my Moon-in-Libra son to choose household things for me, because his 'eye' is far better than mine.

Appearance

Where this is concerned, please take into consideration racial factors and the rest of the birthchart. You are good looking, although not necessarily beautiful. Your features are refined, delicate and attractive. Even if you are plump, you will have a clear skin, beautiful eyes and a lovely smile. In white races, the skin is very fair and the eyes are large, widely set and often a pale luminous grey. You are probably a little below average height with a body which is long in proportion to your legs. Your posture is good and you move with a kind of liquid grace. Your choice of clothing may be conventional or outrageous but it will always be classy, expensive and in keeping with your personality. You like to keep your clothes for a long time and are prepared to spend money on dry-cleaning, therefore you tend to buy quality goods which will last.

Outer manner

You are charm personified. People take to you at once, because of your friendly approach and your genuine interest in what they have to say. Pleasant, humorous and gentle, you are easy to talk to and to get along with, at least on the surface. You enjoy a good old gossip but are rarely sarcastic or hurtful. Your manner of dealing with the world is reasonable, respectful, calm and businesslike, it is rarely brisk or officious. At work you appear to be capable, with an unhurried style which belies your ambition.

Friends drift in and out of your life and though you may forget them for a while, you are always pleased to see them again when they reappear. Unfortunately you lack sincerity, and intuitive people spot this immediately.

Libra characteristics

This section can double up as a brief guide to Libra as a Sun sign *or* as a rising sign, so it can provide a handy reference if you want to check up on someone's Sun sign as well as their rising sign.

Lovely, laid-back Libra – yet another contradictory sign. The evidence from my questionnaires suggests that you didn't enjoy your childhood very much. It is possible that you were afraid of your father, while you may have harboured contempt for your mother. Children from all signs of the zodiac are chivvied by their parents and teachers into making efforts, and many a child is castigated for his or her sloth ('Why are you sprawling in front of the telly when you've homework to do?') Librans seem to be blamed for this more than most. You have a great knack for switching off when asked to do something you don't fancy. You can work very hard, but this will be in fits and starts. You can make a concerted effort when pursuing some money-making scheme or when pursuing a debt, but you cannot keep up the pressure for long because at heart you are lazy.

Librans can be highly ambitious. Remember, this is a cardinal sign. You hate to miss a good opportunity; however your ambitions may not be immediately obvious to others. Many Librans put the minimum effort into their career while working hard at some outside interest. One example is a friend of mine who has served in the Territorial Army for many years without a break while moving around from one job to another. Many of you are musical, continuing to put time and effort into a musical hobby, even when other interests wane.

Your pleasant outer manner may hide contempt for others. It may also hide fear, inhibition and a well-concealed indifference to the needs of others. Some Libra rising subjects, however, are idealistic, truly hoping to make life fuller and better for other people by working in politics or for some worthy cause. You have one really tremendous virtue, and that is your common sense approach to problems. This, coupled with your marvellous ability to listen and give good sensible advice, easily outweighs all your vices. Your talent for listening and advising is terrific but you haven't got the strength, or the patience, to become permanently or heavily involved in the problems of others. You yourself need a listening ear from time to time as your confidence is fragile and you cannot always cope with life.

Libra rising subjects of both sexes are highly domesticated. You may be an excellent cook, a terrific do-it-yourselfer or an inspired antique collector. You may, indeed, be all three. You love your home and enjoy family life. The chances are that you will marry and have children while you are quite young. If you are fortunate in your choice of partner, your marriage will be a great success; however, if it doesn't work out, you will move on and look for someone else. You may be quite hard on your own children, demanding better behaviour and a higher standard of education than you, yourself, achieved. There may be a measure of over-compensation here against your own laissez-faire childhood. You are generous to your partner and also to your children. While it may be true that your children are chivvied to 'perform' well, they are unlikely to be kept short of anything which they need. You, yourself, need a good home, filled with the nicest things for yourself and your family.

As a rising sign even more than as a Sun sign, Libra is concerned with external appearances and the projection of an image. The image may vary from 'yuppy success story' to 'hip musician', but it is always 'cool' in every sense of the word. Confrontations are seen as being uncool and therefore avoided wherever possible. You tend to say what other people want to hear in order to be tactful. Female subjects can project a very feminine or a very sexy image which conceals a cool business head.

I would like to point out something which I have never seen recorded anywhere and that is your gift for spiritual healing. Maybe this is allied to your ability to listen and advise sympathetically. Maybe it has nothing at all to do with it; but I have come across many good healers who have Libra strongly placed in their birthchart. There is another side to the same coin which governs your superb arbitration talents, and that is your ability to argue a point to the bitter end. You may lose sight of reality while you are arguing and end up making absolutely no sense at all but you will win by sheer persistence.

Midheaven

This section and those which follow apply only to Libra rising and not to Sun in Libra. The midheaven shows the subject's aims and ambitions, his public standing and his attitude to work outside the home. In the case of births in the, UK and Europe, most Libra rising subjects have their mid-heaven in Cancer. However those whose ascendant is in the latter part of the sign will have their MC in Leo. For births in the south of Europe and in the United States, almost the whole of this rising sign will have the MC in Cancer and only those with the ascendant in the last few degrees in Libra will have their MC in Leo.

Libra/Cancer

This combination can make for a shrewd businessman or woman. You take your time before committing yourself to anything, carefully weighing up the pros and cons. The Cancerian mid-heaven can lead to an interest in antiques, coin collecting or Egyptology. This may sound peculiar, but it is worth remembering that Cancer is concerned with the past and you may wish to incorporate objects or ideas from the past into your daily life.

Libra, being an air sign, is interested in communicating, keeping up-to-date and being out among people, while Cancer likes to work quietly for himself. This apparent contradiction can be overcome by either doing your own thing inside a large organization or by doing your own thing in some kind of loose association with others. One instance which demonstrates this is a friend of mine who runs a small accountancy business from home, thereby combining her need for autonomy and privacy with her need to communicate with the world at large. Cancer, being a caring sign, can suggest a nursing or counselling career. You may enjoy teaching very young children either in a school or in a Sunday school. This combination is an excellent one for a career in politics, or a quasi-political career such as Trades Union negotiator.

Oddly enough, I have come across a number of electricians and electrical engineers with this rising sign. Maybe the Cancerian MC makes you want to improve people's home and business premises, or maybe it's the presence of air on the ascendant which gives you an affinity to electrical or magnetic forces. Libra is associated with the planet Venus, and this gives you a strong interest in beauty in all its forms, so you may consider working in the field of fashion, cosmetics and design. You may exploit your flair for interior design commercially.

Libra/Leo

This combination suggests a need to leave your mark on the world. You may be attracted to a job which offers you a chance to shine or to use your dramatic flair in some way. The Leo MC seeks the limelight while the Libran ascendant wants to advise others, therefore a position such as a theatrical agent, recruitment consultant or an agony aunt might appeal. Both Leo and Libra are creative signs, so you may choose to work in the fields of design, fashion, jewellery, cosmetics or interior design. Your designs would be both tasteful and opulent.

This combination suggests work in an advisory capacity as, for example, a solicitor, counsellor, consultant, doctor or hypnotherapist. Medical and healing work often appeals to people who have this combination, probably because with a Leo MC so much of the first house is in medically-minded Scorpio. The drawback to this combination is that both the MC and the rising signs denote laziness, so you may have difficulty in finishing the projects which you start.

The midheaven can indicate the type of person to whom you are attracted, both as a personal and a business partner, therefore you could have an affinity with Cancer or Leo types.

The descendant

The opposite point to the ascendant is the descendant or the cusp of the seventh house. Traditionally this is supposed to show the kind of person to whom you are attracted. When Libra is rising, the descendant is in Aries, therefore the enthusiasm and enterprise of Aries types may well attract you. I have noticed that many Librans do actually marry Arians but this union is apt to frustrate both parties because the Arian becomes bored with the Libran's slow, calculating outlook, while the Libran becomes tired of the Arian's childishness. Libra may also object to the Arian's dictatorial manner.

Librans need a partner who enjoys work. You are happy to have them work alongside you, as long as they don't try to make your decisions for you. The cardinal quality of the signs on your ascendant and descendant suggest that you must lead, albeit slowly, rather than follow. You require a fairly calm partner who has a strongly confident centre to his or her personality because you have a habit of taking your everyday frustrations out on your nearest and dearest, or ignoring them when you're in a bad mood.

A clingy, unreasonable or jealous partner is no good for you, as you detest being pinned down or having to account for your movements. Oddly enough, you succeed in one situation where many others fail, and that is in the area of second marriages. You do not trouble yourself to argue with step-children or ex-wives or husbands, preferring to keep the peace if at all possible. Inside your own one-to-one relationship you may be far from peaceful, but to those on the periphery you appear to be decent and reasonable. If you find yourself drawn into a wider family group, you manage very well because you enjoy the fun of family life and all the extra opportunities for conversation and advice-giving. One point which must be made is that you like to experiment with relationships; therefore, you may find commitment and faithfulness impossible.

Love, sex and relating – regardless of the descendant

Despite your cool outer image, relating is never a cool business for you. Somewhere along the line you will fall in love and when this happens you will fall hard. You may not show your feelings to the world but they are strong and deep nevertheless. If you are let down and hurt by this experience you hide your feelings, but they go down deeper than anyone can guess and it is unlikely that you will ever allow yourself to be placed in that situation again. This is a shame because the next person who comes along may be far more worthy of your love, but by then it is too late. Once you have been burned you never place your hand in the fire again.

When you do feel intensely about your partner, your lovemaking can reach magical proportions and even when this is not the case you are a notably good lover. Libra is a hedonistic sign which enjoys any kind of sensual experience, good food, good music and, of course, good sex. You take the trouble to make sure your partner enjoys the experience as much as you yourself and your sensual laziness ensures that you take your time over the process.

There are two further comments which I would like to make about this sign. The first is that you don't like to make love in scruffy or uncomfortable surroundings and the second is that, much as you enjoy sex, you may not want to indulge yourself very often. You may prefer great sex once a month to 'so-so' sex three times a week!

Health

Traditionally, the Libran problem areas are the bladder and the soft organs of the stomach. Your liver and pancreas may be weak, so you should limit your alcohol intake and avoid too much sweet food. You could have a weight problem but your natural vanity might urge you to take action when you realize that you are beginning to look tubby. Libra rules the motor development of the nervous system and, therefore, can be involved with rheumatic or nervous problems, particularly in the spinal column.

Your sixth house is in Pisces, so please also look at the health section on page 586.

11

Scorpio Rising

Give me more Love, or more Disdain;
the Torrid, or the Frozen Zone
Bring equal ease unto my paine:
The Temperate affords me none:
Either extreme, of Love or Hate,
Is sweeter than a calme estate.

Thomas Carew *Mediocrity in Love Rejected*

A few words of explanation

A sign on the ascendant expresses itself in a different way from the Sun sign. However, some of the characteristics, even the childhood experiences will apply if you have the Sun in Scorpio or in the eighth house. There will be some of these characteristics present if you have Mars or Pluto in Scorpio or in the eighth house. If your Moon is in Scorpio, your emotions will have a Scorpionic flavour. If the ascendant is weak (see Chapter 1), the Scorpio overlay will not be so noticeable. If the rest of the birthchart is very different from the rising sign there could be a conflict within the personality. This is because the outer manner, the signals which are given out at first meeting by the subject, is very different from the main character which lies underneath. Another possibility is that the subject rejects all that his parents, parent figures and teachers stood for, and creates a life for himself which is very different from the one which they envisaged for him, or the one which he lived through as a child.

Remember that this is a fixed sign, which implies the ability to stay with a situation and see it through. It is also a water sign, which suggests deep emotions which have a bearing on the subject's behaviour. This is also a sign of long ascension, so there should be plenty of you around.

Early experiences

Scorpio is such an intense sign that one could be forgiven for assuming that this must indicate a particularly difficult childhood. The fact is that there is a wide spectrum of childhood experiences to be found amongst the Scorpio population. Some have truly horrifying childhood experiences, while others seem to have been quite happy. Many Scorpio rising children are naturally cautious and rather withdrawn; they hide their emotions behind a poker face or a blank stare. This makes them hard to read and hard to get close to, which may cut them off from others. If you are a Scorpio rising subject who was ignored as a child, I suggest that you think back to the way *you* behaved and reacted towards others. Did you make any attempt to reach out and touch people? Did you take any interest in their needs or did you simply hide behind your mask, living inside your own head, interested only in your own dreams and desires? This is a difficult situation to explain because there is a chicken and egg aspect here which could have arisen either from a genuine inability to relate to one or more members of your family, or simply because your closed-in manner caused them to withdraw from you. In some cases, there clearly *was* a problem and I shall try to demonstrate some of the difficulties which you may have encountered. I apologize if this explanation is a bit of a list but there are many possibilities.

At the very worst end of the spectrum, some Scorpio rising children are genuinely afraid of one or both of their parents. Some of you feared other relatives or family friends with whom you had to deal. There may, for example, have been an uncle who stood too close to you or a lodger who touched you inappropriately. Even if there was nothing obviously wrong, you may have had an awareness of danger and a sense that all was not as it should have been. Remember that Scorpio is associated with sex, and it is not all that uncommon for children to be taken advantage of. Even if nothing untoward happened, you could have been aware of undercurrents which should not have been present.

Some of you grew up in the kind of home where the father was violent, unpredictable and frequently drunk, while mother was an ineffectual victim. Others had impossible levels of achievement demanded of them by an ambitious mother who lived through her children. Whatever the circumstances, you learned early to keep your feelings under control and never allow your face to betray the thoughts which were running around in your head. This retreat behind the mask, the closed-face withdrawal, is the classic benchmark of this rising sign. One such subject confided to a friend of mine that, when she was nine years old, her truly dreadful, drunken bully of a father died and she had to make an effort to hide her lack of grief. She says that only on rare occasions since has she ever allowed anyone to know how she felt. In some cases, a parent dies and the problem is caused by another adult.

Another possibility is that you developed different values and priorities from the rest of your family and decided that it would be better to keep these quiet. These differing values could have consisted of almost anything; perhaps your parents sought a pedestrian way of life, a humdrum existence, while you yearned for something more exciting and more meaningful. I have come across Scorpio rising subjects who left their parental home at the first opportunity because it was boring and stultifying, mentally and physically cramped, and financially or academically impoverished.

In the years after the Second World War and up to 1960, every young man between the ages of about 18 and 20 had to spend some time in the forces. This took them away from their families and made them see life from a different angle, just at the moment when they were developing into individual adults. For many Scorpio rising youngsters this was a heaven-sent opportunity to get away from home and see something of the world. Girls with this rising sign often 'escaped' into an early marriage in order to have a home and a life of their own. How these youngsters progressed after leaving home depended in part upon their natures and also on the luck of the draw.

There are Scorpionic subjects who got on famously with their families while they were small, only to experience difficulties as they began to grow up and develop ideas of their own. In this case, puberty became a nightmare for all concerned, with the child leaving, or being ejected from the home some time during his teens. Other Scorpio rising subjects have a great time at home with the family but experience problems at school. Sometimes these problems are associated with a particular stage of their schooling, while other Scorpios never seem to get it together where education is concerned. There are Scorpio rising subjects who loved school, and used it as an escape from a mundane or claustrophobic home atmosphere.

I would like to offer the story of my friends, Gillian and Anna, as an example of the subtle difficulties which are associated with this sign on the ascendant. Gillian and Anna are sisters who were born about a year apart. Gill, who was my own special friend, was the elder. Gill was born with her Sun in Gemini and Scorpio on the ascendant, while Anna, the more outgoing of the two girls, had her Sun in Sagittarius but also had Scorpio rising. There had been another much older sister called Tracy who, during the 1950s, met a GI, married him, and emigrated to the United States. I always had a feeling that Tracy was not a natural full sister to the two girls but I have never asked them about this.

Gill and Anna's parents occupied the downstairs part of an old house. Mr Keane, their father, was to my 12 year old eyes, an old man. He had some kind of night-watchman's job and his spare time was spent making their scrap of London-clay-plus-filth front garden into an absolute picture. I have never in all my life seen dahlias like those which Mr Keane so devotedly grew. In bad weather he sat in front of their kitchen boiler fire, sharing the space with strings of washing and reading the *Daily Mirror*. About once every hour he would grunt something incomprehensible through his couple of remaining teeth. I cannot remember him speaking to me or even to the girls very much except to tell them to shut up if they were making too much noise, but apparently (so they later told me) the girls loved him.

Mrs Keane, on the other hand, was a lovely woman. Totally useless in a way many women were in those days, she suffered from angina and agoraphobia and never left the house. To me, growing up in a family where everyone around me died, walked off or ran exciting businesses elsewhere, Mrs Keane's constant presence represented a rare kind of luxury. Needless to say, there was hardly a penny to spare but Mrs K's kettle was always on, and she was always ready for a chat and always interested, in a totally positive way, in everything that we three girls did. She joined in on wet days when we drew or played cards, helping to find string, glue and anything else that we needed for our games. She was a warm, permanent centre to our lives but, in the eyes of the world and, of course, in the eyes of the two growing girls, she appeared far too slow and uninspiring.

Gill and Anna looked increasingly outwards to a world where fun, money, men and the unexpected awaited. Soon after they left school they moved out. The first to go was Gill, who took a live-in job in Cornwall where she became part servant and part trainee horse rider and instructor. She met and married a local man and went on to have a daughter, Rachael. The marriage was a disaster and for a while Gill became a carbon copy of her mother: large, ill and confined to her Cornish home; but now I'm glad to say that she is at work and enjoying her life.

Anna got engaged and, shortly afterwards, became pregnant at the age of 17. The guy who was to be her escape route refused to marry her but, before the baby was born, she met and married Bill, a bus driver, and moved out to a flat a few miles away. Anna has had a couple of husbands since Bill and also several more children, a couple of whom are severely handicapped (more of this interesting phenomenon later). Anna became a nurse and, as far as I know, is now living with yet another guy, working and probably enjoying life a bit more now that her family are at last growing up.

As you can see, neither of these girls' lives are especially remarkable, but they do reflect the Scorpionic disenchantment with childhood and the need to get away at any price. I seriously urge any Scorpio rising youngster who is reading this book to think and plan for your future rather than to run directly towards the first available option, in case the price of escape proves to be just that bit too high. Incidentally, neither Gill nor Anna liked school very much. Gill, in particular, hated her junior school and only learned to read and write properly when she and I were about 12 or 13 years old and needless to say it was I who taught her. I still think back to those two beautiful and imaginative girls whose lives seemed to have been blighted by their lack of sensible planning and their sheer bad luck.

As far as schooling is concerned, I have come across Scorpio rising subjects who were very successful, leaving their contemporaries behind as a result. Some subjects are gifted artists and musicians which, once again, seems to separate them from their contemporaries. Yet others educate themselves out of their social class or have sexual needs which don't fit in with their background. It is this separateness which is at the heart of this rising sign. Sometimes, this separateness is caused by nothing more than the hawk-eyed glare or the flat-faced blank stare emanating from these children's faces which keeps people at a distance and ensures their encapsulation within their own persona.

Finally, back to a subject which I touched upon when talking about Anna. This rising sign is frequently involved with handicaps of one kind or another. I have come across too many instances for it to be mere coincidence. There are Scorpio rising subjects who are mentally or physically handicapped and therefore unable to get around easily or to communicate easily. Some people start out normally enough but by accident, disease or even by their choice of lifestyle, become prevented in some way from living a full life. Others bring up handicapped children themselves. It seems that if Scorpio is strongly shown on a birthchart some connection with helplessness and restriction is inevitable.

Jealousy is very much associated with Scorpio. You may attract envy from others, especially later in life but it is usually you who has to suffer the fires of this most awful and most useless emotion, especially while you are young. Others around you seem to have so much more than you, either in terms of possessions or in their appearance and their status within the group. It is not uncommon for you to burn with jealousy over a luckier or more gifted brother or sister. My Scorpio rising mother cheerfully admits that she loathed her younger sister because she had good looks, the love of their mother and was the recipient of every opportunity that could be mustered for her. My mother, being the elder sister, was sent out to work so that Anne, her younger sister, could have dancing lessons. Many years later, after many ups and downs, Anne, widowed and alone, lost her mind and ended her life in an institution, while my mother, happily married to my lovely step-father is still enjoying a full working and social life at the age of 81! This is typical of the sign, so if you feel that everyone around you is a winner and that you are always cast as the loser, just wait – the tables will surely turn.

Appearance

Taking into account racial and other astrological factors, you are probably shorter than average, broad, stocky and inclined to put on weight easily. Your colouring is sallow and your hair mid to dark brown. Your hair is one of your best features as it is often thick, springy and abundant, keeping its good looks throughout your life. Your hands and feet are small and neat and your movements are economical and quite graceful. You have a lovely smile which lights up your whole face but you have to know someone a little before you favour them with one of your lovely grins. You are light on your feet and a naturally good dancer but as you get older you have to guard against too much sitting about, as you will then begin to gain weight very quickly. Your best feature, a truly hidden asset, is your voice. This is low, quiet but oddly captivating. It commands respect and is a valuable asset to your sexual armoury.

There can be great variations in the appearance of Scorpio rising subjects but one thing is certain, you are not what the computer buffs calls 'wysiwyg'. This term stands for 'what you see is what you get' and, in your case, what we see is definitely *not* what is going on behind your face. Some of you have a strangely flat-faced appearance with broad cheekbones and plenty of width across the eyes. This kind of face may lack expression which helps you to hide your feelings. Other Scorpio rising subjects have a terrifying hawk-like appearance which can be terribly off-putting on first meeting, especially to those with a nervous disposition. To tell you the truth, the hunter-harrier type scares me to death! This too, however, is a disguise which more than adequately conceals a soft heart. Other subjects are extremely good-looking with well defined features and strong bones.

All Scorpio rising subjects have a magnetic appearance but the handsome, dangerous, hypnotic variety of either sex is absolutely irresistible. I have no idea of the birth data but I wouldn't be surprised if the late James Mason, the film actor, had been a Scorpio rising subject – those melting eyes, that magnetic voice, wow! My mother has her Sun on the Scorpio/Libra cusp and also has a Scorpio ascendant. She is a terrifying individual, even now at the age of 81, very athletic, with all her brains intact and a razor-sharp tongue still in full working order. However, like the vast majority of Scorpio rising subjects her appearance hides a soft centre and a deep fund of generosity. Whether you love them or hate them, you cannot overlook a Scorpio rising subject.

Outer manner

Most people who have this rising sign are charming, fascinating and interesting to listen to. As a Scorpio rising subject, you probably have some special ability or interest which makes you stand out from other people in some way. This slight studiousness, coupled with your diffidence, makes you appear clever and mysterious. You don't push yourself forward in social situations, being most relaxed when working on your own particular hobbies. It is always a joy to sit quietly and listen to you when you relax and open out. Your company is so good that time spent with you goes by quickly.

There are some Scorpio rising types who are thoroughly off-putting on first acquaintance, being sharp and forbidding, critical, offensive and rather frightening, but I have found that if I allow myself to slide behind the unpleasant mask there is always a fascinating person tucked safely away around the back of it. You are curious about the motives and behaviour of other people and may tend to put total strangers under interrogation, but even this unnerving trait is far preferable to the type of person who is terminally self-absorbed.

Scorpio characteristics

This section can double up as a brief guide to Scorpio as a Sun sign or as a rising sign, so it can provide a handy reference if you want to check up on someone's Sun sign, as well as their rising sign.

Scorpios are given a notoriously bad press in most astrology books, being written off as drunken sex maniacs with violent tendencies on the one hand, or the kind of mesmeric bodice-rippers so beloved of women's pulp fiction on the other. ('He caught her fragile body within the tensile strength of his muscular arms, the fluttering of her heart as she shivered against his chest meant nought to him as he brought his cruel mouth hard down upon her softly tremulous lips ...) The disappointing fact is that the majority of you are quiet, hard-working, reliable people, good to your families and kind to animals. However there is a powerful side to your nature, an ability to construct, destroy and reconstruct which sets itself into motion when your life begins to go wrong.

Your likes and dislikes are strongly felt. There are no half measures for you, no compromise and no response to coercion other than outright fury. When you approve of something or somebody it goes all the way, whilst no amount of mitigating circumstances will make you bend towards those whom you consider beneath contempt. A very simple example of this phenomenon in action is that of Tony, a Sun in Scorpio guy who cheerfully admits that he dislikes animals. Who but a Scorpio could admit to disliking animals? He even professes to enjoy the sight of spring lambs gambolling around in his freezer. This kind of remark is calculated to shock, and doesn't have to be taken too literally.

You certainly take your likes and dislikes to extremes. You may drink like a fish or be totally abstemious, you may spend money as if it were going out of fashion or use your purse so infrequently that moth larvae reside in it! Whatever your beliefs or values, you would rather lose a job, a lover or £1,000 in cash than change them.

At work, you either remain in a comfortable job which allows you to feel that you belong or you move upwards to become the head of a concern. Many of you run your own businesses, though freelance consultancy work might be too insecure for you. You are quite demanding when in a position of authority but rarely unpleasant or unreasonable (Montgomery of Alamein being a notable exception). You have the uncanny knack of commanding respect from junior employees and they usually continue to work for you over the years. Demanding you may be, but you don't change the rules from one day to the next, so people who work for you always know where they stand and what is expected of them. You, yourself, cannot abide the kind of boss who moves goal posts; you need to know what your duties are and to be left in peace to carry them out. Most of all, you hate being criticized.

Being a water sign you have a long memory. On a practical level this helps you amass and retain data in connection with your job. On a less practical side, you remember those who are good to you and never forget those who hurt or insult you. You remember birthdays, dates, times, places and the gossip and unwise confessions which the unwary let slip into your ears.

Your powers of endurance are incredible, and your health is usually excellent. However, if you *do* fall ill, it is likely to be sudden and dramatic. Your powers of recovery are equally dramatic. You can put up with more hard work, discomfort and exhaustion than any three other signs combined. When you overwork, you may look as if you are coping calmly, but the truth is that you switch to a kind of overdrive facility which consists of determination, stretched nerves and tension. When this happens you may vent your tense feelings on your nearest and dearest. You can be co-operative when you feel like it, but you dislike being taken for granted. You may be helpful on occasion but this does not guarantee that you will be so all the time, and you despise what you see as weakness in others.

Remember that this is a water sign which, despite its fixed quality, denotes moodiness. Scorpios are proud, so your personal standards of behaviour are very high. You don't care much for personal criticism and you dislike jokes which are made at your expense. You can just about accept constructive criticism but are mortally offended by any kind of personal attack. The long Scorpio memory is attached to an ability to keep secrets, a quality which makes you a good choice for any kind of confidential work. Where your personal life is concerned you reveal little. You may appear quite open, even highly opinionated but your real feelings are tucked well away from view. If you find yourself in what you deem to be any kind of challenging or threatening situation, you can be very hostile.

Although this is not a notably intellectual sign, your curiosity about the world gives you a thirst for knowledge. You make sure that you are well-informed on a general level, street-wise even, but you probably have a special interest which holds your attention year after year. Some Scorpios are wonderful amateur historians, others are linguists, while yet others have a great love and knowledge of the natural world. You love to stretch your body so many of you are athletic or interested in dancing or swimming. You tend to keep these interests going throughout life. If other aspects of your chart back this up, you may have a lifelong interest in military matters and be very knowledgeable about military history.

Your need to delve into things can be expressed in a very personal way. You may look through other people's cupboards out of curiosity. Recycling is another Scorpio passion. Like your fellow water sign of Cancer, you prefer articles which have been used before to new ones. 'Waste not, want not' is your watchword; jumble sales and the local Oxfam shop are your spiritual home. Your curious attachment to death may have begun in childhood where you became aware, as a result of the death of someone around you, that life can be nasty, brutish and short.

Your loyalty to your friends and family is intense and you would never abandon an elderly parent or a needy child. Even a wayward spouse is taken care of; although you would probably switch off from them on an emotional level. You don't run away from problems, indeed, you may hang on to bad situations long after they should be abandoned. You are reliable and dependable, very caring and often self-sacrificial with regard to your family and, despite the fact that you yourself are usually robust, you are patient with those who are sick. You are less than patient when you, yourself, are sick, as you either consider it to be an unacceptable sign of personal weakness or an unnecessary interruption to your daily life. Yes, it's true that Scorpios can be cruel, destructive, self-destructive, moody and totally impossible at times, but you prefer to give comfort, affection, love, and care, rather than to dish out pain to those you love. It is worth remembering that you may have been short-changed in terms of physical affection in childhood and you welcome the opportunity to give and receive cuddles and love when grown up. The main thing to remember when this sign is rising is that the outer personality, the messages which are given out at first meeting, is a mask under which there is, modified, of course, by the rest of the chart, a kindly loving person who wishes to leave this world a better place than he found it.

The midheaven

This section and those which follow apply only to Scorpio rising. The midheaven shows your aims and ambitions, therefore it can throw some light on your choice of career. In the case of Scorpio rising in the UK and similar northerly latitudes, the MC is almost equally split between Leo and Virgo. In the USA and southern Europe about two thirds of the MC will be in Leo, with the remainder in Virgo. Either MC will make the subject cautiously ambitious but the drive to achieve will be directed differently.

Scorpio/Leo

These are both fixed signs which denote that the subject finds it hard to adapt to change. If you lose your job or suffer any type of setback which calls for a close look at your situation and your potential, you would view it as a tragedy rather than as a challenge. You would also harbour a deep and abiding resentment for the person or organization who placed you in such a position. However, your tremendous reserves of courage and energy would ensure that you didn't wallow in misery for long.

The fixed nature of this sign makes you reliable and efficient. There is a Scorpio motto which goes 'if you are going to do a job, then for goodness sake do it properly'. You are thorough and painstaking and you hate to be rushed and hassled whilst you are working. The Leo MC gives you a desire for status and glamour, while the Scorpio ascendant adds caution, tenacity and independence, therefore you head slowly towards the top, stamping your personal style upon your surroundings as you go.

You may be found running a business or at the head of a governmental department; you are also able to work alone on creative projects. This Scorpio/Leo combination could denote a winning athlete or a top psychiatrist. Acting is a possibility because here you can use the Leo MC to project emotion and to draw attention to yourself, without the risk of jeopardizing your well-protected persona. Scorpios frequently love music, of both the classical and the pop variety; Leos are also very 'into' music, therefore you could choose to work in the field of music-making, promotion or sales. Musical instruments and the computers and electronics which are nowadays associated with the making of music may interest you as well. As you can see, your career possibilities are diverse; they may include banking, teaching, coal or diamond mining. Many of you are fond of children and will either go into full-time teaching or, and this is more likely, spend some of your spare time scouting, guiding or something similar.

Many Scorpios are drawn to a military career. This gives you the company of people who didn't know you as a child, offering you a fresh start in life so that you can put the pain of your childhood behind you for good. The armed services provide opportunities for travel and sport, plus the opportunity to develop your natural interest in the vehicles and weapons of war. Remember that, before the discovery of the planet Pluto, Scorpio was said to be ruled by Mars, the god of war. Being especially drawn to the sea, you could join the navy or possibly the merchant marines. One Scorpio rising subject of my acquaintance left her awful childhood behind by taking a job on a cruise liner.

Many of you find your way into the police force, this being a job for which you are supremely fitted. You work well within a team and can command the respect of your comrades. Your investigative powers and natural mistrust of fellow humans stands you in good stead here, while your physical strength and well trained body enable you to enjoy exercise and combat. Many Scorpios are drawn to the world of the military and the para-military, just as many more are drawn to the world of medicine and para-medicine. These careers can be viewed as being useful to the community at large, offering aid and protection to the weak, and thus allowing you to express the 'knight in shining armour' aspects of your personality.

Scorpio/Virgo

This combination should lead you towards a medical career, or at least towards a strong interest in all aspects of mental and physical healing. The Scorpio/Virgo combination includes surgeons, doctors, herbalists, spiritual healers and psychiatrists. There is a desire to help humanity and at the same time a fascination with human and animal biology and perhaps even with mental and physical pain. The modest and retiring nature of this combination leads you to choose a job which allows you to stay in the background, therefore you would make a good civil servant, secretary and social worker. You could choose to work in the food or the clothing industry, or even in the trade of butchery. This is partly because Virgo is associated with food and clothing (Scorpio with knives and meat) but also because these jobs supply basic needs to the public. This need to do something which is useful to the public and which is helpful in an impersonal way stems from the same root as the 'knight in shining armour' image which I mentioned a while ago.

Oddly enough you may do well in the world of acting or dancing, as these are jobs which offer opportunities for safe self-expression and which bring influences to bear upon the public while giving pleasure. Spiritual healing might be an attractive interest. You could also be attracted to the use of alternative medicines and therapies; hypnotism is an especially common Scorpio interest. Religion also fascinates you, but the remainder of the chart will determine whether this takes you into the world of the 'respectable' churches, or the wider holistic philosophies of the New Age. It is worth bearing in mind that a late Scorpio ascendant puts a good deal of the first house into the religious and philosophical sign of Sagittarius.

General comments

Don't be too cut and dried with these MCs. The Scorpio/Leo person may be medically-minded while the Scorpio/Virgo person may be the one who runs away to sea. Just bear in mind that this ascendant needs to work and live close to the heart of life and death or at the creative heart of an important project. What you do should *matter*; it should leave its mark on the world and allow you to feel as if you count for something. It is also worth remembering that Scorpio is associated with sex, therefore rape crisis counselling may appeal to you, as might gynaecology – I guess even pornography might appeal, but if you were going to make films which were both artistic and successful, you would need a well placed Neptune in your birthchart!

The midheaven can sometimes indicate the type of person to whom you are attracted both as working partners and as lovers, so you might find yourself most comfortable alongside Leo and Virgo people.

The descendant

The opposite point to the ascendant is the descendant or the cusp of the seventh house. Traditionally, this is supposed to show the kind of person to whom you are attracted. In this case the seventh house cusp is in Taurus. When you find the right partner you settle down to a long-lived and very affectionate relationship, but even this relationship is not without fireworks. It is also worth noting that your most successful relationship is likely to be a second marriage (rather than a first one), coming along when you have learned a bit about living with others. You may 'try out' two quite different types of marriage, one with a sexy firebrand and another with a gentle uncritical homemaker. Assuming that your marriage is a success, you would enjoy becoming a parent, although you may have some unrealistic ideas of what it means to bring up children. It is worth remembering that your fifth house, the one which is concerned with children, is in the illusory and delusory sign of Pisces. If your partner were the Taurean type, you would share an appreciation of music and the sensual joys of good food and good sex. However, trouble could arise from the tendency for both of you to have powerful and destructive tempers.

To be honest, this sign does not carry the best auguries for happy relationships although, if you are not too uncompromising in outlook and the rest of your chart includes some lighter factors, they can work out very well. You take commitments seriously and that is an advantage.

Love, sex and relating – regardless of the descendant

There is no easy description for this. It would be all too easy to fall back on the 'sexy, passionate' image which is the usual theory regarding your sign, but I'm not so sure about this. Scorpio rising subjects can be extremely sexy, using sex as an outlet for bottled-up feelings, as a means to control and dominate a partner or as a form of reassurance. You can use sex to convince yourself that someone loves you, deluding yourself that just because they respond bodily to your efforts, they can't fail to be yours in mind and soul as well. You can use sex to prove that you count or even that you exist and, of course, also for the sheer bloody pleasure of it.

Your patience, endurance and natural desire to give and receive would suggest that you do make an exceptional lover. You're not afraid to experiment, and nor are you easily disgusted, therefore your inhibitions should be few, if any. However, having said all this, I absolutely must point out that Scorpio is such an all-or-nothing sign that some of you are totally uninterested in sex. Some of you may be impotent, while others may be uncertain about your sexuality, while some of you are only interested in sex on a few very rare occasions (anniversaries and similar events). You may choose to remain celibate for religious reasons, or because you wish to save your strength for the athletic field or the boxing ring; yet others of you are fastidious and highly inhibited. Some Scorpios are genuinely terrified of the whole business or just plain unimpressed by it and therefore totally uninterested! As far as relating is concerned, this could go in a variety of directions.

There is a fabulous Sun sign astrology book called *The New Astrology*, written by Poppe Folly. This comically ironic book has this very apt comment in its Scorpio section: 'The casual violence of your successful marriages may appall everyone else, and terrify your children: attacks on your spouse they construe as attacks on themselves. This is why the little things sit at the top of the stairs rocking with horror when they hear you fighting through the night'. True! true! If a Scorpio rising woman marries a man who insists on leaving her at home with small children, too little housekeeping money and a blank refusal to share her burdens or treat her with a modicum of respect, then he is in for a nasty shock. Maybe his mother could be relied upon to lie down under this kind of treatment but his *wife* certainly will not. Violence can arise through jealousy or a fear of abandonment and oddly enough it is not necessarily the Scorpio who is the perpetrator of the violence! The Scorpio could himself be a prey to someone else's unreasonable feelings of possessiveness and jealousy. If you, as a Scorpio, feel threatened or maltreated you could enter into a war of attrition with your partner which could be carried on for years. This kind of relationship needs two warriors to keep it going, it won't work if your partner switches off or walks out.

Very few Scorpios can take criticism. You may take offence even at the most helpful, well-meant and constructive criticism. However you can be an expert at dishing it out. You quickly learn just which of your partner's buttons to push and won't be able to resist winding him up when he is feeling unwell or emotionally vulnerable. Scorpios need a lot of standing up to.

This list of disastrous relationship scenarios is no more than a list of possibilities. There are plenty of good husbands and wives with this sign rising. Many male Scorpios marry large, motherly women. You need affection, reassurance and a feeling of continuity. You appreciate acceptance, even by your spouse's family and you benefit greatly from a wise partner who encourages you to open out and express yourself. If you have the kind of partner who includes you in the mainstream of their life, who genuinely respects your opinions and wants your company, you are the best, the most loyal and hardworking mate in the whole zodiac.

I would like to point out a couple of curious facts relating to the area of children and childbirth. There is often something wrong here. A Scorpio rising woman will often bear at least one child out of wedlock, or she will marry a man who isn't the father of her child. Many of you leave the business of parenthood until relatively late in life and then only have one child. Scorpio mothers are often abandoned by their child's father or left to cope alone. Sometimes your resentment of this situation will be taken out on your children or, alternatively, you could push your children to obtain both the material goods and the status which you were never given the opportunity to have. This can be a very uneasy relationship in some cases, whilst in others, the lone chick and its mother cling together in a mutual outpouring of reciprocal love and affection.

Some astrology books note that Sun in Scorpio subjects are born at the time of a death in the family. My Solar Scorpio husband's elder brother died of complications from measles three months before my husband was born. I don't know whether this thought is relevant to Scorpio rising – perhaps you would like to do some research of your own on this one. One final comment here which neatly takes us forward into the health section, is that there are often problems associated with giving birth.

Health

The sexual organs may cause trouble. We have already mentioned child-birth, but other womb and related areas can present problems, while the male organs may suffer hernias and prostate gland difficulties. Vasectomies can go wrong on the one hand, or there may be something wrong with the sperm count. Scorpios are very healthy as a rule, but you can become sick very quickly and very dramatically from time to time. When this happens you instantly become an excellent patient (at least as far as the doctors and hospital are concerned). You respond to treatment and soon forget that you were ever very ill. Heart trouble is surprisingly common, as are stomach ulcers, or the less dramatic but equally uncomfortable ailment of acidity in the stomach. These illnesses result from your usual state of unre-leased stress and tension. Meditation would be of great benefit to you. Many of you suffer from time to time with problems related to the ears, sinuses, teeth and throat.

Your sixth house is in Aries, so please also look at the health section on page 471.

12

Sagittarius Rising

Slav, Teuton, Kelt, I count them all
My friends and brother souls,
With all the peoples, great and small,
That wheel between the poles.
You, Canadian, Indian,
Australasian, African,
All your hearts be in harmony!

Alfred Lord Tennyson

A few words of explanation

A sign on the ascendant expresses itself in a different way from a Sun sign. However some of the characteristics, even the childhood experiences, will apply if you have the Sun in Sagittarius or in the ninth house. They may also be present if you have Jupiter in Sagittarius or in the first or ninth house. If you have the Moon in Sagittarius or the ninth house, your emotions and reactions will have a Sagittarian flavour. If the ascendant is weak (see Chapter 1), the Sagittarian overlay will not be so noticeable. If the rest of the birthchart is very different from the rising sign, there could be conflict within the personality. This is because the outer manner, the signals which are given out at first meeting by the subject, are very different from the main character which lies underneath. Another possibility is that the subject rejects all that his parents and teachers stood for and creates a life for himself which is very different from the one which they envisaged for him, or the one which he lived through as a child.

Remember that Sagittarius is a mutable, fire sign which implies the ability to adapt to changing circumstances, but also denotes the enthusiasm, energy, intelligence and blind faith which is implied by fire. This is a sign of medium-to-long ascension, which means that there are plenty of you around.

Early experiences

You appear to have been born easily and to have been a wanted child. Your childhood was patchy, with parts of it being good and some parts being diabolical. You learned early in life to switch off and avoid the bad bits. Your parents may have separated from each other but probably not until you had reached a reasonable level of maturity. The problems which you faced could have resulted from situations which were beyond your control, such as a deteriotating relationship between your parents or, on the other hand, conflict between you and your parents. The chances are that, even now, you love them but prefer to live at a distance from them.

You could have found your father too fussy, too disciplinarian or too prejudiced for your free-wheeling taste. There could have been regular rows about the state of your room, your performance at school, or your lack of application to some special interest of theirs ('We spent all that money on violin lessons and now look at you, all you want to do is fish …!'). Your parents may have objected to your tendency to disappear whenever some boring chore loomed up on the horizon or conversely, they may have felt relieved when you *did* disappear, because it offered them a welcome respite from your argumentativeness. Your relationship with your father is ambivalent; you may have hated him while you were young but developed respect for him later on. You may have loved and understood him but never learned to communicate with him except by getting into yet another shouting match.

Your relationship with your mother is even worse. You probably saw her as the archetypal mother, the servant of the family who lived her life in a particularly old-fashioned and limited manner. You may have considered her stupid, useless or powerless. The view of your mother as a person who was incapable of making a decision would inevitably reinforce your natural desire for self-determination and independence. Later in life you may have come to understand the difficulties under which she lived and the compromises which she had to make but, even now, you may lack any real respect for her. Whatever the circumstances, you felt cramped, restricted and even immobilized. It is possible that you were disadvantageously compared to a more conventional brother or sister and maybe you felt that you were growing up in a town or an area which had little to offer ('Nothing ever *happens* here …!'). Maybe you were expected to follow a strict religious regime in which you had no personal belief, or to conform to a restrictive 'lace-curtain' set of values. Maybe your home life was great, but financial or cultural impoverishment irritated you.

Somewhere along the line you switched off, tuned out and began to look outside the home for some kind of escape route. Many of you worked out while you were quite young that education could offer you a useful way out. You were quick to latch on at school, which earned you the praise of your teachers and the admiration of your peers. You were unlikely to be the victim of bullying, due to your strong wiry frame and your natural aggression. School, therefore, was a natural arena which gave you the precious gift of early success and the opportunity to develop a sense of self-esteem.

As you passed the point of puberty, your family became ever more exasperated by you. This mattered less and less to you as time went by, because your eyes and thoughts were drawn ever more outwards to the wider world. Your increasingly (to your family's view) unconventional, indeed unacceptable outlook, plus your absolute conviction that there had to be something bigger, better and, above all, newer out there, set the scene for the classic Sagittarian late-teen leap out of the nest.

Here are a few examples of the 'late-teen leap', as supplied by various Sagittarius Sun or ascendant friends and relatives. My aunt left home to get married at the age of 18. Nothing special in this, you might say, but as the younger sister in a 1929 Jewish household, she had to ask her unmarried older sister for her permission first! After marriage, Aunt Anne moved a good distance away from the rest of the family in order to escape from her demanding mother. Mother, accompanied of course by the rest of the household, decided to move as well – taking a house a few doors away from Anne. Poor Aunt Anne! Fortunately for her the marriage was a great success, so all was not lost.

My daughter, Helen, had a good friend called Sharon who, over a period of five years, spent every Sunday and quite a lot of other days at our home. Sharon's father was not a young man, either in years or outlook. He was fussy about the state of the house and from the moment Sharon began to leave childhood behind he and she were at loggerheads. Sharon's mother tried to keep the peace, but nothing helped. The situation was slightly worsened by the fact that Sharon was the middle child and had a conventional older brother and younger sister. After a year or two of secretarial work and a continuation of the pattern of escaping from the house, Sharon took one of those teenage tours of duty on a kibbutz. She left the kibbutz after a few months and in the intervening years has drifted around the world with hardly any possessions, working casually, sleeping on beaches and sending the occasional postcard to Helen. Sharon never includes an address for replies; she is still moving on.

The story of Sharon leads me on to one further point about your youth, or your childhood, and that is of a 'foreign' influence. You may have been the child of immigrant parents, living in one culture whilst at home and another at school. In your teens you may leave not only the parental home, but the parental *country*; learning another language and becoming part of another culture. You probably had a knack for linguistics and an interest in foreign places, but the two-culture situation may be one of your choosing or simply a matter of family circumstances.

Appearance

The chances are that you are slim and raw-boned, with the characteristically Sagittarian lantern law. Taken separately, your features are nothing special but when viewed as a whole you are good-looking, often in an unusual way. Even the more chubby and round-faced Sagittarian rising subjects have unusually attractive hair and eyes. Your teeth should be white and even, giving you a wonderful carefree smile. The rounder variety of Sagittarian rising women are often top-heavy, with rounded shoulders and a large bust. Your style of dress is probably outrageous, but whichever style you adopt you stick to it throughout life rather than following fashion.

Outer manner

You are friendly, cheerful and outgoing. You seem to lack the natural caution and fear of new people which other signs display, therefore you appear open and non-hostile even on first meeting. Some of you are in a permanent whirl, chasing around like a demented white rabbit while others affect a superior know-it-all attitude. Some of you have a slow-moving, leisurely manner which belies the quickness of your mind.

You are curious about people and therefore may subject perfect strangers to the third degree. This is usually done quite innocently, you have no intention of hurting anybody. Every new person or situation offers you delightful opportunities to further your knowledge. You try to fit in with any company in which you find yourself whilst actually remaining a distinct individual. You may appear eccentric, even crazy, to strangers, especially over-conventional ones, but the messages you transmit on first acquaintance are usually cheerful and friendly.

You may have a knack for making tactless remarks. This is not done in order to hurt; it simply represents the kind of absolute honesty with which you view the world around you. Some Sagittarians tell me that they 'throw out the wrong image'; this may result from the fact that Sagittarius rising sends out signals of confidence and optimism, which may not be backed up by the nature of the rest of the chart. One Sagittarius rising friend says that she appears tough, but is in reality very soft. Another says he is gregarious at work and in social situations but switches off when at home. Yet another sends out signals which are so confusing that he attracts people whom he really doesn't want to be bothered with. One particularly Sagittarian aspect of your personality is your sense of humour. whether dry and droll, broad and deliciously vulgar, witty and sophisticated, or innocently childlike, it is your most wonderful attribute. You can be forgiven anything because you brighten up a dreary world and make all kinds of people *laugh*!

Sagittarius characteristics

Whether you were successful at school or not, you continue to learn throughout your life, either by taking courses which help you to progress in your career, or simply because you enjoy intellectual exploration. You could become fascinated by some particular subject such as astrology, or you could have a broad range of interests. Most Sagittarians live very full lives.

As a child you were rarely at home, being busy with the girl guides, cub scouts, sports, animals or anything else that caught your imagination. As you grew up your interests changed, but your level of involvement remained the same. You are happiest when you are fully stretched and totally involved. You simply cannot live without challenge, whether it be intellectual, creative or physical. You can be very creative yourself, but you excel at inspiring other people. Your life can become overfull, and even when you are at home 'relaxing', you are frequently surrounded by relatives, children, animals and noise. You were probably Chinese in a previous life!

You do occasionally feel guilty when you become aware that you are neglecting some aspect of your life (probably your spouse), but this may only cause you to call a *temporary* halt to your frenetic lifestyle. You don't seek an easy life, you need to be successful, and furthermore, to be *seen* as a success by others, but you also want to be loved and to be the centre of every world which you occupy. This is a tall order because one can only take out of any situation, at best, what one puts in. If you neglect your partner, parents, friends etc. sooner or later, they will wander off in search of more rewarding relationships. Some Sagittarians really do prefer to travel lightly, having plenty of friends and acquaintances but very little in the way of permanent relationships or material goods. You may be an eternal back-packer, the zodiac's version of the wandering Jew. This is all very well, but you still need friends and need to feel accepted somewhere. You must guard against using people and then dumping them when they need you. *Be* a friend – don't just *have* friends.

Not all Sagittarians are the outdoor sporty kind; you may be quiet and shy, but your need to stretch yourself and rise to a challenge will still be expressed. You may, for instance, be very fond of gardening, trying new and better ideas out from one year to another, or you may be of a religious or philosophical turn of mind, experimenting with other-worldly ideas for measure. One attribute which is stressed in all astrology books is your high level of intelligence. To be honest, I have never met a stupid Sagittarius rising subject. You really are clever, but you may lack what a friend of mine calls 'follow-through' unless you are in a particularly determined frame of mind. You are full of inspirational ideas. You don't even resent other people taking up your ideas for development, as long as you receive full credit for them. This is in part due to your generosity, but also to the fact that you are a natural teacher, and no one enjoys seeing his ideas being taken up and put to good use as much as a teacher. There is a kind of vicarious satisfaction to be gained from this. You can put up with difficult or unpleasant circumstances for a while but continued frustration makes you cross. Fire signs are not noted for their patience! If you are not allowed to express your anger you can become extremely depressed. Needless to say, your energy, resourcefulness and natural tendency to look out towards the horizon, coupled with your fabulous sense of humour, ensures that you never stay down for long.

Two attributes which you are almost guaranteed to have are idealism and honesty. You can be devious at times, but rarely crooked, and it would be very hard for you to take advantage of anyone. Your idealism can lead you to keep your head a bit too far up into the clouds. It can be hard for you to come down and get on with the nitty-gritty of daily life. You also have to guard against tactlessness or sheer rudeness in the guise of 'honesty'. Either way, your reluctance to compromise can be your greatest vice or your greatest virtue. You are genuinely broadminded and free from prejudice on grounds of race, religion or colour. You like people who are different because you find them interesting. Your interest in foreigners may lead you to marry someone from a different culture. Even if you don't manage to travel far during your life, you still feel the need to escape, especially if you live in a city. You enjoy the sea, mountains and wide open spaces and if there is nothing better on offer, you enjoy a walk in the country. If you actually live in the country you may choose to work or spend your spare time with animals.

Those of you who are more domestically inclined can be houseproud. However, the usual feeling is that your home is a base, a private retreat and bolt-hole in times of trouble. One aspect of domestic life which you really enjoy is looking after children. You are fond of children and are very loving to your own children, but you cannot spend your life indoors as a house-wife (or house-husband), because you need outside stimulation. As a parent you are reasonable, kind and understanding. There is an element of childishness in your own nature which makes you relate very well to youngsters. Youngsters sense that you respect their dignity because you don't talk down to them. Your acting and story-telling ability comes to your aid here as you can both entertain children and effortlessly enter into their special world.

The midheaven

This section and those which follow apply only to Sagittarius rising. The midheaven shows your aims and ambitions, therefore it can throw some light on your choice of career. In the case of Sagittarius rising births in the UK, and similar northerly latitudes, those of you whose ascendant is in a very early degree of the sign will have a Virgo midheaven while those of you whose ascendant is in the very last degrees of the sign will have a Scorpio mid-heaven. In actual fact, the majority of you have a Libran midheaven.

In the USA and southern Europe, about one third of you have Virgo on the mid-heaven while the remainder have Libra on the MC.

Sagittarius/Virgo

This combination produces an adaptable person who is also very idealistic. You have a strong need to serve mankind, either on an individual basis by caring for an elderly or handicapped relative, or on a group basis by working in one of the caring professions. This caring need may also be expressed in a wider way by working for an idealistic movement. Subjects with this MC may choose to work as teachers, social workers, probation officers or in some aspect of the medical profession. Accountancy is another possibili-ty, due to the Virgoan ability to handle figures and the sign's desire to provide a useful service. The travel and transport industries are popular (remember, Virgo is ruled by restless Mercury). You may be drawn to farming, veterinary work, or anything connected with animal welfare. You may be interested in food and nutrition, or you could help people to keep themselves looking good by working in the cosmetics or clothing industries. This combination makes for a very nervy and restless personality but the practicality and sensousness of Virgo coupled with the Sagittarian imagination and optimism could create outstanding success in any profession.

Sagittarius/Libra

By far the bulk of Sagittarius rising subjects come into this category. You are drawn to ambitious projects and large-scale ideas which, if you have the financial resources and a good team behind you, could be extremely successful. Both Sagittarius and Libra are concerned with advocacy. Both signs like to see justice done. Both signs are fascinated by the workings of the law, therefore a legal career is a possibility. You could be equally drawn to spiritual ideas which could lead you into a religious or philosophical way of life. Even if you don't become directly involved in the spiritual world, an element of this will enter your everyday life. The worlds of astrology or psychic matters might appeal to you. Sagittarius rising subjects are highly intuitive and often very psychic. The desire to help man in a more practical way could lead you into politics.

Many teachers have this combination on their charts, as it is naturally Libran to give advice and naturally Sagittarian to teach. Some astrology books associate Sagittarius with further or higher education and the opposite sign of Gemini with primary or secondary schooling, but I have come across Sagittarius rising subjects in all kinds of educational and training jobs. Another traditionally Sagittarian interest is long distance travel, and there are plenty of you working as couriers, travel agents, translators and airline pilots. You get on well with most people and have no prejudice towards foreigners. In fact, you enjoy meeting people from different cultures and looking into different ways of life.

Last but not least, many of you find your way into show business. You are a natural actor and probably a good singer or dancer too, so you could either spend your life actually working in the business or spend a few years on the stage before settling down to a 'proper' job. Many of you retain your interest in stage work and may even return to it later in life. Here are a few real life Sagittarius rising examples. Jennie is a highly qualified computer expert and she also lectures at the University of Sussex. Every Sunday or religious holiday you will find her singing in her local Church choir. Robin is a teacher who spent a couple of years acting before taking his degree and beginning his teaching career. John is an electronics buyer who has a degree in drama. Tony is a bank manager who is deeply involved in amateur dramatics. He tells me that when he retires, he will try to become a full time 'pro'. Mike is a teacher and administrator in adult education; he is very dramatic and very Welsh. It would be amazing if he *hadn't* done his share of singing or acting and Mike has admitted to me that he would have liked to have been an actor. You may be good at, and very interested in competitive sports. Another interest could be the care of animals.

Sagittarius/Scorpio

There are very few people who have this combination. Such a combination stresses the idealistic side of Scorpio which expresses itself in a need to heal. You may, therefore, work in the medical, psychiatric or veterinary fields and you may be a gifted spiritual healer. There is a natural interest in spiritual and psychic matters. The legal interests which are common in Sagittarians might be used directly in forensic work of some kind. You have more patience and determination than the other two MCs, which suggests that you could haul yourself slowly up to a position of great authority and responsibility. You would use your powerful gifts both wisely and firmly.

You are an excellent communicator, therefore you could find work in journalism, radio or television. You like advising and helping the public, so a media career could well be a very good idea for you. A sporting career is also possible, as many of you are excellent sportsmen and women who can make the grade professionally.

Many of us are attracted to people whose Sun sign is the same as our midheaven, therefore you could be drawn to Librans, Virgos or Scorpios, depending upon the exact position of your own MC.

The descendant

The opposite point to the ascendant is the descendant which traditionally shows the type of person to whom we are attracted. In the case of a Sagittarian ascendant, the descendant is in Gemini. These two signs have even more in common with each other than do most ascendant/descendant combinations. You are a terrific communicator and a hard worker but, being inclined to take too much on, find relaxation difficult. Being idealistic and highly strung, you need a placid and practical partner to create a balanced relationship. You also desperately need the support of a stable home and family environment. You may have the awkward habit of keeping two relationships on the go at once which could make life just a little bit too crowded for comfort.

You need freedom in any relationship, and are also prepared to allow your partner to have the opportunity to be a person in his or her own right. You can be cold hearted at times, even to the point of cutting off completely from other people and disappearing inside yourself. As long as you have a measure of friendship in any relationship you can usually make a success of it. At the very least, you are a *relater*; and you are able to keep your lines of communication open. However, most of all, you need to be taken care of, treated like a child on occasion, cuddled and soothed by a very caring partner. You can't live with a possessive or demanding partner and you need to be able to come in and go out whenever you like; you cannot be chained to the house. For some reason, many of you seem to marry Pisceans!

Love, sex and relating – regardless of the descendant

Your need for affection means that you are unlikely to be alone for long; you are a relater and you need company. If your marriage fails you will soon charm someone else into looking after you. Some of you have surprisingly stable marriages. This is probably due to your ability to choose a fairly self-reliant partner, although I suspect that male Sagittarius rising subjects are luckier in this respect than female ones. Females of the species seem to learn how to cope later in life, probably after jumping impulsively into and out of an early marriage.

Sexually, you like to experiment. You are well-known for wanting to see how far you can go, and this may apply to your sexual nature as well. Curiosity could be the main reason for your numerous sexual partners. You could, in the days before Aids, have been a great one-night-stand merchant. Later in life, when some of your curiosity has been satisfied, you settle down more easily to family life. You are one of those people who can actually live quite happily without sex, as long as your creative urges are being satisfied, although you do need attention and affection. You were not cuddled enough as a child and you really do enjoy the sensation of being held and cared for by another. You can also off-set any missing sex by pouring out your energies into sports, hobbies and even the Church. To be honest, sex isn't your problem: your worst enemy is boredom.

As far as friendship is concerned you can be here today and gone tomorrow. Your friendly, open nature ensures that you make friends easily enough, but you tend to drift away and forget them when you move on to other things.

Health

You are either extremely healthy or extremely unfit. To be honest, the chances are that you are rarely ill, but if you do go through a bad patch it can last for quite a few years before you return to full health. You suffer from sporting injuries and silly accidents due to the speed at which you move. Your vulnerable spots are your hips, pelvic area and your thighs, so arthritis, accidents to the legs, and problems related to the femoral artery are possible, while women may suffer from womb troubles. Your nerves can let you down, giving you sleepless nights, skin and stomach problems. if your ascendant is late in Sagittarius, you could have allergies to certain kinds of food and drink.

Your sixth house is in Taurus, so please also look at the health section on page 481.

13

Capricorn Rising

Nothing to do but work,
Nothing to eat but food,
Nothing to wear but clothes
To keep one from going nude.

Benjamin Franklin King,
The Pessimist

A few words of explanation

A sign on the ascendant expresses itself in a different way from a Sun sign. However, some of the characteristics, even the childhood experiences, will apply if you have the Sun in Capricorn or in the tenth house. There will also be some of these characteristics if you have Saturn in Capricorn or in the tenth house or even in the first house. If your Moon is in Capricorn or in the tenth house, your emotions and reactions will have a Capricornian flavour. If the ascendant is weak (see Chapter 1), the Capricorn overlay will not be so noticeable. If the rest of the birthchart is very different from the rising sign, there could be conflict within the personality. This is because the outer manner and the signals which are given out on first meeting by the subject are very different from the main character which lies underneath. Another possibility is that the subject rejects all that his parents, parent figures and teachers stood for, and creates a life for himself which is very different from the one which they envisaged for him, or from the one he lived through as a child.

Remember this is an earth sign, which is also cardinal in nature and this implies the desire to make things happen plus the patience and determination to make sure that they do. Capricorn is also feminine/negative in nature which implies introversion and shyness. This is a sign of *short* ascension which means that, as far as births in northern latitudes are concerned, there are not many of you about.

Early experiences

Traditionally, Capricorn rising, or for that matter the presence of the planet Saturn, on the ascendant denotes a difficult birth. One could theorize that because Capricorn is associated with old age, you will have been through a number of previous incarnations, and knowing what is ahead, you don't want to go through it all over again! whatever the theory, the evidence is that your mother's labour was protracted, painful and dangerous. In the case of one of my Capricorn rising clients, she was born fairly easily – in an ambulance half-way across Ealing Common in the middle of one of the worst bombing raids of the war.

Many Capricorn rising subjects are born to older parents who didn't want, or expect, to have a child at such a late stage of their lives. I can remember a woman called Paula telling me that when her mother was 43 years old she had a very bad attack of indigestion after eating pickled onions. The attack was so severe that her mother paid a visit to her doctor the next day. He told her that she was in the late stages of pregnancy and sure enough, two weeks later, Paula was born. The birth itself wasn't too difficult, but it was worrying, partly due to her mother's age, and also because there was so little time to get anything organized. This birth also took place in London during the war, although the bombing was not too bad due to the fact that a blizzard was blowing at the time! Shortly after this event her father had his first really serious nervous breakdown.

The sign of Capricorn is traditionally assumed to be a sad one indicative of a life filled with limitations and hard lessons to be learned. There is some truth in this idea but the problems are more likely to stem from difficult circumstances than from cruel or unloving parents. This emphasis on hard circumstances is the benchmark of this rising sign. You may have had a difficult relationship with your parents, but this is most likely to be because they themselves were up against hard times. One of your parents, probably your father, may have been a distant figure, either because he was naturally reserved and withdrawn or because his work took up a lot of his time. Your mother might have been strict, but not unreasonable or uncaring towards you. Circumstances dictated that you remain quietly in the background, making very few childish demands and behaving in an adult manner while you were still very young. I always think of this as an old-fashioned sign, because it is associated with the kind of childhood experiences which were far more common in years gone by. This ascendant is probably found more often in third world societies where opportunities for happiness or for creativity in childhood are still unobtainable luxuries.

During your childhood, your parents may have been short of time and money. There may have been too many mouths for them to feed, together with financial setbacks or family illness. You may have had a parent or a sibling who had some form of physical or mental handicap. You could have had an early introduction to the sadder side of life by losing a family member in a particularly tragic manner. This rising sign is the stuff of which all those best selling 'family saga' books are made.

There is another quite different but still typically Capricorn your parents themselves had risen from obscurity to positively wealthy. If, indeed, one or even both of your parents were especially successful or courageous in some way, you may have considered this too hard an act to follow. The effects of this childhood could have led to a number of different reactions on your part, depending upon your basic nature. One possibility is that you did actually follow in their footsteps, while a second is that you gave up the unequal battle and dropped out all together. A third possibility is that you followed a completely different path, finding values which are equally valid but quite different from those of your parents.

Even in the best circumstances, life was difficult for you. You were shy and withdrawn and inclined to hang back and let others step forward and take all the glory (or make bloody fools of themselves). You had little confidence in yourself and may have been afraid of something or someone, either because there was a genuine threat to your safety or as a result of vague fears and phobias. You were finely-built and small for your age, being completely unable to compete with larger, tougher children either on the sports field or in any kind of physical violence. You were a delicate and timid child, a worry to your parents and hard for them to bring up. The fact that you survived at all says a lot about your inner resources of courage and determination; you didn't give up on life then and have been fighting to overcome difficulties ever since.

I would like to add one final thought about your childhood experiences and that is on the subject of *control*. You could well have been dominated or controlled by one or both of your parents; you were certainly taught the value of self-control. This is a very useful technique in most circumstances but it can cause problems when you enter into relationships later on. On the one hand, you may try to control your future partner or on the other, you may find yourself in a relationship with someone who dominates and controls you in the same way that your parents did. Much as you hate the idea of destroying a relationship, you will have to do so if you find yourself a victim of tyranny.

Appearance

Bearing in mind racial differences and variations in birthcharts, the chances are that if you have Capricorn rising you will have rather bony features, with high cheekbones, large eyes and a nice, if slightly toothy smile. These well-defined features could make you extremely good-looking and incredibly photogenic in a 'Garboesque' way or, if the bonyness is extreme, it will make you appear craggy or 'hawk-like'. There is a characteristically Capricorn smile which turns the corners of your mouth downwards rather than upwards, whilst at the same time lighting up your eyes. Your hair is your worst feature, because it is sparse, fine and of a nondescript colour. Men with this rising sign become 'thin on top', while women spend a fortune in the hairdresser on perms and hair colourants, while cursing this ever-present bane of their lives. Your height and physique is small to medium. You could put on a little weight as you get older but, generally speaking, you will remain perhaps just a little below average in height and weight. You choose conservative clothes which might be either city-smart outfits or something cheap and cheerful, according to your lifestyle and your pocket. To be honest, you don't give much attention to your clothing unless you have a special occasion to dress up for.

Outer manner

You are naturally retiring and are the last person to push yourself to the forefront in any kind of new situation. You appear calm, quiet, gentle and modest in social situations, whilst in business situations you are formal and businesslike. The signals you send out to new acquaintances are gentle, kind and practical. You rarely express your feelings publicly, and are a past master at the art of being non-committal. You are not in the least unfriendly; indeed you go out of your way to make others feel comfortable, but you are reserved. Your dry sense of humour is always a delightful discovery to any new acquaintance and your genuinely non-hostile approach to the world ensures that you are surprisingly popular. However, this popularity can vanish under certain circumstances – but more of that later. You are a good conversationalist partly because you usually have something interesting to talk about, but mainly because you are a good and caring listener.

Capricorn characteristics

This section can double up as a brief guide to Capricorn as a Sun sign *or* as a rising sign, so it can provide a handy reference if you want to check up on someone's Sun sign as well as their rising sign.

Yours is a strangely mixed and multi-faceted sign, with many excellent qualities and a couple of really dodgy ones. To add to the confusion there is a kind of accepted set of theories about this sign which don't always stand up when looked at against real people. One such theory is that you are invariably reliable, practical, determined, capable and thorough and, therefore, heading inevitably for a career in banking. Whilst it's true that many of you *are* just like that, other Capricorn rising subjects are ineffectual, undisciplined, prone to vacillation and inclined to leave jobs half-done! This sign, like Scorpio, seems to have suffered from too much astrology and not enough observation! This disparity can, to some extent, be put down to variations in the rest of the birthchart, but it can also be put down to one particularly Capricornian feature and that is your terrible lack of confidence. You may take on a job and then become unsure that you can cope with it or, if something starts to go wrong half-way through, you may simply walk away from it.

This lack of confidence may stem from simple shyness, but in many cases it can be linked to childhood experiences. It is probable, that your parents, good as they were, didn't spend much time or energy on you or that they didn't teach you how to value yourself. There is sometimes some kind of educational problem when this sign is rising which means that some of you grow up without learning how to read and write properly. Others of you have a very good basic education but may lack the kind of specialized skills or further education which would allow you to get on in the world. You are proud by nature, refined and rather snobbish and therefore a decent job is necessary for your mental health. A particularly menial job would make you feel humiliated and miserable.

If you reach adulthood without the kind of education and training which will allow you to rise to a position in which you feel comfortable, you will find a way to obtain it in your spare time. Capricorn women escape this kind of difficulty by marrying early, a decision which they may, or may not, regret later on according to circumstances. With or without skills, your ambitious determination begins to show itself quite early and, whether you decide to enter the stock exchange or to become a pop singer, your career direction is steadily upwards towards an unassailable position of respect. You view power and money as being useful but the real motivating force behind your ambition is your need for status, self-respect, self-determination and a decent kind of lifestyle.

Your need for security, coupled with your love of money and status, could lead you to compromise your principles. You could find yourself agreeing to advertise a product which you don't believe in. Alternatively you could cultivate friends for their usefulness, rather than simply for the pleasure of their company.

Capricorns are renowned for being hard workers, and this is very true. Even if some project fails badly, you pick yourself up and, confidence or no confidence, you try again, or you turn your hand to something else. Whatever your chosen field, you are patient, reliable and businesslike and your tenacity makes you particularly successful in any form of self-employment. You have a surprisingly independent outlook and although you make a good employee, you are probably happier in the role of employer. Incidentally, I have discovered that those who earn their living by working alone, as artists, musicians or writers, often have Saturn (the planet which rules Capricorn), close to the ascendant in their birthcharts.

One area in which you excel is family life. Although you enjoy and appreciate friendship, your family comes first and foremost. You are not particularly interested in worldly, ecological or humanitarian issues, unless you have a good deal of Aquarius on your birthchart, but you can be drawn into mainstream politics. In this case, you tend to view your party and those who share your ideology and even your country, as part of your 'family', and therefore your own personal responsibility. It was the Capricorn President of the USA, Nixon, who extricated America from the Vietnam war, while the very 'tenth-house' character, Adolph Hitler, put German interests so disastrously before those of everyone else. There can be a 'canny' form of nepotism at work here, a kind of personal or political closing of ranks when trouble looms. It is as if the Capricornian need for status and security is, in this situation, extended to cover the wider political 'family' as well as the personal one.

As a parent, you are dutiful, caring and an excellent provider, but you might object to handing out money for frivolities. You could also fall into the trap of exerting far too much control over your offspring. If one of your offspring appears to have any kind of special talent or ability, you will not stint any amount of money or effort to help develop this. You may be a bit on the strict side, insisting on good behaviour, but there is no doubt at all that you truly love your children. You may moan and grumble when you need to let off steam, but you would be most unlikely to walk away from your responsibilities regardless of any grumbling you may do. Despite all this seriousness, you really do enjoy a good laugh. You have a delightfully dry sense of humour and you genuinely enjoy company and fun.

One subject which is always close to the Capricorn heart is *money*. You can cope with being rich or poor, but you prefer being rich (remember, your eighth house is in sumptuous Leo). You cannot cope under any circumstances with being in debt. Capricorns tend to have a gift for figure work, whether this be balancing the household budget or managing a large organization and you are rarely in the dark about your current personal or business financial position. You are fascinated by money management and are naturally drawn to the world of business, especially the areas of finance and distribution. Unless there are other very outgoing features on your birthchart, you are not really suited to sales work. Even if you work in a field which does not appear at first glance to be particularly businesslike, you still maintain a very sensible and down-to-earth attitude to what you do. Your mind is acute, very shrewd and probably academic but you may have some surprisingly esoteric interests in your spare time. This is the kind of combination which can produce a guy who is an accountant by day and a champion ballroom dancer by night! You may be very fond of animals, bringing to them the same care and consideration that you do to your family members. Here I will quote my long-suffering father as an example. The care and attention she lavishes on Suzie, my parents' half-feral, androgenous and totally uncontrollable cat, has to be seen to be believed. No matter how many times Suzie comes home hours late, covered with fleas and disporting yet another festering relic of some recent cat-fight on his/her body, Sam's gentle love never wavers. I sometimes think that Suzie is the unacceptable face of Gemini with Aries rising! Fortunately, Sam loves my mother and myself just as fiercely, despite the fact that both of us are as awkward in our ways, if not as sexually peculiar, as is his Suzie.

With your excellent powers of concentration you can work hard and study deeply in order to achieve your ambitions. You find it impossible to understand lazy and feckless people and you don't waste any of your valuable time on them. Your own decisions are taken carefully and sensibly and the time and effort which you invest in any enterprise pays off; even if it takes some time to do so. You might be too materialistic for some tastes and you may be mean in stupid and counter-productive ways. Yours is the sign which squeezes the last drop of toothpaste out of the tube.

You cannot bear to be made to look foolish. When confronted by a person whose sense of humour runs to mockery, you just walk away retaining your dignity. Your own sense of humour is not designed to bring pain to others and indeed you only set out to hurt others on those exceedingly rare occasions when you feel that you have been very badly or unfairly treated. However, even in those circumstances, you prefer to simply walk away from such people and forget that they exist. You may hurt others by concentrating too much on their practical needs, and neglecting their emotional ones, or you may infuriate them by your occasional bouts of petty-mindedness or petty meanness. Your pet fear would be to be placed in an embarrassing or humiliating situation. To be in a hospital, helpless and being dealt with by particularly thoughtless people, would be beyond endurance for you.

You are surprisingly easy to live with and to get along with, never making unreasonable demands upon others. You don't require perfection from other people but you can become annoyed if you feel that they are evading what you consider to be their duty. A Capricorn woman who marries an idle and incompetent guy would try to encourage him to change, and if she didn't succeed, would walk away from the situation. Capricorn, for all its shyness and modesty is, after all a *cardinal* sign, and there is a limit to what you will put up with.

You are not particularly tidy or fussy about your surroundings and you will eat almost anything as long as it is well-cooked and presented. Oddly enough, for such a conservative type of person, you really do enjoy exotic foods. You also enjoy exotic places and will travel the world as soon as you can afford to do so. Visitors are made very welcome, and you usually get on well with your family's friends. It would be most unusual for you to become involved in a silly dispute with neighbours or relatives because you prefer to live in peace with those around you, and discord embarrasses you.

This is, of course, an earth sign which suggests a certain level of sensuality. This might be expressed as a liking for good food, good music and, of course, sexual love as well as much-needed affection. Your hobbies may well express your sensuality too, for example in gardening, cooking, dancing or some gentle and pleasant form of sport.

The midheaven

This section and those which follow apply only to Capricorn rising. The midheaven shows your aims and ambitions and therefore can throw some light on your choice of career. In the case of Capricorn rising, in northern latitudes such as the UK the majority of you will have your midheaven in Scorpio, while those of you whose ascendant is in the last couple of degrees of Capricorn will have Sagittarius on the midheaven. In the case of births in the USA and southern areas of Europe, those who have the first few degrees of Capricorn rising will have the midheaven in Libra, whilst the rest will have the MC in Scorpio.

Capricorn/Libra

Both these signs are cardinal in nature which suggests that you prefer to make your own personal decisions, although you are co-operative in working partnerships. The Libran MC modifies your Capricorn shyness to an extent which could allow you to be a capable employment or travel agent, personnel officer or financial adviser. You have a natural affinity for figures, which is useful whatever your line of work. The Libran mid-heaven gives you an artistic outlook and a sense of balance, which is useful in situations which require good presentation. You could succeed in the field of marketing, but probably not in straightforward selling as this requires a brashness and confidence which you don't have. You may not excel as a creative innovator, but you are excellent at judging the work of others. You can see at a glance what will work and what will not, and it is this critical faculty which could successfully take you into the world of fashion or publishing.

Capricorn/Scorpio

This is by far the most common combination in the northern hemisphere, and it makes for an uncomfortable mixture of Capricorn caution with Scorpio manipulation. It is possible that you would be drawn to the Scorpionic interests of medicine or police work, where your careful, methodical mind would come in handy. In theory, you would make a brilliant brain surgeon, detective or spy! However, if you decide to eschew these careers in favour of becoming a secretary, greengrocer or childminder instead, you would tackle those jobs with the same energy and diligence. You can be relied upon to do a job thoroughly, so long as nobody rushes or pressurizes you. Your best bet is to tackle one job at a time and do it properly.

The Scorpio MC encourages you to retreat and reflect, which could take you into some kind of research work. You could make a good investigative journalist or scientific author. You have to take care that your outer manner doesn't offend others, especially at an interview, or when trying to get information out of others. You may put on an aggressive or hostile front in order to hide your vulnerability, but remember that others will take you at face value, and thereby miss your finer qualities. The Scorpio affinity with liquids could take you into the oil industry or shipping.

Capricorn/Sagittarius

This rare combination really doesn't fit comfortably, because the two signs have little in common. However, it is possible that the Capricorn caution, coupled with the Sagittarian optimism and enthusiasm, could combine to make a pretty powerful character. You are drawn to the world of teaching or caring for others in some way. Your practical idealism might lead you into alternative forms of medicine, counselling or even astrology. Your interest in travel and business could lead you to work for an airline or to set up a postal courier service. Alternatively, you could go into some kind of religious occupation or even become a professional mystic or a kind of businesslike Yogi. The sign on the MC can sometimes denote the type of person who we enjoy either working or living alongside. In your case this person might be a Libran, Scorpio or Sagittarian.

The descendant

The opposite point to the ascendant is the descendant. This is traditionally supposed to show the type of person to whom we are attracted. In the case of Capricorn rising, the descendant is in Cancer, which goes a long way towards accounting for the Capricornian love of family life. I have no evidence to suggest that you would go out of your way to choose a Cancerian partner, but I guess that if you did the match would work well because the signs have a great deal in common, both being interested in their homes, families and also in business. However, the emotionalism and moodiness of the Cancerian might irritate you after a while and the combination of these two signs might lead to too much negativity and gloom in the relationship. You'd probably make a better relationship with someone outgoing, who could lift your spirits and also encourage you to stick to your principles.

On the whole, the Cancerian descendant leads you to be very caring towards all those with whom you associate, be they friends, neighbours or working partners. You hate to let anyone down, and therefore are a most reliable person. One black mark which could spoil some of your relationships is your tendency to be mean about small matters. You could be the type who complains about your partner's use of hot water or the way he squeezes the toothpaste tube. However, if your partner is either financially independent, fairly thick-skinned or also rather tight-fisted, none of this will be a problem.

Love, sex and relating regardless of the descendant. This is where contradictions enter the scene. You are able to live without sex when it is not available, and may indeed choose to do so while you are young. This may be due to shyness or to fastidiousness plus a quite reasonable fear of jumping into bed with someone to whom you haven't been properly introduced! When you are with a regular partner with whom you are comfortable, you can really let your hair down. Remember, this is an earth sign which implies sensuousness. You enjoy the sights, sounds and wonderful feelings that sex in a loving relationship can bring.

You may be flirtatious but your strong sense of propriety, not to mention self-preservation, will probably prevent too much actual tomfoolery on your part. Many of you have a peculiar fail-safe device which comes into operation when you feel threatened by the sexual demands of a partner and that is a tendency towards spinal problems. The equation works like this:

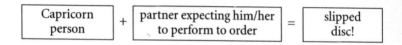

Health

Apart from the sexually-induced slipped disc, this sign is associated with a range of chronic ailments. You may suffer from rheumatism, especially in your knees. Another typical problem is deafness, possibly associated with some kind of bone problem in the ears or tinnitus. Your difficult childhood may leave you with nervous ailments, such as asthma, eczema and psoriasis, together with chesty ailments such as bronchitis. Despite these annoying problems, Capricorns traditionally live to a ripe old age.

Your sixth house is in Gemini, so please also look at the health section on page 565.

14

Aquarius Rising

These things shall be! A loftier race
Than e'er the world hath known, shall rise,
With flame of knowledge in their souls
And light of knowledge in their eyes.

John Addington Symonds (English Critic),
New and Old. A Vista

A few words of explanation

A sign on the ascendant expresses itself in a different way from the Sun sign. However, some of the characteristics, even the childhood experiences, will apply if you have the Sun in Aquarius or in the eleventh house. There will also be some of these characteristics if you have Uranus or Saturn in the eleventh house or Uranus in the first house. If your Moon is in Aquarius or the eleventh house, your emotions and reactions will have an Aquarian flavour. If the ascendant is weak (see Chapter 1), the Aquarian overlay will not be so noticeable. If the rest of your birthchart is very different from the rising sign, there could be a conflict in the personality. This is because the outer manner and the signals which are given out on first meeting by the subject are very different from the main character which lies underneath. Another possibility is that the subject rejects all that his parents, parent figures and teachers stood for and creates a life for himself which is very different from the one which they envisaged for him, or from the one which he lived through as a child.

Remember that this is an air sign which is also fixed in nature and the implication is that you are clever and tenacious. If you become attached to an idea, or accustomed to a particular way of life, you will not willingly change. Aquarius is also masculine and positive in nature, which denotes extroversion and courage. This is a sign of short ascension, which means that, in northern latitudes, there are not many of you around.

Early experiences

Aquarius is the least predictable sign of the zodiac, so it is almost impossible to generalize about any aspect of your life. The chances are that you suffered quite deeply sometime during your childhood. There will have been some kind of dramatic or unexpected event which disrupted your life in some way, and this disruption may have had an unexpectedly beneficial side to it. One Aquarius rising subject told me that as a result of wartime evacuation he received a far better education and, indeed, a far better childhood than he would otherwise have had. It is this element of *unpredictability* which is the hallmark of this rising sign. You were the kind of frustrating child who was obviously clever but unwilling to make an effort except at those subjects which excited you. Despite this waste of early opportunities, you caught up later in life and have done very well in your chosen sphere of work. Despite your inability to be cajoled or coerced, you longed for parental approval, especially from your father.

You may have had an excellent relationship with one parent and a prickly, uncomfortable one with the other. Either parent, (but probably the father), could have been extremely moody, resentful, childish, unpredictable and violent. Yours may have been the kind of childhood where your mother tried to protect you from the worst excesses of your father s temper. In a normal childhood, you could still have been subject to periods of unexplained withdrawal of parental affection. if your home situation was actually quite pleasant, you would have been aware of events within the family circle which appeared to be beyond anyone's control. Here are a couple of examples. Edwin's parents had a second child when he was eight years old and this younger brother was born with a severe mental handicap. Stuart my own son, was terribly upset when his father became severely ill with a heart condition. Happily, the then brand-new operation for a coronary by-pass solved his father's problems. It is interesting to note that the sign of Aquarius is associated with new and experimental ideas and, of course, at that time, by-pass surgery was so new that it *was* experimental.

Your school life could have been disrupted, maybe your family had moved around a good deal which resulted in you attending a variety of schools. Even if this did not occur, the chances are that you didn't do particularly well at school but took up an interest which involved further study later on in life. Some Aquarius rising subjects find it hard to concentrate on anything for long, and if this is your nature you will find that you can grasp new concepts very quickly but then lose interest again just as quickly.

Even as a small child you needed freedom and space and you also needed to be on the move. Like children of the somewhat similar sign of Sagittarius, you were unable to stay indoors for long. You had friends all over the place, and couldn't wait to shoot off out of the house to see them. Yet, despite this need to be out and on the move, you feared the unexpected. It seems that you needed to know that everything was all right at home and in your own private world before you could go exploring. You will have been either very successful or a total failure at school; you were totally incapable of being average. The same situation applied to your outside interests.

There may have been very little pattern to your life. Your parents might have changed their attitude to you from one day to another, or they may have handed out confusing psychological messages. For example they may have told you that they believed in total honesty, whilst fiddling the taxman and pinching envelopes from the office. If your parents were reasonable, they may have been thoroughly unconventional. Perhaps one of your parents was particularly successful or gifted. Maybe one of them was a total failure or even a drunken wreck. You yourself were a jumpy, nervy child, being prone to nervous ailments and bouts of peculiar behaviour. If your parents were the caring variety, they would have found you difficult to bring up. If they were the uncaring sort, it is a miracle that you survived at all!

Appearance

Please take into consideration racial differences and the influence of the rest of the birthchart where this is concerned. You are doubtless very good looking. Aquarian women learn to use cosmetics well, because their complexion is pale or sallow. The bone structure of your face is strong, giving you the kind of features which photograph well. Your eyes are probably quite ordinary, plain brown and slightly prominent, but not especially large. However, your highly arched eyebrows draw attention to your eyes, making them look larger than they actually are. Your nose is prominent, (and maybe bent or twisted) and your teeth regular and very white, so your smile is absolutely lovely.

The effect of these well-developed features with your humorous expression, gives you an appearance which is strong and effective. Your hair may be your worst feature, being either a dull brown or turning grey when you are still very young. Female Aquarians overcome this by tinting and perming their hair and nowadays, so do males! You may only be of average height, but you *appear* tall and you don't carry any excess weight. Your choice of clothes is totally individual and possibly even totally outrageous! You may be the very picture of the smartly dressed business person or a complete slob. You may restrict yourself to one colour, for example, never wearing anything but mauve, or you may choose to wear clothes of a bygone age. Most of you prefer casual, rather 'masculine' clothes such as jeans, track-suits and sweaters. You hate frills, patterns and bunches of flowers on your clothing and you are far happier wearing strong plain colours. However, you could easily turn up at a formal function in a frock-coat and Red Indian head-dress! Where clothes are concerned, I wouldn't put anything past you!

Outer manner

Under normal circumstances, you are friendly, open and totally non-hostile. However, if you are faced with someone who is offensive or other-wise unpleasant, you give them absolutely no quarter. You speak your mind and don't fear the consequences. You may be a little shy when you are in an unfamiliar social setting, but once you feel yourself to be at home, you immediately join in with whatever is going on. You are a real asset to a village-green fete! You love meeting new people, and are not at all put off by unusual ones. Your judgement of people is excellent, and you seem to be able to see through surface impressions to the reality which lies under-neath. You don't judge people by outer appearances and you cannot be taken in by anyone who puts on airs and graces. Your own approach, apart from being friendly, is businesslike and humorous but not pushy. In some circumstances, you can appear arrogant, or you may give the impression that you class yourself above the people with whom you are associating. When you are with people with whom you are really comfortable, especi-ally if the occasion is a social one, you are terrific. You mix with everyone, thoroughly enjoy yourself and help others to do the same. Your most outstanding quality is your quick wit and sense of humour. Aquarius risers are the masters of the pithy comment and the hilarious one liner.

Aquarius characteristics

This section can double up as a brief guide to Aquarius as a Sun sign *or* a rising sign, so it provides a handy reference for you if you wish to check out a person's Sun sign as well as their rising sign.

Despite your super-cool' outer manner, you are quite tense inside. You are a worrier and you hate to feel that any situation is slipping out of your control. You need to be in charge of your own destiny. Like the other fixed signs of Leo, Scorpio and Taurus, you prefer to set your own pace and not to be rushed or hassled by others. When you find yourself placed under severe pressure, you don't crumple up or walk away from the situation but if the pressure is umremitting you become ill. You are capable of running a business of your own, or of having complete charge of a department in a large organization. You can co-operate with others very well, just as long as you are in a position of influence! Where your personal life is concerned, you are a great family member and team worker, just as long as nobody tries to restrict you or dictate to you. Even if you know for certain that you are being stupid, you prefer to be left to make your own mistakes. This doesn't mean that you won't listen to reason; often an opinion given from a person whom you respect is just the thing to help you. However, you are intelligent enough to be able to turn most situations to your own advantage, provided that you don't lose your temper and go at it like a bull at a gate. I know that this next statement is going to come as a surprise to many people, but Aquarians are *moody*!

All fixed signs are moody, because you find it difficult to adapt to changes in circumstances. You can retreat into angry sulking (or become ill) when the world doesn't seem to be going your way. Yours is a very proud sign and you hate to look silly. Perhaps it is just as well that you rarely do act foolishly. You may be surprisingly self-absorbed. You have many friends but you don't enjoy being dragged too deeply into their problems. You have high standards of behaviour but also a high opinion of yourself which can give you an air of arrogance. If someone you respect and care for makes a critical remark obviously you can become upset, but if an outsider criticizes you, it rolls straight off you. Frankly, you are not that interested in the opinions of others. You march to your own drumbeat. You are not easily influenced and will not change the course of your life in order to secure the approval of others. Like all fixed signs, you don't easily abandon either a person or a situation. You cannot be owned or dictated to even by the people whom you most value.

You are a good organizer both at work and at home. Your mind is logical and this is reflected in the way you go about things. There are times when you find it difficult to explain to others why you want things to be done in a particular order or in a particular way, so you may need to pay a little more attention to developing good communication skills. You need to find a career that you enjoy. There must be an element of play involved with your work or you will become bored which will lead you to switch-off completely. You need to be in an environment where you can meet and influence new people. You must have the opportunity to exercise your mind and to use your capacity for lateral thinking. Under normal circumstances you are quite lazy, but when you decide to go after something, or someone, no one is more determined.

Yours is an unusual household. You prefer a clean, tidy and well-appointed home with elegant furniture and fittings and, therefore, you spend a good deal of your time and money on your home. You are a good cook and a good host, making guests feel really comfortable and welcome. The unusual aspect comes from your personal interests. There is a very good chance that you own at least one computer and a variety of other electrical gadgets, especially radio and recording equipment as well as good kitchen equipment. Your bookshelves reflect your esoteric tastes. You accumulate books and you may have a large collection. Your home may be overflowing with magazines, videos, papers, brochures and filing cabinets. There might be a great quantity of equipment stuffed into your garage and kept there 'in case'. This collection of books and other gear reflects the comings and goings, over the years, of your many hobbies and interests.

You enjoy being part of a family and you are an excellent parent. You will probably continue to study in adulthood, and you encourage your partner to do so as well. You will provide your children with as much education as they can stand and will encourage them to take up all kinds of spare-time interests and hobbies. Your rational attitude may be a bit of a drawback in relationships, because you may not find it easy to understand the emotional needs of others. When your partner is looking for sympathy and understanding you may come to respond a little *too* reasonably and logically. You must learn to see the emotional needs, both of yourself and of others. In addition to being logical, you are also intuitive and even, perhaps, psychic. This side of your nature might also take some coming to terms with. Where other family relationships, such as those where parents and in-laws are concerned, you like to maintain good lines of communication with them but not to be over-involved in their lives.

Traditionally, Aquarians are supposed to belong to all kinds of groups and organizations but this is far less so in the case of Aquarius rising. Your independent nature makes you very friendly but not necessarily a good group or committee worker. You may wish to campaign for a particular charity or to make a political point, but once you have achieved your aims, you disengage yourself and sink gratefully back into privacy. Perhaps Aquarius rising subjects dislike having too many obligations and attachments taking up their precious store of spare time. You will help someone on a personal basis, as long as they show some willingness to help themselves; you are impatient with whiners and emotional drainers. You are also not particularly good with sick people, and you may lose patience with them once the immediate crisis is over. You cannot under any circumstances have respect for shirkers, moaners or perpetual 'victims'.

The friendliness of an Aquarian rising subject differs a little from that of the Sun in Aquarius. Both of you are remarkably unprejudiced and have no dislike of people on grounds of race, colour, social class or religion and both like meeting new people, but the Aquarius rising subject lacks patience and may drift away if the friend becomes too demanding. Another slight difference is that the Aquarius rising subject definitely prefers youth to age and will choose his friends from the younger set, whereas the Sun Aquarian isn't so particular.

You are honest and reliable, therefore you keep your promises and hate to let anyone down. You find it hard to understand those who don't share your high standards. You dislike walking away from commitments, but you can be unrealistic in your aspirations. One example might be a woman who takes on a business which lacks any real viability. Another example might be of a guy who goes on loving a girl who doesn't really want him. This inability to separate reality from dreams is typical of an air sign and it can cause you some really awful problems. Your reliability and kindheartedness makes you a truly wonderful friend, but if someone turns against you or begins to laugh at you, you become exceedingly sarcastic and hurtful in self-defence. One final, rather daft point which I would like to make is that all the Aquarian rising subjects whom I have met are extremely faddy about food. Some are vegetarians while others are very plain eaters, while there are others who are totally impossible to cater for.

The midheaven

This section and the ones which follow apply only to Aquarius as a rising sign, and not as a Sun sign. The midheaven is traditionally supposed to indicate the subject's aims and ambitions and, therefore, can show the type of career to which one is attracted. When Aquarius is on the ascendant,

Sagittarius is *always* on the MC. These two signs are very similar, therefore the kind of personality which is projected by the ascendant has a similarity to the subject's ultimate aims in life. To put this into plain English, unless there are a good many planets (including the Sun) hidden in some crafty sign such as Scorpio or Cancer, what you see is, more or less, what you get!

You need freedom and you cannot stand being restricted, dictated to or bullied. You could succeed as a journalist, delivery-driver, racing-driver, travel courier or sales representative; in short, anything which gives you an opportunity to get out and about and meet new people. You look at the world with fresh eyes and bring new concepts to everything you touch, so you are very useful in solving technical problems. Your obsessive nature can be useful here because, when you want to, you can toss aside your languor and work away at a problem until it is solved. Although you can succeed in any technical field, the most obvious ones include electronics, telecommunications and computers. You are intelligent and quick on the uptake and you have a good memory, therefore it would be stupid for you to take a job which didn't stretch your mind.

Your interest in scientific research could take you into the fields of physics, medicine or even horticulture, but your balanced mind and natural arbitration skills could lead you into law. You are a skilled negotiator which could suggest either straightforward legal work or something similar, such as Trades Union negotiations. Another typically Sagittarian career which might interest you is teaching. There is an element of the actor in you which, coupled with your desire to help others, makes you a natural teacher or training officer. The independence of this kind of job would appeal to you as well. There is one more career which might attract you, and that is the world of show business. Many of you are natural actors, singers, dancers or musicians. Your unusual mind could make you a successful inventor or a wonderfully creative and imaginative writer, especially if the rest of your birthchart leans that way too.

Aquarians like to look laid-back and easy-going but this is a pose. You are ambitious and money-minded. You enjoy status. This means that you need a good position within your job and a career which in itself is admired or envied. An eminently suitable position might be the director of an independent radio station! You also like money. You don't need to accumulate money in order to feel secure or to gain power over others, but simply in order to have a comfortable, even luxurious, standard of living.

There is a side to your character which I have left until now, and this is your attraction to mysticism. In your case, this goes beyond the realms of a hobby or vague interest and becomes an integral part of your life's direction. You may become directly involved with a religious organization, either in an established Church or Temple, or you may be attracted to something less orthodox. The Aquarian side will encourage you to take a scientific look at such subjects as astrology, graphology and numerology, while the Sagittarian side will urge you to seek spiritual development. Therefore, you could become minister of the Church, a medium or healer, an astrological counsellor, a holistic or alternative health therapist, or a yoga teacher. There is such a strong pull towards the scientific side of spiritual or metaphysical investigation, which makes it inevitable that you will look for and follow some kind of spiritual path. Whether this remains a part of your private life or whether you decide to make a career of it depends partly upon personal preference, and partly upon the amount of influence your spiritual guides decide to exert upon your life. It is certain that you will go through a number of problems and crises in your life, and it may be at such a time that you begin to feel the need to explore the world of metaphysics and philosophy.

The descendant

The descendant, or cusp of the seventh house, is traditionally supposed to throw light on our attitudes to partnerships and may even indicate the type of person whom we choose to marry. In the case of Aquarius rising, the descendant is in Leo.

There is no evidence that you are especially attracted to Leos, but you do find them easy to understand because you have a good deal in common with them. Your personal standards are high, you are proud, dignified, obstinate and tenacious. It is possible that you could work well together, but I doubt whether two such egocentric people could actually manage to live together for very long. In general, you seek a partner who is intelligent, independent and good-looking! Your partner must have something to offer which is just that little better than the average. You might be attracted to a show-business personality, a high-status business-person or a scientist of high repute. All this will work out very well just as long as your partner can offer you the kind of love, affection, attention and emotional security which you need. You cannot be fettered or smothered and you don't seek to smother your partner but you cannot be ignored and, when your confidence takes a knock, you need to be cuddled, loved and understood. It is possible that your requirements from a relationship are a little unrealistic, and you suffer a certain amount of disappointment. When you learn to adjust your sights a bit lower, your relationships improve. If you are female you will need a career of your own; you can't bear to sit indoors waiting for hubby to come home and slip you a bit of pocket money.

Love, sex and relating – regardless of the descendant

Despite your need for reassurance, you find it hard to give this to others. Your detached attitude and your tendency to give logical answers to emotional questions can leave your partner feeling misunderstood. Your need to travel on an inward, spiritual journey must be understood, and it is best if your partner has the same kind of spiritual interests. If you were to marry an extremely practical and earthy type neither of you would understand each other for one minute. Oddly enough, you have to guard against too much tenacity in relationships because you can hang on far too long to someone who no longer needs you or even abuses you.

You are very active sexually and you are an inventive and exciting lover. However, the most important ingredients in a relationship must be intelligence, humour, shared interests and *friendship*. If the sexual side is good as well, then hooray! You may go through an experimental stage where you separate love from sex, having a variety of partners, some for loving friendship and others for sex. Once you are settled into a permanent relationship, however, you are the faithful type, as long as your partner treats you decently. You are completely turned off by a lack of personal hygiene. I can remember one Aquarius rising subject commenting drily to me that he 'gave the girl up because you could fry fish in the grease on her bra straps'. Finally, you don't fall in love easily but when you do so, you fall very very hard. It's that romantic child-like Leo descendant which catches you out.

Health

The traditional weak points for this sign are the ankles; so you must guard against phlebitis, thrombosis and accidents to the feet and ankles. Apart from this, I have discovered that Aquarius rising subjects have a great deal of trouble with their ears, noses and throats. You may suffer from hay-fever, asthma, allergies which give you runny eyes and thyroid trouble. Your teeth are either very good, or very bad. You do have a nice smile, so if your teeth begin to present problems it would be wise to cultivate a good dentist. You could also be subject to back problems, especially when you are going through a period of stress and tension.

Your sixth house is in Cancer, so please also look at the health section on page 501.

15

Pisces Rising

We are the music-makers,
And we are the dreamers of dreams,
Wandering by lone sea-breakers,
And sitting by desolate streams;
World-losers and world-forsakers,
On whom the pale moon gleams:
Yet we are the movers and shakers
Of the world for ever, it seems.

Arthur O'Shaughnessy, *Ode*

A few words of explanation

A sign on the ascendant expresses itself in a different way from a Sun sign. However, some of the characteristics, even the childhood experiences, will apply if you have the Sun in Pisces or in the twelfth house. There will also be some of these characteristics if you have Neptune in Pisces, or the first or the twelfth house. If you have the Moon in Pisces, your emotions and reactions will have a Piscean flavour. If the ascendant is weak (see Chapter 1), the Piscean overlay will not be so noticeable. If the rest of the birthchart is very different from the rising sign, there could be a conflict within the personality. This is because the outer manner and the signals which are given out on first meeting by the subject are very different from the main character which lies underneath. Another possibility is that the subject rejects all that his parents, parent figures and teachers stood for, and creates. a life for himself which is very different from the one which they envisaged for him or the one which he lived through as a child.

Remember that this is a water sign which is also mutable in nature suggesting emotionalism and changeability. Pisces is also feminine/negative which implies introversion, shyness and a caring nature. This is a sign of very short ascension which means that, in northern latitudes at any rate, there are very few of you around. Oddly enough, even in southern latitudes this sign does not have a particularly long period of ascension, therefore, on our planet at any rate, you are a truly rare fish.

Early experiences

If you have the misfortune to be born with Pisces rising, you could have experienced a truly horrific childhood. As I explained in the previous section, there are technical reasons for there being so few of you around, but there could be a few non-technical ones too. You grew up in a 'mother-dominated' household. Your father may have been severely incapacitated by illness or simply a very weak and ineffectual character. He may have died while you were young, or he may have deserted the family, leaving your mother to cope alone. Your mother was probably strong enough to cope with this, but she may have become embittered or self-pitying as a result.

Some Pisces children have very poor health. The heart, lungs and bronchial tubes are weak, and there may be other problems as well. I have no real evidence of this, but my instinct and intuition tells me that many potential Pisces rising lives may be lost through birth defects, infant mortality and accidents. I suspect that a good many of those children who spend their lives in hospitals or institutions have this ascendant. I am even prepared to bet that a number of children who die from neglect or abuse have this rising sign. The best that one can say about it is that if you survive into adulthood, there will come a time when the ascendant progresses from Pisces into Aries, bringing a change in your luck as well as a change in your attitude to life.

Your problems began while you were still inside your mother's womb! At that point in her life your mother may have been unhappy, unhealthy or short of money and in no shape to have a baby! Your entry into the world was difficult and dangerous, and your survival over those first few weeks was in doubt. Even as a small child you had the look of an 'old soul'. You seem to have entered this world with the remnants of a previous life still clinging to you, although of course, nobody had the time to notice this.

It seems that you are born to fulfil some kind of karmic debt, at least during your early years! The suffering which you underwent as a child could have arisen in a number of ways. If you were the type of Pisces rising child whose health wasn't good, there would have been occasions when you were so ill that you were not expected to recover. You may have spent some time away in hospital, or in a school for delicate children. Even if you were not sent away, you would have spent a good deal of time alone in bed, reading and thinking. It is this enforced withdrawal from life which allowed your creativity and your imagination to develop. The following examples will help you understand the problems.

Eve was the fifth child, born prematurely to parents who needed a fifth child like they needed a hole in the head! In fact, they went on to have a sixth child who, incidentally has the Moon in Pisces, whom they needed even less! Eve was evacuated during the war and this did not prove to be a happy experience for her. She spent her time away from home feeling lonely and desolate. Soon after returning home, she contracted rheumatic fever and was sent away once again, to a special school for delicate children. It was while Eve was at this school that she discovered that she had a talent for sport. She made some friends and really began, for the first time, to enjoy life. Soon after her return to the family, her father left home for good. Eve has told me that she never went short of the basic necessities of life, but there were no luxuries, and little love.

Margaret was adopted under peculiar circumstances (money changed hands). Her adoptive parents were neither young enough nor sufficiently competent to handle the reality of bringing up a boisterous child. Her mother had dreamed of raising a piano-playing, beribboned dolly, whilst Margaret was a gangling, overgrown, uncontrollable hoyden. Her adoptive father was a quiet, withdrawn little man who, in his non-communicative way, actually loved Margaret. Her adoptive mother was the type of woman whose upwardly mobile urges were forever doomed to be frustrated. Mother soon grew to dislike Margaret, and sought various ways of getting her out of the house. Margaret spent a good deal of time with a variety of 'aunties', who were cajoled and bribed into looking after her, until around the age of seven or eight, she developed a 'shadow on the lung' and was sent away to a school for delicate children. It was while she was at this school that Margaret discovered a talent for art and sport. The school strongly favoured the outdoor life and introduced Margaret to horticulture, which developed into a life-long passion. Eventually, Margaret came home. She grew even closer to her father. Her somewhat masculine nature made her a good companion to him, and she learned to share his interests of gardening, do-it-yourself and fixing up the car. However, just as this rapport was firmly established, it was suddenly destroyed due to the fact that her father had a stroke which left him partially paralysed and unable to speak. Both Eve and Margaret 'escaped' into marriage while they were still in their teens, and both went on to have a number of children.

Your health may have been all right, but you would still have been lonely and unhappy a good deal of the time. A Pisces rising girl called Michelle told me that her father left her mother to bring up two children (Michelle and her younger sister) on her own. Her mother had to work, of course, but also enjoyed a great social life with many boyfriends, holidays and outings, leaving Michelle in charge both of the household and her younger sister from a very early age. Despite this, Michelle did well at school, learned to speak a number of languages, and became a courier in the travel trade.

It is just possible that your home life was quite reasonable, but that you were not on the same wavelength as the rest of the family. You may have preferred to laze about in your room, playing music and drawing, rather than helping with the chores or getting on with your studies. If you were this type of Piscean you would eventually have drifted away from the family and made a life for yourself among like-minded people elsewhere.

In your own case, your education may have been good, bad or indifferent. You seem to have had plenty of opportunity to develop your talent for sports, art and dancing, even if the rest of your education was poor. It is possible that you found it difficult to relate either to your teachers or to some of the other children. The children, or worse still, the teachers, might have taken it upon themselves to bully and torment you. Whether this was the case or not, you may have 'switched-off' during childhood, returning to the world of education in adulthood, either through evening classes or by teaching yourself. One can guarantee that you will become an authority on some subject of your own choice later on. With Margaret, it is gardening and the language and culture of Middle-Eastern nations; with Eve it is the psychic and spiritual side of life. Other Pisceans whom I have met are mathematicians, historians, artists, language specialists, or skilled sports and dance teachers.

Appearance

Bearing in mind racial factors and the rest of the birthchart, you should be of medium height and size, with a pale, translucent complexion and fine blonde hair. I have seen Piscean eyes described in an astrology book as 'being like a semitic blowfish'. There is some truth in this. Your eyes are probably very pale grey or grey-blue in colour and they may be large and lustrous, or simply prominent. Women of this sign spend a good deal of time and money perming and lightening their pale, flimsy hair. Nowadays, male Pisceans also perm and colour their difficult hair. You are slim when young but inclined to put on weight later in life, especially if you give up smoking. One of your best features cannot actually be seen, and that is your voice. You have a quiet, gentle and humorous voice which is pleasant and relaxing to listen to. Your choice of clothes is casual and sporty, but not especially unusual. You prefer to put something on and then forget it rather than to try to create an 'image' and you are not especially self-conscious about your appearance. Oddly enough, you may be fussy about the colour of your clothes, preferring to stick to one or two colours which you feel comfortable with.

Outer manner

Under normal circumstances you are friendly, non-hostile and welcoming to new acquaintances. You project a gentle, helpful, kindly openness, and your ready wit and considerable intelligence makes you fun to be with and a very pleasant friend. The problem is that you are not totally reliable, because you prefer to drift in and out of people's lives rather than becoming a permanent fixture. You can be incredibly hostile to anyone who looks as if they might take it upon themselves to talk down to you. In business situations you appear intelligent, sensible, capable and very quick to pick up the essence of the situation. However, you are an excellent actor and, therefore, you can fit into any kind of company or situation. One aspect of your personality which you find hard to hide is your irritation when under pressure. You can become tense, tetchy and surprisingly nasty. Maybe this is the real you!

Pisces characteristics

This section can double up as a brief guide to Pisces as a Sun sign *or* as a rising sign, so it provides a handy reference for you if you wish to check out someone's Sun sign, as well as their rising sign. You may find that other factors on your chart swamp the Piscean influence so that the usual astrological tendency for the ascendant to be on show, while the other features on the chart are hidden, may be reversed. However, for the time being, we will concentrate on the Pisces element in your birthchart.

The sign of Pisces, as we all know, is represented by the image of two fish which are swimming in different directions. I have noticed that there are two distinct types of Piscean, one which represents the practical fish, while the other represents the nebulous, chaotic, dreamy one. Most of you appear to lean towards one of these two natures, whilst having at least a touch of the other one about you somewhere. If you are one of the practical types of Piscean, you will be very attached to your home and family. You have a great longing for a nice home of your own and, if you are lucky enough to eventually obtain one, you will spend a good deal of time and money keeping it in apple-pie order. You may collect antiques, keep a wonderful garden or become the do-it-yourselfer of the century.

Both sexes will be excellent cooks, but you have to watch that your own love of food doesn't spoil your figure. You are surprisingly ambitious, needing to reach a position of status and respectability. This may be a reaction to what you saw as your parents' dereliction of their duty. If your childhood was reasonably normal, then your parents may have made you feel inadequate in some way which, in turn, also leads you to become ambitious. Whatever the childhood situation might have been, the reaction is the same. You want to get on in life! This may be surprising news to those of you who are used to reading astrology books which stress the dreamy, non-materialistic side of the Piscean nature. If you don't have any great ambitions for yourself, you certainly will have them for your children. In the meantime, you need a comfortable, attractive and secure home and will go to great lengths to see that you get this.

Now we will take a glimpse at the other Piscean fish. It is worth remembering that Pisces is a *mutable* sign which denotes restlessness and changeability. You are a dreamer and a fantasizer, and your dreams may take you in any number of different directions. This intuitive and imaginative side of your nature is probably inborn, but your unhappy childhood definitely helped to foster it even more. You spent a good deal of time imagining what life would be like, thinking if only ... 'I were a princess; I won a million pounds; I became the world champion snooker player ...' You may have spent a good deal of time alone, either by choice or by force of circumstances, and this too allowed you to stretch your imagination by reading, dreaming, thinking and generally fiddling around. You may be so emotional that you don't know what you are going to say (or feel) next.

This lonely, introspective childhood will have given you the time and space to develop your creative and intuitive abilities. You may have become an excellent artist or musician, you may make up marvellous children's stories, or you may be able to inspire others in order to make their dreams come true. You could be drawn to the world of metaphysics; perhaps in the form of astrology, mediumship, white (or not so white) witchcraft, or some kind of old religion, such as Druidism. You will be driven to search for a deeper meaning to life and the hereafter. Whether you take the route of deep religious and philosophical thought, or simply a fascination with ghost stories, it is merely a different manifestation of the same urge. You need to escape from our everyday world of practical matters and endless chores in order to delve into the far distant land of beyond. If I do a quick mental round-up of my Sun in Pisces or Pisces rising friends and relatives, I come up with devout Jews, spiritual mediums, spiritual healers, dowsers and ley-line hunters, astrologers and Tarot readers, palmists, regression hypnotherapists, artists, writers and musicians. All of them are canny, sensible, capable and hard-working, but all are equally involved in the search beyond our everyday world for the world which lies hidden beyond the veil.

Now let us take a look at both of the fish on one plate, so to speak! You have a great desire to help others and even to sacrifice your own needs for the sake of others but I'm not sure that your motives for this are altogether altruistic. You may have a need to see yourself as the soul of goodness; you may wish to see yourself as the knight in shining armour. If you insist on continuing to live in unhappy or awkward circumstances, you should look inside yourself and examine your motives in order to see what it is that you are gaining from the situation before bemoaning your fate to everyone around you. Nevertheless, you are absolutely wonderful in a crisis. If anyone, even a new acquaintance, turns to you for help, you immediately understand the problem and act at once to solve it. You can be a great worrier. You may worry about your health, your family or the imminence of a nuclear holocaust and, if you have nothing to worry about, you will go and look for something. You care about small matters and rarely stop to think whether the situation which is currently on your mind is really worth all the anguish. Any form of injustice upsets you and brings you immediately to the defence of the underdog. If it happens that an animal is being ill-treated you really lose your temper and go all out to rescue the poor creature. As it happens, some Pisceans relate better to animals than to people, while most love to own animals and look after them. You have no prejudices against people on the grounds of race, religion or colour. Indeed, you like your friends to come from diverse backgrounds because this makes them all the more interesting.

Where practical matters are concerned you can be surprisingly careful. For example, you hate unnecessary waste and will re-use old envelopes and save paper bags and so forth, for a rainy day. You may never be rich, but you hate to be in debt, and you usually have a few pounds tucked away somewhere for emergencies. You don't like to borrow money, or to be under any kind of obligation to others, but you quite like it when others are under an obligation to you as this fulfils your need for self-sacrifice while, at the same time, giving you a small measure of control over them. One thing you do hate, however, is to be owed money. If at all possible, you will chase up a debtor; if the debt is not repaid you will never forget and never trust the defaulter again. Your strong sense of self-preservation saves you time and again from disaster, and you can be very canny when it comes to making sure that your needs are met

You never forget a hurt, but equally so, you never forget the person who has helped you either. Being a consummate actor you won't necessarily appear to react when you are hurt, but you won't forget either. Your sensitivity and vulnerability are such that you never learn to develop a thick skin. You are just as easily wounded by a nasty remark or by cruelty or treachery in adulthood as you were when you were a child. Your sensitivity to atmosphere is phenomenal, and it is this which makes it possible for you to capture feelings so easily in paint, words or music. Some of you take this sensitivity and awareness and develop it into clairvoyance, mediumship and the ability to 'feel' the future.

Pisceans are relaters. You are probably married (often more than once), or living with someone. You very likely have children around you, and you are in fairly frequent contact with your parents. You also have contact with ex-spouses, ex-in-laws and Uncle Tom Cobbley and all! You are not short of relatives and you get on with all of them amazingly well, just as long as they don't try to remake you or to bully you. Friends are important to you but, much as you like people, you also need time and space for yourself. You need freedom – even if you live the most well-regulated of lives you don't appreciate being asked how long you are going to be away and what time you will be back. You can be both strong and weak, selfish and giving, malleable and obdurate, meek and bossy, reliable and untrustworthy – in fact, a total conundrum. You resent criticism because you rarely see yourself clearly and don't want to be faced with the truth.

Some Pisceans are abstemious, non-smoking, frugal eaters, who never touch as much as an aspirin, while others are deeply into all forms of self-indulgence and self-destruction. Some of you are dreadful hypochondriacs, while others are amazingly forbearing under the weight of truly dreadful ailments. It is a rare Piscean who is truly happy, wealthy or healthy!

One aspect of your personality which is typical of the sign is your moodiness. Another is the duality of your nature; the two fish again, I suppose. Firstly, let us examine the moods. What you wanted passionately on Monday, Tuesday and Wednesday may not suit you at all on Thursday.

You may even change moods each six hours, as the tide turns! The duality of your nature ensures that you can be all sweetness and light on one occasion, and amazingly spiteful on another. You are willing to help others with all your might but when they finally land on their feet you can be consumed with jealousy at their success. You are rarely happy because too much contentment bores you, yet you can be extremely cheerful when living under the most difficult of circumstances. You love a crisis, but cannot take too much strain You are a mass of contradictions, and you react to everything on an emotional level; no one, least of all yourself, can understand you.

The midheaven

The midheaven is supposed to show the subject's aims and ambitions, therefore it can throw light on his choice of career. In the case of Pisces rising, the MC is always in Sagittarius.

You could be attracted to the Sagittarian careers of teaching and training, or the Piscean ones of social and medical work. Both signs have a strong urge to help people and to relieve suffering, therefore you may be drawn to work in some institution, such as a prison, a hospital, a mental hospital or a home for old or disabled people. Your desire to help and care could take you into child care or nursery nursing, while the Piscean attachment to feet could lead to a career in chiropody. Many Piscean subjects make a career out of caring for animals. You are deeply interested in art and music, and may take these up as a career. If you cannot follow a creative career, you will continue to develop your creativity in the form of a hobby. Hobbies and part-time jobs, such as dressmaking and gardening might help to fill this gap, as would self-expression in the form of pottery, metalwork or even singing. You may fulfil your need to care for others by some form of voluntary work, possibly attached to a hospital. Your strong sense of justice could lead you into a legal career, or into one which requires a talent for arbitration and administration.

Both Pisces and Sagittarius are deeply interested in religion and philosophy, so this will figure strongly in your life. You may become involved in some kind of organized religion or take an interest in spiritual and mediumistic work and spiritual healing. You could take up this kind of work on either a full or a part-time basis. Another interest which both these signs have in common is travel. Pisceans are restless and are often drawn to water, so a career on the sea is possible. Fishing is another Piscean interest, so you could take this up as either a job or a hobby. Your talent for languages, combined with your itchy feet, could take you travelling around the world, either in connection with your work or as a hobby. Your restless nature is best suited to a job which takes you around the country rather than one which involves sitting still in one place. You may work from home on some kind of private project, travelling out for purposes of research or observation. Writers and artists of one kind or another would fall into this category. You may teach others from your own home, holding 'workshop' sessions on your own specialized subjects. You need variety in your work and you also need to meet a variety of people. Many of you are not actually suited to work at all, and may be better off with a private income or to being kept by someone else. I have noticed that Piscean subjects have a peculiar kind of love/hate relationship with motor cars. You either love them and are an excellent driver, or you hate to drive and rarely do so. A great many of you never get around to learning this skill and, for all I know, never feel as if you are missing anything. Water is another Piscean oddity, you either love it so much that you include it into your work or your hobbies; or you hate it.

The midheaven can sometimes show the type of person with whom we are comfortable, either in working partnerships or even as marriage partners. In the case of Pisces rising, this would suggest a strong affinity with Sagittarians.

The descendant

The descendant, or the cusp of the seventh house, is traditionally supposed to show the type of person to whom we are most attracted. In the case of Pisces rising, the descendant is in Virgo. This does not mean that Pisceans make a point of marrying Virgoans, but it does suggest that your first experience of marriage will have a Virgoan flavour to it. This situation would involve you in much sacrifice and hard work, in return for very little in the way of respect or affection. After such an inauspicious start, you will probably move on and find another partner who is, at least, a little more affectionate.

The Virgoan influence is also expressed in the way you conduct your marriages. You look after your partner very well, and you will put up with a good deal of restriction or even unpleasantness, if necessary. You cope with this by switching off and letting your mind roam elsewhere away from the reality of your day-to-day life. If you are lucky, you will be able to find someone who represents the better Virgoan values, and who is reliable, competent, hard-working and decent. You may marry initially for security, or in order to escape from your parents. You may even marry for sex! However, if you do make a mistake the first time around, you will look later for someone who shares your interests, is willing to communicate with you and also offer you a peaceful, decent homelife.

Love, sex and relating – regardless of the descendant

Pisces is a very sexy sign! However, you may live for years with a poor lover. You need to give and receive love and affection, possibly because you were deprived of it when you were a child. You are able to divert your sex-drive into some kind of 'higher purpose', such as religion or good works of some kind. Being long-suffering and self-sacrificing, you may continue to live for years with a partner who doesn't please you sexually, or you may learn to live entirely without sex by diverting your love into the care of your children. Given a chance to express your sexuality you can really make the sparks fly. Your vivid imagination and your taste for fantasy may lead you into some very peculiar situations. You are generous and fond enough of play to indulge your partner's need for fantasy, so really, with you, anything goes.

Your partner must take account of your moods, however, because the very thing which you most wanted for the last few months may totally turn you off on the next occasion. Your sensuousness and delicate sense of touch, together with your delight in relaxing and throwing yourself into a whirlpool of sensation, gives you the ability to enjoy the full pleasure of sex in all its forms. If you are the 'water baby' type of Piscean, you will love to make love in the bath!

Health

Traditionally, you are supposed to have bad feet and it is often the case that your feet do give you problems. They are very sensitive, and are apt to swell up when you are overtired or overworked. Other than your feet, almost anything and everything can go wrong with your health. Your lungs and heart may be weak, as may be your spine. Females tend to suffer from menstrual problems, while both sexes will have difficulty in balancing their body fluids. This may result in high blood pressure, cystitis, varicose veins and a host of other problems. However, despite your poor health, you usually manage to live a full and long life.

Your sixth house is in Leo, so please look at the health section on page 586.

Part Three

Deeper and Deeper

If you have an analytical mind and enjoy looking beyond the obvious, you might enjoy exploring some of the ideas which I have set out for you in the following sections. I have taken a look at such features as 'cuspy' ascendants, the decanates of each sign and the influence of the immum coeli plus the effect of planets which are in conjunction with the ascendant.

16

The Immum-Coeli

The immum-coeli (or nadir), usually referred to as the IC, is at the bottom of the birthchart, directly opposite to the midheaven. This refers to the private side of one's life, the home and the family. Traditionally, the IC also refers to the beginning and ending of one's life, the mother or mother-figure, and any kind of ancestral memory. Here is a very brief outline which shows the effects which each of the 12 signs of the zodiac might have when on the IC.

Aries

There may have been some kind of conflict going on in the family at the time you were born. However, your childhood environment was cheerful and your parents helpful and encouraging. Your adult home is an open and friendly place with many visitors and a lot of fun and noise. You could fill your home with gadgets or sports equipment.

Taurus

Your birth should have been comfortable and well arranged and, if your early environment was lacking in either material or emotional comforts, you can rest assured that your later life will make up for this. Your own adult home will be full of music and beauty and probably over-furnished and full of souvenirs.

Gemini

This sign suggests a strange start in life, possibly due to some kind of disruption in your family, or in your schooling. You will probably be active and working right up to the end of your days. You will have either exceptionally good or exceptionally bad relationships with your brothers and sisters. Your own adult home will be full of books, music and people, and you may run some kind of business from it. You need freedom to come and go, but the home you return to will be spacious and full of expensive furniture and equipment.

Cancer

Your early experiences will have a strong impact on your future development. You should remain close to your parents throughout their lives. Your adult home will be very important to you and, even though you frequently travel away from it, you see it as a safe haven. You may work partially or wholly from your home. You may enjoy cooking, and your kitchen should be very well equipped. You could collect odds and ends, antiques or even junk.

Leo

Your early days could have been very difficult, either because you were over-disciplined or because your parents lived a nomadic existence. Later on, you try to make a traditional and comfortable home, but even this may become disrupted in some way. You may want a nice home but somehow find that you are prevented from spending a lot of money on it. If you entertain you will do so in style and if you work from home you will make sure that you have all the latest equipment to hand.

Virgo

Your early life could have been difficult, either in the home or at school. However, your home environment was full of books and music. Your parents would have placed a bit too much importance on good behaviour, a 'proper' diet and cleanliness, and too little on how you felt. Your adult home is spacious and comfortable, with a well-stocked kitchen. If you work from home, you will have all the latest communications equipment.

Libra

Your early life would have been calm, pleasant and loving, with nice sur-roundings and respectable parents. Your adult home should be large and very comfortable, full of artistic objects and music. You probably like cook-ing, so your kitchen will be well-equipped, but any entertaining which you do will be on a small scale.

Scorpio

The circumstances of your birth may have been strange, and there could have been some kind of conflict raging in the family at the time you were born. The atmosphere in your childhood home may have been tense and uncomfortable. Your adult home would be far more pleasant, with an emphasis on good food and a comfortable lifestyle, but you must guard against tension creeping in even there. You may find that you spend a good deal of time alone in your home, either by choice or by circumstances.

Sagittarius

Your early life may have been peculiar, either because your parents were heavily involved in religious activities or because they were immigrants from another culture. You may have lived in two worlds at the same time. Your adult home will be pleasant and open, not over-tidy, but full of inter-esting knick-knacks. You may work from home or use it as a base to travel away from.

Capricorn

Your childhood home may have been happy although lacking in material comforts or it may have been a source of tension and stress. You would have been encouraged to work hard for material success. Your latter days will be very comfortable and you could well end up being very rich. Your adult home will be well-organized and filled with valuable goods, but you may decide to keep animals in preference to having children.

Aquarius

During childhood, your life at home or school may have been very unset-tled or even eccentric. Your adult home could also be rather strange, either being very sumptuous and filled with expensive goods and gadgets, or filled with an odd assortment of junk. Alternatively, your furniture and equipment could be ultra modern. You may work from your home part of the time, but whether this is so or not, your home is often filled with friends and neighbours.

Pisces

There may have been some mystery surrounding the circumstances of your birth or alternatively, you might have been brought up in a nomadic sort of family. Both your childhood home and your later adult one will reflect the many interests of the people who live in it. These may include books and equipment associated with the occult, magic, religion or travel. Your surroundings may be deliberately 'different', perhaps arty, musical, or earth-motherish. Your children will have a good deal of freedom, but they may not actually communicate much with you.

17

Cusps

A cusp is the point where one sign ends and the next begins. We know that to be 'born on a cusp' means that the Sun is located at the very beginning or end of a sign and this can lead to a blending of both signs in the person- ality. For example, someone who was born with the Sun at 29° of Pisces would have a certain amount of Aries energy and enterprise added to their withdrawn and reflective Pisces nature. When the ascendant is 'cuspy', the situation is different. If the ascendant is close to the beginning of a sign, most of the first house will be the same sign; this makes the effect of the ascendant very strong. Figure 5 shows how this looks on a chart.

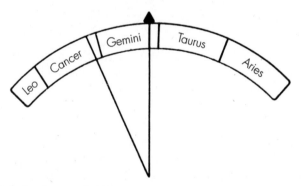

Figure 5: A strong ascendant sign.

If the ascendant is close to the end of a sign the situation becomes cloudy, because the ascendant will be in one sign while the first house straddles the cusp and then spreads itself out over a large area of the next sign. Figure 6 shows how this situation looks on a chart.

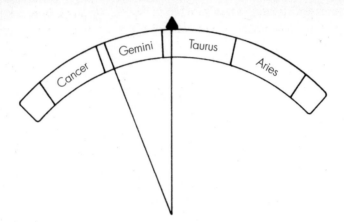

Figure 6: A weak ascendant sign

To add to this confusion, I have an entirely personal theory which deviates from normal astrological thinking. I believe that cusps have a life of their own which goes beyond the simple blending of the two signs which are involved. To test this theory, take a look at the list of cusps below and apply my ideas to anyone who you can find who has the Sun, Moon or Ascendant on or over a cusp.

Aries/Taurus

This belongs to a powerful personality who has the kind of vision which allows him to look forward while retaining strong links to the past. He can be charming when he feels like it, but is also determined, obstinate and even aggressive. He has a strong sexual drive which may or may not be diverted into other activities. He is probably interested in the arts or music and also in architecture and any kind of lasting achievement. He could be a powerful, visionary leader, or a complete mess. Two examples which are different in nature although similar in the kind of arena in which their lives have been lived out are Adolf Hitler and Queen Elizabeth the Second.

Taurus/Gemini

This person can be a creative dreamer, a self-indulgent type of personality who wants the good life and may even make an effort to work for it if pressed. He should be dexterous especially where any form of engineering is concerned. Travel interests him but so does his work, his home and the support of his family. He may move and talk slowly but his mind is quick and shrewd.

Gemini/Cancer

This person is moody, difficult to understand and probably too idealistic for his own good. He is a good listener and also a good talker but his idealism doesn't extend to leaving himself short of money; indeed he has the mind of a creative accountant. Complex; honest but devious, kind but mercenary, independent but desperate for a good relationship; both a mixer and a loner. He may always be on the move, looking for the most advantageous mixture of circumstances. He may carry a chip on his shoulder about past hurts or suffer from a low level of self-esteem.

Cancer/Leo

This subject wants to make a splash; he wants to be noticed and respected but he may be too lazy to achieve this ambition. If he really can't face too much work, he will try to marry someone who has a good income instead. He is probably quite artistic and certainly creative. He has a talent for working in the financial field and may be an excellent accountant or insurance salesman. He may be an excellent sales person as he genuinely likes people, especially young people.

Leo/Virgo

This subject is nervy, a high achiever who never thinks he has done enough. He can become ill when things go wrong or he can punish himself unnecessarily. Emotionally vulnerable, slow to grow up or accept change, he needs to gain confidence. He also needs a stable family life. He is kind hearted and good to others, especially his own family and friends.

Virgo/Libra

This subject is highly sexed and highly charged with many other kinds of energy as well. He enjoys work, especially if it gives him a chance to manage others, and he may travel extensively in connection with his work. He is clever, dexterous and a high achiever, a clever negotiator and a fascinating person, but is not easy to live with. He may dabble at things rather than work properly.

Libra/Scorpio

There may be something physically wrong with this subject, his spine and legs could be affected in some way, even to the point of semi-paralysis. Despite any disability, he overcomes everything and goes on to have an interesting career, often in some form of teaching or media work. This subject is a fighter who goes after what he wants. His marriage and other family or close relationships are likely to be excellent but he may choose not to have children. His outer manner is quite unpleasant on first acquaintance and he needs to work on this if he wishes to increase his popularity out in the world.

Scorpio/Sagittarius

This subject can be very mystical or spiritual in outlook, with a strong desire to help others. He seems to suffer more than most and puts up with it for longer than he really should. He is a reliable and hard worker who will stick to a job until the finish but he likes variety in his work and doesn't mind travelling in order to earn his money. This subject can suffer from accidents to the legs but he seems to overcome everything and keep going. He may be drawn to work in the fields of medicine or religion.

Sagittarius/Capricorn

This subject is fascinated by the occult and may be very psychic; he puts this fascination to use for the benefit of others. He can be very businesslike one minute but quite scatty and unrealistic the next. He needs to relax and have fun as he can find himself on a treadmill of work. He draws the kind of family and friends to him who depend upon him to keep them happy and give them a good life, but he may get little back in return. He is suspicious of others which makes him prefer the company of his family to that of friends.

Capricorn/Aquarius

A strange mixture; outwardly competent and often sarcastic to the point of being offensive, but at the same time idealistic and kind hearted. He is very good to his family and close friends but is often too involved with work to spend much time with them. This subject either identifies himself with his work or he may be heavily involved with committee work. Muddle-headed and somewhat messy administratively, he is at his best when teaching or helping others. His ideas are often wonderful, very clever and truly workable.

Aquarius/Pisces

This subject is a mystic with strong leanings towards religion and/or the occult. He is a terrific teacher with the ability to inspire others. His vision is tremendous, but his ability to cope with day-to-day life may be completely lacking. He is impractical and may get himself into financial muddles. He may be very eccentric and faddy about everything from food, to clothing and the way he lives. To quote a remark made by my friend, Denise, 'such people are fascinating, but out-with-the-fairies!'

Pisces/Aries

Quite a number of people who have this cusp strongly marked on their charts choose to work in the professional astrological or psychic world. Their mixture of superb intuition coupled with their commercial instincts can make them very successful in almost any field of endeavour. However, their high ideals can make them hard to live with.

18

Decanates

Each sign of the zodiac is divided into 300 which can be broken down into three groups of 10°. These sub-sections are called decans or decanates. The first decanate of any sign is ruled by its own sign, the second one is sub-ruled by the next sign along in the same triplicity and the third decanate is sub-ruled by the last sign in the same triplicity. For example, the sign of Aquarius is an air sign. The first decanate is sub-ruled by Aquarius itself, the second by Gemini also an air sign and the third by Libra the other air sign.

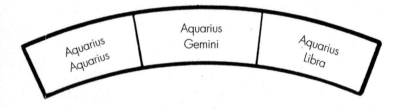

Figure 7: The Aquarius decanates

The influence of the decanates

I'm not sure that decanates are terribly important in themselves but they can have a subtle subsidiary influence on a birthchart. An interesting side issue is to look at your own family's charts and see how the decanates fit together. For instance, I have the Sun in Leo in the third decanate which is sub-ruled by Aries while my father was born with the Sun in Aries in the second decanate which is sub-ruled by Leo.

I have suggested a few key ideas here but you can make up your own list if you prefer.

Aries/Aries	Pure Aries.
Aries/Leo	Leo adds dignity, stability and creativity.
Aries/Sagittarius	Sagittarius adds high-minded idealism, optimism, popularity and political aspirations.
Taurus/Taurus	Pure Taurus.
Taurus/Virgo	Virgo adds an aptitude for hard work and service to others but diminishes the Taurean confidence.
Taurus/Capricorn	Capricorn adds patience, acumen and ambition but also some pessimism and sadness.
Gemini/Gemini	Pure Gemini.
Gemini/Libra	Libra adds charm, calmness, a love of beauty and sex appeal.
Gemini/Aquarius	Aquarius adds academic ability, high-mindedness and eccentricity.
Cancer/Cancer	Pure Cancer.
Cancer/Scorpio	Scorpio adds determination, ambition, depth of feelings and an interest in health or healing.
Cancer/Pisces	Pisces adds vulnerability, mysticism, self-sacrifice and emotionalism.
Leo/Leo	Pure Leo.
Leo/Sagittarius	Sagittarius adds high-mindedness, the need to explore and sporting ability.
Leo/Aries	Aries adds impulsiveness, bossiness and independence.
Virgo/Virgo	Pure Virgo.
Virgo/Capricorn	Capricorn adds ambition, executive ability, practicality and patience.
Virgo/Taurus	Taurus adds calmness, practicality and an artistic eye.
Libra/Libra	Pure Libra.
Libra/Aquarius	Aquarius adds intellect, independence and political ability.

Libra/Gemini	Gemini adds speed of thought and action, wit, dexterity and intellect.
Scorpio/Scorpio	Pure Scorpio.
Scorpio/Pisces	Pisces adds vulnerability, self-sacrifice and an interest in health or healing.
Scorpio/Cancer	Cancer adds shrewdness, a need to care for others and a desire for stable family life.
Sagittarius/Sagittarius	Pure Sagittarius.
Sagittarius/Aries	Aries adds impulsiveness, courage, enterprise and sporting ability.
Sagittarius/Leo	Leo adds stability, love of children and animals, also arrogance.
Capricorn/Capricorn	Pure Capricorn.
Capricorn/Taurus	Taurus adds a love of beauty, music and the countryside together with a need for personal comfort.
Capricorn/Virgo	Virgo adds acumen, analytical or accounting ability, speed of movement and dexterity.
Aquarius/Aquarius	Pure Aquarius.
Aquarius/Gemini	Gemini adds speed of thought and action, mental agility and communication ability.
Aquarius/Libra	Libra adds calmness, sociability and a love of beauty.
Pisces/Pisces	Pure Pisces.
Pisces/Cancer	Cancer adds a need to care for others and a love of family life, but also shrewdness and determination.
Pisces/Scorpio	Scorpio adds stability and determination, plus an interest in psychology, medicine, and mysticism.

19

Planets in Conjunction with the Ascendant

Planets On or Near the Ascendant

Here are some points which the more technically-minded readers might like to consider:

1. Planets which are in the first house have a strong influence on the subject's life and personality. If there is only one planet in this house or close to the ascendant, it will be strongly emphasized. If there is a group of planets, then the first house, and the sign which it occupies, will be stressed. The same could be said for planets in the twelfth house if they are close to the ascendant, except for the Sun which is a little dim in this house.

2. The planet nearest to the ascendant is called the *rising planet*. If there is nothing in the first house, but a planet is situated in the twelfth house very close to the ascendant, then that planet could be termed a rising planet. Please note that in this case the planet would have to be very close to the ascendant; for instance, no more than a degree or two away from it.

3. A planet which is in conjunction with the ascendant is vitally important, both in its effect on the personality, and in its effects on the subject's life. In some cases, a rising planet can be almost as important as the Sun in a birthchart.

If you know that you have a planet close to the ascendant, read the following information and see whether you agree that it influences your life strongly or not.

Sun conjunct ascendant

Assuming that the Sun and the ascendant are in the same sign, (e.g. Sun in Libra, Libra rising), that sign would become an ultra important factor on the chart. If the Sun and ascendant were in adjoining signs (e.g. Sun in Libra, Virgo rising), both signs would be emphasized, but not as much as if only one sign was involved. Transits and progressions over that part of the chart would be exceptionally noticeable. Assuming that the two factors were in the same sign, there would be no need for the ascendant to act as a shield to the personality. This pre-supposes a confident, outgoing, well-integrated person whose childhood experiences were encouraging. If the sign involved were a difficult one (Virgo, Capricorn or Gemini for instance), the childhood might have been hard, but the subject would have the inner strength to rise above the problems and could achieve a good deal of success in spite of them – or maybe because of them.

The subject who has the Sun and ascendant in conjunction has a powerful personality and a strong need to express himself in day-to-day life. He puts his own personal stamp on everything he does and he cannot live or work in a subservient position. He (or she) is strong and healthy, with good powers of recovery from illness. There may be problems in connection with his back or heart, but he would be able to overcome them more successfully than many others. His ego is involved in all that he does and any new beginnings will be initiated by himself, rather than by others. If he finds himself in the hands of fate (or in the hands of other people), he turns the situation to his own advantage as quickly as possible. This subject will have a sunny personality. He will be arrogant and difficult to deal with until he learns to restrain himself and re-channel his powerful energies. In an otherwise introverted or other-worldly chart this Sun placement injects energy, dynamism, cheerful optimism and self-centredness.

Moon conjunct ascendant

The Moon represents the emotions and reactions, therefore this placement denotes a sensitive and vulnerable nature. The feelings are close to the surface and are easily brought into play. The subject reacts in an intensely personal way to every stimulus and he links in easily to the feelings of others.

The ideas, experiences and emotions of the mother will have a profound effect, and the subject will remain close to her, perhaps remaining involved in her life and her work for many years. It is even possible that the subject can remember the things which happened to his mother (and to him), before he was born. Childhood experiences and early training remain in the subject's unconscious mind throughout his life.

There is a strong need to create a home and family as well as to look after others by working in one of the caring professions. The subject may wish to protect the environment, preserve places, buildings and objects from the past, and also to create a better, kinder and safer future for mankind. Psychic ability is almost always present with this placement; there may even be vestigial memories of previous lives. All forms of intuition will be well developed.

The subject may be drawn to a career in travel, especially sea travel. Alternatively, he may wish to run a small business for himself. He is interested in history and tradition, and may try to revive traditional crafts or to collect fine things from the past. He will be able to retreat from the rat race from time to time, in order to calm himself and recharge his emotional batteries. Oddly enough, the Moon is associated with work in the public eye, or for the public good, so he may become a well-known 'personality'.

Being sensitive, he can become depressed or downhearted and may absorb the unhappiness of others. He must take care because this kind of 'psychic absorption' can make him ill. In a notably macho or materialistic chart, this Moon placement lends introspection and sensitivity to the needs and feelings of others.

Mercury conjunct ascendant

Mercury is concerned with communications and the mentality, therefore these subjects are fluent talkers and good communicators. The subject may be highly intelligent or merely bright; active and street-wise. He will choose to work in a job which is directly involved with communications. My cousin, Brian, for example, has Virgo rising with Mercury close to the ascendant in the first house; he has worked as a salesman, tour guide and taxi driver, and is now in the business of selling advertising space. He is communicating with those who wish to communicate!

This subject is a logical thinker and an active worker. He may switch off from time to time, to allow his mind to relax. He is dutiful towards his parents and his family. He feels happy if his work is appreciated and miserable if it is not. This type of subject is restless, easily bored, interesting to listen to, humorous and sometimes very sarcastic. He suffers from nervous ailments when placed under pressure. In a stodgy or over-practical chart, this Mercury placement would add quickness of mind, curiosity and restlessness.

Venus conjunct ascendant

This confers good looks and a pleasant social manner. The subject may have a good singing voice, but even if this is not the case, he will at least have a very pleasant speaking voice. This placement of Venus adds refinement and a dislike of anything which is ugly, dirty or vulgar. This person may take a job in a field where he can create beauty in some way, for example as a gardener, furniture designer, hairdresser or dancer. If he doesn't get the opportunity to express his delight in creating beauty through work, he will take up an artistic or attractive hobby. The subject may be a good arbitrator, with a natural desire to create harmony and understanding all around him. He uses his attractive personality to help him in his day-to-day work.

This subject is materialistic. He enjoys making money and spending it on attractive and valuable goods. He is also concerned about values, both in terms of getting value for money and also in terms of personal values and priorities. He is unwilling to sacrifice anything which he values for the sake of others. Venus on the ascendant can add placidity and pleasantness to an otherwise forceful, dynamic or neurotic chart.

Mars conjunct ascendant

This adds impulsiveness, enterprise and courage to the character. The subject has a strong will and a fierce temper. This 'tough-guy' type can make things happen where other less courageous souls would prefer to run away and hide. This aggressive person stands out in a crowd, dominating and possibly bullying those around him. His influence extends to any sphere in which he becomes involved, and he can become a highly successful, fast-moving achiever. He is best suited for a position of leadership or, if he is too difficult for others to work under, as a self-employed entrepreneur. If the rest of the chart endows sympathy, co-operation and diplomacy, he can really reach the top. To my mind, this typifies the red-haired, red-faced, rugged 'where there's muck there's money' type of businessman. In an otherwise timid, stodgy or lazy chart, this can add enterprise, enthusiasm, energy and will-power.

Jupiter conjunct the ascendant

This adds joviality to the personality because the influence of this planet is cheerful, broadminded and outward looking. The subject is attractive to look at, with a sunny smile and good teeth. This placement adds the kind of broad frame and comfortable shape which looks great on a man, but is unfashionable nowadays for a woman. The subject's outer manner is cheerful, optimistic and confident, he carries authority well and he can be an inspirational leader without throwing his weight about. This subject is not likely to be biased against any class or colour of person and he is not the slightest bit snobbish, but he is highly intolerant of phonies and posers.

Traditionally, this placement gives a love of travel and exploration, plus a touch of studiousness. This person may be particularly interested in philosophy and metaphysical subjects. The subject should also be a lucky gambler, in business perhaps, rather than on the horses. His mind is good, and he can usually see both sides of any argument, but when he chooses to argue a point he becomes very attached to his own opinions. The chances are that the subject will become well-known in his particular field because he enjoys being in the public eye. He is likely to be in contact with many people as a result of working in a personnel, sales or marketing capacity. He could take up a career as a politician, church minister or lawyer if the rest of the chart leans that way. Education is another career possibility because there is a desire to influence others in a beneficial manner.

I have noticed that people who have this planet rising experience quite drastic ups and downs where money is concerned. They are invariably attractive, but the optimism which the old time astrologers associate with this planet can be dampened if there is a good deal of water on the chart. Nevertheless, this placement adds a touch of enterprise, luck and vision to an otherwise stodgy or earthbound chart. Jupiter rising subjects do seem to travel widely, often in connection with their work, and some eventually leave their country of origin altogether.

Saturn conjunct the ascendant

This placement is a real stinker! To be honest, I don't entirely share most astrologers' pessimistic attitudes towards Saturn. On the contrary, I see it as a stabilizing factor on many charts but, when it is on the ascendant or any of the angles for that matter, it takes a lot of living with. This planet brings insecurity, even fear; particularly during childhood. For some reason, the subject's sense of self-worth is crushed by circumstances during his childhood and he has to work long and hard to rebuild it. He may have been rejected by either (or both) of his parents, or deprived of their love and attention due to tragic events. If he was cared for by other people during his childhood he would have been aware that this was done on sufferance. He hides his real needs and feelings and may even deny himself the right to have any needs other than those which other people consider suitable. His natural creativity may be squashed because it doesn't fit in with the requirements of those around him. Depending upon the rest of the chart, this childhood can cause the subject to develop a hard and aggressive attitude to others later in life or on the other hand, he may allow himself (or herself) to become, and to remain a doormat, never making even the most reasonable kind of demands upon others. Another possibility is that he rises above this unpromising start and becomes an outstanding success.

This person is reliable and responsible; he takes all commitments very seriously, he finishes all that he starts and his self-discipline is incredible. He may project an austere image, but underneath will be surprisingly idealistic and, in personal and family life, he is kindly, sensitive and thoughtful, while being tolerant of the foibles of others. His reserve may be hard to penetrate, although this would be mitigated by an otherwise outgoing type of chart. Any appearance of hardness or unfriendliness is caused by shyness and a fear of being hurt. This individual is uncomfortable in social situations, although relaxed with his family and close friends. However, he is frequently most comfortable at work. I guess that it's not surprising that many Saturn influenced people are workaholics.

Traditionally, Saturn on the ascendant or in hard aspect to it (e.g. in opposition or square) at the time of birth indicates a difficult birth. My own theory is that this planet, which is so associated with old age, denotes at least one important previous incarnation and it may be the memory of this which holds the subject back when it is time for him to be re-born. He just may not want to face the whole business again. Another interesting theory is that the mother had to work very hard while the child was young, which gave him an especially diligent parental role model.

As it happens, I was born with Saturn about one degree behind the ascendant and, although my childhood and early life were hard, things are much better now. Saturn is often close to the ascendant in writers' charts, I guess it gives us the necessary self-discipline to get the job done. This placement adds stability, thoroughness, patience and modesty to an otherwise neurotic, unpredictable, lazy or self-indulgent chart.

Uranus conjunct the ascendant

This adds a touch of eccentricity. The subject may be idealistic, unpredictable and quite fascinating. His interests will be unusual; he may be drawn to the world of astrology and the occult, if the rest of the chart has similar leanings. Humanitarian and broad-minded, he tends to opt for an unusual way of life, either following unusual beliefs or making his own up as he goes along. His life takes peculiar twists and turns, partly because he is prey to unusual circumstances and partly because he cannot stand too much normality. He has a good mind which is directed towards the unusual. He may be cranky, strange or visionary in his thinking whilst at the same time being stubborn and determined. The amount of individuality and unusualness will depend on the structure of the rest of the chart. Even an extremely mundane chart will be enlivened by this placement.

Neptune conjunct the ascendant

This fascinating planet can make the subject into an inspired artist, glamorous film star or a complete nut-case. The subject's childhood may have been strange and there could have been some kind of mystery surrounding his birth and parentage. It is possible that one of his parents was very peculiar, even to the extent of being mentally ill. The subject is sensitive, vulnerable, easily hurt and 'destroyed', and he may never have a clear idea of his own needs and feelings. He may try to run his life to someone else's rules, discovering later perhaps, that the rules he tried to follow were abnormal or twisted in some way.

This placement can make the subject psychic, mediumistic, and/or prone to fantasies. In extreme cases, he may lose track of reality altogether. Bear in mind the rest of the chart when Neptune is rising because if it is practical and sensible this will simply add artistry and sensitivity rather than genuine lunacy. The subject may be drawn to a career in the arts, photography, music or the mediumistic side of the occult. He will have a soft spot for anyone or anything which he sees suffering and could either work hard for some kind or charity organization or just be a collector of lame ducks.

Pluto conjunct the ascendant

This subject has great self-control and may seek to control, direct and guide the lives of others. This directing instinct could take him into the world of medicine, the media or teaching, depending upon the shape of the rest of the chart. In personal relationships he could be coercive or domineering and will try to control his partner, either financially or sexually. His own personality is so controlled that it is hard to work out just what he is thinking or what really motivates him. Although very pleasant to the people he works with, he may be very difficult to live with and also something of a loner with no real friends. He is slow to grow up, but when he does he becomes a reliable adult who will never renege on any of his commitments. He is happiest in a career where he is in charge of others, and even happier if he can improve the lives of large numbers of people. He has an exceptionally sharp mind and the kind of insight which may make him uncomfortable to be near. He can pick up even the mildest of undercurrents and 'vibes', and always knows when someone doesn't really like him. He may well appear mild, gentle and amenable but when challenged or hurt, the 'Clark Kent' image vanishes and Superman appears in its place.

His virtues are tenacity and obstinacy, which have the effect of making him extremely reliable and dependable. He finishes all that he starts and does it properly. He arrives in good time for appointments, alert and properly equipped to do what is required of him. He hates to let go of anyone or anything but he will not allow anyone to shackle him or dictate to him. He must be able to come and go as he pleases.

This subject can be idealistic, paternalistic and very sensitive to the needs of others. He tries to improve the world he lives in wherever he can but, altruistic as he is, he cannot explain his motives to others and therefore may sometimes be misunderstood. He has an urge to heal those who are sick at heart or ailing physically, therefore he may choose to work in the medical field. Alternatively, he may help out on a part-time basis as a paramedic. Hypnotherapy might appeal to him, or he may use some of his spare time to work as a spiritual healer.

This planet adds sexuality. Depending upon circumstances and the rest of his chart, he may accept this side of his personality, use it and enjoy it, or he may block it out and try to drive his sexual needs and desires from his mind. If he denies his high-octane sexual needs he may become embittered or depressed. If he can explore this side of his nature he will relax, become comfortable with his strange, obsessive personality, and go on to lead a full and happy life. This placement will add depth and intensity on all levels to an otherwise superficial chart.

Rectification

The term rectification refers to the hunt for an ascendant when the subject doesn't know his time of birth. Every astrology book which I have seen says that this is a job for a skilled astrologer, but even the most skilled astrologer has to start somewhere so why shouldn't you have a go too? There are various ways in which a chart can be rectified. The Aquarian Press publishes a whole book on this subject but, in the meantime, here are a few tips which may prove helpful to the novice.

When the birthtime is given approximately

If your subject gives you an approximate birthtime, for example, between about two and three o'clock in the afternoon, your best bet is to make up a chart for 2.30 p.m. and then try 'fine-tuning' the chart as described a little further along in this chapter.

Dowsing

If a birthtime is completely unknown you could try dowsing, but if you are not into psychic and mystical ideas you will need to find somebody who is. (Rectification dowsers advertise their services occasionally in national astrological magazines). The dowser holds a divining pendulum over each sign while tuning in psychically to his spiritual guides and also to his inner self. Eventually he will come up with a 'yes' movement on his pendulum. This may categorically point to one particular sign, or it might point to two opposing signs, thereby showing the ascendant/descendant axis.

If you feel happier with science, technology, and psychology, then dowsing will not appeal much to you. However, if you already read Tarot, or have mediumistic abilities, you could well become skilled at this line of work.

When the subject has no idea when he was born

It is possible to work out a rising sign by a process of elimination. This is not easy and it requires a thorough knowledge of the energies and characteristics of each rising sign. Firstly, put the chart together or at least list the planets in their signs so that you can see which influences are already in existence on the chart before you begin to hunt for the rising sign. If this points to an obvious type of personality and a specific kind of childhood, then even at this stage some rising signs will begin to fit better than others. If the subject does not resemble his Sun sign, then try to work out what sign he does resemble – the chances are that he will be projecting his rising sign. The second step is to ask a few questions about the childhood and background. The following suggestions may prove helpful.

If the subject was the eldest child or the most responsible one in the family, he may have been Cancer, Leo, Capricorn, Scorpio or even Aquarius on the Ascendant. If he was the youngest or the least likely to take the lead, this would point towards Gemini, Virgo, Sagittarius or Pisces.

If he was loved just because he existed, without having to prove himself to his parents, then his rising sign could be Cancer, Leo, Libra, Sagittarius, Capricorn or Aquarius. If he was only approved of, or even loved, because he behaved in an acceptable manner, or passed exams to order, then he could have Virgo, or Pisces rising.

If he really didn't fit in anywhere as a child he may have had Aries, Gemini or Scorpio rising.

Closeness to the mother (or other nurturing figures), would be shown by Taurus, Cancer, Libra and Capricorn; while closeness to the father would indicate Taurus, Leo, Capricorn and Aquarius. A love/hate relationship with one (or both) of the parents might point to Scorpio or Pisces. Parents who were not interested in the child and fobbed him off with things rather than love suggest Taurus, Leo, Libra, possibly Scorpio or Sagittarius.

A cautious, shy approach during childhood would be shown by a feminine/negative sign on the ascendant, while an extroverted child or one who was expected to act in an extrovert or even rather macho manner, would be Aries, Gemini, Leo or Sagittarius.

If by this process of elimination, you come up with two possible signs, make up two charts with the ascendant placed in the middle section of each of the two signs and then have a go at some fine tuning.

Pre-natal epoch birthcharts

This method was demonstrated to me by Douglas Ashby who had, in turn, been shown how it works by Chryss Craswell.

This idea appears at first glance to be even crazier than dowsing, but it works! In fact, it was by a process of pre-natal epoch work, elimination and finally, fine tuning, that my own ascendant was found. The method is based on the premise that a normal pregnancy takes 280 days or 40 weeks, so it will only work if the subject was born fairly naturally, after a normal length of pregnancy. To find the pre-natal chart, count back 40 weeks (or 280 days) from the date of birth. This will take you back, more or less, to the date of conception. Look at the position of the Moon on the conception date because this will be located on, or around, either the potential ascendant or descendant.

Fine tuning

This can be done in two ways. The first is by moving the midheaven backwards and forwards. The MC moves at roughly a degree for a year, therefore events can be pin-pointed by the aspects it makes to other planets on the natal chart as it progresses. The subject can be asked to mention any particularly memorable events in his childhood and the rectified midheaven can be swung backwards and forwards until it connects with one of the planets or some other feature on the chart at the relevant age. For example, a change in one's direction in life would connect with a progression of the midheaven from one sign to another. An accident might be set off by a midheaven square to Mars or Uranus. Good exam results might be midheaven conjunct, sextile or trine Mercury, while a move of house would connect with the Moon, with a square or opposition, if the subject felt it to be an unhappy event or with a trine or sextile if it was a happy one. A conjunction could go either way. Obviously, this takes a good deal of astrological knowledge, but there are plenty of books on the market which show the effect of planets natally, by progression or when transitting.

Even more fine tuning

The final step is to look back in time at the movement of planets as shown in the ephemeris (or on the computer). Ask the subject what was happening at the times when planets crossed the angles (asc., dsc., MC and IC). A Jupiter transit across the midheaven can bring a terrific expansion in the area of one's work, public life and status. If the midheaven is in a creative sign, such as Pisces or Taurus, this can bring a surge of creativity and recognition for one's work. Saturn crossing the ascendant will cause a slowing down of one's life and a feeling of being restricted and over-burdened with responsibilities. This will last for a couple of years as it transits through the first house, possibly bringing a period of depression and also hard work, resulting in worthwhile long term gains and a definite re-structuring of one's life. If a subject marries under this kind of transit the marriage would be to an older person and/or be based on a need for material security. Venus transits might cause the subject to fall in love, or to become more aware of beauty and harmony. It would also cause the subject to re-evaluate his priorities in life. Marriage resulting from sexual attraction could be due to Mars, Pluto or even Uranus.

I know that rectification is difficult. It really does help if you use a computer because a dozen or more charts might need to be made up in the hunt for the ascendant. It is even necessary to make up separate charts for various times in the subject's past, as they will show by both progression and transit what was going on at that time of his life. If you set these up for those times which were the turning points in the subject's life and also for times of exceptional joy or sadness, this will help in the rectification procedure.

Now you know why the books recommend that you take this problem to a skilled astrologer. I suggest that you take a pocket full of money with you at the same time, because this is hard and time-consuming work and nobody who has spent years of studying astrology should be expected to do it for a pittance. Work out what a highly-trained and skilled accountant or solicitor might want for a few hours' work and give the astrologer the same – he may be an idealist, but he's got to eat and pay his bills too.

Glossary

Ascendant: The actual degree of the zodiac sign which is rising up over the ecliptic at the time of birth.

Cusp: The point where one sign adjoins the next.

Decanate: A ten-degree segment of a sign.

House cusp: The point where one house adjoins the next.

Houses: The division of the chart into 12 segments, each segment is called a house.

IC: Immum Coeli, sometimes called the nadir. The bottom of the chart, also the darkest point of night.

MC: Medium Coeli or Midheaven.

Midheaven: Also called the zenith or the meridian. This is the highest point in the sky at the time of birth. Also the top of the chart in some house systems.